# INDIA'S
# POLITICAL ECONOMY,
## 1947-1977

# INDIA'S
# POLITICAL ECONOMY,
# 1947-1977

## The Gradual Revolution

FRANCINE  R.  FRANKEL

Princeton University Press

Published by Princeton University Press, Princeton, New Jersey
In the United Kingdom: Princeton University Press,
Guildford, Surrey

Library of Congress Cataloging in Publication Data will be
found on the last printed page of this book

This book has been composed in VIP Bembo

Clothbound editions of Princeton University Press books are printed on
acid-free paper, and binding materials are chosen for
strength and durability.

Printed in the United States of America by Princeton
University Press, Princeton, New Jersey

For my mother, Dora,
and in memory of my father, William Goldberg

# CONTENTS

# LIST OF TABLES

# PREFACE

India, like the great majority of new states, has failed to make a significant impact on the problem of mass poverty. Overall gains from huge investments in modern science and technology have made India into the tenth greatest national economy in the world. But this achievement seems to have increased rather than reduced the persistent and deepening dualism between the still limited modern industrial sector and the vast rural hinterland. Within the countryside, a minority of prosperous commercial farmers is swamped by growing numbers of marginal cultivators and landless laborers who have the greatest difficulty meeting even their minimum consumption needs. These impoverished agriculturists swell the ranks of the unemployed and underemployed, mocking earlier promises to make development into an instrument of social welfare.

India's inability to achieve the overall economic transformations that the growth theories were designed to bring about has focused attention on the peculiarities and special conditions that constitute the setting in which economic development must take place. A decade has passed since Gunnar Myrdal advanced the most influential statement of an alternative "broad institutional approach" in his *Asian Drama*, a ten-year, three-volume study that is "mainly about India with numerous and systematic attempts at comparison with other countries of South Asia."[1] Myrdal's critique of the narrowly "economic " framework of analysis rests largely on the argument that Western theories, models, and concepts have distorted the study of economic development in South Asia by separating economic theories from the radically different—and unfavorable—environment in attitudes, cultures, and institutions.

The obstacles to development in the South Asian context turn out to be the very same limitations that were "prominent in the thought of the old European colonial masters."[2] They extend to irrational beliefs sanctified by religion, cultural attitudes deprecating manual labor, styles of living and working accepted as immutable on the strength of these beliefs, all of which are inimical to development. The "inefficiency, rigidity and inequality of the established institutions and attitudes" and the "economic and social power relations embodied in this framework of institutions and attitudes"[3] are considered the primary reasons for the inability to get economic plans effectively implemented. The "precondition" for economic development that logically follows from this kind of reasoning

[1] Gunnar Myrdal, *Asian Drama: An Inquiry into the Poverty of Nations*, I (New York, 1968), 40.
[2] *Ibid.*, p. 20.
[3] *Ibid.*, p. 47.

is that old religious attitudes, cultural patterns, and social structures have to be destroyed before development can take place.

The possibility of achieving such a complete social transformation through democratic processes of government is, of course, remote. Arguments that accept the need for a direct attack on traditional attitudes and modes of economic and social stratification have therefore inevitably stressed the need for compulsion. They have suggested that countries which limit themselves to democratic planning are doomed to failure since they cannot use force to impose obligations. They are, in Myrdal's fashionable terminology, "soft states." Indeed, claims made by the first generation of the post-Independence leadership in India that they were ideologically committed to political democracy are questioned as opportunistic political compromises with powerful propertied classes for the purpose of remaining in office. By contrast, the view is often argued that the litmus test of genuine commitment to development is the willingness to take direct action in a frontal assault on religious attitudes and the institutions sanctified by them which perpetuate inequalities inimical to change.

In this book, I attempt to offer a somewhat different perspective on the extraordinarily complicated problems confronting India. Like Myrdal and a growing number of critics who despair of narrow economic solutions to problems of underdevelopment, I will argue that India's poverty cannot be overcome solely through evolutionary growth models. In India, in the absence of prior institutional change, and no matter how sophisticated the investment plans for "inducing" other investments, if the past is any guide, one set of investments will not lead to another, or to only a few others, and then after a while to a dead end.

At the same time, it is difficult to endorse the opposite view that revolutionary social transformation is a necessary—or perhaps more important—a realistic precondition for breaking down the social barriers to development. The fact is that theories calling for revolutionary action are "non-theories" under Indian conditions once they are tested against political constraints. So far, at least, the poor have shown a weak sense of Indian identity and a strong inclination to seek meaning in traditional relationships based on religion, caste, and family. These living traditions have presented Marxist revolutionaries with seemingly insurmountable barriers in organizing a national movement based on class appeals. It needs also to be remembered that a revolutionary solution in Indian conditions, even if a national movement could be set in motion, holds out the possibility for incalculable levels of destructive violence. An explanation of India's poverty that involves the basic assumptions and structure of the entire social order inevitably raises the most agonizing questions for intellectual analysis and political action. As V. S. Naipaul recently asked, "But where does the system begin and end? Does it take in religion, the security of caste and clan, Indian ways of perceiving, *karma*, the antique serfdom? But no Indian can take himself to the stage where he might perceive that the faults lie within the civilization itself, that the failure and the cruelties of India might implicate all Indians."[4]

Many Indian intellectuals do, in fact, carry out such political self-assessments; but many educated Indians also have good reason for avoiding the issue. Were the problem to be put in this way and then translated into political ideology and action by the masses, it would provide the stuff of nightmares for many members of the educated middle classes. These nightmares are precisely that, once the impoverished millions break through "Indian ways of perceiving" their situation in the age-old obligations of religion, the family, clan, and caste, they will understand only too well the source of their suffering to be in "the system," and not in their *karma*, and will take a terrible revenge. This was Gandhi's nightmare, and in the popular awakening he began during the Independence movement and that has grown in the years since, it has become more than a bad dream: it is a daily reality conveyed in reports of local outbreaks of looting, arson, and murder.

The chapters that follow examine India's political economy by starting from what has been India's basic dilemma: How can a gradual revolution be accomplished, a revolution that can enlarge the possibilities of human development for the poorest of its people without exacting fearful costs in human life by unleashing the unpredictable social chaos of a violent upheaval? They trace the relationship between the economic and political development strategies devised by the nationalist leaders on the premise that the advent of political democracy offered an alternative to revolutionary class struggle in equalizing society. The solution, according to Nehru, was to be sought in using the vote to build up mass consciousness, in holding elections to overcome mass inertia, and in introducing institutional changes at the village level to spur the organization of the most disadvantaged groups in class-based political associations. Political democracy could bring to bear the strength of numbers of the poor in such powerful pressures on the ruling classes that they would be compelled to move in the direction of economic democracy. At the same time, readjustments in the distribution of economic and political power would occur, it was hoped, against the background of increasing productivity, and could therefore be accomplished with a minimum of disruptive violence. These were the expectations of the late 1940s, expectations that can now be evaluated against the experience of thirty years. It is this experience that the book examines.

[4] V. S. Naipaul, *India: A Wounded Civilization* (New York, 1977), pp. 160–61.

The study draws on twenty years of personal and professional involvement in India's dilemma, from the time when I first arrived in Lucknow as a Fulbright student in 1958. Since then, I have returned several times, becoming increasingly indebted to many people, both Indian and American, who extended their friendship and their help, and who made it possible for me to deepen my understanding. These debts cannot ever be repaid: I hope only that my work itself may have some value in redressing the balance of obligation I so deeply feel to all those who made this book possible.

At certain times, some individuals have offered strategic support, help without which a work cannot be completed, and I want specifically to acknowledge this special kind of help. I am indebted in this way to Tarlok Singh, L. K. Jha, Mohan Dharia, and Kuldip Nayar, whose willingness to vouch for my credentials in pursuing a serious scholarly enterprise (without at the same time necessarily agreeing with its conclusions) kept many doors open to me during the later stages of my research.

There are other kinds of strategic support. My husband, Douglas Verney, who since we met in April 1975 has only known me as bearing the burden of an unfinished work, has provided the vital margin of encouragement needed to withstand the strains of completing the book against the background of the most dramatic shifts in Indian conditions, and enduring the separation enforced upon us by a commuting marriage.

Finally, no work of this kind could be accomplished without the free time from normal university responsibilities. I wish to thank the University of Pennsylvania for several leaves of absence, and in particular my chairmen, my colleagues, and the departmental secretaries who did so much of the typing. I also want to express my appreciation for a Ford Foundation Faculty Research Grant in Political Science, 1972-1973; for an invitation to be a Resident Scholar at the Bellagio Study and Conference Center by the Rockefeller Foundation in the Spring of 1975; for grants from the American Council of Learned Societies in 1973 and the American Philosophical Society in 1976 for travel to India; and for the unique intellectual stimulation of my stay as Visiting Member at the Institute for Advanced Study (Princeton) in Spring 1976, where much of the integrating framework and later chapters of the book were completed.

*Philadelphia*
*January 31, 1978*

INDIA'S
POLITICAL ECONOMY,
1947-1977

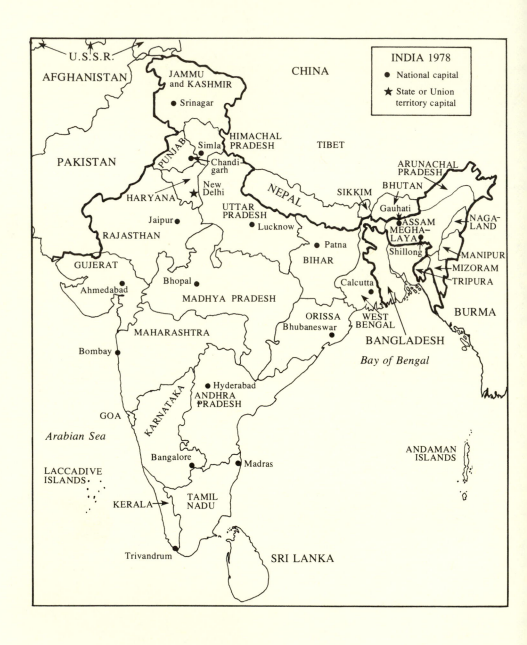

INDIA 1978
● National capital
★ State or Union
  territory capital

U.S.S.R.

AFGHANISTAN

CHINA

JAMMU
and KASHMIR

● Srinagar

PAKISTAN

HIMACHAL
PRADESH

PUNJAB

Simla
Chandi-
garh

TIBET

HARYANA

New
Delhi

NEPAL

ARUNACHAL
PRADESH

BHUTAN

SIKKIM

Gauhati

NAGA-
LAND

UTTAR
PRADESH

● Lucknow

Jaipur ●

ASSAM
MEGHA-
LAYA

RAJASTHAN

● Patna

Shillong

MANIPUR

BIHAR

MIZORAM

GUJERAT

TRIPURA

Bhopal ●

Ahmedabad ●

MADHYA PRADESH

Calcutta ●

BURMA

MAHARASHTRA

ORISSA
Bhubaneswar ●

WEST
BENGAL

BANGLADESH

Bombay ●

Bay of Bengal

● Hyderabad

ANDHRA
PRADESH

KARNATAKA

GOA

Arabian Sea

ANDAMAN
ISLANDS

LACCADIVE
ISLANDS

Bangalore ●

● Madras

KERALA

TAMIL
NADU

Trivandrum ●

SRI LANKA

# ONE

## Introduction: The Paradox of Accommodative Politics and Radical Social Change

India, virtually alone among the new nations, retained a deep commitment to principles of parliamentary government during the three decades after Independence. Its leaders described their approach to planning under a democratic pattern of socialism as a new model for Asian and African development. Jawaharlal Nehru, the nationalist hero and dedicated democrat who set the direction of India's development during the first fifteen years of freedom, pointed to his country as an area of agreement between the opposing ideologies of capitalism on the one hand and communism on the other. It was his experimental framework that enabled a creative approach to be taken toward solving problems of production and distribution, an approach that sought to combine goals of growth and reduction of disparities, while avoiding the violence and regimentation of revolutionary change. Under his leadership, the commitment to democratic social transformation was an integral part of India's economic strategy. It marked India's approach to national development from the earliest days of planning in the 1950s. Nehru spoke of it as "a third way which takes the best from all existing systems—the Russian, the American and others—and seeks to create something suited to one's own history and philosophy."[1]

The optimism of that early period has dimmed. It is becoming more and more difficult to argue that India will manage to avoid the violent conflict and enforced solutions that have accompanied the rapid transformation of agrarian societies elsewhere. The "third way" did not solve India's problems, whether of production or distribution. On the contrary, in the mid-1970s only a small minority of the population had been incorporated into the high-productivity, high-wage industrial sector of the economy. Despite a large expansion of industrial output and social overhead capital, there was little effect on the traditional sector from the creation of more jobs. Eighty percent of the population continued to live in rural areas. Eighty percent of the working members of this vast majority earned their livelihood directly from agriculture.[2] Yet only small

[1] R. K. Karanjia, *The Mind of Mr. Nehru: An Interview*, pp. 100-101.
[2] *Census of India, 1971, Provisional Population Totals*, pp. 3-33, 49.

pockets of rapid growth could be created in the rural sector. Modern agriculture, coexisting alongside much larger subsistence sectors, simply
extended and proliferated the scattered enclaves of development into the
hinterland. During much of the later 1960s and into the 1970s, there were
chronic food shortages, sharp inflationary price spirals, low availability
of domestic raw materials, shortfalls in industrial output, underutilized
capacity in consumer goods industries, stagnant or declining rates of
public investment, and diversion of scarce foreign exchange for imports
of foodgrains and raw materials. All these contributed to the prospect
that India would return to a low-level equilibrium in which growth rates
did not significantly exceed the rate of population increase.

Modest overall increases in per capita Net National Product were substantially neutralized by a demographic explosion that more than doubled population growth rates from about 1 percent during the first half of
the century to a peak of 2.5 percent per annum in the next twenty-five
years. The inability to solve problems of distribution was apparent from
the large proportion of the rural population that continuted to live below
the poverty line. According to estimates made by the Indian Planning
Commission in 1960/61—after the first decade of planning—fifty to sixty
percent of the rural population, or approximately 211 million people,
could not afford minimum levels of consumption, calculated primarily in
terms of caloric intake necessary to avoid the onset of malnutrition.[3]
Available estimates for the early 1970s revealed a reduction in the proportion of the poor, but a moderate increase in their absolute numbers.
About 40 to 50 percent of the rural population, a minimum of 220 million people, were believed to be subsisting below the low poverty line
determined by the Commission.[4]

Economic realities like these, as much as deteriorating law and order,
were invoked by a new generation of India's leaders to justify the imposition of a National Emergency from June 1975 to March 1977. At the time
that the central government acted to suspend the civil liberties guaranteed by the 1950 constitution and to postpone general elections, the ruling Congress party, as it had for most of the period since Independence,
enjoyed secure majorities both in the national parliament and in the legislative assemblies of almost all the states. In the fifth general elections to
the parliament in 1971 and to the state legislative assemblies in 1972, the
Congress had received its largest popular mandate in twenty years of
electoral politics. Despite this vote of confidence, the government appeared powerless to carry out its own program of institutional reform
considered necessary to remove poverty and meet the mounting eco-

[3] Perspective Planning Division, "Perspective of Development: 1961-1976, Implications
of Planning for a Minimum Level of Living," pp. 4-5.
[4] Planning Commission, *Towards Self-Reliance, Approach to the Fifth Five Year Plan*, p. 4.

nomic crisis. It was left to the prime minister, Mrs. Indira Gandhi, the daughter of Jawaharlal Nehru, to argue that economic reforms essential for growth and social justice were impossible to carry out within the limitations of the existing democratic process.

The traumatic experience of the National Emergency raised once again the fundamental paradox of India's political economy. India's leaders had committed themselves to carry out basic changes in the pattern of economic and power relations as an integral part of development. At the same time, they were equally determined to avoid the political costs of a direct attack upon the existing social order. The basic question—and one that provides the analytical focus in this book—was whether there could be any method of transforming the established pattern of wealth, status, and power other than a frontal assault on the beliefs and structures that had institutionalized—and sanctified—a rigid social hierarchy.

This hierarchy was not simply a holdover from the British raj, or even a relic from the distant past that the British had superceded. Hereditary caste groups, each placed in a position of ritual superiority or inferiority to the others, and all governed in their mutual relationships by customary norms of reciprocal, nonsymmetrical rights and obligations, continued to provide the building blocks of social organization in the hundreds of thousands of India's villages. In premodern times, rigorous criteria of pollution and purity had qualified only the upper twenty percent or so of the population for even the rudiments of education, those belonging to elite subcastes or *jatis* grouped under the highest *varna* categories[5] of Brahmin, Kshatriya, and Vaisha—the priest-scholars, warrior-rulers, and traders of the ancient Hindu social order. All schools had been restricted to children of these "twice-born" castes[6] and virtually all instruction was confined to the teachings of the sacred texts. By contrast, the Sudras, the most numerous of the four *varna* strata, including the peasantry and members of the artisan castes, had to be content with opportunities for pursuing their own spiritual merit through service of these superior castes. At the bottom of the religious hierarchy, moreover, one in five persons had no *varna* standing at all. They were considered so

[5] *Varna* refers to the four universal unchanging categories of the Hindu hierarchy— Brahmin, Kshatriya, Vaisha, and Sudra—which are common to all areas of India and provide an overarching ritual ranking system. *Jati* refers to smaller, hereditary, endogamous groups associated with a traditional occupation and related to one another in terms of ritual pollution or purity, but which function as part of a regional-linguistic system. Although the *jatis* in each region number in the hundreds and can be grouped for most ritual purposes within the broad *varna* categories, caste at the local level often contains considerable ambiguity about rank in the context of complex economic and social relations between caste groups.

[6] Only male members of the Brahmin, Kshatriya, and Vaisha *varnas* are entitled to undergo the ceremony of *upanayana* and put on the sacred thread. The ritual is interpreted as a second, "spiritual," birth, after which instruction in the sacred texts may begin.

unclean as to defile caste persons merely by touch, or in some extreme cases, by sight. These pariahs were the miserable outcastes or untouchables whose hovels were segregated at the edges of the village, and whose streets were rarely visited by elite and middle-caste Hindus, who nevertheless depended upon them for menial, and indispensable, services.

The *varna* hierarchy, while paramount even in modern times for allocating religious and ritual rights and obligations among the multitude of caste groups, did not provide the only basis for the actual status ranking of particular local castes. At the village level an additional crucial factor in the exercise of power and authority has been control of a sizable proportion of the agricultural land. In those areas, especially the south, where the highest status group, the Brahmin community, also controlled a large amount of arable land, caste, wealth, and power tended to converge. In other regions, where nonelite peasant castes having strength of numbers also owned a large share of the land, they were able to exercise the authoritative role of "dominant landowning castes."[7] The largest landowners among the locally dominant caste, no less than leading members of the elite castes, wielded significant power over the majority of the poor peasantry. They acted as patrons to provide minimal economic security and protection to land-poor families in return for personal deference and loyalty in situations of social rivalry or factional dispute. Occasionally, a locally dominant Sudra caste might be able to establish a claim to higher *varna* rank after changing group customs, religious ritual, and style of life in imitation of an elite caste. But, this process of "Sanskritization"[8] as a vehicle for social mobility was a prolonged one, extending over one or two generations, and it led only to positional changes within the local hierarchy. The principles of the hierarchical *varna* order and the structure of local inequality remained essentially unchanged. Efforts by untouchable castes to cross the pollution barrier, moreover, by adopting a more Sanskritized way of life were often met with violent attacks by high-caste groups, both on religious grounds and also to preserve the occupational divisions that assured a steady supply of labor for the most polluting tasks.

During the period of colonial rule, the caste-based structure was, of course, challenged by an alternative status system based upon secular norms of individual equality and achievement. The introduction of such

---

[7] See S. N. Srinivas, *Social Change in Modern India*, ch. 1, for the most incisive analysis of the *varna* system and its relationship to caste hierarchies in the rural areas, including the role of landowning peasant castes as the dominant power group in village society.

[8] *Ibid*. According to Srinivas, Sanskritization was the traditional avenue of social mobility for low-caste groups. A low caste or tribal group, usually one that had already experienced some improvement in its economic situation or military power could set out over a long period of time to claim a higher position in the *varna* hierarchy by adopting the customs, ritual, style of life, and occupation of a high, preferably "twice-born" caste.

new principles of justice and administration as equality before the law and recruitment on the basis of merit to the few coveted places in English-medium schools and the prestigious Indian Civil Service injected an unprecedented degree of fluidity into the social system. Although there was substantial continuity between the traditional elite castes and the Westernized class of professionals and administrators created under the colonial regime, at least some members of the dominant peasant castes were able to take advantage of the new educational opportunities. The desire for social mobility outside the traditional system was most clearly evident in the Backward Classes Movement of the 1920s and 1930s, which had its greatest appeal in the Brahmin-dominated areas of the south. Led by powerful peasant castes, it succeeded in gaining British support for caste quotas in admission to colleges and places in the civil service, breaking the monopoly of the small South Indian Brahmin community over these posts. Even so, the new opportunities for mobility were disproportionately concentrated in the coastal areas and towns, where the impact of colonial rule was most directly felt. As in the case of Sanskritization, moreover, the fruits of Westernization rarely reached the untouchable and other low castes in the local rural hierarchy.

Indeed, in the villages the caste basis of social life was only moderately affected by the economic disruption caused by colonial policies. New land tenure arrangements, which eliminated the communal pattern of landholdings and vested full rights of ownership, including those of mortgage and sale, in individual holders, paved the way for the larger peasantry to improve their economic condition at the same time as concentration of landownership widened the gap between the dominant landowning castes and the majority of cultivators. Simultaneously, the self-contained character of the village economy was strained by expanding markets for agricultural commodities that encouraged a shift from subsistence farming to commercial production. Roads and railroads became the conveyer belt for moving an increasing share of agricultural production out of the villages to urban centers and the world market, shrinking the residual pool of grain available to support landless members through customary payments in kind, and increasing the role of money as a medium of exchange. A further blow was the collapse of the balance between agriculture and manufactures, as village artisans confronted severely contracted local demand for hand-crafted products in the face of competition from machine-made goods imported from abroad. Then, as public health measures contributed to spiraling rates of population increase, and competition for fixed land resources intensified, the overwhelming majority of farms, subdivided, fragmented, and encumbered by debt, became uneconomic units of cultivation.

Economic disruption, naturally, was not without social consequences.

The village as a corporate entity, that is, the village councils, virtually ceased to function after they lost collective rights in wastelands and land for grazing, and administrative functions of collecting revenue and carrying out irrigation and road works. After 1870, with the accelerated growth of a money economy and the extensive entry of Indian foodstuffs and commercial crops into world trade, quasi-feudal ties based on mutual, nonsymmetric obligations between high-status landowning castes and landless tenants, laborers, and other service castes began to weaken. Intent on maximizing income, some landowners attempted to extract a larger share of the surplus by reducing the scope of their responsibilities to the landless and, indeed, demanding higher rents and other dues. Nevertheless, in most rural areas, the legitimacy of the traditional norms of unequal, albeit reciprocal, rights and obligations was not effectively challenged as the proper basis of society.

At Independence, caste continued to be associated with cumulative inequalities of status, income, and power. The local caste hierarchy closely, although imperfectly, paralleled the distribution of land ownership in the village economy, and it coincided with the allocation of political authority. Together, these multiple inequalities excluded the majority of citizens in India's new democratic republic from effective participation in either the economic or the political development process. The aim of eliminating these inequalities to ensure that the whole population, not just a handful, participated in the opportunities created by the process of development, was at the outset accorded equal priority with the goal of economic growth.

The refusal of India's leaders to consider the problems of economic development solely in terms of maximizing growth, to the exclusion of other social goals, had its origins in the ideological preferences of the first generation of nationalist leaders. These were most strongly influenced by an unlikely blend of the religious morality preached by Mahatma Gandhi and the materialist philosophy advanced by Marx, including the early achievements reported from the Soviet Union under the new socialist regime.

Gandhi, who assumed leadership of the Indian National Congress in 1920—when he set out to lead the English-educated intelligentsia in a movement of nonviolent noncooperation against the British government—was the first nationalist leader to challenge the middle-class conception of Independence as "English rule without the Englishman." Through his religious life style, his personal austerities, and his voluminous writings, he ceaselessly drew attention to the plight of those "toiling and unemployed millions who do not even get a square meal a day and have to scratch along with a piece of stale [bread] and pinch of salt."[9]

---

[9] M. K. Gandhi, *Socialism of My Conception*, p. 255.

Drawing his inspiration from the popular religious movement of *bhakti*, or devotional Hinduism, dating to medieval times, rather than the "high" tradition of the ancient Vedas, Gandhi reinterpreted the caste system to accommodate egalitarian values. He seized on the central doctrine of the *bhakti* saints that salvation is available to all who seek God in the spirit of love and surrender, regardless of caste rank, to argue that in its uncorrupted form, the caste system made no judgment of superiority or inferiority among the major divisions of society. "All were complementary to the other and none inferior or superior to any other, each as necessary for the whole body of Hinduism as any other." Untouchability, Gandhi insisted, was an excrescence of the caste system; an ugly growth on a healthy body; the product of the "distinction of high and low that has crept into Hinduism and is corroding it."[10] His onslaught on untouchability was, in effect, an attack against this "high and lowness," that is, an assault against the hierarchical order of Hindu society.

Gandhi constantly enjoined Congress workers to take up constructive work activities in the villages and to help the rural masses achieve their own economic, social, and moral regeneration. In most cases, the urban intellectuals had made their first intimate contacts with the villagers after the Indian National Congress, under Gandhi's leadership, became a mass-based political movement. Nehru recorded that it was not until the mid-1920s, when he was active in organizing local units of the Congress party that he first visited the rural areas of his own province. And it was not until 1936, when Congress decided to contest provincial elections, that he traveled to other regions of the interior and literally came to "discover" the hundreds of millions of his countrymen who remained virtually invisible to large numbers of his class prior to the advent of Gandhi. It was the combination of Nehru's socialist language and Gandhi's teachings and techniques that produced the 1931 Resolution of the Karachi Session of Congress, which for the first time widened the definition of political freedom to encompass an "end to the exploitation of the masses . . . and real economic freedom for the starving millions."[11]

The discovery of the Indian masses had an even more far-reaching influence on the political orientation of the Indian intelligentsia. The middle classes "wanted some cultural roots to cling to, something that would reduce the sense of frustration and humiliation that foreign conquest and rule had produced."[12] Accepting Gandhi as their guide, they found strength and encouragement through a vicarious journey into India's past.

Gandhi's impact on the first generation of the nationalist intelligentsia

[10] M. K. Gandhi, *The India of My Dreams*, p. 72.
[11] Indian National Congress, AICC, *Resolutions on Economic Policy and Programme, 1924-1954*, p. 6.
[12] Jawaharlal Nehru, *The Discovery of India*, p. 343.

was so profound that we need to remind ourselves just what it was. As early as 1908, Gandhi described his fundamental philosophical position, which he hardly felt it necessary to alter, as one that assumed that India's ancient civilization, in its "uncorrupted" form, embodied a moral superiority over the advanced industrial societies of the West. He wrote: "True civilization is that mode of conduct which points out the path of duty. Performance of duty and observance of morality are convertible terms. To observe morality is to attain mastery over our mind and passions. So doing, we know ourselves. If that definition be correct, then India, as so many writers have shown, has nothing to learn from anybody else."[13]

In contrast to many liberals and socialists in the West, Gandhi maintained a passionate aversion to modern industrial life throughout his long political career. He blamed modern science and technology for the proliferation of cheap luxuries and easy pleasures that eroded the moral basis of Hindu society. Manufactures from abroad whetted the appetites and strengthened the acquisitive motive. Profit became the sole purpose and only measure of human relationships. Competition corroded the pattern of mutual rights and obligations binding the upper-caste landed and the low-caste landless groups into a cohesive village unit, and injected economic exploitation and class conflict into village life. It sometimes seemed that Gandhi could not find enough pejoratives for modern civilization. It was Satanic; a Black Age; a disease and an affliction. Man, to become well, had to resist the tyranny of the machine; return to manual labor and production for use; forsake the illusory civilization of bodily comfort, and cleave to the real civilization of the spirit and morality.

Gandhi realized that it was not enough simply to condemn industrial society; it was necessary to provide an alternative model, that of a society that had not abandoned its traditional morality. The embodiment of this ancient moral glory, according to Gandhi, could still be found in India, in her hundreds of thousands of village communities that had endured over thousands of years of history. Those who became Gandhi's devoted disciples in accepting his antithesis between material and moral progress also joined in his glorification of village life. They found, along with Gandhi, that "the moment you talk to [the Indian peasants] and they begin to speak . . . wisdom drops from their lips. Behind the crude exterior, you will find a deep reservoir of spirituality. . . . In the case of an Indian villager, an age-old culture is hidden under an encrustment of crudeness. Take away the encrustation, remove his chronic poverty and his illiteracy and you have the finest specimen of what a cultured, cultivated free citizen should be."[14]

[13] M. K. Gandhi, *Hind Swaraj or Indian Home Rule*, p. 44.
[14] Gandhi, *The India of My Dreams*, p. 44.

India's mission after Independence, for those who shared this perspective, seemed clear. It was to restore and rebuild the villages, to purge them of the defects that had corroded but not destroyed the spiritual genius of the ancient civilization. Immediate importance was assigned in this enterprise to rooting out obvious social evils, particularly untouchability, illiteracy, and disease, and debilitating habits such as drunkenness and drug taking. The keystone of village reconstruction was the effort to reestablish traditional handicraft industries that had succumbed to cheaper machine-made products from abroad, but which had kept the villages prosperous and self-sustaining in premodern times.

The Gandhians argued that if these things were accomplished, economic and social inequalities would largely disappear. The adoption of the simple hand technologies of ancient times would again ensure that production, consumption, and distribution were simultaneous and would prevent the emergence of very great differences in wealth. The incentive to economic activity in the absence of a money economy would be production for use rather than the profit motive per se. In fact, virtually an ideal form of cooperative economy would evolve. Gandhi envisaged, for example, that "the land would be held in cooperation by the owners and tilled and cultivated in cooperation. The owners would work in cooperation and own capital, tools, animals, seeds, etc., in cooperation."[15] Cooperative patterns could also be applied to cottage and small-scale industries. Even caste, purified of its hierarchical content, could function as a major pillar of the new egalitarian and cooperative order. It would reconcile natural differences in ability with complete social equality and in so doing protect the organic unity of society from the disintegrative potentialities of competition.

The Gandhians' picture of Indian society as it was to be after Independence was at complete odds with the outline of a modern industrial state. Clearly, for Gandhi and his followers, the path ahead was also the road back. The India of my dreams, wrote Gandhi, "would express the ancient moral glory."[16] It would do this by placing strict limitations on opportunities for the accumulation of wealth. The reconstructed Indian village, using simple hand technologies in agriculture and industry, and engaged mainly in production for use rather than profit, was the nearest approach to a civilization based on religion Gandhi could imagine. It was designed to restore India's traditional identity as a spiritual nation; and to offer hope of redemption from the modern illusion that real meaning could be found in the relentless pursuit of money, machinery, and pleasure.

Nehru and his colleagues were not persuaded. The majority of Indian

[15] N. K. Bose, ed., *Selections from Gandhi*, p. 772.
[16] Gandhi, *The India of My Dreams*, pp. 87-95.

intellectuals, even when they were drawn to Gandhi out of respect for his personal dedication and political acumen, rejected his social vision. Even under Gandhi's leadership, the Indian National Congress never deviated from its long-established goal of developing a modern industrial society in India. Nevertheless, the political orientation of the Indian intelligentsia was significantly and permanently altered by their glimpse of the past. Under Gandhi's tutelage, they thought they saw in the surviving structures of traditional society—no matter how decayed and corrupted they had become—evidence of a system of social morality superior to any found in the advanced countries of the West. Specifically, they discovered in the institutions of the joint family, caste, and the village community, an entire society based on the "security, stability and continuance of the group" in opposition to selfish individual interests. Men such as Nehru identified the vital and enduring element in Indian society, "the worthwhile something" that had preserved India's cultural stability against foreign invasion and colonial rule, in the system of social organization firmly rooted in the group ideal.[17]

Indian intellectuals who began to reappraise traditional values and institutions in the light of Gandhi's critique of modern industrial society did not, on this account, abandon the goal of economic development. They did, however, become seriously concerned about the values and priorities of the modern society they were trying to build. They began to question whether economic modernization was a sufficient end in itself. Science, Nehru finally concluded, said nothing about the moral content or purpose of life. Yet instinctively he felt "some kind of ethical approach to life" was necessary, and it was to the ancient world that he turned for guidance on the set of ethical values that could be applied to modern politics. Significantly, Nehru concluded his "Discovery of India" with a critique of modern industrial society based largely on the absence of social values. He deplored the "excessive individualism of the West" and the conflict inherent in it. He found that "the competitive and acquisitive characteristics of modern capitalist society, the enthronement of wealth above everything else, and the continuous strain and lack of security for many had afflicted entire populations with neurotic anxieties even in the midst of great material abundance." He penned this morbid description of the human costs of modern Western progress:

> It would seem that the kind of modern civilization that developed first in the West and spread elsewhere, and especially the metropolitan life that has been its chief feature, produces an unstable society which gradually loses its vitality. Life advances in many fields and yet it loses its grip; it becomes more artificial and slowly ebbs away.

[17] Nehru, *The Discovery of India*, p. 253.

More and more stimulants are needed—drugs to enable us to sleep or to perform our other natural functions, food and drink that tickle the palate and produce a momentary exhilaration at the cost of weakening the system, and special devices to give us a temporary sensation of pleasure and excitement—and after the stimulation come the reaction and a sense of emptiness.[18]

Gandhi's attack on modern civilization, while it did not convert the intelligentsia to his vision of the future, did focus their attention on the normative aspects of modernization. As a result, in India, the concept of modernity was expanded to add moral to the material elements of economic growth. Indirectly, Gandhi raised the problem of alternative patterns of modern society. As one immediate consequence, the intelligentsia directed their attention to the actual models of development available to India on the basis of the experience of the advanced countries.

As information and propaganda about the Russian experiment began to flood India in the late 1920s and early 1930s, many intellectuals thought they saw in the Soviet pattern of society a more congenial model of modernity. Although Nehru's commitment to socialist ideals has often been traced to his first encounter with Fabianism during his college years at Cambridge, Nehru wrote in his *Autobiography* (and subsequently repeated to his biographer, Michael Brecher), that his early contacts with socialist theory were superficial in nature, and had left no permanent impression on his political attitudes. In fact, Brecher reports that it was twenty years after Nehru left Cambridge, not until 1930 or so, that he actually "began to acquire a serious understanding of and attraction to socialism."[19] Moreover, on Nehru's own testimony, the object of this attraction was not the academic Fabianism fashionable in Edwardian England, but the practical example of socialism in the Soviet Union (before the onset of Stalinism) to which he was directly exposed in contacts with orthodox Marxists in 1927 at the Brussels Conference of Oppressed Nationalities and during a brief four-day visit to Moscow in the same year.[20]

Lenin's polemics against imperialism as the last stage of monopoly capitalism, and vigorous Soviet support for movements of national independence in Asia and Africa certainly predisposed Indian nationalists to think favorably of the Soviet Union. Socialism was also attractive to Congress modernists because of its association, in Russia, with economic planning. It offered a "scientific" approach to the problems of resource

[18] *Ibid.*, p. 567.
[19] Nehru's account of his intellectual interests (or rather lack thereof) at Cambridge is given in Jawaharlal Nehru, *An Autobiography*, pp. 19-26. His remarks to his biographer are found in Michael Brecher, *Nehru, A Political Biography*, p. 48.
[20] Nehru, *An Autobiography*, pp. 161-65.

allocation and investment that seemed instrinsically superior to capitalism's dependence on unpredictable market forces. The strong attraction for Marxism that developed among Indian intellectuals in the 1930s, however, has to be explained primarily in terms of a deeper emotional affinity with its expressed social ideals. There are, in fact, striking similarities between central doctrines of Gandhian thought and the conceptual framework of theoretical Marxism as it relates to the moral basis of economic and political organization.

The writings of Gandhian economists were virtually indistinguishable from Marxist tracts with respect to their basic assumptions about the immoral character of capitalist economic institutions. Private property, and its corollary principle, production for profit, were denounced in both as the fundamental cause of all exploitation in society. Gandhi himself claimed that "socialism was not born in the discovery of the misuse of capital by capitalists," but was an explicit teaching of the earliest Hindu religious texts. He asserted: "Real socialism has been handed down to us by our ancestors who taught, 'All land belongs to Gopal—where, then is the boundary line? Man is the maker of that line, and he can, therefore, unmake it.' Gopal literally means shepherd; it also means God. In modern language, it means the State, i.e., the People. . . . Land and all property is his who will work for it."[21]

Although Gandhi generally expressed his economic theories in traditional language, he left no doubt that he personally subscribed to the labor theory of value. In his view, the capitalist was actually commiting the moral equivalent of theft when he appropriated the greater part of labor's product—the "surplus value" above the minimum needed to sustain the workers' productivity—as profit. Gandhi went so far as to formulate his first economic principle as *asteya* (nonstealing), which he defined as possession for need only. And, he buttressed this further with his concept of "bread-labor," that is, the requirement that every person do some manual labor either in agriculture or handicraft industry to meet his own needs. In principle, Gandhi's vision of a just economic system was indistinguishable from pure communism. His longtime secretary, Pyarelal, has recorded that in Gandhi's ashrams, the ruling principle was "to each according to his needs, from each according to his capacity." Thus, "his ashrams are themselves experiments in communism."[22]

Moreover, Gandhi not only believed that strict limitation of private property and the virtual elimination of the profit motive were basic requirements for a just economic system, he was equally certain that they were crucial to the creation of genuine democracy. In his view, there was an inherent contradiction between a class-based economy and popular

[21] Gandhi, *The India of My Dreams*, p. 96.
[22] M. K. Gandhi, *Towards Non-Violent Socialism*, Appendix to Section XI, "Gandhi's Communism" by Pyarelal, pp. 185-86.

government. Under capitalism, the moneyed class could control political parties, the legislatures, and the mass media so that democracy existed in name only. Gandhi early criticized the British Parliament as "hypocritical and selfish," each member thinking and voting in terms of "his own little interest."[23] According to Gandhi, the only relevent criterion of democratic government was the capacity of the masses to regulate and control authority. In a true democracy, there would not even be any need for political parties or elections in the Western sense of the term. Each individual and group would automatically put the common welfare above his own. The "true democrat" would "think and dream not in terms of self or party but only of democracy."[24] In a "perfect" democracy, consensus and unanimity would replace elections and majority rule. Ultimately, the state would cease to have much importance; law and order could be left in the few deviant cases to organized citizens' groups.

This fortuitous conjunction of "traditional" Hindu values (as they were reinterpreted by Gandhi) and "modern" ethical precepts in theoretical Marxism provided an unexpected basis for active collaboration between the religiously oriented, backward-looking, Gandhian wing of Congress and the secular-minded, modernist intelligentsia. Inevitably, at the same time as the Gandhian-socialist consensus grew, a split began to develop in modernist ranks between the intelligentsia on the one hand and the emerging business classes on the other; the first advocating industrial development in combination with socialist reform, the second, supporting capitalist techniques and showing little sympathy for egalitarian principles. Ultimately, this alignment among the major forces of the nationalist movement exercised a decisive influence on India's basic approach to planning in the post–Independence period.

During the Nehru years, the development strategy was the direct result of Gandhian-socialist collaboration. It therefore becomes important to understand the nature and content of the consensus that evolved.

It is clear that the Gandhian-socialist consensus was predominately value oriented. There was much greater unanimity on the ethical criteria by which social policies should be adopted or discarded than on specific programs of action. First, there was general agreement that economic policy should aim for the progressive removal of inequalities in Indian society, and ultimately result in the complete disappearance of class distinctions. Second, the Gandhians and the socialists concurred on the need to limit sharply the existing scope of the acquisitive instinct in Indian economic life, and to create a new set of cooperative motives. Third, both groups agreed that as far as possible institutional changes should be introduced to substitute cooperative principles of economic organization for the prevailing system based on private enterprise.

[23] Gandhi, *Hind Swaraj or Indian Home Rule*, p. 22.
[24] M. K. Gandhi, *Democracy: Real and Deceptive*, p 36.

Beyond these broad principles, the position was complicated by the fundamental disagreement between Gandhians and socialists about the place of industrial development in post-Independence India. Even here, however, a limited but nevertheless crucial accommodation did take place. In his later writings, Gandhi indicated a willingness to compromise with industrialization, when mechanization did not jeopardize human individuality or social cohesion. In 1940, for example, he wrote: "I do not exclude the industries . . . so long as they do not smother the villages and village life. I do visualize electricity, ship-building, iron-works, machine-making and the like existing side by side with village handicrafts. But, the order of dependence must be reversed. Hitherto, the industrialization has been so planned as to destroy the villages and village crafts. In the State of the future it will subserve the villages and their crafts."[25] Given this formulation, it became possible to treat the Gandhian-socialist controversy over the place of machinery in Indian society as a matter of emphasis, with the Gandhians supporting such industrialization as did not destroy traditional values and patterns of social organization. To the extent that the Gandhians accepted the need for basic industries, moreover, they agreed with the socialists that these should be developed primarily in the public, rather than the private sector.

Socialists, for their part, made an equally critical adjustment in outlook. They continued to rely on public ownership and control of basic industries to prevent the economic exploitation characteristic of capitalist systems. But they admitted that state-operated enterprises could not solve the human problems of psychological distress created by the very process of modernization. In some respects, the Soviet model actually seemed to intensify these costs of economic development. The creation of mammoth industrial complexes in a few urban centers; the large shifts of population to the cities; the breakdown of small local communities; the disintegration of extended kinship groups; the application of mass production techniques; and the impersonal managerial device of a government bureaucracy, all resulted in very much the same sense of personal alienation and anxiety evidenced in advanced capitalist countries. In addition, even in rural areas, peasants were exposed to a similar process of social atomization through the amalgamation of traditional small-scale village communities into huge collective farms, owned by the state and operated in bureaucratic fashion by representatives from the distant Center. Worse still, the concentration of all economic resources in the hands of the state constituted an ever present threat of political abuse, and carried with it the possibility of increasing regimentation.

Indian socialists, in an attempt to avoid the pitfalls of the Soviet model of modernity, decided on two major and related modifications: (1) the

---

[25] Gandhi, *Socialism of My Conception*, p. 127.

decentralization of all economic activity to the extent compatible with overall central planning and direction of the economy; and (2) preservation of the village as the primary unit of social organization. In making these revisions, the socialists implicitly accepted Gandhi's key premise of the moral superiority of the ancient social structure. Even more, they held out the hope of achieving a more humanistic version of modern society than any yet realized, by building on the foundations of the old group values and institutions that still survived. Though the profit motive might dominate the contemporary Indian scene, Nehru reasoned, "There is no such admiration for it in India as there is in the West. The possessor of money may be envied but he is not particularly respected or admired. Respect and admiration still go to the man or woman who is considered good and wise, and especially to those who sacrifice themselves and what they possess for the well-being of the community as a whole."[26] Similarly, he argued that while the village had decayed as a cohesive social unit during the period of British rule,

> still [it] holds together by some invisible link and old memories revive. It should be easily possible to take advantage of these age-long traditions and to build up communal and cooperative concerns in the land and in small industry. The village can no longer be a self-contained economic unit (though it may often be intimately connected with a cooperative or collective farm), but it can very well be a governmental or electoral unit, each such unit functioning as a self-governing community within the larger political framework and looking after the essential needs of the village.[27]

Out of such speculations and hopes, arose the concept of a uniquely "Indian" variety of socialism, a social pattern that could reconcile the modern goals of economic development with the traditional community values of small-scale agrarian societies. The village could no longer be an autonomous and self-sufficient unit, but it could be revitalized as a social organism by making it the primary focus of economic and political development programs in the countryside. India might thereby avoid, Nehru wrote, that divorce from the soil that seemed to condemn all modern industrial societies to spiritual decadence and internal decay. He asserted: "It should be possible to organize modern society in such a way as to keep men and women as far as possible in touch with the land and to raise the cultural level of the rural areas. The village and the city should approach each other in regard to life's amenities so that in both there should be full opportunities for bodily and mental development, and a full, all-rounded life."[28]

[26] Nehru, *The Discovery of India*, p. 512.
[27] *Ibid.*, p. 534.                          [28] *Ibid.*, p. 569.

It was a conception Gandhians and socialists could share. "Socialism," so defined, seemed to ensure that the new pattern would preserve the special "Indian genius" of social organization, by providing for the material advance of the mass of rural people *within* their traditional village setting. In November 1947, the All-India Congress Committee defined independent India's broad political objectives and economic program in the following terms:

> Our aim should be to evolve a political system which will combine efficiency of administration with individual liberty and an economic structure which will yield maximum production without the concentration of private monopolies and the concentration of wealth and which will create the proper balance between urban and rural economies. Such a social structure can provide an alternative to the acquisitive economy of private capitalism and regimentation of a totalitarian state.[29]

This was the first official statement by the national leadership of the "third way" in economic development. Subsequently, the development process was considered in broader terms than economic growth to include ideological preferences for the establishment of an egalitarian, decentralized, and cooperative pattern in agriculture and the rapid expansion of public ownership in the basic industrial sector.

These social goals offered a painful contrast to social realities. On the eve of Independence, India was still stamped with the sharp disparities of the most deeply stratified society in human history. Its predominately peasant economy had been gratuitously exposed to capitalist economic incentives and institutions for over one hundred years. How was the transformation to a modern industrial economy within the framework of socialist norms and patterns of organization to be worked? Above all, how could the goals of economic growth and social transformation be achieved, given on the one hand the rejection of models of evolutionary economic change under capitalism, and on the other constraints imposed by politics and culture against the use of violence for the purpose of sweeping away obstacles to radical social change?

At the outset, the leadership's commitment to social goals of planning led them to reject as inadequate the narrow growth models abstracted from the pattern of industrial development in the West. The growth theories could not be separated from and were predicated upon policies that led to an increase of inequality. They required financial and other incentives to private investment, usually in already favored regions— those having superior infrastructure or other natural resources—and by

[29] *Resolutions on Economic Policy and Programme, 1924-1954*, p. 20.

individuals with sufficient savings to take advantage of new growth opportunities. The resulting increase in economic disparities, whether between "modern" and "traditional" sectors, "advanced" and "backward"
regions, or simply the rich and the poor, was the very mechanism
through which growth had been achieved. They created both the possibility of accumulating the vast amounts of savings essential to capital
formation and the opportunities for profitable investment that established the foundations for future expansion. During the earliest stages of
industrial development, distribution of income between the more and
less privileged regions, sectors, and social classes worsened. Only over
the long run did the process of development accelerate to the point that
surpluses became so large that they generated economic benefits which
"trickled down" to most members of society.

The prospect under Indian conditions was, moreover, much worse.
The adoption of capitalist growth models would have excluded the vast
majority of the peasant population from participating in the gains of development over any foreseeable future. First, there was little prospect that
sufficient additional employment could be created within the modern industrial sector to absorb the rural unemployed and underemployed. The
opportunities for substitution of labor for capital offered by available
technology were limited, especially when contrasted with the massive
numbers of the rural population that needed to be productively employed. In addition, the impoverished peasantry was hardly equipped to
take advantage of new growth opportunities inside the agricultural sector
provided by greater incentives for private investment on improved production practices. They owned either no land or small fragments of land.
Under existing conditions of extreme concentration in the ownership of
physical assets, an undiluted capitalist approach could only benefit those
few who were already reasonably affluent—the members of the dominant landowning castes who had traditionally controlled village life.
Meanwhile, the rapid spread of commercial agriculture would necessarily undermine still further the old caste-based ties of diffuse social obligations that might otherwise have served as a bridge between traditional
and modern forms of reciprocity and cooperation in village economic
life.

Once evolutionary models of capitalist economic growth were rejected, however, it became difficult to distinguish between the economic
means and the social goals of India's development effort. If the majority
of the landless and land-poor peasantry were to be provided with the opportunity of improving their productivity, income and consumption
within the village economy, then economic strategies had to provide for
the prior or simultaneous reduction of disparities, particularly redistribution of land. Once agricultural policies were designed around participation of the majority of small farmers, moreover, some degree of change

in agrarian reorganization from individual to cooperative patterns of
economic activity was essential to provide economies of scale to large
numbers of small holders. Stated this way, the means and ends of development endorsed by the national leadership amounted to no less than a
complete reorganization of the existing village society. They inevitably
evoked political prescriptions, based on historical precedent, for a direct
attack on the old social and economic structure, as the precondition for
reconciling growth and equality goals.

Yet if the evolutionary growth models of the capitalist pattern were in
direct contradiction with the social goals of India's development, alternative revolutionary and communist models of sweeping social change encountered a number of serious political constraints. Not only were such
strategies outside the intention and/or the capability of government or
any organized opposition movement; even worse, they were in practice
prescriptions that could only retard social change on the one hand or
trigger social chaos on the other. Under Indian conditions, a frontal assault on the existing social order, in the best case, would delay or abort
desired egalitarian changes by fragmenting large numbers of the poorer
peasantry among more potent allegiances to language, religion, or caste.
In the worst case, such an assault would be likely to lead to a prolonged
period of disorder and the prospect of national disintegration.

The overriding political constraint was that parochial loyalties far
outweighed national commitments. A myriad of internal cleavages
sharply divided the subcontinent. Within India's boundaries were fourteen major linguistic groupings, each claiming a unique cultural heritage;
a large Muslim religious minority, accounting for one-sixth of the total
population; and, at the core of the social structure, over three thousand
endogamous caste groups. The entire national political structure after Independence was, in fact, built upon accommodation of these linguistic,
religious, and caste sentiments and structures as the only way to accelerate national integration, enhance the legitimacy of the political system,
and maximize the possibility of peaceful adjustments of social conflicts
that arise during the development process.

Language had, by 1956, been granted formal recognition as a legitimate principle of political organization when the states were reorganized
around linguistic boundaries and kept wide federal powers over public
order, welfare, and development subjects, including land reforms. If, for
example, we apply Stalin's definition of nationality, it can be argued that
there were fourteen "nations" in India, in the sense that each linguistic
group is "an historically evolved stable community of people formed on
the basis of a common language, territory, economic life and psychological make-up manifested in a common culture."[30] There is, moreover,

[30] J. Stalin, *Marxism and the National Question* (Moscow, 1950), p. 16.

no dominant national group compared to the Great Russian, nor is the largest linguistic group of Hindi speakers dispersed throughout the country.[31] On the contrary, under a federal constitution, the linguistic state provided a main focus of extended feelings of political solidarity.

Diverse linguistic communities were not the only subnational unit around which the peasantry was politically organized. Indeed, within each "nation" there were multiple centers of personal and parochial loyalty that played an even greater role in arranging peasant participation. Caste, in particular, had been used as a natural building block by party organizations in ways that split the solidarity of the poor.

In general, national political parties did not recruit from among the poor peasantry. Instead, they accommodated themselves to the existing power structures as the easiest way to win votes. The advent of adult suffrage did displace the tiny English-educated upper-caste urban professionals from key positions in party organizations, but the major beneficiaries of the change were the most prosperous sections of the dominant landowning castes, individuals who could exploit a wide network of traditional caste, kinship, and economic ties (of dependent sharecroppers and laborers) to organize a large personal following. The rate of politicization of low caste/class members was by this process slowed down. Such groups did not act independently in making demands on the political system. Rather, they related to the political process only through the dominant caste leadership.

Despite historical precedents suggesting that drastic agrarian reforms could only take place as part of a major revolutionary upheaval of the type experienced in Russia and China, the absence of a class-based party organization among the peasantry made such an approach particularly unrealistic. In contrast to conditions of advanced social disintegration favoring the success of peasant revolutionary movements elsewhere, old beliefs, attitudes, and traditional institutions still retained extraordinary vitality as rallying points for popular loyalties. Class consciousness and the degree of peasant organization was correspondingly low. Any attempt to carry out agrarian reforms on a wave of local peasant revolts risked the danger that large-scale social struggle would spill across class boundaries and trigger civil violence that could threaten national unity.

The potential for widespread social violence was almost boundless. There was, first of all, the "national" issue. To cite Stalin again:

> The bourgeoisie of the oppressed nation, repressed on every hand, is naturally stirred into movement. It appeals to its "native folk" and

---

[31] Whereas Great Russian accounts for the language of over 58 percent of the population, and Great Russian speakers are dispersed throughout the Soviet Union, Hindi users total about one-third of the national population in India and are concentrated in the northern Gangetic plains. See Selig Harrison, *India: The Most Dangerous Decades*, p. 304.

begins to shout about the "fatherland," claiming that its own cause is the cause of the nation as a whole. It recruits itself an army from among its "countrymen" in the interests . . . of the fatherland. . . . As far as the peasants are concerned their participation in the national movement depends primarily on the character of the repressions. If the repressions affect the "land" . . . then the mass of peasants immediately rally to the banner of the national movement.[32]

Second, there was the possibility of large-scale communal violence. Animosity had, in fact, smoldered and sporadically flared between Hindu and Muslim communities throughout the colonial period, ending in the conflagration that consumed half a million lives in 1947, when the subcontinent was partitioned into India and Pakistan. Conflicts between Hindu landlords and Muslim tenants would not necessarily be any easier to contain. Third, in parts of rural India, and particularly in the south, there were possibilities of cruel caste conflict. Cleavages drawn on the basis of landed and landless classes closely paralleled the traditional divisions between pure and polluted castes. In many villages, the landlord was also a Brahmin; the landless farm worker was a Harijan,[33] descendent of the despised untouchables. Finally, even within the lower castes, poor peasants might be divided by different perceptions of their economic interest among those who owned some land and those who owned none at all. Some peasants would simply choose to remain loyal to their old patrons. In such cases, relations between landlords and the landless would settle into a permanent adversary pattern, even while the poor became polarized between "loyal" workers and tenants and those who joined the rebels.

Such political constraints were ultimately decisive in convincing even committed socialists that the multiple goals of development had to be pursued through democratic methods. Yet, this was still mainly to state the dimensions of the problem rather than to suggest a solution. If the cost of social change through violent revolution was likely to be prohibitive in risking the dangers of national disintegration, the pursuit of reforms solely through the electoral process was even more certain to be ineffective.

Some of the same conditions that limited the possibilities of revolutionary change restricted the effectiveness of parliamentary processes in carrying out reforms. The fact that the nation-state had been created without a prior confrontation between the modern leadership and authoritative traditional groups helped to preserve the old leadership pat-

[32] Stalin, *Marxism and the National Question*, pp. 28-29.
[33] As part of his lifelong effort to eliminate discrimination against untouchables, Gandhi called them by the name of Harijans—children of God.

terns. Central power had not been consolidated after a long period of struggle at the expense of local authorities. Rather, the power of the central government complemented and did not replace that of local notables.

Despite their professed aim of carrying out elaborate developmental and welfare functions, the elected governments after Independence were able to establish only a token administrative presence at the village level. Instead, like the colonial regime before them, they relied primarily on the cooperation of established local leaders to organize peasant participation on behalf of national economic and social policies. Similarly, the process of "party building" involved little more than pyramiding alliances among district and state factional alignments that at their base often turned out to be the personal followings of local leaders.

The Congress party, which had dominated politics since the turn of the century, mastered the art of political accommodation to its highest degree. They succeeded by adapting local power structures, using the natural building blocks closest at hand. Within each region, they recruited from among those who were typically members of the dominant landowning castes and who were the leading members of the large landowning caste. Such local notables put together the basic units of the Congress party organization. The units were composed of the leader's kin, caste fellows, and economic dependents. The wider district, state, and national party organization represented a complex pyramiding of these vertical (multicaste and multiclass) alliances. Indeed, the majority of Congressmen retained primary loyalty to their faction, or, if the party dissolved, to the kinship and caste groupings at its core, rather than to the party. The relationship of the local faction leaders and the state and national Congress party was often asymmetrical: the authority of the former was largely independent of party identification; in many cases, the power of the latter depended on the support of the rural elites.[34]

The introduction of electoral politics under these conditions tended at the outset only to reinforce the strategic position of the dominant landowning castes by enlarging their role as intermediaries in relationships between the village and outside authorities in the administration and government. They were the "link men" in the constituencies, whose support was courted by the political parties because they controlled the "vote banks" built on the loyalties of local faction members. During general elections, the faction leader acted as a broker between his village and the political party, delivering peasant votes in return for preferential treatment for his group if the candidate was successful. Similarly, the very fact that a local leader enjoyed access to influential persons in gov-

---

[34] A number of empirical studies have confirmed this general pattern of grass-roots political organization by the Congress party. The model for most of them remains Myron Weiner, *Party Building in a New Nation, The Indian National Congress*.

ernment and administration outside the village enhanced his status and power in attracting a larger local following. The net result was that universal suffrage and an open electoral process *by themselves* could not create the conditions of popular pressure from below to accomplish peaceful implementation of social reforms. Rather, preexisting kinship, caste, and economic ties were projected into vertical patterns of political mobilization by leaders of the dominant landowning castes to reinforce the factional structures that divided the poor and prevented them from using their potential power in superior numbers to pursue common economic interests.

The resolution of the paradox of accommodative politics and radical social change required a substitute for a frontal assault on the strategic position of the dominant landed castes, one that could gradually undermine the vertical patterns of political organization fragmenting the peasantry around ties of kinship, caste, and economic dependence and create the conditions for peaceful mobilization of the poor on the principle of their shared poverty. In fact, the broad outlines of such an approach had been worked out by Gandhi during the early years of the nationalist movement.

Gandhi's point of departure was the notion of appropriate distribution embodied in the traditional recognition of mutual, nonsymmetric obligations by both the landed and landless groups. Even though the ascriptive definition of roles was no longer as decisive in determining the way allocation occurred, the landowners as well as the landless continued to respect the normative ideals on which the system was based. Gandhi, therefore, proceeded by reinterpreting the traditional notion of social obligation as allied to relative standing in the caste hierarchy (*dharma*) from a sacred concept enjoying religious responsibility on the upper castes to use their wealth charitably on behalf of the poor, into a secular ethic of equality in which the propertied castes were no more than trustees of resources given for use of all. Simultaneously, he offered an outline of an action program that could ultimately organize effective power to enforce this egalitarian redefinition. Speaking only in terms of a Constructive Program that would restore the self-sufficient society of the ancient village, Gandhi required Congress workers to alternate political tasks with "village uplift" work for improving the "social" conditions of the peasantry. Despite this formal separation of political and social issues, the penetration of the villages by the Constructive Program was also an organizational device for weakening the links of dependence that bound the peasantry to the dominant landed castes by improving their physical condition, increasing their income through the revival of village industries, and most important, providing basic education. Taken together, Gandhi was convinced that the long-term effects of these methods would be an enlightened and unified peasantry, led by its own cadre, and capable of applying a "nonviolent sanction," such as peaceful strikes, against exploitation by the landowning castes.

These basic premises of Gandhi's approach were not abandoned after Independence. Rather, under Nehru's leadership they were adapted to exploit the new possibilities for peaceful reform created by the advent of democratic political institutions. The strategy that was set down took advantage of the potentiality inherent in the democratic process for converting the superior numbers of the poor into a powerful political resource. It did not, however, rely solely on the dynamics of electoral participation to create new forms of horizontal class organization among the peasantry. On the contrary, the leadership followed Gandhian principles in the attempt to separate the techniques of political organization from the method of social reform. They followed the politics of accommodation in preserving the Congress party as a unifying force. The Congress continued to recruit from among leading members of the dominant landowning castes—notables who had power and influence in local factional groupings—and to organize popular participation in the wider electoral process through a complex pyramiding of vertical factional alliances. The technique permitted Congress to build winning coalitions, provide stable government, and enhance national integration by concentrating power at the Center under a "one-party dominant political system."[35]

The goals of social transformation were pursued outside the arena of party politics. At the same time as the Congress party claimed to represent the interest of all groups, including the propertied classes, the central government advanced development policies that were designed to whittle away at the social supports of economic and political dominance of the landed castes. The approach amounted to an indirect attack on the normative and institutional foundations of traditional, social, economic, and political hierarchies. It was two-pronged. The first point of attack aimed at creating new feelings of class consciousness among the peasantry by challenging traditional beliefs that legitimated ascriptive inequalities sanctified by the religious myths of caste. Under Nehru's leadership, the constitution, the parliament, the ruling Congress party, and the Planning Commission all formally endorsed egalitarian, secular, and socialist goals of national policy that established a consensus at the level of principle on the aim of constructing a "socialistic pattern of society."

[35] This analytical model, which was commonly used to describe India's system of competitive politics before the results of the 1967 election temporarily displaced Congress as the ruling party in several states, is systematically developed in Rajni Kothari, "The 'Congress' System in India" and Gopal Krishna, "One Party Dominance—Development and Trends," in Centre for the Study of Developing Societies, *Party System and Election Studies*.

The second point of attack was designed to establish new institutions at the village level that could ultimately be used by a self-conscious peasantry to mobilize public opinion and organize effective pressure from below for enforcing radical social reforms within the democratic political system.

Under the first three five-year plans, the economic development approach could not be separated from the strategy of peaceful social transformation. In the rural sector, the Planning Commission proposed to establish village cooperatives and panchayats (councils) as the major instruments of agricultural development, to involve the majority of the small peasantry in labor-intensive development schemes and community action projects. At the same time, the new development agencies were constituted on principles of universal membership and adult suffrage, which were intended to make them into major vehicles for democratic social transformation. Over time, they had the revolutionary potential of redefining the participant village community to include all families, regardless of caste and economic standing; and of shifting the balance of economic and political power away from the landed upper castes toward the low-status peasant majority. It was only after the new institutions took root, providing the poor with the rudiments of economic and social services, and creating the skilled popular leadership necessary to transform superior numbers into cohesive electoral blocs, that the conditions for democratic social change were expected to emerge.

The Congress party was not assigned an important role in providing impetus to this process. Rather, as the links of dependence binding the peasantry to the dominant landed castes grew weaker and the capacity of the rural poor for political organization improved, it was anticipated that they would generate their own leadership to challenge the hegemony of the local notables dominating the Congress electoral machines. Under the system of local democracy, the Congress might adapt to the new political realities or it might be swept away. In any case, the ground would be prepared for a peaceful transition in response to the "nonviolent sanction" applied from below for implementation of agrarian reforms. Equally important, given the additional priority of rapid industrialization endorsed by the mid-1950s, it was envisaged that the councils and cooperatives as authentic "peoples' institutions" would liberate new productive energies in the vast rural sector by providing incentives of equitable distribution for popular participation in "human investment" development programs. Inasmuch as substantial increases in agricultural production, savings, and surpluses were crucial to the prospects of the industrial plan, the nonviolent transformation of the traditional social order was placed at the center of both the economic and political development strategy.

The chapters that follow examine the complex interaction between the economic and political strategies that shaped national development over the generation of India's democratic rule. The first part of the book explores the origin of the strategy for peaceful social transformation as it was worked out by Gandhi during the early years of the nationalist movement, and the manner in which these principles were incorporated as an integral part of the economic plans after Independence. The later chapters analyze the dilemmas of the post-Nehru period in the face of mounting evidence that the dual goals of economic growth and radical social change were irreconcilable within the existing framework of accommodative politics. The symmetry between the old arguments of the 1930s and the renewed debate of the 1970s on alternative approaches to social transformation suggests that the basic question of India's political economy remains what it was well over a generation ago. Can there be any method of transforming the entire social structure other than a direct attack on the propertied castes and classes?

# TWO

# Class Conciliation and Class Struggle: Competitive Patterns of Mass Mobilization in Indian Nationalism

It is common to speak of the Indian National Congress after 1920 as a mass organization. In that year, Congress abandoned the program of constitutional agitation it had followed for thirty-five years, and adopted a strategy of nonviolent noncooperation against the British government. The new methods of massive but peaceful civil disobedience, introduced under the leadership of Mahatma Gandhi, were intended to mobilize the passive millions of the rural population for effective boycotts of foreign goods, no-revenue campaigns, and other large-scale civil disobedience movements. An immediate requirement of the new techniques was drastic alteration in the structure and composition of the Congress.

Prior to 1920, the twelve Provincial Congress Committees (PCCs) were organized to coincide with the administrative boundaries of British India. These boundaries, cutting across linguistic regions, imposed knowledge of English as an implicit qualification for active membership in the Congress. The provincial committees, and the few district branches organized by them, were located in major cities and larger towns. Their members were drawn almost exclusively from the professional and business classes. No accurate estimates of Congress membership before 1921 are available. The total, however, was so small that no ceiling needed to be placed on the number of delegates that could attend the annual session. In 1920, the year of greatest controversy and interest in party affairs, fewer than 15,000 delegates attended the annual session.[1]

Striking changes occurred after 1920. Provincial party organizations were reorganized into twenty-one units, mainly in conformity with the major linguistic boundaries. Attempts were also made, as far as possible, to decentralize the party organization by constituting branches in every district and taluka[2] of British India. Simultaneously, Congress created a

[1] B. Pattabhi Sitaramayya, *The History of the Indian National Congress, 1885-1935*, p. 346.
[2] The taluka is a unit of revenue administration below the district level, and includes approximately 100,000 persons.

permanent source of revenue for full-time party work by introducing an annual membership fee of four annas per person.[3] In 1921, the year that Gandhi led the first national civil disobedience campaign against the British, membership in Congress climbed to a total of nearly two million.[4]

The effect of these structural changes on the urban bias of the Congress organization was immediate. It can be gauged from alterations in the membership of the All-India Congress Committee (AICC)—the national executive council of the provincial and district committees. In 1920, some 56.5 percent of the members of the AICC came from major cities and provincial towns in India. By 1923, this proportion was reduced to 34.6 percent, with a decisive majority of party activists hailing from small towns and rural areas.[5] The psychological impact of these changes, moreover, was sharply enhanced by Gandhi's insistence that party workers visibly identify themselves with the masses. Under his leadership, even the more urbane and Westernized nationalists adopted traditional styles of dress (the cotton dhoti instead of trousers), and forms of speech (Hindustani or other local dialects instead of English) at party meetings.

Yet, despite the fact that the constitutional changes facilitated the periodic mobilization of the peasantry in nationwide civil disobedience campaigns, the new party structure did not substantially alter the caste or class characteristics of the political leadership. The membership of the AICC continued to be drawn predominately from among upper-caste Hindus. Virtually all had Western-style education, and most had training in the professions—law, medicine, and journalism.[6]

Even at the local level, the great expansion of Congress membership did not signal any significant devolution of political power to the bulk of lower caste subsistence cultivators, tenant farmers, and landless laborers. The vast majority of four-anna members were admitted solely as "primary" members. Under the 1920 Congress constitution, however, only "active" members who met requirements for enrolling new members, raising funds, and carrying out other political and social welfare activities sponsored by Congress, were eligible to stand for party office. Primary members, moreover, could vote only for representatives to the lowest level of party organization, usually the taluka committee. In most cases, the taluka committees elected the District Congress Committees (DCCs); but the DCCs, in turn, had the greatest influence over the selection of the Provincial Congress Committees. Delegates to the annual session of Congress were elected by the District and Provincial Congress Committees. The All-India Congress Committee was elected by the an-

---

[3] This was the equivalent of about eight cents in 1920.

[4] Gopal Krishna, "The Development of the Indian National Congress as a Mass Organization, 1918-1923," p. 420.

[5] *Ibid.*, p. 423.                                    [6] *Ibid.*, pp. 423-24.

nual session. Further, except for the brief period between 1937 and 1939, when Congress took over the administration of local government in a number of provinces, the day-to-day supervision of the party organization was vested in the High Command—the president, elected by the AICC, and his hand-picked appointees on the Working Committee.

Such demographic data as is available on the Congress party leadership prior to Independence indicates that the new rural recruits were primarily drawn from the dominant landowning castes in the countryside. Indeed, the major effect on patterns of political leadership under the new organizational structure was to limit the power of small Brahmin elites in favor of the more numerous middle-ranking Sudra proprietor castes. This shift occurred in almost all parts of British India, but it was most dramatic in the south, where Brahmins historically were a small and unpopular minority.[7]

While Congress claimed to represent the masses, therefore, it never provided direct access to the party organization for the majority of the rural population. Throughout the pre-Independence period, the Provincial and District Congress Committees remained in the hands of the dominant landowning castes, in alliance with the middle-class urban intelligentsia, businessmen, and merchants.

One result of this was that the national leadership was constantly faced with a tactical (and moral) dilemma. Congress claimed to speak for the masses. In large measure, however, the party organization was controlled by the business classes in the cities and the landowning castes in the countryside. The intelligentsia, most of whom were committed to social and economic reform, feared the effects of splitting the nationalist forces by openly supporting tenants and landless laborers against landlords, and urban workers against industrialists. Under Gandhi's leadership, the dilemma was solved by emphasizing the role of Congress as a nationalist movement that could accommodate all groups and classes committed to achieving freedom from British rule. When class conflicts did erupt, the High Command's characteristic response was to try and arrange a compromise between the opposing groups in the hope that divisive social and economic issues could be postponed for consideration until after Independence.

The greatest challenge to Gandhi's policy of class conciliation developed in the rural sector. The social disruption created by the British decision to introduce private property rights in land resulted in a growing number of peasant agitations. Such conflicts were most common in those parts of British India where the Permanent Settlement (and its variation,

---

[7] The changing religious, caste, and social composition of the Congress party leadership during the pre-Independence period is analyzed in Stanley A. Kochanek, *The Congress Party of India*, pp. 319-41.

the Temporary Settlement) were in force. These land settlements, in large areas of the northern and central regions and portions of Madras in the south, had recognized the exclusive proprietary rights of zamindars. They were local notables who had originally served as tax collectors for the Mughals in return for the right to retain a fixed proportion of the total levy as a fee, but who had become petty overlords in the area under their jurisdiction as the power of the central government declined.[8] The zamindari settlements deprived the cultivator of his customary right to security of tenure[9] and converted him into a tenant-at-will. At the same time, the margin between the "settled" land revenue assessed by government on the zamindar and the competitive rent of land paid by the tenant ultimately became so large that a whole series of intermediaries developed between the peasant and the state, each of whom sold their rights of rent collection to middlemen below. It was estimated that the agricultural classes supporting this chain of rent receivers ultimately paid between fifty percent and sixty percent of their gross produce as rent.[10]

The condition of the peasantry was only somewhat better in the remaining part of British India, most of the southern and much of the

[8] An excellent summary of the Mughal system of tax collection and its collapse is found in Barrington Moore, Jr., *Social Origins of Dictatorship and Democracy*, pp. 314-30. A much more detailed treatment is presented in W. H. Moreland, *The Agrarian System of Moslem India*. The English East India Company, in 1757, recognized the exclusive proprietary rights of the zamindars of West Bengal, partly for reasons of administrative convenience. There were virtually no records of existing land rights and no official agency in the countryside. From the point of view of collecting taxes, therefore, the cooperation of the zamindars was desirable. To gain their support, Lord Cornwallis instituted the Permanent Settlement, vesting full rights of ownership in the zamindars, including those of free transfer and mortgage of land. In return, the zamindars agreed to pay the Company ten-elevenths of the revenue, fixed in perpetuity on the basis of estimates of payments actually collected in the past. The Permanent Settlement was modified in later revenue settlements into the Temporary Settlement. The revised version provided for the reassessment of land revenue rates every thirty years. Altogether, the zamindari system of land tenure was extended to roughly forty percent of British India, including half of Orissa and large parts of the United Provinces, Assam, and Rajputana in the north; Madhya Bharat, Bhopal, and Saurashtra in the central and western regions; and smaller sections of Madras in the south. These areas became part of the post-Independence states of Uttar Pradesh, Orissa, Bihar, Assam, Rajasthan, Madhya Pradesh, Gujerat, and Madras. The most comprehensive treatment of British land-revenue arrangements is B. H. Baden-Powell, *Land Systems of British India*, vols. II and III.

[9] Land rights in pre-British India were not defined by law. The ruler was entitled by custom to a fixed share of the produce in return for providing protection of life and property. At the same time, the cultivator was recognized to have security of tenure as long as he worked the land and paid the revenue. The village community was a third "right" holder. It had collective responsibility for payment of the land revenue; enjoyed ownership rights in uncultivated wastelands and common lands for grazing; and authority over all transfers of land to persons living outside the community. Indeed, individual holdings could not be freely sold or mortgaged, since they were considered to belong jointly to the male members of the family. For a comprehensive survey of landholding arrangements in pre-British India, see Baden-Powell, *Land Systems of British India*, vol. I.

[10] Manilal B. Nanavati and J. J. Anjaria, *The Indian Rural Problem*, p. 105.

western regions, where a ryotwari settlement was introduced vesting property rights directly in the ryot, or cultivator.[11] The smaller land-owner could now command much greater credit on the security of his holding. But spiraling interest charges on loans, ranging up to fifty per-cent or more per annum, condemned him to chronic indebtedness. In ex-tremity, his land was attached for payment and he continued to cultivate it, if at all, as a tenant-at-will of a large landlord or moneylender.[12]

By the late 1920s, objective class conflicts arose that could not be han-dled within the framework of the nationalist ideology. Radical groups emerged to take advantage of these developments and to agitate for revo-lutionary changes in the agrarian structure before Independence as the only real meaning of swaraj (freedom) for the masses. The efforts of socialists within Congress to organize class-based peasants and workers' associations independent of Congress control met with impressive suc-cess after the devastating depression of the 1930s. The push of the socialists within Congress to organize class-based peasants and workers' revolution, and the pull of the Gandhian leadership away from class struggle toward class conciliation, and an indirect attack on the social causes of exploitation under the Constructive Program, constituted the major source of internal tension within the nationalist movement before Independence.

Gandhi's insistence on nonviolent methods of social change has often been interpreted as simple expediency. The major argument advanced for this view is the leading role of Indian businessmen in financing the nationalist movement. Available information on the extent of business contributions to the Congress before Independence is fragmentary. But it is doubtful that the financial support of Indian industrialists was crucial to maintaining the day-to-day operations of the Congress party. Nehru, for one, vehemently denied this. In 1945, he wrote:

> Another frequent assertion almost taken for granted in British cir-
> cles and the British press is that the Indian Congress is heavily

---

[11] The principles of the Permanent and/or Temporary Settlement were abandoned in some areas, such as Bombay, the Punjab, and Madras, mainly because Hindu and Sikh overlords had been directly defeated by the British forces and there were no zamindars with whom to settle. As a result, in slightly more than half of British India, including most of the southern area and much of the regions of Madras, Mysore, Hyderabad, and Bombay, and parts of Assam and Madhya Bharat—areas concentrated in the post-Independence states of Madras, Mysore, Andhra Pradesh, Maharashtra, and parts of Madhya Pradesh and Assam—a ryotwari settlement was introduced, which vested proprietary rights directly in the ryot or cultivator. These settlements were fixed for a period of twenty or thirty years, after which they were revised.

[12] The actual extent of tenancy prior to Independence is uncertain. Nanavati and Anjaria, culling official reports and ad hoc investigations, claimed that as much as seventy-five per-cent of the cultivated area was operated by all classes of tenants in the 1940s. See the *Indian Rural Problem*, p. 197.

financed by the big industrialists. This is wholly untrue, and I ought
to know something about it, as I have been general secretary and
president of the Congress for many years. A few industrialists have
financially helped from time to time in the social reform activities of
Gandhi and the Congress, such as village industries, abolition of untouchability, and raising of depressed classes, basic education, etc.
But they have kept scrupulously aloof from the political work of the
Congress, even in normal times, and much more so during periods
of conflict with government. . . . Congress work has been carried on
almost entirely on the petty subscriptions and donations of its large
membership. Most of the work has been voluntary and unpaid.[13]

Nehru's assertion that the "normal" work of the Congress (for example, running district and provincial Congress offices, recruiting new
members, and distributing party literature) was financed mainly from
membership fees seems reasonable. At the same time, the industrialists
did play a more significant role in smoothing the path of the Congress
than this simple proposition suggests. Even Nehru conceded that in
1937, when the Congress decided to contest national and provincial elections, "some big industrialists" had to be solicited for contributions to
the central election fund.[14] Two other major qualifications to Nehru's
thesis are more important. First, Gandhi's firm refusal to condone an attack on the existing class structure made it feasible for Congress to recruit low-paid and voluntary upper-caste workers who carried the
greatest burden of party work. Second, and perhaps even more important, Gandhi's insistence on peaceful methods of change helped to attract
large ad hoc donations from the capitalist class for use in "nonpolitical"
social welfare work. And except for relatively brief periods, (in 1920-
1922, 1930-1933, and 1942-1945), when the national leadership organized
mass civil disobedience campaigns, day-to-day contacts with the rural
population rested heavily on the ability of Congress to support village-
level workers engaged in "constructive" activity.[15]

[13] Nehru, *The Discovery of India*, p. 495. J. B. Kripalani, who was secretary of the Congress party for twelve years prior to Independence, made virtually the same claim. Kripalani told the Lok Sabha on March 6, 1968, that he wanted to remove the "misconception
that capitalists financed the Congress" during the nationalist struggle. He said that "no
capitalists had given a [cent] to the Congress of those years. And I know it; I was the secretary of Congress for twelve years." Like Nehru, he affirmed that the industrialists had
made donations to Gandhi for welfare and similar activities, but that political work was
carried on by the four-anna subscriptions of the people. None of the full-time workers received more than Rs. 75 a month (about $24) "and we lived with utmost economy." *The
Statesman*, March 7, 1968.

[14] Nehru, *The Discovery of India*, p. 495.

[15] The All-India Village Industries Association was established by Gandhi in 1934. The
AIVIA employed its own cadre to carry on village-uplift activities, centering around the
establishment of hand spinning and supplementary industries; sanitation; health and education. A separate organization, the *Harijan Sevak Sangh*, was also formed by Gandhi to

Gandhi, in any event, was always appreciative of his cordial reception by prominent industrialists. He reported, with evident satisfaction, that at his request the rich "gladly" gave donations to the nationalist cause. He interpreted this generosity as a "triumph of non-violence, which I endeavor to represent."[16] It was Sir Ratan Tata who first came forward with substantial financial assistance for Gandhi's efforts on behalf of the Indian community in South Africa in the early 1900s.[17] Later, in 1917, when Gandhi was still experimenting with nonviolent methods of mass civil disobedience in India, it was the "well-to-do Biharis" and the Bombay merchants who financed the first no-tax campaign in the rural areas of their provinces.[18] After Gandhi took over the leadership of the nationalist movement in 1920, he continued to solicit the industrialists for special donations. Parsi and Marwari merchants of Bombay contributed most of the funds collected in 1920 for the Jalianwala Bagh memorial.[19] Bombay and Calcutta businessmen and merchants also contributed the lion's share of the approximately Rs. 12,450,000 Tilak Swaraj Fund in 1921,[20] which was used to support Congress political activities, including expansion of social welfare programs in village industries, basic education, and removal of untouchability. Indeed, throughout the Independence struggle, Gandhi continued to enjoy cordial personal relations with the major industrialists, including the Tatas, and Birlas, and with scores of lesser businessmen, merchants, and millowners in Calcutta, Bombay, and Ahmedabad.

Still, once all this is said, there is no decisive evidence that solicitude for the purses of the Indian business class is the best explanation for Gandhi's insistence on nonviolent techniques of social transformation. His public statements on the issue were most frequently couched in religious terms celebrating the ideal of *ahimsa* (noninjury), which precluded the use of violence as a moral method of resistance to evil. Related cultural attitudes almost certainly reinforced the religious motivation in his thinking. The traditional Hindu approach to conflict management, which emphasizes the moral superiority of arbitration and compromise in the settlement of disputes, links the preference for methods of class conciliation to religious ideals of self-control and nonviolence. Gandhi's personal attraction to a consensual style of conflict resolution was also consistent with his glorification of ancient village life. In his view, the village councils had protected traditional community values by relying on arbitra-

---

support workers engaged in welfare activities on behalf of untouchables or *Harijans* ("Children of God").

[16] M. K. Gandhi, *Towards Non-Violent Socialism* (Ahmedabad, 1951), p. 65.

[17] *Ibid.*, p. 57.

[18] M. K. Gandhi, *An Autobiography, The Story of My Experiments with Truth*, p. 417.

[19] *Ibid.*, p. 487.

[20] Gopal Krishna, "Development of The Indian National Congress," p. 426.

tional techniques in settling disputes. Judges had always been more concerned with finding a compromise solution acceptable to both sides than with strict enforcement of justice based on the merits of the case. In this way, the village community was spared the group tensions, factional polarization, and decline in social cohesion associated with a direct confrontation between opponents under adversary procedures.[21]

Gandhi's commitment to nonviolence as a strategy of social change was, however, even more complex in motivation than a review of these considerations suggest. Closer examination of his writings reveals an unmistakable strain of political realism in his decision to reject class struggle methods in Indian conditions.

Perhaps the most characteristic—and to many the most puzzling aspect of Gandhi's approach—was his insistence that "political'" and "social" grievances be handled separately. He steadfastly refused to advance the nationalist cause by organizational techniques that capitalized on the economic complaints of tenant-cultivators against British-created landlords; or of factory workers against Indian industrialists, even though the latter often called on English police and other officials to break up strikes and resist unionization. At the same time, Gandhi was unrelenting in requiring all Congressmen to take part in "constructive work" for the uplift of depressed classes in the villages. Indeed, while mass political agitations were sporadic in character, and might be suspended according to circumstance, Congressmen were instructed to carry on constructive work at all times.

This tactical separation of social and political issues appears to have taken shape in Gandhi's mind as a result of his first experience with civil disobedience in an isolated section of rural Bihar in 1917. In the previous year, while Gandhi was attending the annual session of Congress in Lucknow, he had been approached by an agriculturist from Champaran district, who told a grim tale of exploitation of tenant farmers by British plantation owners. Apart from a number of illegal levies that the planters managed to exact, the major cause of the cultivator's distress was the *tinkathia* system—the requirement under law that each tenant plant about one-seventh of every acre with indigo for the landlord. Gandhi agreed to travel to Champaran in his personal capacity and to investigate the grievances of the peasants. When he arrived he was not surprised to discover that the charges of economic exploitation were essentially correct. More revealing was the insight he gained into the cause of the peasants' misery.

[21] In actual fact, as numerous writers have pointed out, the "consensus" reached in such proceedings was often a spurious one, and involved covert favoritism and coercion as a result of the relative differences in status and power among competing groups. Nevertheless, even the appearance of consensus could be highly valued because it protected the legitimacy of solidarity norms. See Ralph H. Retzlaff, *Village Government in India* (Bombay, 1962), pp. 13-26.

In one sense, of course, the explanation was obvious. British planters, with ready access to the provincial government and overriding influence in local administration, had succeeded in getting the *tinkathia* provisions written into law, and could readily enforce them against recalcitrant cultivators by calling on local police power. At a deeper level, Gandhi perceived that such arrangements could indefinitely endure only because the peasants were so crushed and fear-stricken; and that, in turn, the ease with which they were terrorized could be traced to their ignorance and the generally debilitating circumstances of their environment. Apart from the pervasive problem of illiteracy in Champaran, Gandhi found "the villages were insanitary, the lanes full of filth, the wells surrounded by mud and stink and the courtyards unbearably untidy. The elder people badly needed education in cleanliness. They were all suffering from various skin diseases."[22]

Various options were open to Gandhi in these circumstances. He could have responded to the peasants' complaints by interpreting the *tinkathia* system and the general condition of the cultivators as symbols of British exploitation, thereby converting the economic grievances of the tenants into an anti-British or pro-Congress movement. Equally plausible, given his social and economic philosophy, he could have used the occasion to challenge the legitimacy of an entire system of land relations that permitted a handful of land owners to exploit the thousands of landless tenants who worked on the farms.

It is striking that Gandhi did neither of these two things. On the contrary, he decided "not to mention the name of the Congress and not to acquaint the peasants with the organization called the Congress." Second, he made every effort to conciliate the planters by "writing to and meeting such of them against whom allegations of a serious nature were made," and by requesting a meeting with the Planters' Association in order to "know the planters' side of the case."[23] Finally, when the division commissioner, yielding to protests from the planters, threatened Gandhi with arrest if he did not leave the area and abandon his investigation, Gandhi painstakingly made it clear that his sole purpose in coming to Champaran was to investigate any "social" injustice that might exist, with specific reference to the *tinkathia* system.

Gandhi's reasons for adopting this approach emerge from his own account of the episode. Any use of the name of the Congress would have immediately provoked a solid alliance between the government and the planters on resistance to his activities. "For the name of the Congress was the bête noire of the Government and their controllers—the planters. To them the Congress was a byword for lawyers' wrangles, evasion of law

---

[22] Gandhi, *An Autobiography*, p. 421.       [23] *Ibid.*, p. 418.

through legal loopholes, a byword for bomb and anarchical crime and for diplomacy and hypocrisy."[24] If such an alliance had occurred, Gandhi would have been arrested, possibly imprisoned, and certainly deported from the district. His inquiry would have come to naught. The peasants, in their existing state of ignorance and fear, would have experienced even greater suffering at the hands of the wrathful planters. Gandhi's best hope of being effective, therefore, was, as he said, "to see that the Government should remain neutral."[25] This he accomplished in two ways: first, by preventing the struggle from "assuming a political aspect" that would alarm the authorities;[26] and second, by reducing the pressure on the administration from the planters through conciliatory actions that shattered unity within their own ranks so that, as Gandhi reported, while "some of the planters hated me, some were indifferent and a few treated me with courtesy."[27] In Champaran, this strategy proved to be a brilliant success. Within days of his arrival, the police superintendent, as expected, served notice on Gandhi to quit the area or stand trial for disobeying an official order. Gandhi chose arrest and trial—in itself an unprecedented instance of civil disobedience—but before any sentence could be imposed, the lieutenant governor intervened to order the case withdrawn. Subsequently, the district collector wrote Gandhi to say he might conduct his inquiry. As a result, for the first time in living memory, thousands of peasants publicly appeared to give testimony (in the presence of police officers) of abuses they had silently suffered for over a hundred years. Ultimately, the lieutenant governor actually invited Gandhi to sit on an official commission to enquire into the merits of the peasants' case. Finally, on the unanimous recommendation of the members of the commission, the *tinkathia* system was legally abolished.

This was, undoubtedly, a spectacular victory. But as Gandhi was the first to realize, it did not significantly alter the balance of social power in Champaran district, or decisively change the impoverished circumstances of the villagers. As he gained more experience of Bihar, Gandhi concluded that permanent improvement in the situation of the peasantry was not possible without an assault on the social evils that made them such an easy target for intimidation. Any effective program of "village uplift," however, could only be sustained by the villagers' own efforts, and this would take years of patient work to organize. Out of his experience at Champaran, Gandhi developed the idea of the Constructive Program. Immediately after he took charge of the nationalist movement, constructive work became an integral part of Congress activities. It included as many as eighteen different items of self-help, the most impor-

[24] *Ibid.*, p. 412.
[26] *Ibid.*, p. 415.
[25] *Ibid.*, p. 414.
[27] *Ibid.*, p. 418.

tant being revival of khadi (hand-spun cotton) and other village industries, removal of untouchability, basic education, Hindu–Muslim unity, uplift of women, prohibition, village sanitation, and health.[28] Most of the initial work was carried on by Congress volunteers in the villages, who were expected to give simple instruction in medical aid, personal hygiene, sanitation, and even in spinning and weaving or other hand industries. The essential aim, however, was to develop a local leadership cadre capable of taking over the administration of these programs on a permanent basis.

Champaran proved to be a seminal experience for Gandhi in another respect, as well. He believed that the tactic of class conciliation, which had proved so effective in containing active opposition by British planters to "social reform" activities in Bihar, could also be applied to Indian landlords in a way that would advance both the nationalist and egalitarian objectives of the Independence movement, and still avoid a split along class lines. One of Gandhi's first opportunities to test this theory came later in the same year, when reports reached him that severe floods in Kheda district of his native Gujerat had led to widespread damage of the crops. The dominant landowning caste of Patidars were insisting that the crop failure was sufficiently extensive to qualify them for full suspension of revenue assessments under the provisions of the Land Revenue Rules. Local officials denied these claims and insisted on full payment. When petitions to the district collector, the Bombay Legislative Council, and even to the governor were unavailing, Gandhi advised the Patidars to resort to civil disobedience.

In a number of respects, the situation in Kheda was substantially different from Champaran. First, there was no opportunity of blunting the government's opposition to the agitation. Congress had openly sponsored the peasants' cause; and the progress of the dispute was receiving full-scale coverage in the press. Secondly, in Kheda, governmental prerogatives were under direct attack: the agitation was organized against payment of land revenue to the state, not against rents or other levies raised by governmental proxies, such as the planters of Bihar. There was no question, therefore, of conducting the campaign purely as a "social" movement without political overtones.

There was a more serious complication. Whereas the tenant farmers of Champaran had formed a homogenous economic group, the Patidar cultivators of Kheda district were differentiated by varying degrees of affluence based on the size of their landholdings. Even though there had been

---

[28] Other items were adult education, service of backward tribes, propagation of the national language, love of one's native language, working for economic equality, organization of peasant, labor, and student groups, and nature cure.

a universal failure of crops, many of the larger landowners could have paid the land revenue assessment without much strain. Other smaller landholders faced very great economic hardship. The Patidars, potentially at least, were divided by internal differences based on "class" lines. In fact, in some cases, the larger agriculturists faced greater losses through nonpayment of revenue (as a result of government retaliation through attachment of movable property, cattle, standing crops, and fines) than by paying the assessment. At the same time, the success of the no-tax campaign depended on the willingness of all agriculturists to present a united front. Once the larger landlords paid the land revenue tax, local authorities would find little difficulty in intimidating the smaller farmers to do the same. The Congress party would stand discredited. The nationalist cause would suffer. And the poorest cultivators would bear the greatest brunt of the failure. In Kheda, therefore, both nationalist and egalitarian values demanded the subordination of class interests to common goals.

As in Champaran, Gandhi set out to conciliate the larger landlords. This time, however, he was operating in an orthodox Hindu milieu, and he framed his appeal in terms of the ancient Hindu concept of *dharma*— the notion of moral duty allied to relative standing in the caste hierarchy. Using religious language, Gandhi reminded the well-to-do classes of their sacred obligation to do *yagna* or sacrifice, and to use their wealth charitably on behalf of the poor. The Kheda *satyagraha* thus saw the beginnings of what later emerged as Gandhi's theory of trusteeship—his answer to the Marxists who claimed that class war was the only effective instrument of social revolution. On the surface, the trusteeship doctrine appeared painfully naive as an instrument of social transformation. It emphasized voluntary reform through the moral regeneration of the exploiting classes. Gandhi appealed to the religious conscience of Hindu elites, and expressed the belief that the propertied castes could be "converted" into acting as "trustees" of society in the responsible use of their wealth on behalf of the masses.[29]

But the implications of the trusteeship doctrine were more far-reaching than its critics allowed. Even stated in its most innocuous form as a variant of the sacred obligation of *yagna*, it subtly encouraged a shift in the basis of legitimacy of the upper castes. Ascriptive status, standing alone, was no longer sufficient to bestow political authority. This was instead justified according to moral standards of public behavior. Foremost among these was the duty of the propertied castes to use their

---

[29] Gandhi's writings on the theory of trusteeship are scattered throughout his work. A reasonably coherent sampling is contained in Gandhi, *Socialism of My Conception*, pp. 198-306. The term *satyagraha*, coined by Gandhi, refers to nonviolent civil disobedience and is usually translated "holding fast to truth" or "truth-force."

resources to provide for the minimum well-being of the poor. The reciprocal of this duty was the *right* of the low-status landless castes to demand
that the elites allocate resources held for the use of all in equitable fashion.
The trusteeship doctrine, therefore, was the first step in reinterpreting
the traditional notion of social obligation from a sacred concept enjoining
the upper castes to act charitably on behalf of the poor as part of their
religious responsibility to a secular ethic of equality, in which the
propertied castes, transformed into "trustees" of the common pat-
rimony, were by implication subject to removal by the major part of society if they failed to honor their trust.

The trusteeship doctrine, allied to the Constructive Program, moreover, actually held revolutionary implications for the distribution of economic and political power. Once the new (secular) ethic of equality was
accepted at the level of public opinion, the peasantry and workers had
only to develop the strength inherent in their numbers to enforce the
transvalued norm against the propertied classes. The Constructive Program, by weakening the links of dependence binding the peasantry to the
dominant landed castes—by improving their physical condition through
better sanitation and medical facilities, increasing their income through
revival of village industries, and most important, raising their level of
political awareness and capacity for united action through basic education—provided the organizational framework for application of a "nonviolent" sanction for social reform. The propertied castes, their legitimacy eroded, their numbers few, once faced by the organized and potentially overwhelming power of the majority, would voluntarily concede
reforms, and the "conversion" would take place.

The budding theory of trusteeship, stated in its most rudimentary
form, is evident in the pledge that all participants in the Kheda no-tax
campaign were required to sign. It read:

> Knowing that the crops of our villages are less than four annas, we
> requested the Government to suspend the collection of revenue as-
> sessment till the ensuing year, but the Government has not acceded
> to our prayer. Therefore, we, the undersigned, hereby solemnly de-
> clare that we shall not, of our own accord, pay to the Government
> the full or the remaining revenue for the year. We shall let the Gov-
> ernment take whatever legal steps it may think fit and gladly suffer
> the consequences of our non-payment. We shall rather let our lands
> be forfeited than by voluntary payment we should allow our case to
> be considered false or should compromise our self-respect. *Should
> the Government, however, agree to suspend collection of the second install-
> ment of the assessment throughout the district, such amongst us as are in a
> position to pay will pay up the whole of the balance of the revenue that may*

*be due. The reason why those who are able to pay still withhold payment is that, if they pay up, the poorer ryots may in a panic sell their chattels or incur debts to pay their dues, and thereby bring suffering upon themselves. In these circumstances, we feel that for the sake of the poor, it is the duty of those who can afford to pay to withhold payment of their assessment.*[30]

The Kheda *satyagraha* represented the first test in a traditional Hindu setting of nonviolence as a technique of political and social change. The results are therefore particularly interesting to note. They were, according to Gandhi's own admission, less satisfactory than the outcome at Champaran. Many of the landowners did prove vulnerable to government attachments of cattle, other movables, and standing crops, and paid their assessment. Gandhi finally became so discouraged that he doubted the campaign could be continued. He recalled that the people were "frightened and exhausted," and that he was actually "casting about for some graceful way of terminating the struggle"[31] when, through a stroke of good fortune, the collector suddenly agreed to suspend revenue payments for the poorer cultivators if the rest of the well-to-do Patidars honored their pledge to pay back dues. Gandhi agreed, but despite his apparent victory, he wrote, "the end was far from making me happy." The collector retained the prerogative of determining who was to be granted relief. As a result, said Gandhi, "the poor were to be granted suspension, but hardly any got the benefit of it."[32] Nevertheless, he did perceive some gains. The no-tax campaign had produced a new political awareness among the poor cultivators of Gujerat, and an unprecedented sense of social solidarity, if only for a brief period of time. In these two respects, it advanced both the political and social goals of the nationalist movement. Moreover, a few of the most destitute farmers had actually experienced some economic relief.

A second major opportunity to test the advantages—and limitations—of a nonviolent strategy of social reform was provided by the Ahmedabad labor strike of 1919. The situation, Gandhi reported, was "most delicate." On the one hand, the mill-hands' demands for higher wages and better working conditions were demonstrably justified. On the other, the millowners, his personal friends, rejected advice to submit the dispute to arbitration. In the end, Gandhi agreed to lead the laborers in a strike only if they accepted certain conditions. The foremost among these was the pledge of strikers never to resort to violence, and never to attack strikebreakers. Once again, however, after the strike had continued for twenty-one days, and the millowners showed no sign of relenting, Gandhi reported that the strikers showed "signs of flagging." He

[30] Gandhi, *An Autobiography*, p. 435. Emphasis added.
[31] *Ibid.*, p. 439.                        [32] *Ibid.*, p. 439.

wrote: "their attitude toward the blacklegs became more and more menacing as the strike seemed to weaken, and I began to fear an outbreak of rowdyism on their part. The attendance at the daily meetings also began to dwindle by degrees, and despondence and despair were writ large on the faces of those who did attend. Finally, the information was brought to me that the strikers had begun to totter."[33]

At this point, Gandhi adopted a tactic that was not free of a "very grave defect." He declared that he would not touch any food until the strike was settled, even while recognizing that "I enjoyed very close and cordial relations with millowners, and my fast could not but affect their decision . . . to fast against them would amount to coercion. Yet, in spite of my knowledge that my fast was bound to put pressure upon them as in fact it did, I felt I could not help it."[34]

Within three days of the beginning of Gandhi's fast, the millowners announced they would agree to arbitration. Once more, the settlement was celebrated as a victory. But in actual fact, Gandhi's nonviolent techniques had failed to resolve a class conflict. The settlement came about only after he had changed the balance between contending forces by weighing his own life on the side of the strikers.

Even in this instance, however, Gandhi was able to perceive some progress in the aftermath of the 1918 strike. As part of the settlement, the Millowners Association of Ahmedabad recognized the Textile Labor Union, and agreed to set up a permanent arbitration board for the settlement of future disputes. In 1923, the millowners arbitrarily announced a wage reduction of fifteen percent. The labor union demanded full restoration of the cut. The millowners, who had refused to recognize arbitration procedures as a legitimate method of settling employer-labor disputes in 1917, this time did not resort to a lockout, and permitted an umpire to be appointed. The umpire, in his report, established that the average wage of textile workers was about twenty percent less than their expenses, and that even if the entire cut were restored the workers would still not have a living wage. Further, he set down the principle that "when the worker does not get enough wages to enable him to maintain a suitable standard of living, he can ask his employer to pay him wages which would enable him to do so."[35] Paradoxically, however, the umpire recommended only partial restoration of the cut. He cited the mitigating factor that the textile industry was less prosperous in 1923 than immediately after the war, when the previous wage settlement had been made.

Gandhi's reaction to these events is revealing. He found it difficult to understand why the entire cut was not restored, especially since the re-

---

[33] *Ibid.*, p. 430.                                    [34] *Ibid.*, p. 432.
[35] Gandhi, *Towards Non-Violent Socialism*, p. 72.

duced prosperity of the mill industry was a function of only lesser profits, not of loss or encroachment on capital. At the same time, he found that the umpire's endorsement of the *principle* of a living wage was tantamount to a major victory for labor. And he was gratified that some concession had been made without recourse to a long, costly, and divisive strike. He summarized his feelings in the following statement:

> But the men are wedded to the principle of arbitration and therefore they must cheerfully submit to the Umpire's decision even though they do not get the full restoration of the cut. They must thankfully accept what the Diwan Bahadur has allowed, and perseveringly and peacefully work for the balance. Indeed there can be no rest for them or the employers so long as a living wage is not actually reached and better housing and other ordinary comforts are not secured. But it will be a great gain if strikes become unnecessary and the principle of arbitration is strictly adhered to by both parties.[36]

Gandhi went even further toward conciliating the millowners in subsequent advice to the labor union. He praised the workers for dropping their demands for higher pay, citing the "difficult situation of the millowners at the present moment."[37] He emphasized the duty of the laborers to "assure to the mills flawless work" under all circumstances. Nevertheless, he insisted that the workers pursue major improvements in their condition by self-help activities carried out by a strong union in a kind of urban equivalent to the Constructive Program. He suggested, for example, that the Textile Labor Union could lend members credit on easy terms, provide hospital and other medical services, and sell cheap supplies of consumer goods. He even predicted that once the laborers had convinced the millowners of their constructive attitude, they would find their employers more receptive to remedying legitimate complaints. Above all, as in Champaran and Kheda, Gandhi made it clear that the capitalist system was not under attack. Rather, limited "social" and "economic" issues—working conditions and wages for laborers—were being raised. When, for instance, Gandhi praised Sir Ratan Tata "as a human and considerate employer . . . who readily granted . . . all the prayers of the employees at Jamshedpur"—and commended his example to the millowners of Ahmedabad—the concrete concessions he cited were the provision of clean water and proper disposal of sewage for the workers.[38]

It would, of course, be naive to ignore the immediate political considerations that influenced Gandhi's cautious tactics. There is no doubt that class-based nationalist organization would have splintered the independ-

---

[36] *Ibid.*, p. 73.          [37] *Ibid.*, p. 61.
[38] *Ibid.*, pp. 62, 65.

ence movement. There was even the prospect that the propertied classes would join forces with the British government to oppose the Congress. Such an alliance would probably have resulted in much greater—and more effective—use of repressive measures against the poorer peasantry and workers, and substantially retarded the progress of the nationalist cause. Similarly, Gandhi's reluctance to use labor strikes or rural no-rent campaigns for nationalist political purposes can be explained in part by his fear that the class issue, once raised, would release explosive forces in the country that Congress might not be able to control. Again, apart from his moral aversion to violence, Gandhi could not help but conclude that internal war would benefit the British and substantially retard the achievement of Independence.

Yet, even when all these considerations are taken into account, Gandhi's commitment to a nonviolent political strategy appears rooted in more than religious and cultural sentiments, or the pragmatic calculus of short-term political costs and benefits. On the contrary, Gandhi firmly believed that a direct attack on the propertied classes—either in action or words—would in the long run have a disastrous effect on political development in India.

It is certainly worth noting, for example, that Gandhi's glorification of the Hindu peasant as the repository of an ancient spiritual wisdom was inspired mainly by imaginings of what the villager had been and could become again in the absence of both indigenous and imported corruptions. The peasant as he was profoundly distressed, and even frightened Gandhi. He comprehended that once aroused, impoverished millions—ignorant, degraded, and simmering with centuries of pent-up hostilities and hatreds—could easily overwhelm their tormentors and take a terrible revenge. With this haunting vision in view, Gandhi pleaded with the landlord class to "read the signs of the times (and) revise their notion of God-given right to all they possess." He warned bluntly: "there is no other choice than between voluntary surrender on the part of the capitalist of superfluities and consequent acquisition of the real happiness of all on the one hand, and on the other, the impending chaos into which, if the capitalist does not wake up be times, awakened but ignorant and famishing millions will plunge the country and which, not even the armed force that a powerful government can bring into play can avert."[39]

Gandhi was no more sanguine about the capacities of desperate factory workers to resist the appeals of radical rhetoric and take to purely destructive violence. He pointed out: "in the struggle between capital and labor, it may generally be said that more often than not, the capitalists are in the wrong box. But when labor comes fully to realize its strength, I

[39] *Ibid.*, p. 144.

know it can become more tyrannical than capital. . . . The question before us is this: When the laborers, remaining as they are, develop a certain consciousness, what should be their course? It would be suicidal if the laborers rely only on their numbers or brute—force, i.e., violence. By so doing, they will do harm to industries in the country."[40]

Moreover, the most likely alternative to mass violence in a situation of revolutionary threat appeared equally undesirable. Gandhi believed that the propertied classes, frightened by the "unrestrained language" of socialist agitators, could begin to "organize themselves and establish Fascism in our country." In fact, in 1934, he claimed that his insistence on nonviolent techniques had already "checked the advent of Fascism in our country." "In a way," he observed, "Fascism does exist in our country even today, but so far not many of the rich have joined it. Those who have understood I am their friend do not join such organizations. How can they organize against me?"[41]

Certainly, this self-conscious consideration of how to avoid either of these outcomes influenced Gandhi's selection of political techniques. The crux of his analysis was that the approach of class conciliation embodied in the trusteeship doctrine, when combined with an *indirect* attack on the causes of exploitation through the Constructive Program, had both immediate and long-term political and social advantages over class struggle methods in Indian conditions. First, they would win independence for India in the shortest possible time by harnessing the energies of all classes to the nationalist cause. Second, they would ultimately bring about a social revolution through peaceful methods without sacrificing the other goals of the independence movement: social cohesion, economic progress, and political liberty.

Although Gandhi's technique of nonviolent social transformation did not directly attack the economic foundations of mass exploitation, it nevertheless held potentially revolutionary implications for the prerogatives of the propertied classes. The dominant landowning castes might retain their private holdings; but they would find it increasingly difficult to use their monopoly over land against the interest of an informed, united, and organized peasantry. In his later writings, Gandhi elaborated on what he called the "nonviolent sanction" of an enlightened and cohesive tenantry against exploitation by the landowning classes. He posed this case:

> Supposing a landowner exploits his tenants and mulcts them of
> the fruit of their toil by appropriating it to his uses. . . . [The
> tenants] will quit if asked to do so but they will make it clear that the

[40] Gandhi, *Socialism of My Conception*, p. 248. In the wider context of the passage, Gandhi describes the laborers as lacking "intelligence" and "tact."
[41] *Ibid.*, p. 248.

land belongs to him who tills it. The owner cannot till all the land himself and he will have to give in to their just demands. It may, however, be that the tenants are replaced by others. Agitation short of violence will then continue till the replacing tenants see their error and make common cause with the evicted tenants. Thus, *Satyagraha is a process of educating public opinion, such that it covers all the elements of society and in the end makes itself irresistible.*[42]

Elsewhere he was more blunt. He says it "can be asked whether the present Rajas and others can be expected to become trustees of their own accord." Gandhi's answer is a model of political realism. He points out: "if [the propertied class] do not become trustees of their own accord, force of circumstances will compel the reform unless they court utter destruction . . . *public opinion will do what violence can never do. The present power of the Zamindars, the capitalists, and the Rajas can hold sway only so long as the common people do not realize their own strength. If the people non-cooperate with the evil of zamindari or capitalism it must die of inanition.*"[43] Similarly, he says of his approach to labor-employer relations: "the idea is to take from capital labor's due share and no more, and this, not by paralyzing capital, but by reform among laborers from within and by their own self-consciousness; not again through the cleverness and maneuvering of non-labor leaders, but by *educating labor to evolve its own leadership and its own self-reliant, self-existing organization. Its direct aim is internal reform and evolution of internal strength. The indirect result of this evolution, when and if it ever becomes complete, will naturally be tremendously political.*"[44]

The pace of social change envisaged by this strategy was, of course, very slow. In its earliest stages, it amounted to nothing more than piecemeal amelioration of the worst living and working conditions of the masses. Yet, in Gandhi's view, the very gradualness of the process was its greatest advantage. Gradualism was the surest, and in the long run perhaps even the shortest route to achieving equality. "Violence," Gandhi argued, "interrupts the process and prolongs the real revolution of the social structure."[45] He believed that violence in India would lead to a prolonged interregnum of internal war; and that in the process scarce material resources would be destroyed that might otherwise be used to create the conditions of prosperity for all classes.

Gandhi's strategy of nonviolent revolution had two essential prerequisites for success. First, there could be no direct attack on the institution of private property. On the contrary, the propertied classes had to be con-

---

[42] Gandhi, *Towards Non-Violent Socialism*, p. 149. Emphasis added.
[43] *Ibid.*, p. 157. Emphasis added.
[44] Gandhi, *Socialism of My Conception*, p. 215. Emphasis added.
[45] Gandhi, *Towards Non-Violent Socialism*, p. 149.

stantly reassured that social reform did not involve their own destruction. They might even be induced to cooperate by a traditional religious appeal, and contribute their own resources to the "social uplift" of depressed classes. In any event, the strategy of gradualism would minimize immediate losses to the upper classes. They would have a long period of time to adjust to relative changes in social power. At no point would they feel driven to desperate action by the prospect of total disaster. Second, and equally important to a successful outcome, the aspirations of the masses had to be contained. It was necessary to discourage any exaggerated notions of radical betterment on the part of peasants and workers, and to focus their attention on the amelioration of the most pressing social evils. Even for these modest purposes, moreover, Gandhi gave special importance to self-help measures that could be carried out through cooperative action, largely with the resources at hand, and with only marginal infusions of additional wealth, either from the propertied classes or government.

In Gandhi's view, the long-term benefits of this strategy were so great that they more than compensated for any immediate sacrifice in the progress toward egalitarian goals. By reassuring the propertied classes on the one hand, and damping down popular aspirations on the other, the government could mobilize the energies of the entire nation for constructive tasks of development. Part of the additional resources thus created could be set aside to meet the aspirations of the poor, and to modify the sharp cutting edge of social reform on the fortunes of the upper classes. Ultimately, Gandhi believed, the strategy of gradualism, as embodied in the trusteeship doctrine and the Constructive Program, offered India her best hope of defending democratic political institutions against either a communist-led insurgency from below, or a preemptive fascist-style coup carried out by the capitalist classes from above.

The complex of these considerations weighed heavily in Gandhi's selection of political tactics in the organization of the national civil disobedience campaigns. He deliberately attempted to submerge the class issue by confining no-tax campaigns to ryotwari areas, where nonpayment of land revenue, not rent, was made the focal point of peasant mobilization for civil resistance. Yet, after Bardoli,[46] the most widely

[46] Bardoli taluka in Surat district of Gujarat was chosen for a mass civil disobedience campaign in 1927 after the Government of Bombay announced a twenty-two percent increase in land revenue assessment, considered unreasonable by the cultivating castes and the Bardoli taluka Congress Committee. Under Gandhi's leadership, the peasants were advised to suspend payment until the government either appointed an impartial tribunal to investigate the true condition of the taluka, or announced acceptance of the old rates. Congress workers were careful not to attack the class structure, even though the landless and other backward classes were in the majority and the condition of some of the untouchables was close to "bonded serfdom." Even so, the "class" issue was raised when an unexpected split occurred between the Patidars, a cultivating caste, and the Baniyas, a money-lending and

publicized of the no-tax campaigns, it became increasingly difficult to maintain the practical distinction between government oppression in the form of land revenue taxes, and oppression by zamindars and other landlords in the form of high rental and illegal exactions. In Bardoli, "cultivators were told for the first time that it was quite legitimate to refuse to pay land revenue, the payment of which they had come to look upon almost as a religious duty. To them, Swaraj meant freedom from all tax burdens, and especially the abolition of land revenue." After Bardoli, "peasants in other parts of India began spontaneously to refuse payment of land revenue and rent."[47] Moreover, the future prospect of suppressing class antagonism was further compromised by the emergence in the most impoverished region of British India of a militant socialist group within the Congress party organization.

The United Provinces of Agra and Oudh, the poorest area in British India, was characterized by a zamindari form of land tenure and various grades of zamindars. Several hundreds owned vast estates; many more thousands had middle and small holdings. In Agra, the zamindars held about one-fifth of the land under personal cultivation. Another one-half was cultivated by occupancy tenants created under the 1926 Tenancy Act, and the remainder by statutory tenants who had no heritable rights. In Oudh, the situation was worse. About eleven percent of the land was held by the zamindars for personal cultivation. The remainder was farmed by tenants, the great majority of whom did not have permanent or heritable rights in their holdings.

The average tenant-cultivator in the United Provinces worked only between 2.5 and 4 acres of land. An investigation by the United Provinces Provincial Congress Committee in 1931 revealed that after consideration for cost of cultivation per acre, the real value of produce—with only subsistence-level deductions for food and clothing—was not

---

trading community owning considerable areas of land in the taluka, which they generally rented to the Patidars. Unlike the Patidars, the Baniyas did not, in most cases, bear the costs of cultivation, and were not faced with particular hardship if they conceded the government's demand for higher land revenue payments. Rather than suffer immediate loss of property and money through government fines and confiscations if they joined the non-cooperation campaign, many of them deserted their hard-pressed Patidar counterparts, and paid the land revenue assessment. Virtually overnight, however, they found themselves the victims of a general boycott organized by the Patidars, who resolved not to cultivate the land of the Baniyas on lease; and prevented their agricultural laborers from working on it. The boycott was effective, and the Baniyas rejoined the movement. In the end, the government was forced to appoint an official enquiry committee, which conceded virtually all of the peasants' demands, canceling fines and penalties that had already been collected. See Narhari D. Parikh, *Sardar Vallabhai Patel* (Ahmedabad, 1953), I, 157, 314; Peshotan Nasserwanji Driver, *Problems of Zamindari and the Land Tenure Reconstruction in India* (Bombay, 1949), p. 92.

[47] N. G. Ranga, *History of the Kisan Movement*, p. 35.

enough in three major divisions of the province to meet additional charges for rent and debt; in a fourth, the "surplus" was Rs. 24.7 a year.[48] In terms of subsistence alone, the average cultivator in Jhansi, Gorakpur, and Lucknow divisions required an additional Rs. 50-70 per year just to "keep his body and soul together."[49] Further, in addition to rent and debt, the tenants of the United Provinces were liable to all kinds of feudal dues and illegal "taxes," including *begar* or forced labor, placing them among the most exploited cultivators in India.

The Congress was therefore faced with a difficult political decision when it organized a national civil disobedience movement in March 1930. If it called for a general no-tax campaign in rural areas, it would, on the one hand, help the tenants in zamindari regions by indirectly legitimizing the suspension of rent payment as well; on the other hand, it would raise the class issue. This was the decisive point for Gandhi, and he ordered the no-tax campaign confined to ryotwari areas.

In the United Provinces, this decision was immediately questioned. The Provincial Congress Committee contained a strong socialist contingent. Nehru, by then general secretary of the National Congress, was also a member of the Executive Council of the Provincial Congress Committee. He and some of his colleagues in the Allahabad District Congress Committee had previously declared—as early as 1926—that they favored the complete abolition of the zamindari system. The situation was particularly delicate because both the president and the general secretary of the PCC were prominent zamindars. In early 1930, Gandhi's position prevailed. The zamindars were privately urged to grant rent remissions to tenants in situations of extreme hardship. A small number of zamindars did announce voluntary rent remissions as a result of Gandhi's appeal.

Shortly after, both Gandhi and Nehru were arrested for their part in the civil disobedience campaign. When Nehru was released from prison in October 1930, he saw in the desperate situation of the cultivators of the United Provinces an opportunity to dramatize the important social issues involved in Swaraj by extending the no-tax campaign to a zamindari area. With Gandhi still in prison, he acted on his own initiative, and with the support of colleagues in Allahabad, to convene a meeting of the Executive Council of the Provincial Congress Committee. After long debate, Nehru succeeded in obtaining the committee's permission for any district in the United Provinces to announce a no-tax campaign. The committee decided to direct its appeal both to zamindars and tenants in an effort to avoid the class issue, but Nehru was certain that the main

---

[48] Indian National Congress, United Provinces Congress Committee, *Agrarian Distress in the United Provinces*, pp. 29-42.
[49] *Ibid.*, p. 35.

response would come from the peasantry. He subsequently recalled: "our appeal had been addressed both to zamindars and tenants not to pay; in theory, it was not a class appeal. In practice, most of the zamindars did pay their revenue, even some who sympathized with the national struggle. The pressure on them was great, and they had more to lose. The tenantry, however, stood firm and did not pay, and our campaign became practically a no-rent campaign."[50]

In March 1931, after the no-tax campaign had spread into several districts of the United Provinces, Gandhi, in preparation for the Second Round Table Conference, announced the nationwide suspension of the civil disobedience movement. With the end of the nationalist struggle, the zamindars, many of whom had not pressed the peasants for payment, began to demand rent. The Provincial Congress, unwilling to abandon the cultivators, declared they would negotiate with the government for revenue remissions to the zamindars, which could be passed on to the tenants in the form of reduced rent. On March 13, the Provincial Congress Committee adopted a resolution recommending sixty percent remission of rent to statutory tenants, fifty percent to occupancy tenants, and a corresponding reduction in the revenue demand upon zamindars.

These negotiations were unsuccessful. The provincial government, unwilling to add to Congress' prestige, refused to go beyond a token remission of seven percent. At the same time, it gave tacit support to the zamindars for a policy of forcible collection. Many cultivators reported they were beaten by the zamindar and his agents, and saw their cattle and other movable property attached, while police and revenue officials stood by. "Numerous complaints of ill treatment by this allied force, zamindar cum police cum revenue staff" were received by the inquiry committee appointed by the Provincial Congress Committee in June 1931. In one district, for example, it was common for zamindars to be "accompanied in their rent collecting expedition by either the revenue authorities or the armed guard of police, and several instances were proved . . . in which the police and the revenue authorities had beaten the tenants either at the instigation of the zamindars or on their own initiative."[51]

In an effort to control what had undeniably become a "class struggle" between the zamindars and the tenants, Gandhi issued a "Manifesto to the Kisans" on May 23, 1931. He urged all occupancy tenants to pay at least three-quarters of the rent owed by them, and suggested payment of one-half for statutory tenants. He also requested the provincial government to grant a proportionate reduction in land revenue to the zamindars. Finally, Gandhi said, "let me warn you against listening to the ad-

---

[50] Nehru, *An Autobiography*, p. 237.
[51] *Agrarian Distress in the United Provinces*, p. 77.

vice, if it has reached you, that you have no need to pay the zamindar any rent at all. I hope you will not listen to such advice, no matter who gives it. Congressmen cannot, we do not, seek to injure the zamindars. We aim not at the destruction of property. We aim only at its lawful use."[52] Simultaneously, Gandhi addressed a companion "Appeal to the Zamindars." He stressed the necessity for them to become "trustees and trusted friends of the tenants" instead of merely rent collectors. Zamindars should grant cultivators "fixity of tenure, take a lively interest in their welfare . . . and in a variety of ways make them feel that they, the zamindars, are their true friends taking only a fixed commission for their manifold services." "Whatever the law may be," said Gandhi, "the Zamindari system to be defensible, must approach the conditions of a joint family."[53]

This appeal had little effect on either side. After Gandhi left for London to attend the Round Table Conference in August 1931, the situation rapidly deteriorated. Forcible collections, with the connivance of local government officials, increased. On the Congress side, many workers also ignored Gandhi's Manifesto, and advised the tenants not to pay any rent at all. The Provincial Congress Committee observed in its report that many volunteers were preaching "a general non-payment of rent and they further preached that the tenant was the owner of the land and he could do whatever he liked with it, plant gardens, sink wells, build houses thereupon, without seeking the permission of the zamindar. All this was, of course, in defiance of the legal rights of the zamindar and very much to his distaste. . . . One Congress worker specifically asked by us as to what he told the tenants as to the Congress message, said he told them that the land was a gift of God."[54]

The conflict between the zamindars and their tenants threatened to get out of hand after the government announced another round of inadequate remissions in October 1931. Congress leaders feared, moreover, that the cultivators would become increasingly disillusioned with their ability to help. While Gandhi was still in London, therefore, the Working Committee, admitting to "great hesitation" because it "disliked the raising of the tenant versus zamindar question,"[55] finally agreed to Nehru's demand that the United Provinces Provincial Congress Committee be permitted once again to sanction the suspension of rent and revenue payments in any district of the province. The Allahabad District Congress Committee was the first to adopt a tentative resolution stating that in case better terms were not obtained, peasants should withhold payment of rent and revenue. Toward the end of November 1931, the Allahabad DCC actually asked the peasants to suspend payment

[52] Ibid., p. 228.
[53] Ibid., p. 231.
[54] Ibid., p. 86.
[55] Ibid., p. 310.

pending negotiations. By this time, however, the government had issued a far-reaching ordinance prohibiting all political activity, and announcing severe penalties for nonpayment of rent. Nehru was arrested on December 26 and the no-rent campaign was, for all practical purposes, interned with him.

On December 31, 1931, after the failure of the Second Round Table Conference, Gandhi returned to India, and was almost immediately arrested. So concerned was he, however, at the Working Committee's decision to permit a no-rent campaign, that he hastily summoned a meeting and directed the Working Committee to pass a resolution of "Reassurance to Zamindars." Dated January 1, 1932, the resolution affirmed:

> Inasmuch as some misapprehension has been created in the minds of the Zamindars of U.P. in particular, and others, in general that in discussing proposals for non-payment of rent or taxes under given circumstances, the Congress was contemplating a class war, the Working Committee assures the Zamindars concerned that the no-rent proposals referred to were in no way aimed at them but that they represent an economic necessity for the peasantry which is known to be half-starved and at present suffering from unprecedented economic distress. The Working Committee has no design upon any interest legitimately acquired and not in conflict with the national wellbeing. The Working Committee, therefore, appeals to all landed or monied classes to help the Congress to the best of their ability in its fight for the freedom of the country.[56]

Following Gandhi's arrest, and the resumption of civil disobedience, the class issue was again submerged by the need to maintain national unity during the nationalist struggle. From this time onward, however, the Constructive Program, and particularly the concepts of class conciliation and trusteeship, came under increasingly open attack from socialist members of Congress.

The collapse of the civil disobedience movement in the early 1930s convinced the socialists inside Congress that class-based peasants' and workers' associations were necessary to a militant nationalist struggle. Nonviolent noncooperation was discredited even as a political tactic largely because the middle classes proved vulnerable to government pressure. Nehru told the Lucknow session of Congress in 1936 that the middle class, "being too much tied up with property and the goods of the world, . . . is fearful of losing them and it is easier to bring pressure on it and exhaust its stamina. . . . That has been very evident during our

---

[56] *Resolutions on Economic Policy and Programme, 1924-1954*, p. 9.

recent struggle, when our propertied classes were hit hard by the Government's drastic policy of seizure and confiscation of monies and properties, and were thus induced to bring pressure for the suspension of the struggle."[57]

Apart from the question of political tactics, moreover, Nehru was opposed to the strategy of class conciliation in principle, because he did not believe it would win economic freedom for the masses. In an influential series of articles called *Whither India?*, published in 1933, Nehru identified the central issue in these terms: "Congress cannot escape having to answer the question now or later for the freedom of which class or classes in India are we especially striving for? Do we place the masses, the peasantry and workers first, or some small class at the head of our list? In my own mind it is clear that if an indigenous government took the place of a foreign government and kept all the vested interests intact, this would not even be the shadow of freedom."[58]

Having posed the problem, Nehru went on to ask: "And how are we to divest the vested interests?" While he stopped short of a complete endorsement for the tactics of class war, Nehru asserted that some measure of coercion would be necessary. He went on to add: "history . . . shows us that there is no instance of a privileged class or group or nation giving up its special privileges or interests willingly. . . . Always a measure of coercion has been applied, pressure has been brought to bear, or conditions have been created which make it impossible or unprofitable for vested interests to carry on. And then the enforced conversion takes place."[59]

Nehru's political credo found a strong echo in the platform of the Congress Socialist party (CSP), established in 1934 by the younger group of Congress intellectuals. Led by Jayaprakash Narayan and Narendra Deva, the CSP operated within the parent Indian National Congress. Nevertheless, it drew heavily upon Marxist ideology. At its first all-India conference at Patna, it proclaimed two political goals: complete independence from Great Britain; and the establishment of a socialist party. At the second conference in Meerut, June 20, 1936, the CSP declared its endorsement for class-struggle tactics: "Marxism alone can guide the anti-imperialist forces to their ultimate destiny. Party members must, therefore, fully understand the technique of revolution, the theory and practice of class struggle, the nature of the state and processes leading to the Socialist society."[60]

During the same year, moreover, the CSP Executive Committee de-

---

[57] Jawaharlal Nehru, *Toward Freedom*, Appendix B, p. 395.
[58] Jawaharlal Nehru, *Whither India?*, p. 19.          [59] *Ibid.*, p. 34.
[60] Cited in Saul Rose, *Socialism in Southern Asia* (London, 1959), p. 17.

cided to admit communists to membership in an attempt to unify all socialist groups. Individual members of the Communist party (CPI) thereafter joined the CSP, and in this way gained access to the entire Congress organization.

The entry of communists into the Congress party signalled a serious attempt by radical socialists to overturn Gandhian doctrines of nonviolence and class conciliation as the organizational principles of the nationalist movement. The CPI, founded in 1925, had already been exposed as a branch of the Communist International. It received funds from both the Communist party in Great Britain and the Soviet Union. During the first decade of its existence, the CPI had operated on the basis of directives from the Comintern to organize peasants' and workers' associations for the purpose of fomenting demonstrations, strikes, and ultimately revolution, ending in "the overthrow of the sovereignty of the King Emperor in British India."[61] The arrest, trial, and conviction of thirty-one of the most important communist leaders in the Meerut Conspiracy Case (1930-1933), had resulted in a government ban on the CPI as an illegal organization. Nevertheless, the anti-British activities of the accused created sympathy for the communists among nationalists. When the CPI went underground in 1934, they found it easy to maintain contacts with Marxist intellectuals inside the CSP. Communists readily accepted the invitation advanced by the socialists to join the CSP on an individual basis.

Yet, by 1935, the communists were following a more sophisticated approach to nationalist revolution, one advanced by the Seventh World Congress of the Communist International in its call for the creation of an Anti-Imperialist Peoples Front. The new line recognized that the CPI "did not possess sufficient forces independently to organize a powerful and mass anti-imperialist movement."[62] On the contrary, it endorsed the necessity of establishing a united anti-imperialist front with the Indian National Congress. Even so, the communists did not propose merely to join forces with the nationalist leadership. Rather, their purpose was to isolate Gandhi and his conservative colleagues from the rank and file, in the hope of achieving for themselves the dominant position in the direction of the nationalist movement.

The communists' strategy rested on three types of initiatives: the establishment of separate "factions" within CSP party units in order to build up a cohesive parallel organization that could get communists elected to positions of power in the provincial and national executive organs of Congress; the infiltration of mass organizations operating outside Con-

---

[61] For an account of the formation of the Communist Party of India and its activities before 1930, see M. R. Masani, *The Communist Party of India, A Short History*, pp. 19-40.
[62] *Ibid.*, p. 57.

gress in support of nationalist goals, but with a dual commitment to immediate social reform; and the use of strategic positions inside the Congress to bring pressure to bear on the national leadership for recognition of the principle of collective affiliation of mass organizations as the means of altering the balance of power in the Annual Session. This would permit the communists to demand constitutional and policy changes, including the elimination of the dogma of nonviolence and the Constructive Program. The linchpin of this strategy rested on the assumption that the CSP and Nehru—its most powerful patron—would side with the radicals against the conservative High Command in any open confrontation over the principle of collective affiliation. Communist infiltration of peasants' associations became the first step in the strategy to commit the nationalist movement to an active program of revolutionary class struggle.

The first peasants' associations had been started in Andhra in 1923 by N. G. Ranga, the young son of a wealthy landholding family in Guntur district. A Marxist and an active member of Congress, he believed that only a class-based organization strong enough to create physical sanctions in favor of radical reform could secure the socialist transformation of the countryside. The peasants' associations (later called kisan sabhas) supported Congress in the political struggle for independence, but always strove to commit the national leadership to an open break with the large landholding and industrial classes. Ranga argued that social reform could not be postponed until after independence. He reasoned: "so long as feudalism and capitalism are not done away with, real and substantive power cannot come in the hands of the masses. Hence their abolition is a necessity for and condition precedent to Swaraj."[63]

Until the 1930s, the kisan sabhas were largely confined to Andhra, and enjoyed only minor successes in sporadic campaigns against payment of excessive rent or revenue. In March 1933, however, the innovation of kisan marches succeeded in bringing the peasant movement to all-India attention. In less than two years, Ranga organized four large marches, the last two extending to all parts of the Madras presidency. In public speeches and processions, kisan leaders demanded a reduction in rent, occupancy rights for all tenants, a moratorium on agricultural debt, abolition of all feudal dues, and an end to enhanced revenue assessments or assessments on uneconomic holdings. The marches, lasting a number of days, and moving from district to district, often terminated at the office of a local revenue officer or a provincial kisan conference, where peasant grievances were dramatically reviewed. According to Ranga, the marches were deliberately planned to "stir up the whole Andhra coun-

---

[63] N. G. Ranga, *Kisan Handbook*.

tryside and demonstrate the strength of the kisan movement, to convince the various Congress committees that they could maintain their authority only by following our lead or welcoming our assistance."[64] In 1935, the CSP, under the leadership of Jayaprakash Narayan, established provincial kisan sabhas both in Bihar and the United Provinces. During the same year, affiliated peasants' associations also sprang up in Punjab and Bengal. By 1936, the kisan associations were strong enough to form a national organization, the All-India Kisan Sabha (AIKS), which held its first meeting simultaneously with the annual Congress session at Lucknow in April.

At Lucknow, a constitutional subcommittee, with Ranga as president, drafted an *All-India Kisan Manifesto* claiming to represent the small landowners, tenants, and landless laborers. "Minimum demands" advanced by the *Manifesto* included abolition of all zamindari tenures without compensation, abolition of all debts, redistribution of cultivable waste lands vesting in government to subsistence farmers and landless laborers, and a graduated income tax in ryotwari areas, with exemption for all families earning less than a net income of Rs. 500 annually. Other "immediate demands" included reduction of rent by fifty percent; cancellation of rent and revenue arrears; occupancy rights for all tenants; a five-year moratorium on all agricultural debts and attachments; cheap credit, seeds, and fertilizers; marketing cooperatives to eliminate private traders; and the return of communal grazing land to village councils. The *Manifesto*, moreover, concluded with a call for direct action to enforce these demands. It advised all tenants without occupancy rights to refuse payment of rent; it endorsed social boycott of moneylenders and their shops; and it directed landless laborers to strike against the zamindars in order to enforce their demand for a minimum wage.[65]

Ranga introduced the *Manifesto* along with an AIKS appeal for collective affiliation to Congress at a meeting of the Working Committee at Lucknow. Nehru, then president-elect, and a member of the outgoing Working Committee, responded as expected. He pressed hard for the adoption of Ranga's program and the principle of collective affiliation. The conservative majority in the High Command reacted shrewdly. They avoided an outright veto of this suggestion. Instead, they allowed the issue to be considered before the AICC and again in the open session, correctly calculating on carrying a majority of the delegates. The proposal was rejected in each case.

Nevertheless, the *Manifesto* had achieved considerable visibility and could not simply be dismissed without making Congress vulnerable to

[64] *Ibid.*, p. 17.
[65] For the complete text of the *Kisan Manifesto*, see N. G. Ranga, *Kisan Speaks*, pp. 58–65; Calcutta edition, p. 272.

charges of collusion with the zamindars. Gandhi, therefore, did agree to appoint an agrarian subcommittee of the Working Committee to make recommendations for "improving the condition of the kisans." This committee was directed to consult with the Provincial Congress Committees and to report its conclusions to the coming AICC meeting in August 1936. The resolution that established the subcommittee, however, endorsed the preservation of the zamindari system. It defined as one point of reference the "safeguarding of the interest of the peasants where there are intermediaries between the State and themselves."[66]

After Lucknow, left-wing political activity intensified. Numerous peasant conferences were organized to demonstrate support for the *Kisan Manifesto*. Nehru himself spent much time touring the countryside and speaking about socialism.[67] When the AICC met in Bombay in August 1936, the All-India Kisan Sabha again submitted the *Kisan Manifesto* for the consideration of the Working Committee. The Working Committee once again refused to take action, asking for additional time to receive recommendations from the Provincial Congress Committees.

At the next annual session of Congress at Faizpur, in December 1936, a decision on the agrarian platform could no longer be postponed. Pattabhi Sitaramayya, the Congress historian, recalled that at Faizpur the atmosphere was "surcharged with socialist slogans emphasizing the rights of the workers and peasants." One indication of left-wing strength at Faizpur was the surprisingly large vote—more than one-third in both the AICC and the open session—for a communist-sponsored amendment declaring that self-government could be won only after an "uncompromising revolutionary struggle with imperialism."[68] The AIKS achieved maximum impact, organizing a 200-mile peasants' march through the villages of Maharashtra, which ended at an open session in Faizpur attended by some 40,000 peasants. Communist party leaders appeared openly for the first time,[69] and Ranga claimed that "the Kisan Sabha became the real common platform of all the radical forces." Within the short period between Lucknow and Faizpur, said Ranga, the AIKS came to "wield an extraordinary influence upon the Indian National Congress."[70] In his presidential address to the AIKS at Faizpur, Ranga reiterated the sabha's demand for the elimination of all zamindari

[66] *Resolutions on Economic Policy and Programme, 1924-1954*, p. 12.

[67] Nehru's activity so alarmed conservative elements in the leadership that Rajendra Prasad, Vallabhai Patel, and C. Rajagopalachari submitted their resignations from the Working Committee. Gandhi's personal intervention ultimately convinced them to remain, and succeeded in averting a permanent split in the organization.

[68] Cited in Gene D. Overstreet and Marshall Windmiller, *Communism in India*, p. 67.

[69] The Communist party was declared illegal by the Government of India in 1934 and operated as an underground organization until 1942.

[70] Ranga, *History of the Kisan Movement*, p. 43.

and moneylending interests in agriculture, affirming "the eagerness and
readiness of Socialists and Comrades of Kisans and Workers to welcome
the class struggle coming to a head before the contending classes." He
also thanked Nehru, who as Congress president, he said, had "sincerely
and single-mindedly help[ed] us to organize ourselves, to develop our
own class consciousness, and to fight our class enemies."[71]

It seems certain that Nehru, in his turn, was helped by Ranga's demonstration of peasant support. At Faizpur, Nehru finally succeeded in
getting Gandhi's approval for the adoption of a far-reaching program of
agrarian reform that became part of the Congress election manifesto of
1937. In this victory, Ranga claimed credit for the AIKS: "the influence
of the Kisan Sabha upon the National Congress was very great indeed.
The Working Committee which did not expect to formulate any agrarian
program for presentation to the A.I.C.C. felt persuaded to come forward with proposals, which on their acceptance by the Congress, became famous as the Faizpur Agrarian Program, thanks to the stiff fight
put up by our members in the A.I.C.C. and the tremendous success of
our Kisan March and Kisan Congress."[72]

The agrarian program adopted by Congress at Faizpur incorporated
almost all of the AIKS demands. It called for "immediate relief" in the
form of substantial reduction in rent and revenues; exemption for uneconomic holdings from both rent or land tax; cancellation of arrears for
rent; the abolition of all feudal dues and levies; moratorium on debt, including the liquidation of "unconscionable" debts; and occupancy rights
for all tenants. For the first time, Congress also declared that "an effort
should be made to introduce cooperative farming." Most significant, the
Faizpur program came to the very brink of recommending zamindari
abolition, by recognizing the need for "radical change in the repressive
land tenure and land revenue systems."[73] Nehru left no doubt of his own
interpretation. He declared in his presidential address: "The land system
cannot endure, and an obvious step is to remove the intermediaries
between the cultivator and the State," after which "cooperative or collective farming must follow."[74] At the same time, however, when the conservative majority in the Working Committee finally took an open position against any change in the Congress constitution to permit collective
affiliation, Nehru, who continued to speak out in favor of such change,
did not force the issue to the point of a split with the Old Guard.

Subsequently, the tone of AIKS propaganda became more strident.
Although the Kisan Sabha supported Congress in the 1937 elections, the

[71] Ranga, *Kisan Speaks*, p. 7.
[72] Ranga, *History of the Kisan Movement*, p. 65.
[73] *Resolutions on Economic Policy and Programme, 1924-1954*, p. 15.
[74] Nehru, *Toward Freedom*, Appendix B, p. 427.

leadership charged that kisan workers were deliberately excluded from the ticket, and that "pacts and understandings" were being made with the "reactionaries." The AIKS nevertheless managed to take advantage of the elections to intensify recruitment activities. By May 1938, Ranga claimed a total of 572,300 members.[75] Although Congress took office only in August 1937,[76] the October meeting of the AIKS passed a resolution attacking the ministries for the "piecemeal, superficial and perfunctory manner" in which they were dealing with peasant grievances. They charged that Congress had failed to keep its campaign pledges for an immediate reduction of land revenue and rent, exemption on uneconomic holdings, and moratorium on debt collections. Then, in early 1938, the AIKS launched a vigorous agitation for the immediate implementation of the Faizpur program, including zamindari abolition. Peasant marches were organized in Punjab, Bihar, Maharashtra, Bengal, Madras, and the United Provinces. The movement had by this time adopted the red flag as a standard, and was virtually controlled by the Communist party.

By the time of the next annual Congress session at Haripura, in February 1938, hostility between the Congress and the AIKS was so strong that the Reception Committee prohibited any kisan rally within the Congress' meeting grounds. The Congress historian, Pattabhi Sitaramayya, described the dominant feeling at Haripura that the AIKS had grown into a dangerous political rival in the countryside:

> there were the hordes of the Kisans organizing themselves into huge parties marching hundreds of miles along the villages and trying to build a party, a power and a force more or less arrayed against the Congress. They found a cause, a flag and a leader. The cause of the Kisan was not a new one, but had all along been upheld by the Congress. The flag they chose to favor was the Soviet flag. . . . Almost everywhere there were conflicts between Congressmen and Kisans over the question of the height and prominence of the flag, and the virtual attempt of the latter to displace the Tri-color flag symbolized the contest between Socialism and Gandhism. Really it was less of Socialism and perhaps more of Communism that was gradually permeating the atmosphere for the Socialists began already to identify themselves with the Communist group in some provinces or

[75] Ranga, *History of the Kisan Movement*, p. 78. Of this number, 250,000 were in Bihar, although effective provincial organizations also existed in Punjab, Andhra, Bengal, Orissa, and Tamilnad. The enrolled membership in Congress at the beginning of 1938 was about three million.

[76] In the elections of 1937, Congress won a clear majority in five provinces—Madras, United Provinces, Central Provinces, Bihar, and Orissa. In four other provinces—Bombay, Bengal, Assam, and the North Western Frontier Province—Congress was the biggest single party. Only in Sind and Punjab did they have a minority position.

melt imperceptibly into the larger group of nationalists. The leaders of the Kisan movement were many and they toured the country far and wide—and they strengthened and consolidated their party and pitted it against Congress.[77]

By 1938, in fact, the communists had succeeded not only in capturing the AIKS, but were well on their way to establishing control of the CSP. They had one-third of the seats in the CSP executive, and virtually total command over the CSP units in Andhra, Tamil Nadu, and Kerala. They were, moreover, beginning to occupy important posts in the Provincial and All-India Congress Committees.[78]

At Haripura, the conservative membership of the Working Committee found its predominant position directly threatened for the first time. Subhas Chandra Bose, the fiery nationalist hero of Bengal, espousing allegiance to the socialist platform of the CSP, was elected president of Congress. Gandhi and his supporters rushed to protect their control over the nationalist movement by pushing through a "Resolution on Kisan Sabhas," which explicitly dissociated Congress from the activities of Congressmen "who as members of the Kisan Sabhas help in creating an atmosphere hostile to Congress principles and policies."[79]

During the next month, the AIKS launched a virulent attack on the Congress ministries, charging them with favoritism toward the landlords. The new ministries had not made much progress toward implementation of the Faizpur program. Although tenancy acts were passed in Bombay, Madras, the United Provinces, Central Provinces, Bihar, and Bengal to confer occupancy rights on restricted classes of tenants, and to restrain landlords from summary eviction or attachment of property for nonpayment of rent, no substantial reductions or exemptions in rent or revenue, or general moratorium on debts had been declared. On the whole, the basic iniquities of the landlord–tenant relationship remained unchanged. In this atmosphere, the AIKS, meeting in annual session in Bengal in March 1938, suddenly described its ultimate aim as a Kisan Mazdoor Raj (Peasants and Workers State), in which "from each according to capacity to all according to needs shall be the watchword."[80] In a separate resolution, the Sabha specifically denounced the philosophy and techniques of the Constructive Program as reactionary:

This Sabha is convinced that the theory of class collaboration, i.e., the principle that the interests of the exploited classes can be adjusted

[77] Sitaramayya, *History of the Indian National Congress*, II, p. 73.
[78] Masani, *The Communist Party of India*, pp. 66-71.
[79] Sitaramayya, *History of the Indian National Congress*, p. 82.
[80] Ranga, *Kisan Handbook*, p. 103.

and reconciled within the framework of the present society as preached by the Gandhi Seva Sangh and some of the nationalist leaders can only tend to penalize the strength of the masses who are being slowly but progressively awakened to the realization of their historical responsibilities.

This Sabha is convinced that such collaboration even on the excuse that the anti-imperalist struggle demands such a policy for the sake of the so-called national unity, can result only in perpetuation of economic enslavement and checking the growth of the struggle of the masses and therefore, in obstructing the achievement of Swaraj for the masses, and ultimately in a settlement between the traditional exploiters of the masses and imperialism for a more stable and intensive exploitation of the masses.

This Sabha deems its duty to carry on a relentless fight against the advocacy and propagation of such a theory and for that purpose exhorts all kisan comrades all over the country to organize their sabhas as the organs of the kisan struggle, and to pursue their present method of agitation, organization and struggle.[81]

At the Tripuri Session of Congress in March 1939, Gandhi, who was determined to force a showdown with the socialists, decided to convert the election of Congress president into an open test of his strength in the nationalist movement. Acting on Gandhi's instructions, the majority of the Working Committee publicly withdrew their support from the incumbent president, Subhas Bose, and asked him to endorse their own candidate, Pattabhi Sitaramayya, for president. Bose, with the backing of the CSP and the communists, refused and sought a second term. In a stunning defeat for Gandhi, Bose was reelected by a majority of 1,580 to 1,375. At the open session, moreover, he used his presidential address to propose a radical new action program: an ultimatum to the British government for complete independence within a fixed period, followed by a final mass struggle for freedom; and close cooperation with all "anti-imperialist" organizations, including the All-India Kisan Sabha.

Gandhi thereupon decided on one last confrontation. He declared that he regarded Sitaramayya's defeat as his own. Following Gandhi's lead, twelve of the fifteen members of the Working Committee (Bose, his brother Sarat, and Nehru excluded), announced their resignations. At the same time, the Old Guard introduced a resolution at the open session calling on all delegates to reiterate their confidence in Gandhi's leadership by "requesting" Bose to appoint a Working Committee having Gandhi's approval. Barring that act of faith, Gandhi announced, he would break

[81] *Ibid.*, p. 71.

all ties with the Congress. The CSP and their communist allies, faced with that stark prospect, were confronted with a painful dilemma. They could no longer hope to capture the nationalist movement; the best they could do in the circumstances was to split it. This, however, was contrary to the entire united front strategy to which the left wing was then committed in the face of the mounting war threat in Europe. Accordingly, rather than divide the nationalist opposition to Great Britain—still regarded as a potential fascist ally—the CSP and the communists accepted what amounted to a censure resolution against Bose. Subsequently, Gandhi withdrew all cooperation from the president and refused to have any of his followers sit on a "composite" Working Committee. Bose, trapped by the Tripuri resolution, but unwilling to compromise on the principle of a representative committee, finally resigned. In May 1939, the AICC elected Rajendra Prasad, Gandhi's new nominee, president of the Congress.

Shortly after this confrontation, a number of events occurred to isolate the Communist party and the All-India Kisan Sabha from the mainstream of the nationalist movement. In March 1940, the CSP could no longer ignore communist infiltration of local party units, and expelled the communists from membership at the heavy cost of conceding the Andhra, Tamil Nadu, and Kerala units to the CPI. In 1941, as the communists became even more militant, the CSP and Bose's newly formed Forward Bloc seceded from the AIKS. In October 1942, Ranga himself resigned, and acknowledged that he had lost control of the kisan movement. Finally, Germany's attack on the Soviet Union impelled the Communist party and the AIKS to cooperate with the British war effort. Their leadership, released from detention after the British Government of India lifted the ban on the CPI, did not take part in the Congress-led "Quit-India" movement of 1942, and were stigmatized as tools of a foreign power.

Nevertheless, Gandhi's hold on the younger nationalists had been broken. When he and other senior Congress leaders were arrested in July 1942, socialist militants gained control of the "Quit-India" campaign. They went underground, refused to offer themselves for arrest, and engaged in acts of terrorism and sabotage to paralyze the British administration. Jayaprakash Narayan, then the nationalist hero of the left, expressed the prevailing new ethos when he publicly called upon all freedom fighters to "prepare, organize, train and discipline our forces [for] the total revolt of the masses."[82] One of the younger Congress-women to go underground in 1942, Aruna Asaf Ali, remembered that the only restraint on political violence was the "aversion to killing for no reason."

[82] Jayaprakash Narayan, *Towards Struggle*, pp. 25-26.

Apart from that, "everything was attempted. We thought non-violence doesn't yield results. We will show the British we are tired of waiting and that they need our cooperation. We cut telegraph lines; we set fire to houses; we incited people; we asked youngsters to throw bombs now and then, not to kill, but to terrorize."[83]

Those close to Gandhi were appalled. But when they appealed to him to intervene, he no longer had any hope of regaining control. Morarji Desai recalled that "during the forties, after the Socialists got hold of the movement and they used all forms of violence, I went to Gandhi and told him if you let them take over, the whole revolution of Truth and Non-Violence will be lost. But he was desperate, and he had no other program."[84]

The socialists, for their part, believed that the British government, apprehensive of keeping order in India if the masses followed the leadership into open revolt, were pressured by the effects of subversion into acting more quickly to concede the nationalist demands for independence. Without that, and the effects "of those two wars," said Mrs. Ali, "we would have been the way we were. That is why some people left Gandhi in 1942."[85] By June 1945, the members of the Working Committee were released from prison. Less than one year later, Prime Minister Attlee sent a Cabinet Mission to India to negotiate transfer of power.

Independence, when it finally came on August 14, 1947, was accompanied by unexpected trauma. Growing tensions between Hindus and the Muslim minority, the uncompromising demand of the Muslim League for a separate Islamic state, and bloody communal riots in Bengal and Bihar had culminated in the bitterness of Partition. Less than forty-eight hours after a truncated India regained her freedom, unprecedented communal violence erupted in the Muslim-majority province of Punjab, divided between India and Pakistan. In the eastern section, Muslim minorities were slaughtered by Hindus and Sikhs; in the western half, Muslim terrorists turned on Hindu and Sikh minorities. Altogether, some twelve million persons, about equally divided between Muslims on the one side and Hindus and Sikhs on the other, fled their ancestral homes to seek safety in opposite directions. Large numbers never reached their destination. In less than one year, approximately half a million persons were murdered. The most bitter blow of all was yet to come. Gandhi had desperately tried to halt the attacks on the Muslims in Delhi. In January 1948, he announced a fast unto death if peace was not restored. So doing, he earned the fierce hatred of Hindu fanatics. On

---

[83] Interview, New Delhi, March 4, 1959.
[84] Interview, New Delhi, April 8, 1959.
[85] Interview, New Delhi, March 4, 1959.

January 30, 1948, as Gandhi entered Birla House in New Delhi to begin a prayer meeting, a young Hindu stepped into his path and fired three times. Gandhi's death plunged India into a paroxysm of grief and shame, which finally saw the end of communal violence.

It is impossible to measure with any exactness the effect of such events on the political orientation of the socialist intelligentsia. They had only a temporary impact on the dedicated Marxists inside the CPI. After the communal riots, Indian communists who suspected outside agents of provoking the disturbances in order to undermine the authority of the newly independent regime, pledged their loyal support to the government. These pledges did not survive the year. The Second Congress of the CPI, meeting in Calcutta on February 28, 1948, adopted a new "political thesis" that reflected the militant international line approved by the first Cominform meeting several months earlier. Using the language of the cold war, the communists attacked the nationalist leadership for betraying the freedom struggle in "striking a treacherous deal behind the backs of the starving people"[86] to advance the business interests of the Indian big bourgeoisie in alliance with Anglo-American imperialism, and against the democratic camp led by the Soviet Union. The party leadership called on all communists to rally the working class, the peasantry, and the petty bourgeoisie against imperialism and capitalism through tactics that reaffirmed the validity of violent struggle under Indian conditions.

Between 1948 and 1951, the new model for CPI activity was provided by the guerrilla-style agrarian revolution launched in the communist stronghold of Telengana, the eastern part of the princely state of Hyderabad. Armed communists led landless peasants in an orgy of murder, arson, and looting that drove out local landlords and government officials to bring large rural enclaves under the control of a para-political regime of village "soviets." Guerrilla bands were also organized in local communist strongholds of West Bengal, Madras, and Bombay as part of a master plan for seizing power on a wave of peasant uprisings throughout the country.

Such "adventurism," however, proved costly. Several state governments, invoking the measures of Public Safety Acts inherited from the British, declared the Communist party illegal. Large numbers of the leadership were arrested throughout the country. The police action demoralized local party units and resulted in a dramatic decline in membership. Within Telengana, moreover, the Indian army (which moved into Hyderabad state in September 1948 in order to compel the recalcitrant Nizam's accession to the new Indian Union), brought extra force to bear in suppressing the peasant revolt. The communists found they were unable to sustain the momentum of the agrarian struggle. Their appeals

[86] Cited in Masani, *The Communist Party of India*, p. 90.

to violent action degenerated into acts of individual terrorism that exposed the party to further repression.

By 1951, the communists, faced with the real threat of political annihilation if they persisted in armed revolt, were ready to reconsider their earlier assessment of the revolutionary potential in the country. A new lead, moreover, came from abroad, this time from the Communist Party of Great Britain. The British party argued that armed revolution was "not an immediate prospect"[87] in India. They advised that the correct line for the CPI under Indian conditions was to concentrate on building up a more effective party organization by taking advantage of opportunities for legal activity provided under the parliamentary system. Thereafter, the CPI withdrew its program for guerrilla warfare against the government. It changed over to a strategy of peaceful opposition through the organization of united front alliances of leftist parties. The shift, however, was based on tactical considerations alone. It did not rule out resort to violent methods in the future if the situation became favorable.

Congress Socialists, by contrast, underwent a more profound transformation of political outlook. They were deeply shaken by the communal riots accompanying Independence, and even more by the horrible circumstances of Gandhi's death. "If Gandhi had died naturally," Morarji Desai once reflected, "his ideas would have slowly died away. He did more for India with his death than he did alive. The Hindus realized they were responsible for his death because the assassin would never had done it if he hadn't thought the people were behind him. The assassin was an idealist. I knew him. He thought he was saving Hinduism. But after Gandhi's assassination, he was disillusioned because there was a tremendous wave of reaction and the people realized Gandhi was right, that there must always be right means."[88]

Although the socialists reiterated the Meerut program of class struggle as late as 1946, the Nasik conference of the Socialist party—convening less than two months after Gandhi's assassination—resolved to work for a socialist society through peaceful means. Jayaprakash Narayan, then the party's general secretary and chief executive officer, personally placed the new policy before the conference. He gave this explanation of his change of view: "the happenings of the past few months have made me reconsider the whole position. Humanity has been uprooted. There have been mass murders. Women have been raped. Children have been cut to pieces. Blood has flown freely. . . . And the greatest of the tragedies has been the murder of Gandhiji."[89]

Communal tensions, moreover, were clearly not the only source of

[87] Cited in Overstreet and Windmiller, *Communism in India*, p. 303.
[88] Interview, New Delhi, April 8, 1959.
[89] Socialist Party (India), Report of the Sixth Annual Conference, March 19 to March 21, 1948 (Bombay, 1948), p. 12. Narayan's reassessment was also affected by the first reports of massive slave-labor camps in the Soviet Union.

potentially destructive violence in Indian society. Forces of political disintegration were visible on every side. They ranged from demands by some Indian princes for independent status or autonomy; to claims by linguistic and tribal groups for separate states; to insistence by untouchable and backward castes for preferential treatment in government, the civil administration, and schools. Surveying the almost infinite potentialities for internal conflict, Narayan concluded that Gandhi's strategy of nonviolent social transformation was, in fact, the only possible path to socialism in India. He told his old colleagues:

> The greatest thing Gandhi taught us was that means are ends, that evil means can never lead to good ends and that fair ends require fair means . . . nothing but good means will enable us to reach the goal of a good society, which is socialism. . . . It is through intensive constructive activity amongst [peasants and workers] that we will be able to achieve a socialist society and build up democratic socialism. . . . Government should not be the only instrument of social good. We have to train the workers in the fields and factories that they will become strong enough to look after themselves. It should be our aim to educate the mass mind that socialism will become the basis of their life.[90]

It is apparent from Nehru's own writings that he began to experience reservations about the wisdom of class struggle techniques in Indian conditions even earlier. Although he was the most influential advocate of socialism inside the Congress, he had never formally joined the Congress Socialist party. When, in 1936, he was elected Congress president, the Working Committee appointed by him carefully reflected the conservative majority in the AICC. Even in 1939, when with the reelection of Subhas Bose as Congress president in the face of Gandhi's open opposition, the socialists appeared in a position to capture the party, Nehru chose not to go beyond verbal expressions of sympathy with Bose in the critical confrontation with Gandhi that followed.

Nehru's motives must always remain a matter of some speculation. Brecher suggests that there were important psychological pressures affecting his behavior: in particular, that Nehru was so emotionally dependent on Gandhi's esteem and affection that he preferred to give way even on issues of principle rather than risk an irreparable breach in their personal relations.[91] Yet, it is also apparent that Nehru was concerned about preserving the Congress party as a unifying political force. He had, moreover, reason to believe that his personal effectiveness was enhanced by remaining acceptable to the conservative elements inside the party.

[90] *Ibid.*, pp. 96, 11-12.
[91] Michael Brecher, *Nehru, A Political Biography*, p. 140.

Even though he had refrained from packing the Working Committee, and refused to issue an ultimatum on the question of collective affiliation, he did manage to win a free hand in drafting the 1936 election manifesto, which committed the party as a whole to a radical program of agrarian reform. His conciliatory attitude toward the business classes also brought significant gains. When the Working Committee constituted a National Planning Committee in 1938, composed of socialists, communists, and leading industrialists, Nehru as chairman deliberately avoided discussions of basic social policy or principles of social organization that could split the committee, and contented himself with a consensus on the need for central economic planning. Like Gandhi in other circumstances, he reasoned that the committee's endorsement for the *principle* of planning—even without an explicit commitment to the socialist pattern of society—would inevitably lead India "toward establishing some of the fundamentals of the socialist structure." He pointed out, "it was limiting the acquisitive factor in society, removing many of the barriers to growth, and thus leading to a rapidly expanding social structure. It was based on planning for the benefit of the common man, raising his standards greatly."[92]

Perhaps the greatest incentive to Nehru of a conciliatory approach, however, was the prospect of achieving social reform and economic progress with a minimum of disruptive violence. He observed, "if conflict was inevitable, it had to be faced. But if it could be avoided or minimized, that was an obvious gain. Especially, as in the political sphere there was conflict enough for us, and in the future there might well be unstable conditions. A general consent for a plan was thus of great value."[93]

Even so, as late as 1945 Nehru was still not entirely persuaded of the practicability of a nonviolent approach to social revolution. He confessed to nagging doubts: "ends and means: were they tied up inseparably, acting and reacting on each other, the wrong means distorting and sometimes even destroying the end in view? But the right means may well be beyond the capacity of infirm and selfish human nature. What then was one to do?"[94]

Nevertheless, Nehru continued to move toward a conciliatory approach. The Congress election manifesto, which he approved in 1946, finally called outright for zamindari abolition, but also promised payment of equitable compensation to the zamindars. After Gandhi's death, moreover, Nehru became unshakable in his commitment to nonviolence as the only valid policy in approaching problems of social reform in India. Although he did not hesitate to depart from Gandhi's thinking on

[92] Nehru, *Discovery of India*, p. 405.
[93] *Ibid.*, p. 405.                          [94] *Ibid.*, p. 13.

questions of economic policy, he self-consciously kept faith with what he considered the relevant core of Gandhi's teaching in politics, "the most important principle [that] he laid down which is means are as important as ends and in fact are convertible."[95]

Paradoxically, however, in a striking departure from Gandhi's strategy—and his own earlier prudence—Nehru permitted a radical formulation of the Congress party's ultimate goals. In November 1947, at the Jaipur meeting of the AICC, the Committee on Objectives and Economic Program set down the general principle that "land, with its mineral resources and other means of production, as well as distribution and exchange, must belong to and be regulated by the community in its own interests." The committee envisaged that the state would take over responsibility for starting new enterprises in virtually all key industries, and that existing enterprises in these fields would be transferred from private to public ownership after a period of five years, subject to compensation at officially defined rates. The residue of private enterprise in industry was to function under "all such regulations and controls as are needed for the realization of the objective of national policy in the matter of industrial development." Within the rural sector, the committee recommended the elimination of all intermediary tenures; an end to all forms of tenancy; a ceiling on personal ownership of land; the elimination of all private moneylenders and traders; and the formation of village credit, marketing, and processing societies based on the compulsory membership of all cultivators.[96]

The effect of the Jaipur program was heightened by publication in July 1949 of the *Report of the Congress Agrarian Reforms Committee*. This was the first major product of socialist-Gandhian collaboration on an outstanding public issue after Independence.[97] It was also the most threatening document ever drafted by an official committee of the Congress party with respect to the property interests of the landed castes.

The committee set down four standards that it said should determine the government's agricultural policy. They were: the agrarian economy should provide an opportunity for the development of the farmers' per-

[95] Interview, New Delhi, April 9, 1959. Nehru is quoted as defining the core of Gandhi's teaching as "good, pure and truthful" means in R. K. Karanjia, *The Mind of Mr. Nehru: An Interview*, p. 25.

[96] *Resolutions on Economic Policy and Programme, 1924-1954*, p. 18.

[97] The Agrarian Reforms Committee was appointed with Nehru's approval by Congress President Rajendra Prasad toward the end of 1947. It was headed by the Gandhian economist J. C. Kumarappa. Two members with substantial landholdings, N. G. Ranga and O. P. Ramaswamy Reddiar, ex-premier of Madras, issued a "Minute of Dissent" to the main report. Ranga may have been disillusioned by his experience with the communists as president of the All-India Kisan Sabha. In any case, both men argued against virtually all recommendations to restrict private ownership rights in land. They were especially critical of the recommendations for compulsory cooperative farming.

sonality; there should be no scope for exploitation of one class by another; there should be maximum efficiency of production; the scheme of reform should be within the realm of practicability.

The report, which conceded that a capitalist agrarian structure could achieve maximum efficiency in production, rejected such a pattern on political grounds because it would promote exploitation of one class by another. It assumed that full protection for private property rights in land would encourage larger owners to mechanize production, and ultimately to displace smaller and less efficient producers: "to deprive the agriculturists of their rights in land, turn them into mere wage-earners and subject society to capitalist control in such a vital matter as food."[98] At the same time, collective farming, which might improve productive efficiency and eliminate economic exploitation as well, was found unsuitable on grounds of subordinating the individual peasant to a large army of technicians and bureaucrats. On balance, therefore, the committee favored an agrarian pattern of intermediate-size, village-based cooperative associations as the best safeguard for the legitimate interest of both individual and community.

With this central issue decided, the report went on to recommend two types of farming related to differences in the size of holdings. All holdings below "basic" size, that is, uneconomic farms that could not provide full employment and a reasonable standard of living to an average family of five—about forty to fifty percent of the total—were to be amalgamated in joint cooperative farms. This would involve pooling of land, farm implements, and bullocks, with only minimal returns to ownership. The committee recommended family farming only for holdings between "basic" and "optimum" size—a limit defined at three times an economic holding, for purposes of establishing a ceiling on individual ownership of land. They insisted, moreover, on a number of qualifications to full ownership rights, including a ban on subletting, and restrictions on the use of land and free sale.[99] They also stipulated that all farmers must obtain their credit, sell their produce, and buy their supplies only from the village multipurpose service cooperative. Even these arrangements, however, were viewed as an intermediate stage. The report candidly expressed the hope that all land in the village would ultimately come under joint cooperative management, and that family farms would gradually disappear after an indefinite period of transition.

[98] Indian National Congress, AICC, *Report of the Congress Agrarian Reforms Committee*, p. 16.

[99] Owners were expected to conform to standards of good husbandry and the scheme of crop planning set down by a Land Commission, or risk eviction from their fields. They were also required to transfer their holding according to "well defined priorities laid down by an appropriate authority and at a price which is reasonable and not speculative," *ibid.*, p. 11.

To this end, the report noted the need to fix a minimum wage for agricultural labor, which would not only benefit the landless workers, but also drive "the small farms, i.e., the bulk of the agricultural farms out of cultivation, and the small holders into the cooperative farms."[100]

Finally, the authors of the report observed that propaganda, liberal state aid, and other forms of economic inducement might not be sufficient to establish the new agrarian pattern. Some measure of compulsion might well be needed. In one of the more ingenuous passages in the report, the committee reflected: "of course, the scheme of compulsory joint farming would involve an amount of coercion. But we must also consider that by the judicious exercise of coercion by persons of proper perspective, the edge of unpleasantness involved in coercion is greatly taken off."[101]

By 1949, therefore, the propertied classes stood warned of the long-term threat to their economic interests in government initiatives for "social reform" in the rural sector. The mass of illiterate tenant farmers and landless laborers were, of course, only dimly aware of the exact recommendations for changes in the land tenure system. Still, they were also encouraged to hope for a major improvement in their condition as a result of the establishment of a popular government after Independence.

[100] *Ibid.*, p. 123.                          [101] *Ibid.*, p. 25.

# THREE

# Growth and Democratic Social Transformation: Multiple Goals of Economic Planning

In the early years of Independence, two contradictory tendencies were already well advanced inside the Congress party. On the one hand, the national party executive endorsed socialist principles of state ownership, regulation, and control over key sectors of the economy in order to improve productivity and at the same time curb economic concentration. On the other hand, the national Congress government pursued liberal economic policies and incentives to private investment that were justified in terms of the sole criterion of achieving maximum increases in production. The phenomenon reflected a serious attrition in the strength of the socialist and Gandhian intelligentsia at all levels of the party organization, and the inability of the national leadership to command effective support for the implementation of official Congress policies on economic and social reform.

Subhas Bose's decision, in 1939, to lead a majority of Bengali leftists outside the Congress in order to set up a rival vehicle for radical nationalists (the Forward Bloc) had proved to be the first in a series of defections that decisively weakened the socialist wing of the party and splintered the reformist elements. Although most members of the CSP remained in Congress throughout the war years, they never regained their previous strength. Apart from the debilitating effect of the Forward Bloc's defection, there was also the expulsion of the communists in 1940, which revealed that the entire socialist organization in the south—Andhra, Tamil Nadu, and Kerala—was in communist hands. After 1945, when the Congress party resumed its normal functioning, the erosion in the socialists' support was exposed by key votes in the AICC. In July 1946, Jayaprakash Narayan, who doubted the sincerity of Britain's offer to negotiate complete independence, proposed immediate resumption of mass struggle. He was voted down by 204 to 51. Again, in June 1947, the socialists, this time with Gandhi on their side, were badly defeated in their opposition to Partition by a vote of 157 to 20.

Gandhi was himself increasingly bypassed by senior party leaders, once it became clear that independence would be granted by the British government without recourse to another round of mass civil disobedience. Indeed, by 1946 the most powerful man inside the Congress party organization was neither Gandhi nor Nehru. That distinction was enjoyed by Sardar Vallabhbhai Patel, Gandhi's chief lieutenant during the long nationalist struggle in the critical task of building up the local and state party units. It was Sardar Patel, then treasurer of the national party and a staunch conservative opposed to the influence of the socialists, who turned his long years of party building to decisive advantage in virtually dictating the membership of the Working Committee. Gandhi did succeed in having his disciple of long standing, Acharya J. B. Kripalani, elected Congress president. Still, although both Gandhi and Nehru argued for the appointment of a Congress socialist as general secretary of the party, and for a respectable contingent of socialists in the Working Committee, Patel's influence was paramount in the final list of names, which conspicuously omitted the socialists. Again, when Kripalani resigned as Congress president in 1947 and Gandhi suggested either Jayaprakash Narayan or Narendra Deva as his successor, he was firmly rebuffed by the Working Committee.

Just one month after Gandhi's death in February 1948, moreover, Patel succeeded in getting the AICC's approval for an amendment to the party constitution which prohibited the continuation of organized groups within Congress. Subsequently, no member of Congress could be a "member of any other political party, communal or other, which has a separate membership, constitution, and program." The response of the CSP was the intended one. At the Nasik conference of the Socialist party in March 1948, the majority of the membership voted to establish a separate party.[1] While the Socialists did not have more than 8,000 members at the time,[2] even these thin cadres were diluted by the split with Congress. In Uttar Pradesh, where the CSP had established a commanding position in the Congress party organization, less than twenty percent of the membership followed Narendra Deva out of the Congress.[3] The rest decided to remain as individual members. Nehru's socialist support inside the Congress party was sharply attenuated. At the same time, the independent Socialist party lost another crucial element of its organizational base.

The relative strength of radical elements inside the Congress party organization suffered attrition from another source. As early as 1936, when it became clear that the Congress would come to power in the provincial elections, the lure of government patronage contributed to a large influx of new members. Data on the social origins of active members of the

---

[1] An extended analysis of the circumstances surrounding the Congress-Socialist split is given in Myron Weiner, *Party Politics in India*, pp. 42-64.

[2] *Ibid.*, p. 62.

[3] Paul R. Brass, "Uttar Pradesh," in Myron Weiner, ed., *State Politics in India*, p. 80.

Congress party showed that almost half of all Congressmen who joined in the nineteen thirties were recruited from the prosperous proprietor castes, owning holdings between twenty-one and a hundred acres.[4] Moreover, the late arrivals did not scruple about the methods they used to try and gain control of the local organizations. Since primary or "four-anna" members could vote for representatives to the taluka committee—the lowest rung in the party hierarchy—and all other levels of the party organization were indirectly elected, the mass membership held the key to the balance of power in District and Pradesh Congress Committees. As a consequence, competition for control over the party machinery centered around the ability to manipulate the membership lists, either by denying membership to opponents, paying membership fees for supporters, or even enrolling fictitious persons and voting their names. By 1938, the general secretary of the AICC was besieged with "complaints by individuals and parties that those in power and in control of office machinery refused many times to supply books to their personal and political opponents and that in some cases where books were too freely distributed, unreal and bogus persons were enlisted as members to add to the strength of a party or faction."[5]

After Independence in 1947, the efforts of rival factions to gain control of Pradesh Congress Committees became even more frenzied. The AICC's attempt in 1948 to curb the practice of bogus enrollment by amending the Congress constitution to eliminate the four-anna fee for primary membership backfired. The new provision actually encouraged even more massive abuses. Between 1945/46 and 1949/50, primary membership in the Congress registered a phenomenal increase of more than threefold, from 5.5 million to 17 million.[6] Even the Congress president was frank to say that in many provinces it was impossible "for any outsider, however eminent, impartial and farseeing to unravel the tangled web of factious fights and discords and distinguish the genuine from the fictitious amongst the membership rolls. . . . It requires weeks of labor and tons of energy to tell the genuine from the spurious and establish the triumph of truth and morality. Whole districts are sometimes involved in such palpable frauds."[7]

While all party rivals could (and usually did) have recourse to such tactics, the ability to benefit from them was unevenly distributed. In particular, the English-educated urban intelligentsia—the strata from which most socialist and Gandhian workers were drawn—were inevitably disadvantaged in factional fights in predominantly rural districts. By 1949, conservative coalitions built by the dominant landowning castes in al-

---

[4] Stanley A. Kochanek, *The Congress Party of India*, pp. 337-38.
[5] *Ibid.*, p. 215.                                    [6] *Ibid.*, p. 222.
[7] *Ibid.*, p. 223.

liance with urban businessmen had captured effective control over most District and Pradesh Congress Committees.

In addition, over large parts of India, the Congress party's organization had been very weak or virtually nonexistent prior to Independence. This was especially true of the territories of the former princely states, which alone covered some one-third of the subcontinent during the period of British rule. With the integration of the states into the Indian Union after 1947,[8] the Congress party was faced with the problem of creating modern political organizations in areas where ascriptive criteria of authority had barely been challenged. Most of the former rulers were openly hostile to the new regime. Annual privy purses and symbolic privileges of rank were scant compensation for the reality of unlimited power they had enjoyed before Independence. More important, despite the loss of legal authority, the princes, as well as lesser members of the landed aristocracy, were able to exploit traditional vertical ties based on rank, caste, and economic dependence to perpetuate an aura of political legitimacy. In the former princely states, and even in the permanently settled areas of British India, the relationship between Congress party politicians and traditional elites—ex-rulers, jagirdars, and zamindars— was often asymmetrical. The authority of the latter was largely independent of party affiliation, while the power of the former depended on the support of traditional authority structures. In areas such as Rajasthan, Madhya Pradesh, and Saurashtra, the heads of the major ruling houses were often so invulnerable to political challenge that they disdained all formal party ties and entered politics, if at all, as independents. In such areas, the Congress party could only succeed in winning elections by a deliberate effort to accommodate as many of the lesser notables as possible. Still, not all members of the petty aristocracy could be cajoled or bribed into joining Congress. Minor princes, middle-rank jagirdars, and medium zamindars were all in competition among themselves for local political influence. The district and state party "organizations" put together in these circumstances were nothing more than a network of expedient, often ephemeral, factional alliances among traditional elites, each group having a base of local power virtually independent of the Congress party.

During the formative period of the new Indian state, the conservative interests of the diverse local notables that constituted the Congress party were directly represented inside the central Cabinet. Between 1947 and 1950, Sadar Patel, then deputy prime minister, shared responsibility with

[8] Of the 552 states, 216 were merged into former British provinces. Another 275 were combined to form five new states: Rajasthan; Saurashtra; Patiala and East Punjab States Union (PEPSU); Madhya Bharat; and Vindhya Pradesh. The four largest units—Mysore; Travancore-Cochin; Hyderabad; and Jammu-Kashmir were retained without substantial changes.

Nehru for the major functions of government. Patel held the portfolios of Home Affairs, States, and Information and Broadcasting. By contrast, Nehru, who as prime minister was ostensibly the more powerful of the two, held only the portfolios of External Affairs and Commonwealth Relations.

The two men made no secret of the fact that they had serious differences on "the fundamental question of our respective spheres of responsibility, authority and action."[9] Patel refused to recognize Nehru's claim to a superior role as a "coordinator and kind of supervisor" of all government ministries and departments. On the contrary, he considered it "shocking" when Nehru took independent initiatives to collect information[10] or set the broad principles of policy on matters falling within the range of Patel's ministerial responsibilities. Nehru, for his part, rejected such a restrictive interpretation of his functions. He insisted that the prime minister had to be "more responsible than anyone else for the general trend of policy and for the coordination of the work of various Government departments." Otherwise, he pointed out, the prime minister's role would be reduced to that of a "mere figurehead."[11] Even so, Patel did, in practice, provide a rival focus of power inside the Cabinet, one that encouraged the ministries to exercise considerable autonomy on issues of national policy. Nehru complained that he could not impose any close coordination on the decisions taken in different ministries. In particular, his concern that the Cabinet must develop a general economic policy to meet the acute crisis created by the dislocations of Partition found no echo in government actions. The government ignored the 1946 recommendation of the interim government's Advisory Planning Board to establish a national planning agency "responsible to the Cabinet . . . which should devote its attention continuously to the whole field of development."[12] Neither was there any response to the January 1948 recommendation of the AICC's Economic Program Committee that a

[9] Letter from Vallabhbhai Patel to Jawaharlal Nehru dated December 29, 1947. Published in Durga Das, ed., *Sardar Patel's Correspondence, 1945-50*, Volume 6, 12.

[10] Patel described himself as "shocked" at Nehru's decision to send his own observer (his principal private secretary) to Ajmer in order to report on the situation following serious communal rioting in the area. The home minister believed it could only be interpreted as evidence that the prime minister was not satisfied with Patel's account of the incident and/or with the local chief commissioner's handling of the situation, who, he pointed out, "could be subordinate only either to a Ministry or the Secretary to Government concerned," that is, to Patel's own Home Ministry. Letter from Vallabhbhai Patel to Jawaharlal Nehru, dated December 23, 1947; *ibid.*, p. 9.

[11] Nehru asserted this position in a note to Mahatma Gandhi, dated January 6, 1948, in which he insisted that the prime minister's policy-making role must either be accepted by Patel, or if "this is not considered possible, then the only alternative left is for either me or Sardar Patel to leave the Cabinet." Gandhi's assassination a few weeks later caused the two men to subordinate their personal differences in order to meet the political crisis, but it did not resolve the issues dividing them. *Ibid.*, pp. 17-31, 362-67.

[12] A. H. Hanson, *The Process of Planning*, p. 45.

Planning Commission should immediately he established. When, seven months later, Nehru broached the subject of setting up a "Board or Council of expert advisors whose sole function should be to watch every aspect of the economic situation and advise on it," Patel countered with the suggestion of setting up a committee of experts drawn from among industrialists, economists, and representatives of the government departments to achieve their cooperation in the effective implementation of policies that had already been set down to reassure the business community.[13]

Indeed, the years between 1947 and 1950 saw a series of ad hoc economic policies that were designed to create a favorable environment for private investment. Despite expert advice that wartime price controls on foodgrains, sugar, cotton, and cloth should be maintained in a situation of overall scarcity, "especially if our long-term plans involved regulation and direction of economic activity by the State,"[14] the government, in December 1947, removed sugar and foodgrains from control. In the following month, cotton and cloth were also decontrolled. The rise in prices and profit taking that followed was spectacular. From December 1947 to July 1948, the wholesale price index for foodgrains rose by almost 58 percent. The prices of all other consumer goods increased by about one-third. Controls on cloth and cotton had to be reimposed in July and August; on foodgrains in September; and on sugar in December. Meanwhile, however, in the two years between November 1947 and November 1949, the general price index had been permanently inflated by some 23 percent to 29 percent.[15] At the same time, liberal imports of consumer goods during 1948/49 drew down government reserves by over Rs. 600 crores, and added to the pressure for devaluation in September 1949.[16]

In the same period that the business community was taking record profits, the central budget for 1949/50, which showed a deficit of over Rs. 14 crores at existing levels of taxation, provided for a reduction of direct taxes on personal and corporate income amounting to over Rs. 8 crores. The total deficit was to be made up by increases in indirect taxation, especially sales taxes.[17] The Indian National Congress's publica-

[13] *Sardar Patel's Correspondence*, Volume 6, 389-95.

[14] C. D. Deshmukh, *Economic Development in India, 1946-1956*, p. 43.

[15] India, Planning Commission, *First Five Year Plan*, p. 177. For a detailed account of the events leading up to decontrol and its consequences, see Deshmukh, *Economic Development in India*, pp. 43-59. Decontrol has often been attributed to Gandhi's attack on price regulation as leading to dishonesty and corruption. Since the business community was not noticeably influenced by Gandhi's moral injunctions in other cases when their vital economic interests were opposed, it is difficult to interpret their deference to Gandhi's wishes on the issue of decontrol as anything but expediency.

[16] Deshmukh, *Economic Development of India*, pp. 62-63.

[17] Indian National Congress, *Second Year of Freedom, August 1948-August 1949* (New Delhi, 1949), p. 8.

tion, *Second Year of Freedom, August 1948-August 1949*, explained that "The most serious problem before the government was the stagnation in the capital market resulting from a deep underlying fear about the future of that market. Unless this stagnation was checked and conditions were created in which the incentive to save and invest was revived, the industrial expansion in the country and the execution of the plans intended to raise the living standards of the people in general were bound to be delayed. The Finance Minister, therefore proposed certain measures of relief with this fundamental object of reviving confidence in the minds of the public."[18]

Nor was this all. On April 6, 1948, the government published their Industrial Policy Resolution. A public monopoly was to be established only over the manufacture of arms and ammunition, atomic energy, and the railways. The government did reserve the exclusive right to start new enterprises in coal, iron and steel, minerals, shipbuilding, manufacture of aircraft and of telephones and telegraph equipment, albeit qualified by the provision that the cooperation of the private sector would be sought when required "in the national interest." At the same time, the resolution gave assurances to the business community that no existing enterprises would be nationalized. Further, new ventures were to be exempt from all possibility of public acquisition for a period of ten years.[19] Finally, the government assured foreign firms that they could continue to operate under the same conditions as Indian-owned enterprise. No action was taken to break up the big business houses that exercised managerial control over scores of firms through the managing agency system. Rather, negotiations were set in motion with the major British groups to attract additional investment.

Yet, by far the most important initiatives aimed at protecting the interests of the propertied classes were those incorporated into the legal and institutional framework of the new political order. During the period of the "Duumvirate"—which lasted until Sardar Patel's death in December 1950—the government took a series of key decisions on constitutional arrangements that set very narrow limits on the Center's powers for direct implementation of economic and social reforms.

The constitution adopted by the Constituent Assembly on November 26, 1949, established the Democratic Republic of India as a Union of the States (and Union Territories) and provided for a parliamentary form of government at the Center and in the states.[20] The central law-making

---

[18] *Ibid.*, p. 19.                              [19] *First Five Year Plan*, p. 422.

[20] For the text of the 1950 constitution and a useful commentary on its provisions see V. N. Shukla, *The Constitution of India*, 4th edition (Lucknow, 1964). A lucid analysis of the political framework established under these constitutional arrangements is provided in Norman D. Palmer, *The Indian Political System*, 2nd ed., pp. 118-74.

body, including the two houses of parliament and the president, was constituted as an amalgam of American and British patterns of representative government. The upper house, known as the Rajya Sabha or Council of States, could not be dissolved, although the terms of approximately one-third of its members expired every two years. It functioned as the representative of state interests at the Center, with almost all its members elected (on the basis of population), by the elected members of the state legislative assemblies. At the same time, the Rajya Sabha had a weak position relative to the lower house, the Lok Sabha or House of the People. It was more comparable in power to the upper chamber of the British House of Lords than to the American Senate. The Rajya Sabha could not originate any money bills, and any differences on pending legislation with the Lok Sabha were to be resolved in a joint sitting, in which each member of each house had one vote. These provisions gave a decisive advantage to the Lok Sabha, a body having approximately twice the number of members as the Rajya Sabha. In addition, the Council of Ministers was made collectively responsible to the Lok Sabha, which was elected by direct universal suffrage for a period of five years.

The provisions of the constitution on the executive branch of government were similarly a combination of the British parliamentary and American presidential pattern, although the relationship between the president and the Council of Ministers was interpreted within the conventions of British constitutional practice to be analogous to that of the king of Great Britain and the British Cabinet. On the one hand, the president of India—who was indirectly elected by the elected members of both houses of parliament and of the legislative assemblies of the states—was vested with all the "executive power of the Union," including the supreme command of the defense forces. On the other, the president was expected to govern through and with the advice of his Council of Ministers, who were responsible to parliament. Nevertheless, the formal powers of the president were extremely wide. They raised the possibility that the presidency might in the future become the fulcrum of central power. The specific functions of the president included the power to appoint the prime minister and other Cabinet ministers, judges of the Supreme Court and the High Courts, and other important central officials and members of commissions. The president also enjoyed extensive legislative powers. All bills passed by parliament, including money bills, and bills passed by the state legislatures under specified conditions, required the president's signature to become law. He was also empowered, during parliamentary recesses, to legislate through the issuance of ordinances; and under the extraordinary conditions of a State of Emergency, his legislative powers were unlimited either by the federal provisions of the constitution or guarantees for fundamental rights.

In the states, the pattern of parliamentary government replicated the arrangements at the Center. Executive power was formally vested in a governor appointed for a five-year term by the president of India. In practice, the governor was expected to act on the advice of the Council of Ministers headed by the chief minister of the state and responsible to the legislative assembly, which was elected by direct suffrage for a period of five years. A majority of states also had a small and weak upper chamber or legislative council, consisting of members who were either elected by specially qualified electorates or appointed by the governor.

The doctrine of popular sovereignty on which the constitutional framework rested was reflected in the relatively simple amending procedures vested in the parliament and the state legislatures. Under Article 368, most of the provisions in the constitution could be amended by a special majority of the total membership of each house of parliament, requiring a majority of not less than two-thirds of the members of each house present and voting. Amendments to certain specified provisions required, in addition, ratification by resolutions passed by not less than one-half of the state legislatures.

The constitutive powers of parliament were, however, limited in one vital respect. This was the requirement to carry out social and economic reforms through measures that were consistent with the fundamental rights of individuals guaranteed by the constitution. Indeed, the most egalitarian portions of the 1950 constitution were confined to nonenforceable "Directive Principles of State Policy." These enjoined the states to: secure an adequate means of livelihood to all citizens; distribute ownership and control over the material resources of the community to best subserve the common good; operate the economic system in order to avoid concentration of wealth and means of production; and promote the educational and economic interests of the "weaker sections of the people, and in particular, the Scheduled Castes and Scheduled Tribes[21] [to] protect them from social injustice and all forms of exploitation."

The operative portions of the constitution, by contrast, imposed limitations on the power of the central parliament and the legislatures of each of the states against passing any law which "takes away or abridges" the fundamental rights protected under the constitution. These fundamental rights, as enumerated in Part III, included not only the basic political rights such as equality before the law and the freedoms of religion, speech, expression, assembly, association, and movement, but also the

---

[21] The 1950 constitution, as discussed below, abolished the practice of untouchability and enacted special provisions for the former untouchable castes and tribes designed to guarantee their representation in legislative, administrative, and educational institutions in proportion to their numbers in the population. Eligibility for these special privileges was determined by entering the names of the former untouchable castes and of tribes on official central government and state government lists, or schedules.

freedom of property. Article 19 guaranteed the right to "acquire, hold and dispose of property" subject only to "reasonable restrictions" in the public interest. Article 31 stipulated that no property could be acquired for a public purpose unless government paid compensation. The right of individuals to challenge compensation awards in the courts as inadequate (or in violation of the right to equal protection of the laws) was also guaranteed under the general provision of Article 32, confirming the right to appeal to the Supreme Court and/or lower courts for the enforcement of fundamental rights. The Drafting Committee, in fact, was more rigid in insisting on the absolute protection of economic rights than on the inviolability of political freedoms. On the one hand, Nehru's plea that the constitution should clearly exempt the compensation clauses of the Zamindari Abolition Acts from judicial review under the fundamental rights provisions was rejected. On the other, the framers endorsed the principle that it was necessary to qualify the civil rights guarantees by enabling both the Center and the states to pass laws providing for preventive detention "for reasons connected with the security of a State, the maintenance of public order, or the maintenance of supplies and services essential to the community."

The conservative position also prevailed in key decisions to establish constitutional protection for the rights and privileges of pre-Independence elites who had little, if any, commitment to the announced egalitarian and socialist goals of the nationalist movement. Sardar Patel, having successfully presided over the integration of the Indian states as head of the States Ministry, overrode objections by Nehru[22] to convince his colleagues to adopt constitutional guarantees recognizing the rights of the former rulers and their successors to receive tax-free privy purses from the central government and the "personal rights, privileges, and dignities of the Ruler of an Indian State."[23] Similarly, Patel, this time speaking in his capacity as home minister, succeeded in imposing his arguments on the Drafting Committee for constitutional provisions guaranteeing the privileged conditions of service of the officers of the British-trained Indian Civil Service (ICS).[24] As a result, key officials in

[22] Sardar Patel succeeded in reversing a Cabinet decision made during his absence that no constitutional guarantees should be given for the payment of privy purses to the princes, with the argument that such assurances were essential to the stabilization of the new political order. See T. V. Kunhi Krishnan, *Chavan and the Troubled Decade*, pp. 263–64.

[23] The privileges guaranteed to the former rulers under the constitution included the exemption of privy purses from income tax, free medical care, free supply of water and electricity, exemption from customs duty, and other symbolic privileges of rank, including the provision of armed police guards and escorts, military honors at funerals, public holidays in the former states of the rulers on their birthdays, and protection from prosecution in court without prior authorization by the government.

[24] Sardar Patel told members of the Constituent Assembly who were opposed to guaranteeing the privileges of ICS officers: "If you decide that we should not have the service at all, in spite of my pledged word, I will take the service with me and I will go. I will tell the

the central and state administrative apparatus, including district collectors and later development commissioners, continued by virtue of seniority to be drawn from the ICS cadre. Moreover, the successor Indian Administrative Service (IAS) established by Patel (with its own terms and conditions of service also guaranteed under the constitution) retained the structure and style of its elitest forerunner,[25] perpetuating a national administrative system that in numbers and outlook was more suitable to carrying out the narrow colonial functions of law and order than the broad responsibilities for economic development of an independent government.

If the legal and administrative framework appeared to favor the protection of the rights and privileges of diverse local elites, the distribution of powers between the Union and the states also acted as a brake in preventing sweeping changes of the social order by action from above. The strong powers vested in the Union government were more useful as a negative sanction in preventing open opposition by the states to basic principles of national policy than as a positive force for the effective implementation of central programs. The constitution did authorize parliament to form new states or change the boundaries of existing states (Article 3). It also provided that if any law passed by a state legislature was repugnant to any provision of a law made by parliament, then the statute of parliament would prevail (Article 249). But, except in the unusual case that two-thirds of the members of the Rajya Sabha were agreed, parliament could not legislate on any subject on the "State List." Although Article 246 did reserve to parliament the residual power to make laws on any matter not included in the State List, this list was very extensive. It embraced jurisdiction over public order, administration of justice, local government, education, and communications. The state governments, in addition, retained virtually exclusive control over the governance of the vast rural sector, including such key subjects as land reforms, agricultural credit, land revenue assessments, and taxation of agricultural income. Whatever leverage the Center could hope to exercise on state policies in these areas came almost completely from the financial provisions of the constitution. These granted the Union government the right to set down principles by which taxes levied at the Center would be allocated between the Union and the states, and to es-

service men, 'Let us go. The nation has changed.' They are capable of earning their living."
See Kunhi Krishnan, *Chavan and the Troubled Decade*, p. 273.
[25] The size of the entire IAS cadre was kept to fewer than 3,000 by selective recruitment procedures that admitted about 125 university-trained persons annually on the basis of competitive examinations. These officers had to head up the major departments both at the Center and in the states. They also served as commissioners of administrative divisions and as collectors of districts in the states, adding development functions to their older responsibilities for the collection of revenue, the maintenance of law and order, and the dispensation of justice.

tablish similar guidelines for the award of grants-in-aid and loans to the states for development schemes and other purposes. Even then, the structure of government provided mainly for coordination between the Center and the states rather than for central control over state policies, programs, and administration.[26]

There was one dramatic departure from this general framework of Center-state relations. The extraordinary powers conferred on the Center over the states in times of emergency sharply contrasted with the distribution of powers in normal times. Articles 352-355 empowered the president to proclaim a State of Emergency in the case of an "imminent danger to the security of India or any part of the territory thereof," whether from external aggression or internal disturbance. Such a proclamation had to be approved by both houses of parliament within two months, but could be revoked only by a subsequent presidential proclamation at a time determined by the president. During the period that such proclamation remained in force, the federal provisions—no less than the entire constitutional framework for the enforcement of fundamental rights—were, in effect, suspended. The authority of the central government took on an unlimited character. It extended to the power of making laws for the states either by both houses of parliament, or if parliament was not in session, by presidential ordinance. In addition, the Union executive was empowered to give directions to any state on the exercise of its administrative authority on all matters within its jurisdiction, and even allowed the central government to appoint its own officers with special oversight responsibility for executing laws relating to state subjects. Throughout such a period, moreover, the right of citizens to go to the courts to challenge the validity of laws that were inconsistent with the fundamental rights provisions was not recognized.

The sweeping character of these powers was only partly modified under the provisions for a Proclamation of Emergency in any state (or states) arising from a local failure of the constitutional machinery. Articles 356-359 provided that such a proclamation had to be approved by both houses of parliament within two months, reaffirmed every six months, and could not be kept in force for more than three years. During that period, the powers of the state to make laws were to be exercisable by the central parliament and/or the president (or any other authority so designated); and the right to move the courts for enforcement of the fundamental rights conferred by Part III of the constitution could also be

[26] An authoritative report by Paul Appleby on the Indian administrative system concluded that "except for the character of its leadership, the new national government of India is given less basic resource in power than any other large and important nation, while at the same time having rather more sense of need and determination to establish programs dealing with matters important to the national interest." See Paul H. Appleby, *Public Administration in India: Report of a Survey* (Delhi, 1953), p. 16.

suspended in whole or in part, as specified in presidential ordinances. A more limited Proclamation of Emergency was also envisaged at the state level under Article 360. This allowed the central government to take over the financial management of any state in a situation that threatened the "financial stability or credit of India or any part of its territory."

Still, under ordinary circumstances, the federal, legal, and administrative framework imposed severe limitations on the power of the central government to carry out programs of democratic social transformation. These constraints assigned even greater salience to methods of social change that could build up organized popular pressure from below on state governments for the effective implementation of economic and social reforms.

There were, in fact, a number of features in the new constitution that contained the potentialities for carrying out such a decentralized strategy of social change in response to popular pressure. Not least important was the unprecedented provision for the adoption of universal adult suffrage as the principle of election for members of the Lok Sabha as well as for the state legislative assemblies. This was buttressed by the fundamental right to equality before the law and equal protection of the laws under Article 14—a principle of justice once endorsed by independent India's leaders in contradistinction to alien rulers—carried revolutionary implications for the legitimate constituent principles of society. Article 14 put the legal force of the new nationalist government behind the secular ethic that proscribed the application of ascriptive differences on the basis of religion, race, caste, and sex to establish differential rights and privileges. This principle was amplified in Article 15, which prohibited the state from discriminating against any citizen on the grounds of religion, race, caste, sex, or place of birth, and specifically forbade any restriction on this account with respect to access to public places, including the "use of wells, tanks, bathing ghats, roads, and places of public resort maintained wholly or partly out of State funds or dedicated to the use of the general public." Article 16 further guaranteed equality of opportunity in employment and in all appointments to government offices to all citizens. Article 17 was still more explicit. It declared "untouchability" to be abolished under the law and forbade its practice subject to legal penalties.

Apart from establishing a new egalitarian principle of justice, the constitution endorsed a number of practical measures to create more favorable social conditions for the institutionalization of democratic norms over an extended period of time. Special provisions were enacted for a period of ten years under Articles 330-342 to reserve seats in the Lok Sabha and in the legislative assemblies of the state for members of untouchable castes and tribes, in proportion to their percentage in the population, and also for their appointment to reserved posts in the state and Union services. The states were also empowered to create additional reserved posts in state services, schools, and other public facilities for members of the scheduled castes and tribes, and for any other "backward" class that was deemed inadequately represented. The second major positive commitment aimed at speeding up social change was in respect to education. The constitution endorsed the principle of free and compulsory education for all children up to the age of fourteen and directed the states to "endeavor to provide" education for all children of school age within a period of ten years. Further, the constitution paved the way for establishing new institutions of popular participation at the local level. It directed the states to organize village panchayats and "endow them with such powers and authority as may be necessary to enable them to function as units of self-government."

This framework of constitutional arrangements, with its short-term limitations and long-range opportunities for carrying out democratic social reform, was in place by the time that Nehru finally succeeded in winning Cabinet approval for a national program of planned development. The prime minister, whose power was still not predominant in either the government or the Congress party, followed his characteristic political style of getting agreement for broad principles of socialist transformation even while approving the conservative economic policies endorsed in the Draft Outline of the First Plan. This time, however, simply the endorsement of radical economic and social goals proved sufficient to alarm the conservatives inside the Congress party. Nehru found that he could no longer avoid an open confrontation with the opponents to secular and socialist aims of development. The outcome of the conflict, which finally established Nehru's unquestioned authority as the arbiter of national policy, at the same time further weakened the socialist and Gandhian contingent inside the Congress party.

At the end of 1949, Nehru once again revived the question of establishing a planning commission, this time fortified by a recommendation from an American advisor. Once again, the idea met resistance from Sardar Patel and senior government officials. But the inability of private enterprise to deal adequately with the continuing economic crisis strengthened Nehru's hand.[27] On January 25, 1950, the Working Com-

[27] Nehru's hand was also strengthened by the support of Shankarrao Deo, a respected Gandhian and then general secretary of the AICC as well as a member of the AICC's Economic Program Committee. Deo entered the debate with a specific set of recommendations for a Sarvodaya Plan that on the whole followed official party resolutions on major questions of economic policy. In the industrial sector, it endorsed proposals for government control over large private-sector enterprises in consumption goods; public ownershp of all defense industries, power, mining, metallurgy, chemicals, heavy engineering, and ma-

mittee, after acrimonious debate, finally agreed to a resolution calling for the creation of a planning commission. But so far from endorsing government control in industry and land reform in agriculture, Sardar Patel prevailed once again in deleting a passage from the original draft that would have defined the purposes of planning as "the progressive elimination of a social, political and economic exploitation and inequality, the motive of private gain in economic activity or organization of society and the antisocial concentration of wealth and means of production."[28] All that Nehru could manage by way of compensation was a statement linking the work of the planners to the Directive Principles of State Policy contained in the constitution.[29] The final draft of the Cabinet resolution that established the Planning Commission on March 15 singled out three principles as special terms of reference in the preparation of a plan: (1) that the citizens, men and women equally, have the right to an adequate means of livelihood, (2) that the ownership and control of the material resources of the country are so distributed as best to subserve the common good; and (3) that the operation of the economic system does not result in the concentration of wealth and means of production to the common detriment.

The Planning Commission, with Nehru as its chairman, was from the outset relegated to an advisory status. All recommendations on Plan policy had to be submitted to the Cabinet for consideration and approval. The conservative bent of the Draft Outline was evident as early as August 1950, when the planners submitted a six-year plan outline to the Commonwealth Consultative Committee as part of the Columbo Plan for Cooperative Economic Development in South and Southeast Asia. The appearance of the completed Draft Outline a year later confirmed the existence of a wide chasm between statements of principle and programs of action.

The Directive Principles of State Policy were accepted as the guide to the "economic and social pattern to be attained through planning." However, the planners warned in an immediate caveat that "a hasty implementation of measures intended to bring about economic equality, may, in the short run, affect savings and the level of production adversely."[30] Although the Draft Outline endorsed goals of social and in-

---

chinery and machine tools; and nationalization of banks, insurance companies, and foreign trade. In agriculture, it recommended immediate legislation to confer occupancy rights on tenants, reduce rentals, scale down debts, and regulate the operations of rural money lenders. Over the long term, it endorsed the agrarian pattern recommended by the Congress Agrarian Reforms Committee. See Sarvodaya Planning Committee, *Principles of Sarvodaya Plan* (New Delhi, 1950).

[28] Kochanek, *The Congress Party of India*, p. 139.
[29] Tarlok Singh, *Towards an Integrated Society*, pp. 253-54.
[30] *First Five Year Plan, A Draft Outline*, p. 11.

stitutional transformation, virtually all programs included in the plan were justified by reference to a single yardstick: the economic goal of increasing production. The result was an approach to planning that limited the government's role to the creation of social capital and financial incentives for the expansion of private enterprise.

Despite the fact that total tax revenue in 1950/51 was only about seven percent of national income, with less than one-third coming from direct taxes, the planners did not propose any significant new taxation effort except by the states.[31] On the contrary, they were concerned that additional central taxes on personal or corporate income would depress the volume of savings and capital formation in the private sector. Since the inflationary economic climate ruled out any substantial reliance on deficit financing, resources available for development outlay during 1951-1956 were calculated mainly on the basis of normal expansion in governmental revenue and capital receipts, supplemented by withdrawals from India's sterling balances and modest levels of foreign aid. In effect, this approach to fiscal policy eliminated all development projects that were beyond those already budgeted by the states and the central government; that is, it ruled out any large-scale program for industrial development in the public sector. Indeed, industry, including small-scale and cottage industries, was assigned only some Rs. 101 crores out of an estimated total outlay of Rs. 1,493 crores (6.7 percent).[32] The planners did affirm the need to institute a system of controls on capital issues, industrial licensing, foreign exchange allocations, imports and exports, and prices; but they simultaneously conceded that "the expansion of industrial production during the period of the Plan would be largely the responsibility of the private sector."[33] They also extended a warm welcome to foreign capital "when finance is the main handicap in the progress of industry."[34]

The Draft Outline assigned highest priority to agriculture, rural development, irrigation, and power. Altogether, outlays under these heads of development accounted for about Rs. 641 crores, or 43 percent of total expenditure.[35] This emphasis was dictated by the fact that "the shortage of food and raw materials is at present the weakest point in the country's economy"[36] and the greatest break on a faster tempo of development in the future. Here again, there was a large discrepancy between the prescriptive and operational portions of the agricultural development pro-

[31] *First Five Year Plan*, p. 40. The Draft Outline did include provisions for additional taxation by the states amounting to some Rs. 213 crores, composed mainly of increases in land revenue taxes, irrigation rates, estate duties, sales taxes, and luxury taxes.

[32] *First Five Year Plan, A Draft Outline*, p. 39.

[33] *Ibid.*, p. 152.                                    [34] *Ibid.*, p. 159.

[35] *Ibid.*, p. 39. An unspecified amount of the allocation for irrigation and power of Rs. 450 crores was for the development of hydroelectric power only; other schemes were multipurpose; p. 122.

[36] *Ibid.*, p. 75.

gram. The planners, pointing out that the great majority of India's farmers cultivated uneconomic holdings and could not invest in improved practices, defined the solution to the central problem of increasing production as changing "the character of Indian agriculture from subsistence farming to economic farming and [bringing] about such changes in its organization as will introduce a substantial measure of efficiency in farming operations and enable the low income farmer to increase his return."[37] Among other changes, they believed that this would require the reorganization of agriculture into "relatively larger units of management and production than the existing holdings."[38] The "ultimate objective" was described as cooperative village management, under which " all the land in the village is to be regarded as a single farm." In the interim, the smaller holders would be "encouraged and assisted to group themselves voluntarily into Cooperative Farming Societies."[39] All producers, moreover, were expected to belong to a Village Production Council that would frame village production plans, assess requirements for finance and supplies, channel available government assistance from cooperative multipurpose societies (envisaged for groups of ten villages) to individual cultivators, and organize voluntary labor for community works.

In practice, institutional reform was assigned secondary importance in the program for increasing agricultural production. The planners ruled out nationalization of land for collective cultivation on the grounds of "a tradition of free peasant ownership."[40] Next, they rejected the proposal to place a ceiling on existing holdings in order to redistribute land to subsistence farmers, arguing that "on the larger farms production will fall and, for a period at any rate, on other farms also, and it may well be that the decline in production may have a serious effect on the well-being and stability of rural society as a whole."[41] Apart from zamindari abolition, which was already in progress, the only concrete proposals for land reform contained in the Draft Outline centered around recommendations for legislation to protect tenants-at-will and to determine a ceiling on future acquisition of land by individuals.

The greatest emphasis in agricultural programs was placed on the adoption of improved practices, particularly the introduction of irrigation and the application of chemical fertilizer. Since the great majority of cultivators were known to have no surplus for investment in improved techniques, the agricultural development strategy clearly favored the larger landowners. In addition, the planners were so concerned about maximizing the economic goals of planning that they warned the states

[37] Ibid., p. 94.                                         [38] Ibid., p. 98.
[39] Ibid., p. 104.                                       [40] Ibid., p. 99.
[41] Ibid.

against repeating the costly errors of the past in spreading scarce resources and personnel very widely over all districts. Instead, they
stressed, "it is essential that every state should draw up a program of
work for bringing certain areas, one after another, under intensive development, while holding the rest of the State more thinly. Since additional
production is the most urgent objective, those areas should be selected
where, on account of irrigation facilities or assured rainfall, additional effort is likely to produce the more substantial results."[42]

If some socialist and Gandhian intellectuals saw such proposals as "a
great climb-down from the objectives and program advocated by the
Congress till recently,"[43] industrialists and others more sympathetic to
private enterprise viewed the very establishment of a central planning
agency with alarm. Communal elements in the party were also seriously
disturbed by Nehru's conciliatory attitude toward Pakistan; his insistence
on full civil rights for Indian Muslims; and the pending proposals for
basic social reform in the Hindu law code. The upcoming general elections of 1952 acted as a catalyst in stimulating formation of an informal
coalition among conservative and communal groups for the purpose of
curbing Nehru's influence in capturing control of the national party organization, especially the Working Committee and the Central Election
Committee.

In the September 1950 election for Congress president, this coalition,
whose leaders claimed to have the support of Sardar Patel, campaigned
actively for Purshottamdas Tandon, a Congressman from Uttar Pradesh
with strong communal leanings and a pronounced antipathy toward
planning and socialism. Tandon's opponent, J. B. Kripalani, had the
support of the socialists and Gandhians. Nehru characteristically refrained from making a public endorsement in favor of any candidate, although he was believed to be sympathetic to Kripalani. Tandon, with a
margin of some 250 votes in the AICC, proved victorious. Moreover, he
immediately moved to consolidate the power of the conservative elements by naming a Working Committee that drew heavily on state party
leaders, many of whom were known opponents of Nehru's social and
economic policies.[44] Tandon went further: he capitalized on the party
rank-and-file's feelings of neglect to insist that the pre-Independence
practice of consulting the Working Committee on all major issues of policy should be renewed. By September 1950, the socialist and Gandhian
elements, most of whom had already been forced out of key positions in

[42] *Ibid.*, p. 82.
[43] P. A. Wadia and K. T. Merchant, *The Five Year Plan, A Criticism* (Bombay, 1952), p.
78.
[44] Kochanek, *The Congress Party of India*, p. 121.

state party organizations, found that they were also being excluded from decision-making roles in the national party. It was the last desperate effort of this group to preserve their influence at the Center that ultimately precipitated the famous Nehru-Tandon "confrontation."[45]

Nehru, as always, was a reluctant protagonist. On September 20, 1950, Kripalani, and dissident socialist and Gandhian Congressmen from Uttar Pradesh, West Bengal, Andhra, and Malabar organized the Congress Democratic Front in an effort to reform the party from within and safeguard the long-standing commitments to secularism, social reform, and planning. Nehru privately endorsed the Front's aims, but despite Kripalani's hopes, did not join it. By November 1950, partly out of disgust at his attitude, a hundred Congressmen from West Bengal decided to quit the Congress entirely, and form a new party. When Tandon directed Kripalani to dissolve the Democratic Front on December 4, and Kripalani also threatened secession from Congress in response, Nehru still remained silent. It was only after Sardar Patel's death on December 15, 1950, that Nehru took the first tentative step toward intervention by introducing a unity resolution at the January meeting of the AICC that all groups supported. Nevertheless, at the same meeting, Kripalani failed to gain the Working Committee's agreement to a slate of candidates for the Central Election Committee (CEC) that would include representatives of the Democratic Front. Then, in April 1951, the Andhra dissidents also announced they were leaving the party to form a new organization.

In an effort to ward off further defections, Nehru finally promised Kripalani that he would use his influence at the forthcoming Delhi session of the AICC in May to ensure adequate representation for the Front on the CEC. Yet, at Delhi, the prime minister found himself powerless against the conservative majority of the Working Committee. The final list of candidates approved by the AICC reflected Tandon's wishes. Soon after, Kripalani and his supporters also resigned from Congress. In June 1951, the defectors from West Bengal and Andhra announced that they were combining forces with Kripalani's group to form a new party, the Kisan Majdoor Praja party (KMPP), or the Peasants and Workers Popular party, dedicated to "the Gandhian way."

A second attempt by Nehru in July to force changes in the composition of the Working Committee and the CEC in order to win the dissidents back proved no more successful. Finally, at the end of July, Nehru was confronted with the resignations of two of his ministers, Ajit Prasad Jain and Rafi Ahmed Kidwai. Both were longtime party stalwarts from

[45] The most detailed version of the events surrounding the confrontation between Nehru and Tandon is given *ibid.*, pp. 27-53. Other accounts are in Weiner, *Party Politics in India*, pp. 65-97; and Brecher, *Nehru: A Political Biography*, pp. 430-37.

Uttar Pradesh, and one, Kidwai, was a close personal friend. The resignation of Kidwai and his decision to join the KMPP finally jolted Nehru into dramatic action by underscoring the threat to his power as prime minister in the High Command's continuing attacks against his supporters. On August 6, Nehru announced his resignation from the Working Committee and the CEC. Next, armed with a vote of confidence from the Congress party in parliament, he made it known that he was no longer interested in the simple reconstruction of the Working Committee. Rather, he gave tacit approval to suggestions that he assume the party leadership himself. On September 8, despite bitter behind-the-scenes opposition, the AICC accepted Tandon's resignation, and elected Nehru Congress president by an overwhelming majority.

Parallels between the Nehru-Tandon confrontation of 1951, and the Gandhi-Bose conflict in 1939 suggest themselves easily. Brecher observes, for example, that in each case the majority surrendered to political blackmail by a disagreeable national hero whose base in popular support made him indispensable.[46] In 1939, another civil disobedience movement was in the offing, and effective mass struggle required Gandhi's leadership. In 1951, the first general elections were imminent, and party leaders were reluctant to face the electorate without Nehru. Second, the outcomes appear similar. Both Gandhi and Nehru subsequently were established as "super-presidents" of the party. They secured the right of veto over all appointments to the Working Committee. As a result, each is considered to have emerged as the undisputed leader of the party.

Despite these parallels, the differences are at least equally significant. Nehru's triumph occurred in a radically changed political context: that of Independence, a federal constitution, and popular government. In these circumstances, control over the national party amounted to not much more than the power of articulating the broad principles of Congress policy. The Pradesh Congress Committees, which now enjoyed independent access to the patronage of state governments, autonomous sources of finance, and an electoral base among influential local elites, remained in effective control of the action arm of the party. Even to maintain the fragile unity of the national coalition, Nehru felt obliged to follow a conciliatory policy at the Center. He used his new authority to select the Working Committee with characteristic restraint, replacing the organization elements with appointees selected from among Cabinet ministers and chief ministers of the states, partly to facilitate informal coordination of all-India policy. He did not pack the Working Committee with his own supporters. On the contrary, conservative opinion continued to be

[46] Brecher, *Nehru*, pp. 43-45.

well represented.[47] An immediate result was that most dissidents refused Nehru's invitation to return to Congress after Tandon's defeat. Apart from feelings of intense personal resentment aroused by Nehru's prolonged inaction, they realized that he could not alter the composition of local party committees, and he would not purge the national leadership to make way for his own supporters.

On the eve of the 1951 elections, therefore, the socialist and Gandhian forces who together had articulated the fundamental social and economic ideology of the Congress party were widely scattered. Some remained inside Congress; others found a place in the Socialist party or the KMPP. Each claimed to be the true heir to the revolutionary spirit of Gandhism. Those who considered themselves the most orthodox of Gandhi's followers turned their back on the democratic political process entirely. Instead, following the lead of Vinoba Bhave, who had been a constructive worker since 1916, they organized the Sarvodaya Samaj, an all-India confederation of constructive workers to take up the task of nonviolent social revolution. Walking from village to village to emphasize their identity with the poor, Vinoba and his followers asked the larger landowners to contribute one-sixth of their holdings in *bhoodan* (land-gift) for distribution to the landless. The appeal was phrased in traditional terms of *yagna* or renunciation and self-sacrifice, and argued that it was the *dharma* of the upper classes to protect the poor. On April 18, 1951, Vinoba received his first donation of land in the Telegana district of Andhra, where communist-led peasants were still rioting and looting. Subsequently, the Sarvodaya Samaj set out to organize a network of *bhoodan* workers to walk from village to village in all parts of India and to canvass for a whole series of *dans* or gifts: *sampattidan* (money), *shramdan* (labor), *buddhidan* (intelligence), and even *jiwandan* (a pledge of lifelong dedication to *bhoodan* work).

The fact that Nehru could no longer count on a cohesive core of socialist and Gandhian support inside his own party further limited the leverage built into his dual role as leader of the Congress party and the government. He was confirmed as the ultimate arbiter of national party policy. His version of the 1951 election manifesto was accepted without challenge. It reiterated the longstanding commitments to equality, economic planning, secularism, and social reform. He also set down the national criteria for the selection of Congress candidates: proved integrity, devotion to communal harmony, long service in the Congress, and a "progressive social outlook." But he was powerless to enforce these

---

[47] Rafi Ahmed Kidwai was one of the few socialist defectors to heed Nehru's appeal and return to the Congress party in 1951. Though he had been a member of the Working Committee for several years previously, Nehru did not appoint him to the reconstituted Working Committee. He did offer a place to Tandon.

criteria at the level of the state party organizations. His dilemma was dramatized by the lists of candidates recommended to the Central Election Committee. Altogether, about 25,000 individual applications (including those put forward on "official" lists) were received by the CEC for fewer than 4,000 tickets to the state and national legislatures. But "appeals followed these applications, about a lakh of them, almost four on average against each applicant. The complaints made truly distressing reading, alleging about the individuals concerned all possible crimes. Some of the charges were major and serious, many were flippant and frivolous."[48]

Although the AICC secretariat recruited dozens of volunteers to help screen each prospective candidate, it was clearly impossible to conduct a thorough investigation of 25,000 applicants and 100,000 separate charge sheets. In the end, except where the Pradesh Election Committees were internally divided, the CEC had to rely mainly on the recommendations by the state parties. Yet, in the main, the official lists had been carefully constructed to appeal to traditional caste loyalties.

The outcome of the 1952 elections,[49] however, only strengthened Nehru in his conviction that the unity of the Congress party had to be maintained as the only national political force in India. Just 60 percent of the electorate went to the polls. Of this proportion, 45 percent cast their ballots for the Congress in elections to parliament, and little more than 42 percent in the contests for state assembly seats. Opposition groups actually commanded a majority of the total vote, but they were hopelessly fragmented. Altogether, seventy-seven separate political parties took part in the elections. The overwhelming majority of these parties were formed on an ad hoc basis, and drew on local pockets of support based on caste, communal, or regional ties. Fully one-fifth of the electorate cast their votes in state assembly elections for independents, or nonparty candidates, including former princes, and members of the lesser aristocracy.

The Congress party controlled the largest single bloc of voter support in all sections of India. Except in Saurashtra, however, it did not poll a majority of votes in any state. Single-member constituencies and the extreme fragmentation of opposition groups accounted for the ability of Congress to win an overwhelming majority of seats in the national parliament and the state assemblies. Only the Congress party possessed sufficient organizational strength to offer candidates for all contested seats, both at the Center and in the states. The socialists, by contrast, could field candidates for only 1,805 of the 3,205 state assembly seats, and 255

[48] Indian National Congress, AICC, *The Pilgrimage and After* (New Delhi, 1952), p. 6.
[49] For an excellent analysis of the election results, see Asoka Mehta, "General Elections and After," in *Report of the Special Convention of the Socialist Party* (Bombay, 1952), pp. 95-108.

of the 479 Lok Sabha seats. Even then, they managed to win only 128 contests; altogether, they showed significant strength in only 500 constituencies. The second largest party in India, they had polled little more than 10 percent of the popular vote. The KMPP did worse. They were able to contest fewer than one-third of all state assembly and Lok Sabha seats; and won little more than 5 percent of the total vote. Of the remaining parties claiming "national" support, or a following in most states, two were considered communal groups, the Jan Sangh and the Ram Raja Parishad, with 3 percent and 2 percent of the popular vote, respectively. A third, the Scheduled Caste Federation, which appealed exclusively to Harijans, managed to glean another 2 percent of the total vote. Probably the most disquieting omen was the success of the Communist Party of India. Although the communists won little more than 5 percent of the popular vote, their strategy of concentrating on local strongholds proved profitable. Nationwide, they emerged as the largest opposition group in both the Lok Sabha and the state assemblies. They maintained their strong position in the southern states of Madras, Hyderabad, and Travancore-Cochin; in addition, they made an impressive showing in West Bengal, and increased their support in Punjab and Orissa.

On the whole, the results were sufficient to suggest that for the time being only the Congress party could provide a focus for social mobilization on the basis of a common national identity; all other groups would divide the country further along caste, communal, sectional, or class lines. More than ever, Nehru thought in terms of applying Gandhian principles to problems of social change. He reasoned:

It is clear that so far as this country is concerned we cannot attain this ideal [of classless society] by conflict and violence. We have achieved many things by the way of peace and there is no particular reason why we should give that up and take to violent ways. There is a very particular reason why we should not do so, because however high our ideals and objectives may be, if we try to attain them by methods of violence, matters will be very greatly delayed. It will contribute to the growth of the very evils we are fighting against. India is not only a big country, but a varied country, and if anyone takes to the sword, he will inevitably be met by the sword of someone else. Therefore, it becomes a clash between swords, and all the limited energies of the nation required for better ends will be destroyed by the process.[50]

Nehru's "way of peace" in pursuing goals of social transformation drew heavily on Gandhian methods in an attempt to separate the basis of

[50] Jawaharlal Nehru, *Planning and Development*, "Speech to the Lok Sabha," December 15, 1952, p. 6.

political organization from the foundation of social reform. Like Gandhi before him, Nehru maintained the tactical separation between an accommodative party ideology and organization aimed at reassuring the propertied classes, and an economic strategy that incorporated proposals for institutional change designed to speed up popular organization and pressure from below on state governments for the implementation of social reforms.

The final version of the First Five-Year Plan published in December 1952 reflected Nehru's new authority over national questions of economic and social policy. It also contained the first indication of a new approach to economic development that incorporated a strategy for peaceful social change.

Although the First Plan retained the caution of the Draft Outline in its proposals on fiscal policy, there was a discernible change in tone and emphasis on the approach to industrial development. Total Plan outlay was increased from Rs. 1,493 crores to Rs. 2,069 crores, mainly as a result of improvement in the position with respect to receipts from loans, small savings, deposits, and funds.[51] Compared to the Draft Outline, the First Plan raised the allocation to industry from Rs. 101 crores to Rs. 173 crores, or from 6.1 percent to 8.4 percent of total outlay.[52] The bulk of the increase went toward expansion of basic industries, including mineral development, heavy electrical equipment, and a new iron and steel complex. The broad outlines of an indirect attack on the prerogatives and position of private enterprise were, moreover, beginning to emerge. First, the planners announced their intention to increase central supervision and control over the private sector. Private enterprise would subsequently have to operate within the framework of the new Industries (Development and Regulation) Act, 1951, which provided that no new industrial unit or substantial expansions to existing plants could be made without a license from the central government. It also empowered the government to investigate the operations of any industry to make regulations concerning the quality and price of production.[53] Second, there was a new emphasis on overtaking the private sector as the preeminent agency of industrial development. The planners gave notice of a much larger role for the public sector in basic industries in future plans.[54]

[51] *The First Five Year Plan*, p. 54.
[52] *Ibid.*, p. 70.                                    [53] *Ibid.*, pp. 423-24.
[54] The planners asserted: "Whether one thinks of the problems of capital formation or the introduction of new techniques or the extension of social services, or the overall realignment of productive forces and class relationships within society, one comes inevitably to the conclusion that a rapid expansion of the economic and social responsibilities of the State will alone be capable of satisfying the legitimate expectations of the people. This need not involve complete nationalization of the means of production or elimination of pri-

The most striking innovations, however, occurred in the approach to agricultural development. The Draft Outline had offered little by way of practical programs to dissolve the apparent contradiction between the economic and social aims of planning. It had advanced a predominantly technocratic strategy based on incentives to greater private investment on modern inputs and concentration of resources in the irrigated areas having the highest production potential. Such an approach might have yielded maximum gains in output, but only at the social cost of widening the gap between large landowners and the mass of subsistence farmers on the one hand, and the most advantaged and impoverished regions on the other. The final version of the First Plan paved the way for the reconciliation of growth and equity goals by reformulating the problem of agricultural development in terms of eliminating exploitative social and economic relations that inhibited more efficient use of existing labor-intensive production practices to increase output.

The planners this time identified the basic cause of India's backwardness not in the absence of modern technology per se, but in the persistence of "certain inhibiting socio-economic factors which prevent the most dynamic forces in the economy from asserting themselves." In an analysis reminiscent of the "fetters" thesis advanced by Marx, the Planning Commission argued that in Indian conditions, economic progress was inextricably bound up with social change. They asserted the general theory that

> corresponding to each stage of development, there tends to grow a certain economic and social stratification which is conducive to the conservation of gains from the use of known techniques. Such stratification has a part to play in social progress. But beyond a point, it hampers innovation and change, and its very strength becomes a source of weakness. For development to proceed further, a re-adaptation of social institutions and social relationships thus becomes necessary. . . . The problem, therefore, is not one of merely rechanneling economic activity within the existing framework; that framework itself has to be remodeled.[55]

Applying this formulation to the rural sector, it became feasible to argue that higher levels of output depended less on the application of scientific methods to agriculture—which few cultivators could afford—than on the transformation of the institutional framework to provide small

---

vate agencies in agriculture or business or industry. It does mean, however, a progressive widening of the public sector and a reorientation of the private sector to the needs of a planned economy," *ibid.*, pp. 31-32.

[55] *Ibid.*, p. 7.

farmers and agricultural workers with adequate incentives to increase production through more efficient application of traditional labor-intensive techniques.

There was, in fact, substantial evidence of a chronic gap between productivity potential and actual output within the vast agricultural sector. Such a constraint had been apparent since the turn of the century. During the forty years ending in 1946/47, the rate of increase in output of foodgrains, estimated at twelve percent, lagged far behind population growth increases of over forty percent.[56] Yield levels, among the lowest in the world, showed almost no increase. Most remarkable, small negative growth rates emerged, both in output and yield per acre for rice, India's largest crop accounting for about one-half of foodgrain output.[57] India's experience during this period provided a direct contrast to the pattern of "agricultural involution" reported for Java under similar circumstances, where it proved feasible to raise per hectare yields to match population growth rates through the application of more labor-intensive cultivation techniques.[58] In India, the marginal productivity of labor could not be maintained. Per capita availability of foodgrains declined.[59]

The obvious gap between actual average yields and technical possibilities was interpreted as a cause for optimism in assessing India's potentiality for rapid agricultural growth. Grain yields were low, not only in comparison to advanced countries, but with respect to countries at roughly the same stage of development. Average paddy yields per acre in China were estimated at almost twice the Indian level, suggesting that large yield increases per acre were technologically possible with only small changes in production techniques and using mainly indigenous inputs. It was not uncommon to argue that even a one hundred percent increase in yields could be achieved through more careful attention to land levelling, seedbed preparation, weeding, line sowing, interculture, and more efficient techniques in collection and application of organic manures.

The labor force was also inefficiently used for work on land improvement schemes. There was large-scale underemployment in rural areas at the same time as there was substantial scope for capital formation through the construction of land reclamation and irrigation projects. Over the previous forty years, the net acreage sown had not appreciably increased, even though there was significant potential for bringing fallows and new areas under cultivation. Only about eighteen percent of the

---

[56] George Blyn, *Agricultural Trends in India, 1891-1947*, p. 96.

[57] *Ibid.*, pp. 219-24.

[58] See Clifford Geertz, *Agricultural Involution, the Processes of Ecological Change in Indonesia* (Berkeley and Los Angeles, 1963), pp. 28-38, 77-82.

[59] Blyn, *Agricultural Trends in India*, pp. 104-105.

area under crops had assured water from irrigation, although almost fifty percent of the cultivable area could be irrigated. Since 1910, gross area sown had increased by only ten percent, mainly as the result of government initiatives in extending canals from large river-valley projects.

Efforts to raise agricultural productivity within the existing agrarian framework, however, were almost certain to run into direct obstacles in the pattern of land distribution and land tenure. The system of land-ownership based on individual proprietary rights, inherited from the British, imposed severe limitations on the efficient allocation of land, labor, and capital. The characteristic features of the agrarian pattern in the early years of planning could be summarized as follows:[60] (1) the first and overriding constraint was the unfavorable land-man ratio in the rural areas of about .92 acre per capita; (2) this overall scarcity of land was accompanied by extreme inequalities in the distribution of ownership. More than one-fifth of all rural households (22 percent) owned no land at all. Another 25 percent owned fragments of land or less than one acre. An additional 14 percent owned uneconomic or marginal holdings of 1 acre to 2.5 acres (that is, one hectare or less). In brief, the majority of all rural households, approximately 61 percent, either owned no land, or small fragments of land, or uneconomic and marginal holdings of one hectare or less. All of them together owned less than 8 percent of the total area. These were the recruits in the army of the chronically unemployed and underemployed, the millions of the rural poor precariously subsisting just at the border or slipping below the line of poverty. They could be contrasted with what passed for large landowners in India, the upper 13 percent of all households who had more than 10 acres and owned about 64 percent of the entire area, and the even smaller elite of the upper 5 percent having 20 acres or more, and owning 41 percent of the area; (3) even so, the upper 13 percent or so of rural households could be considered "large" landowners only from the perspective of their size relative to the mass of landless and subsistence cultivators. Among this group, for example, fewer than 1 percent owned holdings of 50 acres or more. Even then, there were many fewer large farms than large landowners. Holdings in all size groups were subdivided into separate parcels that were scattered within and between villages.[61] The tiniest fragments were, of course, contained in the smallest holdings. They might be subdivided into one-quarter or one-third-acre plots. Yet, "large" holdings

[60] The first extensive data on landholdings in India was collected in 1954-1955 and is published in *National Sample Survey, Eighth Round*, Number 10, *First Report on Land Holdings, Rural Sector*. The data for distribution on landownership by size of holdings is presented in Table 4.3, p. 14. The average household size was calculated at 4.9 persons, and is presented in Table 7.1, p. 39.

[61] *National Sample Survey, Seventeenth Round*, Number 140, *Tables with Notes on Some Aspects of Landholdings in Rural Areas (State and All-India Estimates)*, Draft, p. 70.

of 10 acres or more were commonly separated into seven or eight parcels of 2, 3, and 4 acres. "Large" landowners, therefore, tended to operate small holdings. They did not enjoy advantages associated with economies of scale; (4) this pattern of land distribution was associated with a complex system of tenurial relationships in which sharecropping played a central role. Landowners with tiny plots leased out their holdings to other cultivators, and sought additional employment outside the village. "Large" landowners leased out part of their holdings because they tended to have several scattered plots that they found impossible to manage without the aid of tenants. The incidence of tenancy was highest in the densely populated rice deltas where land-man ratios were least favorable. It was not unusual for 30 to 40 percent of all cultivators to take some land on oral lease, or for the proportion of the area operated under such sharecropping arrangements to reach levels of 40 percent or more.[62]

Actually, the existing patterns of land distribution and land tenure put major obstacles in the way of increasing per acre yields either through the more efficient application of traditional labor-intensive techniques or the introduction of modern methods. Vast numbers of the landless and those engaged in subsistence agriculture remained unemployed or underemployed for long periods during the year. They had neither the incentive nor the capacity to carry out labor-intensive production schemes that could increase yields within the traditional framework of production. Sharecroppers paying 50 percent or more of their output in rent provided

[62] It is difficult to make accurate estimates of the incidence of tenancy. Most leasing arrangements involve sharecropping agreements that are unrecorded in village records. The method of inquiry used in the National Sample Survey's reports on landholding typically underestimated the size of the problem. Questionnaires were administered to a small number of households per village, selected according to a stratified random sample drawn from four main types of livelihood classes: (1) cultivating owners of land; (2) nonowning cultivators; (3) noncultivating owners; and (4) nonagriculturists and agricultural laborers. However, in assigning each village household to a particular category, the investigator relied mainly on information supplied by "knowledgeable persons," such as the village record keeper or revenue officer, and the head of the village panchayat. Since the interviewer was unfamiliar with the village, and the land surveys were widely associated with the government's proposals for agrarian reform, village officials often collaborated with influential landowners to declare that a given field was in cultivating possession of its owner when it was actually operated by a tenant. Even on the basis of incomplete records, however, data collected in the early 1950s reported a substantial incidence of tenancy. Twenty percent of all cultivators operated "mixed" holdings of partly owned and partly leased land, while an additional seventeen percent were "pure" tenants, cultivating land entirely on lease. Altogether, the proportion of the total area under cultivation of tenants was put at about twenty percent. See *National Sample Survey, Eighth Round*, Number 30, *Report of Land Holdings (2), Operational Holdings in Rural India*, p. 17. According to interview data collected by the Census Commission in 1961, about 23 percent of all cultivators were pure tenants, operating wholly leased-in land; and in many states, 30 to 40 percent of all farmers took some land on oral lease. *The Statesman*, June 1, 1968. Interview materials from local field research in selected regions of the rice areas suggest an even higher incidence of sharecropping. See Planning Commission, *A Study of Tenurial Conditions in Package Districts* by Wolf Ladejinsky.

the most obvious case. They rarely invested in modern inputs and they certainly did not lavish any extra attention on the cultivation of leased-in land. Nor was there much scope for carrying out overhead labor-investment projects—construction and maintenance of water courses, field channels, wells, tanks, drainage systems—which were so critical for increasing productivity through traditional techniques. Individuals were unable to undertake such land improvement schemes, and groups of landless and land-poor cultivators found no incentive to do so.

The patterns of land distribution and land tenure were only somewhat less serious obstacles in achieving higher levels of productivity through the introduction of capital-intensive technologies. Many "large" land-owners, like small and marginal cultivators found it uneconomic to invest in modern agricultural techniques. The large landowner was rarely able to realize the maximum return from his investment because the size of his operational holding was usually less than the optimum area for efficient cultivation using costly modern equipment. This was a pervasive problem in the rice areas, where the installation of minor irrigation works (percolation wells, pumpsets, and tubewells) was desirable to supplement supplies of water from surface irrigation projects, but the command area of the smallest mechanized works were a minimum of five to ten acres. Without assured water, large cultivators, no less than small and marginal holders, hesitated to make higher outlays on the optimum application of fertilizers and pesticides, when the investment was likely to be lost if rains were inadequate or there was flooding. Some landowners, of course, simply had no interest in land development or maximizing output from their holdings. Under existing tenurial arrangements, they effortlessly received reliable income by collecting rent and interest on loans.

Under these circumstances, it appeared plausible that direct obstacles in the pattern of land distribution and tenurial relations were sufficient in themselves to account for a large part of India's problems of agricultural stagnation and mass poverty. It was also reasonable that solutions should first be sought in changing the agrarian pattern. It was, of course, possible to consider a strategy for raising agricultural output that did not go much beyond consolidation of existing ownership holdings aimed at increasing economies of scale. But consolidation, in the absence of any policy for redistribution of ownership rights in land, would only aggravate the problems of technological dualism and income disparities within the agricultural economy. Displaced sharecroppers would swell the ranks of the landless laborers. Meanwhile, even more "surplus" labor would be created as big farmers, operating consolidated holdings, found it more economic to mechanize farm operations.

The final version of the First Plan ruled out the undiluted capitalist

pattern of agrarian reorganization. Instead, it adopted alternative proposals for land reform that made significant redistribution of land and some
degree of change from individual to cooperative patterns of economic activity an integral part of the program for agricultural development.

The most striking departure occurred in the recommendation for ceilings. Reversing their earlier position in the Draft Outline, the planners
announced that they were now "in favor of the principle that there
should be an upper limit to the amount of land that an individual may
hold." Explaining this decision, they assigned overriding importance to
the "social aspect."

> If it were the object of policy to reduce the holdings of the larger
> owners with a view to providing for the landless or for increasing
> the farms of those who now have uneconomic fragments, the facts
> at present available suggest that these aims are not likely to be
> achieved in any substantial measure. The question whether some
> limit should not be placed on the amount of land an individual may
> hold, has, therefore, to be answered in terms of general principles
> rather than in relation to the possible use that could be made of land
> in excess of any limit that may be set. We have considered carefully
> the implications of the various courses of action which are possible.
> It appears to us that, in relation to land (as also in other sectors of the
> economy) individual property in excess of any norm that may be
> proposed has to be justified in terms of public interest, and not
> merely on grounds of individual rights and claims.[63]

The planners endorsed the recommendation of the Congress Agrarian
Reforms Committee to establish a ceiling at three times the "family holding." They set down that the ceiling should apply both to land under the
direct cultivation of owners, and to the amount of land that could be resumed from tenants-at-will for the purpose of personal cultivation. Even
in the case of small and middle owners, the landlord would be permitted
to resume only the amount of land that could be cultivated by the adult
members belonging to his own family. If owners did not act to resume
their holdings, tenants would be protected by a five-year lease, and legal
rents of not more than one-fourth to one-fifth of the produce. Finally,
the planners provided that all tenants of nonresumable land should be
permitted to acquire full ownership rights in return for compensation to
the landlord at rates established by legislation.

The plight of landless workers was expected to be ameliorated but not
removed by the redistribution of land. The planners believed that this
problem could only be solved within the context of "a basic reconstruction of the village economy."[64] As in the Draft Outline, the Planning

[63] *The First Five Year Plan*, p. 188.          [64] *Ibid.*, p. 194.

Commission recommended that small and middle farmers be assisted to group themselves voluntarily into cooperative farming societies. Again, the ultimate goal was defined as cooperative village management. This time, however, the Commission suggested a modest element of compulsion: "if, for instance, a majority of the owners and occupancy tenants in a village wished to enter upon cooperative management of the land of the village, their decision should be binding on the village as a whole. To ensure confidence among all concerned, it could also be prescribed that those who express themselves in favor of cooperative management should as a body hold permanent rights in at least one-half of the land of the village, no individual holding being reckoned for this purpose in excess of the limit prescribed for resumption of personal cultivation."[65]

The recommendations for land reforms and cooperative village management, nevertheless, stopped far short of the generalized attack on private ownership rights in land that characterized the 1949 *Report of the Congress Agrarian Reforms Committee*. The impression of a moderate land policy compatible with the practice of accommodative politics was strengthened by the Planning Commission's projection of an extended time perspective for the organization of cooperative farms of small and middle farmers. The planners gave only a vague mandate to the states to organize a "good number" during the First Plan. They suggested no timetable at all for achieving the ultimate goal of cooperative village management.

Even so, the planners believed that the proposals for land reforms represented an important victory for the goal of a socialist pattern. They had achieved a consensus at the level of principle on the aim of a radical reconstruction of rural society. Recommendations for ceilings on land-ownership and the formation of cooperative farms had been endorsed by the Cabinet, the Lok Sabha, and the Congress party as part of their overall approval for the Plan. The endorsements represented the first step toward a redefinition of distribution norms that was bound in the long run to legitimize resistance to extreme inequalities in economic power. They could be expected to lead, as had earlier victories for more limited principles (for example, the right of workers to a living wage), to a political climate in which informed opinion could be harnessed for the transformation of the social structure in the direction of the new values.

Indeed, the new approach to agricultural development also incorporated a set of proposals for organizational changes at the village level that carried the potentiality for mobilizing effective public opinion as a sanction in enforcing plan policies of agrarian reform. The core of the approach was the recommendation for a Community Development program. Like its predecessor, the Constructive Program, it was designed to

---

[65] *Ibid.*, p. 197.

stimulate popular pressures for social reform from below that would ultimately make institutional change inevitable, while avoiding the destabilizing effects of a frontal attack on the prerogatives of the propertied
classes.

The first fifty-five Community Projects had been started in October
1952, under the supervision of the Planning Commission, with American technical and financial assistance. They were originally conceived
solely as programs of intensive agricultural development, and were, in
fact, allocated only to areas having water from irrigation or assured rainfall. Essentially, the Community Projects provided a multipurpose extension apparatus for coordinating government action on all problems associated with low agricultural productivity. The project staff included not
only agricultural extension workers and subject-matter specialists in crop
production, plant protection, farm management, and fertilizers, but also
extension officers for rural engineering, health, social education, welfare,
panchayats, and cooperatives. Each project area was divided into three
development Blocks of one hundred villages (approximately 65,000 persons), for an intensive development effort. A multipurpose extension
worker was assigned to every five villages to demonstrate the use of improved seeds, fertilizers, pesticides, and implements.

Nehru had been dissatisfied from the beginning with the narrow economic goals of the Community Projects. He particularly objected to the
practice of "pick[ing] out the best and most favorable spots" for intensive development when the majority of agriculturists were economically
backward.[66] But two facets of the Community Projects nevertheless
impressed him as vitally important for the social goals of planning. One
was the approach, patterned after the Constructive Program, of concentrating on all "social" problems associated with low productivity, including basic education, credit, and rural industries. The other was the
community-centered focus of the development projects, that stressed the
principles of cooperation and self-help. The Community Projects
budgeted only one-third of the costs of land reclamation, drainage, irrigation, and road building schemes, and relied on village contributions in
labor and money for the remainder. Matching contributions were also
required to qualify for government grants toward the construction of social amenities projects, including primary schools, community centers,
and drinking-water wells. There was, therefore, an objective justification
for creating and/or strengthening village institutions as grass-roots agencies for organizing the extensive popular participation necessary to carry
out rural improvement schemes. At the center of the Community Development program was a plan to establish cooperative and panchayat

[66] Ministry of Community Development, *Jawaharlal Nehru on Community Development*
(Delhi, 1957), p. 13.

institutions that aimed at reconstructing the whole village as the primary unit of economic and political action.

At the level of ideology, the proposal to use cooperatives as the major instrument of rural economic development appealed to socialist and Gandhian planners alike as desirable in itself for reversing the trend toward individualism and class division. There was still hope that cooperatives would revive and strengthen community values and interests, and restore the corporate character of village life.[67]

The proposal to place the village panchayat at the center of the planning and implementation of rural development projects represented a second aspect of the effort to recreate the community as a cohesive unit of political action. Indeed, the First Plan went as far as recommending that panchayats be given statutory responsibility for developing all resources in the village. They suggested that village panchayats: (1) frame a production plan for the whole village; (2) prepare budget estimates to carry out the plan; (3) act as a channel for government assistance; (4) enforce minimum standards of cultivation; (5) bring wasteland under cultivation; (6) arrange for cultivation of land not managed by owners; (7) organize voluntary labor for community work; (8) make arrangements for cooperative management of land and other resources in the village according to prevailing land management legislation; and (9) assist in the implementation of land reforms.[68]

But the planners were not naive about the practical obstacles to the reconstruction of the village community as the basic unit of social action, given the growth of inequality and the emergence of class interests in modern times. Even Tarlok Singh, the most influential advocate of the community approach inside the commission, had to concede that

> for several decades, as well-knit *social* organization, the village community has been slowly but steadily declining. As the pursuit of individual interest within and outside the village had become more common, the influence of the community over its members had diminished. The growth of inequality in the ownership of land, transfers of land to non-cultivators and migration to towns are evidence of these trends . . . conflict of interest within the village community have sharpened and the process continues. There are now few values which can be said to be common to the whole community, and certainly there is no common purpose which inspires all sections equally.[69]

One of the main attractions of the Community Projects was precisely their potentiality for carrying out a "nonpolitical" organizational ap-

[67] *The First Five Year Plan*, p. 164.      [68] *Ibid.*, p. 148.
[69] Singh, *Towards an Integrated Society*, p. 165.

proach to social reform while avoiding the destabilizing effects of class conflict. Presumably, all castes and classes could agree on the desirability of improving the general standard of life. They could also understand the common interest in pooling local resources of labor and money to carry out development schemes of mutual benefit. Meanwhile, the organizational core of the approach, involving plans to penetrate the village through introduction of primary institutions of cooperatives, panchayats, and schools as the instruments of collective rural improvement, offered wide scope for modifying traditional status norms and vertical caste/class divisions. The proposals for institutional change at the village level followed Gandhi's tactic of maintaining a formal separation between economic and political issues by presenting the new organizational infrastructure as an agency for popular participation in "social" improvement schemes. Indeed, the creation of a national network of village cooperatives and panchayats was represented as the revival and adaptation of traditional group-oriented values and communal institutions. But both the cooperatives and the panchayats were reconstituted on new principles of universal membership and adult suffrage. Over time, they held the revolutionary potential of redefining the effective village community to include all families regardless of caste, and of shifting the balance of economic and political power away from the landed upper castes toward the low-status peasant majority.

All agriculturist families, even uneconomic cultivators, were expected to become members of the village multipurpose cooperative society. The Planning Commission suggested that moral character rather than financial security should be the most important factor in determining the eligibility of members for agricultural loans. In the future, moreover, the cooperatives were supposed to take up supervision and control of all areas of agricultural life, including credit, marketing, distribution, and even cooperative farm management. The planners reasoned that by reducing interest rates on loans, eliminating the fees of middlemen, and facilitating the organization of efficient units of production through cooperative farm management, the societies would increase the income and surpluses from agriculture of millions of small farmers, and set in motion the process through which new norms of equality and cooperation would become incorporated in the village social structure.

The panchayats, recreated on principles of universal suffrage and majority vote, were in complementary fashion visualized as an instrument for redistribution of political power in favor of the peasant and landless castes. Above all, the new panchayat institutions provided the opportunity for a political redefinition of community from narrow notions of caste or faction to the comprehensive category of the village, which broadened the boundaries of solidarity to include the majority of

poor agriculturists. The panchayat, taking root in a period of rapidly expanding education, provided the vehicle through which a heightened
class consciousness could find expression in new horizontal forms of
political organization, and bring the power of numbers to bear in a nonviolent sanction from below for effective implementation of the national
leadership's reform program. The organized demands of the majority for
a greater share in the allocation of rural resources, one hoped, occurring
within an economic environment of expanding production, could be accommodated without a zero-sum conflict between the peasantry and the
propertied classes. Local elites might be persuaded to yield some of their
advantages. Even if a few remained recalcitrant, most would be motivated by the elemental rationality of self-preservation, and realize that
their own interest lay in accepting moderate reform as an alternative to
complete expropriation.

The redefinition of the rural development strategy to reconcile goals of
economic growth and reduction of disparities had an immediate effect on
the priorities of planning in the agricultural sector. The Planning Commission subsequently assigned only secondary importance to the provision of modern scientific inputs in the program for increasing production. Primary emphasis was placed on initiatives for institutional change
that could mobilize local manpower and resources for development. The
Community Development Projects became the "focal centers" of the agricultural strategy.

In the final version of the First Plan, the principle of selective and intensive development was completely abandoned. Instead, the planners
announced the intention to create a national extension organization,
modeled after the Community Projects, which would bring the entire
cultivated area under extensive development within a period of ten years.
The target set down for the First Plan was coverage of nearly one-fourth
the rural population, or about 120,000 villages.[70]

The decision for all-India coverage under the Community Development program was not strictly rational from an economic point of view.
Certainly, the short-term prospect for maximizing agricultural productivity in Block areas was dimmed. Budgets allocated to each Community
Development Block were radically curtailed. The ratio of extension personnel to Block population was drastically reduced. Scarce inputs of improved seeds, fertilizers, pesticides, and equipment were no longer concentrated in the most productive areas of the country, where they could
be expected to bring the highest yields, but were distributed evenly and
thinly over the entire cultivated area.

At the same time, the planners believed that by expanding the Com-

[70] *The First Five Year Plan*, p. 231.

munity Development program beyond the strict limits of economic cost-accounting, they could reap economic and social advantages in the long run, which would mitigate and more than offset the initial sacrifices in production. In exposing all areas of the country to new possibilities of progress, they counted on arousing a "burning desire" for rural better-ment[71] that could make feasible an agricultural development strategy based on the pooled energies and resources of the small farmer; and en-sure to the impoverished majority of cultivators the greatest gains of de-velopment. After 1953, the government's contribution to the Commu-nity Development program was conceived as no more than a catalyst to community action. The official machinery would supply "practical aids"—limited amounts of improved seeds, chemical fertilizers, agricul-tural credit, and technical assistance—but the "very essence of the pro-gram" was "peoples participation."[72]

While a strategy of agricultural development based on the more effi-cient use of labor was at least plausible in 1952, it was no more compel-ling as an approach to rural economic growth than in 1951. Rather, it represented the new leverage of the national leadership in selecting a de-velopment model that conformed to longstanding value goals. The major attraction of an agricultural strategy based on popular participa-tion in Community Development programs was not merely the prospect of harnessing local resources for rural development. On the contrary, rural economic growth through the Community Development program represented the only possible strategy for the accomplishment of the multiple economic, social, and political goals of planning. Subsequently, proposals for institutional reform were incorporated as an integral part of the agricultural development strategy. In the words of the planners, equality and social justice became "both the means and the goal of [India's] development and the entire planning effort."[73]

It was largely on the basis of the new agricultural policies that in 1953 Shriman Narayan, then general secretary of the AICC, claimed there was "no fundamental difference between the ideologies of the Congress, Socialism and Sarvodaya."[74] Writing in a party publication, "Construc-tive Program for Congressmen," he pointed out that the Community Projects were no longer American in conception, but that "they are now based mainly on Gandhiji's Constructive Program."[75] The AICC urged Active Members to resume constructive work as a regular part of party

---

[71] Ibid., p. 224.                          [72] Ibid., p. 228.
[73] India, Planning Commission, The New India: Progress through Democracy (New York, 1958), p. 34.
[74] Shriman Narayan Agarwal, Constructive Program for Congressmen (New Delhi, 1953), p. 3.
[75] Ibid., p. 14.

activity. Congressmen were exhorted to work for *bhoodan*; to take an active role in organizing village industries, panchayats, cooperatives, and schools; and to engage in social welfare work, particularly among the Scheduled Castes. Subsequently, some Congressmen did take up *bhoodan* work, and the Sarvodaya Samaj strengthened its informal ties with the Congress party. The bulk of constructive workers, however, followed Vinoba's lead and remained outside the political process.

Also in 1953, Nehru attempted to forge new ties between the Congress party and the Praja Socialist party (PSP), which had been formed following the 1951 elections by merger of the Socialist party and the KMPP. The results were disappointing. A number of individuals did move back into Congress, but the PSP as a whole rejected the idea of formal cooperation or merger. Jayaprakash Narayan, then president of the PSP presented Nehru with an array of fourteen points as a condition for collaboration. They included demands for constitutional amendments weakening the protection for private property; nationalization of banks, insurance companies, and mines; and "most urgent" of all, a program for "integrated" and far-reaching agrarian reform. Narayan called for immediate redistribution of land to poor peasants and landless laborers; the abolition of all forms of landlordism; and the transformation of the rural sector into a cooperative economy through the creation of multipurpose societies operating on the basis of compulsory membership. Nehru responded by expressing agreement in principle with most of the demands, but confessed his inability as a prime minister operating within the constraints of parliamentary government to give unilateral assurances of action on such controversial issues.[76]

The Sarvodaya Samaj and the Praja Socialist party were actually in broad agreement with each other and with influential members of the national leadership of the Congress party on long-term social and economic goals. But suspicion about Nehru's motives, as well as genuine disagreement on means, prevented the socialist elements from reaching an accommodation that might have restored the noncommunist left as a cohesive force in Indian political life. Ironically, the differences that kept them apart were, to a large extent, rooted in a common legacy—the thought and practice of Gandhi. The question they all tried to answer was how best to adapt Gandhi's technique of nonviolent resistance against foreign rule to India's internal struggle against social and economic exploitation.

The solution favored by the Sarvodaya Samaj fastened on the more utopian and spiritual aspects of Gandhi's thought. In essence, the Sarvodayis argued that social reform could not be effectively accomplished

[76] The correspondence between Nehru and Narayan on the question of collaboration, including Narayan's fourteen-point program, is published in *The Hindu*, March 20, 1953.

by legislation from above. The only reliable method was altering peoples' values by exposing them to proper example and education.[77] In contrast, the PSP, particularly its more militant wing, sought to develop the revolutionary implications o: the Constructive Program and mass civil disobedience. Rammanohar Lohia, who was the leading exponent of a Gandhian-Marxist synthesis along these lines, agreed that constructive work was a necessary part of a political action program, but mainly as an instrument of arousing mass consciousness in preparation for direct struggle. Lohia pointed out that there was, in fact, no opposition between direct struggle and civil disobedience. Rather, civil disobedience was a peaceful method of challenging—and eroding—the adversary's power. In his view, the socialists should be prepared to use peaceful, albeit unconstitutional methods, such as *satyagraha*, whenever it was politically expedient to do so. He argued that as long as the socialists did not advocate the use of force as a political doctrine it was only of secondary importance if violence did, on occasion, erupt.[78]

Nehru sympathized with both points of view, but he accepted neither completely. On the one hand, he did not believe that propertied classes could be converted to a new set of motives and behavior simply by an appeal to traditional religious values. On the other, he was not prepared to weaken India's fragile political unity by an outright attack on the propertied elements through sweeping constitutional changes, or encouragement to civil disobedience as a routine response to injustice. Most important, he believed in the possibility of achieving the multiple economic, social, and political aims of Indian development through pressures generated from within the democratic system. The question confronting Nehru was whether there could be any other method of transforming the entire social structure than a direct confrontation between the classes. His working assumption was that, given the historical innovation of political democracy in India, it was possible to do it "in the Gandhian way."[79] The broad approach he followed, subject to shifting economic and political conditions, was an adaptation of Gandhi's two-pronged strategy of class conciliation and an indirect attack on the social foundations of exploitation.

Nehru maintained Gandhi's "friendly and constructive" approach toward the propertied classes. Apart from the introduction of legislation to bring the private business sector under a more effective public regulation and control, and to eliminate the most exploitative aspects of the zamindari landlord system, he did not launch a frontal attack on the institution

[77] For a statement of the Sarvodaya approach, see Vinoba Bhave, *Swaraj Sastra*.
[78] See Rammanohar Lohia, *Aspects of Socialist Policy*, Part II, *The Doctrinal Foundation of Socialism* (Bombay, 1952), pp. 32-73.
[79] Karanjia, *The Mind of Mr. Nehru: An Interview*, p. 79; also see Jawaharlal Nehru, *India Today and Tomorrow*, p. 13.

of private property. He preferred an incremental approach of whittling away at the social supports of these groups, in the belief that ultimately the government would find it "relatively easy to come to terms with them."[80]

In the agricultural sector, the entire development strategy was conceived as an organizational device for weakening the social pillars of economic and political dominance by the landed castes. The Community Development program was assigned the task of creating in the mass of the rural population an awareness and desire for the implementation of new principles of social justice based on equality and participation, which would find organized expression in the cooperative and panchayat institutions. In this respect, the concept of national extension under the Community Development program came close to Lohia's definition of constructive work as a revolutionary activity. The creation of democratic village institutions was expected to provide the majority of small farmers, tenants, and laborers with effective organizational devices for securing social justice through peaceful means. The new institutions, by mobilizing popular pressure from below, would compel the dominant landowning castes to concede demands for limited reform or face the prospect of total ruin. Speaking at the inauguration of the first Community Projects on October 2, 1952, Nehru visualized "the work we are starting today" as the beginning of a far-reaching social revolution. He asserted: "we are now talking in terms of a big revolution, a peaceful revolution, not of turmoil and the breaking of heads. It is in this manner that we shall transform our country. Peacefully, we shall remove the evils of our country and promote a better order."[81]

Even though Nehru was skeptical about the capacity of rural elites to be inspired by cooperative ideals, he nevertheless counted on a strong response from the peasantry. He was influenced by his memories of the nationalist movement when he had seen Gandhi "work miracles . . . on Indian humanity," raising millions of passive villagers from a "demoralized, timid and hopeless mass, bullied and crushed by every dominant interest and incapable of resistance, into a people with self-respect and self-reliance, resisting tyranny, and capable of united action and sacrifice for a larger cause."[82] The experience made him receptive to Gandhi's view of the average villager as a person with unique moral qualities, and to the belief that a dedicated leadership could regenerate the "elemental force" Gandhi had drawn out of the Indian people.[83]

Although Nehru was scrupulous in denying any comparison between the dimensions of Gandhi's greatness and his own, still the peasant

---

[80] Karanjia, *The Mind of Mr. Nehru*, p. 79.
[81] *Jawaharlal Nehru on Community Development*, p. 22.
[82] Jawaharlal Nehru, *Nehru on Gandhi*, x, 26.
[83] *Jawaharlal Nehru on Community Development*, pp. 17-18.

masses seemed to respond to him with almost the same intensity. He knew that the huge crowds coming out to greet him were divided by myriad communal and caste loyalties, yet he experienced a mystical communion with the people as a whole. Like other socialist intellectuals, he tended to perceive the peasantry in objective terms as a homogenous "mass." Their divisions appeared to him based on ignorance about their own common interests. He was therefore inclined to assume that with proper education this false consciousness would pass. Nehru characterized his own approach as a "mass approach," one that was aimed at changing the "thinking of the masses and produc[ing] the correct mass reaction to any event . . . to making the people at large social-minded."[84] A good part of his hope for a democratic and peaceful solution to social change rested on this assumption that the peasantry could be made to understand their common interest and strength in transcending parochial divisions to cooperate for economic reform. Apart from his own constant efforts, through talks and speeches across the country to educate the population, he clearly assigned primary importance to the impact of institutional change at the village level. He argued, "once the people are given a proper democratic base or moorings, it should be difficult for the mass of the people to be diverted or reversed. The pace of progress could be slowed down or accelerated, of course, but I don't think it would be possible to take a whole people backwards. I cannot think that possible at all."[85]

The keystone of Nehru's faith in the efficacy of the new institutions was his belief that they would gradually generate a popular leadership drawn predominately from among the poorer sections of the peasantry with a capacity to organize the majority for a disciplined drive for social reform. At least for the time being, Nehru believed that the political parties—including the Congress party—had little role to play in providing direction to this process. He asserted, "I am not for a moment thinking about a party like the Congress or any other party sending people to push them on or to organize them. But the real cadres are being built at the village level all the time. They are not party cadres in that sense; they are village level workers, agriculturists, peasants."[86]

Political parties, in fact, were explicitly enjoined not to endorse candidates in the local contests for panchayat elections. Party competition in village contests would only retard social change, by encouraging candidates to mobilize popular support on the basis of existing cleavages organized around the boundaries of caste and faction. It was only after the new institutions took root, and the peasantry achieved higher levels of political consciousness along with the rudiments of economic and social services that weakened the links of dependence binding them to the dom-

---

[84] Karanjia, *The Mind of Mr. Nehru*, p. 62.
[85] *Ibid.*, p. 67.                                              [86] *Ibid.*, p. 72.

inant landed castes, that prospects for genuine democracy would emerge. At this point, the village level leaders, the "real cadres," could lead a movement for effective reform *within* the democratic system by using their bargaining advantage as spokesmen for a cohesive majority to strike the most advantageous alliances with national political parties. The Congress party did not have to lead the movement for social change. Under the system of local democracy, the broad mass of the people would carry the party forward. If it refused to follow the popular lead, it would have to risk being swept away.

It was against these key premises that Nehru could claim that the advent of political democracy offered a realistic hope of achieving a nonviolent social revolution. It is also against the background of these assumptions that Nehru's preoccupation with avoiding premature polarization around sensitive issues of economic reform and his determination to maintain the Congress party as a unifying force at the national level, even at the cost of short-term concessions to the propertied classes, become most convincing.

Yet, from the outset, there was an unavoidable tension between the social and economic goals of planning. In the absence of a dedicated party cadre at the grass-roots level, an active campaign to educate public opinion and organize peoples' institutions fell mainly on the officers of the various development departments. But in the last analysis, the local development officers were themselves drawn mainly from the village population, and responsible to superiors in the administrative services and the ministries of state governments, many of whom had very little genuine enthusiasm for the tasks of social education. For all practical purposes, the prospects of carrying through the nonviolent social revolution rested on the long-term effects of the spread of education in creating a self-aware peasantry, and in the actual experience acquired by villagers over time of their strength in numbers under a system of village democracy.

From Gandhi's point of view, prolonged delays in social reconstruction would not have been undesirable. After all, he wanted to give the propertied classes as much time as possible to adjust to relative changes in the distribution of local power. He was not preoccupied, moreover, with achieving an accelerated rate of economic growth. But by 1954, the Planning Commission was already involved in formulating a design for rapid industrialization under the Second Plan. Very great increases in agricultural production were considered essential to a large-scale effort in industry. At the same time, the agricultural development strategy depended almost entirely on involvement of millions of small farmers in labor-intensive production programs and community action projects. The incentive for such popular participation was progress toward agrarian reform.

The planners were therefore faced with a potential contradiction between the political and economic dimensions of the development approach. On the one hand, they were committed to a gradual process of peaceful reform of the traditional social order. On the other, they recognized the immediate necessity of increasing production—but this could only be done through institutions that were expected to reach their full potential as instruments of rural resource mobilization after the prolonged process of agrarian reorganization was completed.

# FOUR

# The Contradiction of Rapid Industrialization and Gradual Agrarian Reform

After 1955, the Planning Commission became an extension of the prime minister's authority in the area of economic policy. Its status and powers dramatically increased. The demarcation originally envisaged between the advisory functions of the Planning Commission and the decision-making responsibilities of the central government grew blurred. A combination of political influence, superior expertise, and control over formulas for central financial assistance to the states ensured that the economic and social priorities set down by the Planning Commission were adopted in the state Plans.

Nehru's unique position in the government and the Congress party was central to this transformation. As prime minister, he often requested Cabinet approval for recommendations he had already endorsed as chairman of the Planning Commission. In most cases, none of his colleagues had sufficient prestige or popular standing to challenge his advice effectively. The same situation prevailed in the Working Committee and the AICC. Congress party leaders who complained bitterly in private about the prime minister's "doctrinaire" socialist views were among his most vocal supporters at the open annual sessions of the party. Even when the National Development Council (NDC) was created in 1952 specifically for the purpose of giving the chief ministers of the states an opportunity to review and recommend social and economic policies and targets for the National Plan, Nehru's voice as chairman of the NDC was ultimately decisive on questions of national policy.

In addition, Nehru established close links between the Planning Commission and the central government, investing the members of the commission with prestige similar to that enjoyed by Cabinet ministers. From the beginning, the Planning Commission and the central government shared key officials. The Cabinet secretary functioned as secretary to the Planning Commission. The finance ministry's chief economic advisor doubled as economic advisor to the commission. The statistical advisor to the Cabinet was considered a de facto member of the Planning Commission.

The practice of appointing Cabinet ministers as members of the commission also added to its prestige. Starting in 1950, the finance minister was routinely included; in 1956, he was joined by the minister of defense. Either the deputy chairman or a member of the Planning Commission was given full Cabinet rank as minister of planning. Finally, the prestige of the commission was vitally enhanced by the personal role Nehru played in its work. It was his practice to meet the full commission once or twice a month, and to attend all meetings at which major policy issues were discussed. As the Second Plan began to take definite shape, he also read, annotated, and rewrote key sections of the final draft.

From 1955 to 1964, Nehru's pivotal position permitted a handful of men to determine national economic and social policy and methods of development. During this period, the number of full-time members of the Planning Commission, including the deputy chairman, rarely exceeded five. A few part-time members brought the full complement of personnel up to nine or ten. Altogether, no more than twenty persons served on the Planning Commission between 1955 and 1964,[1] all under appointments of open-ended tenure. Those having the longest association with the commission, and also the greatest influence on policy, had no formal economic training. V. T. Krishnamachari, deputy chairman from 1953 until mid-1960, was a lawyer and ICS officer, whose posts before Independence included high administrative appointments in the government of Madras, and seventeen years as dewan of Baroda, during which he initiated a widely admired program of port and industrial development. By contrast, Gulzarilal Nanda, deputy chairman from 1950 to 1953, from 1960 to 1963, and a member and minister of planning from 1953 to 1960, had been a lifelong Congress worker, first joining the noncooperation movement in 1921, and subsequently devoting his energies to trade-union organization. Professor P. C. Mahalanobis, the Cabinet's statistical advisor from 1955 to 1958, member of the Planning Commission from 1959, and leading architect of the development strategy of the Second Plan, was a physicist whose special talent for statistics had by 1931 elevated him to honorary director of the Indian Statistical Institute. Tarlok Singh, additional secretary from 1950 to 1962, member from 1962 to 1966, and a senior advisor on rural policy, with a major role in drafting Plan documents, was an ICS officer who attracted national attention after publication in 1945 of *Poverty and Social Change*. The book drew on observations of peasant life in the Punjab to recommend the reorganization of the rural economy around joint village management as the only solution to the poverty of the small farmer.

The common thread in Nehru's appointments to the Planning Com-

---

[1] A chart showing the personnel of the Planning Commission from 1950 to 1964 and the period of each member's appointment is presented in A. H. Hanson, *The Process of Planning*, p. 54.

mission was the political orientation of the members. The men who served on the commission were firmly committed, or at least sympathetic, to the blend of socialist goals and Gandhian methods that provided the intellectual framework for the approach to planned change. All of them considered the process of development in broader terms than economic growth, to include priorities for transformation of the social order and the establishment of an egalitarian and socialist pattern of modern society.

As preparations for the Second Plan got underway, the commission commanded a number of advantages in imposing these priorities on the states. One was its own superior expertise. The states' facilities for the collection of data and economic planning were extremely rudimentary. State departments of statistics were severely hampered in undertaking independent studies by small research staffs and poorly trained personnel. Newly created state departments of planning or interdepartmental planning committees lacked the data and technical expertise to combine departmental proposals into coherent designs for development. Draft outlines produced by each state for the Second Plan were usually little more than a compendium of projects advanced by each department.[2]

By contrast, during the early 1950s the Planning Commission built up an elaborate secretariat, headed by senior government officials and experts, staffed by a full complement of researchers and statisticians, and organized into general and subject divisions, to provide the members with the best available information on every aspect of the economy. During the first stages of work on the Second Plan, the commission also had the benefit of special studies on each sector of the economy carried out by working groups composed of its own experts and those of the central ministries; and of recommendations by its own panel of economists on broad questions of social and economic policy. On the basis of this information, the commission made its comprehensive recommendations on investment magnitudes, sectoral balances, targets, and economic and social policy for the Second Plan, first in a brief memorandum, and then in the more extended Draft Outline. Only at this advanced stage in the planning process were the chief ministers of the states invited to New Delhi for discussions with the Planning Commission and representatives of the central ministries, and given an opportunity to justify the proposals in the state plans against national priorities.[3]

Apart from superior expertise, the planners enjoyed another major advantage in the discussions with the chief ministers. This was the states' heavy reliance upon the central government for financial assistance in

[2] For a detailed discussion of planning in the states, see *ibid.*, pp. 75-88.

[3] The planning process at the Center is described in detail in India, Planning Commission, *The Planning Process* (New Delhi, 1963). Also, see Hanson, *The Process of Planning*, pp. 50-75.

meeting plan outlay. Under the constitution, the states were assured of
receiving the proceeds from only minor Union taxes (such as levies on
nonagricultural property, railway freights and fares, stamp duties, newspaper and advertisement taxes). They were guaranteed a percentage of
the returns from Union income and excise taxes, but on the basis of a
formula set down by a quinquennial Finance Commission. Some states
also benefitted from central grants-in-aid authorized under Article 275 of
the constitution specifically for "such States as Parliament may determine to be in need." The Union government, by contrast, enjoyed very
broad discretionary power in allocating central assistance to grants-in-aid
"for any public purpose notwithstanding that the purpose is not one with
respect to which Parliament or the Legislature of the States as the case
may be, may make laws." This financial leverage was increased by the
constitutional authority conferred on the Center of making loans to the
states.

The Planning Commission attempted to exploit these financial levers
in a number of ways. Prior to the beginning of plan discussions, only a
preliminary estimate of the Center's total contribution to the Plans of all
states was made known. No ceiling on central assistance to individual
states was announced. The actual amount ultimately assigned to each
state became a matter of negotiation, some states getting more, others
less. In all cases, the total amount of central assistance sanctioned for any
state Plan was made contingent on commitments by the state government to raise a fixed quantum of resources, partly through additional
taxation. Once fixed, moreover, the central assistance available to each
state was disbursed in grant and loan components as "tied" aid, that is,
for specified heads of development or projects, and according to schematic patterns of assistance for different plan programs. The earmarking
of specific proportions of central assistance for various heads of development automatically influenced sectoral allocations of state Plans. The
practice of establishing different proportions of grant and loan assistance
for particular projects influenced the content of development activities
within each sector. In some cases, the Center also specified that central
grants had to be matched in a fixed proportion by contributions from the
states. In addition, the Center advanced loans to the states on the basis of
proposals for the completion of particular projects. Finally, the Center
sometimes decided to meet the full expenditure of "centrally sponsored
schemes" which were included in the central Plan, albeit administered by
state agencies, and for which detailed patterns of construction and staff-
ing were set down by the central government. All these advantages ensured that the Planning Commission encountered little open resistance in
extracting the state leaderships' commitment to the objective of socialism
as the guiding principle for development planning.

The new principles and directions of social and economic policy were settled by late 1954. In a landmark speech to the National Development Council on November 9, Nehru took the initiative in placing the broad questions of economic approach and social policy before the chief ministers of the states. Emphasizing that "we have to be clear about the broad picture we are aiming at," he asserted: "The picture I have in mind is definitely and absolutely a socialistic picture of society. I am not using the word in a dogmatic sense at all. I mean largely that the means of production should be socially owned and controlled for the benefit of society as a whole. There is plenty of room for private enterprise provided the main aim is kept clear."[4]

Two other basic principles of planning were established in the same speech. First, the problem of India's poverty could not be solved by the gradual expansion of consumer goods industries based mainly on imported machinery. Rather, it was necessary to follow an import substitution strategy aimed at a fundamental transformation of the economy to strengthen the domestic capacity for capital formation. Metals, power, and heavy machinery—"the basic things"—had to be produced in India. Second, as far as possible, rising consumer demands should be satisfied by an expansion of village and small-scale industries, both to maximize additional employment opportunities and create the foundations of a diversified and decentralized economy in the rural sector.

As a result of Nehru's initiative, the problem of formulating an economic development strategy was subsequently considered from a dual perspective. It was agreed that over the period of ten or fifteen years, India should advance toward a socialist economy in which the public sector's share of investment and output in organized industries (especially basic and heavy industries in the capital goods sector) was significantly increased relative to that of the private sector; and during this same period, the foundations of a self-reliant industrial economy should be created and the problem of unemployment solved.

Both the government and the Congress party endorsed these objectives. In December 1954, the Lok Sabha affirmed that "the objective of our economic policy should be a socialistic pattern of society; and toward this end the tempo of economic activity in general and industrial development in particular should be stepped up to the maximum extent possible."[5] In January 1955, Nehru personally moved the resolution at the Avadi session of Congress, which finally committed the party as a whole to the principle that "planning should take place with a view to the establishment of a socialistic pattern of society where the principle means of production are under social ownership or control."[6]

---

[4] Jawaharlal Nehru, *Planning and Development*, "Speech Delivered to the National Development Council," November 9, 1954, pp. 15-16.
[5] *Lok Sabha Debates*, Second Series, ix, 3692.
[6] Indian National Congress, *Congress Bulletin*, January 1955.

The prime minister, and the members of the Planning Commission were all aware that the new emphasis on rapid industrialization and expansion of the public sector had far-reaching implications for plan policies in agriculture. Large investment outlays on basic and heavy industries were bound to raise demands for foodgrains and raw materials. In particular, substantial increases in agricultural production were necessary to avoid shortages of foodgrains and essential commodities that would trigger inflationary price rises and distort the entire cost structure of plan projects. Otherwise, there would be pressure to cut down the industrial program in the face of inflated costs and the need to divert scarce foreign exchange from industrial imports to the purchase of foodgrains from abroad. Beyond that, there was the whole question of building up agricultural surpluses from which to finance industrial growth, and of expanding the internal market for the products of industry by generating higher consumer demands from an expanding rural economy. Nehru himself constantly reiterated that the entire program of industrial development depended on achieving adequate increases in agricultural productivity, which he called the "keystone of our planning."[7]

The difficulty was that the large industrial programs preempted the lion's share of available resources for investment on costly modern technologies. There was no possibility of increasing agricultural output by providing tens of millions of small peasant households with capital-intensive production inputs such as mechanized irrigation, farm machinery, or even chemical fertilizer. Instead, agricultural productivity had to be increased by more efficient use of available land and labor resources within the rural sector.

The ramifications of the large industrial programs went beyond the immediate problem—raising agricultural output with the actual resources at hand—to affect the feasibility of the long-term strategy for gradual social transformation in the rural sector. The decision to speed up the process of development and to put an end to unemployment "in about ten years"[8] meant that basic changes in the agrarian pattern to bring about a cooperative economy similarly could "not be slow."[9] Nehru was convinced that the Community Development Program could only succeed in raising food production through mobilization of local

---

[7] *Fortnightly Letters to the Chief Ministers, 1948-63*, dated May 5, 1957, unpublished.

[8] This was Nehru's estimate in a letter to the chief ministers dated December 24, 1954. He asserted, "We have practically committed ourselves to rapid industrial development and to put an end to unemployment in about ten years time." *Ibid*.

[9] Nehru wrote to the chief ministers on August 12, 1956, that "I am convinced it is essential for us to have cooperative farming . . . the principle and essential elements of practice have to be accepted and acted upon. It has also to be remembered that, in the world of today, the pace is fast. Those who lag behind get left to fend for themselves in a world against them. These changes to bring about cooperative farming cannot be slow." *Ibid*.

manpower and resources if one and two-acre farmers became owners of the land, and supported by the services of village multipurpose coopera- tive societies, combined together with other small peasants in joint farm operations. Indeed, he believed that cooperative farming was "essential from the economic and social point of view" once the decision had been made to reject both a capitalist agrarian pattern and collective farms. He reasoned that

> it is true from the economic point of view, a large farm will . . . also be very productive. But once we give up these large farms and have relatively small holdings, or farms, it becomes inevitable for cooperation between a number of small farmers. This is the eco- nomic aspect. From the social point of view, cooperative farming is equally necessary. . . . In the world today, there is an inevitable tendency for everything to be done on a larger and more centralized scale. . . . It has many advantages, more especially if these large- scale operations are controlled by a few private individuals . . . de- centralization by itself is not likely to succeed unless we bring to it the advantages of large-scale cooperative working through co- operative processes. The alternative is State ownership . . . we have no other choice but cooperative farming. The real alternative is collective farms owned by the State which most Communist countries have.[10]

Apart from its potential for increasing agricultural productivity with minimum new capital investment, basic agrarian reorganization prom- ised to solve the problems of building up linkages between the modern industrial sector and the vast rural hinterland, setting in motion the dynamic process of overall increases of income, consumption, employ- ment, and production at the core of self-sustaining economic growth. According to Nehru,

> the whole policy of land reform, apart from removing the burden on the actual tiller, was to spread the income from land more evenly among the peasantry and thus give them more purchasing power. In this way, the internal market would expand and the productive forces of the country would grow. We cannot go on increasing our production unless we increase our consumption. . . . We cannot in- crease our consumption unless there is the wherewithal to buy among large numbers of people. . . . Once this wheel of greater pur- chasing power got going, there is no limit to it. This applies, of course, not only to land but even more to industry. It applies espe- cially to small industries which should produce many of the articles needed in the villages.[11]

[10] *Ibid*.                    [11] *Ibid*., letter dated August 5, 1954.

Cooperatives had still other advantages. They provided an organizational infrastructure that was particularly suitable for the mobilization of agricultural surpluses through compulsory state trading and price controls. As the planners observed, the problem was not merely one of finding resources to finance a bigger Plan, but also of "mobilizing more effectively the surpluses which became available with the producers."[12] This problem was compounded by building the agricultural development program on tens of millions of subsistence cultivators who were generally not responsive to market conditions, but, on the contrary, responded to higher prices by selling less of their output to increase consumption.[13] Unless the government could locate and collect agricultural surpluses, they could not insure the rational disposition of available supplies. Artificial shortages and uneven distribution could wreak as much havoc with the price structure as absolute scarcities of foodgrains and essential commodities.

The economic rationale for speedy reorganization of the agrarian sector in the context of the large industrial programs projected for the Second Plan were highly persuasive. Such an approach, as the planners were keenly aware, appeared to be bringing major gains in neighboring China. The difference was that in India these changes had to be carried out without authoritarian methods, and in "a peaceful, democratic way." Nehru, in fact, accepted the implicit challenge of competition with China's communist methods of change. He affirmed that "the most exciting countries for me today [are] India and China. We differ, of course, in our political and economic structures, yet the problems we face are essentially the same. The future will show which country and which structure of Government yields greater results in every way."[14]

But neither Nehru nor the other members of the Planning Commission squarely faced the emerging contradiction between the requirements of the industrialization strategy and those of peaceful social and political development. As originally envisaged, the strategy of nonviolent social transformation assumed a long period of transition, during which the impact of education and popular suffrage could create a well-informed and united peasantry capable of generating its own leadership at the local level to organize collective pressures for agrarian reform through the

---

[12] *The First Five Year Plan*, p. 176.

[13] Preliminary studies indicated that almost one-half of the produce marketed was sold by 75 percent of cultivators with holdings of less than ten acres, and that such supplies represented mainly "distress" food sales, that is, not true commercial surpluses responsive to market conditions. See Dharm Narain, *Distribution of the Marketed Surplus of Agricultural Produce by Size-Level of Holding in India, 1950-51* (Delhi, 1961). For a discussion of the distinction between commercial surpluses and distress surpluses, see Gorakh Nath Sinha, *An Introduction to Food Economics* (Allahabad, 1956).

[14] *Fortnightly Letters to the Chief Ministers, 1948-63*, letter dated November 15, 1954.

new village institutions. But on the eve of the Second Plan, the vast majority of the rural population were still outside the organized economic or political sectors, and were splintered along traditional communal, caste, and factional lines. The decision for rapid industrialization and an accelerated pace of agrarian reorganization demanded that the process of social mobilization be speeded up. It required an infusion of leadership at the village level to take the initiative in the political education and organization of the peasantry. But the only "cadres" in place were the district and Block development officers and their poorly trained, badly underpaid, and painfully overextended "village level workers," all of whom, moreover, functioned in a line of command responsible to mostly conservative IAS officers and agriculture ministers of the states. It was, in addition, unrealistic to expect that the dominant landed castes would accept the challenge of the projected cooperative institutions to their hegemony over agricultural credit, marketing, distribution, and, ultimately, productive land, without offering any resistance.

Indeed, by 1955 the link between the immediate aim of organizing multipurpose village cooperative and panchayat institutions on the one hand, and the ultimate goal of imposing restrictions on the prerogatives of private ownership of land on the other, became an increasingly explicit element in the formulation of development policy for the rural sector. Traditional elites quickly perceived the recommendations for new principles of "social" organization in the "reconstruction of the agrarian economy" as the entering wedge of a revolutionary shift in the distribution of economic and political power, that they were intended to be. The approach to democratic social transformation was therefore trapped in a basic contradiction as soon as its goals were broadened to include the aim of rapid industrialization.

The political strategy could only proceed through a process of gradual restratification of the traditional social order, which offered sufficient concessions on the scope and pace of change to reassure the propertied classes against the threat of expropriation and prevent their active opposition to effective implementation of agrarian reforms. The economic approach required immediate increases in agricultural production through the very institutions that were expected to achieve their full potential as instruments of rural resource mobilization only after the long process of basic agrarian reorganization was completed.

The planners therefore approached the Second Plan with considerable uncertainty about the appropriate mix between economic and political goals of development. Nehru, particularly, was impressed with the need for compromise on both dimensions, even while he was apprehensive of the costs in terms of preserving the integrity of the basic approach. He reflected in retrospect, in a democracy, a leader may put forward policies he considers right, but he has to take into account the ability of his followers to implement them. In a democracy, the most important thing is not an individual [leader's] principles. The important thing is to build up the people to them. Will they accept them? A leader can have principles, but if only he has them, he will be isolated. Sometimes you have to compromise. If you compromise too much and you lose the principle, that is not good. If you can compromise and still keep the principle, that is what we try to do, but we don't always know if we will succeed.[15]

Two preliminary outlines of the Second Plan, one prepared by Professor Mahalanobis ("Draft Recommendations for the Formulation of the Second Five Year Plan"), the other by the economic divisions of the Planning Commission and the finance ministry ("Tentative Framework for the Second Five Year Plan"), were circulated for discussion in March 1955.[16] Both drafts were based on working papers prepared at the Indian Statistical Institute under Mahalanobis' supervision, and were virtually identical with respect to outlay, sectoral allocations, targets, and recommendations on social and economic policy. Inasmuch as Mahalanobis was considered the major architect of the Plan design, his version, referred to as the Plan Frame, monopolized public attention.

The Plan Frame was constructed to achieve the mixture of economic and social goals outlined by Nehru: (1) to increase "the scope and importance of the public sector and in this way advance to a socialist pattern of society"; (2) to develop heavy industries and "strengthen the foundations of economic independence"; (3) to increase production of consumer goods through an expansion of labor-intensive village and small-scale industries, thereby increasing employment, especially "among the poorer sections of the people so that a greater proportion of the increase in income would go to them"; (4) to eliminate unemployment after a period of ten years; (5) to increase agricultural productivity; and (6) to improve the quality of social services in housing, health, and education, "especially for the poorer sections of the population." All of these measures together were expected to increase national income by about twenty-five percent, and also "to achieve a more equitable distribution of income."

Fundamental structural changes in the economy were envisaged. Modern manufacturing and mining were expected to account for a much larger share of the gross domestic product. Within the modern sector, there was to be a shift away from the production of consumer items to-

[15] Interview, Jawaharlal Nehru, New Delhi, April 8, 1959.
[16] Both drafts are published in Planning Commission, Panel of Economists, *Papers Relating to the Formulation of the Second Five Year Plan*.

ward the output of intermediate and capital goods. In the organized industrial sector as a whole, the size of public investment was to increase both absolutely and relatively to that of private enterprise. These proposals were combined with recommendations for transferring large investment resources from the private sector to the state. The planners called for nationalization of the Imperial Bank and the life insurance industry, the creation of a State Trading Corporation, and revisions in the tax structure to increase income taxes and introduce new taxes on wealth, expenditure, and capital gains.

Even so, the new approach raised formidable problems of domestic resource mobilization. Both the Plan Frame and the Planning Commission's "Tentative Framework for the Second Plan" proposed a total expenditure in the public sector of Rs. 4,300 crores, more than twice the total outlay of the First Plan. Apart from deficit financing, which the Planning Commission considered safe only up to Rs. 1,000 to Rs. 1,200 crores, and resources to be raised through foreign aid amounting to an estimated Rs. 400 crores, the remainder of the Plan had to be financed by the state and central governments from taxation and other forms of public savings. But at 1955/56 rates of taxation, only Rs. 700 crores was expected to be available out of current revenues for developmental expenditure. Allowing for another Rs. 1,000 crores in borrowing from the public, and Rs. 200 crores in receipts from railways, Mahalanobis and the planners conceded there was a gap in Plan resources of about Rs. 800 to Rs. 1,000 crores.

Neither Mahalanobis nor the Planning Commission believed that the resource gap could be filled by additional taxation alone. Among other problems, the majority of subsistence farmers could not be reached through the tax system. Some other method of restricting mass consumption had to be devised. Apart from the possibilities of imposing compulsory savings on the public, and generating additional profits from state enterprises, the planners believed that the most effective means of regulating consumption and increasing the proportion of savings to national income was through a system of price controls and state trading in foodgrains and essential consumer commodities. In the rural sector, members of the Panel of Economists urged, "More can be achieved through the price system than through orthodox tax machinery. The general character of the products consumed by the vast majority of the rural sector is fairly well known. If a network of State trading institutions can be built up and appropriate policies are followed . . . it should be possible to get more from the rural areas than we are at present getting."[17]

[17] C. N. Vakil and P. R. Brahmananda, "Institutional Implications of a Bolder Plan," ibid., pp. 422-35.

Another important consideration also favored state entry into the trade of essential commodities: the need to stabilize the general price level and prevent any serious distortion in the pattern of planned development. The planners were concerned that inflationary pressures would raise the costs and reduce the returns of capital projects in the public sector; and that sharp fluctuations in the price index would dampen the incentive for private investment. Inasmuch as fifty percent of national income originated in agricultural commodities, the planners proposed that government should build up a buffer stock of foodgrains, and during the Second Plan undertake open market operations, buying when prices were low to establish a floor, selling when prices were high to enforce a ceiling.

The recommendation for state trading in foodgrains raised the practical problem of how to establish effective supervision over the market transactions of some sixty million cultivators. It was clearly impossible for a state trading organization to deal individually with each farm family. Cooperatives offered a far more convenient organizational device. Instead of sixty million agriculturist families, government could deal with some 300,000 village societies. The First Plan had already assigned a key role to multipurpose service cooperatives in village community development, albeit primarily on grounds of their redistributive effect in raising the income of the majority of small farmers, while limiting the profits of private moneylenders and traders. But there were also important precedents for using cooperatives as instruments of government supervision and control over the disposition of agricultural savings and surpluses. In fact, in the early 1950s the planners had a concrete example before them in the pattern of agrarian reorganization then being carried out in China.

India's planners were keenly interested in China's economic progress because of what they considered to be striking similarities in the experience and problems of the two nations. Both had suffered foreign economic domination and imperialism. Both also shared basic problems of severe population pressure on the land, a large volume of unemployment and underemployment and low levels of productivity; and as a result of these factors, both faced enormous obstacles in the way of accumulating sufficient surpluses for rapid industrialization. Not least important, the two nations appeared dedicated to similar social goals, especially the elimination of economic disparities, and the creation of a socialist pattern of society. In 1951, feelings of solidarity with China were so high that Nehru even acquiesced in the Chinese takeover of Tibet, signing the Sino-Indian Treaty, which elaborated the famous principles of *panchsheel* (mutual respect, nonaggression, nonintervention, equality, and peaceful coexistence) as the basis of foreign relations between the two countries.

Between 1952 and 1955, high-ranking officials of the Congress party,

Parliament, the Ministry of Food and Agriculture, and the Planning Commission visited China and consulted with their counterparts in the Chinese Communist party, the ministries, and the Planning Commission. Both Nehru and Mahalanobis visited China during this period. Both were impressed. Mahalanobis came away convinced that "China provided a better model of development for India than the advanced western countries."[18] In his view, China had shown the way to rapid industrialization from a subsistence agricultural base by its program for cooperative reorganization of the rural sector. Nehru also found "one of the most impressive things that is happening in China is the rapid growth of agricultural and industrial cooperatives." He was sufficiently persuaded of the relevance of the Chinese experience for India to recommend in late 1955 that a special study team be sent there to enquire into the causes of "the phenomenal growth in agricultural cooperatives."[19]

Earlier reports from China had indicated remarkable progress, despite the difficulties involved, of increasing agricultural savings and surpluses for investment. Among the techniques reported by Professor Ganguli, a member of the Panel of Economists who visited China in 1952, were the use of rural grain taxes and compulsory procurement of grain by government at low prices. Ganguli pointed out that both of these practices were facilitated by the formation of multipurpose cooperatives "which lend or sell seeds, prescribe the methods of cultivation, determine the time of harvest, buy the crops, fix prices, sell salt, fertilizers and industrial products which the farmer needs, and when funds are short, lend them money." He observed, "The cooperatives are the subordinate agencies of the Government departments of food, taxation and trade. Their operations are coordinated with Government state trading agencies handling cloth, food and other essential products."[20]

The striking success of the cooperative movement in China, moreover, offered a sharp contrast to the limited progress that had been achieved in India. The Reserve Bank's all-India rural credit survey, published in 1955 after an exhaustive study of the condition of the cooperative movement revealed that fewer that ten percent of all cultivating families belonged to one of the approximately 100,000 agricultural credit societies in the country. The overwhelming majority of the societies were dormant or functioning in an unsatisfactory way. Fewer than twenty percent were considered economically viable. Altogether, the cooperatives were meeting less than three percent of the cultivators' total annual credit requirements. The survey cited a number of reasons for this failure: the small size of credit cooperatives, which were organized on the principle

[18] Interview, P. C. Mahalanobis, Philadelphia, April 8, 1964.
[19] *Fortnightly Letters to the Chief Ministers, 1948-63*, letter dated December 30, 1955.
[20] B. N. Ganguli, *Economic Development in New China*, pp. 71-72.

of one village, one society; insistence on land as security for most loans; a low turnover of funds; inadequate supervision over recovery; and a large proportion of overdue loans.[21]

Nevertheless, even if cooperatives had failed in the past, their vital role in the development strategy required that they should be made to succeed in the future. The recommendations of the Committee of Direction of the rural credit survey were, in fact, designed not only to remedy the economic weaknesses of agricultural cooperative societies, but to refashion them so that, like their organizational counterparts in China, they might facilitate government regulation and control over agricultural savings and surpluses.

It was clear that small cultivators, with their meager resources, could not finance the necessary expansion of cooperative credit, marketing, and distribution, or compete successfully with facilities offered by private moneylenders and traders. The Reserve Bank, therefore, proposed that government should contribute to the share capital of cooperative associations as a means of strengthening the financial structure of the cooperative movement. At the same time, they recommended that government participation should be fifty-one percent or more of the share capital of rural credit, marketing, and processing societies from the primary to the apex level. At the apex level, government partnership would be direct and involve state contributions to share capital, while at the district and primary levels such participation would ultimately derive from contributions by the apex society. In the case of marketing and processing societies, direct government participation in the share capital of primary units was envisaged, as well. Moreover, in all cooperative institutions in which the government was a major shareholder, the committee asserted that the state should control one-third of the seats on the boards of directors, and "on certain specified matters have overriding power, e.g., power to reverse or modify decisions on those matters or power to impose decisions of its own insofar as they are related to those items."[22]

A second major recommendation also had the double advantage of strengthening the economic position of the cooperative societies and enhancing opportunities for state control. The Committee of Direction presented a new scheme for "integrated" rural credit, under which primary cooperative societies would advance loans to members on the basis of an approved production plan and repaying capacity in kind (instead of land or real security) *on condition* that borrowers agree to sell their produce through a primary marketing cooperative affiliated to the credit society. Production-oriented loans would not only ensure adequate credit

[21] For a comprehensive analysis of the condition of the cooperative movement in the early 1950s see Reserve Bank of India, *All-India Rural Credit Survey,* ii, *The General Report*.
[22] *Ibid.*, p. 435.

to the small farmer and help eliminate the problem of overdues, but they would facilitate the collection of the rural surplus and thereby make it possible to use the price mechanism as a lever of regulation and control over rural savings and consumption. The integrated scheme of rural credit, when combined with proposals for price controls and state trading, promised to solve the government's problem of acquiring sizable quantities of foodgrains for planned distribution in urban centers, and to create the conditions of an effective price stabilization policy.

The main recommendations of the rural credit survey were approved by the Reserve Bank's Standing Advisory Committee on Agricultural Credit in January 1955. During the same month, they were endorsed, at Nehru's insistence, by the annual session of the Congress party at Avadi. Both the Plan Frame and the Planning Commission's "Tentative Framework for the Second Plan" placed the proposals of the rural credit survey at the center of the agricultural strategy. According to the Panel of Economists, "the State partnered cooperative [was] generally accepted as the most important type of organization in the future development of India."[23] This was reiterated by the minister of planning, G. L. Nanda, who emphasized that "the development of cooperative forms of organization in [agriculture and small industries] and in respect of internal trade, especially in the rural areas, should be the most important single objective in a program for achieving the socialistic pattern of society."[24]

Despite the apparent consensus both in the Congress party and government, the reformulation of the central role of the cooperatives as the pattern of economic organization in the rural sector profoundly disturbed influential elements in the local Congress party organizations. The explicit purpose of the new approach was distressing enough. Proposals for large-scale government participation in the purchase and sale of foodgrains at controlled, that is, lower-than-market prices threatened the profits of larger producers, and directly struck at the source of livelihood of private traders and millers who dominated the foodgrains market. The implicit goal was more menacing. Recommendations for reorganization of virtually all business activities in the rural sector along cooperative lines once again raised the specter of a general attack on private forms of production, through pressures for the compulsory formation of cooperative farms—a proposal that had earlier been endorsed in the *Report of the Congress Agrarian Reforms Committee*. While the planners had since avoided all talk of coercion, they nevertheless did endorse pro-

[23] "The Second Five Year Plan, Basic Considerations Relating to the Plan Frame" in *Papers Relating to the Formulation of the Second Five Year Plan*, p. 11.
[24] Gulzarilal Nanda, *Approach to the Second Five Year Plan: Some Basic Considerations* (New Delhi, 1955), p. 4.

posals for the Second Plan aimed at "tak[ing] such essential steps as will provide sound foundations for the development of cooperative farming, so that over a period of 10 years or so a substantial proportion of agricultural lands are cultivated on cooperative lines."[25] Indeed, as a result of the key economic role assigned to cooperatives in the strategy for resource mobilization, measures for agrarian reorganization that had seemed to be projected over an indefinite time period in the First Plan, were suddenly to be implemented within a fixed timetable. Mahalanobis spoke of completing the fixation of ceilings on landownership and the redistribution of surplus land by 1958. The planners envisaged that all economic activities in the rural sector would be reorganized along cooperative lines within a period of ten or fifteen years.

If local elites refused to be persuaded to hasten their own decline by acquiescing in an accelerated timetable for the implementation of land reforms and the formation of cooperatives, however, the obstacles to agrarian reorganization were virtually insurmountable so long as the constitutional structure prevailed. As Mahalanobis himself recognized, the central government enjoyed much less leverage over events in agriculture than in industry. Standing between the central government and the millions of agriculturists in the villages were state governments with exclusive jurisdiction for the subjects of agriculture, cooperation, panchayats, and land reforms. While central decisions concerning the "concentrated" sector of large-scale industry could be implemented without much difficulty, "as it would involve only a small number of persons," the position was entirely different in agriculture. In the rural sector, a national policy decision "by itself would not be sufficient because the implementation would depend on securing the willing cooperation or at least concurrence of millions of persons in the villages. In the beginning, the organization of agriculture and small scale production which can be called the 'diffuse' sector would be far more difficult than establishing large scale industries."[26]

The final version of the Second Plan revealed that while the planners had successfully resisted the business community's demands for major concessions on key issues of industrial policy, they were unable to ignore the pressures applied by state party leaders for a series of compromises on the content and pace of agrarian reorganization. These concessions seriously undermined the rationale of the agricultural strategy and the entire approach to economic planning.

Throughout the summer of 1955, the Plan Frame was the target of a steady barrage of criticism from the business community. The only as-

---

[25] *The Second Five Year Plan*, p. 201.
[26] P. C. Mahalanobis, *Talks on Planning*, p. 69.

pect of the approach with which the industrialists agreed was the emphasis on larger investment outlays and higher allocations to basic and heavy industry. Otherwise, they challenged the entire framework of the plan documents. The Federation of Indian Chambers of Commerce and Industry (FICCI) charged that the planners had ignored basic economic criteria of efficiency in favoring the public sector as the major agency of industrialization. They predicted that "unrealistically high" taxes on the private sector would weaken initiative; that the proposed restrictions on the expansion of factory production in favor of inefficient cottage and small-scale industries would result in an acute shortage of consumer goods; and that the whole structure of the Second Plan would collapse in the face of strong inflationary pressures and rising prices. Actually, the industrialists wanted nothing less than a complete reversal of roles between the public and private sectors. FICCI argued: "the proper spheres of activities for the public sector in the future are the formation and maintenance of social capital. In an underdeveloped country like India, the task of providing the basic requirements such as power, or from a long-term point of view, education, health, etc., and also the institutional framework within which private enterprise is to work is in itself sufficient for any government administration to be fully occupied with. A revision in the official approach on the subject is urgently called for."[27]

The government, however, did little to alter its basic policy in the industrial field. Instead, it sought to reassure the business community about its own future role in the development process. The new Industrial Policy Resolution of April 30, 1956,[28] reiterated the principle that "industrial policy, as other policies" would be governed by the objective of achieving a socialist pattern of society. Accordingly, the state was to "progressively assume a predominant and direct responsibility for setting up new industrial undertakings and for developing transport facilities. It will also undertake State trading on an increasing scale." At the same time, the private sector was to have "the opportunity to develop and expand." The government then went on to classify industries into three categories, depending on the state's role in the development of each of them. All new units in seventeen industries of "basic and strategic importance,"[29] including public utilities, were to be set up only in the pub-

[27] Federation of Indian Chambers of Commerce and Industry, *Second Five-Year Plan: A Comparative Study of the Objectives and Techniques of the Tentative Plan-Frame* (New Delhi, 1955), p. 16.
[28] The text of the 1956 Industrial Policy Resolution is published in the *Second Five Year Plan*, pp. 43-50.
[29] Schedule A industries of basic and strategic importance included arms and ammunition; atomic energy; iron and steel; heavy castings and forgings of iron and steel; heavy plant and machinery required for iron and steel production; mining and machine tool manufacture; heavy electrical plant; coal and lignite; mineral oils; mining and processing of specified ores, metals, and minerals; aircraft; air and railway transport; shipbuilding; electricity; and public communications.

lic sector, although existing privately owned units were not precluded from expanding, or even establishing new enterprises in cooperation with the state, when "the national interests so require." The future development of another twelve "essential " industries[30] was also to be left predominately to the public sector. Within this field, however, the private sector was to have the "opportunity to develop . . . either on its own or with State participation." All remaining industries were left open to both the state and the private sector. The government expected, however, that "their development will be undertaken ordinarily through the initiative and enterprise of the private sector," albeit subject to controls imposed by the 1951 Industries (Development and Regulation) Act and other legislation. Complaints by the private sector against government policies to support both cottage and village industries and small-scale industries by restricting the volume of production in large-scale consumer industries, or by differential taxation and subsidies, were treated sympathetically. In the future, state policies were to rely more heavily on "measures designed to improve the competitive strength of the small scale producer," including the organization of industrial cooperatives.

Apart from these assurances to the business community that they would have ample opportunity to expand within the context of national economic and social priorities, the Planning Commission explicitly rejected the industrialists' view that the proper role of the state in economic development was the creation of social capital for the expansion of private enterprise. In an extended discussion of the "Approach to the Second Five Year Plan," they once again asserted the overriding objective of establishing a socialist pattern of society, to insist that "major decisions regarding production, distribution, consumption and investment—in fact, all socio-economic relationships—must be made by agencies informed by social purpose." Inasmuch as the state was the principle representative of the community interest, the public sector "has not only to initiate developments which the private sector is either unwilling or unable to undertake; it has to play the dominant role in shaping the entire pattern of investments in the economy . . . it is inevitable, if development is to proceed at the pace envisaged and to contribute effectively to the attainment of the larger social ends in view that the public sector must grow not only absolutely but also relatively to the private sector."[31]

Plan outlay and allocations conformed to this set of priorities. Total expenditure was estimated at Rs. 4,800 crores. New investment in the public sector was put at Rs. 3,800 crores, about two and one-half times

---

[30] Schedule B industries included nonferrous metals, machine tools, ferro-alloys and tool steels, basic and intermediate products required by chemical industries, essential drugs, fertilizers, synthetic rubber, carbonization of coal, chemical pulp, road transport, and sea transport.

[31] *Second Five Year Plan*, p. 22.

the level achieved in the First Plan. By contrast, investment in the private sector was expected to reach Rs. 2,400 crores, an increase of only fifty percent over the First Plan.[32] The main point of departure, however, was not simply the increase in the absolute size of public outlay: investments in power, transportation, and communications were in any case necessary to create the infrastructure necessary for modern industry. Rather, the essential difference was "the precedence that is accorded to the public sector in industrial and mineral development."[33] Under the First Plan, private investment in organized industries had been more than twice the amount of public outlay. The Second Plan reversed this order, and established the public sector as the more important instrument of industrialization. Compared to a projected outlay of Rs. 575 crores for industries and mining in the private sector, new investment of Rs. 690 crores was allocated for large-scale industries and mining in the public sector, including iron and steel, coal, heavy engineering, and heavy electricals.[34]

The relative shift in public investment priorities between the First and Second Plans is shown in Table 4-1. Outlays on industry and mining, as would be expected, showed the greatest proportional and absolute increase between the two Plans—from 7.6 percent to 18.5 percent, and Rs. 179 crores to Rs. 890 crores, respectively. Since large investments in capital projects would not immediately increase the supply of consumer goods or create substantial new job opportunities, the planners proposed to rely on labor-intensive village and small industries to the extent possible in meeting consumer demands. The Second Plan provided allocations of Rs. 200 crores, more than six times the level in the First Plan, for the development of village and small industries.

The decision in favor of rapid industrialization sharply reduced the proportion of total outlay allocated to agriculture and irrigation, from 34.6 percent in the First Plan to 17.5 percent in the Second Plan. In absolute terms, total expenditure on agriculture as a whole did rise by over 25 percent. But within this category, outlay on agricultural production programs, that is, schemes contributing directly to increased output, actually declined from Rs. 197 crores in the First Plan to Rs. 170 crores in the Second Plan. Expenditure on irrigation fell slightly in absolute terms, and showed a sharp relative decline in total Plan outlay, from 16.3 percent to 7.9 percent. As a result, reliance on the mobilization of local resources—voluntary contributions of labor and money to carry out labor-intensive development projects in agriculture—was even more pronounced. Between the two Plans, allocations to the National Extension and Community Development projects increased by more than two times.

[32] Ibid., p. 57.       [33] Ibid., p. 66.
[34] Ibid., p. 67.

# TABLE 4-1

## Distribution of Outlay in the First and Second Five Year Plans by Major Heads of Development

| | First Five Year Plan total percent provision (Rs. crores) | | Second Five Year Plan total percent provision (Rs. crores) | |
|---|---|---|---|---|
| *Agriculture and Community Development* | *357* | *15.1* | *568* | *11.8* |
| A. Agriculture | 234 | 10.0 | 294 | 6.1 |
|    Agricultural programs | (197) | (8.3) | (170) | (3.5) |
|    Animal husbandry, forests, fisheries and miscellaneous | (37) | (1.6) | (124) | (2.6) |
| B. National extension and community projects | 90 | 3.8 | 200 | 4.1 |
| C. Cooperation and other programs | 33 | 1.4 | 74 | 1.6 |
|    Cooperation | (7) | (0.3) | (47) | (1.0) |
|    Village panchayats | (11) | (0.5) | (12) | (0.3) |
|    Local development works | (15) | (0.6) | (15) | (0.3) |
| *Irrigation and Power* | *661* | *28.1* | *913* | *19.0* |
| A. Irrigation | 384 | 16.3 | 381 | 7.9 |
| B. Power | 260 | 11.1 | 427 | 8.9 |
| C. Flood control and other projects | 17 | 0.7 | 105 | 2.2 |
| *Industry and Mining* | *179* | *7.6* | *890* | *18.5* |
| A. Large and medium industries | 148 | 6.3 | 617 | 12.9 |
| B. Mineral development | 1 | — | 73 | 1.5 |
| C. Village and small industries | 30 | 1.3 | 200 | 4.1 |
| *Transport and Communications* | *557* | *23.6* | *1,385* | *28.9* |
| A. Railways | 268 | 11.4 | 900 | 18.8 |
| B. Roads | 130 | 5.5 | 246 | 5.1 |
| C. Ports, shipping, civil aviation, posts and telegraphs, etc. | 159 | 6.7 | 239 | 5.0 |
| *Social Services* | *533* | *22.6* | *945* | *19.7* |
| A. Education | 164 | 7.0 | 307 | 6.4 |
| B. Health | 140 | 5.9 | 274 | 5.7 |
| C. Housing | 49 | 2.1 | 120 | 2.5 |
| D. Social welfare and rehabilitation schemes | 180 | 7.6 | 244 | 5.1 |
| *Miscellaneous* | *69* | *3.0* | *99* | *2.1* |
| *Total* | *2,356* | *100.0* | *4,800* | *100.0* |

SOURCE: Adapted from *Second Five Year Plan*, pp. 51-52.

Yet, despite attempts to minimize the capital costs of increasing agricultural productivity, the problem of raising adequate domestic resources had still not been solved. Even in the brief period between preparation of the Plan Frame in March 1955 and the completion of the final version of the Second Plan in February 1956, estimates of the costs under all heads of development had climbed from a total of Rs. 4,300 crores to Rs. 4,800 crores. By contrast, allowing only for "minimum" increase in expenditure on nondevelopmental items (defense, administration, and maintenance of existing projects and services), surpluses from current revenues were estimated at no more than Rs. 350 crores, about one-half the level projected a year earlier. Moreover, despite the fact that receipts from public borrowings, the railways, provident funds, and other deposits had all been revised upwards in the interim—with no specific justification—budgetary resources at 1956/57 levels of taxation amounted to no more than Rs. 1,950 crores. After taking credit for the maximum limit of deficit financing at Rs. 1,200 crores, and for foreign aid amounting to Rs. 800 crores, the planners were left with a resource gap of Rs. 850 crores. Estimates of financial resources for the Second Plan are shown in Table 4-2.

The Planning Commission proposed that Rs. 450 crores should be raised through additional taxation, the burden of which was to be evenly distributed between the Center and the states. The possibility of raising even larger resources through taxation was to be "investigated fully." Nevertheless, the planners emphasized that the remaining gap of Rs. 400

### TABLE 4-2

#### Sources of Finance for the Second Plan

|  | (Rs. crores) |
|---|---|
| *Total budgetary resources* | *2,400* |
| Surplus from current revenues at 1955/56 rates of taxation | 350 |
| Revenues from additional taxation | 450 |
| Borrowings from the public | 1,200 |
|    Market loans | (700) |
|    Small savings | (500) |
| Railways | 150 |
| Provident funds and other deposit heads | 250 |
| *Deficit financing* | *1,200* |
| *Foreign aid* | *800* |
| *Gap* | *400* |
| *Total* | *4,800* |

SOURCE: Adapted from *Second Five Year Plan*, pp. 77-78.

crores could be covered only if "other measures and techniques" were adopted to control public consumption. Obliquely citing the Chinese experience with state trading in comsumer items, the planners asserted:

> It must be recognized, of course, that taxation has its limits, and this means in turn that it has to be supplemented by institutional arrangements which bring directly into the public exchequer the surpluses which accrue from the sale of goods and services to the public. It it through devices of this type, that is through appropriate pricing policies in respect of the products of public enterprises, and through state trading or fiscal monopolies in selected lines that some of the underdeveloped countries with levels of living not much higher than those in India are raising the resources required for their developmental effort.[35]

State trading was simultaneously assigned a major role in stabilizing the domestic price level. The planners warned that in cases of acute scarcity or shortage of foodgrains and other essential commodities, price controls and rationing of necessities might become necessary to preserve the structure of the plan. They envisaged that during the Second Plan, government would build up adequate reserve stocks of foodgrains to undertake open market operations for the purpose of moderating sharp seasonal fluctuations in prices or any inflationary pressures arising from a large investment program.

As in the Plan Frame, a central role was assigned to the organization of state-partnered cooperatives in agricultural credit, marketing, and processing. A number of National Funds[36] were created to permit the states to subscribe to the share capital of apex (state) banks, central (district) banks, and large-size primary credit societies, as well as to the share capital of noncredit institutions, especially marketing and processing

---

[35] *Ibid.*, p. 91.

[36] The National Agricultural Credit (long-term operations) Fund, with a capitalization of Rs. 35 crores, was to extend loans to the states to permit them to subscribe to the share capital of apex (state) banks, central (district) banks, and large-size primary credit societies. A second fund, the National Agricultural Credit Stabilization Fund, set up by the Reserve Bank with a capitalization of Rs. 5 crores, was to advance medium-term loans to state cooperative banks (under government guarantee) for the purpose of repaying short-term dues to the Reserve Bank when drought or other natural calamity interfered with timely repayment. The newly created National Cooperative Development and Warehousing Board also administered two other centrally financed funds, the National Cooperative Development Fund and the National Warehousing Fund. Loans from the National Cooperative Development Fund were to be advanced to the state governments to enable them to subscribe to the share capital of noncredit institutions, especially marketing and processing societies, and to subsidize their operating expenses. The National Warehousing Fund was to finance federal government contributions to share capital of a central warehousing corporation, as well as loans to the state governments for subscriptions to the share capital of state warehousing corporations.

societies. In addition, the Second Plan provided for the establishment of a National Cooperative Development and Warehousing Board (composed of officers from the Reserve Bank, the State Bank, the Government of India, and nonofficial representatives of the cooperative movement) to act as the all-India planning, organizing, and coordinating agency for cooperative policy in marketing, processing, and warehousing.

Nevertheless, having created what appeared to be a national financial and administrative apparatus for the supervision of the cooperative sector, the planners were unable to avoid numerous concessions on the scope and pace of agrarian reorganization that seriously undermined the utility of the cooperatives as instruments of government regulation over the agricultural economy. In response to objections raised by the state leadership, the Planning Commission declined to press the Rural Credit Survey's proposals for formal state control over appointments to the boards of directors of cooperative banks; or official veto power over lending policies and appointments by the cooperatives. They did reiterate the Rural Credit Survey's recommendation that all members of cooperatives be eligible to receive loans on the basis of production plans and the capacity to repay in kind, but they retreated from the position that members could receive production loans only on condition that they agreed before hand to market their produce through the cooperative society. The Second Plan entirely eliminated this element of compulsion. Instead, the planners provided that "members of credit societies will be persuaded to agree in advance to market their produce through the primary marketing society."[37]

A critical concession also was made to the state leadership on the question of a timetable for cooperative reorganization of agriculture. Although the planners believed that agrarian reorganization—with the exception of cooperative farming—should be completed within a period of ten years, the state ministers of cooperation, meeting in April 1955, argued that even with government participation in share capital and other financial and managerial assistance to the cooperatives, it would not be possible to organize more than fifty percent of agricultural credit, marketing, and processing activities in the cooperative sector over a period of fifteen years. Actual targets adopted for the Second Plan implied an even more prolonged period of transition.[38] It was estimated that only fifteen

[37] *Second Five Year Plan*, p. 226.
[38] The Second Plan provided that 10,400 larger-sized societies would be formed either through the formation of new societies or the amalgamation of existing ones. Targets for short-term credit, medium-term credit, and longer-term credit were put at Rs. 150 crores, Rs. 50 crores, and Rs. 25 crores, respectively. In addition, it was proposed to organize 1,800 primary marketing societies, 35 cooperative sugar factories, 48 cooperative cotton gins, and 118 other cooperative processing societies. There was also to be construction of 350 warehouses of central and state corporations, 1,500 godowns of marketing societies, and 4,000 godowns of larger-sized societies. *Ibid.*, p. 227.

million agriculturalist families—about one-fourth of the total—would be
covered by agricultural cooperatives at the end of the Plan. Little more
than ten percent of the total requirement for agricultural credit would be
met. Marketing cooperatives were expected to be able to handle only ten
percent of the marketable surplus. Finally, although the planners believed that a buffer stock of five million tons of foodgrains was the
minimum size necessary to have any impact on the domestic price level,
less than two million tons of storage capacity was actually proposed to be
constructed by the Central and State Warehousing Corporations during
the Second Plan. About the only proposal that survived intact in the transition from the Rural Credit Survey report to the Second Plan was the
recommendation to establish large-size cooperatives in the interests of
economic efficiency. The Planning Commission provided that primary
credit and multipurpose service societies should include a number of villages in order to achieve an average membership of five hundred families,
a minimum share capital of Rs. 15,000, and an annual turnover of Rs. 1.5
lakhs. Existing small societies were to be reorganized according to this
pattern. Yet, even this proposal represented a setback for the commission, which reluctantly sacrificed its preference for the village as the basic
unit of cooperative organization—a part of its policy for the gradual transition toward joint village management.

Other concessions on the pace of land reforms were hardly less serious
in weakening the "keystone" of the economic approach for increasing
agricultural production through the mobilization of local manpower and
resources. Land reform was essential to large-scale mobilization of idle
manpower in two ways: to supply the social incentives needed for
motivating voluntary labor; and to pave the way for a more rational pattern of land utilization, allowing the release of large numbers of underemployed farmers and agricultural workers for full-time construction
work on capital projects. Although the Second Plan reiterated proposals
for tenancy reforms and ceilings on landownership, the planners were
unable to extract any firm commitment from the states on a time
schedule for completing legislation. Moreover, while the Planning
Commission believed that a substantial proportion of the land should be
cultivated under cooperatives within ten years, they could not achieve
any agreement with the state governments on targets for the formation
of cooperative farms. This question had to be left open for determination
during the first year of the Plan.

The result was that the Second Plan was allowed to begin with a glaring discrepancy between estimated requirements for agricultural production during the Plan period, and the actual targets adopted. On the basis
of a number of considerations, including an estimated population growth
rate of 1.2 percent per annum, increases in the urban population, the need

to improve standards of per capita consumption, the necessity of containing inflationary pressures, and an anticipated increase in demand arising from higher purchasing power and redistribution of income, the planners concluded that the requirement for foodgrains production would double over a ten-year period. Yet, by the Planning Commission's own calculations, direct investment outlay on agricultural production programs was sufficient only to increase total production by 15 percent, from 65 million tons in 1955/56 to 75 million tons in 1960/61.[39] The final version of the Second Plan endorsed the goal of "a doubling within a period of ten years of agricultural production, including food crops,"[40] at the same time that it accepted a target for the increase of foodgrains production for the five-year period, 1956-1961, of 15 percent. At the root of this contradiction was the ongoing political struggle between the planners and the state leadership on the pace of agrarian reform.

The Planning Commission believed that "appreciably higher targets of agricultural production"[41] could be achieved within the investment outlay provided. In 1955, while the Second Plan was still in the early stages of preparation, V. T. Krishnamachari, then deputy chairman of the Planning Commission, had urged the states to accept a target of forty percent increase in foodgrains production over the five-year period, 1956-1961. The planners argued that more extensive mobilization of local labor and resources through the Community Development and National Extension programs could substantially increase the scope for raising productivity within existing levels of investment. Although the states refused to be persuaded, the planners continued to insist that "by harnessing voluntary effort and local manpower resources physical targets in the plan can be supplemented in many fields and even greatly exceeded." The Second Plan suggested that the National Extension Service could "organize the systematic use of manpower resources in a number of ways, for instance, in constructing local works such as village roads, fuel plantations, tanks, water supply and drainage, and maintaining existing minor irrigation works. Where a large work is undertaken, such as an irrigation project, the national extension and community project personnel, should take the initiative, with the support of nonofficial leaders, in organizing labor cooperatives of villages interested in work on the canal system and connected activities."[42]

Even before the publication of the Second Plan, moreover, there was mounting concern that the low agricultural target would create serious inflationary pressures. As early as October 1955, prices of all cereals

[39] Ibid., p. 268.                              [40] Ibid., p. 62.
[41] Ibid.                                           [42] Ibid., p. 141.

showed a steady rise. Even the favorable harvest of 1956/57 did not stimulate a decline in prices as was expected.

By the spring of 1956, the Planning Commission renewed its campaign to get the agricultural targets revised upwards. Nehru reminded the chief ministers that despite the emphasis on heavy industry in the Second Plan, "the fact remains that agriculture is the solid foundation on which we have to build. It is from agriculture and from the increasing production on the land that we can build up our surpluses for future growth." He drew a pointed contrast between the planned rate of progress in India and in China: "Our original estimate [in India] was for a fifteen percent increase in agricultural production during the Second Plan. This manifestly is too little. The Chinese estimate is between 35 and 40 percent in five years and they start with a higher yield per acre. There is absolutely no reason why, if we are serious enough and work hard, we cannot equal the Chinese rate of progress in this matter. Our Food and Agriculture Ministry is giving fresh thought to this question and I have no doubt that they will put forward fresh targets well in advance of the old ones."[43]

Within three months after the beginning of the Second Plan, the planners scored their first success. The AICC took the unusual step of adopting a "Resolution on the Second Plan" that suggested that the "targets laid down in the Plan for agricultural production are capable of being and should be considerably raised."[44] Shortly after, at the meeting of the National Development Council, V. T. Krishnamachari "raised a hornets nest"[45] by circulating a note in which he reiterated the view that there could be an increase of 40 percent in agricultural production during the Second Plan without any increase in investment outlay, simply by more efficient use of labor-intensive techniques. Krishnamachari's position, however, met with vigorous objection from the Union food and agriculture minister, A. P. Jain, who insisted that within the existing allocation, the maximum possible increase was little over 15 percent. A conference of state food ministers convened by Jain in late June 1956 upheld his position, and suggested that foodgrains production could be boosted to 80 million tons—an increase of about 28 percent over 1955/56 levels—but only with an additional outlay of about Rs. 120 crores.

The Planning Commission, nevertheless, remained unpersuaded that any additions to financial outlay were needed to increase agricultural production beyond Plan targets. They were, moreover, once again confirmed in their views by reports from China of very large increases in

[43] *Fortnightly Letters to the Chief Ministers, 1948-63*, letter dated May 10, 1956.
[44] AICC, *Congress Bulletin*, May-June 1958, p. 191.
[45] *Hindustan Times*, July 13, 1956.

agricultural output as a result of agrarian reorganization and mobilization of idle manpower.

As early as 1954, accounts from China had indicated that a new movement was underway to reorganize all agricultural land into primary cooperative farms and collective farms. Members from the Indian Trade Union Delegation visiting Peking for the May Day celebrations in 1955 reported there were 60,000 producers' cooperatives in China, covering 15 million out of a total of 116 million cultivators. Six months later, in December 1955, Professor Chen Han Seng, accompanying Madame Sun Yat Sen on a visit to India, told the Planning Commission that the over-whelming majority of Chinese cultivators had joined cooperative or col-lective farms, and as a result of more efficient utilization of manpower and bullocks, China would be able to increase agricultural production 35 to 40 percent over the next five years.

In June 1956, at the height of its campaign to commit the states to higher targets of agricultural production, the Planning Commission an-nounced it was sending a Delegation on Agrarian Cooperatives (referred to as the Patil Committee) to China "to study in greater detail the methods adopted . . . for development of agrarian cooperatives."[46] Very soon afterward, the Union Ministry of Food and Agriculture announced the appointment of its own Delegation to China on Agricultural Plan-ning and Techniques, also to study "the scheme and programs which the Chinese authorities are adopting for increasing the productivity of their agriculture."[47] The ministry explained its decision by referring to the "strong feeling" that targets for agricultural development under the Sec-ond Plan were inadequate, and reports from China of much higher rates of growth.

The Patil Committee and the delegation appointed by the food minis-try reached China at about the same time. The Patil Committee arrived

[46] Planning Commission, *Report of the Indian Delegation to China on Agrarian Cooperatives*, p. 1. The seven-member delegation was composed mainly of workers in the cooperative movement and politicians and administrators known to favor the cooperative pattern. They included R. K. Patil, a Gandhian constructive worker and leader of the cooperative movement in Gujerat, leader; D. K. Barooah and H. V. Tripathi, M.P.s; K. D. Malaviya, secretary, Economic and Political Research Department, AICC; B. J. Patel, honorary secre-tary, All-India Cooperative Union; F. N. Rana, IAS registrar, cooperative societies, Bom-bay State; and M. P. Bhargava, cooperation advisor, Ministry of Food and Agriculture, member-secretary.

[47] Ministry of Food and Agriculture, *Report of the Indian Delegation to China on Agriculture Planning and Techniques*, p. 1. The food ministry's delegation was more of an "expert" group. The membership included M. V. Krishnappa, deputy minister of food and agricul-ture, Ministry of Food and Agriculture; P. N. Thapar, secretary, Ministry of Food and Ag-riculture; Tarlok Singh, joint secretary, Planning Commission; Dr. R. J. Kalamkar, addi-tional agricultural commissioner, Indian Council of Agricultural Research; Dr. S. R. Sen, economic and statistical advisor, Ministry of Food and Agriculture.

in Peking on July 25, 1956, remained two months, and visited nineteen producers' cooperatives and eight provinces of China. The Delegation on Agricultural Planning and Techniques reached Peking on July 20, 1956, and left China August 8. The delegation visited an unspecified number of cooperative farms, but spent most of its time in discussions with technical experts from the Ministry of Agriculture, related ministries in Peking, and the Chinese Planning Commission.

As V. T. Krishnamachari acknowledged, the reports of the two delegations to China "confirmed what the Planning Commission was thinking all along."[48] The Patil Committee reported that foodgrains production had increased by 15 to 30 percent over a two to three year period in those Chinese villages where cooperative farms had been formed. They attributed most of this increase to more rational patterns of agrarian organization that released large numbers of underemployed farmers for construction of physical assets. Among other projects, they cited reclamation of wastelands, construction of roads, contour bunds, irrigation channels, and new wells; they also reported mass "drives" for such things as the collection of organic manures. As a result of such programs in one province alone, the Patil Committee reported, 300,000 wells and 10,000 small dams had been constructed in one season, raising the total irrigated area by a hundred percent. Other accomplishments attributed to the mobilization of idle manpower included collection of seventy percent of the total manure requirement for the next season and intensified methods of cultivation to raise yields. On the basis of its observations in China, the Patil Committee recommended that 10,000 cooperative farms should be organized in India during the Second Plan.[49] The food ministry's delegation actually reached broadly similar conclusions. They reported that

[48] Interview, V. T. Krishnamachari, New Delhi, August 26, 1963.
[49] These recommendations were not unanimous. In a sharp "Minute of Dissent" to the majority report, two members of the delegation, B. J. Patel and R. N. Rana, argued that the Chinese pattern was incompatible with Indian democracy, and that agrarian transformation had been achieved only after "great stress and violence." Patel and Rana charged that the land reforms of 1949, which redistributed almost forty percent of the cultivated area in tiny one acre plots to tenants and laborers, had been accomplished at the cost of the liquidation of some two million landowners. They also disputed the majority finding that the cooperative sector had been built up on the principles of "gradualness and voluntariness." They pointed out that "when the State has a complete monopoly on the purchase of agricultural produce, when it imposes prohibitory taxes and delivery quotas on individual farmers and denies them essential supplies and credit which are again in the hands of the State, the so-called freedom of the peasants to continue individual farming can only be illusory and temporary." *Report of the Indian Delegation to China on Agrarian Cooperatives*, p. 204. In the main, however, the Indian planners accepted the majority finding that "the masses were overtaken by the idealist aspect of the movement under the leadership of the Communist Party and the propaganda carried by it." *Ibid.*, p. 36. They were convinced that physical coercion had only been used during the first stage of land reforms, when the victims were landlords living on the labor of others, and by definition "exploiters." This underlying assumption that the landlords were antisocial elements who ought to be re-

"Chinese experience shows that given certain conditions, it is possible through cooperatives to organize rural manpower resources so as to ensure a high level of employment for all members of the community and not merely those who happen to have fair-sized agricultural holdings. This is significant for our future development." The delegation also recommended a "bold program of experiments in cooperative farming" during the Second Plan.[50]

The reports reinforced the planners in their conviction that new patterns of agrarian organization could create the conditions for more efficient use of available resources and achieve adequate increases in agricultural production during the Second Plan. Nehru scored the state agriculture ministers who "take it for granted that additional increase in agricultural production cannot be had unless additional funds are available." He was, on the contrary, convinced that "the increase should certainly be 30 percent," and that this rate of growth could be achieved "without any large additional expenditure" through more labor-intensive techniques in the Community Development and NES Blocks. Once more, he cited the example of China, "where millions of cooperative farms have sprung up," and asked,"How then, are we to increase this [agricultural] production? We know for a fact that some other countries have rapidly increased their food production in the last few years without any tremendous use of fertilizers. How has China done it? China's resources in this respect are not bigger than ours. China is at the same time laying far greater stress on industrial development and heavy industry than we are. Yet, they are succeeding in increasing their agricultural production at a faster pace than we are. Surely, it should not be beyond our powers to do something that China can do."[51]

The food minister, A. P. Jain, was constantly reminded of China's achievements. He recalled, not without exasperation, that in 1956,

the Planning Commission had adopted the idea that you can raise any amount of food by utilizing surplus labor power. Our people

moved in the interests of the community as a whole, helps to explain why both delegations and the Planning Commission chose to minimize the violence and intimidation associated with the Chinese land reforms of 1949. For example, Shriman Narayan, general secretary of the AICC, commenting on the divergent reports of members of the Delegation on Agrarian Cooperatives asserted: "Whether the agrarian cooperatives of China were formed voluntarily or not through coercive pressure is a matter of controversy. But truth perhaps lies in the fact that while there was a certain amount of coercion in the beginning, the farmers in China are now experiencing the benefits of cooperation and are therefore, quite enthusiastic about agrarian cooperatives." "Note on Cooperative Farming Prepared and Submitted by Shriman Narayan to the AICC Informal Session on September 1 and Discussed," AICC, *Congress Bulletin*, September 1957, p. 432.

[50] *Report of the Indian Delegation to China on Agricultural Planning and Techniques*, p. 193.

[51] *Fortnightly Letters to the Chief Ministers, 1948-63*, letter dated August 12, 1956.

were going to China. Delegations were coming and going. My Minister of State made fantastic statements in Parliament that the Chinese were ploughing four feet deep. He showed a photograph of a man climbing up the leaves of tobacco plants to show how tall it was. Children were shown dancing on the top of paddy crops. All of this the planners were convinced came from mobilizing surplus manpower. We had begun to believe that by the sheer utilization of the waste labor power, you can achieve anything and everything.[52]

In December 1956, the Planning Commission enjoyed a partial success in its campaign to commit the states to higher agricultural targets. The National Development Council finally voted to adopt a target of 80.5 million tons of foodgrains production for the Second Plan—an increase of 25 percent over 1955/56 levels—without any increase in investment outlay. But the planners considered that this was still inadequate. Soon after, the AICC again called for a higher target. Asserting that industrial development would require a large increase in agricultural production "far beyond the figures initially adopted in the Second Five Year Plan," they proposed that "during the next five years, the present agricultural production must be raised by at least 35 percent."[53]

The states proved more recalcitrant, however, in accepting any large-scale program for the organization of cooperative farms during the Second Plan. In replies to the Planning Commission and the Ministry of Food and Agriculture concerning the recommendations of the two delegations to China, state leaders agreed only to a small experimental program in cooperative farming on condition that membership remain entirely voluntary. In November 1957, the National Development Council voted to establish 2,000 cooperative farms during the Second Plan period.

By the summer of 1957, however, economic pressures for more rapid reorganization of the rural sector increased. Agricultural production fell below the high level of 1953/54, and food prices jumped as much as 50 percent between October 1955 and August 1957. Reflecting the sharp upward trend in agricultural commodities, the wholesale price index rose by 14 percent in the first fifteen months of the Plan. During 1956/57, government imported two million tons of foodgrains, about one-third the total amount allowed for the five-year period. Then, in April 1957, the monsoon failed in north India and the wheat crop was badly damaged, aggravating an already strained situation. Foodgrains production fell by almost 10 percent, from about 69 million tons in 1956/57 to 63 million tons in 1957/58. The food minister, A. P. Jain, speaking in the

[52] Interview, A. P. Jain, New Delhi, April 17, 1963.
[53] AICC, *Congress Bulletin*, November 1956, p. 452.

Lok Sabha admitted, that "we have passed through a very bad year, a year of scarcity the like of which did not occur in living memory." Although the government imported another four million tons of foodgrains in 1957/58, he continued, "we could not make up the total deficit [and] prices did go up to a level which was quite unprecedented."[54]

The report of the Foodgrains Enquiry Committee appointed by the Ministry of Food and Agriculture in 1957[55] only heightened the atmosphere of crisis. On the basis of discussions with the state governments, the committee estimated actual achievement of foodgrains output at the end of the Second Plan "in the neighborhood of 60 percent of the targets laid down."[56] Price controls, government procurement of foodgrains, and rationing of available supplies seemed an absolute necessity for preserving the structure of the Plan. In addition, the Planning Commission was convinced that hoarding activities by traders, who profited from creating artificially severe scarcities during the lean season, had seriously aggravated the sharp upward spiral in food prices. They warmly endorsed the Foodgrains Enquiry Committee's conclusion that "until there is social control over the wholesale trade we shall not be in a position to bring about stabilization of foodgrains prices. Our policy should therefore be that of progressive and planned socialization of the wholesale trade in foodgrains."[57]

Starting in the spring of 1957, the Planning Commission began to press the food ministry for rapid implementation of the Foodgrains Enquiry Committee's recommendation to establish a Foodgrains Stabilization Organization (FSO), with branches in all important market towns, to undertake purchase and sale of wheat and rice at controlled prices. Yet, in the absence of cooperative marketing societies that could act as procurement agents for the state, the proposed FSO was to operate through government-licensed millers and wholesale merchants in foodgrains. The new agency was to have the authority to restrict movements of rice and wheat on private account outside of designated districts; undertake monopoly procurement in surplus states or districts for export outside the state; and in the absence of voluntary offers of rice and wheat at fixed prices, requisition the stocks of millers and traders. The Planning Commission envisaged that the food ministry could build up sufficiently large

[54] *Lok Sabha Debates*, Second Series, xiv (1958), 8135.
[55] The Foodgrains Enquiry Committee, under the chairmanship of Asoka Mehta, then leader of the Praja Socialist party, was reluctantly appointed by A. P. Jain in May 1957, in response to sharp criticism in the Lok Sabha of the food ministry's handling of food shortages and rising prices. The committee was charged with studying the reasons for rising prices since 1955 and recommending measures to stabilize foodgrain prices at reasonable levels.
[56] Ministry of Food and Agriculture, *Report of the Foodgrains Enquiry Committee*, p. 12.
[57] *Ibid.*, p. 86.

buffer stocks through these means, even in a period of scarcity and rising prices, so that by the end of the Second Plan the government would emerge as the dominant trader in the economy.

Such optimism, however, failed to take account of the reaction of the Union food minister. A. P. Jain, a former chairman of the Uttar Pradesh Congress Committee, was completely unsympathetic to a policy of price controls and state trading, both of which he judged would antagonize the large landowners and traders who still formed the backbone of the Congress party organization in his state. In a statement to the Lok Sabha on July 30, 1957, Jain did not hesitate to attack the Planning Commission (albeit obliquely) for worrying too much about rising prices and consumer interests, and too little about price incentives for the farmer. He observed acidly:

> There is also a school of thought in this country consisting of economists and persons mostly confined to their rooms. They think that you can finance the Plan by depressing the agricultural prices. Some of them go to the length of saying: "Fix the price of wheat [at a very low level] and the price of rice and other agricultural commodities at a parity. Procure all the wheat and rice and other commodities compulsorily in the market and that will solve the problem of prices. Wages will not go up and the Plan will progress smoothly." These people seem to forget that there is also some such thing as agricultural sector in our economy and that it all forms part of the Plan. . . . If we adopt any policy of low prices for agriculture, it is a regressive policy. If our policy does not give any incentive to the farmer, he is not going to produce and if the Plan fails it will wreck on the policy of depressing agricultural prices.[58]

Jain was more colorful, but perhaps more candid, in explaining his real objections in private. Commenting on his assignment to implement state trading in foodgrains, he pointed out, "state trading meant that the surplus had to be taken over by the state and redistributed to the consumers. In practice, it meant that there had to be marketing cooperatives in every state that would compulsorily collect the surplus so that the state could then redistribute it. I felt I was not the man to do it. It requires a bit of pressure. It was Stalin and Mao who enforced it in Russia and China."[59]

Throughout 1957, Jain, citing administrative and organizational obstacles to rapid implementation, delayed in carrying out the Planning Commission's recommendation to establish a Foodgrains Stabilization Organization. Under his leadership, the Union ministry and the state

[58] *Lok Sabha Debates*, Second Series, IV (1957), 6066.
[59] Interview, A. P. Jain, New Delhi, April 17, 1963.

Departments of Agriculture complied only with the least controversial recommendations of the Foodgrains Enquiry Committee's report. Between 1957 and 1959, restrictions were imposed on the free movement of rice outside the "Southern Zone"—the two surplus states of Andhra Pradesh and Madras and the two deficit states of Mysore and Kerala—although rice was permitted to move freely among the four states. Similarly, all exports of rice and paddy on private account were banned from Orissa and Bihar, from Assam and West Bengal, and finally, from Madha Pradesh, Uttar Pradesh, and Punjab. The same pattern was followed with respect to private trade in wheat. In 1957, three wheat zones were constituted: Himachal Pradesh, Punjab, and Delhi; Uttar Pradesh; and Rajasthan, Bombay state, and Madhya Pradesh. Under this system of zonal restrictions on the free movement of foodgrains,[60] the food ministry assumed responsibility for supplying localized food shortages that still remained after pairing surplus and deficit states in one trading area. In addition, beginning in 1957, the Union government undertook to meet the rice requirements of Bombay and Calcutta to avert an unreasonable drain on rural surpluses toward urban centers with greater purchasing power.

Until late 1957, however, the food ministry successfully resisted pressure by the Planning Commission to undertake state trading in foodgrains. Instead, central government wheat stocks were accumulated through commercial imports from Australia, and under the first PL 480 agreement signed with the United States in August 1956. Rice stocks were procured through commercial imports from Burma, Cambodia, and Thailand. These stocks were then moved on government account to the deficit states, and subsequently were released through nonprofit fair-price shops in the larger cities, operated directly by government, government-licensed foodgrains dealers, or cooperatives.

Toward the end of 1957, however, a growing shortage of foreign exchange prevented the Union ministry from supplying all of the rice deficit from commerical imports. In November, the Union ministry, already under pressure from the Planning Commission, agreed to begin procurement operations on its own account in Andhra Pradesh, Mysore, and Orissa. The Punjab government also entered the market on behalf of the central government. In Assam and West Bengal, the state govern-

[60] The zonal restrictions were designed to make the southern states self-sufficient in rice, and to prevent exports from Andhra and Madras outside the Southern Zone to the more prosperous states of West Bengal and Bombay, both of which, buoyed by the purchasing power of the big cities of Calcutta and Bombay, could afford to outbid Mysore and Kerala on the open market. At issue were costly cross-shipments of rice involved in landing larger quantities of imported rice from Burma at ports in Madras and Kerala instead of nearby Calcutta, while Andhra rice moved to Bombay and West Bengal by rail. Economy of transport also favored landing overseas rice at Bombay rather than Madras or Kerala, and this obviated the usefulness of rail movements of rice from Andhra to Bombay.

ments attempted to procure part of the rice surplus on their own account in order to supply the deficit districts in their states. Still, no attempt was made to replace the private traders with a state trading organization. Rather, the traders continued to act as purchasing agents for the central and state governments, along with the cooperatives, in making purchases on government account in return for a commission; and they continued to make purchases on their own behalf.

In the main, these first attempts at "state trading" in foodgrains were unsuccessful. In Orissa and Mysore, government restricted its activities to voluntary procurement at the average of prices that prevailed in the three months prior to November 1957. Rice offered for sale at these prices, which were lower than the open market price in most districts, was 56,000 tons and 13,000 tons, respectively. In Andhra Pradesh and Punjab, very low levels of procurement ultimately convinced the state government to fix maximum controlled prices for wholesale purchases and sales of rice, and a compulsory levy on rice mills. Total procurement under these regulations reached 200,000 tons in Andhra and 100,000 tons in Punjab. In West Bengal and Assam, where maximum controlled prices on all wholesale transactions were applied to surplus districts only, government was able to procure only 77,000 tons and 22,000 tons, respectively.

The failure of these first tentative efforts at state trading was apparent from rising food prices throughout 1957/58, and from chronic food shortages in the deficit states and larger cities. The Planning Commission blamed the shortages on the failure of the food ministry and the states to establish monopoly procurement of foodgrains and price controls at all levels of the distribution process. The planners charged that a system of partial controls, which applied only to wholesale transactions of foodgrains, and in some cases, only to surplus districts in the states, was designed to facilitate evasion. Although the procurement price established by government was simultaneously declared the legal maximum controlled price for all wholesale transactions in the affected district or state, many middle and large producers managed to smuggle their stocks into uncontrolled districts or states for sale; and many sold rice in smaller than wholesale quantities to retailers and consumers who were not affected by price controls. In the states that imposed a compulsory levy on a fixed proportion of the wholesalers' and millers' stock, the trader was still free to sell the remaining portion to a retailer who was not subject to controls. This encouraged the trader to hold back supplies until the post-harvest "lean" season, and when government stocks were exhausted to sell at very high prices that helped recoup the losses suffered under the levy. The planners were convinced that traders were also evading the levy orders and controls by paying higher than maximum fixed prices to the farmers, and arranging with them to hold stock in the villages until later in the season, when it could be sold at very high margins of profit either in the black market or to retailers in the large urban centers.

The food ministry and the states rejected outright this analysis by the Planning Commission of the causes of food shortages and rising prices. They insisted that market factors, including static production levels, higher income generated by development outlays, and rising population growth, rather than hoarding, were mainly responsible. The food ministry's solution to the food crisis, which it argued before the Planning Commission, was a reorientation of agricultural policy to restore the priority for the introduction of scientific practices over changes in organization as the foremost instrument of increasing agricultural productivity and surpluses. Among other policies, they pressed for greater investment outlays on agriculture for improved seeds, pesticides, and especially fertilizer; and remunerative prices for rice and wheat in order to provide an incentive for increased private investment in improved inputs. In the short run, the food ministry proposed to meet the requirements of the deficit states by importing wheat and some rice under PL 480, supplemented by commercial imports of rice. Indeed, in September 1958, the ministry signed another PL 480 agreement with the United States to provide for 3 million tons of wheat imports over a two-year period.

The conflict between the Planning Commission and the states assumed more critical dimensions with the deepening financial crisis in 1957/58, and strong pressures to reduce the size of the Plan. By March 1958, the foreign exchange position had dramatically deteriorated. Originally, the total aggregate deficit in the balance of payments had been estimated at Rs. 1,120 crores over the five-year period. The Planning Commission provided that Rs. 200 crores of this amount would be met from India's sterling balances, and the remainder from external assistance. In the first two years, however, the aggregate deficit in current accounts climbed to Rs. 821 crores. India drew down her foreign exchange assets by Rs. 479 crores. It appeared that the five-year deficit in the balance of payments would ultimately total Rs. 1,700 crores.[61]

A number of circumstances contributed to the crisis. Growing needs for defense imports, a general rise in the prices of iron and steel, and higher foreign exchange costs than anticipated for some new industrial projects all played a part. Another significant factor was the need to im-

---

[61] A summary statement of the dimensions of the foreign exchange shortage is found in Planning Commission, *Appraisal and Prospects of the Second Five Year Plan*, pp. 14–16. For a more detailed analysis, see Council of Applied Economic Research, Occasional Papers, No. 1, *Foreign Exchange Crisis and the Plan* (New Delhi, 1957).

port twice the amount of foodgrains than originally envisaged. In addition, the failure of the finance ministry to impose adequate controls over import licenses led in the early years of the Plan to larger than expected numbers of licenses sanctioned to the private sector for imports of capital goods and iron and steel. All of these factors together lowered the ceiling on the total quantum of foreign exchange available for expansion of the public sector during the remainder of the Plan. As early as 1957/58, the planners were forced to limit allocations of foreign exchange to a small list of "core" projects in iron and steel, coal, power, railways, and ports. Completion of a number of other industrial schemes in the public sector, including the large fertilizer plants, had to be delayed.[62]

The scarcity of foreign exchange was not the only source of strain on the completion of public-sector programs. It soon became evident that domestic inflationary pressures had pushed up the rupee costs of some industrial projects, and that the financial requirements for achieving the physical targets of the Plan would be substantially higher than the Rs. 4,800 crores originally envisaged. In 1957/58, the Planning Commission, conceding that higher financial outlays were not feasible, acquiesced in a lowering of the physical targets and decided to maintain the financial ceiling of Rs. 4,800 crores. Still, the "core" projects were protected through a reallocation of outlays under the major heads of development that provided an additional Rs. 190 crores for industry and mining. With great effort, allocations to agriculture and Community Development and village and small-scale industries were maintained at the original level. Cuts were, however, imposed on allocations to social services of Rs. 82 crores; irrigation and power, Rs. 53 crores; transport, Rs. 40 crores, and to other miscellaneous expenditures, Rs. 15 crores.

Nevertheless, the appraisal of Plan outlay and resources in April 1958 clearly indicated that even the financial ceiling of Rs. 4,800 crores would have to be reduced. During the first two years, serious shortfalls in

[62] The foreign exchange shortage and the bias of import licensing toward the private sector in the first two years intensified pressure for a smaller Plan outlay in still another way, by diverting internal resources from the public sector. In January 1958, Professor D. R. Gadgil presented an analysis of the economic crisis to the Planning Commission's Panel of Economists, which stressed that the liberal licensing policy had stimulated "almost an overfulfillment in the large private sector," partly at the expense of public enterprise. On the whole, the high level of demand for funds by the private sector and its capacity to offer more attractive dividends had reduced the ability of the government to mobilize domestic resources through market loans. In particular, the large imports of capital goods in 1955/56 and 1956/57 triggered a great expansion in building and construction activities, with the result that the banks committed large funds in commercial credits to private firms that might otherwise have come to the state in the form of subscriptions to government issues. Meanwhile, the private sector was also benefiting from its ability to attract foreign private capital for investment in joint ventures, even while the government's leverage was reduced by increasing reliance on foreign aid from countries generally opposed to a socialist approach for completion of industrial projects in the public sector. See D. R. Gadgil, "On Rephasing the Second Five Year Plan," paper prepared for the Economists Panel for consideration at its meeting in January 1958, *The Indian Economic Journal*, v (April 1958).

budgetary resources had depressed aggregate Plan outlay far below the levels originally envisaged. During 1955/57, total Plan expenditure was Rs. 635 crores, compared to budget provisions of Rs. 828 crores, a shortfall of over 23 percent. In 1957/58, actual Plan outlay did show an increase to Rs. 861 crores, compared to budget estimates of Rs. 966 crores; but the entire increase in Plan expenditure had to be met by deficit financing. The budgetary gap jumped from Rs. 238 crores in 1956/57 to Rs. 464 crores in 1957/58. Within two years, the economy had to absorb Rs. 700 crores in deficit financing, compared to the maximum limit of Rs. 1,200 crores considered safe for the entire five years. As a result, during 1958/59, the upper limit on deficit financing was put at Rs. 215 crores. Together with external assistance of Rs. 300 crores (an increase of three times the 1957/58 level), an annual Plan outlay of almost Rs. 1,000 crores might be achieved. Still, over the first three years of the Plan, little more than fifty percent of Plan outlay—Rs. 2,456 out of Rs. 4,800 crores—would have been financed.[63]

A detailed analysis of the resources position over the first three years again focused attention on the need to mobilize higher domestic savings from the rural sector. An examination of the tax effort made at the Center and the states revealed that contributions from current revenues for financing Plan outlay came mainly from central taxes levied on the urban sector. By contrast, the states had generally failed to meet their commitments under current revenues; and this failure was most striking with respect to measures for additional taxation on the rural sector.

During the first three years of the Second Plan, the Center had actually over fulfilled its target for the mobilization of domestic resources from taxation. Originally, the Center's aggregate contribution to the Plan from current revenues was estimated at Rs. 420 crores—Rs. 252 crores at 1955/56 rates of taxation, and Rs. 168 crores from additional taxation.[64] By contrast, during the first three years of the Plan, central receipts from new taxes on income, company dividends, capital gains, wealth, and excises were as high as Rs. 376 crores; over the five-year period they were expected to reach Rs. 725 crores. Even so, the largest part of the additional revenues were not available for central Plan outlay. Rs. 160 crores had to be transferred to the states under an unexpectedly generous award by the Finance Commission. Another Rs. 225 crores was absorbed by rising outlays on defense. After subtracting the costs of other miscellaneous nondevelopmental expenditures, the Center's aggregate contribution to the Plan from current revenues was estimated at Rs. 465 crores, higher by just Rs. 45 crores than the original target.[65]

[63] *Appraisal and Prospects of the Second Five Year Plan*, pp. 7-9, 31-32.
[64] The actual target for additional taxation by the Center was Rs. 225 crores, of which an estimated Rs. 57 crores was earmarked for transfer to the states as their share.
[65] *Appraisal and Prospects of the Second Five Year Plan*, pp. 10-13.

This modest gain was more than cancelled by serious shortfalls at the states in budgetary resources for the Plan. Altogether, the states had been expected to find Rs. 370 crores from current revenues. In addition to funds drawn down from the Finance Commission's award, and the devolution of Union taxes, the states were supposed to contribute Rs. 98 crores from current revenues at 1955/56 rates of taxation and Rs. 225 crores from measures of additional taxation. During the first three years of the Plan, however, the states' aggregate contribution to total Plan outlay from these sources was about Rs. 135 crores. Over the five-year period it was not expected to exceed Rs. 295 crores.

An examination of the resources position in the states revealed that the expected surpluses from current revenues at pre-Plan rates of taxation had evaporated. In fact, the states were running a deficit of Rs. 10 crores to Rs. 20 crores under this head, mainly because of an increase in non-developmental expenditures. The yield from additional taxation over the first three years of the Plan, moreover, was only about Rs. 79 crores. Aggregate yields over the five-year period were estimated at Rs. 173 crores, Rs. 52 crores less than the target of Rs. 225 crores set out in the Plan.[66] Most of this shortfall represented failures to meet Plan commitments for enhancing taxes on the rural sector, including land revenue rates, irrigation rates, betterment levies, and agricultural income tax. The yield from measures of additional state taxes adopted during the first three years of the Plan compared to Plan targets is presented in Table 4-3.

The serious shortfall in current revenues at the state level, combined with a decline in receipts from market loans and shortfalls in collections from small savings (mainly because of the failure of cooperatives to mobilize agricultural savings) not only left the original resource gap of Rs. 400 crores uncovered, but added to it. In April 1958, even after taking credit for an additional Rs. 283 crores of deficit financing during the last two years of the Plan, and an increment in external assistance of Rs. 238 crores above the amount originally envisaged, the Planning Commission concluded that Plan resources at the Center and the states would not total more than Rs. 4,260 crores for the five-year period. The gap in Plan finances stood at Rs. 540 crores.[67]

The pressure of reducing Plan outlay to this low level became even more painful against the background of new data from sample surveys that indicated a much higher rate of population growth than had originally been estimated—over 2 percent per year compared to earlier projections of 1.2 percent. At the May meeting of the National Development Council, the Planning Commission suggested that total Plan outlay might still reach Rs. 4,500 crores if the states and the Center undertook new efforts of resource mobilization. The finance minister proposed

[66] *Ibid.*                                              [67] *Ibid.*, pp. 16-19.

TABLE 4-3

Yields from Measures of Additional Taxation Adopted
by the States from 1956/57 to 1958/59

*(Rs. crores)*

| | Yields from measures adopted in the first three years | | Targets as set out in the Plan |
|---|---|---|---|
| | 1956/57 to 1958/59 | Five-year yield | |
| General sales tax | 39.6 | 83.2 ⎫ | 112.0 |
| Tax on motor spirit and diesel oil | 2.9 | 7.0 ⎬ | |
| Land revenue | ⎫ | | 37.0 |
| | ⎬ 4.0 | 9.6 | |
| Irrigation rates | ⎭ | | 11.0 |
| Betterment levy | 0.8 | 2.2 | 16.0 |
| Agricultural income tax | 3.3 | 7.5 | 12.0 |
| Electricity rates and duties | 3.4 | 8.4 | 6.0 |
| Tax on motor vehicles | 5.3 | 13.1 | 10.0 |
| Stamp goods and registration | 1.2 | 3.0 | 4.0 |
| State excise duties | 1.8 | 3.6 | — |
| Others | 17.0 | 35.3 | 17.0 |
| Totals | 79.3 | 172.9 | 225.0 |

Source: *Appraisal and Prospects of Second Five Year Plan*, p. 20.

measures of additional taxation of Rs. 100 crores (Rs. 40 crores at the
Center and Rs. 60 crores at the states); an increase in market loans and
small savings of Rs. 60 crores; and economies on nondevelopmental expenditure of Rs. 80 crores to yield an additional Rs. 240
crores in internal resources for the Plan.[68] Both the Center and the states
accepted these new commitments. Nevertheless, the lower financial outlay[69] meant new reductions under all heads of development, this time in-

[68] *Ibid.*, p. 19.
[69] Actually, the National Development Council did not formally adopt the lower Plan
outlay of Rs. 4,500 crores as the financial target. Instead, the state leaders, fearing the "bad
psychological effect" of a cut in Plan expenditure, followed Nehru's suggestion of dividing
the Plan into two parts. Part A, involving a total outlay of Rs. 4,500 crores, was to include
the core projects, other schemes in an advanced stage of implementation, "inescapable"
projects, and programs directly related to increasing agricultural production. Part B, accounting for Rs. 300 crores, would only be taken up if additional resources became available. The actual list of projects assigned to either category was left for determination
through consultations between the Planning Commission, the states, and the central ministries. See Planning Commission, Tenth Meeting of the National Development Council,
*Summary Record* (New Delhi, May 1958), pp. 1-30.

cluding industries, minerals, agriculture, and community development.
The changes in allocations under major heads of development as adopted
in May 1958 are shown in Table 4-4.

TABLE 4-4

Original and Revised Estimates of
Allocations for the Second Plan by Major Heads of Development

*(Rs. crores)*

| | Allocations as originally made in the Plan | Percent of total | Revised allocations (to accommodate the higher cost of some projects within the ceiling of Rs. 4,800 crores) | Percent of total | Outlays now proposed to correspond with the resources position, April 1958 | Percent of total |
|---|---|---|---|---|---|---|
| Agriculture & community development | 568 | 11.8 | 568 | 11.8 | 510 | 11.3 |
| Irrigation & power | 913 | 19.0 | 860 | 17.9 | 820 | 18.2 |
| Villages and small industries | 200 | 4.2 | 200 | 4.2 | 160 | 3.6 |
| Industries and minerals | 690 | 14.4 | 880 | 18.4 | 790 | 17.5 |
| Transport and communications | 1,385 | 28.9 | 1,345 | 28.0 | 1,340 | 29.8 |
| Social services | 945 | 19.7 | 863 | 18.0 | 180 | 18.0 |
| Miscellaneous | 99 | 2.0 | 84 | 1.7 | 70 | 1.6 |
| Total | 4,800 | 100.0 | 4,800 | 100.0 | 4,500 | 100.0 |

SOURCE: *Appraisal and Prospects of Second Five Year Plan*, p. 23.

The feasibility of even this reduced level of financial outlay depended
in "a large degree on the success achieved in increasing agricultural production."[70] Unless foodgrains output was stepped up and food prices
brought down, additional deficit financing on the scale envisaged for the
last two years of the Plan would only accelerate the inflationary pressures
on the economy. At the same time, the planners informed the National
Development Council that domestic output of fertilizer was expected to
reach only one-half the projected level, and "on account of the foreign

[70] *Appraisal and Prospects of the Second Five Year Plan*, p. i.

exchange shortage, supplies of chemical fertilizers were bound to fall short of the demand which was itself increasing." The gap had to be filled through "greater efforts in the direction of green manures and other manurial resources."[71] In fact, given the stringent financial situation, it was more important than ever that "local participation and community effort . . . be enlisted on the largest scale possible in support of agricultural programs."[72]

Shortly after the May meeting of the National Development Council, V. T. Krishnamachari, writing in the AICC's *Economic Review*, once again argued for a more rapid pace of agrarian reorganization. He pointed out that there was a gap of 3.5 million acres in the utilization of irrigation potential because the construction of field channels had lagged behind schedule. According to official estimates, some 160,000 miles of field channels would have to be dug by the end of the Plan to make use of the full irrigation potential available. But it was "impossible to expect any government machinery, however well organized, to dig 16 lakh miles of canals and all those things in thousands and thousands of villages within a short time." On the contrary, the Planning Commission was convinced that "responsibility had to rest squarely on the villages." If the village cooperatives and panchayats were given statutory powers to initiate and implement local development projects with village monies and labor, production could be raised through a wide variety of labor-intensive schemes, such as contour bunding and soil conservation, planting of seed farms in every village, and the collection of local manurial resources. Speaking for the Planning Commission, Krishnamachari asserted, "our thinking on this is that the responsibility for organizing all these efforts in villages must rest on the Village Panchayats and village cooperatives. Each village being made responsible for its own requirements for its own obligations through a Village Panchayat and a village cooperative. . . . The state governments should bring these bodies into existence and see that they are so organized as to carry out these functions."[73]

Even if agricultural production could be increased by such bodies there was still the problem of mobilizing farm surpluses for equitable distribution. As early as August 1957, Nehru told the chief ministers that he saw no other solution to the problem of food shortages than compulsory government purchase of foodgrains at controlled prices. He argued that

> next to food production, the question of the price of foodgrains is of vital importance. Indeed, the two are intimately connected. If the prices of foodgrains go up, then the whole fabric of our planning

[71] *Ibid.*, p. 40.                          [72] *Ibid.*, p. ii.
[73] V. T. Krishnamachari, "Agricultural Production and Role of Village Institutions," AICC *Economic Review*, x (May 1, 1958), 7.

suffers irretrievably. . . . How can we keep the price of foodgrains at
reasonable levels? The only course appears to be to have a large
stock of foodgrains at every time and even be prepared for natural
calamities, droughts, etc. That has been our objective for a long
time. But, we have failed to achieve it. It is not possible to maintain
large stocks if the Government has to buy them in the open market.
It is well known that the moment the Government goes into the
open market, prices shoot up. The only other course, therefore, is
for Government purchases of foodgrains to take place compulsorily
at fixed and reasonable prices. . . . I see no way out except this
way.[74]

Throughout 1958, there was increasing evidence that the government
was preparing to mount a major effort for more rapid agrarian reorganization. The Planning Commission, which had reluctantly endorsed the
Rural Credit Survey's recommendation for large-size cooperatives on
grounds of economic efficiency, reverted to its original preference for
societies organized around the village as the primary unit. Under this
pattern, cooperatives and panchayats would cover identical jurisdictions,
and be able to combine more effectively for mobilization of village resources for development. Village-based service cooperatives, moreover,
could more easily provide the foundation for an advance toward
cooperative management of village lands.

In April 1958, the Planning Commission succeeded in persuading the
states once again to accept a modest upward revision in the targets for
formation of cooperative farms—from 2,000 to 3,000—during the Second Plan. In May, when it became apparent that the National Extension
Service would achieve all-India coverage only in 1963 (not at the end of
the Second Plan, as initially envisaged), it was proposed to rephase the
program in order to prolong the period of intensive development in each
Block. More important, actual administration of the Community Development program at the Block level was to be transferred from government officials to popularly elected Block Panchayat Samitis in an effort to stimulate local enthusiasm and mass participation in development
projects. Finally, during the summer of 1958, Krishnamachari began to
argue for a comprehensive upward revision in the targets for the
cooperative sector. In another article for the AICC *Economic Review* in
September 1958, he blamed shortfalls in agricultural production upon
India's failure to follow the Chinese example in organizing village
cooperatives with powers to persuade, advise, or compel villagers to take
up construction of capital projects. He wrote,

[74] *Fortnightly Letter to the Chief Ministers, 1948-63*, letter dated August 1, 1957.

In China, with which we always try to compare ourselves, two years ago, it was said that the villagers—there are 110 million agriculturist families in China, as against 65 million in India—are organized in agricultural cooperatives. Individual cultivation is negligible in China. We were told that these cooperatives, by their own labor, added 21 million acres to the irrigated area of the country by small irrigation schemes on which they worked; they put up voluntary labor and that was in one year. During last year, they claimed they had 15 million acres. There is no doubt that an enormous amount of voluntary work like this is done in the villages of China to strengthen the community assets. This factor is very important in the development of economically underdeveloped countries. As you know, in most villages of India, work in connection with agriculture is available only for four months in a year. Whether we can harness the unutilized time and energy of the villager in these months of waiting between one crop and another for producing community assets, assets of value to the community as a whole, is the most important question facing the Community Development organization today.[75]

By the summer of 1958, the planners' determination to save the core industrial projects of the Second Plan, and, indeed, the entire economic development strategy, seemed to leave them little option than to try and force the pace of agrarian reform, especially implementation of ceilings on landownership and the organization of cooperatives.

[75] V. T. Krishnamachari, "Facts about Agricultural Production," AICC *Economic Review*, x (September 15, 1958), 9.

# FIVE

# Failures of Implementation

The serious economic cost of slow progress toward agrarian reform in undermining the foundation of the Second Plan was compounded by the first signs in the late 1950s of emerging political discontent. The results of the 1957 elections both at the Center and in the states revealed weaknesses in the performance of the Congress party relative to the opposition that were interpreted by the national leadership as disappointment over the slow pace of implementation of longstanding promises for improved living standards.

Initially, the political scene had appeared to hold fewer challenges to Congress control than at the previous election. The Praja Socialist party (PSP) was weakened on the eve of the elections by a division in the central leadership. Rammanohar Lohia and a group of his followers, protesting the policy of collaboration with the Congress party adopted in response to the Avadi Resolution, were expelled from the PSP for breach of discipline. The split cost the party about thirty percent of its popular following and most of its active workers in the south and central states. In addition, Jayaprakash Narayan, the PSP's most popular leader, had withdrawn from active politics in 1953 to join the *bhoodan* movement.

The Communist party also appeared to be weaker than in 1951. The revelations of the Twentieth Party Congress, the active policy of de-Stalinization that followed, the Hungarian revolt of 1956, all were thought to have undermined the moral position of the party. At the same time, the Congress party's commitment to a socialistic pattern of society, and Russia's support of Nehru as the architect of nonalignment, seemed to rob the communists of convincing ideological issues. The communal groups, including the Jan Sangh and the Ram Raja Parishad, were fragmented, and did not appear to pose a serious threat.

In aggregate terms, the results of the election[1] confirmed the original optimism. Both at the Center and in the states, the total vote polled for the Congress party showed a modest improvement. Almost 48 percent of the electorate voted for Congress candidates in elections to the Lok Sabha in 1957, compared to 45 percent in 1951. Over 45 percent of the voters selected Congress nominees for the state assemblies in 1957, com-

---

[1] For a review of the election results, see Sadiq Ali, *The General Election 1957: A Survey* (New Delhi, 1959), p. 6.

pared to 42 percent in 1951. The expected also happened in the case of the socialists, whose strength at the national level seriously declined. Compared to over 16 percent of the popular vote, which the Socialist party and the KMPP had commanded between them in 1951, the successor PSP won little more than 10 percent. Yet the Communists managed to demonstrate unexpected strength. They almost trebled their popular vote from 3.3 percent in 1951 to 8.9 percent in 1957, and reinforced their position as the largest opposition party in the Lok Sabha. In addition, the communally oriented Jan Sangh demonstrated growing vote-getting powers, increasing its popular vote from a little over 3 percent in 1951 to almost 6 percent in 1957.

A similar pattern was repeated in the assembly elections. The Congress party's lead was unexpectedly eroded in a number of states. The central government, having conceded the demand for the reorganization of states on the basis of linguistic boundaries in 1956, found that it had opened a Pandora's box of parochial and communal claims. In many areas, communal and regional parties successfully opposed Congress candidates by exploiting the unsatisfied aspirations of religious, linguistic, and tribal minorities. The combined strength of opposition parties relative to Congress increased in Uttar Pradesh, Bihar, and Bombay. In Orissa, the Congress party failed to win a majority of seats and had to form a government with the help of independents. The most disturbing outcome occurred in Kerala. Congress lost its position as the largest single party in that state, and had to stand by as the first Communist ministry in India was formed.

The CPI's victory in Kerala was perceived as a springboard for further conquests. The Communists had begun to experiment with a potentially effective electoral strategy, reviving the tactic of united front alliances to weaken the major advantage of the Congress party in the multiplicity of candidates. In West Bengal, a united Leftist Election Committee led by the CPI showed striking results. The Communists increased their share of the popular vote from little over 10 percent in 1952 to almost 18 percent in 1957. The parties of the leftist alliance among them captured roughly one-third of the seats in the legislative assembly. As a result, the strength of the independents was substantially reduced, the communal parties were virtually eliminated, and politics in the state moved in the direction of a confrontation between conservative and radical forces. The CPI's electoral alliances in Bombay and Madras were less successful. Nevertheless, in U.P. and Bihar, even where no electoral arrangement proved possible, the CPI was strong enough to win representation in the state assemblies for the first time. In Punjab, it succeeded in doubling its popular vote. Viewed against the almost uniform decline of the PSP in all states on the one hand, and the growing strength of regional and communal parties on the other, the CPI emerged from the 1957 elections as the only potential alternative on a national level to the Congress party.

The national leadership was generally inclined to interpret the pattern of voting as a sign that the "Congress hold on the loyalty of the people is weaker than before and it is exposed to attack from many quarters."[2] The official AICC election review focused attention on a widening gulf between local Congress party organizations and the rural masses. It found that Congress workers had abandoned virtually all constructive work. In addition, they were often so preoccupied with factional feuds that they neglected even routine party activities, visiting the villages only at election time, with the result that "the love and respect of the people [for Congress] diminishes as we go down the rungs of the Congress ladder."[3]

The dominant direction of the shift in voter sentiment was perceived as a move toward the left. The major issues raised by all opposition groups, regional or communal, socialist or communist, centered around economic discontent, including "rising taxes, corruption, poverty, unemployment and centralization."[4] The election review concluded that adult suffrage had "released forces which no party could control" or use for buttressing vested interests:

> So evident is this lesson of democracy that even communal organizations in the country cannot hope to win the ear of the people unless they talk the language of radicalism and socialism. It might be a cover for communal and reactionary designs but that such a cover is necessary for approaching the electorate is a tribute to the transforming power of adult suffrage. . . . Two lessons emerge which it would be well to bear in mind. One is that all parties will have to move more and more to the Left if they wish to survive and serve the country. The second lesson is that the people will judge parties less by their written and spoken word and more by their action and performance and inner structure.[5]

The official party view echoed Nehru's own assessment. Reviewing the election results before new members of the Congress party in the Lok Sabha, he warned that "if the forces released by democracy and adult franchise were not mastered, they would march on leaving the Congress aside."[6]

This was not merely a hypothetical concern. In Kerala, the CPI had already started to experiment with a new strategy of "peaceful transi-

[2] *Ibid.*, p. 82.      [3] *Ibid.*, p. 66.
[4] *Ibid.*, p. 72.      [5] *Ibid.*, p. 76.
[6] Quoted in *Keep the Flame Alive: A Thesis by a Group of Congress Workers* (New Delhi, December 1, 1957), p. 9.

tion" to communism.[7] They adopted their own "minimum program" based on the blend of growth and distribution goals that provided the policy framework of the Second Plan. Although the Communists promised to work within the limits of the 1950 constitution, they set out to exploit its implicit contradiction between the Directive Principles of State Policy that endorsed goals of radical social change and the fundamental rights provisions that provided guarantees of individual rights including property. On the one hand, the CPI-led united front government enacted an ambitious program of social reform, including a new agrarian relations act that embodied the recommendations for security of tenure and ceiling on landownership set down in the Second Plan; and an education act that extended state control over the influential network of Christian private schools in the state. On the other, the Communists used the party media to rally popular support against "reactionary" interests that were using the device of majority rule under a "bourgeois democratic" constitution to prevent the adoption of more sweeping measures. Their appeal to popular opinion was combined with aggressive organization of workers' and peasants' associations at all levels of government to carry out "direct action" for enforcing the class interests of workers and agricultural laborers. The police and the courts, which had previously invoked constitutional guarantees for individual rights and private property to protect the victims of mass demonstrations and illegal strikes, were directed to remain neutral in conflicts between employers and workers or landlords and peasants arising from "class struggles." The result was a steady increase in rioting, political assaults, and both rural and urban unrest as the number of strikes against plantation owners, landlords, and factory employers sharply increased. After 1958, an escalating confrontation between the government and the powerful noncommunist student community organized in the Kerala Students Union intensified the growing tendency to take politics into the streets. Both sides, the Communists and their opponents in the newly created joint front of opposition parties, set out to mobilize their own popular militias in preparation for open combat. Nehru, who had originally prevailed against his senior colleagues in inviting the CPI to form the first Communist-led state government in India, finally yielded to their urgings and recommended the imposition of President's Rule on the state.

The small group of Gandhian and socialist intellectuals inside the Congress party seized on the evidence of emerging popular discontent provided by the election results and the Communist agitations in Kerala to

---

[7] The argument that the Communist party in Kerala was experimenting with a model of "peaceful transition" to communism that could be adapted for the establishment of the dictatorship of the proletariat at the all-India level is presented in Victor M. Fic, *Kerala, Yenan of India*, ch. 5. See also Jitendra Singh, *Communist Rule in Kerala*, chs. 2, 3.

buttress their case for a more rapid pace in carrying out promised social reforms. Writing in the AICC *Economic Review*, Shriman Narayan, then general secretary of the national party, insisted that the only way to regain the confidence of the people was to bridge the gap between Congress principles and practices. The question of land reforms was a major case in point. Asserting that the pace of implementation had been slow and unsatisfactory, Narayan blamed Congress legislators belonging to the landowning classes for "trying to put spokes in the wheel," and argued that as a result, "the Congress has been losing its hold on the tenants and landless laborers, particularly the Harijans." He insisted that the time had come to recognize the existence of objective class conflicts in India and to come down firmly on the side of the underprivileged:

> We have within the organization persons belonging to the landlords as well as the tenant class; there are businessmen, industrialists as well as representatives of the working class. When natural differences arise as a result of existing conflict of class interest we try to strike a balance in order to satisfy both the sections. Time has come when these attempts to balance the conflicting interests and viewpoints must give place to a clear and bold policy of bringing about the socialist order through the democratic process. We must recognize that there do exist class conflicts and it is necessary to resolve them, not through hatred and violence but through persuasion and democratic legislation. The Congress stands for the ultimate welfare of all sections of the population and desires to hate none. But it cannot continue to run with the hare and hunt with the hound. We have to be clear in our minds that the Congress must necessarily sponsor and safeguard the interests and the underprivileged classes as against those of the privileged and richer sections.[8]

By December 1957, a small band of Gandhian and socialist Congressmen, composed mainly of members of parliament and led by S. N. Mishra, then deputy minister of planning, proposed to organize the Congress Socialist Forum as a "ginger group" inside the party to "make this idea of socialism seep into the ranks of Congressmen."[9] They insisted that it was necessary to define the content and policy implications of the socialist pattern; educate the public at large about Congress principles and purposes; and most important, indoctrinate party workers in these principles through study groups and training programs. Their initiative, however, failed to gain the active support of Nehru.[10] The prime

[8] Shriman Narayan, "Need for Ideological Clarity," AICC *Economic Review* (June 15, 1957), pp. 9-10.

[9] Interview, S. N. Mishra, New Delhi, February 23, 1963.

[10] According to Mishra, Nehru was displeased to hear that the Congress Socialist Forum

minister was still hesitant to endorse any political move that could undermine the umbrella character of the Congress party as the best guarantor of national cohesion. But even he found the economic compulsions for speeding up the pace of agrarian reform more difficult to resist as the resources position for the Second Plan rapidly deteriorated.

The National Development Council, which met in November 1958, was once again confronted by the unpleasant prospect of having to reduce Plan size, this time below the revised May estimate of Rs. 4,500 crores. The finance minister, in a review of the economic situation, strongly advised against further deficit financing unless there was reasonable assurance of an increase in agricultural production and lower food prices. This was Nehru's opening, and he took it. The prime minister argued that additional deficit financing could be absorbed and the Plan maintained at Rs. 4,500 crores if the states accepted the approach of the Planning Commission to mobilize rural resources for increased agricultural production through an acceleration of the cooperative movement; and also acted to stabilize the general price level by a program of state trading in foodgrains. Specifically, Nehru recommended that the NDC endorse an upward revision in the targets for the organization of cooperatives; and the recommendation of the Foodgrains Enquiry Committee for the socialization of the foodgrains trade.

The members of the National Development Council appeared to accept Nehru's lead. They gave formal approval for a new and expanded program of cooperative development to organize multipurpose cooperative societies on the basis of the village community as the primary unit; and to complete the process of reorganization by the end of the Third Plan. Simultaneously, the NDC endorsed the immediate introduction of state trading in foodgrains, beginning with wheat and rice. The food ministry was directed to draw up a two-stage scheme: (1) during the first year or more, all wholesale foodgrains dealers were to be licensed and strictly regulated. They would be required to purchase foodgrains at prices fixed by government, and to sell some or the entire stock procured by them to government, also at controlled prices; (2) at the second stage, when government had trained an adequate number of personnel, and constructed sufficient storage facilities, a state-sponsored trading corporation would begin to procure the marketed surplus directly.

The November 1958 resolutions of the National Development Council were, in fact, part of a carefully orchestrated campaign initiated by Nehru to push the Congress party toward a major new program of

---

had been organized, and acquiesced in the move because the leaders were adamant in carrying on their activities unless a formal ban was voted by the AICC. Interview, S. N. Mishra, New Delhi.

agrarian reform in support of the requirements of the basic approach of the Second Plan. At the October 1958 meeting of the AICC, Nehru had already set the process in motion with the appointment of an agricultural production subcommittee, to prepare a draft resolution on an integrated program of agricultural development for consideration at the forthcoming annual session of Congress, scheduled for January 1959 at Nagpur. The subcommittee, whose membership was drawn primarily from among state party leaders, was influenced in its deliberations by the fact that Nehru, who was not a member, "took an active part" in its work.[11]

The subcommittee's report, which was completed for presentation to the Working Committee at Nagpur on January 6, 1959, endorsed an agricultural strategy that was almost entirely confined to institutional change as the instrument of growth in the rural sector. In a "Resolution on Agrarian Organizational Pattern," approved and edited by Nehru, the Working Committee, the Subjects Committee,[12] and the open session unanimously approved an agricultural program that called for the immediate transformation of the agrarian structure. The resolution envisaged the completion of all land reforms, including ceilings on land-ownership, within one year, by the end of 1959. It then went on to link land reforms to the formation of cooperative farms, and recommended, in a departure from the Second Plan, that surplus land should vest in the village panchayat rather than individuals and be managed through cooperatives of landless laborers. The core of the resolution was an elaboration and expansion of the decisions taken by the National Development Council in November. According to the resolution, "the organization of the village should be based on village panchayats and village cooperatives," both of which were expected to become the "spearheads of all developmental activities in the village." The key passage of the Nagpur resolution was the following:

> The future agrarian pattern should be that of cooperative joint farming, in which the land will be pooled for joint cultivation, the farmers continuing to retain their property rights, and getting a share from the net produce in proportion to their land. Further, those who actually work the land, whether they own the land or not, will get a share in proportion to the work put in by them on the joint farm.
>
> As a first step, prior to the institution of joint farming, service cooperatives should be organized throughout the country. This

[11] *Indian Affairs Record* (January 1959).
[12] The AICC constitutes itself as the Subjects Committee at the Annual Sessions to consider official resolutions introduced for party approval.

stage should be completed within a period of three years. Even within this period, however, wherever possible and generally agreed to by the farmers, joint cultivation may be started.[13]

The resolution ended with an endorsement for the introduction of state trading in foodgrains, including a recommendation to assure a fair return to the farmer by setting minimum floor prices at which crops might be sold directly to the government.

Although the Nagpur resolution only reiterated the broad policy goals accepted under the five-year plans, it suddenly advanced a concrete timetable for agrarian reorganization that significantly shortened the transition period to cooperative village management. While the National Development Council had spoken of universal membership in service cooperatives at the end of the Third Plan, the Congress party suggested a new three-year deadline, ending in 1962, the second year of the Third Plan. In contrast to the Second Plan, moreover, which envisaged three distinct agricultural sectors—cooperative farms, family farms, and the common lands of the village—with an indefinite period of transition toward cooperative village management, the Nagpur resolution accepted cooperative village management as the only and the immediate goal of agrarian reorganization.

The Congress party, which had unanimously endorsed the agrarian policies in deference to Nehru, was, however, far from united. Many delegates opposed and even feared the new programs as a prelude to collectivization. It was apparent from the debate in the Subjects Committee and even in the open session that the opposition was widespread. The same uneasiness prevailed in the Working Committee, which formulated the resolution. Nehru frankly admitted: "Some of our colleagues [on the Working Committee] were opposed to the idea of cooperative farming in the beginning. The idea had to be slowly absorbed by all."[14]

Yet, neither Nehru nor the other members of the Planning Commission were prepared for the enormous wave of criticism that followed. Three of the four basic programs outlined in the resolutions—ceiling on landownership, service cooperatives, and cooperative farming—were already incorporated into two five-year Plans, and the fourth—state trading in foodgrains—had been accepted by the National Development Council in November. But the accelerated timetable and Nehru's show of determination in achieving effective implementation of agrarian reforms galvanized the conservative elements into action.

[13] *Congress Bulletin* (January-February 1959), pp. 22-23.
[14] "Congress Resolution on Agrarian Organizational Pattern," *Indian Affairs Record*, 5 (January 1959), 5.

As the *Eastern Economist* observed:

The tremendous concern comes because promises and theories are now on the point of being committed to action. It was not believed that a government which has not shown any pointed revolutionary fervour in the last few years, would rush through what is properly described as a revolutionary programme. The withdrawal of land from a large number of landholders and its distribution is undoubtedly a revolutionary thing. Whether the landless laborers are cooperatively grouped or otherwise is not at the moment fundamental. The point is that a major property redistribution is taking place under cover of a sweeping land reform policy.[15]

The Nagpur session considered as a whole, moreover, sounded a clear danger signal not only to the landlords and traders within the Congress party, but also to the industrial and financial elements. An official "Resolution on Planning," drafted by Nehru, accepted the principle of an absolute ceiling on profits in the private sector (in addition to indirect controls through taxation), while recommending the organization of public enterprise to yield a planned profit for development.[16] In addition, the "ginger group," led by the deputy minister of planning, S. N. Mishra, presented a "nonofficial" Plan Outline that projected a total expenditure of Rs. 9,000 crores during the Third Plan—almost double the amount of the revised Second Plan. In order to help finance the increased outlay, the Plan Outline suggested the socialization of the "vital sectors of trade and commerce" and the extension of state trading to import and export activities. Finally, the election of Nehru's daughter, Indira Gandhi, as president of the Congress party, was widely interpreted as a shift to the left within the national organization. Mrs. Gandhi, who signed the manifesto of the "ginger group,"[17] was expected to "introduce new blood into the Congress leadership and check a drift toward the rightist trend of thought."[18]

The Nagpur resolution violated an essential requisite for reconciling accommodative politics and radical social change. It departed from previous assurances to the propertied classes that social reform did not in-

[15] *The Eastern Economist*, 32 (January 15, 1959), 205.
[16] The text of the "Resolution on Planning" adopted at Nagpur is published in *Congress Bulletin* (January-February 1959), p. 20.
[17] Mrs. Gandhi did not formally become a member of the "ginger group" because she did not want it "to grow into some kind of group as such within the Congress." *Hindustan Times*, February 19, 1959.
[18] This statement, attributed to A. S. Raju, then general secretary of the Congress party, appeared in the *Hindustan Times*, January 14, 1959.

volve their own destruction. Instead, it presented the landed castes with the prospect of immediate loss of some land and of effective control over the rest of their holdings—changes that many interpreted as tantamount to expropriation.

During the months that followed Nagpur, the press gave wide currency to the charge that "Sino–socialist minded planners" were plotting to collectivize Indian agriculture. There were bitter attacks against cooperative farming within the Congress party. Respected elder statesmen, including C. Rajagopalachari, the retired chief minister of Madras, began to write and speak out against agrarian cooperatives as the entering wedge of totalitarianism. N. G. Ranga, then parliamentary secretary, became active in organizing the dissidents inside the Congress parliamentary party with the apparent intention of breaking from the party. In a speech to a farmers' convention in Mysore state in March 1959, Ranga charged in effect that Congress had been captured by the Communist party: "It is the irony of things that the very political parties in which we reposed our confidence because of their patriotic traditions as against the internationalist parties, have now accepted the credit so far as our peasants and rural economy are concerned, and the communists and socialists of Marxist inspiration are now running their suicidal race with the Communist Party in their attempts to liquidate our freedom and independence, enterprise and initiative, which are all embodied in our self-employed status."[19]

The disagreements over cooperative farming inside the Congress party entered into national debate when the issue was injected into the Lok Sabha soon after the beginning of the Seventh Session in early February 1959. The disparity between Nehru's forceful statement on ceilings and cooperative farming at a press conference on February 8,[20] and the omission of any reference to the Nagpur resolution in the President's Address to the Lok Sabha[21] on February 9 indicated that the Congress party was badly divided. President Prasad, who summarized the decisions of the National Development Council of May and November 1958 to reduce the size of the Second Plan and stabilize expenditures at Rs. 4,500 crores, commented only that the government would seek to promote agrarian

[19] Cooperative Farming, The Great Debate (Bombay, 1959), p. 28.

[20] At his press conference, Nehru described the Nagpur Resolution as the product of "mature consideration." He elaborated: "Many months previously, the AICC met and appointed a special committee on planning and another one on agriculture and land reforms. They met at some length day after day. They coopted or invited eminent people from outside Congress, economists and others. They gave very full consideration to it. Finally, it was the culmination of numerous discussions, talks, circulars and replies in the Congress organization for the last two or three years." Hindu, February 9, 1959.

[21] The President's Address is similar in focus to the American State of the Union Message.

reforms, cooperation, and devolution of responsibility to village panchayats in order to increase production, and that village cooperatives would be organized in all Community Development Blocks.[22]

Even this pale statement precipitated a bitter attack upon government policy. Minoo Masani, by then spokesman for the Independent Parliamentary Group, and a founder-member of the Forum for Free Enterprise (a Bombay-based businessmen's association dedicated to the elimination of government controls over private industry), supported two amendments to the motion of thanks to the President's Address. They expressed the hope that "the reference to cooperation and agrarian reforms in the President's Address do not have specific reference to the proposals for joint cooperative farming and for ceilings which have recently been adopted by the ruling party." Masani charged that joint cooperative farming as envisaged in the Nagpur resolution would put an end to private property rights and pave the way for forced collectivization. In a long and emotional speech he argued that

> when the boundaries of the farm have been uprooted, when tractors are running over that land which was once six, eight, ten or twenty farms, the right of property will mean a mere piece of paper given to the peasant to console him by saying, "You once owned so many acres; your property is still intact. . . ." But after a while, the question is raised, "Why should this man who is not working hard or not doing as much as the other fellow draw a large share because he once owned some land?" In other words, you start by saying that the people in the farm will be remunerated partly in proportion to the labor contributed. This is fair enough. But this can never last because the functionless owner is no owner. His property has actually been taken away from him without telling him so and he is

---

[22] "President's Address Given to the Lok Sabha," February 9, 1959. *Lok Sabha Debates*, Second Series, 25 (February 9, 1959), 1188. The omission of any mention of the Nagpur Resolution or the NDC's decision to accelerate the cooperative movement prompted S. A. Dange, leader of the Communist party in parliament to challenge the sincerity of the Congress leadership in offering the new program at Nagpur. Dange sarcastically observed: "I should like to know despite what has been said about the Congress Resolutions in Nagpur whether even one-tenth of the Resolutions is anywhere hinted at in this Address. . . . No, they do not want to talk about it. They are not even decided about it. They are quarreling about it. Even Hon. Ministers sabotage land reforms on the matter of ceilings. . . . Their own organization talks of ceilings and their own Ministers go denouncing it. . . . What are we going to do with these gentlemen? They are in a majority in the States. They are in a majority in the Centre. If you pass a resolution about ceilings on land holdings, you cannot keep Ministers who are opposed to that in principle. . . . You must remove those Ministers who oppose that. But here a peculiar situation exists. When suddenly the Hon. Prime Minister takes up an issue they start opposing it, then they pass it and say: 'It does not matter. Let him talk, we can sabotage him in action.' " *Ibid.*, p. 1207.

being fobbed off with a scrap of paper which a future government will have no hesitation in tearing up, because his use to society ends on the day on which the farm ceases to be his. . . . I have no hesitation in asserting that the resolution passed at Nagpur, whether those who passed it are aware or not, is a resolution for collective farming of the Soviet-Chinese pattern, and not for genuine cooperative farming.[23]

Masani's attack against cooperative farming was well received in the press. It established the fixed points of the national debate that recurred throughout the year. The government, and particularly the prime minister, were increasingly constrained to adopt a defensive posture. Although Nehru clearly did not envisage Soviet or Chinese-style coercion to implement the Nagpur resolution, he was nevertheless painfully aware that "one peasant could not be given the power of veto to prevent any change being effected."[24] Yet, faced with the possibility of splitting his own party as the crescendo of criticism mounted, Nehru, in his answer to Masani in the Lok Sabha on February 19, 1959, felt compelled to promise that "no Act is going to be passed by Parliament. . . . There is no question of coercion. There is no question of a new law." Having thrown away this card at the outset, Nehru could only fall back on his own firm belief in the correctness of the cooperative pattern and his faith that the peasantry could be educated to this view. He told the members of parliament, "But I do believe in cooperation and I do firmly and absolutely believe in the rightness of joint cultivation. Let there be no doubt. I do not wish to hide my own beliefs in this matter. I shall go from field to field and peasant to peasant begging them to agree to it, knowing that if they do not agree, I cannot put it into operation."[25]

Then, in mid-March, a completely unexpected and extraneous event —China's suppression of the Tibetan revolt in transparent disregard for the doctrine of *panchsheel*—began to exert a critical, if indirect, influence upon the national debate over accelerated social and economic reform. Not only did the Chinese action in Tibet—and more important, encroachments on the border after 1959—call into question fundamental assumptions of India's foreign policy, but it also put the Planning Commission on the defensive with respect to the Chinese agrarian model. As one senior officer of the Planning Commission put it, "we had been emphasizing 'look at the Chinese cooperatives, see how wonderful they are,' and after Tibet, everything Chinese became taboo. Even those persons who still believed cooperative farming was the best sort of organiza-

[23] *Ibid.*, p. 1216.          [24] *Cooperative Farming: The Great Debate*, p. 63.
[25] *Lok Sabha Debates*, Second Series, 25, February 19, 1959, 1415.

tion dared not say it. Only the prime minister could say it, but hardly anyone else."[26]

Nevertheless, Nehru had become vulnerable to attack on a basic principle of national policy for the first time. As the architect of India's foreign relations, his personal prestige was most directly affected by the Chinese action. Almost immediately he began to execute a tactical retreat, tempering his support for the more radical features of the Nagpur resolution by minimizing the immediate threat to large landowners of the Congress party's commitment to cooperative farming. Toward the end of March, when U. C. Patnaik (Ind., Orissa), moved a private member bill in the Lok Sabha, affirming, "this House recommends that the question of introducing cooperative farming be given top priority in the program of land reforms and agricultural development of the country," Nehru supported a substitute amendment introduced by Ram Subhag Singh (then secretary of the Congress parliamentary party), which gave greater prominence to service cooperatives than cooperative farms. The amendment stated: "This House recommends that during the next three years every possible effort should be made to organize Service Cooperatives all over the country and to develop the spirit of cooperation in general so that cooperative farms may be set up voluntarily by the people concerned wherever conditions are mature."[27]

At the same time, Nehru also modified his position at Nagpur that cooperative farms should be organized simultaneously with service cooperatives "wherever possible." On March 15, 1959, the Working Committee deliberately distinguished two phases of agrarian reform, the first of three years' duration, involving the organization of service cooperatives; and the second or final stage, consisting of joint management of village lands. In a "Resolution on Implementing the Nagpur Resolution," the Working Committee asserted:

[26] Interview, director, Land Reforms Division, Planning Commission, New Delhi, May 9, 1963.

[27] *Lok Sabha Debates*, Second Series, 27, March 28, 1959, 8366. In supporting Ram Subhag Singh's version, Nehru rejected a number of other amendments brought to substitute for the original resolution, one of which closely paraphrased the text of the Nagpur Resolution. Moved by Shri N. B. Maiti, it read:

> This House is of the opinion that the future agrarian pattern should be that of cooperative joint farming in which land will be pooled for joint cultivation, the farmers continuing to retain their property rights and getting a share from the net produce in proportion to their land. Further, those who actually work on the land whether they own their own land or not will get a share in proportion to the work put in by them on the joint farm.

> As a first step prior to the institution of joint farming, service cooperatives should be organized throughout the country. This stage should be completed within a period of three years. Even within this period, however, wherever possible and generally agreed to by the farmers, joint cultivation may be started.

There has been an attempt on the part of the opponents of the Nag-pur Resolution to concentrate their attack on Joint Cooperative Farming and divert the attention of the people from Service Cooperatives which were essential for a number of reasons, and whose success would also open the way for the introduction of Joint Cooperative Farming. Joint Cooperative Farming was envisaged in the Nagpur Resolution as the ultimate pattern. For a period of three years, our main task should be formation of service cooperatives.[28]

Simultaneously, the Working Committee announced an AICC decision to establish a training center for Congress workers who were expected to take an active role in organizing the service cooperatives. They also directed the Pradesh Congress Committees to organize state-level training programs "so that these trained workers may start organizing service cooperatives in different districts."

The organizational effort required was a formidable one. In order to establish service cooperatives covering every village in India by 1962—the target date of the Nagpur resolution—it was necessary to set up about six thousand new cooperatives every month for a period of three years, and to train about 70,000 workers annually.[29] Yet, when the Congress president, Mrs. Gandhi, attempted to recruit volunteers for the AICC training programs, only six hundred Congressmen came forward. The Working Committee's directive to the Pradesh Congress Committees, moreover, instructing them to organize their own state training programs was almost universally ignored. By early May, the Working Committee was compelled to execute another step backward on the issue of agrarian reform. In a "Note on Cooperatives" dated May 8, the committee tacitly reverted to the National Development Council's timetable announced in November 1958, of bringing 20 million families into the cooperative movement at the end of the Second Plan. This downward revision implied—according to the NDC's calculations—that universal membership would not be achieved before the end of the Third Plan, compared to the Nagpur target date of 1962.

Also, by implication, no serious attempt would be made to implement joint farming until after the Third Plan. As if to compensate for this concession, the Working Committee reaffirmed its commitment to the principle of joint cooperative farming, and recommended a program of pilot projects in selected areas to establish a relatively small number of cooperative farms during the Third Plan. They declared,

[28] *Congress Bulletin* (March 1959), p. 128.
[29] This was the estimate of L. C. Jain, then general secretary of the Indian Cooperative Union, the peak organization of voluntary workers in the cooperative field.

an impression is growing that for the time being we are shelving the question of joint cooperative farming, but this is far from the truth. Service cooperatives can mobilize internal and external resources in money and material while joint cooperative farms can, in addition, mobilize labor, which happens to be the most abundant resource and can also reduce farming costs. It is necessary that simultaneously with the program of setting up service cooperatives, we have a program to organize joint cooperative farming in related areas to begin with. If each State Government can attempt in one Block area, an integrated land reforms program immediately, it would be easier to set up joint cooperative farms.[30]

The first AICC training camp in cooperation was scheduled to be held in Madras on June 1, and accommodate one hundred state-level trainees so that "one or two men in each State may soon be in a position to carry forward the program and themselves undertake to a certain extent the training of other classes of workers."[31] Each of the state-level workers was subsequently expected to work full time for at least one year in promoting the cooperatives through the organization of propaganda and training programs at the district, mandal, and village levels. The training course at Madras was to be six weeks long, and to include forty-two lectures on Congress, socialism, and the cooperative movement, as well as a number of field trips to cooperative institutions.

Long-term plans were also announced for a series of three to four-month AICC training camps for district and mandal-level party workers, during which trainees would receive theoretical instruction in socialist ideology and cooperative development, and visit a number of primary, district, and state-level cooperative institutions. According to the announcement,

the duty of the Congress workers in fact will be to build up and sustain the enthusiasm of the public for the cooperative cause and help to keep the tempo of progress at the pace and in the direction indicated in the national plan. This will mean: (1) helping the organization of societies by providing local leadership; (2) ensuring efficient workings of societies by (a) assisting them in mobilizing local capital; (b) helping them to draw up a production plan, expressed in terms of resource requirements; (c) seeing to it that production requirements including credit, are received and distributed to the cultivator in time; and (d) helping activity in the linking up of credit with production and credit with marketing; (3) preparing the ground for more active collaboration of the members in the pro-

[30] *Congress Bulletin* (April–May 1959), p. 297.        [31] *Ibid.*, p. 299.

cesses of farming which will quicken the progress towards full-scale cooperative joint farming.[32]

None of these camps were held. The projected AICC training programs were completely abandoned after June 1959 for lack of support at all levels of the Congress party organization.

The record of implementation on state trading in foodgrains was hardly more encouraging than the performance on cooperative policy. At the outset, a tendency toward conciliation of the landowning and trading interests in the party was evident in the modified Scheme for State Trading in Foodgrains[33] presented to the Lok Sabha on April 2, 1959. A. P. Jain, the Union minister of food and agriculture, cited several administrative and organizational obstacles in the way of undertaking full state trading immediately, including lack of storage space for large buffer stocks. The scheme, as presented, provided for two stages of implementation. During the first or interim period, of unspecified duration, wholesale traders would be permitted to continue as licensed traders and to make purchases from the farmer on their own behalf, but only at fixed maximum prices. The government would then have the right to acquire a portion or the whole of these stocks at controlled prices. Traders would be permitted to sell the remainder, also at controlled prices, to retailers. At the same time, during the initial stage, government would not in practice attempt to purchase the entire marketed surplus. Rather, during the first two years of state trading, the food ministry envisaged that only fifteen percent of the wheat and rice surpluses would be procured. During this period, the government did plan to establish a state trading agency to make direct purchases in the rural areas from the farmers, although cultivators would be free to sell either to the government or to private traders at uniform prices fixed for the whole region or state. Retail prices, moreover, were not controlled under the scheme. Instead, it was planned to multiply the network of government-supplied fair-price shops in the large urban centers. In a final reassurance to the larger producers and traders, it was announced that all state trading operations would be undertaken on a no-profit, no-loss basis.

The "ultimate pattern" of state trading in foodgrains was postponed until the second stage. At that point, farm surpluses would be collected through "the marketing cooperatives and the apex marketing cooperatives for distribution through retailers and through consumers coopera-

[32] *Ibid.*, p. 303.
[33] The scheme was initially developed by a group of officers from the Ministry of Finance, the Planning Commission, the Reserve Bank, and the Food and Agriculture Ministry. It was approved by the Cabinet in January, circulated to the states for comment, subsequently revised, and then submitted to the Lok Sabha for approval.

tives," thereby eliminating private traders from the wholesale trade. No time limit, however, was set for achieving the ultimate pattern. In practice, the pace of progress toward this goal depended on the rate at which the states organized marketing cooperatives and consumers cooperatives and constructed godowns for storage.[34]

The state governments accepted the watered-down version of the Planning Commission's scheme with relief, but little enthusiasm. Many of the chief ministers, particularly those of the surplus states (Andhra Pradesh, Madras, Punjab, and Orissa), were reluctant to implement the new policy. They hesitated to take any action at all against the larger producers, millers, and traders, many of whom were members of the Pradesh Congress Committees or the state legislative assemblies, and often heavy contributors to the party. In this general reluctance, the chief ministers were supported by the Union food and agriculture minister, A. P. Jain, who as former president of the Uttar Pradesh Congress Committee, was sympathetic to the problems of the state leadership.

During the remainder of his tenure as food minister, until his resignation in August 1959, Jain made almost no effort to establish a state trading organization, a price stabilization board, or to build government godowns in which large buffer stocks might be stored. In all these areas, he attributed his ministry's inaction to organizational and administrative difficulties.

During the 1958/59 crop season, the food ministry and the state departments of agriculture did little more than elaborate upon the policy of ad hoc controls first adopted in 1957. Zonal restrictions on the movement of rice and wheat were retained for the remainder of the Plan, with periodic changes in zonal boundaries to facilitate government procurement and food distribution.[35]

The state governments demonstrated a minimum level of compliance with national policy. They began to license wholesale dealers, roller flour mills and rice mills from the end of 1958. Wholesale traders were required to have a license for the purchase, sale, and/or storage of foodgrains, and to keep records for government inspection, including names of places at which foodgrains were stored, minimum quantities stored, opening stocks on each day, purchases and sales, price per maund

---

[34] The text of the government's Scheme for State Trading in Foodgrains is published in the *Lok Sabha Debates*, Second Series, 28, April 2, 1959, 9290-95.

[35] In February 1959, the Wheat Zone, encompassing Rajasthan, Bombay, and Madhya Pradesh, was dissolved, and each of these states was established as a separate zone to facilitate government procurement. In December, the surplus rice-producing state of Orissa was combined with the deficit state of West Bengal to form the Eastern Zone and alleviate food shortages in West Bengal. Subsequently, the zonal boundaries were altered many times either to facilitate movement on private account or to restrict movement and facilitate government procurement, depending on current market conditions.

charged, and closing stocks each day. Several state governments acting on behalf of the central government, and in some cases on their own account, also undertook procurement of foodgrains in surplus districts at maximum fixed prices, either on the basis of voluntary offers or compulsory levy.[36]

It was soon apparent that the introduction of partial controls on the purchase and sale of rice and paddy actually contributed to a decline in market arrivals, which in almost all states failed to increase proportionately with output. Although the Center and the state governments were able to procure over 1.4 million tons of rice in 1958/59 (roughly half of this through open market purchases and the remainder through compulsory levy),[37] this was not sufficient to supply the needs of deficit states. Between March and August 1959, rice prices continued to rise in the Southern Zone, and were higher than in the previous year, while the all-India wholesale index of prices rose from 91.5 percent in March 1959 to 112.7 percent in August.

Virtually the same situation developed in the major wheat-producing states when the state governments introduced statutory price controls for the 1958/59 season. Despite a bumper crop, market arrivals were reported to be only a small fraction of normal. Government procurement reached only 216,000 tons. Prices were prevented from rising only by large releases of PL 480 wheat from the fair-price shops.

Continuing food shortages and rising prices throughout the 1958/59 crop season, in spite of a record harvest, discredited the government's program for state trading in foodgrains by the end of 1959. Although the Planning Commission privately blamed the food ministry and the state governments for the failure effectively to implement state trading in

---

[36] In the Southern Zone, Andhra Pradesh announced maximum controlled prices for the purchase and sale of rice and paddy in January 1959, but only in respect to wholesale quantities, and for eight surplus districts. Maximum controlled prices were also imposed for wholesale quantities of foodgrains throughout the state of Madras in January 1959; and throughout Mysore in February. During the first six months of controls, the Andhra government received assurances from the Andhra Pradesh Rice Millers Association that their member mills would cooperate with government by surrendering 40 percent of their production to the state at the controlled prices. When the mills failed to honor this agreement, government imposed a compulsory levy in June 1959. In Madras, a 50 percent levy on mills, 25 percent levy on wholesale dealers in rice, and 50 percent on wholesale dealers in paddy was imposed in January 1959. Subsequently, millers were required to sell an additional 25 percent of their production at controlled rates to bulk customers. In Mysore as well, the state government imposed a 50 percent levy on all rice mills and wholesale dealers. However, the state governments did not attempt to institute monopoly procurement or to apply price controls at all levels of the distribution system.

[37] Government procurement was most successful in Madhya Pradesh (550,000 tons) and Orissa (220,000 tons) where the price structure was most favorable. At the same time, government was able to procure only 100,000 tons of rice in Andhra Pradesh, 130,000 tons in Madras, and 30,000 tons in Mysore; "State Trading in Rice and Wheat," *Agricultural Situation in India*, 14 (December 1959).

foodgrains, mounting political dissatisfaction in the states among the larger producers and traders caused Nehru to suspend the scheme. Jain was finally forced to resign ₂s food minister in August 1959. But Nehru apparently felt constrained to replace him with another powerful state party leader, S. K. Patil, the head of the Congress party organization in Bombay. Patil immediately made it clear that he would not implement state trading in foodgrains except as a last resort.

Shortly after Patil took office, orders relating to price controls and compulsory levy on rice were withdrawn in Mysore, Madras, Bihar, and West Bengal, and all purchases on government account were suspended. In Punjab, Madhya Pradesh, and Orissa, government purchases were continued on the basis of voluntary offers at competitive prices. In Andhra and Uttar Pradesh, ad hoc price controls and levies continued to be applied from time to time in the surplus districts, but Assam became the only rice-producing state to establish monopoly procurement through the Cooperative Apex Marketing Society of the state.

Uttar Pradesh also stood alone in retaining maximum controlled prices and levy with respect to wheat. Punjab, Rajasthan, and Madhya Pradesh confined their purchases mainly to the open market on the basis of voluntary offers. They subsequently imposed price controls and levies in the surplus districts only during periods of acute shortage.

For the remainder of the Second Plan, the food ministry under S. K. Patil openly abandoned all attempts to implement state trading in foodgrains, and relied instead upon wheat imports under PL 480 and some commercial imports of rice to build a central buffer stock that could be used to stabilize foodgrains prices. In May 1960, under Patil's leadership, India signed a new agreement with the United States to supply 16 million tons of wheat and one million tons of rice over a four-year period.

Toward the end of 1958, as the first position papers on the Third Plan appeared, the national leadership was becoming more deeply entrapped in the contradiction between the economic and political development strategies. It was clear that the overall pace of agrarian reorganization had to be accelerated if the economic strategy were to be saved. At the same time, the needs of the Plan were in conflict with the requirements of maintaining political consensus inside the Congress party on the rate and scope of institutional change.

The preliminary proposals on the approach to the Third Plan revealed the growing dimensions of this dilemma. The domestic resource base was more narrow than had been anticipated. The increase in aggregate national income by the end of the Second Plan was expected to be closer to 20 percent than the 25 percent targeted. In per capita terms, the gain was reduced to about 9 percent (one-half the projected level) by population growth rates of over two percent compared to the original estimate of 1.2 percent. In addition, forced reductions in financial outlay for the Second Plan inevitably created a shortfall in the employment target. This, together with a larger increase than anticipated in the labor force, meant that India would begin the Third Plan with a backlog of unemployment approaching some 9 millions, and new entrants into the labor force estimated at 17 millions. Finally, until basic capital goods industries could be established, the continuing foreign exchange shortage meant that a large industrial plan would require much higher levels of external assistance than earlier envisaged.

Against this background, the planners calculated that a Third Plan outlay of Rs. 10,000 crores (of which about two-thirds was in the public sector) was the minimum necessary to maintain "satisfactory results in terms of increases in national income [of 5 to 6 percent annually] and employment."[38] Yet, there was virtually no possibility of raising this amount from conventional budgetary sources. The "Dimensional Hypotheses Concerning the Third Five Year Plan," prepared in the Perspective Planning Division of the Planning Commission in December 1958, once again linked the high target for net investment with "massive mobilization of surplus manpower for carrying out projects of permanent improvement." According to the planners, "if this [could] be done on a sufficiently large scale all over the country, in the main without recourse to normal wage payments, not only the main difficulty of employment but of investible funds would be substantially eased."[39] In addition, the Planning Commission's calculations of major sources of government investment also placed primary importance on greater taxation of the rural sector, both directly through levies on agricultural production and/or land, and indirectly, through profits from state trading.

The same themes were echoed in the Planning Commission's formal memorandum on "Main Issues Relating to the Third Five Year Plan" presented to the National Development Council in April 1959. The resources position was bleak. A preliminary examination indicated that no surpluses were available to government at existing rates of taxation. Current account deficits would begin to appear as some of the plan expenditures in the Second Plan became "committed" revenue expenditures in the Third. Sizeable fresh taxation would be necessary just to balance the revenue accounts. Imports for industrial projects would have to be met almost entirely from external assistance, and the "utmost care will have to be exercised to avoid generating inflationary pressures that might upset internal price stability and react adversely on the balance of payments by reducing exports and increasing imports."[40]

[38] Hanson, *The Process of Planning*, p. 173.     [39] *Ibid.*, p. 176.
[40] Planning Commission, *Main Issues Relating to the Third Five Year Plan*, p. 20.

According to the planners, the most important factor in maintaining the delicate financial balance required for the success of the Third Plan was the "order of increase achieved in agricultural production." Their calculations indicated that the magnitude of necessary growth was no less than an annual rate of 8 to 9 percent per year,[41] compared with past performance of little over 3 percent. The tight resources position further intensified the need for increasing agricultural production through "administration and organization and enthusing the people."[42] On the production side, major emphasis had to be placed on building up capital assets through making use of idle manpower. Even in fulfilling requirements for primary schools, drinking-water wells, roads, and other amenities, it would be necessary for local governments to share the financial burden with the state by raising taxes to qualify for matching grants. The primary responsibility of providing credit for production, and of undertaking sale of production inputs as well as marketing of foodgrains had to be shouldered by village multipurpose service cooperatives linked to primary marketing societies. Finally, against the background of dangerously high levels of inflation during the Second Plan, state trading in foodgrains was essential for stabilizing the prices of essential commodities. Such economic compulsions made it impossible to postpone any longer effective implementation of plan policies for basic agrarian reorganization. Nehru once again applied pressure against the chief ministers of the states. At the April 1959 meeting of the National Development Council, he summed up the thinking of the planners in the proposition that the "main aims" of the Third Plan had to be "bring[ing] about institutional change."[43] V. T. Krishnamachari, deputy chairman of the Planning Commission, elaborated on this goal by expressing the hope that "eventually the village cooperative would take up cooperative farming as the general form of management of agricultural land."[44]

The state leaders once again publicly deferred to Nehru. They accepted the main principle of pursuing rural development through large-scale mobilization of local capital and manpower by village cooperative and panchayat institutions. They went on record to support the Planning Commission's position that cooperatives should subsequently be formed on the basis of the village as the primary unit (barring cases of very small villages, when the scope of the societies might be expanded to include a population of about 1,000). They gave explicit recognition to the link between the decision to organize village cooperatives and plans for cooperative farming, and agreed that "in implementing cooperative pol-

[41] *Ibid.*, pp. 20–21.                          [42] *Ibid.*, p. 20.
[43] Planning Commission, *Summary Records*, Twelfth Meeting of the National Development Council, New Delhi, April 3 and 4, 1959.
[44] *Ibid.*, p. 64.

icy . . . it was also essential to keep in view the fundamental objectives of cooperation at the village level, more especially the objective of joint cooperative farming on a village basis."[45] Neither was there any challenge to the policy of state trading in foodgrains as the key to price stabilization. Altogether, dissent was so restrained that Nehru appeared to believe he had finally gained the active support of the state leadership. His assessment of the discussions was that they revealed "a considerable measure of agreement with the broad approach" and only "slight variations of emphasis here and there."[46]

The appearance of a united party was reinforced during the week-long Ooty Seminar organized by the AICC in June 1959 to discuss strategy, resources, and economic and social objectives of the Third Plan.[47] Both Nehru and V. T. Krishnamachari were present to underline its importance as a strategy-making meeting. An important part of the deliberations of the conference was devoted to defining the implications of the socialist pattern for a strategy of resource mobilization.

As in 1955, most of the discussion on financial resources for the Third Plan revolved around the implementation of institutional change as the most effective method for mobilizing agricultural savings and surpluses. The notion that organization of cooperatives and state trading in foodgrains could create and mobilize much higher levels of agricultural output and savings permeated all discussion about resource mobilization in the rural areas. Asserting that "the establishment of a network of Panchayats and service cooperatives in the rural areas and development of joint farming and State trading in foodgrains have a key role to play in the creation and mobilization of surpluses in the agricultural sector,"[48] the seminar reiterated support for the major elements of the agricultural development strategy: (1) service cooperatives should be organized rapidly; (2) credit should be extended on the basis of an approved production plan; and (3) marketing and the distribution of supplies should be undertaken by the village society in conjunction with state trading in foodgrains and other consumer articles. In contrast to the food ministry's earlier assurances in April 1959 that state trading in foodgrains would be conducted on a no-profit, no-loss basis, the Ooty Seminar recommended

[45] *Ibid.*, p. 85.                    [46] *Ibid.*, p. 70.
[47] According to the official report, the seminar considered and rejected the view presented by "some of the participants" that the Third Plan should give higher priority to stimulating production in both agriculture and industry than to the redistribution of income, and should devise fiscal policies as incentives to investment whether or not they favored the private sector. Instead, the Ooty Seminar reiterated the official position that the aim of the Third Plan should be to take the country "a significant step forward to its goal of a socialist society." All India Congress Committee, *Report of the Congress Planning Sub-Committee* (New Delhi, 1959), p. 21.
[48] All India Congress Committee, Congress Planning Subcommittee, *Ooty Seminar, May 30 to June 5, 1959, Papers Discussed* (New Delhi, 1959), p. 106.

maximum fixed prices for foodgrains and other essential commodities to earn a profit for development.[49]

The seminar also endorsed V. T. Krishnamachari's position that utilization of idle manpower resources could make a "significant" contribution to the finances of the Third Plan. The deputy chairman of the Planning Commission suggested four different ways in which panchayats might use local labor for development activities: (1) to enforce customary obligations upon the community or the beneficiaries of development projects to excavate field channels and carry out contour bunding; (2) to undertake community projects to build up assets belonging to the village as a whole (tanks, fisheries, fuel plantations, and common pastures) through voluntary contributions of capital as well as labor; (3) to construct social amenities projects under the Community Development program and qualify for matching government funds by donating an equivalent of money or labor; and (4) to form labor cooperatives of skilled or semiskilled workers to execute Plan projects at the village level in the place of private contractors. With the exception of the fourth category of rural works projects, for which villagers would be paid at village rates, every other program that Krishnamachari proposed envisaged the mobilization of surplus manpower without payment, or with only token payment. All of these schemes depended on local institutions for effective implementation and presupposed the reorganization of the village economy around cooperatives and panchayats.

The recommendations of the National Development Council and the Ooty Seminar, coming on the heels of the Nagpur resolutions, intensified the growing sense of alarm. The greatest apprehension was voiced by the Forum of Free Enterprise (FFE). Minoo Masani, the FFE's most articulate spokesman, warned that the ruling party had now embarked on a direct assault to cripple the free enterprise system. He urged the immediate necessity of forming a new political party capable of offering a viable conservative alternative at the national level to the Congress party.

This was not entirely a new idea. The FFE had experimented in this direction during the 1957 elections by endorsing selected candidates, almost all of whom were defeated. The experience alerted them to two major obstacles in the way of organizing a free enterprise party. First, public attitudes toward private business were either too negative or apathetic to expect a popular response to a capitalist appeal. Second, the

[49] The seminar stated plainly that the state trading corporations' "contribution to the resources will be determined by the difference between purchase price and sale price." According to one estimate, by the economist V.K.R.V. Rao, profits from state trading could be made to yield between Rs. 500 and Rs. 700 crores for development over a five-year period.

business community itself, while favorably inclined by ideology and interest, was also reluctant to extend open support for fear of jeopardizing relatively profitable working relationships with the government. Then in 1959, the Nagpur resolutions suddenly presented the FFE with "something of a godsend."[50] The proposals for cooperative village management appeared to offer the first opportunity for organizing a mass-based free enterprise party by exploiting the fears of large and small land-owners alike. Almost immediately, the FFE set out to identify themselves with the interests of the landowning classes by arranging a series of open meetings whose main purpose was to denounce the Nagpur proposals as harbingers of collectivization.

The first signs of a positive response to Masani's initiative from inside the Congress party came from expressions of support by prominent dissidents. By May 1959, both C. Rajagopalachari and N. G. Ranga were ready to join Masani in the call for the formation of a new party. At the June meeting of the All-India Agricultural Federation (a small interest group hastily organized by large landowners in 1958 to protest the Nagpur proposals), Ranga and Rajagopalachari joined hands with Masani to announce the creation of the Swatantra (Freedom) party. The role of agriculturists in the formation of the new party was deliberately emphasized by the selection of Ranga, a veteran peasant leader, as president, and in the official slogan, devised by Rajagopalachari, "freedom of man, freedom of the farm and the family as against the attack by totalitarianism on the freedom of everybody."[51] By far the most disturbing aspect of the challenge to the national Congress leadership was the similarity between Swatantra's aggressive antagonism to government controls over the economy, and deep-seated resentment among strategic elites of the Congress party over the same policies.

As preparation on the Draft Outline got underway, the impact of domestic political dissent was suddenly magnified by a reinforcing set of pressures from external sources. The Planning Commission's increasingly radical rhetoric also raised apprehension among Western aid-givers, including the World Bank and Consortium powers. They expressed the view that India's public sector program was overly ambitious and that private enterprise in collaboration with foreign private capital should be assigned a larger role. The United States, in particular, opposed the primary emphasis on heavy industry in the pattern of investment allocation, and urged a revised set of priorities to give first claim on resources to agriculture. The most influential statement of the American position appeared in April 1959, with the publication of the Ford Founda-

---

[50] Howard L. Erdman, *The Swatantra Party and Indian Conservatism*, p. 69.

[51] *Ibid.*, see chapter 4 for detailed account of the FFE's tactic of identifying the founders of Swatantra with the AIAF and the rural sector.

tion's *Report on India's Food Crisis and Steps to Meet It*. Asserting that India would have to increase the rate of growth of foodgrains by two to three times existing levels merely to meet minimum requirements at the end of the Third Plan, American experts argued: "It is clear to us that food production increases at the rate required . . . cannot be realized unless an all-out emergency programme is undertaken, and adequate resources are made available. This means that agricultural development must be given the highest priority among all categories of development for the remainder of the Second Five Year Plan and for the entire Third Plan period."[52]

Although Indian planners were in agreement with the experts' assessment that the success of the Third Plan required doubling or trebling the rate of growth of foodgrains production, there was obvious divergence on the question of how best to achieve this target. The Ford Foundation report implicitly criticized the entire approach of institutional change as the keystone of the agricultural strategy. Instead, it echoed the food ministry's position in favor of a technocratic approach based on price incentives to individual farmers for higher private investment in modern inputs, especially fertilizers. Simultaneously, the report recommended the formula, abandoned in 1952 on the grounds of social equity, of an intensive and selective development strategy, involving the concentration of a combination of modern practices—improved seeds, chemical fertilizers, and pesticides—in irrigated areas of the country. It argued the case solely from the perspective of maximizing growth goals:

> The immediate potential for increased wheat and rice production lies in certain districts which have previously shown appreciable increases in yields. These districts have irrigation facilities and the farmers are anxious to apply technological knowledge in order to further increase yields. *Special consideration would be given to about 25 rice districts in Punjab, parts of Uttar Pradesh, Madhya Pradesh and Bihar. In many of these specified districts, yields of rice and wheat can be doubled, if the scientific approach is utilized and all factors of production are made available in optimum quantities.*[53]

The effect of these mutually reinforcing pressures on the planners as they worked to give final shape to the Draft Outline was to once again strengthen the tendency toward political compromise on the pace of structural change. Even so, the planners resisted the pressure to redefine basic socialist principles of economic policy or methods of development.

The Draft Outline published in June 1960 kept total Plan outlay high, at an estimated Rs. 10,250 crores, of which Rs. 7,250 crores (70 percent)

---

[52] Ministry of Food and Agriculture and Ministry of Community Development and Cooperation, *Report of India's Food Crisis and Steps to Meet It*, p. 13.

[53] *Ibid.*, p. 56. Emphasis in original.

was in the public sector. The Planning Commission did make an important concession on the public-to-private investment ratio in industries and minerals. The initial projection of the Dimensional Hypotheses of a 67 : 33 percent balance in favor of the public sector was lowered in the Draft Outline to approximately 60 : 40 percent, the same target adopted in the Second Plan. Against the actual division of public-to-private industrial investment, which averaged 56 : 44 percent over the preceding five-year period, the reduced ratio meant that in the last year of the Third Plan the share of the public sector in organized manufacturing industries would still be somewhat less than one-fourth of the total, and in mineral production, approximately one-third.[54]

The planners also made substantial revisions in favor of the partisans of agriculture in the distribution of investment outlay. As late as October 1959, working estimates of agriculture, community development, and irrigation had amounted to only 16 percent of total Plan outlay.[55] By the time the Draft Outline was published eight months later, the share of these three heads of development accounted for more than 23 percent of total investment. In addition, the planners projected very large increases in outlay on fertilizers, from less than Rs. 30 crores in the Second Plan to Rs. 240 crores in the Third Plan. Public sector capacity was expected to increase from about 144,000 tons of nitrogen in 1959 to 800,000 tons in 1961. The private sector was also expected to provide 200,000 tons, to bring total capacity for the production of nitrogen to one million tons by the end of the Third Plan.

The increase in the ratio of agricultural investment to total Plan outlay (from the initial projection of 16 to 23 percent), raised the absolute amount of expenditure by 70 percent over Second Plan levels. At the same time, output of foodgrains was expected to grow 33 to 40 percent over the Third Plan period, about 6 to 8 percent annually; as opposed to the actual achievement of approximately 16 percent (3.3 percent per annum) during the Second Plan. The Planning Commission, therefore, was proposing to more than double the rate of growth in foodgrains production, while increasing total expenditure on agriculture by about 70 percent. This might have been compensated by much larger expenditures projected for fertilizer, except that the planners refused to alter their basic approach to the distribution of agricultural inputs. Specifically, the Draft Outline reiterated the principle of all-India coverage under the Community Development program. Available resources were to be spread thinly and evenly throughout the country in an effort to reach all farmers. The Ford Foundation's recommendation for an intensive and

[54] Planning Commission, *Third Five Year Plan*, p. 14.
[55] The working paper from which this figure is taken is cited by John P. Lewis, *Quiet Crisis in India*, pp. 86–87.

selective development program in irrigated areas was accepted only as an experimental pilot scheme to be started sometime during the five-year period in one district in each state. The Intensive Agricultural Development Program (IADP), moreover, was clearly tacked on to the existing development strategy as an additional technical element that did not represent a reorientation of the basic community approach. Indeed, the planners made a special point of their intention in the selected districts to make "a concentrated effort . . . to reach all farmers through cooperatives and panchayats and to organize village production plans which will involve all agricultural families."[56]

As in the Second Plan, the Planning Commission emphasized that financial outlay would have to be supplemented in the rural sector by the use of idle manpower "to the maximum extent possible." The planners made detailed recommendations for five categories of rural works projects, which corresponded almost exactly to the proposals offered by V. T. Krishnamachari at the Ooty Seminar. Commenting on these programs, the Planning Commission returned to a familiar theme: "In the main, it is through the participation of millions of peasant families in village production plans and in large-scale programs of irrigation, soil conservation, dry farming and the development of local manurial resources that the major agricultural objectives are to be reached. The question, therefore is, how in the conditions prevailing in India, the manpower resources available in the rural areas can be effectively harnessed for development."[57]

Institutional change, especially the organization of village cooperatives and panchayats, was once again assigned the central role of rural resource mobilization. The planners envisaged that each panchayat would prepare a village production plan to ensure all cultivators a supply of credit for improved agricultural inputs; and to involve the entire community in the construction of capital assets through the digging of field channels, digging and maintenance of tanks, and contour bunding. Conversations with state governments were reported to be in progress to determine whether a number of compulsory labor days could be prescribed, and how "with the maximum consent possible, this system can be brought into operation on a large enough scale."[58] The village panchayats were to be vested with executive powers, especially the authority to undertake construction and maintenance of field channels and minor irrigation works when the beneficiaries failed to do so, and to realize the costs from the farmers concerned. The Planning Commission's formal endorsement of the new scheme of democratic decentralization or Panchayati Raj—the creation of indirectly elected Block Panchayat Samitis and District

[56] Planning Commission, *Third Five Year Plan, A Draft Outline*, p. 150.
[57] *Ibid.*, p. 66.                          [58] *Ibid.*, p. 71.

Parishads to administer the Community Development program—reflected the hope that more active popular involvement would result in greater support for agricultural development schemes requiring local contributions in manpower and other resources.

Cooperatives were again assigned primary responsibility for arranging credit and supplies. Altogether, primary agricultural societies were expected to provide short-term production loans amounting to some Rs. 400 crores, more than double the amount achieved by the end of the Second Plan. Credit was to be linked to marketing, and village societies were expected to serve as channels for the disposal of the agricultural surplus. The planners reiterated that cooperation in credit was only "the beginning of cooperation." Cooperation had to be extended from credit to "a number of other activities in the village, including cooperative farming, until it encompasses all aspects of rural life."[59]

The critical questions of a timetable for land reforms, the organization of cooperatives, and the introduction of state trading in foodgrains nevertheless went unanswered. The planners did no more than note the record of ineffective implementation of land reforms, and reiterate the need for regulation of rents, security of tenure, ownership rights for tenants, and a ceiling on landownership. Tentative targets for the organization of cooperatives revealed that the Planning Commission and the Ministry of Food and Agriculture were still locked in disagreement on the pace of agrarian reorganization. According to the Draft Outline, each state was expected to work out programs for cooperative development "with due regard to the objectives of bringing all rural families within the cooperative movement by the end of the Third Plan."[60] At the same time, the planners reproduced targets for the organization of cooperatives to be considered "illustrative" by the states, which had been recommended by the Ministry of Food and Agriculture's Working Group on Cooperative Policy in December 1958. They envisaged that only 74 percent of the agriculturist population would be members of primary village cooperatives at the end of the Third Plan.[61] No detailed program for the introduction of state trading in foodgrains and other essential commodities was included in the Draft Outline at all. All of these questions were left for negotiation between the state chief ministers and the Planning Commission in the discussions on the state plans that followed the publication of the Draft Outline.

The final version of the Third Plan revealed that the Planning Commission had been completely unsuccessful in convincing the state leaders to accept an accelerated pace of agrarian reorganization. On the contrary, the chief ministers prevailed in making their case for even greater conces-

[59] *Ibid.*, p. 166.                                     [60] *Ibid.*, p. 164.
[61] *Ibid.*, p. 164.

sions to the landed classes as the price of party unity. The state chief ministers, who still did not openly oppose the new agrarian policies in principle, argued privately for a cautious approach to implementation. They cited a number of administrative and organizational difficulties in the way of immediate application of ceilings and formation of cooperative farms. Above all, they warned that precipitous action could force large-scale defections from the Congress party only months before the next general elections.[62]

Contradictions between Plan policies and programs in the rural sector not only remained, but grew worse. The planners failed to get the state leadership's recognition of land reforms as a positive program of development and an integral part of the community-based effort to increase agricultural production. Yet, they endorsed proposals for a comprehensive rural works program that envisaged very little government assistance and only limited wage employment, amounting to subsistence payments in cash or kind for particular projects. Under the Third Plan, moreover, mobilization of idle manpower remained a voluntary program. The planners, in deference to the state leadership, dropped their earlier proposal for establishing a labor tax in rural areas.

Some of the worst discrepancies occurred in the provisions for organization of cooperatives. Although the Planning Commission emphasized that "all families in the village, especially those engaged in cultivation, must be involved in the agricultural effort through the village cooperative,"[63] actual membership targets were substantially lower than the National Development Council's November 1958 projection, and even less than the food and agriculture ministry's "illustrative" figure of 74 percent cited in the Draft Outline. The target accepted by the Planning Commission, after consultation with the states, was membership of 37 million cultivators in primary cooperatives by 1965/66, more than double the 1960/61 membership levels, but only some 60 percent of the agriculturist population. Despite the fact that the pace of organization had been significantly slowed down, an even greater burden was placed on the cooperatives for financing agricultural production. Short-term loans were expected to reach Rs. 530 crores in 1965/66, compared with Rs. 200 crores in 1960/61, and the original target of Rs. 400 crores projected in the Draft Outline.

The political compulsion of conciliating the larger farmers and traders was also apparent in the gap between the statement of Plan policy and

[62] Minoo Masani, the Swatantra leader, was convinced that the Nagpur Resolutions "if properly explained [could bring] to the landed peasants in the villages who constitute 53.7 percent of our greater population, and to the middle classes in the city an awareness of their common interests and perils." Erdman, *The Swatantra Party and Indian Conservatism*, p. 79.

[63] *Third Five Year Plan*, p. 304.

proposals for government action on state trading in foodgrains. The planners envisaged "a network of cooperative and governmental agencies close to the farmer, licensing and regulation of wholesale trade, extension of State trading in suitable directions and a considerable sharing by Government and Cooperatives in distribution arrangements at retail stage."[64] Such a vigorous state trading program was necessary to assure the government's ability to influence the course of prices and "[mop] up the excess purchasing power which tends to push up demand above the level of available supplies."[65] But despite proposals to establish primary marketing societies and storage facilities in almost every *mandi* or marketing town, the total volume of agricultural business conducted through the cooperatives was expected to reach only Rs. 400 crores. Even if all this were to be made up by foodgrains purchase, it would still represent just 20 percent of the marketed surplus. By contrast, the Planning Commission believed that the government must procure at least one-half the marketed surplus in order to have effective control over the price level.

The accommodations made by the Planning Commission in the final version of the Third Plan increased the sources of contradiction in the basic approach to the point of almost complete immobilization. Concessions to the propertied classes, designed to win their cooperation for moderate reforms were, in fact, so large as to prevent the possibility of carrying out institutional change on any meaningful scale. But in the absence of effective implementation of proposals for basic agrarian reform, there was little likelihood of mobilizing the additional rural resources that were considered necessary to augment planned financial outlays. The entire rationale of national development planning was put into question. The Third Plan as it stood offered little hope of meeting either goals of rapid progress toward a self-reliant economy, paced by public investment in the basic capital goods sector, or the aims of reducing social inequalities and improving the standard of living of the majority of the peasant population.

The outlook appeared even more bleak in the light of new estimates of population growth derived from the 1961 census. These showed that the Central Statistical Organization's 1959 projections, which had formed the working basis for preparation of the Third Plan, were too conservative. Population was growing at an annual rate closer to 2.3 percent than 2 percent.[66] Apart from depressing the projection for per capita gains arising from the budgeted expenditure, the census figures called attention to the deteriorating employment situation. Over the previous five years, development programs had been too small even to create sufficient jobs

[64] *Ibid.*, p. 131.                    [65] *Ibid.*, p. 127.
[66] *Ibid.*, pp. 50–51.

for all new entrants into the labor force. As a result, the backlog of unemployment was steadily growing. At the end of the Second Plan, about
nine million persons were unemployed—some 6.5 million outside agriculture. During the Third Plan, the labor force was expected to increase
by 17 millions. Against these magnitudes, only an additional 14 million
new jobs, 10.5 million outside agriculture, were provided. This was
three million fewer than necessary to absorb only the new entrants into
the labor force. Another three million jobs had to be created just to avoid
adding to the backlog.[67]

The pressing need to find additional finances in order to mount a larger
Plan was satisfied at the symbolic level only. The final draft of the Third
Plan actually increased public outlay to Rs. 8,098 crores, compared to the
original estimate of Rs. 7,250 crores projected in the Draft Outline. The
increase reflected upward revisions under all major heads of development. Yet, the new figure mainly represented an attempt to satisfy both
the partisans of agriculture and the advocates of heavy industry, each of
whom believed that still larger allocations were necessary to achieve the
high production targets. Each side was accommodated, but only at the
expense of raising the cost of the Third Plan above the most optimistic
estimates of available resources. Even after assuming more than a 62 percent increase in revenues from additional taxation over amounts realized
during the Second Plan, and another Rs. 550 crores of deficit financing,
the resources available for financing Plan outlay were estimated at no
more than Rs. 7,500 crores, as shown in Table 5-1.

The final version of the Third Plan at the outset faced a "gap" of over
Rs. 500 crores between the figure for the estimate of financial resources at
Rs. 7,500 crores, and the requirements for meeting the financial costs of
the physical programs calculated at Rs. 8,098 crores. The result was that
in terms of the resources at hand, allocations under major heads of development both in absolute and percentage terms conformed closely to the
pattern of the Draft Outline, allowing only modest upward revisions in
agriculture, power, industry and minerals, transport and communications, and social services. Table 5-2 shows the distribution of Plan outlay
in the Draft Outline compared to the financial provisions of the Third
Plan, and the estimated costs of implementing the physical programs envisaged.

The private sector, by contrast to the public sector, had distinctly better prospects of meeting its investment targets, especially in the strategic
area of industries and minerals. The overall cost of the public sector programs in industries and mineral production was estimated at Rs. 1,882
crores. The Planning Commission was able to provide only Rs. 1,520
crores, and this exceeded by Rs. 50 crores the amount considered likely

[67] *Ibid.*, pp. 156, 159-60.

## TABLE 5-1

### Financial Resources for the Third Plan

| Item | Rs. crores |
|------|:---:|
| Balance from current revenues (excluding additional taxation) | 550 |
| Contribution of railways | 100 |
| Surpluses of other public enterprises | 450 |
| Loans from the public (net) | 800 |
| Small savings (net) | 600 |
| Provident funds (net) | 265 |
| Steel equalization fund (net) | 105 |
| Balance of miscellaneous capital receipts over non-Plan disbursements | 340 |
| Additional taxation including measures to increase the surpluses of public enterprises | 1,710 |
| Budgetary receipts corresponding to external assistance | 2,200 |
| Deficit financing | 550 |
| Total | 7,500★ |

SOURCE: *Third Five Year Plan*, p. 95.

★ The actual sum of the items listed is Rs. 7,670. No explanation for this discrepancy appears in the Planning Commission's estimates; and the figure of Rs. 7,500 crores is used throughout the Third Plan as the official estimate of available financial resources.

to be available.[68] At the same time, the cost of the private sector programs in industries and minerals was estimated at Rs. 1,185 crores; of this amount, fully Rs. 1,100 crores was expected to be forthcoming.[69] Taking into account only the estimates of resources "likely to be available," the ratio of public-to-private investment in industries and minerals actually declined from about 60 : 40 in the Draft Outline to 57.2 : 42.8 percent in the Third Plan. This unstated, but implicit, change was underlined by the allocation of higher targets to private enterprise in "reserved industries," especially chemical fertilizer.

In agriculture, similar compromises resulted in the paradoxical outcome of a development strategy that was inimical to the goal of increasing production. Political guidelines still mandated principles of extensive coverage that prevented concentration of scarce funds and modern inputs in the most productive areas or among the most efficient producers. Larger farmers who appreciated the profitability of modern techniques were often hobbled by severe shortages of supply. In addition, during the 1950s, such "progressive" cultivators had little to learn from agricul-

[68] *Ibid.*, p. 461.  [69] *Ibid.*, p. 461.

## TABLE 5-2

### Distribution of Third Plan Outlay in the Public Sector

(estimates for the Draft Outline, and for the Third Plan in terms
of available financial resources and the costs of physical programs)

(*Rs. crores*)

| | Outlay | | | Percentage | | |
|---|---|---|---|---|---|---|
| | *Draft Outline* | *Third Plan financial provisions* | *Third Plan costs of physical programs* | *Draft Outline* | *Third Plan financial provisions* | *Third Plan costs of physical programs* |
| Agriculture and minor irrigation | 625 | 666 | 687 | 8.6 | 8.8 | 8.5 |
| Community development and cooperation | 400 | 402 | 402 | 5.5 | 5.4 | 5.1 |
| Major irrigation | 650 | 650 | 660 | 9.0 | 9.0 | 8.2 |
| Power | 925 | 1,012 | 1,019 | 12.8 | 13.0 | 12.6 |
| Village and small industries | 250 | 264 | 254 | 3.4 | 4.0 | 3.1 |
| Industries and minerals | 1,500 | 1,520 | 1,882 | 20.7 | 20.0 | 23.2 |
| Transport and communications | 1,450 | 1,486 | 1,654 | 20.0 | 19.8 | 20.4 |
| Social services | 1,250 | 1,300 | 1,416 | 17.2 | 17.0 | 17.4 |
| Miscellaneous | 200 | 200 | 110 | 2.8 | 3.0 | 1.2 |
| Grand Total | 7,250 | 7,500 | 8,098* | 100 | 100 | 100 |

SOURCE: *The Third Plan: A Draft Outline*, p. 27; *Third Five Year Plan*, p. 58, Annexure II, pp. 85-88.

* The discrepancy in column 3 between the grand total of Third Plan costs set down at Rs. 8,098 crores and the actual sum of the figures under each head of development, which totals Rs. 8,084 crores, is a result of the transformation from the estimates presented in the *Draft Outline* as lakhs into crores, with the elimination of remainders.

tural extension officers and village-level workers, whose training was directed to educating poor peasants in improved practices using traditional techniques. Meanwhile, Community Development, initially conceived as no more than a catalyst or "practical aid" in supplying technical assistance, agricultural credit, and limited amounts of improved inputs to spark large-scale peasant mobilization for labor-intensive projects, found its village programs more and more confined to the availability of central government funds. Yet a budget that provided an annual per capita expenditure of about Rs. 4 could not be expected to have a significant impact on growth.

Efforts to mobilize local manpower and resources for construction of capital projects met with little success. While richer farmers generally could contribute cash to village projects, subsistence cultivators and land-less laborers, of necessity, were asked to donate labor. Local officials quickly discovered it was not possible to mobilize idle manpower for unpaid work on a "community" project in minor irrigation or soil conservation when the benefits were disproportionately skewed toward the larger landowners. Difficulties arose even with respect to use of surplus manpower for the construction of social amenities projects, such as approach roads, drinking-water wells, community centers, and libraries. Cultivators were also the greatest beneficiaries of new roads linking the village to nearby markets; and in situations of social discrimination, lower castes might be excluded from the full enjoyment of a community center, panchayat house, or a drinking-water well. Poorer families were also illiterate; they had no need for libraries, and in some cases they could not afford to send their children to school. Even official figures—which were inflated by a variety of practices—showed that public donations to community development schemes were steadily declining both in absolute terms and relative to government expenditures throughout the period of the three five-year plans.[70] Whatever voluntary contributions in money and labor did come forward, moreover, were almost entirely restricted to the construction of social amenities projects, particularly roads, schools, drains, and drinking-water wells. The Blocks, with very few exceptions, were not able to organize collective efforts to improve and construct small irrigation works and channels, bring new land under reclamation, or carry out soil conservation measures. On the contrary, in practice, the main role of the Block agency in minor irrigation, land reclamation, and soil conservation schemes was to act as a lending agency to individual cultivators who could afford to invest on land improvement schemes.

The Planning Commission, taking account of the economic and social costs of conciliating the propertied classes inside the Congress party,

[70] Block Development Officers, faced with the dilemma of fulfilling targets of "peoples participation" (usually fifty percent of the expenditures on any village project) resorted to a number of expedients. Labor contributions and money were made in ad hoc fashion for each Community Development project; and records of public contribution, kept by the panchayat secretary or village-level workers, were not inspected or audited. In many cases, the cost of a village project could be overestimated to ensure that government funds were sufficient to complete the project or most of it. In such cases public contribution, although actually very small, was noted as half the cost of the project in official records. In other instances, sums paid by the panchayat out of their normal income from taxation or even from government grants were counted as public contributions. Such practices made it virtually impossible to make an accurate estimate of the value of peoples' contributions to community projects. Even so, official figures showed a steady decline in the value of peoples' contributions to community projects over the period of the three five-year plans.

were unhappy with the terms of the political bargain they had struck. They once again stressed that development on the scale provided in the Third Plan "must be indeed improved upon in actual achievement" mainly through "an intensive and continuous effort to utilize fully the manpower resources of the country, to make the most efficient use possible of resources available for investment, to mobilize domestic savings and channel them into appropriate directions."[71] The planners appeared to regard the concessions they had made as a temporary expedient to be reconsidered after the pressures of the election had safely passed. But the ability of the central government to impose its own principles of socialistic economic policy on the states was eroding. Failures in implementing institutional change had not only impaired the entire economic strategy, but produced social effects opposite of those intended. By the early 1960s, disparities in income, status, and power between the larger landowners and the majority of subsistence cultivators and landless laborers perceptibly began to widen.

The national leadership's inability to enlist the support of state leaders for effective implementation of land reforms resulted in defective legislation that actually aggravated existing inequalities in the distribution of protected land rights enjoyed by landowners and those without land. Similarly, the failure to activate party workers in setting up new village institutions left a leadership gap at the local level that was quickly filled by members of the dominant landed castes. They proved adept at manipulating the diffuse loyalties of the peasantry based on kinship, caste, and factional ties to mobilize their followers and gain control of village cooperative and panchayat bodies. The dominant landed castes, increasing both their economic and political leverage, gained access to additional sources of credit and scarce modern inputs introduced into the villages by the Community Development program, and enlarged their role as intermediaries in relationships between the village and outside authorities in the administration and ruling party.

The abolition by state legislation between 1950 and 1954 of intermediary rights and tenures[72] did accomplish major changes in the pattern of landownership in those areas (Assam, Bihar, West Bengal, Orissa, Uttar Pradesh, Rajasthan, Saurashtra, and Hyderabad) where the zamindari system had existed on a large scale. Proprietary rights over vast agricultural estates extending over several villages, even talukas, were transferred from a handful of absentee landlords to state governments. Even so, zamindari abolition fell far short of an agrarian transformation.

[71] *Third Five Year Plan*, p. 28.
[72] A collection of the Zamindari Abolition Acts is published in Ministry of Food and Agriculture, Directorate of Economics and Statistics, *Agricultural Legislation in India*, Vol. IV, Land Reforms (Abolition of Intermediaries), 1953.

The land reform laws bore obvious marks of political compromise. While they abolished the zamindari system, the provisions stopped well short of expropriating the zamindars. On the one hand, the zamindars' proprietary rights were vested in the state governments; on the other, the zamindars were permitted to keep land in their direct occupation for personal cultivation, and in most cases no ceiling was placed on the size of the "home farm" so retained. In Rajasthan and Saurashtra, where large numbers of intermediaries were absentee landlords with no land in their possession, or *jagirdars* enjoying rights of revenue collection only, the state governments went so far as to permit any intermediary to apply for an allowance of *khudhasht* (land for personal cultivation) subject to a ceiling limit.

The acts, moreover, conferred full ownership rights on the ex-intermediaries with respect to their home farms. By contrast, tenants in direct occupation of land on resumed estates were confirmed only in the legal rights they enjoyed on the date immediately preceding vesting. In Assam, Bihar, Orissa, West Bengal, and Hyderabad, the acts made no provision for tenants to acquire full ownership rights, thereby perpetuating the cultivator's inferior status in relation to former zamindars. In Uttar Pradesh, Rajasthan, and Saurashtra, occupancy tenants as well as inferior rights holders were permitted to acquire ownership or occupancy rights in their holdings, but only after paying compensation to the government.

Further, "landlordism" was not ended. In Assam, Bihar, and Orissa, many of the tenants who came into relationship with the state had not been cultivating the land directly. Rather, they leased out some or all of their holdings to subtenants and sharecroppers. Even in states such as West Bengal and Saurashtra, where all tenure holders were subsequently forbidden to let or sublet their holdings, the word "lease" was carefully defined to exclude sharecropping arrangements. The fact was that the process of zamindari abolition mainly benefitted the intermediate peasant classes, those larger occupancy tenants—many of whom belonged to the middling Sudra peasant castes—who were elevated in economic standing relative to resident upper-caste ex-zamindars left with reduced estates. By no means did all who actually cultivated the land improve their position. On the contrary, the weakest sections of the rural poor were often adversely affected. The provision in the state acts allowing intermediaries to keep land in their home farms without any upper limit proved a direct incentive to zamindars for evicting unprotected tenants-at-will from their holdings in order to exaggerate the proportion of the estate under "personal cultivation." Except in Uttar Pradesh, moreover, virtually no land records existed at the village level to verify the actual distribution of holdings between zamindars and tenants. As a result, many small holders who customarily leased land lost this land or part of it to the ex-intermediaries under the provisions for personal cultivation. In the absence of accurate land records, it is impossible to establish the actual numbers of agriculturists evicted in this way. The Planning Commission, however, believed the number had been substantial in almost all states.[73]

The balance of social costs and benefits of zamindari abolition were skewed even further to favor the ex-intermediaries by generous formulas for compensation in the loss of ownership or revenue rights on resumed estates. The great absentee landlords were, in general, not ruined by zamindari abolition. Many remained men of considerable wealth. Those with superior education and skills were able to rebuild their fortunes by taking up new activities in commercial agriculture, trading, or manufacturing—or, by entering politics.[74] Meanwhile, compensation payable to intermediaries proved a substantial burden on state budgets. Although the states had relied on rising land revenue collections to finance compensation, these were usually insufficient in the face of new charges for survey, settlement, and land revenue administration that became necessary after zamindari abolition. Between 1950/51 and 1960/61, state expenditures on land revenue collections alone increased more than five times. Even before payment of compensation, a number of states experienced a net decline in revenues as a result of zamindari abolition. Once compensation payments are taken into account, the net impact on revenue receipts of a majority of states was negative.[75] In effect, most of the agricultural revenues collected in the ex-zamindari areas well into the 1960s had to be earmarked for nonproductive expenditures, limiting outlays for development in rural areas.

A similar pattern emerged in the aftermath of ceiling legislation. The principle of imposing ceilings on landholdings was first announced in 1953; detailed recommendations for legislation were not made until 1956;

[73] For an official assessment of the impact of zamindari abolition on the status of unprotected tenants, see India, Planning Commission, *Implementation of Land Reforms: A Review*.

[74] The situation of large landlords after zamindari abolition in Uttar Pradesh is explored in Thomas R. Metcalf, "Landlords without Land: The U.P. Zamindars Today," *Pacific Affairs*, 40 (Spring and Summer 1967). Metcalf reports that most of the largest zamindars of Uttar Pradesh adjusted very comfortably. Although the greatest talukdars (owning 500 square miles or more) were often too removed from the daily operation of their estates to protect themselves against the machinations of land managers, those with "middling size estates" (50 to 300 villages) were not only able to retain very large farms, ranging up to 2,000 acres, but also used their capital for agricultural improvements that added considerably to their income. In addition, by virtue of their social prestige as leaders of local Rajput lineages, they could mobilize support of fellow caste members and members of dependent lower castes to become powerful political figures, often shifting allegiance from one party to another for maximum leverage.

[75] See M. L. Dantwala, "Financial Implications of Land Reforms," *Indian Journal of Agricultural Economics*, 17 (October-December 1962), 2. Altogether, compensation payable to intermediaries in all states amounted to more than Rs. 641 crores. India, Planning Commission, *Progress of Land Reforms* (New Delhi, 1963), p. 4.

and most states did not actually pass enabling legislation until 1960 or 1961. The landowners, therefore, had a period of seven or eight years to arrange partitions and transfers of holdings to escape the impact of the new laws. Even while some states were still in the process of formulating legislation, the Planning Commission concluded that excessive ceilings in state laws, combined with transfers and partitions of land, "have tended to defeat the aims of the legislation." By 1961, the planners reported that ceiling legislation "was not likely to yield any appreciable surplus for redistribution."[76] The overwhelming majority of tenants discovered they held land from an owner with a holding below the ceiling level. In some cases, the ceiling legislation encouraged landowners to resume land from tenants in order to increase the size of their home farms to the permitted limit.

Worse still, legislation to provide security of tenure and reasonable rents to tenants included loopholes that not only deprived cultivators of promised benefits, but in some cases actually jeopardized the customary rights they already enjoyed. The most immediate obstacle to tenancy reform was the lack of reliable land records and the failure of most state governments to undertake a complete reconstruction of the record of rights to establish the identity of tenants and the extent of the land held by them. Yet, without documentary proof of tenancy, cultivators were unable to claim the protection of the tenancy acts that were passed. At the outset, therefore, the great majority of tenants and virtually all sharecroppers cultivating under oral lease were excluded from any new benefits under state tenancy acts.

Many landlords were, nevertheless, alarmed. Land records might be revised in the future. The safest course, therefore, was to show as much land as possible under personal cultivation. Two glaring loopholes in the tenancy acts[77] were particularly useful for this purpose. First, "personal cultivation" was not defined to require manual labor. It was sufficient if the owner, or a member of his family, supervised cultivation carried on by farm servants. Except in Assam, a landowner did not even have to be resident in the village during the greater part of the agricultural season to qualify as a "cultivator." The laws left the way open for owners to operate agricultural holdings either with hired laborers or through disguised tenancies, as in sharecropping "partnerships" between owner and cultivator. Second, most tenancy acts also provided that tenants could "voluntarily surrender" their holdings in favor of the landlord, and that in such cases no ceiling restriction on the right of resumption would apply.

---

[76] Planning Commission, Panel on Land Reforms, *Report of the Committee on Ceiling on Land Holdings* (New Delhi, 1961), pp. 5, 8.

[77] The provisions of the States' Tenancy Acts are summarized in two Planning Commission publications, *Implementation of Land Reforms: A Review* and *Progress of Land Reforms*.

Together, these two provisions virtually invited the landlords to evict tenants from their holdings under the guise of voluntary surrender in order to show the maximum area under personal cultivation. By 1961, the Planning Commission reported such extensive evictions of tenants in all states that "unless [voluntary] surrenders of land are severely regulated, the provisions for security of tenure cannot be enforced effectively."[78]

The state governments, however, with few exceptions, made virtually no effort to stop such abuses. On the contrary, they rarely appointed additional staff to supervise implementation. Land records continued to be prepared by village officers who had traditionally kept the revenue rolls. These record keepers, struggling with a jurisdiction extending over several villages and on a salary of some Rs. 30 to Rs. 60 per month, not infrequently found it convenient to collaborate with the landowners in protecting the latters' interest. Superior officers were too few in number to exercise effective supervision. It was rare to have one revenue inspector for every ten villages, common to have one inspector for every 25 or even 50 villages. Higher supervisory personnel, the tehsildar at the taluka level (with responsibility for 100 to 200 villages), the revenue officer at the divisional level (with a charge of two to three talukas), and the collector at the district level (with jurisdiction over six to nine talukas), had too many other responsibilities to conduct more than a few ad hoc checks into the accuracy of village records. But even if these officers had been more freely available for the collection of land data, it is doubtful that their exertions would have been rewarded. Under the provisions of the tenancy acts drafted by the states, primary responsibility for initiating enforcement procedures rested with the tenants rather than the revenue agency. The tenant was expected to claim his rights against eviction or to a regulated rent by filing application with the taluka or district revenue officer, or even in some instances, by bringing suit in district court. Predictably, in the absence of a political party to carry out propaganda publicizing the provisions of land reform laws and to organize tenants to claim their rights in ways that assured protection against retaliation, very few felt confident in coming forward. Indeed, it is a sound assumption that the relatively small numbers of tenants who acquired superior occupancy or ownership rights in land under the land reform legislation were outweighed by the numbers of tenants who lost their holdings to landlords under provisions permitting resumption for personal cultivation. Comparative data presented in the National Sample Survey's reports on landholdings for 1954 and in the early 1960s strongly support such a conclusion. Although village records showed little change in the distri-

[78] Planning Commission, Panel on Land Reforms, *Report of the Committee on Tenancy Reforms*, p. 11.

bution of landownership between 1954 and 1961, striking differences were noticeable with respect to leased-out land. Only 7 percent of all rural households were recorded as leasing out any land in 1961, compared to 12 percent in 1954.[79] The number of cultivators reported to be operating "mixed" holdings of partly owned and partly leased-in land, moreover, had declined from about 23 percent in 1954 to 15 percent in 1960, while those classified as "pure" tenants fell from about 17 percent to 8 percent.[80] The area under cultivation of tenants also registered a marked drop from about 20 percent of the total in 1954 to a little over 12 percent in 1962.[81] Given the failure of land reforms to vest ownership rights in tenants, the only logical explanation for the sharp decline in recorded tenancies is the eviction of tenants from their holdings, and resumption of land for personal cultivation. There is, however, little reason to believe that the actual incidence of tenancy decreased. Rather, it appears that registered leases were simply converted into informal, oral agreements that effectively deprived the cultivator of any protection under state tenancy acts. According to interview data collected through household sampling techniques for the Census Commission in 1961, about 23 percent of all cultivators were actually pure tenants, operating wholly leased-in land, and in many states, 30 to 40 percent of all farmers took some land on lease. Over 80 percent of these tenancies were described as oral agreements unrecorded in village records.[82]

The results were little more encouraging in the progress of the cooperative movement. The responsibility for establishing the cooperative bodies that were expected to function as strong "peoples institutions" was similarly left in the hands of bureaucrats who staffed the state Departments of Cooperation. Administrative and supervisory personnel rapidly proliferated. Headed by an IAS officer as acting registrar, the headquarters staff in the state capital was typically expanded to provide assistants in charge of various functional specializations, including activities such as audit, marketing, and processing. These officers, in turn, were provided with a staff of deputies. An entirely new tier of cooperative administration was created at the divisional level, with its own inspectorate and clerical staff. District-level administration was strengthened to provide additional officers and supporting staff for at least every eight hundred to a thousand cooperative societies. Another level of cooperative administration was created in the Blocks, entailing recruitment of five thousand extension officers for cooperation deputed to the

---

[79] *National Sample Survey, Seventeenth Round*, Number 140, *Tables with Notes on Some Aspects of Landholdings in Rural Areas (State and All-India Estimates)*, Draft, p. 34.

[80] *Hindustan Times*, April 28, 1964.

[81] *National Sample Survey, Sixteenth Round*, Number 122, *Tables with Notes on Agricultural Holdings in Rural India*, p. 27.

[82] *The Statesman*, June 1, 1968.

Block staffs. Finally, a supervisory staff of some seventy thousand persons—one for a maximum of every thirty societies—was created to oversee the operations of primary societies of all kinds.[83]

This far-reaching administrative apparatus was vested with formidable powers. State acts gave the registrar and his organization extensive regulatory and executive authority over the whole range of operations of cooperative societies. These powers included control over registration of new societies, inspection of finances, arbitration of disputes, supersession of negligent managing committees, annual audit, and even liquidation. In most states, the registrar could refuse to register a society on such nebulous grounds as that the aims of the society are not consistent with the principles of "social justice," or are not in keeping with "cooperative principles."[84] In several states, the registrar could order compulsory amendments to the bylaws of cooperative societies, including provisions for extending crop loans to link credit with marketing. Beginning in 1956, officers of the state Departments of Cooperation also served as executives in state and central (district) cooperative banks. Finally, the state was empowered to bring financial sanctions against recalcitrant societies. Applications by primary agricultural credit cooperatives and central banks for loans from apex financing institutions had to be recommended and approved by senior officers of the cooperation departments.

Altogether, these powers provided more than adequate leverage for the implementation of the Planning Commission's policy linking credit to an approved production plan and repayment in kind through crop deliveries to a cooperative marketing society. But the Department of Cooperation, functioning in local environments of entrenched hierarchies, and generally unsympathetic to the egalitarian goals of national policy, preferred to operate in ways more congenial to the interests of the existing power structure. With few exceptions, cooperatives continued to follow, with impunity, conservative banking principles requiring land, jewelry, or personal surety by a landowner as security for all loans. Crop loans, a crucial ingredient in the government's plan to organize production programs around the participation of millions of small cultivators, rarely became available. Those with very small landholdings, especially tenant cultivators, were, in fact, often excluded from membership, and in any case, found little reason to want to join. As a result, the president and other elective members of the managing committees of the cooperative societies were disproportionately drawn from among

[83] The practical difficulties of meeting these targets contributed to problems of inefficient administration, placing untrained, unreliable, and even incompetent personnel in important technical and organizational positions. See National Cooperative Development Corporation, *Report of the Committee on Cooperative Administration* (New Delhi, 1963).

[84] India, Ministry of Community Development and Cooperation, *Cooperation in India* (New Delhi, 1965), p. 199.

"the big people of the villages [who] had their fingers in many other pies as well as cooperation, including trade, government contracts, local politics and rice-milling among others."[85] A number of the leaders of the cooperative movement were active party workers in the district Congress committees. Some were MLA's whose influence extended directly to the state level of government. Indeed, control over the management of agricultural credit cooperatives became an important new source of economic patronage and political influence for the propertied castes.

The failures of the cooperatives to implement the crop loan system inevitably distorted the intended flow of credit from the majority of subsistence cultivators to the upper 20-30 percent of agriculturist families able to satisfy conventional banking criteria for credit-worthiness. This was true even though the active membership did not necessarily use production loans for development purposes only, or even prove reliable in repaying outstanding debts.[86] Meanwhile, the managing committees demonstrated little interest in strengthening internal resources of share capital and reserves to expand the lending capacity of the primary cooperatives. Instead, after the Second Plan, they relied primarily on outside borrowing from central banks.[87] In practice, the volume of short-term loans advanced by primary societies was closely tied to the level of available credit for production loans supplied to the apex (state) cooperative banks by the Reserve Bank of India. Contrary to the basic intention of the government's policy in using the cooperatives to mobilize local resources for investment, schemes for cooperative credit were being transformed into public subsidies on the cost of private investment (and in some cases, consumption and moneylending activities) for the more affluent landowning classes.

This was not all. As the only cultivators with access to sufficient resources either from savings or low-interest loans to experiment with and risk adoption of improved methods of cultivation, the more substantial landowners early acquired the additional prestige of being identified by

[85] Daniel Thorner, *Prospects for Cooperation in Indian Agriculture* (n.p., 1960).

[86] A 1961 study by the Planning Commission's Programme Evaluation Organization reported that over one-quarter of the total amount of short and medium-term credit advanced by cooperatives was annually diverted from production to consumption expenditures. *Study of Utilization of Cooperative Loans*, p. 88. Other studies conducted in 1961/62 showed that only 2.6 percent of cultivator households in the lowest asset group (less than Rs. 500) had reported any borrowing from cooperatives, while the proportion rose to 19 percent for the highest asset group (Rs. 20,000 and above). The percentage of overdues to outstanding loans in 1960/61, moreover, was 20 percent. Reserve Bank of India, *Report of the All-India Rural Credit Review Committee*, pp. 128, 138.

[87] In 1960/61, the total working capital of agricultural credit societies amounted to Rs. 273.9 crores, of which more than 60 percent (Rs. 174.7 crores) represented borrowing from central cooperative banks. Ministry of Community Development and Cooperation, *Cooperative Movement in India, Important Statistics, 1963-64*, Part I—Credit Sector (New Delhi, 1965), p. 5.

the Block Development staff as "progressive" farmers in the villages. From this vantage point, it was a short step to assuming the role of intermediary between the Community Development administration and the more "backward" farmers to control access to "community" funds and services.

By the latter 1950s, the Block extension staff, hampered by serious shortages of trained personnel, began to concentrate contact visits on "village leaders," the biggest "adopters" of the new techniques, and men who could in their turn "talk to their neighbors and become each in his own sphere a kind of voluntary worker."[88] In 1957, this informal bias was institutionalized with the initiation of the Gram Sahayak (Village Helper) program. Under this scheme, special training was provided to "village leaders" in agriculture, animal husbandry, minor irrigation, panchayats, and cooperatives, at the three-day training camps organized by Block-level officials for every circle of ten villages. A profile of persons attending these camps, provided in a 1961 study conducted by the Planning Commission, indicated that about 90 percent were owner cultivators, with almost two-thirds being classified as "big" and "medium" holders; about half of all trainees were also members of the village panchayat or managing committee of the village cooperative, or both.[89] While it is unlikely that the participants acquired much significant new expertise during a three-day training camp, after a lifetime of farming experience, the Gram Sahayak program did provide quasi-official standing for influential members of the village as legitimate channels of communication between the mass of the cultivators and the government-operated Community Development program.

The larger landowners, moreover, were able to use their strategic position in the village economy to strengthen their role as intermediaries in wider markets through their virtual monopoly over the disposition of agricultural savings and surpluses. The failure of cooperatives to provide low-cost credit and services to the majority of cultivators (while expanding resources available to larger landowners) meant that subsistence farmers and laborers were more than ever dependent on village landlords and moneylenders for production loans, consumption credit, and other marketing and distribution facilities. Small peasant "savings" continued to be transferred to landlords and moneylenders in the form of high-interest rates on loans, while the bulk of the marketable crop passed to these creditors along with other middlemen and traders either as payment for past accommodations or to satisfy immediate cash needs. Neither could the government harness the surpluses of the larger land-

[88] Planning Commission, Programme Evaluation Organization, *Evaluation of the Gram Sahayak Programme*, p. 9.
[89] *Ibid.*, pp. 22-26.

owners who enjoyed lower-cost credit through the cooperative societies. Although primary marketing societies were being established in all major marketing centers of India, failure to link credit with crop loans and repayment in kind rendered the cooperative structure virtually useless as an instrument for controlling the disposition of agricultural surpluses. Indeed, the great majority of primary cooperatives were not affiliated with a marketing society. Those cooperatives that did include provisions in loan bonds requiring members to sell their produce through an affiliated marketing society did not enforce such provisions. Under these conditions, government attempts to establish maximum controlled prices for foodgrains and to procure rice from millers and traders through compulsory levy were easily evaded. By the late 1950s, lower market arrivals reflected extensive hoarding and smuggling activities, in which the more substantial peasants collaborated with traders in holding back stocks to avoid government levies, force up the price level, and sell supplies in flourishing black markets.

As the national leadership searched for new institutional devices to outflank the intermediaries and break their stranglehold over village institutions, attention was drawn to proposals for devolution of administrative control over the Community Development program from development officers and officially appointed advisory groups to indirectly elected Block and district panchayat bodies. At the Block and district levels, indirectly elected councils promised to raise the stakes of winning local contests so that eventually rival leaders would be forced to appeal for the support of backward and Scheduled Castes with promises of more effective implementation of government policy on economic reform. Once again, however, the first set of elections to Panchayati Raj bodies resulted in the phenomenon of the selection of pradhans (presidents) of Block Panchayat Samitis and pramukhs (chairmen) of Zilla (district) Parishads, who were less representative of their constituencies than presidents of village panchayats. Under the system of indirect elections to Block and district panchayat institutions, local notables, mobilizing their followers through the familiar pattern of vertical factional alignments cross-cutting class lines, won the village elections and then simply chose representatives from among their own ranks to pyramid their influence at higher levels of government. They were joined, under the provisions of the state acts, by coopted members, including representatives of the "weaker sections" (women and Scheduled Castes and Tribes), but also persons with "experience in public life," representatives of the cooperative movement and members of the legislative assemblies.[90] Indeed, the

[90] Data available for Rajasthan, the first state to implement Panchayati Raj in 1959, revealed trends typical of an emerging all-India pattern. Compared to estimates showing over 68 percent of the rural population in Rajasthan having an annual income of less than

most that even the community development ministry hoped for was evolutionary change toward more representative leadership after several rounds of elections. S. K. Dey, minister since the inception of the program, likened the introduction of Panchayati Raj to "building the roots of a tree":

> I am attempting today to create an institutional pattern for the growth of democracy. The longer we keep the institutions going, the more people will get used to them and habit will support them. Secondly, education is coming on a large scale. But most important, in history the leader of the oppressed class has never been one of the oppressed class. I am dividing the forces and putting one against the other. If the landowners win places on the panchayat, some will be left out. They will try to build an opposition on the basis of the oppressed class.[91]

But experience had already shown that attempts at social transformation through institutional change that stopped short of direct peasant organization only compounded the problem of democratic reform. At least in the short run, the dominant landed castes were successful in manipulating the majority of subsistence cultivators and landless workers fragmented by vertical factional structures to capture the village institutions. They increased their access to scarce development resources and strengthened their position as strategic intermediaries, linking local markets and power structures to the state and national economic and political systems.

---

Rs. 1,000, 84 percent of all presidents of village panchayats enjoyed an annual income of Rs. 1,000 or more. Although Scheduled Castes and Tribes accounted for approximately one-fourth the population of the state, only ten village panchayat presidents out of 7,394 belonged to these communities. *Pradhans* of Block Panchayat Samities were, however, less representative. In 1961, only two thirds of all *pradhans* were even agriculturists: 17 percent were businessmen, 13 percent lawyers, and 5 percent "social workers." Two-thirds had received a high-school education, and more than one-third were college graduates. None was a member of the Scheduled Castes or Tribes. At the district level, data for 24 of the 26 *pramukhs* showed that only 7 were engaged in agriculture, 9 were lawyers, 4 businessmen, and 4 were in social science or other occupations. Seventeen of the *pramukhs* lived in towns. Of the 26, 11 had LL.B. degrees, 9 were graduates, 5 matriculates, and only 1 was a nonmatriculate. Data collected by the Government of Rajasthan Evaluation Organization, 1960 and the Development Department, 1961, and cited in David C. Potter, *Government in Rural India* (London, 1964), pp. 53-55.

[91] Interview, S. K. Dey, New Delhi, July 26, 1963.

# SIX

# Attack on Socialist Principles
# of Planning

Since the early days of the independence movement, the separation between "political" and "social" issues had produced national gains in
maximizing consensus, stability, and integration. On the eve of the
Third Plan, however, it was becoming apparent that the politics of
accommodation had accomplished these goals only at the cost of the social and economic aims of planning. In particular, it seemed impossible
to maintain the conciliatory style of the national and state Congress party
organizations that claimed to represent the interests of all groups, including the propertied classes, and at the same time to build up popular pressure from below for social reforms. The establishment of village development bodies in which the majority could apply their potential power
in the strength of numbers to force implementation of plan policies was
by itself inadequate to undermine the existing power structure.

Expectations that the landless and land-poor peasantry could use the
new village cooperative and panchayat institutions constituted on principles of universal membership and mass suffrage to shift the balance of
income, status, and power away from the dominant landed castes proved
to be unjustified. On the contrary, the propertied classes, far from being
outflanked by popular majorities, showed themselves adept at manipulating the fragmented peasantry along divisions of kinship, caste, factional,
and economic lines. They mobilized their followers and gained control
over village cooperative and panchayat bodies. Hopes that an informed
popular opinion operating through strong "peoples institutions" would
innovate new patterns of horizontal organization to apply a "nonviolent
sanction" in favor of agrarian reforms were disappointed. Deprived of
outside leadership and organization, the peasantry continued to acquiesce
in the domination of proprietor groups. Indeed, existing vertical structures were actually strengthened. The dominant landed castes, increasing both their economic and political leverage, gained access to additional resources of credit and scarce agricultural inputs introduced into
the villages by the Community Development program. They enlarged
their role as intermediaries in relationships between the village and outside authorities in both the administration and the ruling party.

Failures in implementation of institutional change not only produced social effects opposite of those intended, but impaired the entire economic and political strategy. Plan policies for agrarian reform and reorganization were at the heart of the economic framework for increasing foodgrains production, raising the level of savings, and mobilizing surpluses essential to financing large-scale industrial development schemes. As concessions to the propertied castes slowed down the tempo of institutional change, the government's capacity to raise additional rural resources for development programs declined. Growth rates fell to levels that barely kept pace with the gain in population. Related increases in the expansion of governmental functions and payrolls also showed signs of slowing down. Meanwhile, the proliferating political claims on stagnant government resources reduced the capacity of the one-party dominant system to accommodate the demands of new participants for a share of power and patronage without seriously threatening the gains of groups already in advantaged positions. Particularly destabilizing, the low ceiling on the number of new participants that could be accommodated without breaking apart the Congress party, set in at a time when lower caste groups did begin to realize the power of numbers in contesting state and national elections. In some instances, backward castes organized themselves into caste associations—embracing essentially comparable *jatis* over extended geographic areas—that deserted the dominant landowning leadership to demand independent access to the status, resources, and power controlled by state and national governments.[1]

The limitations of political accommodation as an integrative device, given an economy of scarcity and weak national commitments, took on tangible form by the early 1960s. Even though the multiplicity of factional and parochial groupings ensured that none had a clear majority, expectations that the largest groups would compromise to win power did not always prove correct. On the contrary, growing demands on static resources led to bitter internal disputes inside the Congress party. Factional alliances frequently broke down. There were constant rivalries for control over the party machinery, particularly the Pradesh Election Committees, which nominated candidates to coveted offices. Dissident elements were also active in the state legislative assemblies, using the lure of ministerial posts to induce members to "cross over" to their ranks and topple the existing ministry. Maintaining party cohesion became a full-time job. General secretaries of the national party in New Delhi as well as district and pradesh secretaries devoted more and more of their time to arbitrating factional disputes. They kept the peace by dividing and redividing among rival groups the limited resources of patronage and power available.

[1] The most influential analysis of the role of caste associations in Indian politics was developed by Lloyd and Susanne Rudolph, *The Modernity of Tradition: Political Development in India*, pp. 17-154.

This was not the only sign of political decay. At the same time as attempts to service growing demands from static resources strained the stability of the one-party dominant political system, standards of honest and efficient administration precipitously declined. Officers of the police, the judiciary, the state and local revenue and development services, and even the vaunted Indian Administrative Service, were all engaged in selling influence (often at fixed prices and graded fees) to individuals ranging from industrialists, contractors and suppliers, traders and large agriculturists, to the chief ministers and ministers of the state and central governments. As corruption became institutionalized into a distributive device, those who could not afford to pay found themselves at the bottom of the list in the allocation of access to "public" goods and services.[2]

By the early 1960s, therefore, social goals of reducing disparities and economic aims of rapid industrialization were both being sacrificed, even while the achievement of political consensus began to be imperiled by economic failures and visible signs of growing corruption. The very fact that Congress promises of rapid economic growth and reduction of disparities failed to materialize was successfully used by all opposition groups, radical and conservative, regional or communal, to denigrate the policies for democratic socialist reform embodied in the Five Year Plans. The leadership's resolve to maintain the tactical separation between techniques of "social" and "political" transformation was further tested by the conservative opposition's direct attack on the principle of planning and the Planning Commission itself. The assault, which also challenged Nehru's preeminent authority in determining principles of national policy, appeared finally to persuade him to reconsider the role of the Congress party in the process of social change.

On the eve of the third general elections, amid talk that the entire political system was falling into disrepute, Nehru gave the first sign of reassessing the accommodative style of Congress political organization. At the risk of provoking the conservative rank and file, the prime minister approved a restatement of the party's goal in the Congress election manifesto to replace the Gandhian formulation of a "cooperative commonwealth" with a more Marxist-sounding commitment to the "establishment of a socialist state." Then, reversing an earlier decision against extensive campaigning, he set out on another marathon tour, covering 14,000 miles by road, rail, and air, appearing before an estimated 20 million people, about 10 percent of the electorate. For the first time, moreover, Nehru campaigned not merely for the party as a whole, but selectively, giving his personal endorsement to candidates committed to the socialist creed.[3]

[2] See John B. Monteiro, *Corruption*, pp. 28-69.
[3] Congress Socialist Forum, *Looking into the National Mirror*, p. 9.

Yet, the results of the national elections[4] showed that even Nehru's efforts could not entirely compensate for the fact that in many areas, lack of educated and trained cadres made Congress committees ineffective as campaign organizations. Indeed, the outcome highlighted a growing dilemma of the one-party dominant system. On the one hand, Congress was ill-equipped to play a direct, mobilizing role. On the other, it was losing its capacity to perform an aggregative function as an umbrella party accommodating the demands of newly politicized groups. Party leaders reported that the "Congress was more disunited in many states this time than in the previous general election"; that Congressmen not infrequently "worked with crusading zeal to defeat a Congress candidate who would not support their choice in the leadership contest" (for leader of the Congress party in the state assembly); and that it was "more a case of Congressmen vs. Congressmen than a fight against an opposition party."[5] Altogether, partly because of such infighting, forty-nine Congress ministers were defeated, including four at the Center, as well as the chief minister of Madhya Pradesh and two potential chief ministers in Gujerat and Mysore.

The causes of the party's reverses, moreover, also had deeper roots. At the national level, about 45 percent of the electorate voted for Congress candidates to the Lok Sabha in 1962, compared to 48 percent in 1957, with a net loss to the party of 18 seats. In the states, the total vote polled by Congress for the legislative assemblies also declined somewhat from almost 45 percent in 1957 to little over 43 percent in 1962. More disturbing, the party's lead over the opposition was eroded in its strongholds of the Hindi-speaking north. In Madhya Pradesh and Rajasthan, Congress failed to win a majority, and the deterioration in neighboring states was so marked as to cause concern that "a small gust of wind may turn the scale in the next election."[6] There were also disconcerting reverses in the more highly politicized urban constituencies, particularly in major industrial centers such as Calcutta, Jamshedpur, Kanpur, Bhopal, and Madras, where workers were organized by opposition parties through their trade union affiliates. Closer analysis of the election returns did indeed show that Congress was losing its momentum, managing to win only one out of three additional votes cast in 1962 over 1957, with the greatest erosion of voter support evident among the young, illiterate, and lowest-income groups.[7]

The decline in popular support pointed up previously hidden costs to

[4] For a summary of the results, see Myron Weiner, "India's Third General Election," *Asian Survey*, 2:3 (May 1962).

[5] *Looking into the National Mirror*, p. 10.          [6] *Ibid.*, p. 9.

[7] Indian Institute of Public Opinion, Monthly Public Opinion Surveys, *An Analysis of Indian Political Behavior, 139, 140, 141*, Vol. 12, nos. 7, 8, 9 (April, May, June 1967), 12, 23.

the party of relying on "key men" in the constituencies to deliver the votes of personal followings. Not only had the party failed to organize its own loyal cadre on the basis of commitment to Congress policies, but it had neglected mass education in the specific content of Congress programs. But rural voters enjoyed wider lattitude in exercising their own opinions and choices in contests for state and national legislative bodies than they did in those for local panchayats, since the interests or personal position of village leaders usually were not directly at issue. The results of the election suggested, in fact, that vaguely defined promises of progress toward equality and social justice excited expectations of improvement, which when weighed against growing income disparities, food shortages, rising prices, unemployment, and corruption, stimulated general discontent that could as well be turned against the Congress as any other party. Indeed, the 1962 elections demonstrated that when opponents of the Congress, regional or communal, conservative or radical, could attract better disciplined and committed party workers and/or wean away alienated members of the traditional power structure, including princes, ex-zamindars, and large landowners, they could use the very slogans advanced by the Congress to win support at the polls for a direct attack on national principles of policy in failing to realize the promises made by the ruling party.

Among the more ominous signs, as all opposition parties exploited regional, communal, and caste grievances in their attempt to build up anti-Congress sentiment, was an apparent resurgence of subnational political loyalties. In Madras, the Dravida Munnetra Kazhagam (Dravidian Progressive Association), articulating longstanding resentments of the Tamil community against northern domination, launched an appeal to feelings of regional nationalism that not only attacked Hindi as the national language and demanded communal quotas in recruitment to public services, but raised the cry for separation of Dravidistan (Kerala, Andhra Pradesh, Mysore, and Tamil Nadu) from the Union of India. The campaign brought a response from the electorate that saw the DMK double its 1957 poll.[8] Similar tactics were used in the Punjab. There, the Sikh-based Akali Dal, forsaking the intercommunal alliances that had extended to merger with the Congress party between 1955 and 1960 reconstructed itself as an independent party and began a militant new drive for the creation of Punjabi Subah, a Sikh majority state. The pattern was also repeated in Assam, in the sensitive border area with China, where the Hill Leaders' Conference, agitating on behalf of demands by tribal groups pressed for local autonomy within the state.

The most serious long-term danger to the development of a national

[8] See P. Spratt, *D.M.K. in Power* (Bombay, 1970), pp. 44-46.

consensus around principles of equality, planning, secularism, and non-alignment was apprehended from the growing strength of national parties that directly challenged the Congress aim of establishing a socialist pattern of society. In particular, the Jan Sangh began to make unexpected gains. The party, formed in 1951, did not hesitate to identify its objectives in traditional terms of building a powerful nation-state around the revival of the ideals of Hindu culture (Bharatiya Sanskriti), including the religious precepts of the ancient Sanskrit tradition and the "age-old scientific principles of social organization." At the outset, moreover, the Jan Sangh had a ready-made cadre in the members of the Rashtriya Swayamasevak Sangh (National Volunteer Association). The RSS, a Hindu nationalist organization founded in 1925 to mobilize youth in the fight for India's freedom, continued to attract young men through vigorous physical strengthening and cultural education programs that also hammered away at the need to "nationalize" all non-Hindus, especially Muslims, in Hindu language and culture as the condition of building a strong and united nation. The Jan Sangh, in fact, had originally been organized as a surrogate of the RSS, when that organization had been briefly banned by the Government of India after the assassination of Mahatma Gandhi by one of its former members, and allowed to resume activities only upon a pledge that it would confine its work to cultural and social programs. Altogether, the RSS was estimated to have some 700,000 to 1,000,000 dedicated—some believed fanatic—members, organized into state, division, district, tehsil, and town units. Key posts were filled by locally influential persons nominated by a national "supreme leader" to ensure a ready response to directives from above. As individuals, moreover, RSS workers were still permitted to join any political party. They provided the backbone of the Jan Sangh organization, once the party leadership adopted virtually the entire RSS ideology.[9]

During the 1952 and 1957 elections, this cadre, drawn mainly from among urban shopkeepers, traders, professionals, and the lower ranks of the civil service, including the police, provided the election funds and campaign workers responsible for the party's modest successes in the main areas of RSS strength: the urban constituencies of Madhya Pradesh, Uttar Pradesh, and Punjab. In 1962, the party had larger ambitions. It aimed to achieve the status of official opposition in Uttar Pradesh and Madhya Pradesh, the areas of the Hindi-speaking heartland where it had previously shown its greatest strength. By this time, moreover, the party was making vigorous efforts to extend its organization outside the

[9] For a discussion of the ideology and organization of the RSS and its relationship to the founding of the Jan Sangh, see Craig Baxter, *The Jana Sangh: A Biography of an Indian Political Party*, chs. 3, 4.

Hindi-speaking areas and down to the village level. They set out to attract a more broadly based cadre of workers, enlisting college youth as
party activists by aggressive recruitment for its student affiliate, the Akhil
Bharatiya Vidyarthi Parishad. In addition, the national leadership experimented with a more cosmopolitan appeal, endorsing full guarantees
for freedom of faith and worship (albeit still stressing the importance of
Hindu culture), and giving greater importance to economic issues. Although the Jan Sangh advocated economic policies that were little different from the free enterprise program advanced by Swatantra, the party
nevertheless adopted a populist rhetoric in calling for more equitable distribution of wealth. Still, the populist slogans were advanced side-by-
side with a bitter attack on the Congress party's proposals for agrarian
reform, especially the Nagpur program for cooperative farming. That
policy was denounced as one that would both impoverish agriculturists
and deliver India to a godless political system of communism. Indeed,
Jan Sangh propaganda launched a campaign of vilification against the
Congress party—including personal attacks on Nehru—that accused the
national leadership of undermining resistance to communism at home
through secular policies that weakened religious values, while betraying
the motherland abroad in concessions to Pakistan and China that could
have been avoided by suspending doctrinaire insistence on nonalignment
and seeking American support.[10]

Improved organizational strength, more careful recruitment of local
notables as candidates (including big ex-zamindars and talukdars in rural
areas), and populist rhetoric had a positive, albeit modest effect at the
polls. Overall, the increase in popular vote for the Jan Sangh was less
than 1 percent at the Center, rising from 5.9 percent in 1957 to 6.4 percent in 1962; and 2 percent at the state level, up from 4 percent in 1957 to
6 percent in 1962. The major difference, however, was the party's growing effectiveness as an electoral organization in maximizing the number
of seats won. Jan Sangh representatives increased in the Lok Sabha from
4 to 14 members; and in the state assemblies from 46 to 116 MLAs. The
party achieved its main goal, moreover, of emerging as the official opposition (with at least 10 percent of the seats) in both Uttar Pradesh and

---

[10] Jan Sangh propaganda—as described by Congressmen—was said to portray leaders of
the ruling party as "anti-Hindu," men who had no respect for Hindu temples or sacred
places; fostered intercaste and intercommunal marriage; encouraged large-scale cow slaughter to supply government-owned hotels with beef; and were cowards who betrayed the
national interest in acceding to Pakistani and Chinese occupation of Indian territory. Nehru
himself was often the personal target of such villification. One story told was that the
government-owned Asoka Hotel in New Delhi had been built especially to prepare beef for
his meals. "For this purpose, a cow in very advanced stage of pregnancy is brought and five
people jump on it. The ejected calf is then cooked for the P.M.'s meals." See H. D.
Malaviya, *The Danger of Right Reaction*, A Socialist Congressman Publication, pp. 36,
42-43.

Madhya Pradesh. In Uttar Pradesh, the key state in Indian electoral politics, the Jan Sangh managed to win over 17 percent of the popular vote. More significant, it made its greatest inroads in rural areas.[11]

Among the national leadership, the Jan Sangh's successes were received with special alarm that went beyond chronic concern about the resurgence of "communal tendencies." Congress socialists, in particular, perceived the Jan Sangh as a quasi-fascist organization using communal, populist, and militarist appeals to focus resentment for economic hardships at home and losses of Indian territory to enemies abroad against a religious minority, while relying for finances and leadership on upper-caste Hindus, including "a number of Zamindars, Rajas, Maharajas and other rich landed interests in our country" eager to exploit communalism as a diversionary tactic in resisting demands for social reform.[12] Such apprehensions were reinforced, moreover, by the impressive performance of the conservative Swatantra party in its first effort at the polls.

Swatantra, a new organization lacking its own cadre, was nevertheless able to attract locally influential leaders of the opposition who previously had put together small regional parties or entered local politics as independents. One fertile recruiting ground was among the former princes. In Orissa, the Ganatantra Parishad, then the second strongest party in the state, merged with Swatantra after its leadership found the principles of the new party "remarkably similar to the ideals of the Ganatantra Parishad."[13] Similarly, in Bihar the Janta party, at that time the third largest in the state, led by the Raja of Ramgarh, merged with Swatantra in an effort to expand its power for a continuing assault against the state Congress leadership over the abolition of zamindari rights. Ex-princes and former zamindars also provided the leadership core for Swatantra party units in Rajasthan, Uttar Pradesh, and Punjab. The party, in addition, attracted substantial support from upper-caste groups, especially the landed Rajput castes organized in Kshatriya caste associations in northern India. Individually and collectively, the ex-rulers, ex-zamindars, and large landowners put their "vote banks" built on traditional ties of kinship, caste, and economic dependence at the disposal of the Swatantra party. Like the Jan Sangh, moreover, the Swatantra leadership echoed the Congress in promising greater equality and social justice for the common man, while simultaneously waging a relentless attack on the Nagpur proposals "to defend the interest of the people oppressed by the State."[14] Swatantra leaders accused the Congress party collectively and Nehru personally of preparing the ground for com-

[11] Baxter, *The Jana Sangh*, pp. 217-23.
[12] Malaviya, *The Danger of Right Reaction*, p. 38.
[13] Erdman, *The Swatantra Party and Indian Conservatism*, p. 117.
[14] Malaviya, *The Danger of Right Reaction*, p. 51.

munism in India by adopting policies for joint farming that amounted to confiscation of property and an end to political freedom.

Such propaganda was effective. Congress workers traveling in rural areas reported growing support for the Jan Sangh and Swatantra among peasant landowners. Longtime national leaders found themselves on the defensive. G. L. Nanda reported he was "appalled to see that half my energy during the five weeks or so of the campaign had to be spent simply defending myself and the Congress on the question of cooperative farming. In that area, everybody was told the Congress wanted to take away the peasant's land."[15] In the end, Swatantra polled about 8 percent of the popular vote in the national election, to become the third largest party after Congress and the CPI in the Lok Sabha. At the state level, where it won about 7 percent of the votes polled, Swatantra secured the second largest total of assembly seats, emerging as the largest opposition party in four states: Bihar, Gujerat, Rajasthan, and Orissa.[16]

Assessing the combined gains of Jan Sangh and Swatantra, some Congress leaders believed they were witnessing the emergence for the first time of "a right reactionary opposition in an organized way" that signalled the determination of the propertied classes to "fight with all resources at their command and resort to all means and methods without any scruples" to protect their position. Ex-princes, former zamindars, and large landowners, after ten years of seeming quiescence, "somehow felt themselves strong enough to cast off their masks of meekness and come out openly and defiantly in opposition to Nehru and the Indian National Congress."[17] The prospect of more formal collaboration between the Jan Sangh and Swatantra could also not be ignored. Although Swatantra's leaders were generally repelled by the blatant communal appeal used by Jan Sangh, the two parties shared a broad area of agreement in challenging Nehru's policies on socialism and planning. Together, they might maximize their political impact. The resources of capitalism potentially available to Swatantra in the vast financial assets of the major business houses and control over important English-language newspapers, joined to the grass-roots organization of the Hindu communalist movement commanded by the Jan Sangh through its RSS cadre, raised the specter of a strong party on the right that could attract sufficient mass support to mount a serious challenge to Congress dominance. Separately or in combination, moreover, the Jan Sangh, as well as Swatantra, had already demonstrated their ability through manipulation of traditional ideals and power structures to "utilize the ignorance and subservience of

[15] G. L. Nanda, "Origin of Congress Forum for Socialist Action," *Journal of the Congress Forum for Socialist Action*, 1:1 (August 15, 1962), 22.

[16] Indian National Congress, *The Fourth General Elections, A Statistical Analysis*, pp. 71, 79.

[17] Malaviya, *The Danger of Right Reaction*, pp. 117, 122.

the erstwhile beneficiaries [of socialist reforms] to defeat the Congress and Congress programs."[18] In fact, in the absence of any effort by the Congress party at direct political propaganda and organization, the bulk of the peasantry could probably be kept fragmented almost indefinitely along caste and communal lines. The Congress party's own organizational pattern of vertical mobilization through leaders of the dominant landowning castes was a powerful contributing factor in strengthening the traditional system. It reinforced factional structures that perpetuated the division of the lower castes and excluded them from direct access to external sources of power. It even seemed possible that the Congress system might ultimately frustrate whatever potential did exist for peaceful social mobilization of the peasantry through the democratic process. Assuming that universal suffrage and an open electoral process ultimately did expand effective participation to accelerate the emergence of class consciousness among the most impoverished sections of the peasantry, new horizontal alignments could be expected to seek political expression through parties of the radical left rather than those committed to democratic socialism.

An incipient polarization was already discernible. By the early 1960s the share of the democratic Socialist parties (other than Congress) in the total vote had noticeably declined. The PSP's percentage of the popular vote was reduced from more than 10 percent in 1957 to 6.4 percent in 1962. The newly formed Socialist party, a splinter group of the PSP led by Rammanohar Lohia, contributed to this attrition, although by itself it was able to attract less than 3 percent of the vote.[19] By contrast, the communists held their own, improving their poll slightly from almost 9 percent in 1957 to approximately 10 percent in 1962, and maintaining their position as the largest opposition in the Lok Sabha.[20] At the state level, although communist strength declined somewhat from more than 9 percent of the votes cast in 1957 to 8.5 percent in 1962,[21] more effective electoral strategies, including united front alliances to minimize the advantage of Congress against a fragmented opposition, succeeded in consolidating regional bases of support. In West Bengal, the United Left Front (the CPI-led alliance) commanded almost one-third of the popular vote. The CPI alone, concentrating its efforts in local strongholds, in-

[18] Nanda, "Origin of the Congress Forum for Socialist Action," p. 22.

[19] R. Chandidas, Ward Morehouse, Leon Clark, and Richard Fontera, *India Votes*, pp. 256, 261-62.

[20] *Ibid.*, pp. 256-57.

[21] The apparent decline in the vote for the communists at the state level is actually an artifact created by excluding from the valid votes cast during the Third General Election votes won by the CPI in the February 1960 mid-term election in Kerala, which did not go to the polls in 1962. Once these votes are added to the total won by the communists at the state level, they register a modest improvement from 9.3 percent in 1957 to 10.6 percent in 1962. *Ibid.*, Table ii-5, p. 718.

creased its vote from approximately 18 percent in 1957 to almost 25 percent in 1962, closing part of the gap between itself and the Congress party, whose support remained relatively constant at 47 percent.[22] The CPI's gains in West Bengal, moreover, were not confined to urban constituencies. The returns indicated the party's growing ability to expand the base of its popular support into rural areas.[23] In Andhra Pradesh and Kerala, the two other areas of CPI strength, the party's support in rural constituencies was already well established. The situation in Kerala, moreover, despite the success of the anticommunist opposition's "Liberation Struggle" against the Communist ministry that had forced imposition of President's Rule in July 1959, did not justify the general impression that communism in Kerala had been defeated. The mid-term election in February 1960, which saw the Congress party enter into an electoral alliance with the PSP and the Muslim League, did inflict major losses of seats on the CPI, and effectively prevented the formation of another united front government. Yet the CPI, which campaigned on its accomplishments in introducing the agrarian relations act and passing the education act, was able to rely on loyal village cadres from among the landless and Harijan classes to maintain and even increase its voter support in the rural areas. Although Nehru had personally spearheaded the Congress electoral campaign in Kerala, the 1960 poll revealed that in the three years since 1957, the proportion of the total vote won by the Congress party decreased from 37.4 percent to 34.5 percent. At the same time, the share of the Communists rose from 35 percent to 36.7 percent. If votes polled for communist-supported independents were included, moreover, the CPI had managed to mobilize almost 44 percent of the popular vote.[24]

Meanwhile, at the national level, there were signs that the communists were attempting to use the tactical line of peaceful transition first tested in Kerala to rally support of disillusioned supporters of Congress and other democratic socialist parties. As in Kerala, the CPI emphasized that its immediate aim was to execute Congress policies the government had failed in carrying out. Indeed, the CPI leadership expressed solidarity with "progressive" Congress candidates in constituencies where it had no candidate of its own, and even offered to support Congressmen of more conservative stripe who were thought to be in a fight against "reactionaries."

Thus, by 1962, there was an emerging pattern which showed the opposition vote slowly polarizing around conservative communal and

[22] Marcus F. Franda, *Radical Politics in West Bengal*, pp. 116, 126.
[23] Myron Weiner and John Osgood Field, "India's Urban Constituencies."
[24] Fic, *Kerala: Yenan of India*, pp. 70, 497.

capitalist parties on the one hand, and the Communists on the other. The rationale for the Congress party's role as an instrument of national consensus was significantly weakened. The socialists inside Congress envisaged that popular support for the principles of the party would shrink at both ends of the political spectrum, so that "Congress would appear as a party of the Centre which will have to fight two diametrically opposed forces at the same time."[25] Assessment of the meaning of the election results by the more conservative opinion represented in the English-language press was broadly similar. Political observers linked together the strong showing of Swatantra and Jan Sangh as evidence of voter disaffection with the Congress variety of democratic socialism. The *Hindu* noted signs of a "developing contest between pragmatic socialism of the Congress . . . and the extremism of the Communists on the one side, and on the other, the progressive liberalism of the Swatantra and Jan Sangh parties, with their emphasis on limits to the State's incursions in the economic field and greater realism in planning."[26]

Almost immediately after the elections, the socialist and Gandhian contingent inside Congress once again approached Nehru about the necessity of taking "energetic efforts to bring about greater ideological awareness and homogeneity in the ranks of the Congress."[27] Earlier hopes that the Congress Socialist Forum, organized in December 1957, would take up this task had been disappointed. The Forum, which failed to attract more than a dozen MPs, functioned only as a discussion group in socialist theory, mainly with reference to planning. By contrast, the need was for an action-oriented body that could exert pressure within the party on behalf of effective implementation of plan policies. In May 1962, Gulzarilal Nanda, then home minister, began to canvass support for the formation of a new Congress Forum for Socialist Action, one that would consider the content of the socialist pattern in terms of specific measures and programs and assist in the implementation of resolutions adopted by the Congress, especially the programs embodied in the Five Year Plans. Nanda's suggestion found support among several longtime socialist and Gandhian MPs, as well as a small nucleus of young "radicals" just succeeding to positions of leadership in the state PCCs. The younger members, who took their lead from the Congress party's 1962 election manifesto calling for the establishment of a socialist state, believed that immediate action was imperative to arrest the loss of popular support for the party, especially among younger voters disillusioned by the gap between Congress promises and performance. Al-

[25] *Looking into the National Mirror*, p. 11.
[26] Cited in Baxter, *The Jana Sangh*, p. 231.
[27] *Looking into the National Mirror*, p. 11.

though Nehru was still uneasy that the Forum might function in a "group way,"[28] this time he appeared receptive to arguments in favor of consolidating a socialist core. Indeed, he endorsed the Working Committee's approval of the organization of the Forum in August 1962, and inaugurated its first meeting.

Nehru's motives in lending his personal prestige to the formation of a separate socialist group inside the party must remain a matter of speculation. The younger socialists, at least, regarded the organization of the Forum as the first step toward redefining the role of the Congress party in the strategy of social transformation.

The "nonpolitical" approach to social and economic reform through institutional changes aimed at improving the position of the poor peasantry relative to larger landowners, launched under cover of the Community Development program, was widely recognized to have failed. Well-entrenched elites, exploiting traditional peasant ties to caste, community, and faction, captured control of the people's institutions and immobilized them as agencies for redistribution of income, status, and power. Certain elements of the peasantry realized the advantage of large numbers in organizing for united action within the framework of universal suffrage and party competition. But even they were fearful of defying local notables who could retaliate with impunity as long as they monopolized access to external sources of political authority. Class conciliation methods had to rely on the local administration to carry out mass-oriented rural improvement schemes. However, under these circumstances, with the Congress party claiming to represent all interests, including those of the propertied castes, conciliation worked only to deprive the village poor of leadership and organization in demanding effective implementation of plan policies. The best possibility of bringing to bear the primary resources of the poor in their superior numbers rested on outside intervention by a committed party cadre. An attempt at direct peasant mobilization could raise mass consciousness through propaganda aimed at introducing issue-oriented politics. It could also spearhead effective grass-roots organization by recruiting from among members of the poorer castes with the greatest stake in change; and most important, it could provide protection for local cadres by building reliable new relationships between them and sources of power beyond the village.

The younger socialists in Congress saw no alternative but to end the tactical separation between "social" and "political" issues that had characterized the national leadership's approach to social transformation since the early days of the independence movement. They were convinced that

---

[28] Nehru's letter endorsing the forum is cited in G. L. Nanda, "Origin of the Forum for Socialist Action."

the Congress party would have to give up its umbrella character. The leaders of the Forum envisaged a fundamental change in the composition of the party to "face squarely the consequences of the acceptance of socialism."[29] The Congress, according to this view, had to weed out "capitalist men, casteist-orthodox men, feudal men" and to create a committed cadre "imbued with the spirit of socialism."[30]

In the summer of 1962, steps were taken which only years later were to appear critical to the development of the Congress party. The Congress Forum for Socialist Action, working out of AICC headquarters in New Delhi, took some preliminary initiatives toward setting up the new framework of its organization inside the party. Starting with an initial membership of some 17 MPs in the central "section," the Forum envisaged the organization of sections corresponding to the various levels of party organization, reaching down to the state, district, and mandal units. Each section was to have its own steering committee drawn from persons whose "principal source of income is earnings from personal work," and who were either full-time workers in the Congress party or in some field of constructive work. Initial plans called for a small cadre of paid full-time workers, two or three at the Center, at least one in every state, a minimum of ten workers for a district, and three or four workers per Block to act as an auxiliary team to official personnel in implementation of national plan policies.[31] The organizational task, which fell to Nanda as the founder of the Forum, was pursued through a series of visits to the states that enlisted at least the formal support of the chief ministers and the presidents of the Pradesh Congress Committees. By the early months of 1963, Nanda reported successes in organizing units of the Forum in several states, including Madras, Punjab, Bihar, and Uttar Pradesh.

Confrontation between the leadership and those who opposed the socialist pattern developed much sooner than the socialists expected, however, and not by their choice. Moreover, it led at least temporarily to the virtually total eclipse of their influence inside the party. The precipitating factor, as in 1959, was another external challenge mounted by China on India's borders, this time with devastating effect. A large-scale Chinese offensive, launched on October 23, 1962, in both NEFA and Ladakh, inflicted major casualties on an ill-equipped Indian army, and resulted in Chinese occupation of some 14,500 square miles of territory claimed by India.

Overnight, Nehru's policy of *panchsheel* and the essential principles of

---

[29] G. L. Nanda, "Address to the Inaugural Meeting of Delhi State Unit of Congress Forum for Socialist Action," in *Socialist Congressman*, 2:8 (August 1, 1962), 6.
[30] Malaviya, *The Danger of Right Reaction*, pp. 357, 360.
[31] Nanda, "Origin of the Forum for Socialist Action."

nonalignment were exposed to public ridicule. Indeed, by the time the Chinese announced a surprising unilateral withdrawal on December 1, Nehru had himself felt compelled not only to request immediate American military aid to India, including an airlift of infantry weapons and light equipment for troops fighting on the border, and even American-piloted transport planes, but had authorized a formal request to Washington for consideration of a joint air defense, involving American air cover for Indian cities in order to free India's air force for tactical raids against the Chinese. As hundreds of U.S. military advisors and air force personnel descended on New Delhi, the American ambassador recorded that "even the word non–alignment has disappeared from everything but the Prime Minister's speeches and the left wing press, and there is lively discussion as to whether we will insist on it" (that is, on formal repudiation of nonalignment).[32]

The most ferocious assaults were directed at Nehru's friend of thirty years, the defense minister, V. K. Krishna Menon, a staunch leftist, with an inappropriate preference not for mountain divisions but for investment in highly advanced technologies, including supersonic planes that were still on the drawing boards. But the attacks went further, this time to challenge the prime minister's role as the arbiter of national policy. Nehru's judgment in endorsing the policies of his defense minister was called into question. Some critics suggested that the prime minister's "doctrinaire socialist thinking" was to blame for government's failure to recognize the necessity of preparedness for a land war against China, which as an avowedly socialist state had been considered by definition to be a peaceful neighbor. Members of the national Congress party leadership including the Working Committee and the Congress parliamentary party, all of whom had routinely deferred to Nehru on all major decisions since 1950, were adamant in insisting that Menon be dismissed as minister of defense. Within two weeks of the first Chinese offensive, Nehru, unable to resist the demands of colleagues, removed Menon from all positions inside the government. The forced ouster of the defense minister, moreover, was followed within a few months by the exit of the minister of mines and fuel, K. D. Malaviya, after a concerted attack by the opposition raised a barrage of charges that he had misused election funds. Malaviya, the architect of the public-sector oil industry and a founder of the Congress Forum for Socialist Action, had long been, with Menon, Nehru's mainstay inside the Cabinet on domestic policies of socialism and economic planning. Indeed, almost from the first day that a National Emergency was declared in response to the Chinese attack, the issue of military preparedness was used by opponents of the

---

[32] John Kenneth Galbraith, *Ambassador's Journal*, p. 512.

public sector to undermine the entire planning effort through arguments for a major reduction in expenditure on industrial projects in favor of defense during the Third Plan.

Purely in economic terms, the rationale for a reorientation of national development policy toward a primary role for private enterprise was powerful. There were clear signs that the Third Plan was falling into deepening crisis. Progress in the vital agricultural sector was stalemated. Foodgrains production in 1961/62 showed no improvement over the previous year, and in 1962/63 registered a decline. Production of sugar cane, oilseeds, and cotton also dropped below previous levels. Progress in the industrial sector was somewhat more encouraging. Even so, the rate of increase in production of 6.5 percent in 1961/62 and 8 percent in 1962/63 was well below the average annual target of 14 percent. Shortages of imported materials, coal, and power, as well as transportation bottlenecks delayed both public and private-sector projects. The failure to increase agricultural production once again had the greatest negative impact, affecting raw materials supplies and depressing demand for products of major consumer goods industries. Indeed, the static production levels in agriculture were mainly responsible for pushing down the overall gains of the economy in the first two years of the Plan to an average annual increase of 2.5 percent, roughly the same rate as that of population growth. By the first half of 1962, there were warning signs of another inflationary price spiral that could threaten the cost structure of Plan projects. Between March and August, the level of wholesale prices rose by over 6 percent, led by the increase in foodgrains prices of more than 9 percent. Added to these pressures was a growing strain on the balance of payments, starting toward the end of 1962.[33]

Even before the Emergency, the finance ministry had run into difficulties in providing for planned development outlay within the limits of deficit financing considered safe for the five-year period. In the first year of the Third Plan, total Plan outlay of Rs. 1,130 crores was achieved at the cost of deficit financing amounting to Rs. 168 crores, almost one-third of the total of Rs. 524 crores visualized for the entire five-year period. Part of the problem was the increasing dependence of the states on central grants and loans to finance aggregate expenditures, as they failed to levy measures of additional taxation that could tap the resource potential of the rural sector. Compared to the First and Second Plans, when central assistance had contributed approximately 41 percent and 48 percent, respectively, of total budgetary expenditure at the state level, this proportion climbed to 52 percent in 1961/62—with the proportion of de-

[33] For a detailed review of economic performance during the first two years of the Third Plan, see Planning Commission, *The Third Plan, Mid-Term Appraisal*.

velopment expenditure financed by transfer of resources from the Center to the states reaching 56 percent.[34]

The impact of the Emergency on the already strained budgetary position appeared devastating. The 1962/63 budget, which had managed to increase total Plan outlay to Rs. 1,414 crores, while holding deficit financing to Rs. 90 crores, provided Rs. 376 crores for defense. But in November, a supplementary provision of Rs. 95 crores had to be voted, and an additional Rs. 13 crores was spent. In addition to this extra burden, the Center was once again called upon to increase its assistance to the states to 54 percent of total expenditure, and a record 62 percent of development expenditure. The overall budgetary deficit climbed to Rs. 240 crores. In the first two years of the Third Plan, deficit financing totalled Rs. 408 crores, or 70 percent of the amount considered safe for the entire five-year period.[35] The long-term prospect, moreover, was for a substantially enlarged defense effort at more than double 1962/63 levels of expenditure of well over Rs. 800 crores per annum.

The chief ministers of the states who gathered for the November 1962 meeting of the National Development Council to discuss the Annual Plan for 1963/64 were therefore confident in arguing for a substantial reduction in Plan outlay, and much greater reliance on the private sector to carry out development schemes, while stepping up public outlays on defense. This time, however, Nehru refused to give way. In an impassioned speech that defied the opposition, he insisted that the Plan as a whole, and in particular the program of development in heavy and intermediate industries, was vitally connected to defense efforts, and that allocations to these projects should in fact be increased. The chief ministers, still sufficiently uncertain at the outcome of taking differences with Nehru to the public, decided once again to acquiesce. It was only this show of determination by Nehru, "in set[ting] his face firmly against any attempt to nibble away at the Plan from within that made it possible to continue the Plan."[36] At the subsequent meeting of the National Development Council in January 1963, the chief ministers reaffirmed that the Plan was essential for defense, and even agreed to adjustments in the allocation of total investment that reduced expenditures under social services, major and medium irrigation projects, and village and small-scale industries, to provide a modest increase in outlays on power, industry, and minerals.

Even if Nehru had once again succeeded in enforcing a "consensus" within his own party, the unprecedented effort at resource mobilization

[34] *Reserve Bank of India Bulletin* (Bombay, May 1966), p. 507.
[35] *The Third Plan, Mid-Term Appraisal*, pp. 32-39; Ministry of Finance, *Budget for 1963-64* (Delhi, 1963), p. 142.
[36] Tarlok Singh, *Toward an Integrated Society*, p. 264.

needed to finance both development and greatly increased defense expenditures set him on a collision course with the business community
that rapidly assumed the character of a confrontation on basic principles
of economic policy. The 1963/64 budget, presented to the Lok Sabha on
February 28, 1963, by the finance minister, Morarji Desai, reflected
Nehru's mandate that the full claims both of defense and development
must be met. Total outlay essential to the defense effort was estimated at
Rs. 867 crores, an increase of Rs. 491 crores over 1962/63 levels. At the
same time, a step-up in total Plan expenditure of Rs. 237 crores (from
Rs. 1,414 crores in 1962/63 to Rs. 1,651 crores in 1963/64) was required to
maintain the momentum of development. A review of all sources of revenue revealed a budgetary gap of Rs. 454 crores, "aris[ing] almost entirely from the increase in Defense outlays."[37] The finance minister, citing the "chaos of inflation" that would be caused by leaving the gap
uncovered, soberly informed the members of parliament, "Earlier in the
year, it was my hope and expectation that having raised taxation in the
first two years of the Plan to meet nearly 80 percent of the target for the
Third Five Year Plan, it would be possible to provide for all essential requirements this year without any significant additional taxation. But the
new threat on our borders had made it necessary for me to come to the
House with proposals for a much higher order of taxation. . . . I am
deeply conscious of the fact that the scale of taxation I am about to propose is going to impose an unprecedented burden."[38]

The finance minister at first had recourse to conventional methods—a
general surcharge on all import duties and selective additional increases
on a number of articles; selective surcharges on central excise duties over
a wide range of articles consisting mostly of "luxury items consumed by
the more well to do classes"; an additional surcharge on the incomes after
tax of individuals and Hindu joint families; a surcharge on the income tax
payable by registered firms, and an absolute limit on tax deductions by
companies for expenditures on remuneration and perquisites for employees. Yet, with all this, the budgetary gap still yawned wide at over
Rs. 200 crores.

Desai's solution to this dilemma was to propose new forms of taxation
that appeared finally to unleash the long-feared attack on the prerogatives
of private property. In proposals that evoked the recommendations endorsed by the Congress party in the Nagpur Resolution on Planning, the
budget called for an absolute ceiling on returns to capital; and a nationwide scheme for compulsory savings. The first proposal, the super-
profits tax, was presented as a remedy for the shortcoming of the existing system of corporate taxation, namely that "there is no correlation
between the rate of tax and the percentage of profits."[39] The super-

[37] *Budget for 1963-64*, p. 146.          [38] *Ibid*.
[39] *Ibid*., p. 153.

profits tax was to be imposed on companies when their income, after deducting the income tax and surcharges payable by them, exceeded 6 percent of their capital and reserves. The rate of tax was a minimum of 50 percent of the income above six percent but under ten percent, and 60 percent of the income above 10 percent. The second proposal, for a compulsory deposit scheme, provided for the collection of progressively scaled compulsory deposits (subject to specified maxima), withdrawable after five years, and bearing simple interest of 4 percent per annum, from individual taxpayers, urban property owners, and landowners liable to land revenue payment.[40] Inasmuch as the collection of compulsory savings in the rural sector depended on the introduction and enforcement of legislation by the states, however, the immediate and effective focus of the scheme was once again the urban taxpayer.

The business community was outraged. Assaulted by the combination of additional indirect taxes, surcharges on income, and the punishing super-profits tax—all of which were expected to raise the entire cost structure of industry and depress incentives for investment—they reacted with an attack on the economic policies of the government that went beyond these specific measures to indict the very principle of planning and the Planning Commission itself. The Federation of Indian Chambers of Commerce and Industry, accusing the Planning Commission of being more interested in meeting high investment targets than ensuring that expenditures led to commensurate increases in production, charged the government with failure on all economic fronts. Demanding recognition for the dominant role of private enterprise in development programs, they insisted on an end to limitations on spheres of activity, and elimination of the multiple rules and regulatory arrangements under which private companies had to operate.

The Jan Sangh and Swatantra vigorously joined in the attack. Spokesmen for Swatantra issued a blanket indictment of all government intervention in the development of nondefense industries. According to Swatantra:

> Apart from defense industries, on which Government should concentrate in this period of emergency, it would leave the development of large-scale industries largely to private enterprise. Private enterprise which put up the great Tata Steel Factory and the textile and cement factories can be trusted to starting large-scale industries in steel and machine tools and heavy machines, according to the proved needs of the country. The Swatantra Party feels that Government must keep out of business and industry. . . . But, while keeping out of industry, Government, according to the Swatantra

---

[40] The text of the Super Profits Tax Bill, 1963, and the Compulsory Deposit Scheme Bill, 1963, are reproduced *ibid*., pp. 377-404.

plan will help private enterprise, giving facilities and aids in regard to the securing of capital from inside and outside the country, raw materials, technical equipment, by the abolition of the system of permits, licenses, quotas.[41]

Nehru's initial reaction to his critics was only moderate concern, in the belief that they could be discredited through a vigorous restatement of his personal determination to continue basic Plan policies and programs. In April 1963, he used the occasion of the AICC debate on the Chinese invasion to warn his detractors that he was well aware of their tactics in using India's military difficulties for a general attack on longstanding principles of national policy, and served notice that such efforts would be firmly resisted. The official AICC Resolution on the "Chinese Aggression" included this strong passage:

> While the Government of India are striving hard to meet the Chinese menace, certain elements in our country are taking advantage of this difficult situation to launch an attack on the cherished ideals and policies for which the Congress Organization has all along firmly stood and which form the basis for the various programmes and policies of the Congress Governments at the Centre and in the States. We are pledged to establish a socialist society to be achieved within the framework of a democratic pattern through a planned economy. In international affairs we have adopted the policy of non-alignment and it is our objective to work for the establishment of world peace. Attempts are now being made to cast doubts on the soundness and validity of these policies and programmes by reactionary and vested interests. The All-India Congress Committee wishes to reaffirm its unflinching faith in these policies and programmes which are not only good in themselves but are in the best interests of the country.[42]

The assault on government policies led by business interests and the conservative opposition nevertheless suddenly assumed more serious dimensions. A series of parliamentary by-elections in the spring of 1963 revealed further evidence of general discontent. More striking, it appeared that popular disappointments could be harnessed by consolidated opposition parties for a successful attack against the faction-ridden Congress, to undermine the credibility of the ruling party and by extension to challenge Nehru's preeminent leadership role.

[41] M. Ruthnaswamy, "The Swatantra Idea of Planning," *Swarajya* (November 9, 1963), p. 11.
[42] All India Congress Committee Meeting, New Delhi, 6 and 7 April, 1963, "Chinese Aggression," mimeographed, p. 3.

The contests occurred in three constituencies that were considered "safe" for the Congress party: Amroha and Farukhabad in Nehru's home state of Uttar Pradesh, and Rajkot in Gujerat. The opposition, determined to use the elections as an opportunity to challenge and ridicule both the military and economic policies of the government, put up their most outstanding candidates. Each was also known to be a prominent personal adversary of Nehru: Rammanohar Lohia of the Socialist party in Farukhabad; Acharya J. B. Kripalani, running as an independent in Amroha; and Minoo Masani, representing Swatantra in Rajkot. The Congress party, accepting the challenge, gave nominations to figures of national prominence, including ministers in the Union Cabinet (in Amroha and Farukhabad), and a sitting member of the Rajya Sabha (in Rajkot). They then called upon the electorate to vote for the Congress and demonstrate their support of the prime minister and the government.

In each case of the by-elections, the Congress party candidate was defeated. The opposition exulted that the result demonstrated a popular vote of no confidence against the government for its inept handling of military and economic affairs. In fact, attempts to explain Congress policies and problems of implementation to the voters had been, at best, superficial. Factionalism was increasingly paralyzing the local Congress party organizations and undermining the entire structure of mass support for the national leadership. In all three constituencies, Congress workers demonstrated greater loyalty to local factional leaders than to the national party, and canvassed for the official nominee only if he was also the faction's preferred candidate. Even then, with district Congress organizations badly divided by personal rivalries, it was difficult to mount a vigorous campaign. Workers in the field, cut off from a unified election command, made half-hearted efforts at direct voter contact, rarely visiting villages off the main roads, or even arranging public meetings, and relied instead on "key men" (whose loyalty to the nominee was itself uncertain in the context of local rivalries) to "deliver" the popular vote. By contrast, the opposition forces made strenuous efforts to cooperate and to mobilize a large contingent of campaign workers. In Amroha, all of the opposition parties, except the Communists, rallied around Kripalani, with the Jan Sangh in particular providing disciplined volunteers, including RSS cadres, for sustained village work. The pattern was similar in Farukhabad. Lohia, drawing support from the Jan Sangh no less than the socialists, was able to deploy thousands of workers in the rural areas during the final week of the campaign. In Rajkot, logistics were even better. Swatantra managed excellent coordination of its campaign through a well-funded and staffed district election office. It arranged separate meetings with leaders presenting all different sections of the voters and factions within these sections, and also imported prominent party workers from outside the constituency to make contact with voters sharing common regional, linguistic, caste, and professional backgrounds. In addition, Masani rallied the support of both the PSP and Jan Sangh, the latter once again supplying RSS volunteers for sustained campaigning in the villages.[43]

The most incisive analysis of the organizational weaknesses contributing to Congress defeats was offered in an election post-mortem carried out by the AICC's own By-Election Committee. The report drew a vivid picture of the organizational decay undermining the effectiveness of national policies. It concluded:

> The most decisive single factor in determining the outcome of elections to the legislatures in the present circumstances, so far as the Congress is concerned, is the state of its own organization. Allied to it is the question of the image of the Congress as reflected in the minds of the people. In both these directions we are confronted with serious deficiencies and a considerable setback.
>
> . . . wherever Congress has had to face defeat, it was in most cases due to the fact that in these areas it had no organization worth the name at various levels which could assemble the pro-Congress forces and direct the operations effectively. . . . What is worse the Congress personnel is hopelessly divided. Factionalism is so pervasive that one can see only the groups and there is little left of the Congress in these places. The dissensions and mutual vilifications create on the one hand a revulsion of feeling against the Congress among the people and lead to a paralysis of Congress activity on the other.
>
> . . . The ideology of the Congress, its economic and social goals, and short and long term strategy, figures very little in the thinking and day to day life of the Congress. The pivot around which Congress activity revolves is the personality through whom preferment can be obtained and not the aims and purpose of the party. . . . The influence of the Congress in such cases is restricted to the personal hold of some leaders who are associated with the Congress. The campaigns of Congress candidates are thus not backed by an efficient machinery. Ad hoc arrangements have to be made and the elections have to be fought on almost a personal basis. The workers who go

[43] For a detailed analysis of the three by-elections see: Bashiruddin Ahmed, "Congress Defeat in Amroha—A Case in One Party Dominance"; Ramashray Roy, "Congress Defeat in Farukhabad—A Failure of Party Organization"; and Rushikesh Maru, "Fall of a Traditional Congress Stronghold," all in Centre for the Study of Developing Societies, *Party System and Election Studies*, pp. 164-242.

about canvassing on behalf of the candidate are mobilized for the occasion and in many cases cease to be workers of the Congress for normal work.[44]

Whatever the real causes of the party's defeat, Nehru's personal prestige, already shaken by the challenge to nonalignment in the aftermath of the Chinese attack, was further undermined by evidence of slippage in popular support for government policies. The opposition was encouraged in its frontal assault on Nehru's preeminent leadership role. In August 1963, for the first time since he assumed office, Nehru found himself the target of a no-confidence motion introduced into the Lok Sabha. The thrust of the opposition's attack this time aimed at failures in national economic policy. The theme of debate, amplified by members of the conservative as well as socialist opposition, was that Nehru's brand of socialism had failed to achieve the primary goal of improving the well-being of the overwhelming majority of the population. Rammanohar Lohia, dramatizing the charge, cited estimates that two-thirds of the population continued to earn an average of three annas a day (approximately four cents). Nehru, attempting to offer a rebuttal, could do no better than to argue the figure was five times as high, about fifteen annas a day (almost twenty cents). The Planning Commission, drawn into the Lok Sabha debate with the request to issue an authoritative estimate, disputed Lohia's figure as too low, but had to concede it was closer to reality than the one used by Nehru.[45]

Meanwhile, Nehru's authority within his own party to command even formal support for the basic principles of economic and social policy was dramatically eroding. Indeed, in May 1963 he was subjected to public humiliation when a large number of Congress MPs failed to support the government on a vital constitutional amendment to protect the validity of legislation for ceilings on landholdings challenged by a Supreme Court decision the previous year. The issue arose out of the court's ruling that the Kerala Agrarian Relations Act (1961) did not come under protection of Article 31A of the constitution, which excluded all laws for the state acquisition of "any estate or rights therein" from the guarantees of property contained in Articles 31, 14, 19, and 25 (1). The court argued that Article 31A referred only to such tenures as were estates in local law on January 26, 1950, when the constitution came into force. Since ryotwari tenures were not "estates" under Keralan law, the court proceeded to rule that the compensation provisions of the Kerala Agrarian Relations

[44] AICC, *Bye-Elections Committee Report*, pp. 2-5.
[45] According to rough estimates worked out in the Planning Commission, two-thirds of the population were earning an average of 7.5 annas a day, approximately 10 cents. Interview, Joint Secretary, Planning Commission, August 27, 1963.

Act were ultra vires of the constitution on grounds they violated the guarantees of Article 14 granting every person equality before the law. First, the compensation formula, based on a graduated scale of multiples of net income, was discriminatory among persons. Second, the artificial definition of the family as mother, father, and minor sons, was discriminatory of minor children inasmuch as they lost the right to an equal share of the family property with adult sons who had already attained their majority.

The Supreme Court's decision struck at the heart of all existing land ceiling laws. In most states, the term "estate" had only been used in local law with respect to intermediary rights and tenures, and did not include land under ryotwari settlement. Compensation provisions tended to follow similar formulas to that used in the Kerala act. The government, outraged at what it believed to be the willful misinterpretation of Article 31A (after extended court battles following zamindari abolition had led to a constitutional amendment aimed at settling this very question),[46] reacted by introducing another Constitution (Seventeenth Amendment) Bill on May 6, 1963, which explicitly widened the definition of the expression "estate" to include any land held under ryotwari settlement. In the Lok Sabha debate that followed, several Congress MPs joined with members of the Swatantra party, charging that the government's bill would curtail the rights of private property in land, and discriminate against rural property and income. Then, in an unprecedented occurrence, the bill was declared lost at the first stage of discussion, when the law minister called for a division on the motion to take it under consideration. Although the division favored the bill by 206 to 19, it was nevertheless defeated because fewer than two-thirds of the members of the Lok Sabha were present and voting, whereas a quorum of two-thirds was required at all stages of consideration on a constitutional amend-

[46] During the 1950s, the compensation clauses of the Zamindari Abolition Acts were challenged in the courts as ultra vires of the constitution, either on the ground that the award was inadequate or that the rate of compensation, determined according to sliding scales of multiples which declined at higher levels of income, was discriminatory. Three clauses of the Indian Constitution were most frequently cited: Article 14, granting every person equality before the law and equal protection of laws; Article 31, stipulating that no person could be deprived of property unless the law provided for compensation; and Article 25 (1), declaring the right of compensation justiciable. In 1950, the Patna High Court upheld the zamindars' case, and ruled that the Bihar Land Reforms Act was unconstitutional because the sliding scale of compensation introduced discrimination among persons in violation of Article 14. Under the First Amendment, passed in 1951, two new amendments (31A and 31B), were appended to Article 31. Under Article 31A, no law providing for the state acquisition of any estate or any rights therein could be declared void on the ground that it abridged any of the rights conferred by Article 31. Article 31B removed all existing Zamindari Abolition Laws from the purview of judicial review by listing them in a new (Ninth) Schedule of the Constitution. Although the zamindars also challenged the constitutionality of the First Amendment, it was upheld by the Supreme Court in 1952.

ment. A roll call revealed that only 225 out of a total of 510 members were present at the time of the division, and that more than 125 members of the Congress party were absent. Commenting the next morning, the *Statesman* reported that "Congress whips could not muster the requisite number to get the bill passed at the introductory stage."[47] The government was portrayed as stunned, helpless, and humiliated.

The full measure of Nehru's declining authority was most evident in the virtually independent policies followed by his own ministers on vital economic issues, in disregard of the Planning Commission's directions, even when reinforced by personal intervention of the prime minister. As in 1957, the Planning Commission responded to the growing economic crisis by pressing for more effective implementation of the policy requirements of the approach. In particular, they stepped up pressure on the concerned ministries to undertake a vigorous price control and procurement policy. Although the finance minister, Morarji Desai, enjoyed wide executive powers, both under the Essential Commodities Act (1955) and the Defense of India Rules (DIR) invoked for the duration of the Emergency, to issue orders controlling the price of any essential commodity, his assurances to the Planning Commission of an active price policy resulted only in the announcement of maximum controlled prices for kerosene. S. K. Patil, the minister of food and agriculture, was equally uncooperative. Apart from issuing an order (under the DIR) to regulate the supply and prices of sugar cane, he insisted that the only solution to the food crisis lay in incentives for greater production. Patil countered the Planning Commission's proposal for meeting the shortage through building up administrative machinery for government purchase and distribution of available supplies at maximum fixed rates, with recommendations for increasing production by providing incentives to private investment in agriculture. He especially advocated higher guaranteed prices for the farmer, and as much money as necessary for irrigation, primarily in the form of loans to individual producers for investment in tubewells and other minor irrigation facilities.

Unlike his predecessor, A. P. Jain, Patil refused to accommodate the Planning Commission even to the extent of carrying out the initial first steps of a state trading program. He made no effort to license wholesale traders; to set fixed minimum prices at which they must make purchases from farmers; or to arm the government with the right to acquire a portion or the whole of these stocks at controlled prices. On the contrary, Patil allowed the mechanisms of the market to operate freely. He did announce that starting in March 1962, the government would be prepared to purchase rice and wheat from the farmer at minimum "support"

[47] *The Statesman*, May 7, 1963.

prices in order to create an incentive for production. But since the "support" prices were generally lower than the prevailing open market prices, Patil was simply following a policy of noninterference in the foodgrains trade, while representing it as a step to aid the farmer. Indeed, far from undertaking a serious procurement program to build up government buffer stocks, the ministry in 1961/62, and again in 1962/63, released almost all of the wheat imported under PL 480 for sale at subsidized rates through the fair-price shops. As a result, when inflationary pressures, aggravated by large increases in defense expenditures and declining levels of production, reached an acute phase in 1963, buffer stocks were already close to exhaustion and the government found it impossible to stabilize prices through release of additional supplies. Per capita availability of foodgrains for consumption fell to levels of the mid-1950s,[48] and shortages of food and other essential commodities once again threatened the entire cost structure of the Plan.

The impasse between the Planning Commission and the Food and Agriculture Ministry took on the character of a showdown when, in May 1963, a policy decision had to be taken on one of two alternatives to meet the acute food shortage. The first was the Planning Commission's recommendation for building a permanent buffer stock of 5 million tons—3 million tons of rice and 2 million tons of wheat—partly through imports, and partly through internal procurement involving state trading, controls, and rationing. The other approach, advanced by the ministry, relied almost exclusively on a fresh agreement for PL 480 imports after the current arrangements for import of 16 million tons of wheat and 1 million tons of rice expired at the end of 1964. The question took on special urgency because Patil was scheduled to attend the World Food Congress in Washington toward the end of May, and to have conversations with American authorities on PL 480 assistance.

At a Cabinet meeting on the eve of Patil's departure, Nehru once again supported the Planning Commission. Their view prevailed that a fresh agreement for the import of wheat under PL 480 would be injurious to internal efforts at achieving food self-discipline. The Cabinet authorized Patil to discuss only two questions with the Americans: (1) an extension of the current agreement for one year to permit delivery of the balance of the wheat and rice that had been delayed in arrival by inadequate port facilities and storage capacity; and (2) a possible agreement for supplies of about two million tons of rice under PL 480 to help government build up its buffer stock.[49] With these instructions in hand, Patil met with the U.S. secretary of agriculture, Orville Freeman, on June 9, 1963. He arranged both for an extension of the current agreement and a tentative

[48] Ministry of Finance, *Economic Survey 1963-73*, p. 242.
[49] *The Statesman*, May 16, 1963; *Times of India*, May 18, 1963.

understanding on the import of rice under PL 480. Then, unaccountably, he went beyond his instructions to initiate agreements for detailed discussions later in the year for a new agreement.[50] The information was received by an obviously angered prime minister. Recalling his reception by Nehru after his return, Patil was indignant: "I was given no credit. Nobody else could have gotten the American agreement to build a rice stock of two million tons. America itself does not have such big rice surpluses. But I came back from America and instead of congratulating me the Prime Minister gave me a lecture and said it would be better for me to leave the Food Ministry."[51]

Nehru was, in fact, reacting to more than the defiance of one minister. He was confronted with rapid erosion inside his own party of the personal authority to determine major policy decisions and to set India's course permanently on the path of planned development under the principles of the socialist pattern. The challenge, moreover, was more serious than any temporary setback created by the damage to his prestige following the Chinese invasion. The prime minister was in his seventy-third year, and visibly tired. He could not seem to recover fully from the effects of a kidney ailment that flared up in the spring of 1962. The question of succession was already being raised.

Speculation focused mainly on the prospect that Morarji Desai, second in Cabinet rank to Nehru, would succeed him as prime minister. Desai, who had joined the Cabinet in 1956, after a lifetime commitment to the nationalist cause and the Congress party, including a term as chief minister of Bombay, was moreover, by temperament and party standing, perhaps best placed to mount a far-ranging attack on the basic principles of Nehru's approach. A self-described anticommunist who took some delight in pointing out that the "Communists have always considered me their enemy no. 1,"[52] his attack on Marxism was all the more credible because difficult to associate with self-interest. Indeed, Desai's scorn for socialist ideology was ultimately an expression of essentially religious convictions that moral and spiritual development rather than material progress were the true yardsticks of human civilization. A man of ability as well as integrity, his challenge to Nehru's approach came less from a well-articulated liberal philosophy than a life style of personal austerities, religious devotion, and "social" work that evoked memories of Gandhi and gained for him a substantial personal following inside the Congress party.

Desai was, in fact, the most influential opponent inside the govern-

[50] *Times of India*, June 21, 1963.
[51] Interview, S. K. Patil, New Delhi, August 27, 1963.
[52] This self-assessment and views on economic planning were stated by Morarji Desai in interviews in New Delhi, August 22 and August 23, 1973.

ment of the predominant role of the public sector in the development strategy. The finance minister, who lost the debate for a smaller Third Plan in the National Development Council once "Nehru spoke and almost incited the members to accept a bigger Plan," followed a correct policy in public of supporting the prime minister's policies. Nevertheless, he did not hide his own strong private conviction that the socialist approach was bound to fail because it did not take into account basic motivations of human behavior. Believing that "99.9 percent of people require incentives—power, wealth, fame," Desai preferred government to make "discriminating use of these in order to see that society develops properly." Scoffing at the possibility of a classless society, his approach to social policy was "not to put handicaps in anybody's way to improve himself," but to link material rewards with production, so that "those who work more, get more." The premises were clearly consistent with the business community's demand for a free enterprise approach, and indeed, Desai, pointing to the experience of the Second Plan, and the "picture of the public sector in the doldrums" was concerned not with finding more resources to expand public investment, but to "stem our losses." His approach to planning, apart from providing incentives to private investment, gave priority to projects that had the immediate potential of providing more employment and generating the daily necessities of life. Even so, he relied mainly on the "trusteeship system of Gandhi" for progress toward reduction of economic disparities. A favored suggestion was a ceiling on personal income—to be established by consensus—with earnings above this level to be put in charitable trust and used for financing public services such as hospitals and education.

Nehru, who recognized Desai's integrity as well as his strong-minded determination, and was aware of his appeal to a large section of the party, characteristically avoided a direct challenge. Yet in 1960, at the prime minister's instance, the Congress parliamentary party did alter its procedure of proposing the senior Cabinet minister—by this time, Desai —as deputy leader of the party in parliament, and decided instead to have two deputy leaders, neither of whom was a minister. Meanwhile, Nehru increasingly brought his own daughter into positions of national prominence both inside the Congress party and on government councils. Nevertheless, in the early 1960s Desai, on the basis of his seniority, experience, all-India stature, and party following, was already being treated on official visits abroad, including one to the land of his ideological adversary, the Soviet Union, as the next prime minister of India.

Belatedly, in 1963, Nehru attempted a counterattack on his conservative opponents inside the Congress party. Facing personal reverses that were tantamount to final defeat of his entire development approach, he finally took the offensive in a drive to reassert his paramount position as the source of authority on major policy matters and to ensure the permanence of his policies. The first round of the struggle began with the prime minister's dramatic initiative in August 1963, known as the Kamaraj Plan. Named after K. Kamaraj, then chief minister of Madras, the plan originated in discussions among a number of chief ministers who agreed on the need to revitalize the party organization in the wake of the humiliating by-election defeats of the previous spring. As endorsed by Nehru and adopted by the Working Committee on August 8, the plan provided in general terms for the resignation of senior Congressmen from government office to take up full-time organizational work. Approved two days later by a special session of the AICC (convened to consider deficiencies in the party organization revealed by the by-election defeats), implementation of the plan was left solely to Nehru's discretion. Although the original authors had apparently not envisaged the resignation of central ministers, Nehru's own lead in immediately seeking permission to resign (which was inevitably rejected) set the example that mandated offers of resignation from Cabinet ministers as well as the chief ministers of the states. On August 24, Nehru announced the final disposition to the Working Committee. Altogether, he accepted the resignation of six ministers at the Center and six chief ministers in the states. As Brecher points out, multiple considerations undoubtedly influenced the final selection.[53] A few of those chosen genuinely desired to step down, including the two chief ministers, K. Kamaraj of Madras and Biju Patnaik of Orissa (among the initial authors of the plan), and the home minister, Lal Bahadur Shastri. Others were removed either because they were ineffective ministers at the Center or a source of factional quarreling in the states. But there is little doubt that Nehru also used the opportunity to purge the Cabinet of his most powerful critics. The six resignations accepted included those of both Morarji Desai and S. K. Patil, removing the two major obstacles inside the Cabinet to effective implementation of economic policies considered essential by the Planning Commission to salvage the Third Plan. Whatever Nehru's intentions, moreover, the Kamaraj Plan was perceived by his opponents as a calculated effort to save the socialist pattern. Patil's interpretation was blunt: "The prime minister doesn't like violence, but he is a 100 percent communist in my mind. He wants a leftist pattern. He practically gave everything to the leftists. All six [Cabinet ministers] removed were considered from the communists' side to be on the right. All these things that are being done are not honest. They are camouflage. They are not really to strengthen the [Congress party] organization at all."[54]

Nehru's determination to reassert the basic principles of Plan policy

[53] See Michael Brecher, *Nehru's Mantle*, pp. 9-17.
[54] Interview, S. K. Patil, New Delhi, August 27, 1963.

was also evident in the appointments he made to fill the vacancies created by the Kamaraj Plan. The new finance minister, unlike Morarji Desai, was not drawn from the ranks of powerful state leaders. Instead, Nehru reappointed Desai's predecessor, T. T. Krishnamachari, a distinguished administrator and expert on fiscal management who was known to support the rapid development of basic and heavy industries in the public sector. Similarly, S. K. Patil's place at the Ministry of Food and Agriculture was taken by Swaran Singh, a Congress party leader with a relatively weak power base in the localized support of the minority Sikh community in (undivided) Punjab. Then, when Gulzarilal Nanda stepped down as deputy chairman of the Planning Commission to assume the office of home minister vacated by Lal Bahadur Shastri, Nehru named Asoka Mehta to the post. The selection of Mehta, a leading figure in the Praja Socialist party at the time of his appointment, had obvious symbolic significance in placing a well-known socialist at the head of the Planning Commission. Nehru's support inside the Congress party was, in addition, reinforced when Mehta led a group of his followers out of the PSP to rejoin the Congress.

Simultaneously, Nehru advanced more direct efforts at strengthening the party organization as an instrument for carrying out Plan programs and policies. At the same time that the Working Committee endorsed the Kamaraj Plan, it also set up an Organizational Affairs Committee to prepare a detailed program of work to be pursued by the party; and a committee to consider changes in the Congress constitution to accomplish greater mass participation, along with popular contributions to party funds. On September 15, at a meeting to which Nehru was especially invited, the Organizational Affairs Committee made its recommendations. These included new arrangements for coordination between the national and state Congress committees and between the governmental and organizational wings of the party in order to activate workers on behalf of national developmental programs. They provided that in addition to consultations between the prime minister and the president of the Congress party, each state should set up a coordination committee consisting of the chief minister and any two representatives of the organizational wing, and a representative of the Central Parliamentary Board. The coordination committee was to concentrate on eliminating groupism inside the party in order to direct attention toward matters of policy and program, especially the task of organizational participation in carrying out development activities. The Working Committee suggested the formation of study circles among party workers on subjects relating to the socialistic pattern of society, planning, foreign affairs, agriculture, cooperation, and industrial growth; the creation of new machinery at the local level for "giving publicity and propagating the basic policies and programs of Congress in regard to national, international, social and economic matters"; and the formulation of a "scheme for training workers for different activities including national and administrative responsibilities, suggesting targets of work for legislators and Congress representatives in local bodies, and suggesting machinery for assessing their performance."[55] These initiatives were followed in October by the announcement that the Working Committee had appointed another committee to prepare a definitive new statement of the party's objectives for consideration by the AICC at its next meeting in November.

The delegates who assembled on November 4 at Jaipur gave enthusiastic endorsement to both the Working Committee's report on the Kamaraj Plan and the recommendations for follow-up party work to carry out training of cadres; the organization of youth, women, and labor; work among minorities, Scheduled Castes and Tribes; and general publicity and propaganda about Congress policies and programs. The 2,000-word draft statement on democracy and socialism submitted by the Working Committee restated the Congress party's commitment to "democratic socialism, based on democracy, dignity of the human individual and social justice," and reiterated the goal of eliminating "privilege, disparities and exploitation by peaceful means." The document did not, however, consider specific policy actions to carry out its declared support for a "revolution in the economic and social relationships in Indian society."[56]

Although the statement was approved by unanimous vote of the AICC, members of the Congress Forum for Socialist Action led by K. D. Malaviya, then also a member of the Working Committee, pressed for revisions in the final draft to indicate a positive program of action. Malaviya's position, strongly supported in the general debate, stressed that promises of social revolution could only be redeemed by concrete proposals for state intervention in the economy. Nehru also appeared dissatisfied with the lack of substantive content. Arguing that "the masses must be made to realize what socialism meant and that the salvation of the country lies only in socialism,"[57] the prime minister joined Malaviya to underline the urgent necessity of translating promises into action. He reminded the delegates that "time [is] of the essence, and there [are] inherent dangers in slowing the pace of progress toward the socialist goal. It is possible that 10 to 15 years hence, people may lose faith in peaceful means and the problem may get more complicated."[58]

Once again, a firm initiative by Nehru provoked fresh expressions of support. Among the proposals for policy action recommended during

[55] *Congress Bulletin* (August-September 1963).
[56] *Hindustan Times*, November 4 and 5, 1963.
[57] *Hindustan Times*, November 5, 1963.          [58] *Ibid*.

the debate were immediate implementation of state trading in food and essential commodities, and nationalization of banks, and even of the press. At the same time, the Constitution Committee, headed by none other than S. K. Patil, recommended the reorganization of the party to ensure greater participation of workers in development activities. He endorsed suggestions for establishing party committees below the District Congress Committees in every Community Development Block, with the additional provision that active workers enroll at least fifty "ordinary" members and collect Rs. 12 in order to raise funds for the party "from the masses instead of depending on the rich." More startling, considering its chairman, the committee suggested a revision in the Objectives clause of the Congress constitution from the aim phrased in Gandhian language adopted in 1957 of establishing by "legitimate means of a socialist cooperative commonwealth" to a more Marxist-sounding formulation of establishing by "peaceful and constitutional means of a socialist state based on Parliamentary democracy."[59]

At the annual session of Congress at Bhubaneswar in January 1964, a revised version of the Resolution on Democracy and Socialism was introduced that represented virtually a new draft. It had been prepared by a second committee, this one headed by Nehru. Although it bore marks of the effort to compromise between the conservative and socialist elements, it was, nevertheless, a "radical advance" on the Jaipur statement.[60]

The resolution[61] began by summarizing the essential continuity of the social objectives of the Congress party, starting with Gandhi's Constructive Program and the 1931 resolution of the Karachi Congress, and proceeding to efforts after Independence aimed at giving "concrete shape" to these goals in the Directive Principles of the Constitution and the Avadi resolution. The "basic ideas underlying the Congress approach" were described as at Jaipur in terms of a "revolution in the economic and social relationships in Indian society." This time, however, the statement included the first time-bound commitment to "substantially" provide the "basic needs of every individual in respect to food, clothing, housing, education and health," by 1976, the end of the Fifth Plan. It also indicated that such a revolution "is to be brought about through radical changes in the attitudes and outlook of the people as well as the institutions through which they have to function." The bulk of the resolution was devoted to the political-action implications of the party's socialist commitment.

In terms of overall strategy, the document was a lengthy restatement of the correctness of the planners' approach to economic development

---

[59] *Hindustan Times*, November 4, 1963.          [60] *Times of India*, January 1, 1964.
[61] The text of the "Resolution on Democracy and Socialism" is published in both the *Times of India* and *Hindustan Times*, January 1, 1964.

aimed at achieving the multiple goals of a satisfactory growth rate, a strong industrial base, the removal of poverty, and a socialist society. This reaffirmation was combined with an analysis of the slow pace of progress that clearly attributed the primary "faults and shortcomings" to "failures of implementation." The resolution once more endorsed the 1956 Industrial Policy Resolution, emphasizing that the "public sector must grow progressively in large-scale industry and trade, particularly in the field of heavy and basic industries as well as trade in essential commodities." On this core issue, the resolution endorsed the "left" position of the necessity for more extensive state controls, including recommendations for a ceiling on individual income and private property, and social control over banking institutions that, however, stopped short of nationalization. On these issues, the resolution affirmed:

> It is necessary to bring about a limitation of incomes and property in private hands. This limitation should apply especially in respect of inherited wealth and urban property. The State should secure a large share of capital gains and appropriate a much larger proportion of unearned income than is done at present.

> The Government should place itself in a position more effectively than is now the case to direct the means of credit and investible resources of the country along the lines of national priorities and our social purposes. At present, small entrepreneurs and new-comers are placed under serious disadvantage in respect to the availability of financial resources. There is also need for further steps for the removal of abuses and malpractices in financial institutions.

The strategy recommended for achieving growth and equity in the rural sector similarly reasserted plan policies in providing that "the cooperative method of organization will occupy an increasingly important place in the field of agriculture, small scale and processing industries and retail trade." The resolution reiterated once again that "the community through suitable agencies should assume full responsibility for timely provision of the means, material and other facilities needed for the farmer for increasing production to the maximum extent. Special institutions should be set up at the national and other levels down to the panchayat for the supply of all forms of credit to the farmer. Creditworthiness should depend on capacity for production and not necessarily on the ownership of assets. In case of uneconomic holdings it is important that the unit of cultivation is enlarged on cooperative basis to be adopted voluntarily."

Other sections of the resolution made specific recommendations for completion of land reforms within a two-year period; progressive state takeover of rice mills and other processing units, pending arrangements for cooperative management; imposition of price controls when required by the public interest; readjustment of the administrative system for the tasks of implementing the programs and policies of the five-year plans; and finally, "if the administrative machinery is found wanting," the creation of "party cadres to shoulder the responsibility in the various fields."

The revised Resolution on Democracy and Socialism was passed by unanimous vote of the Working Committee, the Subjects Committee, and the open session. But this time it proved impossible to prevent an open confrontation in debate that revealed publicly the existence of serious divisions among senior members of the Working Committee. S. K. Patil, who as chairman of the Constitution Committee was in the uncomfortable position of piloting the recommendations for party reorganization that included the new definition of the party's objective as a "socialist state," warned obliquely that the change had "revolutionary" implications. The former food and agriculture minister had no inhibitions, however, in his criticism of the key recommendations on agricultural policy in the resolution. He heaped special scorn on such long-standing—and sacrosanct—principles of policy as the notion that credit-worthiness should depend on capacity for production and not necessarily on ownership of assets. Referring to this as a "new concept which was not followed anywhere," Patil predicted it would never be accepted by "a single banker or cooperative credit society." He further questioned the capacity of the states to take over the 43,000 rice mills in the country, and to mobilize the capital and administrative machinery necessary to replace the hundreds of thousands of middlemen and millowners engaged in the rice purchasing and processing business. Indeed, Patil ridiculed the entire effort to apply social controls over the agricultural sector. He argued that "whether it was Russia, America, or India, experience has shown that any increase in agricultural production could be brought about only through incentives to the individual." His own prescription for solving the food shortage, which he shared with the delegates, was to extend price subsidies to the farmers on the model of the United States and Japan.[62]

If Patil found the policy proposals at Bhubaneswar too radical, Malaviya still did not find them far-reaching enough. While endorsing the principles of Nehru's draft, he put forward a substitute resolution that was more explicit in calling for an immediate action program. The proposals demanded introduction of state trading in foodgrains and price controls on farm products; cooperative credit facilities for farmers; ceilings on the value of industrial licenses given to individuals; the separation of the press from business and industrial ownership interests, and the na-

[62] *Hindustan Times*, January 1, 1954; *Hindustan Times*, January 9, 1964; *Hindu*, January 9, 1964.

tionalization of banks. Malaviya's draft brought strong statements of approval in the debate, along with recommendations for even more extensive nationalization extending to basic consumer goods industries and the press—and though he was finally persuaded to support the official motion, his position was firm in insisting on the necessity at least of bank nationalization within the year.[63]

Shortly after the Bhubaneswar session, the more radical wing seemed to win a victory at the conference of state food ministers called by Swaran Singh on February 24, 1964. Against a background of growing urgency—as reports of looting of grain shops in villages of Bihar and Uttar Pradesh increased anxiety over the maintenance of law and order—the Union food and agriculture minister offered full support to the plan policy of imposing state controls over the agriculture sector. A new draft foodgrain dealers' licensing order, prepared by the Union ministry and circulated to the state departments for approval, provided for greatly tightened controls over the operations of private dealers. It required persons engaged in the wholesale trade to identify all sites used for storage of grains; to exhibit prices at all shops; to sell at rates no higher than the official maximum prices that might be fixed by the central and state governments; and to confine sales to registered retailers in accordance with directions issued from time to time by government-designated marketing authorities in local markets or *mandis*. Swaran Singh, moreover, clearly told the state food ministers to anticipate large-scale government regulation and distribution of stocks held by the wholesale trade. He announced the time had come to set a maximum price on foodgrains, and to enforce it through compulsory levies on the stocks of private dealers, in order to build up government supplies for equitable distribution of available quantities. Finally, he proposed that the conference endorse the policy recommendation of the Bhubaneswar resolution to bring rice mills under state control and to construct all new milling capacity in the cooperative sector. The conference ended with an agreement of the state food ministers to meet again after two months to present their schemes for implementation of state controls.[64]

Nevertheless, there were signs that the reassertion of essential principles of plan policy was ineffective. The state food ministers failed to reconvene within the planned two-month period. No new government initiatives for the procurement of foodgrains and the introduction of price controls was announced.

It was not long before the limitations of Nehru's victories became glaringly apparent. His gains, while dramatic, had been superficial. After the

[63] *Times of India*, January 1, 1964; *Hindustan Times*, January 9, 1964.
[64] *Times of India*, February 24, 1964.

Kamaraj Plan, the critical job of reconstructing the party organization remained to be accomplished. Yet, while Nehru appeared to have reestablished his power in defining the national policy commitments of the Congress party, the authority at his command to carry out the organizational changes required for effective implementation of plan programs had, in fact, forever slipped from his grasp. During the final days of the Bhubaneswar session, on January 8, 1964, Nehru suffered a mild stroke. The momentum he had painstakingly generated by forcefully moving to give substantive content to the goal of socialism within a time-bound program of action was lost. All that could be done or was attempted, in the absence of effective party machinery to mobilize grass-roots support on behalf of institutional changes at the core of the plan approach, was to ensure Nehru's legacy by a holding operation aimed at protecting the public sector from further attack.

Over the next several weeks, during the period of preparation of the 1964/65 budget, most of Nehru's work had to be delegated to subordinates, none of whom approached his position of independent political power. The home minister, Gulzarilal Nanda, and the finance minister, T. T. Krishnamachari, took on primary responsibility for running the government. Within days, they were joined by Lal Bahadur Shastri, the lone "Kamarajed" minister to be brought back into the Cabinet as a minister without portfolio, and the vague mandate to "perform such functions . . . as may be assigned to him by the Prime Minister from time to time."[65]

The budget presented to the Lok Sabha on February 29, 1964, was the work primarily of Krishnamachari in consultation with Shastri. Its main feature was an effort to maintain adequate investment outlays on the core industrial projects of the Third Plan, while meeting the requirements of defense, and to do both in a way that would avoid further attacks on the public sector.

Altogether, the budget provided for total Plan outlay of Rs. 1,984 crores, an increase of Rs. 333 crores over the 1963/64 level. Expenditure on defense was maintained at the high level of Rs. 854 crores. The finance minister, in an effort to appease the opponents of the public sector, avoided any new initiatives for the implementation of government controls. He was, on the contrary, deliberately conciliatory to the private sector in his proposals to "temper" the budgetary gap of Rs. 176 crores. Modest increases were envisaged in excise duties and customs duties. Changes in direct taxation were approached in the spirit of meeting the "primary need of the hour to infuse some confidence."[66] Krishnamachari announced he would respond to criticism from the corporate sector on

[65] Brecher, *Nehru's Mantle*, p. 23.
[66] Ministry of Finance, *Budget for 1964-65* (Delhi, 1965), p. 171.

the super-profits tax. He retreated, in effect, from the principle of an absolute ceiling on returns to capital. As a substitute, he proposed a surtax on the profits of companies at the rate of 40 percent after tax, allowing for a deduction of 10 percent on the capital base. Companies engaged in preferred forms of industrial investment were also to receive rebates on income tax and surtax. Finally, although a graduated expenditure tax was introduced above the level of Rs. 36,000, the compulsory deposits scheme was completely withdrawn. In its place, Krishnamachari proposed a graduated annuity deposit scheme, to be levied only on income-tax payers above the income level of Rs. 15,000 per annum, and repayable in ten annual installments at 4 percent interest. The result of the proposed changes in the tax structure was to reduce the overall budgetary gap to Rs. 86 crores.

The finance minister, having acquitted his chief task of protecting the core industrial projects in the public sector, was willing to be guided on matters of agricultural policy by the political pressures that converged on his chief consultant in the Cabinet, Lal Bahadur Shastri. Although Krishnamachari personally found the "most disturbing feature of the economic situation"[67] to be the price rise of over 7 percent between March 1963 and January 1964 (led once again by the price of foodgrains) he made no proposals for the introduction of state trading or regulation and control over prices and distribution of essential commodities. Instead, the finance minister turned for advice to the newly created Agricultural Production Board, a coordination committee of the Ministries of Food and Agriculture, Irrigation, and Community Development. This group, impressed with the political obstacles confronting the states in carrying out institutional and administrative reforms, and preoccupied with ensuring rapid increases in production to damp down the price spiral, advised an emphasis on quick-yielding schemes. The board recommended higher agricultural prices and incentives to producers; and a selective program of intensive development in 20 to 35 percent of the cultivated area of the country. This was essentially the program adopted by Krishnamachari in the 1964/65 budget. The finance minister, who told the Lok Sabha that the "main emphasis will have to be on production," announced a generalized extension of the Ford Foundation approach of concentration of resources in irrigated areas: "The experience of intensive agricultural production in certain selected areas through what is known as 'package programs' has led us to decide that we should concentrate our efforts in about 80 selected Districts or roughly about 1,500 development blocks which hold out the promise of quickest results."[68]

By 1964, the entire planning approach was in jeopardy. The attempt to reconcile growth and equity goals through institutional changes aimed at

[67] *Ibid.*, p. 160.                                    [68] *Ibid.*

transfer of land and other resources to millions of subsistence and land-less cultivators as the condition of their effective participation in the efforts and gains of development was rapidly being abandoned. A discussion paper prepared by the Perspective Planning Division of the Planning Commission as early as August 1962, to consider the "Implications of Planning for a Minimum Level of Living," pointed out that any commitment to radical redistribution of incomes would be "operationally meaningless unless revolutionary changes in property rights and scale and structure of wages are contemplated."[69] Significantly, the planners' working assumption throughout the exercise was that *no* redistribution at all would be carried out. According to their projections, "the distribution of income in the upper 80 percent of the population in 1975 may not be very different from the present pattern."[70] The only method of ensuring a minimum income to the poorest segments of the population, once this constraint was accepted, was to achieve a high enough rate of overall growth so that the amount of income earned by the lowest deciles (although calculated as a constant proportion of total income) would rise in absolute terms to meet modest consumption standards. But taking into account "past achievements, the emerging experience of the Third Plan, our capacity to mobilize domestic resources and foreign exchange of the requisite magnitude, our ability to realize an adequate rate of growth of farm output and to design, construct and operate large complex projects,"[71] the planners could not project more than a maximum rate of growth of 7 percent per annum during the decade 1966–1976. At best, this might support per capita monthly consumption expenditure for the top 80 percent of the population at Rs. 20 ($4.40) by 1975/76, compared to the top 40 percent of the population that enjoyed at least this "bare minimum" standard in 1960/61.[72] The condition of the bottom 20 percent, some 125 millions out of an estimated population of 625 millions, comprising in the main landless laborers, subsistence cultivators, and other marginal producers "isolated from the mainstream of the economy," was expected to remain "stagnant or any rate to improve much less than average unless specific steps are taken to deal with their problems."[73]

[69] Planning Commission, Perspective Planning Division, *Perspective of Development: 1961-1967, Implications of Planning for a Minimum Level of Living* (August 1962), mimeographed, p. 6.

[70] *Ibid.*, p. 10.                                    [71] *Ibid.*, p. 12.

[72] The estimate of the minimum consumption provided only for foodgrains, clothing, and fuel sufficient to rise above "abject poverty." It fell considerably short of the cost of approximately Rs. 35 per capita per month for a balanced diet, as recommended by the Nutrition Advisory Committee, together with a modest standard of consumption of other items. It also excluded expenditures on health and education that were expected to be provided by the state, *ibid.*, p. 11.

[73] *Ibid.*, p. 9.

Nothing in these assumptions appeared to have been changed by Nehru's eleventh-hour offensive to restore the program of institutional reform as an integral part of the development strategy. The publication in April 1964 of the Perspective Planning Division's guidelines for the Fourth Plan, "Notes on Perspectives of Development, India: 1960-61 to 1975-76," revealed the overriding concern with maximizing growth rates. The basic objectives of the program only appeared to conform to the goals of the Bhubaneswar resolution. These were described as four-fold: "(a) to ensure a minimum consumption of Rs. 20 per capita per month to the entire population by the end of the fifth five year plan and in particular to improve the amenities of life in the rural areas; (b) to en-sure that the economy will be capable of sustaining the average annual rate of growth of the order of 7 percent even after 1975-76 without de-pending on foreign aid; (c) to achieve a significant increase in employ-ment opportunities during the next decade; and (d) to promote a social order which affords equality of opportunity and which at the same time prevents excessive disparity of income and wealth."[74] The approach, method, and substance of the notes (reminiscent of the gap between Plan principles and programs in the First Plan), contrasted sharply with the policy measures recommended in the Bhubaneswar resolution.

The planners, in practice, concentrated almost exclusively on protect-ing the role of the public sector in key areas. They were hard pressed to find sufficient resources for a large expansion in domestic production of intermediate and capital goods. Nevertheless, this priority was dictated by the need to manufacture import substitutes in order to relieve pres-sures on the balance of payments, given the policy goal of reducing net foreign aid in 1970/71 (exclusive of debt repayment) to two-thirds of the amount in 1965/66 and to virtually zero in 1975/76.[75] During the Fourth Plan period alone, total net investment, public and private, of Rs. 22,000 crores was necessary to finance the "minimum effort required" to achieve self-sustained growth and make any significant impact on living standards.[76]

The pool of resources for financing investment in the public sector was shrinking. The central government was approaching the legal and practi-cal limits of imposing additional taxation on individuals and organized business, while the states failed to adopt measures tapping new poten-tialities for resource mobilization in the rural sector. Even on the basis of generous estimates for savings out of current revenues, large surpluses

[74] Planning Commission, *Notes on Perspectives of Development, India: 1960-61 and 1975-76*, p. 2.

[75] *Ibid.*, pp. 12-13.

[76] *Ibid.*, pp. 9, 22. Per capita consumption was expected to rise between 3 and 3.5 percent per year, given an average annual rate of growth in national income of 7.5 percent.

from public enterprises, greater market borrowings, and "non-inflationary levels of deficit financing," it was only possible to project some Rs. 14,200 crores as the upper limit on total public investment, *after* allowing for a gap of about 17 percent of the total to be filled from unspecified sources of additional taxation.[77] The overall share of investment allocated to the private sector was of necessity large, totaling over Rs. 7,900 crores. In the core areas of industry and mining, total new investment of Rs. 6,440 crores, or 30 percent of total net investment during the Fourth Plan period, had to be provided to meet the targeted growth rate of over 11 percent per annum. On the basis of available resources, the planners were unable to project more than investment of Rs. 3,580 crores in the public sector. The remainder, Rs. 2,860 crores, was assigned to private enterprise. The result was a public-to-private sector investment ratio of approximately 56 : 44 percent—a decline over Third Plan levels.[78]

The effort to maintain even these reduced ratios of public investment in industry and mining, while increasing allocations in health, education, and other social services as part of the effort to raise mass consumption standards, further eroded the amount of resources available for agriculture. Altogether (apart from investments allocated for the manufacture of fertilizers in the industrial sector), direct investment in agriculture, including major and medium irrigation projects, was envisaged at Rs. 3,200 crores, or only 15 percent of total net investment.[79] Still, in order to secure the minimum progress necessary in the core industrial sector, the planners had to guarantee an annual average growth rate in agriculture of more than 5 percent, over twice the rate achieved during the Third Plan. This time, they indicated a willingness to consider the agricultural strategy solely in terms of short-run growth-maximizing goals. Apart from the investments on irrigation, land improvement, and other infrastructure, they gave greatest emphasis to provision of fertilizer and other modern inputs, and to improvement in the efficiency of the extension service and the organization of supplies, credit, and marketing. Most important, they endorsed the long-resisted capitalist methods of "well thought out policy of price supports and subsidies" as incentives to surplus producers for investment, along with the "careful selection of products and areas to increase production in the relatively short period."[80] As a result of rapid improvements in production associated with these efforts, the planners even predicted that state trading in foodgrains for the purpose of creating stockpiles as a hedge against inflation would be unnecessary after 1965/66.

In the months following Bhubaneswar, speculation on the question "After Nehru, Who?" insistently filled the press. Despite repeated pres-

[77] *Ibid.*, p. 28.
[79] *Ibid.*, p. 232.
[78] *Ibid.*, pp. 232-33.
[80] *Ibid.*, p. 15.

sure during his illness to name a deputy prime minister and indicate his choice of a successor, Nehru maintained his longstanding position that in a democracy the people must choose. At the same time, no successor was in view who enjoyed a decisive advantage in an independent base of popular support. The next prime minister would be selected by the men in control of the party machinery, the state leaders to whom the Congress MPs owed their place on the party ticket and in parliament.

Nehru could not help but be aware of this prospect. It appears that, characteristically, his last efforts were aimed at influencing the outcome in an indirect way. Although many of his colleagues believed Nehru's real, but unspoken, preference was to have his daughter, Indira Gandhi, succeed him, he made no overt attempt to promote her candidacy. Instead, his immediate aim seems to have been negative, to prevent the succession from falling to the man most likely to do lasting damage to his legacy. This goal was tantamount to minimizing the prospects of Morarji Desai as the choice of the state party leaders.

Ironically, the evidence suggests that Nehru's notion of reducing the chances of his most potent adversary coincided with that of many of the state party leaders, who for reasons of their own, involving the desire to protect new-found influence against the inroads of another strong-minded prime minister, were interested in finding an alternative choice. It further appears that at the outset Nehru's judgment of the least dangerous candidate was the same as that of the state party leaders, and that the two sides tacitly helped each other in engineering the succession of Lal Bahadur Shastri.

Nehru's assessment of Shastri rested on a long political association during which the younger man had displayed high standards of integrity along with loyalty and personal diffidence toward the prime minister in the various posts to which he was successively elevated. In fact, Shastri's rise in national politics was to a significant extent the result of Nehru's interest in his career. Shastri, who came from Nehru's home state of Uttar Pradesh, had left school at the age of 17 in 1921 to join the non-cooperation movement, and had assumed an important organizational role in the province that brought him into early contact with Nehru. By the mid-1930s, Shastri had achieved the position of general secretary of the Uttar Pradesh Congress Committee. Eventually, he was to spend nine years in prison for his nationalist activities. After Independence, he was rewarded with election to the Uttar Pradesh legislative assembly and appointment in the state government as minister of police and transport. It was Nehru, however, who selected Shastri for a pivotal position at the Center in another party assignment, this time as general secretary in charge of the national Congress campaign during the first general elections. In 1952, Nehru elevated Shastri to a position in the Union Cabinet, where he served as minister of transport and railways. After Shastri's resignation in 1956 (when he assumed personal responsibility for a series of railway accidents), Nehru quickly brought him back into the Cabinet, this time as minister of industry and commerce. In 1960, Nehru promoted Shastri to home minister, where he continued until his resignation in 1963 under the Kamaraj Plan.

Shastri could certainly be expected to have personal feelings of loyalty and gratitude to Nehru. It was even possible to imagine, and some believed Nehru did, that Shastri would, perhaps after an interim period, step down as prime minister in favor of Mrs. Gandhi.[81] At the least, he appeared sympathetic to his mentor's goals. One of the few men among the national leadership to come by his compassion for the common man through experience rather than ideology, he was for most of his life poor, a man whose integrity had sometimes meant material sacrifices for his family.

The state party leaders were attracted to Shastri by other of his qualities. He was the archetypical "conciliator," the man who after spending decades in political life had not made a single enemy. He was "a moderate . . . a conciliator, compromiser and coordinator, above all a shy, modest, humble and unpretending man who hardly ever made an enemy during his entire career."[82] He was, in short, a man completely unlike Morarji Desai, one who could be safely entrusted with the office of prime minister by a group of state party leaders intent on establishing a consensus style of government under new patterns of collective leadership.

The first initiatives designed to influence the outcome of the succession struggle appear, in retrospect, to have been launched under cover of the Kamaraj Plan. S. K. Patil, among others, discerned at the time a "sinister intention, an attempt to make the line of succession clear [to eliminate Morarji], and make Nehru's daughter prime minister."[83] Desai himself, ten years after the event, was still convinced that "the Kamaraj Plan was designed especially to get me out. Nehru wanted his daughter to succeed him."[84] Although there is no direct evidence that Nehru was paving the way for Mrs. Gandhi—the most obvious symbol of continuity with his policies—there is certainly sufficient reason to believe that the removal of Morarji Desai as the second-ranking minister in the Cabinet gravely weakened his lead in the contest for succession. The move was particularly shrewd in exploiting the personal rivalries and ambitions within the conservative coalition, and emboldening that group of leaders who came to be known as the Syndicate in their efforts to keep Desai from power.

---

[81] Desai, for one, was of this view. Interview, New Delhi, August 18, 1973. S. K. Patil also believed Nehru harbored this hope. See Kuldip Nayar, *India, The Critical Years*, p. 24.

[82] *Times of India*, January 11, 1966.

[83] Interview, S. K. Patil, New Delhi, August 27, 1963.

[84] Interview, Morarji Desai, New Delhi, August 18, 1973.

In October 1963, consultations between five state party chiefs (K. Kamaraj, Madras; Atulya Ghosh, West Bengal; Sanjiva Reddy, Andhra Pradesh; S. Nijalingappa, Mysore; and S. K. Patil, Bombay), on the question of electing a new Congress president for the Bhubaneswar session ended in an agreement to thwart Desai in his bid to return to national office. It was agreed to support the candidacy of Kamaraj instead, a suggestion that Nehru had personally endorsed at the first signs of an emerging struggle between Desai and the Syndicate on the question of the nomination. Writing Atulya Ghosh, Nehru flatly stated, "I [think] that Kamaraj would be the best person for us to choose."[85] Meanwhile, the Syndicate took a decision which it did not communicate to Nehru. "At the same time, at that meeting," Atulya Ghosh later revealed, "we considered it desirable that as Pt. Nehru was getting old, Shri Lal Bahadur Shastri should succeed him as the Prime Minister."[86] Even so, when the Syndicate suggested to Nehru within a few days of his stroke that he should invite Shastri to return to the Cabinet as minister without portfolio, Nehru readily agreed in an action that inevitably created the impression he had chosen his successor.[87]

Nehru's death at his official residence in New Delhi on May 27, 1964, after apparent recovery, was not unexpected. Only the inability to know the exact time and place endowed the event with the shock of surprise. The question of succession was taken up informally even before the cremation ceremonies were completed on the following day.[88] Those whose personal loyalty to Nehru was especially strong found the spectacle distressing. It is unlikely that Nehru anticipated much else. Indeed, his maneuvers during the final year of his life appeared directed toward that moment.

[85] Nehru's letter to Atulya Ghosh is reproduced in Atulya Ghosh, *The Split in Indian National Congress*, Annexure A.

[86] *Ibid.*, p. viii.

[87] Nayar, *India, The Critical Years*, p. 25. There are, however, some indications that Nehru developed misgivings about Shastri. Nayar reports that after Nehru recovered from the acute stage of his illness, he stopped the flow of important papers and files to Shastri, who complained of being treated as a "glorified clerk." *Ibid.*, p. 26. Desai's interpretation suggests that Nehru grew disillusioned with Shastri when he came to believe that his former protégé had developed personal ambitions to succeed him as prime minister and was collaborating with the Syndicate to prevent any possibility that Mrs. Gandhi would ultimately be elevated to that office. According to Desai, shortly before Nehru's death, he was approached by emissaries from the prime minister with an offer to rejoin the Cabinet as deputy prime minister, on the understanding that Desai would do as Nehru wished on any further questions involving a difference between them. Desai, who found such a condition objectionable and did not explore the substance of the offer, nevertheless believed it related to the succession, and was meant to extract a personal commitment from him (which Nehru knew would be honored once given), either to make Mrs. Gandhi prime minister immediately, or to step down in her favor after an interim period. Interview, New Delhi, August 18, 1973.

[88] For a detailed account of the maneuvers surrounding the succession, see Michael Brecher, *Nehru's Mantle*, ch. 3.

The structure of power Nehru helped shape worked against Morarji Desai. It is true that there was no serious discussion of Mrs. Gandhi as a candidate for the succession. An initiative on her behalf by K. D. Malaviya was aborted when Mrs. Gandhi refused categorically to be drawn into a contest during a period of deep mourning. But Nanda, Krishnamachari, and Shastri, the three men Nehru had deliberately brought back to key positions in the Union Cabinet, constituted the effective leadership of the national government. It was they who decided to recommend to the president that Nanda, as home minister, be appointed interim prime minister until the Congress party in parliament could meet to select a new leader. Desai, who as the senior member of the Cabinet would have inevitably acceded to this position in the absence of the Kamaraj Plan, was instead relegated to the political sidelines, deprived of any official role, and of the symbolic and patronage advantages of national office in pressing his candidacy on the party. By contrast, Kamaraj, who with Nehru's support had helped prevent Desai's selection as president of the Congress party, now enjoyed a pivotal role in that position. He announced, with approval from the Working Committee—including members of the Syndicate—his responsibility to canvass the views of the chief ministers and the Congress MPs to discover the party's choice of successor, and to advise the Congress parliamentary party on the "consensus." In the process, Kamaraj and the state leaders made known their own preference for Shastri to the MPs from their states, and attempted to ensure a majority for their candidate by resisting a secret ballot in the CPP on the choice of their new leader. When, on June 1, Kamaraj formally reported to the Working Committee his finding of a party consensus on Shastri, Desai agreed to withdraw. The next day, at a meeting of the Congress parliamentary party, Shastri was unanimously elected. He appeared to justify Nehru's gamble that he was the safest choice. In his acceptance speech, Shastri took special care to praise Mrs. Gandhi and to extend to her an open invitation to join the new government. Then he went on to declare his commitment, at the level of national policy, to continuing Nehru's work. "Socialism," he asserted, "is our objective. Our policy has already been defined and enunciated. What is essential is its proper and quicker implementation."[89]

A more reliable harbinger of things to come, however, was the special session of the Lok Sabha called as an act of ritual homage to Nehru for the purpose of reintroducing the Constitution (Seventeenth Amendment) Bill. When the bill was reported out of the Select Committee, the Congress leadership issued a very strong whip. This time, the bill was enacted into law by a vote of 389 to 30.

[89] *Ibid.*, p. 67.

But the Select Committee had made a crucial change. A new provision appeared, stipulating that in all future land reform acts, cultivating owners of land would be entitled to compensation for loss of land or any rights therein on the basis of full market value. The provision did not apply to existing ceiling legislation, which was allowed to stand. What it did accomplish, however, was to rule out in practice a significant land redistribution program through future legislation for lowering ceiling limits by making it financially impossible for the government legally to acquire a substantial proportion of the cultivated area. The intention and ability of conservative groups inside the Congress to resist any further attempts at reform had been made unmistakably clear.

# SEVEN

# Retreat from the Social Goals of Planning: Domestic Constraints and Foreign Pressures

At the time of Nehru's death, the Congress party leadership reaffirmed its commitment to democratic social transformation as the national aim of development planning set down in the Five Year Plans. Yet, the critical task of reconstituting the party organization as an instrument of popular involvement in the implementation of Congress policies had hardly begun. This task proved to be completely outside the capacity of Nehru's successor to accomplish. Lal Bahadur Shastri did not have an independent base of popular support at the time he took office. On the contrary, he was the creature of the party bosses who derived their power from the dominant landed groups that reorganization would have displaced. Proposals for party reform were set aside. Instead, Shastri took exactly the opposite route than the one charted by Nehru in the last years of his life. Conceding the virtual impossibility of transforming the rural power base of the Congress party in the support of the proprietor castes, he abandoned the social goals of planning.

The departure from past principles of policy was all the more complete because the prime minister as an insecure head of government was vulnerable not only to domestic attacks on plan policy, but to criticism by international aid-giving institutions of overly ambitious industrial plans in the public sector and inefficient methods of development both in industry and agriculture that ignored incentives to private (domestic and foreign) investment. The two currents of criticism, one internal, the other foreign, combined to reinforce each other in increasing pressure for a complete reorientation of the economic approach. Failures to carry out agrarian reforms capable of increasing agricultural output and mobilizing larger rural surpluses for public investment left India even more dependent on higher levels of external assistance to finance future plans. Increasing insistence by the major aid-giving nations that India alter her investment priorities and methods of development, in the face of continuing resistance by state leaders to carry out agrarian reorganization, left the government with little room for maneuver.

During the brief twenty months of Shastri's tenure, a series of undramatic initiatives in economic policy that went virtually unnoticed at the time cumulatively altered the entire approach to India's development strategy. Among the results of decisions taken during this period were the eclipse of the Planning Commission as a policy-making body; a shift from controls to incentives as major instruments of development planning; a reorientation of public investment from basic industries to agriculture; a new agricultural strategy to concentrate modern inputs in irrigated areas of the country; and an enlarged role for private domestic and foreign investment in the development of the industrial sector. In sum, in less than two years, the key pillars of Nehru's strategy of self-reliant growth and social transformation through expansion of basic and heavy industries in the public sector, and land reforms and cooperative reorganization in agriculture, were virtually overturned. The Shastri interregnum saw the beginnings of the sharp contradiction between pledges of economic and social reform endorsed by the national party leadership and policies of active encouragement to private investment both in industry and agriculture pursued by Congress governments. The new policies ultimately failed to accelerate the process of economic growth, even as they inevitably increased disparities and eroded the legitimacy of the Congress party as well as the entire system of democratic government.

Shastri was, on the face of it, an unlikely person to have initiated such a major policy reversal. Indeed, the general view at the time of the succession was best summed up in the estimate that a man of his background and temperament would "never take new or daring decisions or put the stamp of his leadership on his inheritance."[1] It is, moreover, doubtful that Shastri intended to introduce a decisive break with past principles of economic policy, if only because his own legitimacy as successor was publicly linked to at least formal affirmation of continuity with Nehru's basic approach.

At the same time, Shastri had neither the ideological commitment nor the political power necessary to insist, like Nehru, that shortfalls in Plan performance had been failures of implementation rather than strategy. His endorsement of socialism represented a statement of personal empathy for the problems of the common man in securing the necessities of life, rather than a comprehensive world view that provided a guide to the selection of policy instruments. The new prime minister was, moreover, lacking in any formal economic training or even practical experience in planning. Confronted by authoritative explanations of economic difficulties that emphasized defective Plan methods rather than poor implementation, his tendency was to accept expert opinion.

Glaring shortages of essential commodities and the spiraling cost of

[1] Pran Chopra, *Uncertain India*, p. 284.

living lent further common-sense credibility to the business community's claim that economic problems were due mainly to the penchant of
leftist-minded planners for large outlays on projects requiring long gestation periods, which caused neglect of agriculture and consumer industries. Indeed, Shastri's own perception of the public sector was critical.
He confided in his colleagues that the public sector was not operating to
capacity and had failed to justify the enormous sums spent on it. Plans
for more rapid expansion against past experience of long gestation periods and poor production results would only intensify the problems of
exhaustion of foreign exchange reserves and dependence on foreign aid,
while aggravating the rising domestic price level as demands for scarce
consumer goods increased. In contrast to Nehru, who had insisted that
these difficulties be absorbed as the price of maintaining the momentum
of industrial development required for achieving the long-term goal of
self-reliance, Shastri inclined toward greater emphasis on more efficient
use of existing capacity rather than construction of new projects, except
in a few "core" industries considered absolutely essential for self-
reliance. He was, further, unsympathetic to what he believed was a hostile view toward private business by the planners. His own approach was
to emphasize the complementarity of the private and public sectors; to
impose the minimum a priori restrictions on the expansion of the private
sector consistent with the 1956 Industrial Policy Resolution; and to rely
on the public sector mainly when it could demonstrate greater comparative advantage in efficient production.[2]

Above all, Shastri was concerned to make immediate progress in ensuring the basic necessities of food and primary consumer items to the
poorest sections of the population. Unlike Nehru, he was uncertain
about his ability to cope with both foreign and domestic pressures arising
from continuing shortages of essential commodities. He was particularly
sensitive to the potential vulnerability of India to foreign pressures as
long as the economy remained dependent on imported foodgrains. His
discomfort at continuing reliance on PL 480 supplies assumed an acute
dimension when, in April 1965, President Johnson abruptly inflicted a
national humiliation on the new prime minister by canceling an invitation for a well-publicized trip to the United States. Meanwhile, at home,
Shastri still had to prove his credibility as prime minister through evidence of his ability to solve the economic crisis, and most especially to
increase production in agriculture and bring down the price of food. Indeed, within three months of taking office, Shastri was confronted with

[2] Shastri's views are reconstructed from conversations with some of his principal advisors, especially T. N. Singh, then member (Industries), Planning Commission, New
Delhi, June 3, 1973; Asoka Mehta, then deputy chairman, Planning Commission, New
Delhi, May 25, 1973 and June 15, 1973; and L. K. Jha, then principal secretary, prime
minister's secretariat; Washington, D.C., June 21, 1972 and September 21, 1972.

the challenge of a nationwide agitation against rising prices led by the Communist party. Demonstrators appeared in the thousands; some called angrily for the resignation of the government. Altogether, some 1,300 arrests were necessary to keep the situation from getting out of control. Even then, there were instances of rioting by students in towns and states as widely separated as Orissa and Kerala.[3]

Perhaps the greatest constraint on Shastri's personal initiative in economic policy came from a sense of political insecurity inside his own party. The future offered an uncertain prospect. Morarji Desai had refused to join the Cabinet, amid indications that the former finance minister's supporters in the Congress parliamentary party remained unreconciled to his defeat. Meanwhile, Shastri's political fortunes rested in the hands of the state party leaders who controlled the blocs of votes in the CPP necessary to his continuation as prime minister after the general elections scheduled in 1967.

In contrast to Nehru, who had removed the most vocal critics of Plan policy from the Cabinet under the Kamaraj Plan, one of Shastri's first acts as prime minister was to return them to positions of power at the Center. Although Desai refused Shastri's invitation to join the Cabinet, S.K. Patil accepted appointment as minister of railways. Sanjiva Reddy, a powerful Congress party boss of Andhra Pradesh, was given a key portfolio as minister of mines and engineering, and became the unofficial spokesman in the Cabinet for the chief ministers of the southern states (including Nijalingappa of Mysore, Bhaktavatsalam of Madras, and Brahmananda Reddy of Andhra). In addition, Kamaraj, as Congress president and the "strong man" of the party, with the ability to put the power of the organization behind a new prime minister in 1967, was accorded an important advisory role. At the highest level, an appearance of continuity with the Nehru years was pursued with the appointment of Indira Gandhi as minister of information and broadcasting.

Against the background of these diverse considerations and pressures, Shastri approached the Fourth Plan convinced that highest priority in public expenditure should be given to agriculture, even if this involved concessions to domestic and foreign private investment in the expansion of large-scale industry. He nevertheless tried to find middle ground acceptable both to the planners and his colleagues in the Cabinet and the chief ministers of the states. At his very first meeting with the Planning Commission on June 24, 1964, Shastri had to take a decision on the Perspective Planning Division's tentative guidelines for the Fourth Plan, approved by Nehru less than three weeks before his death. The new prime minister endorsed the PPD's projections of outlays at double Third Plan levels to preserve continuity of past policy and ensure the momentum of

[3] *Times of India*, October 20, 1964 and November 7, 1964.

development in basic and heavy industries. At the same time, however, he insisted on giving highest priority in the allocation of resources to agriculture. In an appeal for a "common man's plan," one that would bring immediate benefits in food, clothing, and shelter,[4] the prime minister suggested priorities for quick-yielding projects in the rural sector, with special attention to minor irrigation, fertilizers, and medium and small-scale industries. Taken together, the changes he favored suggested a reduced role for detailed planning in the development process; but something less than a major departure from established goals and methods of development. They were, in fact, presented as a shift of emphasis within the existing framework to meet the acute production crisis.

The Planning Commission, however, had lost its most effective shield against a direct attack from its opponents inside the government and the Congress party. The planners' influence on the formulation of national development policy had all along rested on the commitment of the prime minister as chairman to ignore criticism from his own party leaders. As long as the prime minister and the chairman of the Planning Commission had spoken with one voice—and that voice was decisive on questions of national economic policy—there was every incentive for the ministries to negotiate directly with the planners to reach an agreed position before an issue was considered at Cabinet level.

During the Nehru years, the consensus on economic policy was achieved by consultations between the deputy chairman and members of the Planning Commission, and the ministers and senior officials concerned. Most of these contacts developed informally over the years. The ministries submitted proposals to the Planning Commission for comment, and the commission made its own recommendations on policy to the ministries. The deputy chairman, or his representative, participated in interdepartmental meetings of ministers and secretaries and other senior officials. In addition, the secretary of the Planning Commission served in the dual capacity as Cabinet secretary (and chairman of the Committee of Secretaries). He presented the Planning Commission's point of view to the secretaries of the ministries, providing guidance on drafting formal policy proposals, and alerting the planners, in turn, to any objections that might arise. If differences involving policy remained unresolved after informal discussions, senior officials and the ministers concerned were invited to a formal meeting of the Planning Commission for further talks. At such meetings, the Planning Commission was strengthened in its bargaining position by its generally close working relationship with the finance minister, who as a member of the commis-

[4] *Times of India*, June 24, 1964.

sion was accustomed to seeking the views of the planners before accepting proposals for new expenditures from the ministries. Finally, when
differences between the Planning Commission and a ministry could not
be resolved, the deputy chairman and the members of the Planning
Commission could press their views against an uncooperative minister
before a usually sympathetic prime minister.[5]

Within the first few months of Shastri's leadership, the balance of
power between the Planning Commission and the ministries was transformed. The new prime minister quietly introduced a number of administrative and procedural changes in the policy-making process that
had the twofold effect of creating a clear separation between the Planning
Commission and the office of the prime minister, while shifting the balance of influence within the decision-making networks from the Planning Commission to the ministries, and by extension, to the chief ministers of the states.

One of Shastri's first acts was to divest the members of the Planning
Commission of their longstanding privilege of indefinite tenure and to
place them on fixed term (albeit renewable) contracts. The new formal
arrangements effectively reduced the status of the Planning Commission
from its position as an extension of the prime minister in the area of economic policy to a subordinate group of advisors. This effect was enhanced by the decision to terminate the link between the Cabinet secretary and the secretary of the Planning Commission, and to appoint a
separate secretary (and additional secretary) attached solely to the Planning Commission.

The separation between the prime minister and the Planning Commission took on more substantive meaning after Shastri's decision in July
1964 to constitute his own prime minister's secretariat. This innovation
had the effect, desired by Shastri, of strengthening the prime minister's
office against the pressures advanced by senior members of the party
(both from their positions in the Cabinet and on the Working Committee). It provided him with his own set of experts who could be consulted
independently on major questions of economic policy and foreign affairs.
The initiative, which grafted some of the elements of a presidential style
of government onto the cabinet system, established the preeminence of
the prime minister beyond the conventional norm maintained by Nehru
(albeit in fiction, not fact), of the prime minister as the "first among
equals."

The selection of L. K. Jha, the former finance secretary and the ranking ICS officer in the Government of India, as head of the secretariat di-

---

[5] For an authoritative summary of the relationships between the Planning Commission
and the ministries during the Nehru years, see Tarlok Singh, *Towards an Integrated Society*,
pp. 440-43.

rectly undercut the policy-making role of the Planning Commission.[6] It placed a high-powered economic adviser in the prime minister's office. Unlike Nehru's personal secretaries, including Tarlok Singh and Pitambar Pant, both of whom had simultaneously held senior positions on the Planning Commission, Jha had no such affiliation. He sat on committees at the secretary level as the representative of Shastri in the latter's capacity as prime minister. Apart from the special prestige Jha enjoyed as head of the prime minister's secretariat, moreover, his views were respectfully solicited by senior members of government on the basis of impressive professional credentials in the field of finance. Within a short time, Jha became the most influential official adviser in the government. Equally important, through his close personal ties with other senior civil servants, especially in the finance ministry, he played a major role in reestablishing the influence of the bureaucracy in the formulation of economic policy. In particular, those officials who had argued since 1963 that the resource position mandated a virtual moratorium on new development schemes to meet the requirements of defense achieved direct access to the prime minister. In turn, their allies among the chief ministers who also advocated limitations on expansion of the public sector in favor of greater reliance on incentives to private enterprise found a new route to participation at the highest levels of decision-making, one that permitted circumvention of the Planning Commission on questions of economic policy.

The decline in the Planning Commission's policy-making role was further aggravated by Shastri's political style. In contrast to Nehru, who used his authority as chairman of the Planning Commission to concentrate responsibility on economic matters in that body, Shastri emphasized his powers as prime minister to decentralize the policy-making process and encourage independent inputs in the formulation of development programs from members of his Cabinet. His very first alteration in the Cabinet, the decision to transfer the successful minister of steel, C. Subramaniam, to the Ministry of Food and Agriculture, signaled his own wish to accord highest priority to agriculture in planning, and his political style of widening the decision-making sphere to assign a major role to individual ministers. In general, Shastri's approach to decisions on economic policy was to seek a consensus solution by encouraging extensive informal consultations between ministers, senior administrators, advisors, and planners. He himself preferred to consult individually with the ministers and officials concerned, rather than to meet with the full Planning Commission. In most cases, differences in point of view were

⁶ For an extended discussion of the impact of the prime minister's secretariat on the policy-making process, and the role of L. K. Jha, see Michael Brecher, *Nehru's Mantle*, pp. 115-20.

reconciled before they reached the stage of Cabinet discussion. When differences persisted, Shastri invited the deputy chairman of the commission and/or his representative to a meeting of the Cabinet or Cabinet committee at which alternatives were debated and a common solution found. The style was an almost complete reversal of the pattern established under Nehru, when the preeminence of the Planning Commission was demonstrated by the practice of making all important decisions on economic policy at meetings of the Commission to which the concerned ministers were invited.

The difference held more than symbolic meaning. The Planning Commission, cut loose from the power of the prime minister, was most often represented in informal consultations and Cabinet meetings by its deputy chairman, Asoka Mehta. Mehta, who did not enjoy ministerial rank, operated from a weak position. A politician without a secure base of support after leading his own faction of the PSP back into the Congress party in 1963, he had relied for influence on his association with Nehru as the latter's hand-picked adviser. In the new circumstances, he had to be concerned as much with projecting his personal influence among his powerful colleagues, as with advancing the position of the Commission. On other counts as well, Mehta, who had played no role in establishing the independent authority of the Commission, agreed with many critics of the planners who argued they had exceeded their proper mandate as an advisory body in moving toward a policy-making role. Indeed, Mehta, who shared the view that "the Planning Commission had been throwing its weight around and causing annoyance to the ministers" advised Shastri favorably on proceeding with both of his early initiatives to introduce fixed term contracts for the members, and to end the secretarial link between the Cabinet and the Planning Commission. In fact, he went further. He argued the desirability of a basic reorientation in the role of the Planning Commission from that of arbiter of national economic policy—better left to the judgment of the central government ministries—to that of spokesman for state interests. Perhaps most important, although his public image as a socialist persisted, Mehta's thinking, according to his own account, had undergone substantial change by the time he was appointed deputy chairman in 1963. He was convinced that India lacked the political capacity and administrative machinery to operate a controlled economy, and was converted to the view that the only option corresponding to economic and political realities was a shift in planning toward a market approach, involving greater reliance on incentives to private investment. His thinking in this respect was hardly different from that of L. K. Jha and the senior officials of the finance ministry, although he retained a strong concern for keeping up the momentum of expenditure on heavy industries, partly out of desire to keep pace with China. Similarly, he had virtually no commitment to a continuation of the community development strategy in agriculture, on the ground of inadequate political and administrative infrastructure to carry out the agrarian reorganization of village panchayat and cooperative institutions, including joint land management, required for its effective implementation.[7]

Much of the burden of advancing the Perspective Planning Division's point of view on economic policy fell, under the new circumstances, on the finance minister, T. T. Krishnamachari, a longtime associate of Nehru who had shared his commitment to basic industrial development and the regimen of physical and price controls necessary to implement a large public-sector plan. But he was a political appointee whose power rested solely on his personal ability to retain the confidence of the prime minister. By contrast, the opponents of the Planning Commission tended to represent powerful constituencies in the state Congress party organizations, and could press their arguments from positions of independent political strength. Indeed, the shift of emphasis from the Planning Commission to the ministries in the formulation of economic policy meant that the representatives of the Commission had to counter not only the proposals advanced by the ministries, but the pressures applied by the chief ministers of the states through their allies in the Cabinet.

The first test of the Planning Commission's influence in the new power structure occurred at the October 1964 meeting of the National Development Council called to consider the *Memorandum on the Fourth Five Year Plan* prepared by the Perspective Planning Division. Citing the necessity of meeting commitments on improved living standards and levels of employment, and the desirability of reduced dependence on foreign aid, the memorandum provided projections for achieving "much higher rates of growth than was originally envisaged for the next two Plan periods"[8] at 6.5 percent per annum, including a 5 percent rate of growth in agriculture and 11 percent in organized industry. Despite formal endorsement for the principle of assigning highest priority in the allocation of resources to agriculture, the actual pattern of sectoral outlays envisaged was almost identical to that anticipated under the Third Plan—21.8 percent compared to 21.2 percent in agriculture, and 20.5 percent compared to 20.3 percent in industry.[9]

The size and pattern of investment were also associated, as before, with "certain directions of policy."[10] Total Plan outlay, projected at Rs. 15,520 crores, was tied to a major effort of additional resource mobilization, estimated at Rs. 2,500 crores to Rs. 3,000 crores. This required a

[7] Interview, Asoka Mehta, New Delhi, May 25, 1973 and June 12, 1973.
[8] Planning Commission, *Memorandum on the Fourth Five Year Plan,* pp. 3-4.
[9] *Ibid.*, p. 11.                        [10] *Ibid.*, p. 21.

multiple strategy of augmenting revenues by ending large-scale tax evasion, which was also responsible for the circulation of growing amounts
of "black money" in the economy with its dangerous inflationary impact; a price policy in the public sector based on a 12 percent return on
invested capital; and a dramatic increase in receipts from taxation of agricultural income. Equally important, the "highest attention" had to be
given to price stabilization.[11] Once again, the Planning Commission underlined "the necessity for the country to keep in readiness to contain the
prices of basic commodities through direct measures of controlled distribution," and recommended stronger efforts to "bring within state control the distribution at regulated prices of foodgrains, common varieties
of textiles and other primary consumer goods articles."[12]

The planners, still secure in the precedents of previous meetings of the
National Development Council, presented the memorandum for consideration in the expectation of pro forma discussion and approval. From
the beginning, however, the prime minister himself invited open dissent.
He described the draft "as essentially a first approximation" that would
have to take account of the need for a program of concrete action in agriculture geared to immediate results in ensuring a better life for the
common man. Simultaneously, moreover, Shastri announced that in
consultation with the deputy chairman, he had decided to constitute a
National Planning Council with the deputy chairman as head—but excluding the other members of the Planning Commission—to bring together some 15 to 20 scientists, economists, and other experts "who
could help the Planning Commission" in carrying out this task.[13]

The chief ministers, thus encouraged, gave strong expression to their
own reservations on a number of basic points. They questioned the
feasibility of additional resource mobilization by the states on the scale
envisaged, citing rising levels of committed expenditure and obligations
of debt repayment to the central government. They objected to the principle of large profits in the public sector, especially in industries serving
agriculture. They insisted on the importance of giving higher priority to
the allocation of investment to agriculture over industry, including larger
outlays on minor irrigation, rural market roads, and transport. Finally,
they asserted serious administrative weaknesses in implementing proposals for state procurement of foodgrains.

Shastri, who shared many of the misgivings of the state leadership
about the size, objectives, and priorities of the Fourth Plan memorandum
seized the opportunity to make an unprecedented suggestion. He proposed that the National Development Council establish five committees

---

[11] *Ibid.*, p. 92.                          [12] *Ibid.*, p. 6.
[13] Planning Commission, *Twenty-first Meeting of the National Development Council, Summary Record* (New Delhi, October 27 & 28, 1964), p. 2.

(Agriculture and Irrigation; Industry, Power and Transport; Social Services; Resources; and Development of Hill Areas) to "go into and advise on *policy issues* relating to programs in the respective sectors of the Fourth Plan."[14] By one stroke, the chief ministers of the states were accorded a formal role in the definition of national economic policy. For the first time since it was created, recommendations of the National Development Council to the Planning Commission on aspects of Plan policy took on the force of an official guideline. The impact was immediate. Although the council finally endorsed the broad outlines of the memorandum, it specifically instructed the Planning Commission to "provide *resources and inputs* sufficient to achieve a rate of growth [in agriculture] of not less than five percent per annum."[15]

The decisive shift of power on questions of economic policy from the Planning Commission to the ministries, and from the central government to the states, was dramatically demonstrated in the struggle over state trading that once again erupted as the government sought to meet the growing food crisis. The planners, while conceding the existence of real shortages created by stagnant output since 1961/62, insisted that price increases on the scale experienced could not be explained by shortfalls in production. They assigned greater blame to hoarding activities by the "farmer-trader axis"—larger producers and grain dealers accused of holding back stocks to convert marginal and local scarcities into large artificial shortages. The Commission urged an interventionist state role of stringent regulation of the private trade, including price controls, government procurement, and rationing of available supplies.

The prime minister, the Cabinet, and even the Congress Party's Working Committee[16] all accepted the Planning Commission's assessment that the immediate cause of rising foodgrains prices was a decline in market arrivals rather than an acute shortfall in supplies. They also believed that hoarding activities by the private trade were mainly responsible. But the food minister insisted that proposals for price controls and state trading offered, at best, only a short-term solution to meeting the food crisis. The real answer, according to Subramaniam, was to increase production. The method urged on the government was a return to the market approach of providing price incentives to private investment and much

---

[14] *Ibid.*, p. 12. Emphasis added.

[15] *Memorandum of Fourth Five Year Plan*, Annexure, Suggestions of the National Development Council, p. 195. Emphasis added.

[16] S. K. Patil was among those who conceded that the immediate cause of the food shortage was hoarding by farmers and traders, albeit in an interview in the United States. See *New York Times*, July 28, 1964. Subramaniam also publicly endorsed this view, *Times of India*, July 28, 1964. The Congress Working Committee, meeting in late August, similarly found "the speculative tendency and incentive for hoarding the two factors responsible for the current scarcity." *Hindustan Times*, August 20, 1964.

higher Plan outlays on yield–enhancing inputs, especially chemical fertilizer. In the short run, the ministry once again proposed to meet the
requirements of the deficit states by importing wheat and some rice
under PL 480, and arranging supplementary commercial imports of rice.
Subramaniam did not oppose the Planning Commission's suggestion to
establish a food trading organization for purchase of foodgrains from
domestic production; but in a major departure from previous policy, he
suggested that the state agency engage only in competitive open market
purchases with the private trade, and build up stocks by attracting voluntary offers of foodgrains at incentives prices.[17]

The argument over appropriate economic policies to meet the food
crisis, conducted in the context of ongoing preparations for the Fourth
Plan, reopened basic questions of national policy that Nehru had sought
to settle with his political counteroffensive in the year before his death.
The proposals advanced by Subramaniam had long been advocated by
his predecessors in the Union Cabinet, with the tacit support of the chief
ministers of the states. They had just as consistently been rejected by the
Planning Commission. The planners not only believed that a strategy of
agricultural development based on incentives to individual investment
would aggravate disparities between the minority of commerical farmers
and the mass of subsistence cultivators, but would require such large outlays on physical inputs, particularly chemical fertilizers, as to jeopardize
minimum investment levels required to maintain the momentum of the
industrial program. This was also the view of the finance minister.
Krishnamachari agreed on the need for a viable food economy, but argued that attention to increasing production was only one component of
an effective policy. The additional requirement, in periods of persistent
shortage, was for a national food distribution system to prevent pockets
of high demand from triggering a general price rise. Such a distribution
system, according to Krishnamachari, could only be established if the
government acquired a commanding position in the foodgrains trade
through policies of price control and monopoly procurement.[18]

Shastri, confronted with an urgent economic crisis that threatened to
degenerate into political disorder, but unable to work out a compromise
on national food policy once divergent ideological orientations complicated the debate, quickly accepted Subramaniam's suggestion that an expert committee headed by L. K. Jha might provide the best chance of
finding an acceptable solution to tide over the immediate crisis. In June

[17] *Hindustan Times*, June 29, 1964.

[18] Krishnamachari advanced this argument in an interview with Michael Brecher in July
1964. Michael Brecher, *Nehru's Mantle*, p. 144. One year later, he presented his analysis of
the key role of government procurement of foodgrains in preserving the approach to
planned development in a comprehensive note on economic policy circulated among members of the Working Committee at the AICC meeting in Bangalore. *Times of India*, July 24,
1965.

1964, Shastri appointed a Prices Committee under the leadership of his chief secretary to make recommendations on price policy for the 1964/65 season. As Subramaniam confidently expected, Jha's expert opinion coincided almost exactly with that of the food minister and the chief ministers of the states. He agreed that proposals for price controls, state trading, and rationing might have some utility as crisis measures, but that the basic solution to the food problem demanded a substantial increase in production.[19] Impressed with the efficiency of the technocratic approach in maximizing immediate growth goals, he was sympathetic to the view that past policies aimed at social transformation of the rural sector should be reversed to provide price incentives to commercial farmers, and much larger investment outlays on improved inputs.

Jha, who had to present the recommendations of his committee to a divided Cabinet, prepared his proposals in language that was carefully chosen to conciliate the planners and imply a continuation with the previous approach. The Jha Committee accepted the proposition of establishing a government trading organization at some future time. In the present period of scarcity, however, it recommended against any step that might further dislocate established trade patterns. The committee suggested, instead, that private traders continue to act as purchasing agents for the central and state governments, albeit subject to tighter regulation, including officially fixed profit margins. Purchases on behalf of government were to be carried out within the framework of the market mechanism, with one modification—the introduction of a central government monopoly over the movement of foodgrains across state boundaries—as the inescapable minimum restriction on the operation of the free market to improve government's competitive position relative to the private trade in purchasing foodgrains in surplus areas.

The core of the Jha Committee's report was its recommendations on price policy for the 1964/65 season. The language conformed to previous policy in fixing a two-tiered price structure for paddy: a guaranteed minimum or support price to protect farmers against an artificial drop in prices in isolated rural areas; and a maximum purchase/procurement price to impose a price ceiling in urban markets with high effective demand. In substance, however, the recommendations represented a basic departure from past policy in pegging support and purchase prices so high that they satisfied the food minister's redefinition of state trading as a mechanism for the voluntary purchase of foodgrains by government agents acting in competition with the private trade.

The minimum (guaranteed support) prices at the producers' level recommended by the Jha Committee as "fair and reasonable" exceeded the

[19] Interview, L. K. Jha, Washington, D.C., January 11, 1973.

average open market postharvest prices in all except two states over the previous three years—even though these prices were already higher than usual, in a period of scarcity. The government stood ready to purchase all paddy offered to it at the guaranteed support price. In addition, it was ready to compete with the private trade in open market purchases by offering a premium of Rs. 1 per quintal above the support price.[20] The recommendations for a higher minimum price structure were represented as a crisis measure, justified by the immediate need of government to attract additional stocks and meet its commitments to supply the fair price shops in urban areas. The impression that the Jha Committee's recommendations were an ad hoc response to a pressing food crisis, and not a statement of new policy, was strengthened by the agriculture minister's announcement of the intention to appoint a permanent Agricultural Prices Commission to make long-term recommendations on price policy and relative price structure. The proposals of the Jha Committee, placed before the Cabinet as an administrative solution to a managerial problem of rationalizing the distribution of available foodgrains aroused no serious opposition. They became the basis of government price policy for the 1964/65 season.

In July 1964, Subramaniam scored a more far-reaching victory. The agriculture minister announced a Cabinet decision to establish a foodgrains trading corporation, with branches throughout the country, to begin operations during the next harvest of January 1965. In a reversal of official policy, however, the new Food Corporation of India would not rely on price controls and compulsory procurement to acquire stocks, but was expected to compete with private traders in purchases on the open market by offering attractive prices to producers. Following the strategy of a modified market mechanism favored by Jha, the FCI was to be established with a competitive advantage of monopoly control over the movement of foodgrains between states and over long distances within states. Although the corporation was formally charged with the acquisition of wheat as well as rice, primary reliance for accumulation of wheat stocks in practice continued to be placed on imports under Pl 480. In July, S. K. Patil once again journeyed to the United States, and started negotiations for a new agreement to provide about 20 million tons of grain over a five-year period. In September, a fresh agreement was signed to cover the fiscal year ending June 30, 1965, for four million tons

---

[20] See Ministry of Food and Agriculture, Department of Agriculture, *Report of the Agricultural Prices Commission on Price Policy for Kharif Cereals for 1965-66 Season* (New Delhi, May-July 1965). The minimum prices of coarse paddy in the major rice-growing states recommended by the Jha Committee for 1964/65 ranged from a low of Rs. 33.50 per quintal to a high of Rs. 39.00 per quintal. The range of the average post-harvest prices for the three preceding years was Rs. 28.56 per quintal to Rs. 38.36 per quintal, p. 3.

of wheat and 300,000 tons of rice, and talks were scheduled to complete a similar agreement the following year.

But the issue was not settled. On the contrary, immediately after the Union government's announcement of the new maximum fixed prices for purchase and sale of standard varieties of paddy and wheat for the 1964/65 season, a fall in market arrivals forced an immediate reappraisal. Despite the fact that the states had endorsed the new price structure as remunerative, they quickly found that "the prices fixed by Government [had become] unreal and paddy and rice are being sold in the open market at much higher rates."[21] It soon became apparent that the private trade, dissatisfied with the narrow profit margins allowed,[22] was refusing to cooperate. As open market prices pushed up beyond the government's announced purchase price, the acquisition of rice in the surplus states on state and central government account became increasingly difficult. Government supplies available for distribution in the fair-price shops in the deficit states and large cities fell dangerously close to exhaustion.

By the end of October 1964, Shastri was finally convinced of the Planning Commission's view that the government's effort to stabilize food prices through the market mechanism was unrealistic. He found that the "traders are not prepared to cooperate with us. They want complete freedom and they will not play the game."[23] Subramaniam also appeared to shift his position, and agreed to the need for stringent controls on the private trade in order to stop the price rise. On the eve of the October 28 meeting of the National Development Council, Shastri, supported by Subramaniam, called a special meeting of the chief ministers to discuss the food situation. He took a strong position in recommending a comprehensive price control policy, including summary trial of private traders and heavy penalities for hoarding; the cordoning off of Bombay, Calcutta, and cities with a population of one million or more, as well as the entire state of Kerala, for the purpose of introducing statutory rationing; and the introduction of informal or partial rationing in urban areas with a population of 100,000 or more. The proposals had the effect of placing an additional responsibility on the central government for meeting the full deficit of Kerala and the requirements of all large urban centers. They therefore required a major additional procurement effort by the states. Shastri's recommendations ended with the request to the state governments to establish machinery for the procurement of foodgrains in surplus districts and states, including effective powers to requisition

---

[21] *Times of India*, October 19, 1966.

[22] Profit margins prescribed for the wholesale trade ranged from 1.5 to 2 percent, and for rice retailers from 4 to 7 percent, including transportation costs.

[23] *Times of India*, October 28, 1964.

stocks at maximum fixed prices when sufficient supplies were not forth-coming as voluntary offers of sale to state purchasing agents.

At the October meeting, the prime minister failed completely to convince the state chief ministers to carry out an active procurement policy. The only agreement taken was to cordon off Kerala and impose statutory rationing in that state. Decisions on all other aspects of the Union government's proposals for price control and rationing were deferred to the November 7 meeting of the AICC at Guntur, when the chief ministers agreed to a further review of the situation. On the eve of the Guntur session, the central government attempted to regain the initiative on food policy with promulgation of an ordinance under the Essential Commodities Act to provide for summary trial of traders involved in infringement of orders by the central and state governments for sale of foodgrains at controlled prices. The ordinance was hard-hitting. It provided that district collectors might seize the stocks of dealers suspected of contravening price control orders; conduct trials allowing no appeals; and impose sentences of fines of Rs. 2,000 or one month's imprisonment. State governments were requested to act immediately in empowering at least one magistrate at each district headquarters to try offenders.[24]

The Guntur session met in a crisis atmosphere amid reports of starvation deaths in Kerala. Rice in the open market was being sold at a hundred percent above the maximum price fixed by government, and the Center was unable to supply sufficient stocks to meet the minimum ration requirement for each card holder. Once again, Shastri and Subramaniam appealed for a formal commitment from the state governments for a program of compulsory procurement.[25] Once again, the chief ministers rejected their appeal.

Shastri's remaining option in restoring the primacy of the Center's decision-making role was a showdown confrontation with the states. The Union government, armed with emergency powers under the Defence of India Rules, was in a position to issue orders directing the states to enforce the central policy on procurement. At a final crisis meeting of the Working Committee and the chief ministers of the states held in New Delhi on November 19, 1964, however, Shastri pulled back from an open conflict. Instead, he surrendered the initiative to the chief ministers in allowing food policy to become a matter of negotiation between the

[24] *Times of India*, November 7, 1964.
[25] The impression of a powerless central leadership unable to impose a national food policy on the states was underscored in the press. A *Times of India* editorial on November 11, 1964, commented: "The failure of Shastri and Subramaniam to push through the AICC a Resolution endorsing the Government's professed food policy in regard to procurement and rationing creates the impression that the States are steadily becoming stronger at the expense of the Centre. It is known that only a handful of Chief Ministers are opposed to the food proposals of Mr. Shastri. In effect, these Chief Ministers are exercising a power to veto while the Centre looks on with apparent helplessness."

Center and the states. After two days of bargaining, the surplus states agreed to procure a total of two million tons of rice on central account during the 1964/65 season, mainly through the imposition of levies on the stocks of rice dealers, millers, and producers. The amount was the minimum necessary to meet prior central government obligations to supply the requirements of deficit states under the policy of government monopoly over interstate movement of rice. It was inadequate to support any major new commitments under proposals for the introduction of rationing in Kerala and the large urban centers. The result was a decision to limit statutory rationing to Calcutta and the urban areas of Kerala, and to acquire supplementary stocks through commerical imports.

For the remainder of the Third Plan, the actual enforcement of even such minimal commitments by the states depended less on what the chief ministers had undertaken to do in negotiations with the Union food minister than on considerations of political feasibility at the local level. Virtually all the state governments went through the motions of establishing machinery for enforcement of the antihoarding ordinances promulgated under the Essential Commodities Act. But the total number of prosecutions launched under the provisions of summary trial in more than two years was little more than 6,000. Convictions were obtained in about one half those cases, accounting for fewer than two percent of the 178,500 licensed foodgrains dealers.[26]

The record of the state governments in meeting their commitments to the Center for procurement was only somewhat better. Although virtually all states engaged in the purchase of foodgrains after 1965, the decision of whether or not to initiate some degree of compulsory levy was left to the political determination of the state leadership. In at least six states, there was no attempt to establish maximum controlled prices or compulsory levies, and all government procurement was carried out in the open market at announced purchase prices. In these states (Punjab, Uttar Pradesh, Rajasthan, Bihar, Mysore, and Orissa), government preferred to absorb the popular discontent created by steadily rising prices than to enforce a price control policy resented by larger landowners and traders in strategic positions at the local levels of the Congress party organizations. In other states, government procurement operations were a mixture of open market purchases and compulsory levy. Depending on the political influence of private wholesalers and millers, the size of the levy imposed varied widely from state to state. Altogether, in 1964/65,

---

[26] "Statement Showing Number of Prosecutions Launched and Convictions Obtained under the Essential Commodities Act in Respect of Foodgrains, December 1963–September 1966," Ministry of Food and Agriculture, Department of Food, 1966, mimeographed.

the state governments procured about 1.4 million tons of rice on central account, approximately 70 percent of the target.[27]

The establishment of the Food Corporation of India on January 1, 1965,[28] did little to overcome the problem of central dependence on the states for enforcement of a national food policy. On the contrary, the powers of the corporation were exercised in such a way as to make it an instrument of state policy, rather than an independent arm of the Union government.

The FCI and its state branches were expected to take over a progressively larger share of the responsibilities for financing, procuring, and arranging shipments of grain on central account from surplus states to deficit areas. Nevertheless, the states were left free to designate their own procurement agents: they could choose to authorize the corporation to carry out foodgrains purchases or continue to operate through their own licensed dealers, millers, or cooperatives. In the latter case, the stocks purchased by private agents were turned over to the corporation, which then took responsibility for storage and transportation. The FCI was, in addition, empowered to acquire its own stocks through open market purchases (at government-fixed maximum prices) either directly or through contracts with intermediaries. Arrangements for moving all stock acquired on behalf of the states and central governments to deficit districts within surplus states, or to deficit states, were made by the corporation on the basis of its monopoly control over long-distance shipment of grain.

A major limitation on the FCI as an agent of central government policy was imposed at the outset by its purely advisory role in discussions to determine the proportion of the marketed surplus that should be procured in each state. The decision on such questions remained a matter of negotiation between the Union food minister and the state chief ministers. Only after these political decisions were made, and each state indicated how much it was prepared to procure from its own marketed surplus, did the FCI begin to assume an operational role. Even at that point, the FCI could engage in actual procurement operations only at the invitation of the state government. In those cases when the corporation was invited to undertake procurement on behalf of the state, it was generally obstructed in efforts to develop its own local purchasing organization by pressures to contract for deliveries through intermediaries, either

[27] *Report of the Agricultural Prices Commission on Price Policy for Kharif Cereals for 1965-66 Season*, p. 17.

[28] The bill providing for the creation of the FCI was passed by the Lok Sabha on November 26, 1964. The corporation, which is wholly owned by the central government, includes representatives from the Ministries of Agriculture and Finance, the Central Warehousing Board, and six other nonofficial members.

the private trade or cooperatives. Under these conditions, private traders and millers who acted as middlemen between the producer and the corporation actually retained a strategic position of control over food stocks. In periods of acute shortage, traders were able to pay higher than maximum fixed rates, and have stocks held on their behalf in the villages, while limiting their deliveries to the corporation, and citing lower-than-average market arrivals. Then, as postharvest stocks declined, and open market prices rose, the larger producers, traders, and millers, having acquitted their formal obligations to the government, could exploit their ability to hold back stocks by arranging sales at premium prices in the black market or to retail dealers.[29]

The failures of the government in food policy resulted in increasingly virulent political attacks. In September 1964, the opposition was able to mobilize sufficient numbers to force a debate of no-confidence in the Lok Sabha against the Shastri government. Simultaneously, Congress ministries in the states were bombarded with a spate of no-confidence motions that charged them with "abject failure to tackle the food situation" and accused them of "shielding" the dealers in their failure to impose price controls.[30] Even dissident factions inside the Congress party did not hesitate to bring the same charges of incompetence and corruption against their own leadership. In Kerala, this tactic resulted in defections from the ruling Congress party, and the collapse of the ministry, paving the way for new elections and the resurgence of the Communist opposition.

The most chilling aspect of the political scene, however, was the first sign that economic discontent might be used to spur mass violence in the countryside. In December 1964, the newly formed CPI (Marxists), a radical left faction of the CPI that had broken with the parent body the previous July, met in congress at Calcutta to draft an action program. According to the government, booklets secretly circulated among the rank-and-file members indicated that the Marxists had determined on organizing a revolutionary party in the rural areas, based on "class strug-

---

[29] Even in good crop years, the FCI was bound to operate at a disadvantage as long as it could not establish its own procurement organization at the local level. The corporation's ability to attract stocks, and the period in which it concentrated active purchase operations, was limited to the first few months after harvest, when farmers were eager to make voluntary offers in return for slightly higher than open market prices. But there was no way to guarantee that private traders actually paid the statutory support price to cultivators, especially to subsistence farmers with small supplies to sell and immediate cash needs to satisfy, who sold their grain in their own villages or neighboring hamlets. Dishonest traders could increase their profits—and their control over the marketed surplus—by paying less than the minimum support price to subsistence cultivators, while holding back the extra stock they accumulated at the lower rates. The major beneficiaries of high support prices—apart from the traders—were the large farmers, who could deliver their grain to corporation depots in the towns and collect the statutory wholesale price.

[30] *Times of India*, July 28, 1964.

gle and communism," and were proceeding to create small primary cells among the landless peasantry, and to coordinate them on a regional basis.[31] This threat was considered sufficiently serious—especially in face of the upcoming elections in Kerala—that the Shastri government authorized large-scale arrests of active organizers of the CPI (Marxists) under the Defence of India Rules. In an extraordinary radio address to the nation, Home Minister Nanda explained the action by asserting that "the leaders of the party have been preparing the rank and file for armed revolution and guerrilla warfare. They have been exhorting their followers to organize a massive agitation designed to create an atmosphere of disorder in which the party can resort to violent methods."[32]

At the annual session of the Congress party at Durgapur in early January 1965, the tension created by feelings of political frustration and fears of popular disorder found expression in "the most ruthless criticism of the Government [by the rank and file] ever to be witnessed at a Congress session."[33] The effort of the Working Committee to defuse the debate by confining the content of the official resolution on the economic situation to a factual summary of current difficulties and assurances by the government of action to meet them failed when a barrage of protests was unleashed from all sides during the discussion of the Subjects Committee. The small group of radicals, now loosely organized in the Congress Forum for Socialist Action, and claiming to be the real guardians of Nehru's legacy, took the lead in pressing for formal reaffirmation of the goals of democracy and socialism adopted at Bhubaneswar, and the policy measures essential to their implementation. Their domination of the debate ultimately persuaded the Working Committee of the necessity to redraft the resolution as a restatement of faith in the "basic concepts and programmes" of economic policy laid down at Bhubaneswar. The victory was, however, only partial. Although the revised resolution reiterated the goal of "progress towards a socialist society . . . measured in terms of the success achieved in creating adequate employment opportu-

[31] Excerpts from a booklet written in Bengali, identified as circulated by the Marxists, and calling for the creation of a revolutionary party organized for class struggle, were published in *Times of India*, January 5, 1965.

[32] The text of Nanda's radio address is published in *Times of India*, January 2, 1965. The situation was made to appear even more grave by Nanda's attempt to link the formation of the CPI (Marxists) with aggressive designs by China on Indian border areas, and the intention to synchronize a fresh attack with a Marxist-led internal revolution. According to Nanda, "There was reason to believe that the left Communist party was formed under Peking's inspiration and was to serve as Peking's instrument in creating conditions of instability in the country and to facilitate the promotion of Chinese designs against India in furtherance of her grand strategy of establishing hegemony over Asia and her declared aim of world revolution. . . . The object of the party now is to promote internal revolution to synchronize with a fresh Chinese attack, destroying the democratic Government of India through a kind of pincer movement."

[33] *Times of India*, January 11, 1965.

nities and in ensuring for every family a minimum standard in respect of the essential needs of life," the action programs suggested avoided the issue of institutional change by emphasizing projects aimed at "quickening the pace of production, both in industry and agriculture." The resolution, reverting to generalities, called for measures to "minimize disparities and prevent the concentration of economic power and monopoly in all its forms," without direct reference to the specific proposals at Bhubaneswar for limitations on private income and property, and social control of banks. Similarly, while it noted the "crucial importance" of evolving a national plan for the distribution of foodgrains, it made no explicit endorsement of the introduction of price controls and state trading, or government control over agricultural processing industries.[34] On the whole, the Durgapur resolution gave visible manifestation to the quickening internal contradiction in the development of the Congress party: the conflict between the foundation of its legitimacy in the pledges of economic and social reform endorsed by the national leadership and the practical constraints on their implementation created by the dominant role of the landed and business classes at all levels of the organization. The dilemma was perhaps best symbolized by the resolution's call, on the one hand, for a "bold Fourth plan and at the same time [speedy advance] towards the goal of socialism"; and on the other, for a "period of consolidation" over the next two years.

Even this ambivalent endorsement of planning was immediately challenged at the highest level of the party leadership. Within less than forty-eight hours of the publication of the new draft resolution, Kamaraj, making his presidential address to the plenary session, unexpectedly delivered a major statement on economic policy that questioned the feasibility of the entire Fourth Plan. Beginning with a tribute to Nehru as the "last giant among the national leaders . . . with the vision and the authority to draw up the framework of policy in national and international affairs and to impart to events a sense of direction"—a not-too-subtle reminder to Shastri that he was not of the same stature and could not presume similar authority—Kamaraj justified his intervention by evoking a new principle of collective leadership that clearly assigned a coequal role to the party organization on decisions involving national policy. He asserted, "it became clear to all of us that no single leader of the eminence of Gandhiji or Jawaharlalji was available for shaping the affairs of the country and a collective leadership of workers who had imbibed the ideals of these leaders and who had worked under their guidance had to bear the responsibility of guiding the nation."[35]

[34] The text of the Durgapur Resolution on the economic situation is published in *Times of India*, January 8, 1965.

[35] The text of the Congress president's speech is printed in *Times of India*, January 10, 1965.

Having thus paved the way, the Congress president went on to assert that "the present food situation in the country leads us all to ponder over the Fourth Plan proposals of the Planning Commission." In particular, he found that projected outlays (of Rs. 21,500 crores to Rs. 22,500 crores) were of such magnitude that they would release even greater inflationary pressures and impose more severe hardships on the poor, and on this account, were unwise. He questioned, in addition, the feasibility of financing such a large Plan, given the limited opportunity for taxation "in new fields." He appeared to hint at an alternative approach in his observation that "there is plenty of room for the private sector to grow." Most of all, he underlined the political authority implicit in his criticism, by expressing the "earnest hope that the Governments at the Centre and the States will give their most careful consideration to the anxieties which I have expressed." Shastri responded immediately. He announced a decision to call a full meeting of the Planning Commission to review the Cabinet's decision on the size of the Fourth Plan, in view of the Congress president's advice.

At the January 19 meeting of the Commission, over which Shastri presided, the planners, buoyed by the support of the finance minister and the mood of the rank and file at the Durgapur session, refused to give ground. While noting the Congress president's concern over the inflationary potentialities of a big plan, they argued that the appropriate solution rested on greater financial discipline, especially price control measures and food rationing in the cities. Subramaniam, who was present, and by this time convinced that adequate enforcement machinery for control of the private trade could not be created in the absence of state support, did not press the argument. At the end of the meeting, the Planning Commission announced it did not favor a cut in the size of the Fourth Plan.[36]

The Commission's ability to resist further encroachments on its policy-making role was rapidly crumbling. The business community was now able to circumvent the planners by exploiting alternative access routes to the prime minister at the highest levels of the Congress party and in his secretariat. They found powerful advocates to advance the arguments that India could protect herself from the Chinese military threat and also find sufficient resources for development only through an expanded role for domestic private enterprise in collaboration with foreign private investment.[37] By January 1965, in fact, a whole series of negotiations to attract foreign capital were in progress. Starting in late 1964, the petroleum ministry entered into negotiations with the American-owned Bechtels International for a joint government-Bechtels project to set up

[36] *Times of India*, January 19, 1965.
[37] For a discussion of the political inspiration behind this argument see K. N. Raj, *Indian Economic Growth*, Lecture 2: "Industrial Growth and Foreign Aid," 1964, mimeographed.

five large fertilizer factories in India. Although Bechtels finally conceded the government's demand for a majority share in the capital structure (of 51 percent), they insisted on complete technical and managerial control during construction, and control over prices, marketing, and distribution for an indefinite period thereafter. T. T. Krishnamachari, who found the terms prejudicial to India's economic independence, ultimately succeeded in vetoing the agreement. Yet, teams of industrialists continued to be invited to visit India to study the possibilities for investment. The most dramatic sign of the change in political orientation came when FICCI arranged to host the annual meeting of the International Chambers of Commerce in New Delhi—which brought more than 1,000 representatives of international business corporations to India—and the inaugural session was attended by the prime minister.

Indeed, Shastri was increasingly influenced by his official advisers to accept the business community's arguments in favor of a period of "consolidation" in the public sector. Significantly, at the same meeting in which the planners affirmed their commitment to a big plan, Shastri took two further initiatives to dilute the commission's authoritative position. He finally announced the appointment of a National Planning Council, headed by the deputy chairman, and composed of seventeen "expert" nonofficial members, including industrialists, trade unionists, and workers connected with the rural sector, to "work in close and continuous association with the Planning Commission." The innovation, represented as a measure to promote support for planning by involving outside experts in the Commission's work, was bitterly resented by the members. Shastri's attempt to conciliate them through inclusion as full participants in the new body met with little success. Although the expert members of the NPC were supposed to be assigned according to their competence and interest to work with individual members of the Commission, and to meet together with them two or three times a week, the new arrangement never worked as intended, partly because of the hostility of the planners.[38]

Shastri's second unprecedented initiative was his announcement appointing a Business Advisory Council to act as a panel of consultants to the Planning Commission in the formulation of the industrial program of the Fourth Plan. At the end of January, the council, including the president of FICCI and eleven other representatives of Indian and foreign business, were accorded a full-dress meeting with the Planning Commis-

[38] See A. H. Hanson, "Power Shifts and Regional Balances," in Paul Streeten and Michael Lipton, eds., *The Crisis of Indian Planning*. Although the National Planning Council did not play an important policy-making role in the formulation of the Fourth Plan, it did provide an additional forum for the expression of group interests, and imposed the further burden on the planners of considering the recommendations of the twelve study groups created by the NPC on various aspects of development policy.

sion, the ministers of petroleum and chemicals, commerce, industry, and heavy engineering, and the heads of major government financial institutions. The meeting produced assurances by Asoka Mehta that the process of consultation would be continued until the Plan was completed, and the scope for development in the private sector "will continue to be very large and in fact much larger in the Fourth Plan than in earlier plans."[39] The growing estrangement between the deputy chairman and the members of the Planning Commission was highlighted by the failure of the planners to extend a second invitation for a meeting to its Business Advisory Group.

Nevertheless, the pressures on the planners mounted. The Commission, preoccupied with staving off its domestic critics in an effort to prevent a major departure from the aims, strategy, and methods of development of previous plans, was unprepared to fight on the second front that soon opened. In the early months of 1965, a special World Bank Mission, conducting a six-month study of economic policy under the Third Plan, tacitly joined forces with the opponents of the Commission in an assault on their competence that finally ended in the complete collapse of their authority to establish the basic principles of plan policy.

World Bank experts had been arguing at least since 1958 that India's public-sector programs were too ambitious, and a larger role should be assigned to Indian private enterprise and foreign private capital in industrial development. They also endorsed the United States' point of view that agriculture should receive priority in the allocation of investment resources, and that incentives to farmers for the adoption of modern inputs, especially fertilizers, in the irrigated areas of the country, represented the optimal production strategy. Although the Third Plan had made some accommodations to these criticisms, the concessions, as authorized by Nehru, were granted on the understanding that there would be no departure from the social goals of planning. When the Bank's experts arrived for their appraisal of the Indian economy in late 1964, however, Nehru was dead; the competence of the Planning Commission was under widespread attack; and the economy was caught in an accelerating food crisis that threatened to spill over into political violence. The prospect of restoring economic progress under the Fourth Plan, moreover, rested heavily on the ability to continue to attract high levels of foreign aid. In fact, the failure to achieve the projected targets for the manufacture of capital goods and components in India during the Third Plan meant that foreign aid requirements were higher than ever. Compared to little over $1 billion per annum received during the Third Plan, India's needs were estimated at $1.6 billion per year,[40] or almost one-fourth the

[39] *Times of India*, January 30, 1965.          [40] *Times of India*, April 17, 1965.

total outlay in the public sector projected by the *Memorandum on the Fourth Plan*.

The Economic Mission's criticism of Indian planning,[41] expressed in the technical language of detached experts concerned with maximizing efficiency in the use of scarce resources, nevertheless involved an attack on the Planning Commission for allowing political objectives of institutional change to determine the development approach. It questioned the practicability of village-based agricultural programs and the efficiency of extending cooperation to all economic activities, particularly to cultivation of land. Above all, the Bank's experts did not believe that cooperation ought to be pursued for its own sake. Rather, if some other method were more efficient in raising agricultural productivity, then that method should be adopted. The Economic Mission laid special stress on the need for pragmatism in the formulation of development policy. If the objective was to achieve accelerated agricultural growth, and if non-co-operative institutions could contribute to this end more effectively, in credit, in marketing, provision of inputs and farming, these institutions ought to be used. In particular, from this point of view, it would be much more efficient to focus on the individual farmer rather than the village as the decision-making focus of agricultural policy. Indeed, the Mission's experts argued that within the existing constraints of technical knowledge, land tenure and farm size, it was possible to achieve substantial increases in agricultural production by providing price and cost incentives to individual farmers for higher private investment on modern inputs. The major components of the new approach urged on the Indian government were a reorientation of overall investment priorities toward agriculture; incentive prices at levels high enough to guarantee profitability to individual farmers using the most advanced techniques; and the concentration of modern inputs, especially pure seeds, pesticides, power, implements, and above all, fertilizers, in areas with assured water from irrigation.

The implication of the new policies for the social goals of Indian planning were clearly spelled out. The Bank's experts had little illusion that their recommendations for achieving rapid agricultural growth were reconcilable, at least in the short term, with the aim of reducing disparities. Apart from the obvious consequences of aggravating inequalities between irrigated and rain-fed areas, there was also the recognition that initial adoption trials with fertilizer were made for the most

---

[41] The mission's critical evaluation of India's economic policy was presented in the Report to the President of the International Bank for Reconstruction and Development and the International Development Association on *India's Economic Development Effort*, Vols. II, III, IV, *Agricultural Policy* and *Appendices*. 1964/65 Economic Mission Headed by Bernard R. Bell, October 1, 1965. Following is a summary of the major points made by the Economic Mission in the Bell *Report*.

part by owner-cultivators with larger size holdings of 8 to 25 acres. Only such farmers, by virtue of their superior economic standing, education, and social status at the top of the village hierarchy could afford to take the economic and social risks of innovation.

In the case of the improved practices recommended by the World Bank Mission, the economic assets of the individual farmer became a primary consideration for an additional reason. Major irrigation schemes, constructed to provide drought protection over maximum areas, generally could not supply the higher water levels per acre necessary for the most efficient use of modern inputs, especially chemical fertilizer. On the whole, the new technology required supplementary water from a tubewell. Accordingly, the Mission leaned toward the view that in many areas the best result would come from encouraging private investment in tubewells, where the nature of the water resources permitted this.

Finally, the Mission acknowledged that the new agricultural policy was competitive with a program of industrial expansion in the public sector, requiring not only a much larger share of domestic investment, but foreign exchange for the import of modern inputs, especially chemical fertilizer. It therefore combined its recommendations on agriculture with renewed emphasis on the necessity of greater efforts by government to attract higher levels of domestic and foreign private investment in industry. The package of policies recommended included proposals for relaxation of controls on industrial licensing; and an import liberalization program to stimulate investment in priority industries. As part of the strategy for strengthening price incentives in the promotion of export-oriented industries, moreover, the mission made its first recommendation for the devaluation of the rupee. Attributing India's chronic trade imbalance to an overvalued exchange rate that reduced the competitiveness of exports in foreign markets, the Mission argued that devaluation, supported by relaxation of industrial licensing controls and import liberalization, would work to stimulate investment in the more profitable export sector by freeing the market mechanism to operate efficiently in allocating scarce resources. The step also had the ancillary advantage of creating more attractive terms of exchange as incentives to foreign private investment.

The package of economic reforms recommended by the World Bank, taken together, represented a fundamental departure from basic principles of planning laid down by Nehru and followed by the Planning Commission. It was, however, presented to the Indian government as the condition of substantial inflows of aid, along with informal assurances of a significant increase in foreign assistance to levels reaching $1.5 billion annually during the period of the Fourth Plan.

Expert opinion in the finance ministry and the prime minister's secretariat was generally favorable. The policy changes recommended by the Bank were in broad agreement with their own assessment that a reorientation of economic planning toward greater reliance on incentives to the private sector was the only realistic course in the situation of highly constrained resources. They also viewed the prospect of devaluation as virtually inevitable. Indeed, they pointed out that the growing reliance, since 1962, on export promotion policies involving a wide variety of subsidization schemes and rising import duties to counteract the negative effect on exports of an overvalued exchange rate had already added up to a partial de facto devaluation of the parity rate of the rupee. Within the government, Asoka Mehta and Subramaniam took a similar view: both advocated a quick positive response to the Bank's proposals in order to maximize the proffered inducements of rising levels of foreign aid.

At the highest levels of the government and the Congress party, even when opinion was favorable on other items of economic reform, there was, however, resistance to the idea of devaluation. Some objections grew out of immediate and relatively narrow concerns over the impact of such a step on the Congress party's chances at the forthcoming election. Others reflected more general political resentment at foreign pressure on a matter considered integral to the independence of the nation. There was finally, an emotional resistance to the step, as a confession of failure of the previous ten years of economic policy. Probably no one felt this last sentiment more keenly than T. T. Krishnamachari, who as finance minister in the late 1950s had helped Nehru lay the foundations of a modern industrial structure meant to take India to the goal of self-reliance. In a major radio address on July 18, 1965,[42] he flatly stated his determination to resist devaluation of the rupee. Asserting that devaluation was "no answer to our problem," he argued that, on the contrary, it would increase India's long-term foreign exchange difficulties by slowing down import substitution programs in the industrial sector through imposition of a "sharp, sudden and indiscriminate increase in the prices of even those imports which could not be conceivably produced at home in the immediate future." Conversely, the price of India's exports would be lowered, including the bulk of traditional items such as jute and tea that faced an inelastic world demand. The alternative, which the finance minister later advanced in the form of a supplementary budget, was to apply even more stringent controls on imports in an across-the-board tariff increase.

Krishnamachari was, however, alone in suggesting that if necessary India should be prepared to do entirely without World Bank or Consortium aid, and seek bilateral aid arrangements with friendly countries, even at the cost of declining net inflows. The policy implications of following this approach were outlined by him at some length in a note on

[42] The text of Krishnamachari's speech is published in *Times of India*, July 18, 1965.

the current economic situation submitted to the AICC meeting in Banga-lore on July 24.[43] Stressing the need for "every possible endeavor . . . to channel future investments so as to increase import substitution and im-prove the export capability of the country," the finance minister outlined a program for reducing dependence on foreign aid that emphasized the necessity of establishing a public distribution system based on price con-trols, monopoly procurement of foodgrains, and strict rationing of avail-able supplies.[44] Assaying the most efficient mechanism for ensuring gov-ernment control over agricultural surpluses, Krishnamachari reverted to the original approach of the Planning Commission in advocating reor-ganization of the rural sector into cooperatives, in order to link credit to marketing through repayment in kind, with the "objective of substantial procurement by Government." The finance minister, who received a sympathetic hearing from both the prime minister and the Congress president in his arguments against devaluation, found no response to his proposals for institutional change at the core of the programs recom-mended to reduce India's dependence on foreign aid. The AICC session ended without passing any resolution on economic policy.

Longstanding pressures by the major aid-giving powers, applied against a new and insecure government uncertain of its prospects at the next poll, and anxious to deliver on the economic front, were, in fact, having their effect. The national leadership, already alarmed at the first signs of popular discontent erupting into violence, found further reason for worry in the emergence of the Marxists as the largest single party in the mid-term election in Kerala in March 1965.[45] By April, moreover, Shastri was challenged within his own party by threats of defection from

[43] *Times of India*, July 24, 1965.

[44] At almost the same time, the Food and Agriculture Ministry's own Agricultural Prices Commission used the occasion of its first report to argue that government control over the foodgrains market was necessary to an effective price stabilization program. The commis-sion presented statistics to show that government (central and state) requirements of rice, simply to meet rising demands on the fair price shops serving the cities would reach 14 percent of the marketed surplus in 1966, and climb to 22 percent by 1971. When meeting the entire requirements of deficit states was taken into account under the new policy of government monopoly over movement of rice across state boundaries, the ratio of required purchases to marketable surplus was much higher, amounting to 4 million tons and almost 30 percent of the surplus in 1966. Assuming a persisting overall shortage in food supplies, the commission argued that "voluntary methods may not enable the Government to pur-chase the quantities it required except at a very high price. . . . If the States make purchases at the market price and make most of its sales at lower prices, it will have to incur an enor-mous expenditure to subsidize its operations." It therefore saw "no escape in the immediate future, from the use of the levy system—or compulsory purchases at fixed prices which may be lower than the market prices." *Report of the Agricultural Prices Commission on Price Policy for Kharif Cereals for 1965-66 Season*, pp. 24-25.

[45] For a detailed review of the comparative strength of the Congress party, the CPI, and the CPI (Marxists) in the state elections of 1965, see Bashiruddin Ahmed, "Communist and Congress Prospects in Kerala," in Centre for the Study of Developing Societies, *Party Sys-tem and Election Studies*.

dissident Congressmen who met to discuss the formation of a new party,
possibly in alliance with Swatantra, to enlist support for private enterprise at home and full alignment with the "Western democratic parties"
in foreign affairs.[46] Despite his reluctance to endorse a formal departure
from Nehru's approach, Shastri was nevertheless confronted with the
confluence of two mutually reinforcing pressures, which when combined made the continuation of past policies virtually impossible: the
growing strength of the chief ministers of the states relative to the Center
in their effective opposition to social reform; and the sharp criticism of
the World Bank that development policies requiring institutional change
were unrealistic instruments of growth, and should be corrected in order
to demonstrate India's claim to continued consideration by the large aid-
givers.

   In the event, Shastri did not take personal responsibility for the break
with past economic policy. By the spring of 1965, he was almost wholly
preoccupied with foreign affairs involving first the confrontation with
Pakistan over incursion of Pakistani troops into the Rann of Kutch, and
the full-scale war that erupted in September over the disputed status of
Kashmir. The shift in economic policy was managed mainly by the
ministries, as Shastri relied even more heavily on the view of the executive departments in the preparation of action programs to achieve production goals.
   The initiative on agricultural policy passed to Subramaniam. The agriculture minister was impressed by the arguments of World Bank and
American experts that the food problem could be solved through application of modern technology, supported by large investments on modern inputs and price incentives to farmers to adopt them. As early as
January 1, 1965, at the first meeting of the NDC's Committee on
Agriculture and Irrigation, Subramaniam outlined a comprehensive program of raising production that included proposals for "administrative
reorganization from top to bottom" to ensure a "common approach . . .
[and] common objective of achieving results" among the various ministries involved with agriculture, especially at the central level—the first
bid to dismantle the separate identity of the Community Development
Ministry. Other items recommended strengthening agricultural research
and training in modern techniques with the help of American technical
assistance; a sharp increase in the domestic production and import of
physical inputs; and price incentives to farmers. On this last point, Subramaniam stressed the need to get away from "mere slogan shouting and make pragmatic approach to the problem [of credit and distribu-
tion]," appearing to echo World Bank opinion in posing the rhetorical

[46] *Times of India*, April 30, 1965.

question: "Where cooperation is not in a position to deliver the goods, shall we wait indefinitely for the cooperatives to become effective instruments?"[47]

The same message was delivered to the Lok Sabha in April 1965 with publication of a 71-page pamphlet by the Department of Agriculture to provide extended argumentation for the minister's view that "scientific knowledge is available and technological conditions also exist to achieve this goal [of a 5.6 percent rate of gowth per annum in output], provided the requisite supplies are arranged, the administrative organizations are streamlined and adequate financial provisions are made."[48] By this time, Subramaniam had taken the first step toward formal reorientation of the agricultural strategy from a community-oriented labor-intensive approach to an entrepreneurial pattern emphasizing high levels of private investment in modern inputs. He announced a change in the central government policy on subsidies to the states from one allowing only for expenditures on general agricultural infrastructure, to a program of direct payments to individual farmers for costs of investment in tubewells and other improved implements and inputs. According to the Agriculture Department, detailed examination of the possibilities for using subsidies as incentives to farmers for private investment showed that "subsidies have an important role in spearheading development efforts in new directions and accelerating the use of new inputs as also encouraging larger use of inputs which lead to increased production. Subsidies are an important means of encouraging new investment by lowering net cost of additional inputs, reducing the risk of investment and promoting capital formation."[49]

Then, in August 1965, as the Planning Commission entered the final stages of preparing its comprehensive approach document on the Fourth Plan for presentation to the September 1965 meeting of the National Development Council, the Ministry of Food and Agriculture published its own detailed outline of a strategy and program for agricultural production, which it described as "the new approach of the Government of India."[50] The strategy was advanced under three heads: (1) new policies, (2) incentives to farmers, and (3) special intensive production in selected areas. The new policies were mainly an amalgam of the dominant strains in foreign expert advice represented by the World Bank, USAID, and the Ford Foundation then enjoying maximum influence on the thinking of the agriculture minister. They repeated the recommendations for combi-

[47] Subramaniam's speech is reprinted as Appendix I of Ministry of Food and Agriculture, *Agricultural Development: Problems and Perspective*.

[48] *Ibid*., p. 2.                                    [49] *Ibid*., p. 53.

[50] Ministry of Food and Agriculture, *Agricultural Production in the Fourth Five Year Plan: Strategy and Programme* (cited hereafter as *Strategy and Programme*), p. 1.

nation and concentration of modern inputs, based on the application of "scientific techniques and knowledge of production at all stages, particularly in the fields"; and the selection of "a few areas with assured rainfall and irrigation for concentrated application of [a] package of practices." The second element, incentives to farmers, emphasized the necessity of making a long-term commitment to the favorable price structure represented by the ad hoc decisions taken in 1964/65 to "fix prices of agricultural commodities on remunerative basis" and to set up the Food Corporation to "ensure the availability of this price to the farmers" through arrangements for procurement.

The third prong of the approach for special intensive production in selected areas, however, appeared in a dramatic new form. Anxious to clinch the argument in favor of a major reorientation of investment priorities toward agriculture, and eager to offer more hard evidence in favor of his case that application of scientific techniques could in fact solve the food problem, the agriculture minister was receptive to the first reports of a new technology that could guarantee remarkable results. Starting in the early 1960s, the Rockefeller Foundation, in collaboration with the food and agriculture ministry's Indian Council of Agricultural Research, had succeeded in developing new hybrid varieties of maize suitable to Indian field conditions that were able to double the maximum yield of local varieties. By 1964, there were also reports of a breakthrough in wheat pioneered by the Rockefeller Foundation in Mexico. Hybrids of Mexican wheat and dwarf strains from Japan produced new shorter varieties capable of absorbing much higher doses of chemical fertilizer without lodging (falling over), to give yield levels of 5,000 pounds per acre, more than twice the potential output of local Indian varieties. Similar advances were reported for rice in the Philippines, where "miracle" seeds produced as a result of hybridization between indigenous tall varieties and dwarf strains from Taiwan were highly fertilizer-responsive and gave yields of 5,000 to 6,000 pounds per acre—approximately three times the maximum of local varieties. The difficulty was that, with the exception of maize, a minor foodgrains crop, data on the performance of the high-yielding varieties under Indian field conditions were still insufficient to establish their value. Intent on winning the policy debate with the finance ministry and the Planning Commission, and buoyed by the enthusiastic reports of foreign experts, Subramaniam took a decision, involving in part "an act of faith"[51] to base the planning for the special intensive programs around the high-yielding varieties. According to the calculations of the Department of Agriculture (built on production co-

[51] In 1966, Subramaniam's personal secretary characterized the planning for the new agricultural strategy as very crude. He described the high-yielding varieties programs as involving, to some extent, "an act of faith" on the part of the ministry. Interview, New Delhi, June 12, 1966.

efficients worked out in cooperation with American experts), the new seeds in combination with optimal dosages of chemical fertilizers were capable of yielding additional output of one ton per acre of paddy and wheat; one-half ton per acre of jowar and maize; and one-quarter ton per acre of bajra. On the basis of these technical yardsticks, the ministry proposed a special intensive program for the cultivation of the high-yielding varieties on 12 percent of the area under food crops, to provide as much as five-sixths of the total increase necessary to meet consumption targets in 1970/71. In absolute terms, intensive cultivation based on the new seeds was expected to add 25 million tons of foodgrains to production, out of the 30 million needed during the Fourth Plan.[52] Total output would be boosted from the base level of 90 million tons in 1965 to 125 million tons in 1971. The projected increase approached 38 percent over a five-year period, or over 7 percent per annum. By contrast, between 1949/50 and 1964/65, the annual increase in foodgrains production averaged approximately 3 percent.

The advantage in bargaining power to the agriculture ministry of adopting the high-yielding varieties program as the core of the new agricultural strategy was considerable. It allowed Subramaniam to offer scientific evidence that his ministry had found "a formula [and] a programme which would take us toward self-sufficiency"[53] within a time-bound period, provided only that the planners made concessions in the salience of social goals of development. Speaking to the Lok Sabha on December 7, 1965, Subramaniam argued that the major "concrete lesson" of past failures was the policy under the Community Development program of insisting on all-India coverage in the distribution of inputs, which diluted scarce resources below the critical level needed to achieve significant increases in output. The continuation of this pattern would be all the more damaging in the case of the new seed varieties, where prospects of achieving optimal levels depended on the availability of assured water supply and the application of a "package" of modern inputs, especially very high doses of chemical fertilizers and pesticides. Therefore, the agriculture minister asserted, "if we concentrate our efforts in a given area where we have assured water supply and we have the necessary extension services also concentrated in that area, then it should be possible for us to achieve much better results than by merely dispersing our effort in a thin way throughout the country."[54]

[52] On the basis of the technical yardsticks used by the Ministry of Food and Agriculture, it was proposed to cover 12.5 million acres under paddy; 8 million acres under wheat; 4 million acres under maize; 4 million acres under jowar; and 4 million acres under bajra, to get an additional yield of 25.5 million tons of foodgrains of all the varieties in this area (of 32.5 million acres) alone. See *Strategy and Programme*, pp. 5-6.

[53] India, Lok Sabha Secretariat, *Lok Sabha Debates*, Third Series, Vol. XLIX, No. 24 (December 7, 1965), 6075.

[54] *Ibid.*

Equally important to the success of the new approach, the cultivator had to be provided with incentives to adopt the new practices. Once again, the agriculture minister insisted this required a reversal of past approaches to price policy, from a preoccupation with providing low-cost foodgrains for the urban poor, to a firm commitment to "remunerative and incentive prices to make this production process reasonably safe for farmers."[55] In practice, this meant long-term guarantees of profitable minimum support prices for foodgrains, as well as higher incentive prices for government purchases of surplus produce.

Above and beyond the advantage of providing empirical support for a basic shift in plan priorities from multiple social goals of development toward an exclusive emphasis on growth, the availability of more sophisticated technical data showing strong positive complementarities on production coefficients from the combined use of high-yielding varieties, fertilizer, and irrigation allowed the ministry to base its claims for much higher allocations of foreign exchange on input-output ratios that were "scientifically" as respectable as the technical yardsticks used to justify the resource requirements of the industrial program. This was, in fact, the major purpose of the exercises carried out in the ministry as part of Subramaniam's crusade to break through the finance ministry's objections to higher allocations of foreign exchange for agriculture.

In almost all cases, domestic production of essential inputs for the agricultural program fell far short of the total requirement. The most serious gap occurred in the availability of chemical fertilizers. According to projections based on the (much higher) fertilizer response ratios for the new varieties, the likely consumption level of nitrogenous fertilizer (taking into account both the increased application rates in the areas selected for the high-yielding varieties program, and the amount needed to maintain and moderately increase consumption levels in the rest of the country) was 2,400,000 tons in 1970/71.[56] By contrast, domestic production in 1965/66 was 450,000 tons.[57] Even by 1971, India's capacity for production of nitrogen was expected at best to reach 1,800,000 tons.[58]

Indigenous capacity for manufacturing other key inputs was similarly limited. Indeed, there was virtually no modern seed industry. During the Second and Third Plans, nucleus/breeder's stock of the best local varieties grown on government research farms were multiplied as foundation seed on Block seed farms. But the severe scarcity of trained personnel to supervise the growing process and a paucity of modern equipment to carry out scientific roguing, drying, and cleaning operations to ensure

---

[55] C. Subramaniam, "New Agricultural Strategy in a Socialist Society," mimeographed, p. 5.
[56] *Strategy and Programme*, p. 7.
[57] Fertilizer Association of India, *Fertilizer Statistics, 1965-66* (New Delhi, 1967), p. 6.
[58] *Ibid.*, pp. 8-9.

good germination and trueness to variety, resulted in foundation seed that was not pure. These difficulties were aggravated by the practice of having the seed multiplied further on the fields of registered growers at the village level. In many instances, there was little difference between the "improved" seed sold in government stores and the grains that farmers customarily kept back from their produce for sowing. But the whole rationale of the high–yielding varieties program rested on assuring supplies of pure varietal materials, which had to be replaced with fresh seeds at least every four years.

Another supply bottleneck was pesticides. The total requirement for plan protection materials starting in 1968/69 was estimated to be over 76,000 tons,[59] compared to an installed capacity of less than 26,000 tons in 1966.[60] The same magnitude of discrepancies in supply and consumption requirements appeared with respect to the availability of agricultural machinery. According to the ministry, requirements for application equipment for pesticides by 1971 included about 1,500,000 manually operated sprayer/dusters and over 300,000 power sprayers.[61] In contrast, during the Third Plan, domestic industry produced approximately 100,000 hand-operated sprayer/dusters and only 900 units of power sprayers annually.[62] Similarly, compared to an estimated demand for 150,000 tractors in 1971,[63] all-India production in 1965/66 was about 2,000.[64] Some 400,000 power tillers were also needed,[65] but Indian industry was equipped to produce fewer than 35,000.[66]

The foreign exchange component of the new agricultural strategy was, in fact, very high. In August 1965, the Ministry of Agriculture estimated the foreign exchange costs of implementing the new strategy at Rs. 1,114 crores for the five–year period 1966–1971.[67] By contrast, the total amount allocated to agriculture during the Third Plan period was approximately Rs. 191 crores.[68] The practical import of the ministry's calculations, therefore, was that the essential inputs for the production program in agriculture could only be provided by a major shift of priorities in the allocation of foreign exchange, involving a sharp reduction, if necessary, in the amounts available for expansion of the core industrial sector.

[59] *Strategy and Programme*, p. 11.

[60] Ministry of Food and Agriculture, Department of Agriculture, *Report of the Working Group for the Formulation of the Fourth Plan Proposals on Plant Protection* (New Delhi, 1965) (cited hereafter as *Plant Protection*), p. 34.

[61] *Strategy and Programme*, p. 12.        |        [62] *Plant Protection*, p. 3.

[63] *Strategy and Programme*, p. 13.

[64] Estimate provided by deputy secretary (Pesticides, Agricultural Machinery), Department of Agriculture, Ministry of Food and Agriculture, New Delhi, July 17, 1966.

[65] *Strategy and Programme*, p. 13.                [66] Estimate provided as in n. 64 above.

[67] *Strategy and Programme*, p. 24.

[68] Estimate of value of imports into India of fertilizers and agricultural machinery during the Third Plan provided by the Planning Commission, July 1966.

There was only one other available source: foreign private investment. Not so clearly stated, but nonetheless implicit in the approach, was an enhanced role for private enterprise, both domestic and foreign, in fields of production and marketing previously closed to them or made unattractive by government controls over pricing and distribution. This was, in fact, the solution urged on India by the United States and the World Bank, along with recommendations for relaxation of controls and maximum reliance on the market mechanism.

The major case in point was fertilizer. Until 1965/66, virtually all the installed capacity for the production of fertilizers was in the public sector. Although the private sector was not completely excluded, government policies on price and distribution effectively discouraged private enterprise from meeting even the modest targets allocated to them. High operating costs in public-sector factories—a function of inefficient technology and low rates of utilization—led government to the practice of subsidizing the costs of fertilizers by placing both high-priced indigenously produced products and less expensive imports into a central fertilizer pool, and setting pool prices for all fertilizers at rates below the actual procurement price for the domestic product. In addition, during the three five-year plans, the cooperative sector enjoyed a monopoly over the distribution of nitrogenous fertilizers. The allocation from the central government to the Departments of Agriculture in the various states were distributed through the district cooperative societies, which acted as wholesalers in selling fertilizers to taluka primary marketing societies, which in turn distributed nitrogen to affiliated primary credit societies, or in cases where the local village society was not a member of the marketing society, kept supplies for direct sale to consumers at taluka godowns. The local cooperatives, moreover, were allowed a standard margin of only ten percent above the purchase price to cover the costs of warehousing, unloading, loading, wastage, and commission, and in many instances were engaged in unecomonic operations.

Actually, there were sound technical arguments in favor of inviting foreign private investors to come in and set up the necessary facilities. Foreign contractors were expected to be able to put new fertilizer factories on stream within three years from date of first construction, compared to the five or six years commonly taken by public-sector factories. The foreign chemical companies were also considered to have the skills and equipment necessary to operate fertilizer factories at or near full capacity, compared to the average of sixty-one percent achieved in public-sector factories during the Third Plan.[69] A more immediate consideration was that advances in fertilizer technology originating in the United

[69] Department of Agriculture, Ministry of Food and Agriculture, *Report of the Committee on Fertilizers* (New Delhi, 1965), p. iii.

States held out the prospect of building new plants capable of manufac-turing higher-analysis products at savings in total production costs of about ten percent. The economies on the costs of production were in turn expected to permit some reduction in the sale price of chemical fer-tilizer, to make it more economical for the farmer to apply optimum doses and get maximum yields from the adoption of the high-yielding seed varieties.

Indian and foreign businessmen, moreover, expressed interest in par-ticipating in new fertilizer projects. The Tatas, Birlas, and several other Indian firms presented plans for fertilizer factories to the government. Among foreign investors (in addition to the Bechtel Corporation), Standard Oil, Armour and Company, Phillips Petroleum, Allied Chem-icals Corporation, and American International Oil Company indicated an interest in establishing fertilizer projects. Their price, however, was considerable. Indian companies demanded complete freedom to fix their prices; to sell where and when they chose; and to select their own selling agents and dealers. Foreign firms demanded majority control of equity in all projects supported by them and/or a majority on the Management Board; monopoly rights over marketing in the zones assigned to them; freedom from price control for an indefinite period of time; and mutually agreeable formulas, negotiated in advance, for setting the price of any sales to the government. This was not all. In 1965, during negotiations between the Union Ministry of Petroleum and Chemicals and a number of international oil companies, the latter also insisted that fertilizer fac-tories in which they participate should also operate with imported am-monia. Representatives of the international oil companies argued they could supply ammonia from their subsidiaries in the Arabian Gulf and North Africa at less capital expense than the cost of manufacturing nitro-gen in India from indigenous sources of naptha. Indian experts, even those who accepted this estimate, pointed out that imported ammonia would have to be paid for entirely in foreign exchange, whereas the pro-duction of ammonia in India ensured that foreign exchange expenditures on maintenance imports—and reliance on foreign aid for that purpose—would diminish in the future.

As the full range of concessions in ideological and social goals of plan-ning demanded by the new agricultural strategy came into sharper focus, the Planning Commission, which had at first been enthusiastic about the potentiality of the new technology to increase production, began to resist any restatement of plan policies that suggested a major departure from the past approach. V.K.R.V. Rao, then member (Agriculture) of the Commission, refused to accept the food and agriculture ministry's ver-sion of the draft chapter on agriculture in preparing the revised approach document of the Fourth Plan, presented to the National Development Council in September 1965.[70] Although the draft prepared by the Agricultural Division of the Planning Commission was amended to take into account many of the recommendations of the food and agriculture ministry, Rao nevertheless succeeded in changing the tone of the policy statement. As presented in the final document, *Fourth Five Year Plan— Resources, Outlays and Programmes*, the ministry's proposal for a special intensive program in selected areas was treated as an additional technological element to existing policies made possible by "the discovery of some very high-yielding, fertilizer responsive, and non-lodging varieties of paddy, wheat, maize, jowar and bajra."[71] No mention was made of the size of the new program, its contribution to the physical targets of agricultural production, or the actual magnitude of the essential inputs required. The Plan confined itself to the bland statement that "the Ministry of Food and Agriculture has proposed an upward revision of the programme targets for fertilizer consumption and plant protection measures."[72] The proposals for intensive agricultural development, moreover, were linked with universal participation by cultivators in selected areas through an emphasis on "the concerted and well-coordinated efforts of the Community Development organization, Panchayati Raj institutions and Cooperatives,"[73] and a renewed exhortation to the states to implement land reform measures as soon as possible.

There were other, more tangible, signs of the planners' resistance. According to the Commission, the feasible target for agricultural production in 1971 was only 120 million tons, compared to the higher figure of 125 million tons set down by the ministry.[74] The lower target reflected the commission's appraisal, pressed in arguments with the ministry, that it was unwise to rely so heavily on the high-yielding varieties in the production program when they had still to be extensively tested under Indian conditions. The lower target, which also implied a smaller intensive program for foodgrains, permitted the Planning Commission to reduce the target for consumption of nitrogenous fertilizers from the 2.4 million tons in 1971 advanced by the Food and Agriculture Ministry to 2 million tons,[75] thereby making the strain on the balance of payments somewhat more manageable. On the whole, moreover, while claiming to meet the National Development Council's mandate of providing sufficient resources and inputs for agriculture to achieve a 5 percent rate of growth, the planners slashed by over 46 percent the total financial outlay on ag-

[70] Interview, V.K.R.V. Rao, New Delhi, August 17, 1966.
[71] Planning Commission, *Fourth Five Year Plan—Resources, Outlays and Programmes*, p. 27.
[72] *Ibid.*, p. 28.                                    [73] *Ibid.*
[74] *Ibid.*, p. 29.                                    [75] *Ibid.*

ricultural production programs proposed by the ministry—with the cut rising to about 58 percent in the case of manures and fertilizers.[76]

Even so, the Planning Commission could not solve the problem of financial resources for a large plan within the political constraints imposed, on the one hand, by the National Development Council regarding measures to mobilize additional internal resources; and on the other, by the World Bank for higher levels of foreign assistance. At the outset, the planners felt compelled to respond to the National Development Council's criticism that total outlay of Rs. 22,500 crores during the Fourth Plan as proposed in the October 1964 memorandum was bound to result in inflationary financing. The revised document, which kept the private sector's investment target of Rs. 7,000 crores intact, reduced the size of public-sector investment from Rs. 15,620 crores earlier projected to Rs. 14,500 crores, with no adjustment for inflationary changes in the price level during the preceding year. Constricted by the directive of the NDC to provide adequate funds for agriculture, the planners were able to make only marginal reductions in the allocations proposed for agriculture and irrigation; in fact, the revised draft showed a slight increase over the memorandum of 1 percent in the proportionate outlay for the agricultural sector, reaching 22.8 percent, compared to 21.8 percent in the earlier version. By contrast, investment funds for organized industry were reduced from 3,200 crores to Rs. 2,866 crores, depressing the proportionate share of industry in Plan outlay to 19.8 percent, somewhat below Third Plan levels.[77] The cut was rationalized as having no adverse effect on industrial growth rates during the Fourth Plan, with the main impact falling on output from programs and activities whose benefits were expected to accrue in the Fifth Plan period.

Even then, the size of the Fourth Plan at Rs. 14,500 crores depended on efforts to mobilize additional internal resources amounting to Rs. 3,650 crores, an increase of Rs. 650 crores over levels recommended in the memorandum.[78] Additional resource mobilization of this magnitude required a sharp increase in domestic savings,[79] a good part of which had to be raised from additional taxation.[80] The effort inevitably required new tax measures in the rural areas to siphon off some significant proportion of the additional income generated by the large investments planned

---

[76] *Ibid.*, p. 30.          [77] *Ibid.*, pp. 4-7.

[78] The increase arose mainly from the Fourth Finance Commission's unexpectedly generous award to the states.

[79] Additional resource mobilization of the magnitude envisaged in the September 1965 version of the Fourth Plan implied an increase in domestic savings from about 10.5 percent at the end of the Third Plan to approximately 15 percent at the end of the Fourth Plan. *Fourth Five Year Plan—Resources, Outlays and Programmes*, p. 21.

[80] The planners aimed at boosting tax receipts as a proportion of national income from less than 13 percent in 1965–66 to 18 percent at the end of the Fourth Plan, *ibid.*

on improving agriculture. According to Asoka Mehta, the continuation of past patterns had become untenable. During the three plans, of the Rs. 4,142 crores in additional taxation raised by both the Center and the states, only Rs. 95 crores—or 2.6 percent—had been contributed by direct agricultural taxes or in irrigation rates. By contrast, the extra taxation effort required to mobilize adequate internal resources for the Fourth Plan demanded that at least "one fourth of the additional mobilization of resources should come from the rural sector as without that the Plan would not be sustained."[81]

The other resource bottleneck was foreign exchange. According to the planners, India's export earnings during the five-year period were not likely to be more than Rs. 5,100 crores. Against this, requirements of maintenance imports amounted to Rs. 5,300 crores. In addition, outflows of foreign exchange to meet debt reservicing obligations climbed to Rs. 1,350 crores. Exclusive of expenditures on imports for new projects and programs included in the Plan, therefore, India's foreign exchange resources were deficit by about Rs. 1,550 crores, simply to meet current expenses.[82] If, on top of this, the food and agriculture ministry's estimate of its import requirement at about Rs. 1,100 crores were allowed to stand as the first charge on foreign exchange resources for the Plan, then external assistance in the amount of about Rs. 2,650 crores was from the outset preempted. Yet, during the Third Plan, gross assistance had not exceeded the level of Rs. 2,600 crores.[83] Confronted with this reality, but unable to enforce its own priorities on the National Development Council, the Planning Commission avoided the issue by indicating that the Fourth Plan could be financed only if external assistance of the "order of Rs. 4,000 crores is available."[84] In practical terms, this meant that the level of foreign assistance would have to be increased from approximately $1.1 billion dollars per annum during the Third Plan to $1.7 billion per annum during the Fourth Plan. Barring an increase in aid of roughly this magnitude, the requirements of the production programs under the new agricultural strategy were clearly competitive with plans for expansion of industrial programs in the public sector.

Shastri, explaining the implications of attracting much higher aid levels to the September 1965 meeting of the National Development

---

[81] Planning Commission. *Twenty-Second Meeting of the National Development Council, Summary Record*, New Delhi, September 5 & 6, 1965, p. 47.

[82] *Fourth Five Year Plan—Resources, Outlays and Programmes*, p. 25.

[83] *Ibid.*, p. 25.

[84] *Ibid.*, p. 15. The growing burden of debt repayment, which increased from Rs. 500 crores during the Third Plan to Rs. 1,350 crores during the Fourth Plan, meant that the projected increase in gross external assistance of about 54 percent from Rs. 2,600 crores to Rs. 4,000 crores provided a gain in net assistance of only about 26 percent, from Rs. 2,100 crores to Rs. 2,650 crores. *Ibid.*, p. 25.

Council, did not mince words. He told the members that India's ability to attract external resources of this magnitude "all depended on the goodwill of countries that had been helping India and also institutions like the World Bank, etc. Naturally, they would expect that India should do something of her own."[85] Yet the issue was not clearly faced. The session coincided with escalation of the conflict between India and Pakistan into full-scale air and ground battles. Although the NDC gave perfunctory approval for the overall size of the Fourth Plan at Rs. 21,500 crores, the state leaders clearly gave top priority to defense needs in ensuring a "war-oriented" plan. Indeed, the council voted sweeping authority to Shastri as chairman "to reorientate, alter and amend the Plan as necessary to meet the emergent situation and safeguard the country's security and long-term interests."[86] Unlike Nehru, when confronted with similar circumstances in 1962, Shastri made no impassioned appeal for preserving the Plan as the best safeguard of national security. On the contrary, he immediately ordered the Commission to determine "the changes that were needed to be made in the programmes proposed for the Fourth Plan to ensure that the requirements of both defense and development are met, so far as possible, by the development of productive resources in the country."[87] Simultaneously, moreover, Shastri directed the Commission to formulate the Annual Plan of 1966/67 in advance of preparation of the Draft Outline of the Fourth Plan, and to emphasize quick-yielding schemes in agriculture and better utilization of industrial capacities already created.

The fate of the Fourth Plan, which was already behind schedule as a result of the additional tasks imposed on the planners, subsequently became even more precarious as several events combined to increase the leverage of the agriculture ministry. By September, the country was feeling the first impact of the failure of the monsoons, which ultimately saw unprecedented decline in agricultural production of 17 percent between 1964/65 and 1965/66.[88] Within a year, wholesale prices of foodgrains jumped almost 14 percent.[89] Yet despite the sharp increase in demand for supplies by the deficit states, the central government remained powerless to force the surplus states to procure at higher levels than in the previous year, even though the favorable maximum price structure was continued. The chief ministers were, nevertheless, finally compelled to agree on a scheme for statutory rationing in cities with a population of over 100,000. The difficulty, as Subramaniam explained to the Congress par-

[85] *Twenty-Second Meeting of the National Development Council, Summary Record*, p. 45.
[86] *Ibid.*, p. 58.
[87] Planning Commission, *Fourth Five Year Plan: A Draft Outline*, p. xii.
[88] *Ibid.*, p. 172.
[89] India, *Economic Survey, 1966-67* (Delhi, 1967), Appendix, Statistical Tables, 5.1, "Index Number of Wholesale Prices."

liamentary party in November 1965, was that all government buffer stocks were exhausted.[90] The only alternative was to arrange for substantial imports. By this time, however, the United States, as a sign of displeasure at the waste of scarce resources in an unproductive war, had indefinitely suspended all aid to both India and Pakistan. It had, moreover, refused to sign a fresh long-term agreement with India under PL 480 when the existing agreement expired in August 1965. Instead, the Johnson administration, egged on by growing Congressional opposition to concessional food aid for India, adopted a "short-tether" policy of doling out stocks sufficient only to meet requirements a few months at a time, and explicitly tying the continuation of food aid to the adoption by India of policies aimed at increasing agricultural production and curbing population growth. Against an estimated overall requirement of about 8 million tons in 1965/66, the United States, between September and December 1965, released an additional two million tons.

The shift in the American approach to foreign aid which made "specific aid offers contingent upon the institution of particular adjustments in indigenous rural policy,"[91] strengthened Subramaniam's position in the ongoing policy debate. The agriculture minister, who traveled to Washington in November 1965 and submitted his ministry's program for comment to the U.S. Department of Agriculture, came away with assurances that the new agricultural strategy would satisfy the basic conditions for a resumption of American food shipments. In December, in another meeting in Rome between Subramaniam and U.S. Secretary of Agriculture Orville Freeman, the specific policy proposals were reviewed item by item, including the plans for incentives to foreign private investment, especially in fertilizer.

By early December, all of these pressures finally overwhelmed the objections raised by the finance minister and the Planning Commission. After discussions between Subramaniam and Shastri, the agriculture ministry's scheme for achieving self-sufficiency in foodgrains through the three-pronged approach of intensive cultivation of the high-yielding varieties, concentration of improved inputs in irrigated areas, and price incentives to producers, was placed before the full Cabinet. Despite vehement objections by the finance minister, the Cabinet voted to give its approval. Almost at the same time, the central government announced a new policy of concessions to foreign private companies willing to invest in the fertilizer industry in India. Any foreign company signing a contract before March 31, 1967, would enjoy the freedom to set its own prices and establish its own distribution apparatus for a period of

---

[90] *Times of India*, November 11, 1965.
[91] The new aid philosophy was expressed by John Lewis, then USAID administrator in New Delhi, and is cited in Chopra, *Uncertain India*, p. 348.

seven years, subject to the qualifications that the Indian collaborator (whether the Government of India or a private entrepreneur) would control the majority of equity, and the government would enjoy the option to buy thirty percent of the annual output at negotiated prices.

A final condition of the resumption of large-scale foreign aid had still to be met, that of devaluation. Krishnamachari, as the responsible minister, still refused to consider such a step. Shastri's view remained unclear, and no formal decision was taken. Yet there is some indirect evidence that the prime minister, despite his dislike for appearing to yield to foreign pressure, had become persuaded by his expert advisors. On the eve of his departure for Tashkent and negotiations with President Ayub Khan on an accord to end the Indo–Pakistan War, Shastri took a decision that had the predictable effect of precipitating T. T. Krishnamachari's resignation from the Cabinet.

Starting the previous February, Krishnamachari had been the target of charges alleging improper use of his office in favor of a firm, T. T. Krishnamachari and Sons, then managed by his sons. The charges, circulated in anonymous pamphlets to members of parliament, were attributed by the finance minister to "some of these businessmen who have openly said that if only I ceased to be in the Government they could prosper."[92] By the end of November, the charges suddenly surfaced in a formal memorandum to the president presented by several members of parliament, which demanded an official inquiry. Krishnamachari, who was by that time defending a minority position in the Cabinet on the question of economic controls, battling with the ministries to enforce budget cuts, and fighting to impose financial discipline on the states in the face of pressure to expand currency and credit and allow large unauthorized overdrafts—all at the same time as he was embroiled in the dispute with the World Bank on the question of devaluation—clearly required a show of support from the prime minister to sustain his influence. The finance minister's view, which he expressed several times to Shastri, was that it was necessary for the prime minister personally to dismiss the charges against him and express faith in his integrity. Shastri, meanwhile, was being advised against clearing Krishnamachari on grounds that he would become personally responsible for answering the charges, and vulnerable to future attacks if the campaign persisted. On the eve of his departure, Shastri took his decision. He informed Krishnamachari of his intention to submit the charges to an independent judicial authority for an impartial examination. On December 31, Krishnamachari announced his resignation from the government. In a press conference on January 4, he defined the issue as ultimately "one of confidence between the Finance Minister and his Prime Minister. . . . I can only interpret the Prime Minister's desire to consult someone else as indicating that the confidence he had in me is not the kind or the degree which I should expect."[93]

Within less than twenty-four hours, Shastri announced the name of Krishnamachari's successor. His choice, Sachindra Chaudhuri, was an MP from West Bengal with little experience in public finance. He was, in fact, the nominee of P. C. Bhattacharjea, then Reserve Bank governor, and a strong proponent of devaluation as the best means of breaking the bottleneck that had appeared during discussions with the International Monetary Fund on additional loans to India. Chaudhuri was expected to lean heavily on Bhattacharjea and the experts in the prime minister's secretariat for advice. He was, moreover, well regarded by the World Bank. An authority on company law, and a director of several private companies at the time of his appointment, he had previously negotiated with the Bank on behalf of the Government of India. Within a few days, the first agreement with the United States since the suspension of American economic aid was announced, to lend India $50 million to purchase fertilizer and fertilizer raw materials.

On January 11, 1966, the news of Shastri's sudden death at Tashkent shocked New Delhi. Although the immediate transition was smoothly handled—Gulzarilal Nanda, as the senior minister in the Union Cabinet once again acceded to the role of acting prime minister—the unexpected turn of events found the party leadership unprepared to coalesce around a common candidate for the succession. The members of the Syndicate were united mainly by the negative consensus that the first priority was to stop Morarji Desai from assuming power. The alternatives were limited. Nanda was so lacking in political stature as to raise doubt he could defeat Desai in a contest within the Congress parliamentary party or provide the positive national image needed to galvanize voters in the upcoming 1967 elections. The other serious candidate, Y. B. Chavan, then defense minister, had a secure political base in Maharashtra, a progressive image, but a relatively limited regional appeal. He was, moreover, unacceptable to Patil on the basis of a longstanding rivalry in Bombay politics, and had also irritated Nijalingappa by what the latter considered a partisan intervention from the Center on behalf of Maharashtra against Mysore in the border dispute between the two states.

At the outset, the Syndicate made urgent efforts to arrange a consensus around the candidacy of Kamaraj himself. The Congress president, who kept his own counsel, and was conscious of his personal limitations as a national leader unable to speak either Hindi or English, refused to be per-

---

[93] The text of T. T. Krishnamachari's statement made to the press conference is published in *Times of India*, June 4, 1966.

suaded. The logic of the situation, in which the overriding criteria were to find a candidate capable of defeating Morarji Desai in the event of an open contest in the CPP and of projecting a popular national image in an election year, pointed to the selection of Indira Gandhi. This was, in fact, the assessment Kamaraj made.[94]

Mrs. Gandhi enjoyed several advantages. First she was Jawaharlal Nehru's daughter, carrying the aura of having been his closest confidante. In addition, she was in her own right an authentic symbol of continuity with the Congress party's commitment to nationalist goals. A young activist during the 1942 Quit-India movement, she had been the third generation of her family to suffer imprisonment for India's independence. Further, although Mrs. Gandhi's rapid rise in the party— starting in 1955, when she was named to the Working Committee, the Central Parliamentary Board, and the Central Election Committee, and culminating in 1959 in her election as Congress president—came about initially at Nehru's instance, over the years she developed her own group of supporters, especially among younger party workers. Finally, her popularity appeared to extend beyond the party and to survive her father's death. During the Shastri period, Mrs. Gandhi was the only national figure who could rival the prime minister in the ability to draw large crowds simply by virtue of her presence. She was, moreover, acceptable to the nation's minorities, including the Muslims, as a trustee of the Nehru family's commitment to secular values. In fact, during the time Shastri served as prime minister, Mrs. Gandhi continued to be cast in the role first assigned to her as a young woman by Mahatma Gandhi during the Hindu-Muslim riots at the time of Independence, that of national peacemaker in situations of local communal conflict.

Actually, Shastri had recognized Mrs. Gandhi's utility in enhancing the legitimacy of his government. Although he ignored suggestions that she be offered the senior portfolio of external affairs, and invited her to join his government as minister of information and broadcasting, he indirectly conceded her unique personal role not only by elevating the minister of information and broadcasting to Cabinet status, but assigning her fourth rank in the Cabinet as a whole. In another departure from precedent, Shastri included Mrs. Gandhi in the Emergency Committee of the Cabinet, along with the ministers of home affairs, finance, external affairs, and defense.

Mrs. Gandhi also appeared useful to the conservative government in deflecting criticism from the left. She had a "progressive" image in the party, having supported the younger activists in their efforts to organize Socialist Forum groups since the late 1950s. She was, indeed, accessible

---

[94] For a detailed account of the round of political discussions and maneuvers that resulted in the elevation of Mrs. Gandhi as prime minister, see Brecher, *Nehru's Mantle*, ch. 8.

to leaders of the left opposition parties, maintaining friendships since her student days in London with men such as Bhupesh Gupta and Mohan Kumaramangalam, who later cast their political fortunes with the CPI. Like her father, she was reputed to be a firm proponent of planning, somewhat suspicious of private enterprise, and well disposed toward the Soviet Union.

The Syndicate was, nevertheless, uneasy. Its most conservative member, S. K. Patil, found Mrs. Gandhi's reputation for left-leaning views unpalatable. Others resented her manner. They felt she had adopted an imperious attitude in her personal relations with the older party leaders that was especially inappropriate when measured against her real accomplishments; and that she nurtured an arrogance about her antecedents as a Nehru that led her to demand the same degree of deference accorded her father for great sacrifices and achievements.[95]

Kamaraj, however, found both of these qualities less threatening. He was in his political outlook less conservative than other members of the Syndicate. Indeed, by contrast to Patil and Nijalingappa, and even to Mrs. Gandhi, Kamaraj was often described as holding radical views.[96] More important, he felt confident of controlling Mrs. Gandhi. Her performance as the fourth-ranking member of the Shastri Cabinet suggested no reason for alarm. As Brecher reported, Mrs. Gandhi was not among "the people who matter in the broad spectrum of Cabinet deliberations." She spoke "rarely in Cabinet as in Parliament, and has not made a mark on either."[97] At the outset of the second succession debate, moreover, when Mrs. Gandhi's name was first suggested, and she was sounded on her reaction, she limited her response to the modest intimation that "if there is near unanimity and Kamaraj asks me, I would stand."[98] After the January 14 meeting of the Working Committee failed to produce a unanimous choice of the new leader,[99] and Mrs. Gandhi for the first time publicly acknowledged that she would be a candidate, it was again with the caveat "only if the Congress President asked her to do so."[100]

Ultimately, the Syndicate responded to pressures generated by Kamaraj. The Congress president not only encouraged Mrs. Gandhi's younger supporters to come to Delhi and lobby for her in parliament; but through constant personal consultations with the chief ministers of the states, during which he expressed his own preference, he helped

[95] This attitude of personal irritation experienced by members of the Syndicate is reported by Kuldip Nayar, *India, The Critical Years*, p. 21.

[96] Of 63 politicians, including 36 Congress MPs, interviewed by Michael Brecher in March 1967, 30 ranked Kamaraj first in commitment to the implementation of a socialist program; 20 awarded the first place to Mrs. Gandhi. Michael Brecher, *Political Leadership in India, An Analysis of Elite Attitudes*, p. 83.

[97] Brecher, *Nehru's Mantle*, p. 113.              [98] *Ibid.*, p. 202.

[99] *Congress Bulletin*, Nos. 1, 2, 3 (January–March 1966).

[100] *Times of India*, January 14, 1966.

create the climate in which a breakthrough was achieved. On January 15, eight chief ministers, meeting at the headquarters of D. P. Mishra, then chief minister of Madhya Pradesh and Mrs. Gandhi's strongest supporter among the state leaders, issued a public statement calling for her election as leader of the CPP. Nijalingappa, the only member of the Syndicate who was also a chief minister at the time, joined in signing the statement. Subsequently, Atulya Ghosh and Sanjiva Reddy signified their acquiescence in the decision. Although the press declared "the succession was practically settled" once the chief ministers had made their declaration, Mrs. Gandhi still continued to accept numerous new pledges of support by telling journalists she "would do what Mr. Kamaraj tells me."[101]

Desai himself believed he "would not win because these people had gone around and cornered everybody and promised them everything." Still, he remained firm in pressing the decision to an open contest in the CPP in an affirmation of the principle of an election by free vote. The most he permitted himself by way of campaigning was a telephone call to every MP, followed by a letter saying in effect they "should support the best person to run the Government, and if they believe I am the best person, they should vote for me."[102] In the end, when the election was held on January 19, Mrs. Gandhi won easily with about two-thirds of the vote, polling 355 out of a total of 526. Nevertheless, Desai, who had spurned even the more innocent forms of bargaining for support common to democratic politics, had through the force of his personality managed to retain the allegiance of about one-third the CPP.

The outcome and the process preceding it contributed to a certain ambiguity about the source and scope of the new prime minister's power. On the one hand, Kamaraj, and later the chief ministers of the states, gravitated toward Mrs. Gandhi's candidacy on the basis of their assessment that she alone possessed the qualities necessary to win a decisive victory in the CPP and in the country at large. On the other, Kamaraj, through his maneuvers in manipulating the consensus of the chief ministers, was credited with converting Mrs. Gandhi's potential appeal into actual power, putting pressures on MPs in an election year during which party tickets would be distributed by state leaders. The elevation of Mrs. Gandhi, therefore, was subject to the interpretation that power had shifted even more sharply toward the Congress president (if somewhat away from the Syndicate) and to the chief ministers of the states.

The expectation that Mrs. Gandhi would be a convenient instrument for the influence of the Congress president and state party leaders appeared at first to be amply rewarded. Before announcing the composition of her new Cabinet, Mrs. Gandhi held long consultations with, among others, Atulya Ghosh, Sanjiva Reddy, Y. B. Chavan, and S. K.

---

[101] *Ibid*.          [102] Interview, Morarji Desai, New Delhi, August 30, 1973.

Patil.[103] The changes she announced, moreover, seemed minor. Ironically, they included a reorganization of the administrative departments concerned with food production to satisfy Subramaniam's demand for a common approach among the central ministries involved in agriculture were merged. The subjects of Community Development and Cooperation into an enlarged Ministry of Food and Agriculture. Thereafter, the Ministry of Community Development, which Nehru had once believed would become the focal center of the peaceful transformation of the countryside, ceased to have an independent existence or input in the decision-making process on agriculture. Subramaniam achieved even greater authority over economic policy through appointment as a full member of the Planning Commission. Asoka Mehta was similarly elevated in influence by appointment as minister of planning.

[103] *Times of India*, January 24, 1966.

## EIGHT

# Crisis of
# National Economic Planning

At the outset, Mrs. Gandhi's new government had to cope with severe failures in virtually all sectors of the economy. Signs of stagnation were apparent on all sides. During the Third Plan (1961-1966), per capita income did not increase at all as population growth rates neutralized the low overall gains in the rate of growth of national income. Per capita availability of foodgrains and other essential articles of consumption were at or slightly below levels achieved in 1956. Agricultural output, relatively stationary in the first three years of the Plan, spurted upward after a good monsoon in 1964, but then precipitously declined in the drought year that followed. Despite record imports of 25 million tons of foodgrains over the Plan period, prices of food articles increased by 32 percent, signaling the onset of a serious inflation.

The repercussions were felt throughout the economy. Although substantial additional capacity was created in a number of industries, including steel, engineering goods, and chemicals, shortages of domestic raw materials, compounded by low levels of demand, slowed down the overall increase in industrial production. Average growth rates of 8 to 10 percent during the first years of the Third Plan declined to little more than 4 percent in 1965/66.[1] No progress at all could be made in solving the problem of unemployment. On the contrary, the backlog of unemployed, estimated at 12 millions at the end of the Third Plan, was expected to increase to 15 million persons by 1971.[2] Any prospect of making up the shortfalls in Plan performance by expanding future development programs was, moreover, seriously diminished by the shrinking share of budgetary resources available for investment. During the Third Plan, the proportion of domestic budgetary finances to total finances for Plan outlay declined to 59 percent. The balance was funded by foreign aid, which accounted for 28 percent of total Plan outlay, and deficit financing, which contributed the remaining 13 percent.[3]

The food crisis continued to worsen. Despite imposition, in the early months of 1966, of statutory rationing in Kerala and all large cities and

[1] A review of the economic situation at the end of the Third Plan is presented in Planning Commission, *Fourth Five Year Plan, 1969-74, Draft*, pp. 5-7.
[2] Planning Commission, *Fourth Five Year Plan, A Draft Outline*, pp. 106-108.
[3] Planning Commission, *Fourth Five Year Plan, 1969-74* (July 1970), p. 78.

towns, to cover a population of some thirty million persons, and the extension of fair price shops to bring another two hundred million persons under informal rationing schemes, the central government could not arrest the price rise. The strained distribution system, which continued to rely mainly on wheat imports was directly threatened, moreover, by the refusal of the United States Congress to renew Public Law 480 authorizing the sale of surplus commodities for local currencies when the law expired June 30, 1966. Instead, the Johnson administration proposed a Food for Peace Program, which over a five year period envisaged that all U.S. shipments of food would be financed by long-term credits, repayable only in dollars.

The pressure on the balance of payments intensified. Suspension of American aid began to effect the government's ability to import sufficient raw materials, machinery, and spare parts to meet the maintenance requirements of industry. A personal appeal by Mrs. Gandhi to President Johnson for immediate resumption of American economic assistance had only partial success. The United States responded by announcing release of $100 million out of the balance of $388 million covered by agreements signed before the aid freeze.[4]

Despite all these warning signs that the momentum of the national development effort could not be maintained in the absence of effective implementation of longstanding plan policies for much higher levels of agricultural taxation and state regulation of the procurement and distribution of foodgrains and other essential commodities, the new government, like its predecessor, did not attempt any programs involving economic reforms. On the contrary, it completed the policy reorientation initiated during the Shastri period of relying mainly on increased incentives to private investment within the existing framework of production and distribution.

Actually, the new government went further to overturn completely the Planning Commission's position as a national policy-making body on economic issues. A new Commission, constituted in March 1967, was formally circumscribed to the narrow function of expert advisory body. Sweeping reforms of the planning agency's operation were adopted to dismantle most of its de facto controls over the allocation of investment outlays in state Plans.

Notwithstanding the comprehensive reversal of past policies completed in the first years of Mrs. Gandhi's rule, the endorsement of a new entrepreneurial approach could not inject sufficient stimulus to investment to push the economy out of its continuing stagnation. In agriculture, with the exception of wheat, technical and tenurial problems combined to prevent the productivity breakthrough in major foodgrains

[4] See *New York Times*, February 12 and February 18, 1966.

crops promised by the new agricultural strategy. In the industrial sector, sluggish demand and low rates of profit dulled the impact of relaxed licensing controls on private investment, even while shortfalls in foreign aid made it difficult to ensure imports of raw materials, components, and spare parts needed for production. The new policies, which could not accomplish rapid increases in growth, did, however, succeed in accelerating the increase of disparities. The nation, which faced an economic crisis of stagnation by the early 1960s, confronted an economic and political crisis of stagnation compounded by growing inequalities and discontent at the end of the decade.

The economic policies charted by Mrs. Gandhi's government were foreshadowed by the provisions of her first budget, presented to the Lok Sabha in March 1967. Sachin Chaudhuri, then finance minister, provided total Plan outlay for 1966/67 of Rs. 2,081 crores, Rs. 144 crores less than the amount budgeted in 1965/66. It was the first time since the beginning of planning that developmental activity was allowed to fall to a lower level than in the previous year. The finance minister, arguing that "every effort has to be made to restrain Government expenditure"[5] in order to dampen inflationary pressures, attempted to compensate for the cutbacks by measures to increase the flow of private savings to industrial investment. These included greater assistance to private entrepreneurs from public financial institutions; tax reliefs, including credits for the purchase of plant and machinery; and import entitlement schemes tied to investment in export industries.

The new pattern and approach to development was elaborated further in the Annual Plan for 1966/67. The low level of financial resources for the public sector meant that funds could not be stretched much beyond the "expeditious completion of projects which are already underway and on which substantial investments have already been made."[6] The few exceptions included the Bokaro steel project financed by credits from the Soviet Union, the program for construction of new fertilizer plants, and expansion of capacity in existing projects.

The agricultural plan reflected Subramaniam's victory as a member of the Planning Commission in gaining formal endorsement of the food and agriculture ministry's new policies. It acknowledged the adoption of a "new agricultural strategy and an approach that marks a certain departure in the strategy for agriculture." According to the planners, "the new strategy for agriculture is also founded . . . and in fact constitutes the main feature of the approach—on the premise that the problems of raising agricultural production is not so much the backwardness of the

[5] Ministry of Finance, *National Budget, 1966-67*, p. 15.
[6] Planning Commission, *Annual Plan, 1966-67*, p. 7.

farmer as the insufficiency of modern inputs like chemical fertilizers, irrigation, pesticides and new crop varieties of proved genetic capabilities."[7] The acreage to be covered under the high-yielding varieties, the additional yield from the special intensive programs, and the quantities of essential inputs required, including fertilizer, were all drawn from the calculations of the food and agriculture ministry. The Planning Commission accepted the ministry's projection for agricultural production in 1971 at 125 million tons of foodgrains, and endorsed consumption targets of nitrogenous fertilizers at the higher rate demanded by the ministry of 2.4 million tons.

Even these modest Plan programs were heavily dependent on resumption of foreign economic assistance. The planners took credit for budgetary receipts corresponding to external assistance of Rs. 581 crores or over $1.2 billion, representing almost 28 percent of the total financial resources available for the Plan. Such aid inflows were of course still contingent on devaluation. The step, blocked by T. T. Krishnamachari until his exit from the Shastri Cabinet late in December, was approved at the level of policy during the first weeks of Mrs. Gandhi's government.[8]

The issue had become acute by the time of Shastri's death. On January 1, 1966, B. K. Nehru, then ambassador to the United States, returned to New Delhi for consultations following a conversation with the director general of the International Monetary Fund that indicated the IMF would insist on devaluation as the condition of further loans. Nehru, who did not have time to raise the issue formally with Shastri before the latter's departure for Tashkent, was anticipating full discussions with the prime minister after his return. The unexpected having intervened, Nehru instead broached the topic with Sachin Chaudhuri, now finance minister in Mrs. Gandhi's new government. The result was the appointment of a committee by the prime minister, consisting of Asoka Mehta, Subramaniam, and Chaudhuri, with L. K. Jha as rapporteur, to make a formal recommendation. The committee, which consisted of the most committed advocates of devaluation inside the government, made a positive recommendation. Mrs. Gandhi offered no objection. Indeed, in a show of independence that once known created outrage and alarm, she did not consult any senior party leaders on the decision, although the issue had previously caused serious controversy and Kamaraj was known to be opposed. The day before B. K. Nehru returned to Washington he was given Jha's report, initialed by Chaudhuri, as a formal instruction indicating India's intention to devalue. This decision was communicated

---

[7] *Ibid*., p. 32.

[8] The events surrounding the decision to devalue have been reconstructed from interviews with B. K. Nehru, London, October 12, 1973; Asoka Mehta, New Delhi, June 12, 1973; and L. K. Jha, Srinagar, October 3, 1973.

to the International Monetary Fund soon afterward by India's director of the Fund on cabled authorization by the governor of the Reserve Bank. Although the magnitude and timing of the adjustment remained questions for further negotiation, the policy commitment by the Government of India was considered a sufficiently firm undertaking by the IMF after it was reiterated at the annual meeting of the Fund in March that a substantial new credit of over $187 million was subsequently approved.

During the next few months, Mrs. Gandhi continued to follow the path chalked out by her advisors and to cooperate in carrying on the new economic policies initiated during the Shastri period. In March, she traveled to the United States, where she was warmly received by President Johnson. Although the visit was not intended to produce an immediate American commitment for resumption of aid, Mrs. Gandhi set out to underline India's goodwill for the United States. She both avoided any criticism of American policy toward Vietnam (then under sharp attack in India by the Communists), and agreed to an announcement endorsing a proposal for a joint Indo–U.S. Educational Foundation in India to be financed by American holdings of unconvertible PL 480 rupees. Serious negotiations on aid were left to Asoka Mehta, who followed Mrs. Gandhi to Washington in late April for three weeks of intensive discussion. The planning minister had two meetings with President Johnson, talks with senior Cabinet officials, including the secretaries of state, commerce, and agriculture, and held lengthy discussions with George Woods, then president of the World Bank. Mehta, believing that the United States was "concerned to know if they were dealing with competent people after Nehru" considered his mission one of reassuring the aid-giving countries that India now had a government of "forward looking people" prepared to carry out a whole new series of policies to solve the main problems alarming the World Bank and Consortium countries about the prospects of India's development. The minister of planning, who placed virtually all of India's major Fourth Plan schemes before George Woods for his consideration and approval, pointed to the progress in carrying out the new agricultural strategy; a major new commitment to family planning, with the creation of a separate Department of Family Planning in the Ministry of Health; new opportunities for foreign private investment in fertilizers and petroleum; and the first steps toward relaxation of industrial licensing policy and price and marketing controls. Against these clear signs of a shift toward greater reliance on market forces in development policy, Mehta argued for a five-year aid commitment of $1.5 billion per annum, including levels of non-project aid reaching $1.1 billion annually. The higher assistance levels were justified as necessary to get India "over the hump" to a self-sustaining economy by removing bottlenecks to full utilization of industrial capacity created by shortages of imported components, spare parts, and raw materials. During the discussions with Woods, Mehta did get oral assurances of a five-year commitment, plus annual aid levels of about $1.2 billion a year, a figure he interpreted as a floor that could be easily raised once India substantially revamped the economy in the indicated direction.[9] Even so, Mehta left the United States without any firm commitment either on the resumption of American assistance or the size of new Consortium aid for the Fourth Plan. By late May, it became clear that aid would be forthcoming only after India acted on her earlier promise to devalue the rupee. The government then went ahead to complete negotiations with the IMF on the exact parity value of the rupee, which was changed relative to the dollar from Rs. 4.75 to Rs. 7.50.

It was only on the weekend before the formal announcement of devaluation that Mrs. Gandhi consulted senior colleagues in the Cabinet and the president of the Congress party about the decision. Virtually all were opposed. They not only doubted any substantial benefit to India from the step, but were also concerned about its effects on the prospects of the party in the national elections if government were attacked for yielding to foreign pressure. Kamaraj, who was in addition outraged at not having been consulted, argued that the question had to be put before either the Working Committee or the Parliamentary Board for consultation before an official decision was made. Mrs. Gandhi apparently wavered. One day before devaluation was supposed to take place, her chief secretary, L. K. Jha, cabled B. K. Nehru in Washington advising him to withhold any announcement, and citing a possible change in policy. Nehru, who believed India had gone too far to turn back without severe loss in international credibility, responded with a brief reply pointing out the political realities that if India did not devalue, she would not get any more aid.[10]

On June 6, 1966, with the government and party bitterly divided, Sachin Chaudhuri informed an unprepared public by special radio broadcast of India's decision to devalue the rupee by 36.5 percent. Describing the step as "one of a number of economic decisions of great consequence to the health and progress of our economy," he went on to announce significant reductions in import duties and elimination of the major export promotion policies, including tax credits, direct subsidies, and import entitlement schemes. The finance minister, noting the "upward adjustment of the cost of imports" expected as the consequence of devalua-

---

[9] This account is based on discussions with Asoka Mehta, New Delhi, August 18, 1973.

[10] The political opposition to devaluation within the Congress party and the last-minute hesitation of the government are described in *Link*, June 12, 1966, and in Nayar, *India, The Critical Years*, p. 114. These accounts are confirmed in an interview with B. K. Nehru, London, October 12, 1973.

tion, welcomed the change as "reflect[ing] more accurately than before the scarcity value of foreign exchange to the Indian economy." He predicted that rising prices of imports would generate powerful incentives for private investment in import substitution industries, improve efficiency in the allocation of resources, and reduce the necessity for an extensive control system. On that account, the government moved toward a liberal import policy, allowing market forces a much larger role in the allocation of foreign exchange. Chaudhuri announced that fifty-nine priority industries, accounting for about eighty percent of industrial production, were to be granted import licenses as and when needed for components, raw materials, and spare parts.[11]

Although it would take some time for the potential benefits to the Indian economy from all these measures to take effect, one gain was immediate and glaringly apparent. Within ten days of the finance minister's announcement of devaluation and the liberalization of foreign exchange controls, the United States announced resumption of economic aid to India. The implication was unmistakable. The government had devalued in response to pressures by the major aid-giving nations in order to get further assistance.

Attacks on devaluation cut across ideological lines. Opposition leaders, including those in the conservative Swatantra party and the Jan Sangh, could find neither "sound economics nor honorable politics" in the decision.[12] Even the major industrial and business groups were skeptical, welcoming the step only if it paved the way for the complete dismantling of government regulations and controls over the economy. Many industrialists were, in fact, hard hit. Overnight, the rupee costs of repayment obligations on foreign exchange credits advanced by collaborators abroad appreciated in value by amounts of more than one-third.

The left perceived more sinister results. *Link*, the pro-CPI weekly newsmagazine, denounced the decision to devalue as a "craven surrender" to the United States that dealt the final blow to Nehru's strategy of economic independence built on rapid industrialization and agrarian reform. It asserted:

> Devaluation of the rupee under American pressure is the end of one chapter of our economic effort and the beginning of another. The chapter that has ended began with Jawaharlal Nehru's vision of economic independence achieved through quick industrialization and agricultural progress. The party he led had no use for his vision. . . .

[11] The text of the finance minister's speech is published in *Times of India*, June 7, 1966.
[12] Jagdish N. Bhagwati and T. N. Srinivasan, *Foreign Trade Regimes and Economic Development, India*, p. 8. For an extended analysis of the political response to devaluation, see ch. 14.

Almost from the day of his death retreats from affirmative objectives began. One by one the principles that served as foundation for the Industrial Policy Resolution and for an agricultural revolution were discarded. Devaluation of the rupee is the final admission by an abject administration that it has not got enough belief in itself to go to the people and make them work for their independence.[13]

The National Council of the CPI meeting in Hyderabad from June 9-15, 1966, formally called for "the immediate resignation of the Central Government."[14] Leaders of the CPI in parliament, condemning devaluation as the "greatest betrayal of national interest since Independence"[15] moved to censure the government by introducing a no-confidence motion in the Lok Sabha.

Attacked on all sides, the government found it impossible to offer a convincing economic argument in favor of devaluation. The opposition enjoyed the advantage of the commerce ministry's own annual report, which argued against devaluation on the ground that only eighteen to twenty percent of India's exports—mainly those in the modern manufacturing sector—required government subsidies and could be helped by devaluation. The bulk of India's traditional exports confronted conditions of inelastic demand and could only be adversely affected.[16] The finance ministry, moreover, in a burst of candor, circulated a question-answer note to all members of parliament that clearly attributed the decision to devalue to pressure from the aid-giving countries. Answering its own question, "Why have we acted now?" the ministry explained:

> Action could not be postponed as all further aid negotiations hinged on it. It is extremely doubtful whether without demonstrable evidence of our determination and capacity to push up our exports and improve the internal viability of our economy, we shall continue to get external credits, particularly as we are already at a stage when we have to incur fresh debt in order to pay off old ones. Without reasonable prospects of aid forthcoming on the scale contemplated by us, the finalization of the Fourth Plan will be still further postponed. A truncated plan without aid or aid in much smaller amounts will not meet the requirements of the situation and enable us to deal with our deep-rooted economic problems satisfactorily.[17]

The outcry against devaluation, combined with the experience of the "recent emergency, when there was a sudden suspension of certain non-

[13] *Link*, June 12, 1966.
[14] The text of the resolution entitled "Demand for Resignation of the Central Government" is cited in Fic, *Kerala: Yenan of India*, p. 341.
[15] Bhagwati and Srinivasan, *Foreign Trade Regimes*, p. 8.
[16] *Ibid*.                                              [17] *Ibid*., pp. 19-20.

commercial credit,"[18] actually fortified the Planning Commission in making one last attempt to restore Nehru's approach of achieving self-reliance. The Draft Outline of the Fourth Plan published in August 1966 did not make any further concessions to critics of planning. On the contrary, it marked a reversal of earlier accommodations to the liberal economic doctrines introduced during the Shastri period. In objectives, strategy, and pace of advance it was consistent with the principles of the Perspective Planning Division's April 1964 "Notes on the Perspectives of Development" approved by Nehru shortly before his death.

The planners once again assigned "overriding importance" to basic industrialization as the cornerstone of economic independence. They proposed to achieve a self-reliant and self-sustaining economy capable of ensuring "a steady and satisfactory rate of economic growth without dependence on external aid"[19] within a ten year period, by 1976. In concrete terms, the perspective presented required an increase in the investment rate from the Third Plan target of 14 percent in 1966 to 19-20 percent by 1976, and an even more rapid increase in the rate of savings from 10.5 percent to 20-21 percent; a reduction in the rate of population growth during the same period by 20 to 30 percent; an increase in the real value of exports by 7 percent per annum; and "the creation of a domestic economic structure capable of meeting the physical requirements of capital formation, maintenance needs and a substantial increase in mass consumption availabilities."[20] During the Fourth Plan alone, by 1971, these broad aims required an increase in the rate of investment to 18 percent and in the rate of savings to over 16 percent. Finally, the planners obliquely reasserted Nehru's thesis that previous plan failures had been mainly those of implementation rather than policy. They asked, "Can this perspective be realized or is it a matter of setting the sights high in order to urge the nation to greater effort?" The commission found the answer to its own question in "what will be done by the people; and what the people will do will depend on the leadership, the clarity and definiteness of the measures it proposed to follow for the development objective and drive with which it operates these measures."[21]

The measures required of the political leadership for achieving the program of self-reliance placed before them rested mainly on their capacity to implement the recommendations for resource mobilization described as the "kingpin of the Fourth Plan."[22] The Planning Commission proposed a total Plan outlay of Rs. 16,000 crores, compared to the estimate of Rs. 14,500 crores set down in the September 1965 Draft. The revised estimate, at postdevaluation prices, still involved a reduction of

---

[18] *Fourth Five Year Plan, A Draft Outline*, p. 17.
[19] *Ibid*., p. 24.                                  [20] *Ibid*., p. 29.
[21] *Ibid*.                                          [22] *Ibid*., p. 32.

about 5 percent in physical terms over targets envisaged the previous September. Nevertheless, as shown in Table 8-1 below, the planners altered priorities for allocation of national resources to provide much larger outlays on organized industries and mining both in absolute terms and relative to other heads of development. Plan outlays on industries and minerals increased by more than Rs. 1,000 crores, from Rs. 2,866 crores in the 1965 document to Rs. 3,936 crores in the Draft Outline. The change pushed up the share of the industrial program in total Plan outlay from less than 20 percent in the earlier draft to almost 25 percent in the revised version. The new calculations once again raised the ratio of public to private investment in the key sector of basic and heavy industries to 62.6 : 37.4 percent, well above the Third Plan levels.

By contrast, the slight increase in outlay on agriculture and irrigation from Rs. 3,296 crores in the 1965 note to Rs. 3,374 crores in the 1966 Draft Outline had the overall effect of depressing the total share of the rural sector in development outlay from 22.8 to 21 percent. The Planning Commission, moreover, returned to its argument against excessive reliance on the untested high-yielding varieties in the agricultural production program to hold the target for foodgrains output to 120 million tons and the corresponding fertilizer requirement to two million tons.

TABLE 8-1

Size and Pattern of Outlays Proposed for the Fourth Plan
in 1965 and 1966

*(Rs. crores)*

| Head of development | 1965 | | 1966 | |
|---|---|---|---|---|
| | Total outlay | % of total | Total outlay | % of total |
| Agricultural programs, including community development and cooperation | 2,372 | 16.4 | 2,410 | 15.0 |
| Irrigation and flood control | 924 | 6.4 | 964 | 6.0 |
| Power | 1,828 | 12.6 | 2,030 | 12.7 |
| Industry and minerals | 2,866 | 19.8 | 3,936 | 24.6 |
| Small industry | 395 | 2.7 | 370 | 2.3 |
| Transport and communications | 2,768 | 19.1 | 3,010 | 19.4 |
| Social services | 3,051 | 21.08 | 3,210 | 19.5 |
| Other programs | 296 | 2.0 | 70 | .04 |
| Grand total | 14,500 | | 16,000 | |

SOURCES: *Fourth Five Year Plan—Resources, Outlays and Programmes* (September 1965), p. 506; *Fourth Five Year Plan, A Draft Outline* (August 1966), p. 41.

The problems of finding financial resources for a Rs. 16,000 crores Plan, however, appeared virtually insurmountable. On the most generous estimates for revenue receipts, including a ceiling of 5 percent on the increase in non–Plan expenditures per annum, resources in sight, exclusive of external assistance, amounted to Rs. 9,494 crores. The sharp rise in prices of food and essential commodities created by persistent shortages of food articles and raw materials during the Third Plan ruled out any significant recourse to deficit financing. A minimum of Rs. 1,800 crores in additional domestic resources from new measures of taxation was required. A large portion of the increased tax intake had to come from agriculture, which at existing rates of both direct and indirect taxes contributed only 13 percent of the revenue from additional taxation of the states.[23] The planners confined themselves to restating the dilemma. They asserted that "the existing structure of agricultural taxation is not such as would enable any significant part of the increase [in agricultural incomes] to flow into financing of development expenditures," and stressed the need for a "bold restructuring of the tax system and a greater resort to taxation at the source."[24] Assuming the bottleneck of domestic resource mobilization could be broken, the problem of preventing a further inflationary spiral from large governmental outlays in a situation of persistent food shortages remained. The recommendations for a large Plan, therefore, once again rested on implementation of effective price controls, this time involving extensive "State participation and control in regard to both wholesale and retail trade"[25] in respect to a whole range of consumer items, including food, textiles, edible oils, and other essential commodities.

The political constraints on carrying out such an approach extended beyond the demonstrated opposition of strategic elites inside the Congress party. Paradoxically, the long–term goal of self–reliance required larger commitments of foreign aid over the short run than amounts earlier extended. Against Rs. 8,033 crores in export earnings in postdevaluation rupees envisaged for the Fourth Plan period, India's requirements for foreign exchange on account of maintenance and project imports and external debt servicing charges amounted to Rs. 14,333 crores. The "gap" of Rs. 6,300 crores had to be made up almost entirely by loans and grants from developed countries and international institutions. Gross aid requirements were therefore calculated at $8.4 billion during the Fourth

[23] According to Asoka Mehta, of the Rs. 4,142 crores in additional taxation raised during the three Plans, both at the Center and the states, only Rs. 95 crores, or 2.6 percent, had been contributed by increments in direct agricultural taxes and irrigation rates. Planning Commission, *Twenty Second Meeting of the National Development Council, Summary Report*, New Delhi, September 5 & 6, 1965, p. 47.

[24] *Fourth Five Year Plan, A Draft Outline*, pp. 33, 87.

[25] *Ibid.*, p. 18.

Plan period.[26] Even allowing for about $1 billion in aid inflows from the USSR (negotiated by Asoka Mehta in July 1966), the lion's share of $7.4 billion had to be raised from World Bank and Consortium countries. The projection of gross aid inflow of $1.5 billion per annum from Western aid-givers, in contrast to the average under the Third Plan of about $1.1 billion annually, indicated the planners were working with the most optimistic estimates mentioned by the World Bank in discussions about the possible quid pro quo for devaluation. Yet, the Commission was proposing a Plan aimed at more rapid expansion of public-sector heavy and basic industries in the face of contrary advice from the aid-givers to emphasize investments in agriculture and agriculture-related industries and to allow a larger role for foreign and indigenous private capital in industrial growth.

The Draft Outline, which received Cabinet approval on August 19, quickly ran into strong opposition. In a brochure issued by FICCI, the industrialists proposed a sharp cut in public outlay from Rs. 16,000 crores to Rs. 10,500 crores as the maximum feasible expenditure, given the resources in sight. They once again advised the government to concentrate on the development of agriculture and social overhead projects, and to leave industrial development to private enterprise in cooperation with foreign private capital through further relaxation of controls, reduction in taxation, and protective tariffs for new industries.[27]

At the meeting of the National Development Council on August 20-21 that considered the Draft Outline, Mrs. Gandhi attempted to deflect further criticism by conceding at the outset past "failures and mistakes" in planning. All the same, she argued the necessity of proceeding with the Fourth Plan, including high priority for projects in industry, since "even agriculture needed industrial production and the urgent needs of defense were also dependent on industry."[28] Asoka Mehta, this time underscoring the prime minister's arguments, defended the large import substitution programs as the means of achieving self-reliance by the end of the Fifth Plan in 1976.

The chief ministers failed to be persuaded. They not only questioned the ability of the states to mobilize additional resources from new measures of taxation, but this time went further to demand "more equitable reallocation of available resources between the Center and the states." They suggested that Rs. 750-800 crores in additional funds should be found for state outlays in agriculture, irrigation, power, and social

[26] Ibid., p. 83.

[27] The Statesman, August 19, 1966.

[28] Planning Commission, Twenty Third Meeting of the National Development Council, Summary Record, New Delhi, August 20 & 21, 1966, p. 2.

amenities by reducing the amount earmarked for centrally sponsored programs—a cut amounting to well over eighty percent of the funds provided. The criticism, in fact, was cumulatively so far-reaching that it constituted an attack on the authority of the Planning Commission to set down the principles according to which the size, sectoral outlays, and programs of state plans were fixed. The state leaders, denouncing the use of extremely general guidelines for the allocation of central assistance to the states—a device that enhanced the planners' bargaining power— argued for a fixed set of criteria that should be uniformly applicable to all states and serve as mandatory guidelines to the Planning Commission in allocating central assistance. In addition, they challenged the Center's continuing control over patterns of assistance, which extended to earmarking central loans and grants for particular projects, programs, or schemes under the various heads of development. Rather, they asserted that central assistance should be prescribed for sectors as a whole, and preferably allocated to the states in the form of bloc loans and grants to be distributed according to local priorities.[29]

Asoka Mehta and Mrs. Gandhi both gave way. The planning minister suggested that the "National Development Council might consider appointing a Committee of the Chief Ministers and the Central Ministers concerned to help the Planning Commission in deciding what should be the nature and pattern of central assistance and what programs should be included in the centrally sponsored schemes."[30] This suggestion was promptly acted upon by Mrs. Gandhi. The prime minister ended the meeting by summing up the sense of the session in an unconvincing conclusion that "the N.D.C. had given its general approval to the Draft Outline."[31]

The Plan met with still further attacks when it was discussed in parliament in early September. Congress, as well as opposition MPs, attacked the sectoral allocations in the Draft Outline as a "travesty" of the official commitment to give top priority to agriculture, and charged that the Fourth Plan held out no hope for any improvement in fulfilling the basic needs of the poor. In an unusual show of solidarity between Congress party and opposition MPs, the House gave unanimous support to a resolution calling for top priority to irrigation, electrification, and water supply schemes in the rural sector.[32]

Finally, on the eve of national elections, leading industrialists launched a fierce attack on planning. J.R.D. Tata blamed "unsound planning, and specifically . . . wrong priorities and inaccessible targets which have led

[29] The comments of the chief ministers expressing these criticisms are summarized *ibid.*, pp. 26-34.

[30] *Ibid.*, p. 25.                                    [31] *Ibid.*, p. 47.

[32] *Hindustan Times*, September 3, 1966.

to target missing" for the country's difficulties. Citing the "prevailing mood of frustration and despair," he bluntly underlined the precarious position of the planners by suggesting the popular disillusionment was "reflected in the cry for the abolition of the Planning Commission which has begun to be raised." Tata's advice to the government was to drastically reduce the role of the planners in the formulation of economy policy. He suggested that government concentrate on a few key plan targets headed by agriculture, family planning, and industries directly serving agriculture, "leaving remaining areas to forces of demand and supply."[33]

G. D. Birla, by turns vituperative and threatening, also found the reasons for economic setbacks in "the kind of stupid plan that is prepared in this country by amateurs without knowing what is planning." He charged the government with clinging "to the most out-dated methods of planning. They are still talking in terms of socialism about which they themselves do not know what they are talking about. Therefore, all these slogans which are made up of false notions must be made to disappear." Then, warning that the business community would make Plan failures a major issue at the polls in an election that he characterized as "crucial" for the Congress party, he expressed his personal hope that

> the Congress will come back to power, at least in the Centre but with a highly reduced majority. And if they come back with a reduced majority, then they will have to be alert.
>
> Now, leading from that argument, I believe there will be a stronger Cabinet. Some of our Ministers, who are talking in slogans and leftist language, have not yet realized that it is 1967 and not 1952. The world is talking in different slogans now. These slogans have become out of date and therefore I personally believe from the way in which elections are going that we can reasonably expect a better Cabinet, pragmatic, practical and interested in increasing production.[34]

The crescendo of criticism had its effect. Mrs. Gandhi, confronting the electorate on her own for the first time, and insecure in the support of her own party after the disaster of devaluation, appeared increasingly undecided on how to proceed. The dilemma was resolved by delaying formal discussions in the Cabinet and in the National Development Council on the final draft of the Fourth Plan. When, in November 1966, the planners informed the prime minister that the finished version could be readied for Cabinet consideration within six weeks, well before the national elec-

[33] J.R.D. Tata, "The Implementation of Plans," speech delivered to the Ahmedabad Management Association, *The Economic Times*, February 5, 1967.

[34] G. D. Birla, "Bad Planning, Bad Fiscal Policy, Root Cause of Economic Failure," inaugural address at the Annual Session of the Engineering Association of India, January 2, 1967, printed in *The Economic Times*, February 14, 1967.

tions scheduled for February 1967, she agreed orally to set a date for the meeting of the National Development Council. Yet, the formal instructions for sending out a letter of notification to the chief ministers were never issued.[35]

Mrs. Gandhi's decision to "do nothing" until after the elections had profound repercussions for the fate of the planning approach. As early as August 1966, shortly after the difficult meeting with the National Development Council, the prime minister instructed Asoka Mehta to circulate a memorandum to members of the Commission, indicating her intention to dissolve the existing Commission and reconstitute its membership within a year, by August 1967.[36] Postponement of the Fourth Plan therefore implied that the final version would be formulated without participation of the leading architects of Nehru's development strategy.[37] Indeed, by the end of 1966, it was clear that the changes contemplated extended beyond the matter of personnel. The structure and functioning of the Planning Commission was called into question with the government's decision to create a special study team under the Administrative Reforms Commission charged with studying the "planning organization and procedures of the Centre and the States and the relationship of the Planning Commission at the Centre and the planning agencies in the States with other agencies." The study team was charged to "ascertain facts, locate the principal problem areas, examine solutions for the problems and make recommendations to improve the working of the planning process."[38]

The results of the 1967 elections,[39] which stunned the Congress party (see Chapter Nine), made G. D. Birla's prepoll warnings sound prophetic. Congress was returned to power at the Center, but with a greatly reduced margin. Accustomed to governing with an unshakable majority of well over 100 seats, the party resumed the tasks of national leadership after 1967 with only 25 seats to spare. At the state level, the Congress debacle was even greater. The party lost a total of 264 seats in the legislative assemblies to opposition candidates. In eight states— Bihar, Kerala, Madras, Orissa, Punjab, Rajasthan, Uttar Pradesh, and West Bengal—they failed to win legislative majorities.

[35] Interview, Tarlok Singh, Princeton, December 13, 1969; also see *Economic and Political Weekly*, Annual Number, February 1967.

[36] Interview, Asoka Mehta, New Delhi, June 12, 1973.

[37] P. C. Mahalanobis, the architect of the plan approach during the Second Plan was then a member of the Planning Commission. Tarlok Singh, who played a major role in drafting the first three plans and also served as advisor on agricultural strategy was then member-secretary of the Planning Commission.

[38] Administrative Reforms Commission, Report of the Study Team, *Machinery for Planning*, Final Report (New Delhi, December 1967), introduction, pp. ix-x.

[39] See AICC, *The Fourth General Elections, A Statistical Analysis*, pp. 2-3.

Even more encouraging to the business community, the major beneficiaries of Congress losses in terms of seats won were the Swatantra party and the Jan Sangh. In the Lok Sabha, Swatantra increased its standing from 18 seats in 1962 to 42 seats in 1967, and emerged as the largest opposition party. The Jan Sangh, now second only to Swatantra, similarly improved its performance from 14 seats won in 1962 to 35 seats won in 1967. By contrast, the CPI, which since 1952 had enjoyed the position of largest opposition party, slipped to fourth place overall (behind Congress, Swatantra, and Jan Sangh) in the aftermath of the 1964 split that divided communist supporters between the CPI and the CPI (Marxist). At the state level, similarly, Swatantra and Jan Sangh, of the national parties, emerged as the major beneficiaries. Swatantra improved its overall position from 171 seats won in 1962 to 256 seats captured in 1967. The Jan Sangh made even greater gains, from 116 seats in 1962 to 268 seats in 1967. Together they won more than twice the number of legislative assembly seats as the two communist parties. Except in Kerala and West Bengal, moreover, where communist-led electoral alliances succeeded in forming state governments, the Swatantra and/or Jan Sangh came to power as constituent members of multiparty coalition governments.

Expectations of business leaders that such circumstances would bring about a "better Cabinet, practical and interested in increasing production" were realized in at least one important respect. The election results, which created alarm among Congress leaders about the prospects for political stability at the Center, resulted in efforts to arrange a close working relationship between the two rivals for power inside the party, Mrs. Gandhi and Morarji Desai. Desai's condition for entering Mrs. Gandhi's new government was nothing less than number two position in the Cabinet as home minister. Mrs. Gandhi, reluctant to affront Y. B. Chavan by removing him from that post, proposed to solve the problem by naming Desai minister of finance, but with the additional title, deputy prime minister.[40] From that position, and during the period when the reorganization of the Planning Commission was in progress, Desai assumed the dominant role in the formulation of economic policy. The triumvirate of Mrs. Gandhi's first year in power was disbanded. Sachin Chaudhuri was, of course, replaced by Desai as finance minister. Subramaniam, one of the scores of Congressmen defeated in the 1967 polls, temporarily left government and was succeeded by Jagjivan Ram as minister of food and agriculture; and Asoka Mehta was named minister of petroleum and

[40] Interview, Morarji Desai, New Delhi, August 30, 1973. The demand was consistent with Desai's position since the succession of Shastri that he would only rejoin the government at the same rank of "number two next to the prime minister" he had achieved under Nehru. His own estimate of the power structure in 1967 was that this required appointment either as home minister or deputy prime minister, since finance was a "thankless job."

chemicals while serving as interim head of the Planning Commission.

The new Planning Commission, constituted in September 1967, reflected Desai's growing influence. Despite the preference of Asoka Mehta and others for Subramaniam as the new deputy chairman, Desai's choice for the post, D. R. Gadgil, was selected. Gadgil, a prominent economist, was a well-known critic of the Planning Commission who attributed glaring economic failures to the low level of technical competence of the members. According to the new deputy chairman, the planners lacked expertise to carry out rigorous examinations of the validity and internal consistency of key physical estimates in the plans. This neglect of technical and empirical examination of the relationships between targets, outlays, quantities of essential inputs, and sectoral requirements was associated in Gadgil's mind with the political character of the Commission. It was his own firm conviction that the Planning Commission should function solely as an expert advisory body to make recommendations exclusively in terms of economic feasibility to be evaluated by the appropriate—and separate—political authority, either the concerned ministry or the Cabinet. Indeed, Gadgil went further than Asoka Mehta in arguing for a complete separation between the government and the Planning Commission in order to eliminate the "unnatural kind of prestige and importance" attached to the planners' decisions.[41]

Gadgil was, in fact, persuaded to accept appointment as deputy chairman only after receiving assurances of full scope for reorienting the planning process around technical and advisory functions concerned solely with objectives of advancing growth. Accordingly, the men he recruited to fill the empty posts on the Commission were selected to emphasize its changing role from a "political" to an "expert" body. They included R. Venkataraman, former industries minister of Madras state, who had earned a reputation for attracting private investment to Madras; B. Venkatappiah, a retired ICS officer and former deputy governor of the Reserve Bank with expertise in agricultural credit; Nag Chaudhuri, a physicist and former director of the Institute of Nuclear Research, Calcutta; and Pitambar Pant, the former head of the Planning Commission's Perspective Planning Division. The appointment as secretary of B. D. Pande, another ICS officer, completed the roster. Mrs. Gandhi, in her capacity as prime minister, continued to act as chairman of the Commission. Morarji Desai was the only other member of government to be appointed ex-officio member.

The reconstitution of the Planning Commission effectively eliminated all remaining opposition inside the central government to the liberal eco-

[41] Gadgil wrote extensively about the shortcomings of the Planning Commission and his recommendations for reform. See D. R. Gadgil, *Planning and Economic Policy in India*, pp. 88-111.

nomic policies set in motion during the Shastri years. Within months, moreover, the Planning Commission lost much of its authority to set priorities for the allocation of plan resources at the states.

The final report of the Administrative Reforms Committee (ARC), published in March 1968, recommended a series of changes in the functions and scope of planning that aimed at dismantling most of the mechanisms of central control over the allocation of investment outlays at the state level developed during the Nehru years. According to the ARC, the Planning Commission was in the future to be constituted exclusively as an expert advisory body, with responsibilities "only for formulating the objectives, laying down priorities, indicating sectoral outlays, fixing basic targets and approving main programs."[42] These tasks were circumscribed by the provision that detailed work in the formulation of the Plan should proceed in the light of guidelines given by the National Development Council. The Planning Commission was to present minimum and maximum rates of growth along with the policy implications of each for the investment program, including rates of domestic resource mobilization and the likely availability of foreign exchange from exports and aid. The NDC would then decide on the broad magnitudes of the plan program, taking into account "the extent to which they would be prepared to go in discharge of that responsibility, particularly in matters which would involve sacrifices on the part of the people."[43] Once having received the NDC's guidelines, the Planning Commission could proceed to the formulation of the Plan, but this work was confined to "the broad aspects." Detailed planning of programs and schemes within the sectors was to be carried out within the concerned central ministries by newly created "planning cells." Manned by the ministry's own technical and professional personnel, the planning cell was to operate under the overall supervision of the secretary of the ministry—an organizational innovation that transferred effective control of planning to the senior members of the bureaucracy. The almost total exclusion of the planners from the operational side of the planning process was underlined by the recommendation to terminate the existing practice of having officers of the Planning Commission attend meetings of government committees concerned with the implementation of economic policies. Indeed, the ARC stressed that "not only should the Planning Commission avoid getting involved in implementation, it should also see to it that no impression is created that it is getting so involved. All that is necessary is that the Commission should continuously be supplied with all the relevant information regarding the progress in the implementation of Plan policies and programmes."[44]

[42] Administrative Reforms Commission, *Machinery for Planning*, p. 34.
[43] *Ibid.*, p. 8.                                    [44] *Ibid.*, p. 35.

Similarly, at the state level, the task of plan formulation, involving an assessment of state resources, the determination of plan priorities, and the policies and measures necessary to implement plan programs was to be carried out by newly formed planning boards. The state planning boards, no less than the central Planning Commission, were also to be constituted as nonpolitical expert advisory bodies. Departmental planning cells were to take operational responsibility for preparing detailed schemes and projects for inclusion in the Plan.

More crucial, the ARC went beyond recommendations for decentralizing the planning process to proposals for transferring effective decision-making powers over the content of plan programs in the matter of state subjects from the Center to the states. Citing "the need for allowing full initiative and freedom of action to the States,"[45] they echoed the chief minister's arguments in favor of new rules for allocating central assistance that virtually ended the Planning Commission's dominant role. According to the ARC, the total amount of central assistance to be given each state should be settled at the outset. Subsequently, the bulk of all grant aid and all loans was to be made available as bloc grants and loans that could be freely distributed by the states among all schemes according to local priorities. The earmarking of funds for specific programs was to be confined to centrally sponsored schemes, and these were restricted to a "minimum number" having "basic national importance."[46]

Finally, citing the diminished responsibilities of the Planning Commission under the new organizational pattern, the ARC discovered substantial opportunities for reducing the Commission's annual expenditure. It suggested that under the new machinery for decentralized planning "the Commission can very well work with about half of its present staff strength."[47]

The recommendations of the Administrative Reforms Committee were rapidly carried forward, with the exception that Mrs. Gandhi, as prime minister, retained her position as chairman of the Planning Commission, and Morarji Desai, as finance minister, continued as a full member. But the Commission's staff of economic investigators was retrenched, and its special technical sections dismantled. Meanwhile, planning cells were established in the central ministries, and directives went down to the state governments to set up planning boards, as well as district planning bodies.

The major departure, and one that signaled the end of an era of national planning, came with formal revision of the principles governing

[45] *Ibid.*, p. 20.
[46] The Commission's recommendations for changes in the principles of central assistance to the states are summed up *ibid.*, pp. 30-31.
[47] *Ibid.*, p. 38.

the distribution of central assistance for Plan outlay to the states. The Planning Commission put forward

> far reaching proposals which, at the stroke, sought to abolish the practice of tying Central assistance with Centrally "approved" schemes and envisaged the allocation and flow of Central assistance predetermined on the basis of certain broad socio-economic considerations, irrespective of the sectoral allocations or the nature of the schemes adopted in the plans of the States. These measures it was felt would enable the States to evolve their plans without any *dictation* from the Centre either about the contents or the nature of the plan schemes, of course within the overall availability of plan resources. It was realized that this would reduce the Centre's control of the Planning process in the States, but this was nevertheless gone through partly because the Administrative Reforms Commission had urged the loosening of the Centre's control over States planning and partly because the Commission hoped to influence the States through the publication of an "Approach" paper as also through the intensification of formal and informal interaction between the Central Ministries, the Division of the Commission and the State authorities.[48]

The "Gadgil formula" for allocating central assistance to the states was considered at the September 1968 meeting of the National Development Council's Committee of State Chief Ministers, a committee of the whole, including the deputy chairman of the Planning Commission as chairman. The formula as finally endorsed set down objective criteria for determining the principles of allocation of central assistance to the states. Apart from the requirements of sensitive border states (including Jammu and Kashmir, Assam, and Nagaland) to be met by setting aside an ad hoc lump sum of total central assistance, the distribution of the remaining amount was to be apportioned among the states to the extent of 60 percent on the basis of their population; 10 percent on the per capita income if below the 1962-1965 national average; 10 percent on the basis of tax effort in relation to per capita income; 10 percent in proportion to commitments on major continuing irrigation and power projects, and 10 percent for special problems of individual states (such as metropolitan development, flood control, and tribal areas development).

The committee also decided to "untie" central assistance from specified heads of development or schemes, and to eliminate all schematic patterns of assistance for different plan programs. Instead, they

[48] Planning Commission, "Preparation of States Plans, An Appraisal of the 4th Plan Experience," mimeographed, p. 4.

provided that central assistance should be distributed in the form of bloc loans and grants in the proportion of 70 : 30 to all states. Only an attenuated earmarking procedure was retained, which sought to restrict the transfer of resources from certain schemes or heads of development without prior approval of the Planning Commission, including agriculture; certain continuing irrigation and power projects; specified projects involving foreign contractual obligations and interstate payments; elementary education; and rural water supply programs.

Finally, the committee endorsed proposals to limit overall outlay on centrally sponsored schemes to one-sixth or one-seventh of the five-year central assistance available to each state, and provided that each scheme must receive a hundred percent central funding, eliminating the element of matching state contributions frequently required in the past. Even then, centrally sponsored schemes could be taken up only under restricted conditions: that they relate to demonstrations, pilot projects, surveys, or research; that they have a regional or interstate character; that they require lump sum provisions to be made until they could be broken down territorially; and that they have overall national significance.[49]

The meaning of the new criteria was clear. The states were "free to formulate their own plans on the basis of their own appreciation of the local problems, priorities, potentials, and past experience,"[50] in respect to state subjects that included almost all development activities in the vast rural sector. Subsequently, "national" planning referred in practice to expenditures proposed in the central sector. Yet, with the growing constraint on government resources, even these activities were increasingly confined to the provision of economic infrastructure rather than an expansion of industrial capacity. On the eve of the Fourth Plan, the Planning Commission's role was so reduced in scope as to virtually satisfy the demands of the business community, reiterated since the mid-1950s, that the proper sphere of activity for the public sector was to promote social overheads and incentives supportive of private investment. In most other aspects as well, the economic programs endorsed by the planners carried the impression of a reversion to policies predating the Second Plan in an almost total obliteration of Nehru's approach.

One of the first decisions taken by the new economic directorate was to scrap the Draft Outline of the Fourth Plan. "After a careful review of the position the Commission felt that with the lapse of time, many of the assumptions and estimates of the Draft Outline were no longer valid

---

[49] *Ibid*., pp. 4–5. The new formulas for central assistance to the states are also summarized in *Fourth Five Year Plan, 1969-74*, pp. 54–57.

[50] "Preparation of States Plans," p. 6.

[and] fresh exercises would have to be undertaken."[51] The start of the Fourth Plan was delayed until 1969.

The decision set in motion what amounted to a three-year "Plan holiday," although the Planning Commission continued the practice of formulating annual plans. The Annual Plans of 1966/67 and 1967/68, prepared by the lame-duck Planning Commission, and the 1968/69 Plan formulated by the Gadgil Commission displayed considerable homogeneity in size, goals, approach, and programs, a reflection of objective constraints on the policy choices available. Yet, the two earlier plans preserved the principle that smaller developmental outlays on industrial projects and concessions to private enterprise were mainly a response to immediate financial and physical shortages that, once solved, would allow a return to the long-term strategy for self-reliance set down in the Draft Outline. The 1968/69 Plan, by contrast, explicitly tailored the development approach to fit the "prevailing economic situation"[52] in a departure from past policies that was meant to be permanent.

Worsening food shortages and a new price spiral that by early 1967 threatened starvation deaths in the hardest-hit areas of Bihar, and triggered large-scale food riots in West Bengal and Kerala, reinforced the new priorities of giving greatest importance to agriculture "and those developmental activities which directly cater to the growing needs of agriculture."[53] The high-yielding varieties program, which covered only four million acres in 1966/67 was expanded to 15 million acres in 1967/68 and to 21 million acres in 1968/69. The Annual Plans, constructed with this strategy of agricultural development as their base, projected an increased production potential from 90 million tons in 1965 to 125 million tons in 1971, and the achievement of self-sufficiency in foodgrains.

Limitation of resources made it impossible to meet both the large expenditures necessary for the agricultural production programs and the minimum investment levels required for maintaining the momentum of new investment on industrial projects. Annual Plan outlay in the years 1966-1969 remained more or less stationary, somewhat below Rs. 2,300 crores, the level achieved in 1965/66, the last year of the Third Plan. Against increases in the wholesale price index during this period of approximately 30 percent, development outlay experienced a significant decline in real terms.[54] The constraint on resources was so great that, as shown in Table 8-2, absolute amounts of Plan expenditure on irrigation, transport and communications, and social services fell below 1965/66 levels. The increase provided for organized industries and mining was

[51] Planning Commission, *Annual Plan, 1968-69*, p. 1.
[52] *Ibid*.                                    [53] *Annual Plan of 1966-67*, p. 2.
[54] *Fourth Five Year Plan, 1969-74*, p. 8.

## TABLE 8-2

### Plan Expenditure by Heads of Development, 1965/66 to 1968/69

*(Rs. crores)*

| Head of development | 1965/66 | 1966/67 | 1967/68 | 1968/69* |
|---|---|---|---|---|
| Agricultural programs | 231.98 | 268.89 | 284.87 | 270.24 |
| Community development and cooperation | 80.66 | 77.66 | 70.02 | 57.54 |
| Irrigation and flood control | 167.51 | 143.76 | 147.16 | 154.69 |
| Power | 382.95 | 399.27 | 400.56 | 338.80 |
| Village and small industries | 54.20 | 45.53 | 44.94 | 41.41 |
| Industry and minerals | 455.43 | 542.84 | 520.85 | 539.33 |
| Transport and communications | 495.32 | 431.87 | 424.09 | 426.16 |
| Social services | 407.19 | 292.18 | 328.25 | 369.24 |
| Miscellaneous | 22.12 | 18.71 | 21.25 | 21.85 |
| Grand total | 2,297.36 | 2,220.71 | 2,241.99 | 2,119.26** |

SOURCES: *Annual Plan, 1966-67*, pp. 11–13; *Annual Plan, 1967-68*, pp. 26–27; *Annual Plan, 1968-69*, p. 13.

* Estimates for 1968/69 represent Plan outlay and provide only rough estimates of actual expenditure.

** Plan outlay for 1968/69 was officially estimated at Rs. 2,337.41 crores, but the higher figure includes a provision of Rs. 140 crores for government purchases of foodgrains, the first time such expenditures were counted as part of Plan outlay.

sufficient only to support major new projects in fertilizers, and relatively limited expansions of existing capacity in petro-chemicals, petroleum refining, and the development of iron ore and other minerals schemes. Greater reliance on the private sector to stimulate the growth of industrial production was reflected in a series of measures to relax controls under the 1951 Industries (Development and Regulation) Act. By 1967, forty-two industries, drawn mainly from those producing agriculture-related equipment, or light industries with a high export potential were exempted from licensing provisions, and existing units were allowed to increase or diversify production up to 25 percent beyond the licensed capacity without government approval. Controls on the prices and distribution of several industrial commodities were also lifted, including coal and iron and steel.[55]

An even greater casualty of the constrained resources position was the Community Development program. Against provisions of Schematic Budgets for the Community Development blocks accepted as guidelines

[55] A summary statement of changes in policy and administrative controls with respect to private industry is given in *Fourth Five Year Plan, 1969-74, Draft*, pp. 231-34.

for Plan outlays since the initiation of the program, central assistance to states in grants, loans, and other advances earmarked for Community Development were, by 1968/69, less than one-half of its entitlement, sufficient to support the salaries of development staff in place but not to finance any new Community Development schemes.[56] The importance of governmental institutions as a source of funds for financing individual investments in land improvement projects, by contrast, sharply increased. Between 1966 and 1969 alone, loans for minor irrigation to individual cultivators by land development banks, agro-industries corporations, and other agencies amounted to Rs. 229 crores, compared to Rs. 100 crores during the entire Third Plan.[57]

The retrenchment of funds had a further effect on rural development that was not so directly apparent. It compromised the experiment in democratic decentralization still in the early stages of organization in several states as an instrument for activating the peasantry through participation in powerful local government bodies. The major purpose of the new Panchayati Raj institutions (based on indirectly elected Block Samitis and District Panchayat Councils) was to vest administrative control over Community Development schemes in representative bodies. Yet, the new local development councils suffered severe budget cuts almost at the moment they came into being. Combined with the failure of the states to route other departmental development funds through the panchayat system, and their own inability and/or unwillingness to raise significant resources through the powers of taxation granted them, the panchayat structure was undercut at the outset as an important political arena in which large numbers of small peasant farmers and landless laborers might have become involved in rural development schemes.

Ironically, almost at the same time as the institutional supports of the earlier community-oriented approach were dismantled, doubts arose that the new agricultural strategy based on incentives to individual investment could achieve the productivity gains expected from it. By 1969, it seemed unlikely that the high-yielding varieties program would meet the production target of 125 million tons by 1971, and achieve the goal of self-sufficiency in food grains promised by the Ministry of Food and Agriculture. After an initial spurt in foodgrains production from the peak level of 89 million tons achieved in 1964/65 to 95.6 million tons in 1967/68, production in 1968/69 under less favorable weather conditions remained at 94 million tons.[58]

Expectations of a rapid agricultural transformation in the intensive areas were realized only in the wheat region accounting for approxi-

---

[56] *Annual Plan, 1968-69*, p. 39.
[57] *Fourth Five Year Plan, 1969-74, Draft*, p. 185.          [58] *Ibid.*, p. 117.

mately 13 percent of the acreage and output of foodgrains. Seven states—Bihar, Gujerat, Haryana, Punjab, Madhya Pradesh, Rajasthan, and Uttar Pradesh—containing 88 percent of the area under wheat and 95 percent of the irrigated area, contributed 93 percent of production. The heartland of the "green revolution" was more narrowly defined. Three states, Punjab, Haryana and (western) Uttar Pradesh, accounted among them for fully 69 percent of the irrigated area.[59] By 1969, Mexican seeds covered almost the entire irrigated acreage and spurred a spectacular increase in production. Total output between 1966 and 1969 registered a gain of more than two-thirds over 1964/65 levels.[60]

By contrast, the high-yielding varieties program could make little progress in raising the production of paddy, India's largest foodgrains crop, accounting for approximately 31 percent of the total area under foodgrains and over 40 percent of total output. By 1969, the area planted under high-yielding varieties of paddy was 6 million acres, about one-fifth the irrigated paddy acreage and approximately 6 percent of the total paddy area.[61] Average yields from the new varieties remained far below the levels forecast on the basis of production yardsticks. Overall, rice output showed virtually no improvement, rising in 1967/68 and 1968/69 only to levels achieved in 1964/65, the last year of good weather.[62]

There were unexpected technical problems. Reports that dwarf paddy varieties imported from Taiwan faced serious difficulties under Indian field conditions reached the Food and Agriculture Ministry in the spring of 1966, only after it was decided to use these strains as the mainstay of the new agricultural strategy. State officials cited a number of practical problems.[63] The growing cycle of the Taiwan varieties was basically un-

[59] USAID, New Delhi, "Outline for Country—Crop Papers, Country, India, Crop, Wheat," March 3, 1969, p. 4.

[60] Wheat production reached a peak output in 1964/65 of 12.2 million tons, and had increased by 1968/69 to approximately 18 million tons. Directorate of Economics and Statistics, *Area, Production and Yield of Principal Crops in India, 1949-50 to 1967-68*, p. 7; *Fourth Five Year Plan, 1969-74*, p. 184.

[61] *Fourth Five Year Plan, 1969-74*, p. 122. The total area under rice was approximately 91 million acres, and the irrigated rice area was more than 32 million acres. USAID, New Delhi, "Outline for Country—Crop Papers, Country, India, Crop, Rice," March 10, 1969, p. 5.

[62] Rice production reached a peak of 39 million tons in 1964/65 and declined during the drought years of 1965/66 and 1966/67 to approximately 30 million tons. Rice production in 1967/68 and 1968/69 once again approached 39 million tons. *Area, Production and Yield of Principal Crops in India*, p. 30; *Fourth Five Year Plan, 1969-74*, p. 184.

[63] The Department of Agriculture in the Union ministry selected three Taiwan varieties—Taichung Native 1, Taichung 65, and Tainan 3—for use in the first year of the high-yielding varieties program on the basis of their reported performance in Taiwan. However, at the Conference of State Officials held in New Delhi, March 18-19, 1966, to consider the operational details of the high-yielding varieties program, representatives from Madras and Andhra Pradesh reported that the Taiwan varieties were not suitable for the major rice-growing season in their states (July-August to December-January). Cultivators

suited to the monsoon patterns of the major growing seasons in the rice-producing states. When planted in mid-June, the new seeds flowered and came to maturity by mid-October, the worst period of the northeast monsoon. Cultivators not only found it difficult to harvest the crop in heavy rain, but suffered large losses unless mechanical drying equipment was immediately available.

Farmers planting a winter rice crop also faced serious disadvantages. Very heavy rain during the early part of the growing season in September and October sometimes submerged seedlings and caused serious damage to dwarf plants; water shortages at the end of the crop season in March inflicted losses in yields. In both seasons, moreover, the heavy cloud cover of the monsoon deprived the paddy plants of the strong sunlight needed for photosynthesis at the end of the growth cycle to achieve optimum yields. These problems were compounded by the discovery that the most popular Taiwan seeds also showed higher vulnerability than conventional varieties to bacterial leaf blight and other insect diseases during the high humidity of the monsoon season. Finally, all the imported varieties had coarser, less desirable grain quality than local varieties, and commanded lower market prices.

The prospect, as it emerged in 1966, was for a major effort in adaptive research before the imported paddy varieties could be extensively introduced. The All-India Coordinated Project in Rice Research was, however, only in the initial stages of organization. It was ultimately expected to cover all the rice-growing areas of the country and to conduct large-scale programs of hybridization with the purpose of evolving shorter-duration varieties suitable to basic monsoon patterns, and having the high yield potential of imported strains as well as the blight resistance of Indian plants. Except for a breakthrough by local researchers in Tanjore (Madras), where a short-duration, fine-grained Japonica indica hybrid was developed that was also resistant to lodging in heavy rain and suita-

---

customarily planted their seedlings sometime in June with the arrival of the southwest monsoon, transplanted in mid-July, and then harvested in December, after retreat of the northeast monsoon that brings particularly heavy rains during September and October. Local varieties, long duration and photoperiod sensitive, were specially adapted to these monsoon patterns. They flowered only when day length reached a critical number of minutes, and came to maturity after an interval sufficient to allow for retreat of the monsoon and harvesting under clear skies. By contrast, the high-yielding varieties of paddy were short duration and nonphotoperiod sensitive. When planted in mid-June, they came to flower and reached maturity within a fixed period of about 107 to 115 days, by mid-October, or during the worse period of the northeast monsoon. These problems are reported in India, Ministry of Food and Agriculture, "High-Yielding Varieties Program for 1966-67," mimeographed, pp. 1-2. The first press reports of disappointing performance of the new grain varieties were published in the summer of 1966. See *The Statesman*, September 1, 1966. Subsequently, technical difficulties inhibiting rapid introduction of the high-yielding paddy as well as hybrid bajra, jowar, and maize were more thoroughly detailed in "A Note on High-Yielding Varieties Program" prepared by the Ministry of Food and Agriculture, November 2, 1968, mimeographed.

ble for immediate introduction,[64] it was expected to be three to four years before the results of this research could be taken to farmers' fields.

The constraints on achieving a breakthrough in productivity went beyond technical problems to more intractable structural limitations of the land-distribution and land-tenure pattern. Experience showed that except in areas where landholdings were consolidated and were two or three times the size of the national average—conditions that existed in the "green revolution" wheat areas[65]—"large" landowners, like small and marginal farmers, found it uneconomic to invest in modern agricultural techniques. Their holdings, separated into two, three, and four-acre parcels and scattered within and between villages, were usually less than the optimum area required for the efficient cultivation of the high-yielding varieties. This was a pervasive problem in the irrigated paddy areas where the installation of minor irrigation works became necessary to supplement inadequate and/or uncertain supplies of water from surface irrigation projects,[66] but the command area of the smallest percolation

[64] The new hybrid variety, ADT 27, was introduced in 1965 and soon earned such extravagant names as the "seed of destiny" and "heavenly gift." Although not as high yielding as the exotic varieties, it gave reliable yield increases over the local variety of about 45 percent; required minimum changes in cultivation practices; was relatively disease resistant; produced fine grain; and most important of all, was more resistant to lodging than the local variety in heavy rains.

[65] Punjab and Haryana, the heartland of the green revolution wheat area, are the only two states in which consolidation operations were carried out over the entire sown area. In the majority of states, land consolidation was still in the early stages of implementation. Planning Commission, *Report of the Task Force on Agrarian Relations*, p. 97. There were also fewer small-size operational holdings in these states than in India as a whole. According to data collected in 1960, the average size of operational holding in India (that is, all lands that are part of the same economic unit, including leased-in land) was 6.6 acres; almost three-quarters of all holdings were less than this size. By contrast, data for the undivided Punjab (the state was bifurcated into Punjab and Haryana in 1966) showed that 42 percent of all holdings were 10 acres or more. In Ludhiana, the showcase district of the green revolution in the Punjab, fully 80 percent of cultivating households operated holdings of 10 acres or above. "Data Collected in the 16th Round of NSS on Operational Holdings," mimeographed, p. 1; Francine R. Frankel, *India's Green Revolution*, p. 17.

[66] The existing canal irrigation systems are inadequate for the efficient cultivation of the high-yielding varieties on several counts. They were initially designed with traditional cultivation techniques in mind to spread water as widely and thinly as possible, and provide protection in time of drought, rather than to supply the higher water levels per acre necessary for the introduction of scientific agriculture. In addition, the canals have no cross regulators to allow for controlled rotation of watering. They also lack channel systems that reach directly into the farmer's field. The result is that cultivators cannot be certain of receiving supplies at the exact time and in the amounts required. None of the irrigation systems, moreover, has master drainages. Finally, irrigation water is usually sufficient for only one wet-rice crop during the main growing season. But the growth cycle of the high-yielding varieties is basically unsuited to the monsoon patterns of much of the rice-growing area. The new varieties are best cultivated as a second crop during the sunny, dry season. In practice, therefore, the efficient adoption of modern techniques requires the installation of minor irrigation works to tap underground water as an assured source of supply all year round. See B. Sivaraman, "Scientific Agriculture is Neutral to Scale—The Fallacy and the Remedy," Dr. Rajendra Prasad Memorial Lecture, December 27, 1972, Indian Society of Agricultural Statistics, 26th Annual Conference, Kalyani.

wells or tubewells was a minimum of five to ten acres. It was, moreover, financially impossible for even large landowners to duplicate such facilities, costing $400-$1,000, on several scattered holdings. But without assured water, cultivators would not make the increased outlays for modern inputs, especially the higher dosages of fertilizer required by the high-yielding varieties, when the investment was likely to be lost if rains were inadequate.

Some landowners, of course, had little interest in land development or maximizing output from their holdings. Under existing tenurial arrangements they were able to lease out their scattered plots to sharecroppers willing to pay sixty or seventy percent of the gross product as rent. Meanwhile, they viewed their land in irrigated areas as an investment that was bound to appreciate steadily in value.

Unlike the situation in the wheat belt, conditions in the paddy-growing areas required significant changes in the agrarian pattern for the full realization of the production potential of the high-yielding varieties. Two logical alternatives existed: consolidation of ownership holdings, including expropriation of sharecroppers to provide large farmers with economies of scale capable of supporting profitable investments in land and water development, including the full complement of modern technology; or a redistribution of landownership to ensure minimum levels of viability to larger numbers of small holdings, combined with some form of cooperative organization to provide opportunities for land improvement and water utilization schemes that cut across the boundaries of individual fragments and farms.

The first option, by 1969, seemed to hold serious political dangers of increasing rural discontent (see Chapter Nine). It also had broader economic limitations. A process of agrarian modernization that left behind some seventy to eighty percent of the peasantry as income differentials widened was bound to aggravate the problem of dualism within the agricultural economy and to have very narrow spread effects in stimulating the growth process in other sectors. There were, in fact, signs that under such conditions new government policies for increasing incentives to private industrial investment could be only partially effective. Although in 1968 and 1969 agricultural production reached record levels, there was an incomplete recovery in industrial production and a pronounced increase in unused capacity, especially in capital goods industries.[67] Meanwhile, despite further tax incentives to the private sector, there was a slowdown in investment except in industries directly catering to modern agriculture. The retrenchment was only partly explained as a symbiotic response to the reduction in public spending. Available data suggested

[67] The index of industrial production increased by 0.3 percent in 1967-68 and 6.2 percent in 1968-69. *Fourth Five Year Plan, 1969-74*, pp. 7, 8.

declining rates of return on industrial investment since 1963, with the rate of increase in industrial costs exceeding the rate of increase in industrial prices. The inability of industry to pass on rising costs to consumers was due in some cases to the persistence of price controls, but another important factor was sluggish demand.[68]

Under such circumstances, investors were able to find more attractive alternatives. By the late 1960s, the accumulation of "black money"—from tax evasion on unrecorded production, black-market transactions in scarce commodities, illegal payments for licenses and permits, bribes to avoid the application of controls, trade in smuggled imports, and illegal exports of foreign exchange and other goods—had become so extensive that it constituted a "parallel" economy to the official monetary system. The effects of "black money" on government economic policies were nothing short of "disastrous." Not only did the availability of alternative funds from "underground" banks frustrate government attempts to impose selective credit controls on nonpriority economic activities, but it reduced the resources forthcoming from the private sector for development. Such money was instead diverted to unproductive but highly profitable activities. These ran the gamut from speculation in real estate to hoarding and black marketing of scarce commodities, to smuggling and purchase of gold, gems, and other luxury import articles. In 1968/69—a year when total new private investment in industry was well under Rs. 500 crores—the money value of transactions involving black income was estimated to have reached Rs. 7,000 crores.[69]

Apart from these deep structural problems, plan policies emphasizing the new agricultural strategy also faced immediate limitations in the shortages of key inputs either from domestic production or imports. The high-yielding varieties program, insofar as it depended on higher availabilities of chemical fertilizer than could be produced by indigenous factories, was dependent on increasingly precarious assumptions about the ability to attract foreign private investment and/or import the necessary quantities with foreign exchange provided through aid. The Indian fertilizer industry was expected to have an installed capacity of about 1.7 to 2 million tons by 1970/71,[70] compared to requirements estimated at 2.4 million tons in 1970/71 and 4 million tons by 1975. Yet by 1969, the ear-

[68] A useful analysis is presented in Samuel Paul, "Income Shifts and Recession," *Economic and Political Weekly*, April 3, 1968.

[69] The most detailed description of the size and dimensions of the parallel "black money" economy is provided in Ministry of Finance, Direct Taxes Enquiry Committee, *Final Report*, pp. 5-12.

[70] India's capacity for production of nitrogen in 1966 was about 450,000 tons. New projects with a capacity of some 900,000 tons were under construction, and additional plants with a capacity of 495,000 tons had been "approved in principle" but not started. Five to six years were ordinarily required to get fertilizer plants into operation. Fertilizer Association of India, *Fertilizer Statistics, 1965-66* (New Delhi, 1967), pp. 6, 8-9.

lier optimism about attracting large-scale foreign private investment had largely disappeared as the government found the terms and conditions put forward by prospective collaborators more and more politically difficult to accommodate. Although the deadline on pricing and marketing concessions was extended from the end of March to December 1967 in order to allow additional time for processing applications from eight American, British, and West German firms, the negotiations faltered once the government proved unwilling to accept the proposals of international oil companies for operating fertilizer factories with ammonia imported from their subsidiaries in the Middle East. The memory of public outcry over devaluation was still fresh. The Cabinet, advised by its own experts that factories could be successfully operated using the byproducts of indigenous refineries while saving foreign exchange, hesitated to approve the import of ammonia that could be similarly interpreted as yielding to foreign pressure by international oil companies and the World Bank. The government found such political considerations sufficiently persuasive, moreover, that it did not change its policy even after the experts revised their previous projections to show that India would begin to suffer shortages of naptha, the indigenous feedstock for fertilizer production, by 1975.[71]

At the same time, the prospect that adequate fertilizer supplies could be imported with the help of American aid grew dim. By November 1967, the Johnson administration, facing Congressional cuts on its foreign aid bill, had to inform the Consortium it could not keep its April pledge to provide $380 million of the $900 million already promised for 1966/67. Thereafter, actual new commitments by the United States for nonproject aid to India showed a steady decline from about $300 million in 1966/67 to $250 million in 1967/68 and $200 million in 1968/69. Reflecting America's reduced role, total new commitment for nonproject aid (exclusive of food) fell from $888 million in 1966/67 to $534 million in 1967/68 and $594 million in 1968/69 (including debt relief during this period of $34 million, $90 million, and $100 million, respectively).[72]

India's earnings from exports failed to take up the slack. On the contrary, the immediate impact of devaluation proved unfavorable. Although mineral and manufacturing exports did increase, stagnant or declining sales of traditional items produced an overall decline of real foreign exchange earnings of about 8 percent in 1966/67.[73] This situation was somewhat improved by the imposition of countervailing duties on

[71] *The Statesman*, December 27, 1967.

[72] During the same period, project aid declined from $722 million in 1966/67 to $107 million in 1967/68 and $164 million in 1968/69. New commitments in both projects and nonproject aid, therefore, dropped from a total of $1.6 billion in 1966/67 to $641 million in 1967/68 and $758 million in 1968/69. India, Ministry of Finance, unpublished data.

[73] India, *Economic Survey, 1966-67* (Delhi, 1967), p. 42.

traditional exports of staples such as jute manufactures and tea, in order to protect the prices of commodities with relatively inelastic world demand; and by the introduction of large cash subsidies on commodity exports for which world demand conditions were favorable, but in which India had not acquired a strong competitive position. Even so, export earnings for 1968/69 were only about 4 percent higher than the previous peak in 1964/65.[74]

The result was that the overall level of imports could not be increased to meet the additional requirements of the agricultural sector. In fact, the value of total imports actually declined between 1965/66 and 1968/69, amounting to Rs. 2,218 crores in the first year of this period and Rs. 1,862 crores in the last.[75] Expansion of agricultural imports had to be met from shrinking foreign exchange resources. Between 1965/66 and 1968/69, imports for the modern agricultural sector, including fertilizers, fertilizer raw materials, pesticides, and machinery, increased as a proportion of the total import bill from less than three percent to more than ten percent.[76] Yet the absolute level of expenditure was about one-half the amount earlier demanded by the food and agriculture ministry for effective implementation of the new strategy.[77]

Despite all these signs that liberal economic policies would soon run into structural and foreign exchange constraints, no reassessment of the entrepreneurial approach was attempted on the eve of the Fourth Plan. On the contrary, the development process became more dependent than ever on private initiatives, as the government's ability to raise resources for Plan outlays progressively diminished. This erosion in the resources position emerges from a comparison of original estimates and revised estimates of finances for the Annual Plans, 1966 to 1969, presented in Table 8-3.

During the period 1966-1969, the lion's share of current revenue balances initially earmarked for Plan outlays had to be diverted to meet non-Plan expenditures. During the first year, 1966/67, extraordinary financial and physical shortfalls caused by the impact of two bad-weather

[74] *Fourth Five Year Plan, 1969-74, Draft*, p. 93.

[75] Imports in postdevaluation rupees totalled Rs. 2,218 crores in 1965/66, and thereafter declined to Rs. 2,078 crores in 1966/67; Rs. 2,008 crores in 1967/68; and Rs. 1,862 crores in 1968/69. *Fourth Five Year Plan, 1969-74*, p. 103.

[76] Data provided by the foreign exchange section, Planning Commission, unpublished.

[77] The estimated foreign exchange costs of implementing the new agricultural strategy over the five years 1966-1971 was Rs. 1,114 crores, as calculated by the Ministry of Food and Agriculture in August 1965. *Agricultural Production in the Fourth Five Year Plan: Strategy and Programme*, p. 24. After adjusting for devaluation, the cost rose to Rs. 1,754 crores. The value of imports for the modern agricultural sector in the three years 1966/67, 1967/68 and 1968/69 was Rs. 133 crores, Rs. 191 crores, and Rs. 201 crores, respectively. Data provided by the foreign exchange section, Planning Commission, unpublished.

## TABLE 8-3

### Financing of the Annual Plans: 1966-1969

(Rs. crores)

| Item | Original estimates Center | States | Total | Latest estimates Center | States | Total |
|---|---|---|---|---|---|---|
| *Domestic budgetary resources* | *2,737* | *1,158* | *3,895* | *2,397* | *1,251* | *3,648* |
| Balance from current revenues at 1965/66 rates of taxation | 621 | 245 | 866 | 184 | 119 | 303 |
| Surplus of public enterprises at 1965/66 fares, rates, and tariffs | 381 | 206 | 587 | 215 | 194 | 409 |
| Additional taxation, including measures to increase the surpluses of public enterprises | 635 | 425 | 1,060 | 611 | 299* | 910 |
| Loans from public (net) | 244 | 327 | 571 | 384 | 335 | 710 |
| Small savings | 115 | 276 | 391 | 125 | 230 | 355 |
| Annuity deposits, compulsory deposits, bonds | 41 | — | 41 | 65 | — | 65 |
| State provident funds | 157 | 96 | 253 | 176 | 125 | 301 |
| Miscellaneous capital receipts (net) | 543 | (−)417 | 126 | 637 | (−)51** | 586 |
| *Budgetary receipts corresponding to external assistance (net)* | *2,435* | *—* | *2,435* | *2,426* | *—* | *2,426* |
| Other than P.L. 480 | 1,650 | — | 1,650 | 1,507 | — | 1,507 |
| P.L. 480 | 785 | — | 785 | 919 | — | 919 |
| *Deficit financing* | *313* | *22* | *335* | *644* | *38* | *682* |
| *Aggregate resources* | *5,485* | *1,180* | *6,665* | *5,467* | *1,289* | *6,756* |
| *Central assistance for state Plans* | *(−)1,714* | *1,714* | *—* | *(−)1,763* | *1,763* | *—* |
| *Resources for the Plan* | *3,771* | *2,894* | *6,665* | *3,704* | *3,052* | *6,756* |

SOURCE: *Fourth Five Year Plan, 1969-74*, p. 74.

* Inclusive of share in additional taxation by the Center of Rs. 148 crores.

** After allowing for ad hoc loans from the Center to the states of Rs. 226 crores.

years and the dislocations of devaluation partly accounted for the negative balance that emerged. Recessionary trends in industry reduced receipts from the collection of taxes; rising prices imposed higher non-Plan expenditures on the central and state governments for increases in dearness allowances to government employees. In addition, the central government decided to absorb the immediate impact of devaluation on the cost of imported foodgrains and fertilizers by providing large subsidies on the prices of these commodities. But persistent shortfalls in balances from current revenues during 1967/68 and 1968/69 reflected sharp increases in non-Plan expenditures representing more permanent commitments, including provisions for budgetary maintenance of already completed Plan schemes; the rising proportion of debt service charges as a percentage of total government expenditure; and increasing administrative costs of government as a result of inflation. Among other problems, moreover, public-sector enterprises failed to yield the internal surpluses projected, while the railways, suffering from prolonged neglect, began to operate at a deficit.

The most alarming aspect of the situation was the growing difficulty of mobilizing additional resources from new measures of taxation. The Center's earlier ability to compensate for budgetary shortfalls under other revenue items by extracting higher resources than originally estimated from measures of additional taxation sharply declined. Compared to its performance during the Third Plan, when the Center exceeded its own target by two times—managing to raise more than Rs. 450 crores a year from additional taxes alone—revenues under this head in 1966-1969 sank to an average of Rs. 200 crores per annum. During 1968/69, the last year of this period, the extent of income tax evaded was estimated to have reached Rs. 470 crores.[78]

At the same time, the states, far from acting to pick up the burden by improving upon their own poor performance in the past, actually moved to reduce taxes in a bid to cement the popular support that brought opposition parties to power for the first time. Starting in 1967, state governments variously abolished or reduced land revenue taxes and betterment levies, and delayed the collection of *taccavi* loans. As a result of these concessions, the net additional resource mobilization by the states in 1966-1969 was less than one-half the amount they undertook to raise. Their performance in mobilizing no more than Rs. 151 crores from this source over three years represented a decline of well over 50 percent compared to levels achieved during the Third Plan. Overall, taxation as a percentage of national income declined from 14 percent in 1965/66 to less than 13 percent in 1968/69.[79] Altogether, almost 58 percent of Plan out-

[78] Direct Taxes Enquiry Committee, *Final Report*, p. 8.
[79] *Fourth Five Year Plan, 1969-74*, p. 47.

lay at the states had to be financed by central assistance, and even then, it became necessary for the Center to extend ad hoc loans to the states to cover large budgetary deficits on non-Plan expenditure.

The deteriorating resources position was reflected in other basic economic indicators. The rate of savings, which achieved a peak of about 11 percent in 1965/66, compared to more than 8 percent in 1961/62 hovered between 8 and 9 percent during 1966-1969.[80] Investment rates, which reached almost 14 percent in 1965/66 were maintained with difficulty at between 10 and 12 percent[81] by increasing reliance on foreign aid and deficit financing. Overall, the share of domestic budgetary resources in total resource mobilization for the three Annual Plans declined to 54 percent from 59 percent during the Third Plan. Net external assistance, which fell short of the original estimate by over Rs. 300 crores, nevertheless accounted for 36 percent of public outlay during the three Annual Plans, compared to 28 percent in the Third Plan. Deficit financing was somewhat reduced over Third Plan levels of 13 percent, but remained high at 10 percent of Plan outlay. Both these sources of extrabudgetary finance, however, were being exhausted. The major aid-giving countries, experiencing chronic balance-of-payments strains, appeared unwilling to continue to extend aid at existing levels during the Fourth Plan. At the same time, the worsening inflation made it more and more dangerous to continue deficit financing.

As the pool of public finances contracted, the Planning Commission carried out a formal revision of the economic approach that for the first time explicitly endorsed a growth strategy built on incentives to private investment, even at the cost of concentration of economic power. They conceded, in yet another draft of the Fourth Plan, that government did not have sufficient command over the resources of the country to carry out programs for accelerating growth while mitigating inequalities and regional imbalances. Rather, in the present phase of development, the planners argued, inequalities had to be expected as the natural outcome of policies designed to increase production. They asserted:

> The concern for achieving the desired increase in production in the short run, often necessitates the concentration of effort in areas and on classes of people who already have the capability to respond to growth opportunities. This consideration shaped the strategy of intensive development of irrigated agriculture. Output increases more rapidly in areas which have the basic infrastructure. The operation of programmes of assistance related to size of production tend to

[80] The rate of saving (and investment) is expressed as the ratio of net saving (net investment) to net national product at market prices. See Planning Commission, *The Fourth Plan Mid-Term Appraisal*, I, 36; also India, *Economic Survey, 1973-74*, p. 2.

[81] *Ibid.*

benefit the larger producers in the private sector. A small number of business houses with experience and resources have been able to take greater advantage of the expansion of opportunities for profitable investment.[82]

According to this new economic realism, it was necessary to postpone goals of increasing mass consumption until some future time when the surpluses generated through investment could be more equitably distributed. The planners urged, "it is important to lay far greater stress on positive steps for ameliorating the conditions of the poorer people through planned economic development. In a rich country greater equality could be achieved in part by transfer of income through fiscal, pricing and other policies. No significant results can be achieved by such measures in a poor country, where whatever surpluses can be mobilized from the higher income of richer classes are needed for investment in the economy to lay the basis for larger consumption in the future."[83]

There was no prospect of meeting the promise given by the Congress party to provide by 1976 the basic needs of each individual in respect of food, clothing, housing, education, and health. On the contrary, according to the Planning Commission's calculations, the average per capita private consumption at 1967/68 prices would reach Rs. 690 by 1980/81, or about Rs. 57 per month. Allowing for the persistence of inequalities in consumption levels, the planners estimated that the second poorest decile would have a per capita consumption level of Rs. 320 per annum, or about Rs. 27 per month. "This would be equivalent to the consumption level of Rs. 15 per month in terms of 1960/61 prices which is appreciably below the Rs. 20 per capita per month which was deemed a minimum desirable consumption standard."[84]

Within these parameters the goals set down for the Fourth Plan were intended to avoid the mistakes of earlier years, when overly ambitious public outlays had led to increasing reliance on inflationary deficit financing and uncertain foreign aid, without accomplishing sufficient increases in economic output. The priorities of the Fourth Plan included efforts to increase agricultural production and stabilize foodgrains prices and prices in general; liberate Indian planning from dependence on foreign aid by eliminating PL 480 imports after 1971, and reducing foreign aid net of debt charges and interest payments to about one-half the Third Plan level by the end of the Fourth Plan; improve the balance of payments by increasing exports at the rate of 7 percent per year; and limit resort to inflationary financing by linking Plan outlay more closely to domestic budgetary resources.

---

[82] *The Fourth Five Year Plan, 1969-74, Draft*, p. 9.
[83] *Ibid.*, p. 14.                                    [84] *Ibid.*, p. 33.

The determination to limit inflationary financing and reliance on foreign aid was reflected in a total investment outlay described by the planners as modest. Compared to the 1966 version of the Fourth Plan Draft Outline, which provided public outlay of Rs. 16,000 crores, the March 1969 version reduced Plan outlay to Rs. 14,398 crores—against a rise in the wholesale price index between 1966 and 1969 of approximately 30 percent. The lower outlay was expected to generate an average annual increase in national income of 5.5 percent (the same rate as projected in the larger Plan), on assumptions of "relatively favorable capital to output relationship during the Fourth Plan." According to the planners, this was feasible as the result of considerable idle capacity in manufacturing industries; sizeable investments on projects initiated in previous years and expected to reach completion in the near future; and the "possibility of securing relatively large increases in agricultural output based mainly on high-yielding seeds and the expansion of fertilizer use."[85]

The guiding principle of growth with stability prompted maximum reliance on initiatives by the private sector. As shown in Table 8-4 below, the largest cuts in Plan outlay, with the exception of social services, were directed at industry and minerals. Altogether, public outlay under this head was trimmed by Rs. 846 crores, reducing its share of the total from 24.6 percent in the 1966 Draft Outline to 21.5 percent in the 1969 version. Actual outlay of about Rs. 2,800 crores was not more than 60 percent above Third Plan levels in unadjusted prices. The major share of this investment had to be reserved for completion of projects "already under implementation and projects for which investment decisions have been taken."[86] New projects were envisaged only in high-priority fields such as fertilizers, pesticides, petrochemicals, nonferrous metals, nuclear power, and development of mineral ores. Only a few small projects could be taken up in the engineering industries. Overall, the cuts in financial outlay depressed targets for industrial growth from 11 percent as proposed in the Third Plan to 9 percent during the Fourth Plan.

The role of the private sector, by contrast, was expanded. The target for new investment of Rs. 2,400 crores in industries and minerals[87] was more than double the Third Plan level. As a result, the ratio of public to private investment in organized industries dropped to the lowest value since the First Plan, 53.8 : 46.2.

Projections of a larger role for the private sector were combined with a wider array of incentives to investment, including stepped-up availability of institutional credit from new financial agencies created since 1964. In addition, by 1969 a total of forty-one industries had been exempted from licensing provisions; existing firms were permitted to diversify or

85 *Ibid*., p. 41.
86 *Ibid*., p. 244.                                    87 *Ibid*.

## TABLE 8-4

Public Sector Outlay by Heads of Development as Estimated in the
*Fourth Plan Drafts* of August 1966 and March 1969

*(Rs. crores)*

| | 1966 | | 1969 | |
|---|---|---|---|---|
| *Head of development* | *Total outlay* | *% of total* | *Total outlay* | *% of total* |
| Agricultural programs, including community development and cooperation | 2,410 | 15.0 | 2,217 | 15.4 |
| Irrigation and flood control | 964 | 6.0 | 964 | 6.7 |
| Power | 2,030 | 12.7 | 2,085 | 14.4 |
| Industry and minerals | 3,936 | 24.6 | 3,090* | 21.5 |
| Small industries | 370 | 2.3 | 295 | 2.1 |
| Transport and communications | 3,010 | 19.4 | 3,173 | 22.0 |
| Social services | 3,115 | 19.5 | 2,091 | 14.5 |
| Family planning | 95 | .06 | 300 | 2.0 |
| Other programs | 70 | .04 | 183 | 1.2 |
| Grand total | 16,000 | | 14,398 | |

SOURCES: *Fourth Five Year Plan, A Draft Outline*, August 1966, p. 41; *Fourth Five Year Plan, 1969-74, Draft*, March 1969, p. 48.

* Includes Rs. 250 crores for transfer to private and cooperative sectors through financial institutions and Rs. 40 crores for supporting plantation programs and for state Industrial Development Corporations.

expand production up to twenty-five percent of capacity without being required to secure a new license; and price controls, with the exception of some articles of basic consumption such as vegetable oil, drugs, and kerosene, were generally lifted.

Even so, the Planning Commission proposed a comprehensive review of licensing policy in order to allow "the market much fuller play" in accomplishing the efficient allocation of investment. Arguing that previous practice of setting specific targets for a wide range of industries had led to creation of excess capacity in certain sectors and inadequate capacity in others, the planners recommended that except for basic or strategic industries, or industries requiring more than ten percent of their capital equipment from purchases involving foreign exchange, entrepreneurs should be exempted from the need to secure industrial licenses. While recognizing that freedom from industrial licensing could have some "adverse consequences," including diversion of productive resources to inessential consumer goods and greater concentration of economic power, the planners attached greater importance to achieving an improved equilibrium between supply and demand. They recommended only that definite production targets be set for a limited number of high-priority industries, and that private investments should be canalized in desired directions by appropriate fiscal policies.[88]

The agricultural plan similarly gave full scope to market forces in providing conditions for a sustained increase in foodgrains production of about five percent per annum over a ten-year period. The core of the agricultural strategy continued to be the high-yielding varieties program. During the Fourth Plan, it was to be extended over 53 million acres, nineteen percent of the total area under food crops, and virtually the entire irrigated area. Of the total increase in food output envisaged between 1969 and 1974 (from 98 million tons to 129 million tons), the high-yielding varieties were expected to contribute nearly two-thirds of the additional production.[89]

Plan outlay in agriculture of Rs. 2,217 crores, a cut in expenditure over 1966 estimates, appeared modest. Nevertheless, a substantial step-up in agricultural investment was envisaged from loans to individuals by financial institutions in the agricultural sector. In fact, Rs. 435 crores of Plan outlay was earmarked for the support of land development banks, agro-industries corporations, the Rural Electrification Corporation, and other agencies. Altogether, the investment in agriculture to be financed by these institutions was estimated at Rs. 1,450 crores between 1969 and 1974, amounting to forty-five percent of total expenditure (exclusive of investment from private savings) on agriculture.[90]

The agricultural corporations, established since 1965, were expected to operate in ways that would encourage private investment. The Rural Electrification Corporation, set up in the public sector to provide loans to state electricity boards, was directed to focus its schemes on the "pumpset to be energized rather than the village which is to be electrified."[91] Altogether, an additional 740,000 irrigation works were expected to be activated during the Fourth Plan.[92] Similarly, the agro-industries corporations established in the states as joint ventures of the central and state governments were to act as central stockists for agricultural machinery for sale and on hire-purchase agreements.

Other incentives were offered to avoid bottlenecks in the supply of modern inputs. Tractor and power tiller industries were delicensed to provide manufacturers with attractive opportunities for increasing production. At the same time, the government sought to spur private in-

---

[88] *Ibid.*, pp. 238-40.                    [89] *Ibid.*, p. 125.
[90] *Ibid.*, p. 52; an additional Rs. 800 crores of investment in agriculture was expected to come from household savings and commercial banks. *Ibid.*, p. 118.
[91] *Ibid.*, p. 135.                    [92] *Ibid.*, p. 205.

vestment in the manufacture of fertilizers, pesticides, and seeds by removing price subsidies on these inputs except in remote backward areas.
Starting in January 1969, indigenous manufacturers were also given the
freedom to market fertilizers in areas of their choice, subject to the right
of government to acquire up to thirty percent of their production at
negotiated prices.

Actually, the planners were not unconcerned about the need to enable
small farmers to participate in the new technology. They attempted,
however, to find solutions within the existing agrarian pattern that could
satisfy the norms of profitability and enhance the entrepreneurial approach by helping larger numbers of cultivators to move from subsistence farming to commercial cultivation. Approximately Rs. 235 crores
under minor irrigation was allocated for expenditure by state governments on community tanks, tubewells, and river pumping projects considered to offer special benefits to small farmers unable to afford private
schemes.[93] In addition, the planners provided for a pilot experiment in
twenty districts to establish Small Farmer Development Agencies
(SFDA) aimed at indentifying those farmers whose business, including
subsidiary activities, was potentially viable, and to assist them in obtaining credit, supplies, and services from the existing cooperative structure
necessary for investment on minor irrigation and improved practices.[94]
Consistent with its market approach, the new agencies specifically
excluded from their area of responsibility the needs of "sub-marginal"
farmers and agricultural laborers as requiring assistance that extended far
beyond credit, and greatly exceeded available resources.

The impression of tough-minded pragmatism that the planners sought
to convey in tailoring development programs to fit existing economic
and political realities was less easy to sustain in overcoming the obstacles
to providing finances for even a modest Plan. The attempt to come to
terms with contracting sources of funds from deficit spending and
foreign aid was only partly successful. As shown in Table 8-5, the Fourth
Plan outlay of Rs. 14,398 crores allowed Rs. 850 crores of deficit financing, compared to Rs. 1,133 crores during the Third Plan, reducing
finances from this source to less than six percent of total outlay. Similarly, the planners set out to eliminate PL 480 imports within two years,
taking credit for Rs. 380 crores of external assistance under this item,
compared to Rs. 1,084 crores received during the Third Plan. Aggregate
project and nonproject assistance, estimated at Rs. 2,134 crores, compared to Rs. 1,339 crores (in pre-devaluation rupees) during the Third

[93] *Ibid.*, p. 190.
[94] *Ibid.*, p. 116. The prototype for the creation of Small Farmer Development Agencies
was initiated in Reserve Bank of India, *Report of the All-India Rural Credit Review Committee*,
ch. 18.

TABLE 8-5

Financing of the Third Plan and Estimates
of Resources for the Fourth Plan

(*Rs. crores*)

| Item | Third Plan (actual) | | | Fourth Plan (estimates) | | |
|---|---|---|---|---|---|---|
| | *Center* | *States* | *Total* | *Center* | *States* | *Total* |
| 1. Domestic budgetary resources | 1,223 | 906 | 2,129 | 6,868 | 1,457 | 8,325 |
| 2. Budgetary receipts corresponding to external assistance | 2,423 | | 2,423 | 2,514 | | 2,514 |
| Other than P.L. 480 | (1,339) | | (1,339) | (2,134) | | (2,134) |
| P.L. 480 | (1,084) | | (1,084) | (380) | | (380) |
| 3. Total budgetary sources (1+2) | *3,646* | *906* | *4,552* | *9,382* | *1,457* | *10,839* |
| 4. Deficit financing | 1,004 | 129 | 1,133 | 850 | | 850 |
| 5. Additional resource mobilization | 2,277 | 615 | 2,892 | 1,600 | 1,109 | 2,709 |
| 6. Aggregate resources (3+4+5) | *6,927* | *1,650* | *8,577* | *11,832* | *2,566* | *14,398* |
| 7. Assistance for state Plans | (−)2,515 | 2,515 | | (−)3,500 | 3,500 | |
| 8. Net resources Plan outlay (6+7) | *4,412* | *4,165* | *8,577* | *8,332* | *6,066* | *14,398* |

SOURCE: *Fourth Five Year Plan 1969-74, Draft*, pp. 78, 82-83.

Plan, was justified as representing disproportionately high aid requirements during the first two years of the Fourth Plan, after which an
increasing proportion of the foreign exchange bill could be met from export earnings, allowing India to reach the target of a fifty percent reduction in net aid inflows in the last year of the Fourth Plan. This magnitude
of aid was consistent with the planners' goal of reducing foreign assistance as a proportion of development expenditure from about twenty-
eight percent during the Third Plan to seventeen percent during the
Fourth Plan. The lion's share of resources, according to these estimates,
was accounted for by domestic budgetary resources, both from current
revenues and measures for additional resource mobilization.

The difficulty was that the financial estimates were based on a number
of questionable assumptions. The calculations of foreign aid, while holding estimates of gross external assistance below $1 billion per annum,
somewhat under the levels achieved during the Third Plan, still represented a significant increase in assistance from Consortium countries during the first years of the Fourth Plan, against the decline in new commit-

ments during the previous three years. This time, moreover, any shortfall in foreign aid was bound to have broader repercussions than those of slowing down new schemes. The major assumption of the production programs in the Fourth Plan, that adequate levels of growth could be achieved by exploiting favorable capital output ratios in major sectors of the economy, depended on ensuring sufficient imports of raw materials and components to make maximum gains from underutilized and newly completed capacity in industry, and higher production coefficients in agriculture created by the introduction of highly fertilizer-responsive varieties of seeds. The vulnerability of the approach to any contraction of Consortium aid, moreover, was increased by problematical estimates of foreign-exchange earnings from exports, which assumed a rate of growth of 7 percent per annum, an advance never previously achieved.

An even more glaring deficiency was evident in estimates of available budgetary resources. At the outset, the planners appeared to accept an artificially low rate of likely increase in non–Plan expenditures by making no provisions for food imports beyond 1971, for food subsidies, or for further increases in dearness allowances of central and state government employees. If estimates of balances from current revenues were suspect, the projection of finances from additional resource mobilization proved totally unwarranted. The reduction in foreign aid, especially the elimination after 1971 of budgetary receipts from sales of PL 480 foodgrains, made it more urgent than ever to mobilize additional internal resources to finance development outlay. The planners therefore provided for additional resource mobilization of Rs. 2,709 crores, somewhat below levels achieved during the Third Plan—but at much higher rates than realized during the previous three years. In addition, the decline of the Center's ability to raise new resources meant that a much larger proportion of the revenues to be mobilized from tax measures had to be levied by the states. The Center's target for new taxation was Rs. 1,600 crores, compared to its achievement during the Third Plan of Rs. 2,277 crores. The states, by contrast, were charged with raising an additional Rs. 1,109 crores, in comparison with their achievement during the Third Plan of Rs. 615 crores, and between 1966 and 1969 of Rs. 151 crores. Inevitably, and compounding the political difficulty, the measures suggested to the states for mobilizing additional resources once again concentrated on proposals for taxing the rural sector.[95]

[95] Among other steps suggested to the states as a means of mobilizing additional resources were measures for the increase of irrigation rates to 25 to 40 percent of the additional net benefit to farmers from irrigated crops; for floating rural debentures for financing agro–industries; for irrigation schemes; for rural electrification and other services of direct benefit to the rural population; for the introduction of a progressive income tax aimed at raising resources from well-to-do farmers; and for general commodity taxation to restrain conspicuous consumption. *Fourth Five Year Plan, 1969-74, Draft*, pp. 88-89.

The state chief ministers, who discussed the Draft Outline at the April 1969 meeting of the National Development Council, refused to make any commitment about the magnitude of resources they might be expected to raise, at least until after the October 1969 award of the quinquiennial Finance Commission. On the contrary, pleading financial distress, they demanded that the Center arrange to reschedule debt repayments, and provide an additional Rs. 1,000 crores in Central assistance for the states' Plans.[96] When the long-delayed Fourth Plan began its first fiscal year in March 1969, it was without any agreement between the Center and the states on the crucial question of additional resource mobilization.

A final revision carried out under altered political circumstances in July 1970 (see Chapter Eleven) once again raised total outlay to Rs. 15,902 crores, and provided increased expenditures under all heads of development.[97] The revised estimates of the final version of the Fourth Plan were even more unrealistic than the projections of the 1969 Draft. Apart from maintaining the artificially low level of growth in non–Plan expenditures, the planners projected higher revenues from domestic budgetary sources, along with increased contributions from external assistance and the mobilization of additional resources by the central government. At the same time, they reduced by a small amount estimates of additional resource mobilization by the state governments, even as the chief ministers continued to reject the Center's recommendations for imposing direct taxes on the rural sector.[98]

The entrepreneurial approach adopted in the mid–1960s ended with the worst possible result from the point of view of the multiple economic and social goals of planning. The new economic policies appeared unlikely to achieve goals of economic growth; and they were certain to increase economic disparities.

At the end of the Third Plan, the private sector's contribution to the output of organized industry was still approximately 80 percent of the total.[99] Data prepared in the late 1960s indicated that the licensing system not only had failed to prevent the growth of capacity in less essential industries, but actually had worked to provide a disproportionate share of new licensed capacity to the few firms belonging to the larger business houses.[100] Over the years, the share of total approved investment allo-

---

[96] India, Planning Commission, Twenty-sixth Meeting of the National Development Council, April 19 & 20, 1969, *Summary Record*.

[97] *Fourth Five Year Plan, 1969-74*, p. 66.     [98] *Ibid.*, pp. 76-77.

[99] Ministry of Industry, *Industrial Planning and Licensing Policy*, by R. K. Hazari, p. 15.

[100] This outcome occurred largely as the result of "the lack of clarity about Plan targets and their implications in terms of creation of capacity, the failure of the planning authorities to work out *inter se* priorities among different industries, the uncertainty about resources

cated to the four largest business houses—the Birlas, Tatas, J. K., and
Shri Ram—actually increased. The Birlas, in particular, submitted such a
multitude of applications in almost every product as to prompt serious
questions that they were trying to "foreclose" licensable capacity to
other potential entrepreneurs.[101]

An additional source of striking increases in economic disparities was
provided by the new agricultural policies. Inequalities widened not only
between the irrigated and rainfed lands, which was only to be expected,
but between the northern wheat-growing states and the paddy-pro-
ducing areas of the east and south. Severe regional disparities in the
pace of agrarian modernization were evident over a wide range of indicators. Between 1966 and 1969, as the proportion of all fertilizers used on
foodgrains increased from 70 percent to 80 percent of the total, the percentage absorbed by wheat rose from 10 percent to 25 percent.[102] Similar
disparities emerged between the wheat and paddy areas in the development of minor irrigation facilities. In the three years between 1966 and
1969, 67 percent, 49 percent, and 53 percent of total Plan outlay on minor
irrigation was concentrated in the wheat-belt states.[103] In addition, investment from private sources, which had amounted to less than one-
half the sum provided under Plan outlay in 1966/67, jumped to more than
140 percent by 1968/69.[104] Of the more than 552,000 pumpsets energized
during 1966-1969, approximately 226,000, or 40 percent, were installed
in wheat-belt states.[105] In addition, about 50 percent of all tractors were
in the wheat-growing tract, along with 30,000 to 50,000 power wheat
threshers and 3,000 seed-fertilizer grain drills.[106]

Inequalities were compounded further by disparities within intensive
agricultural areas that quickly widened among the different classes of cultivators in their ability to take advantage of the new techniques. Even in
irrigated areas, large capital investment on a supplementary minor irrigation facility was generally prerequisite to the efficient use of the package
of high-yielding seeds, fertilizers, and pesticides. Usually, only the class
of cultivators with ten or more owned acres, mainly those who had al-

---

that prevailed, and the non-availability of any properly worked out industry Plan on the
basis of which individual decision on licensing could be taken within a rational
framework," all compounded by the lack of any clear directives to the licensing authorities
and financial institutions regarding the treatment of the larger houses. See Department of
Industrial Development, Ministry of Industrial Development, Internal Trade and Company Affairs, *Report of the Industrial Licensing Policy Inquiry Committee* (Delhi, July 1969),
pp. 183-86.
[101] *Industrial Planning and Licensing Policy*, pp. 8-12.
[102] "Country Crop Paper—Wheat," p. 16.
[103] *Ibid*., p. 22. Also *Annual Plan, 1966-67*, p. 32; *Annual Plan, 1967-68*, pp. 52-54; *Annual Plan, 1968-69*, p. 34.
[104] "Country Crop Paper—Wheat," p. 22.
[105] *Fourth Five Year Plan, 1969-74*, pp. 214-15.
[106] "Country Crop Paper—Wheat," p. 24.

ready adopted a wide variety of modern inputs to increase production
and income under the Community Development programs, were in a
position to afford the capital outlay on land improvement from their own
savings. They were also the major beneficiaries of loans from Land Development Banks, which even under the most liberal credit terms required the mortgage of at least two, and more often four to seven acres of
land as security for loans. In the heart of the wheat belt, especially in Punjab and Haryana, where over forty percent of the holdings were ten
acres or above, opportunities for participating in the gains from modern
technology were opened to large numbers of cultivators. But in the
rice-producing states, where over eighty percent of cultivating households operated holdings of less than ten acres, and the majority of agriculturists farmed uneconomic holdings of two and three acres—part of
which was frequently cultivated on a crop-share basis—the overwhelming majority of cultivators were, from the beginning, excluded from the
modernization process.[107]

Small farmers faced additional handicaps. They found it difficult to
meet the higher production costs of the "package" of practices, especially
fertilization, recommended for the most efficient cultivation of the
high-yielding varieties. Unlike larger landowners, they could not rely on
savings to finance the increased costs of modern inputs. They were also
less likely to receive producion credit advanced by the cooperatives. The
1969 report of the All-India Rural Credit Review Committee revealed
both the slow growth of the cooperative movement relative to Plan
targets and the continuing disadvantages suffered by small landowners
and tenants in gaining access to the limited credit that was available.

The survey data, presented in Table 8-6, showed that almost all villages were covered by agricultural credit societies in 1966/67. Yet fully
one-third of the societies could not meet modest standards of "viability"
prescribed by state governments.[108] Membership as a proportion of cultivator households was estimated at about 45 percent of the agriculturist
population.[109] The percentage of borrowing members to the total membership was no more than 40 percent. The ability of the cooperatives to

[107] This conclusion is supported by interviews conducted in 1969 with small farmers and
tenants in four intensive agricultural development program areas for paddy in different
parts of the country. Frankel, *India's Green Revolution*, chs. 3-6.
[108] Unpublished estimate supplied by the Joint Secretary, Ministry of Community Development and Cooperation (Department of Cooperation), August 1966.
[109] An estimate of the percentage of cultivator households covered by membership of
agricultural credit societies is calculated by dividing the membership of societies by the estimated number of cultivator households in any given year. The cooperatives do not keep
any figures on membership of cultivator households as differentiated from others. The
figure, in any case, is considered inaccurate because large numbers of noncultivators may be
enrolled to meet membership targets, and the figures are also inflated by enrolling more
than one member from the same family. *Report of the All-India Review Committee*, p. 147.

TABLE 8-6

Progress of Agricultural Credit Societies,
1951–1967

|  | 1951/52 | 1960/61 | 1965/66 | 1966/67 |
|---|---|---|---|---|
| Number of societies (lakhs) | 1.08 | 2.12 | 1.92 | 1.79 |
| Number of villages covered (lakhs) |  | 4.23 | 5.03 | 5.07 |
| Membership (lakhs) | 48 | 170 | 261 | 267 |
| % of membership to rural households |  | 23.7 | 32.3 | 32.0 |
| % of dormant societies to total |  | 19.3 | 12.3 | 14.0 |
| % of borrowing members to total membership |  | 52.6 | 41.6 | 39.7 |
| Share capital (Rs. crores) | 9 | 58 | 115 | 129 |
| of which Government contribution (Rs. crores) |  | 6 | 10 | 11 |
| Owned funds* (Rs. crores) | 18 | 76 | 149 | 165 |
| Deposits (Rs. crores) | 4 | 15 | 34 | 39 |
| *Loans issued* |  |  |  |  |
| Short term (Rs. crores) |  | 183 | 305 | 325 |
| Medium term (Rs. crores) |  | 20 | 37 | 40 |
| Total (Rs. crores) | 24 | 203 | 342 | 365 |
| Loans outstanding (Rs. crores) | 34 | 218 | 427 | 477 |
| Overdues (Rs. crores) | 9 | 44 | 125 | 160 |
| % of overdues to outstandings | 25.3 | 20.3 | 29.4 | 33.5 |
| *Average per member* |  |  |  |  |
| Share capital (Rs.) | 19 | 34 | 44 | 48 |
| Deposits (Rs.) | 9 | 9 | 13 | 15 |
| Loans advanced (Rs.) | 51 | 119 | 131 | 137 |
| *Average per society* |  |  |  |  |
| Membership | 44 | 80 | 136 | 149 |
| Share capital (Rs. thousand) | 0.8 | 3 | 6 | 7 |
| Deposits (Rs. thousand) | 0.4 | 0.7 | 2 | 2 |
| Loans advanced (Rs. thousand) | 2 | 10 | 18 | 20 |

SOURCE: Reserve Bank of India, *Report of the All-India Rural Credit Review Committee* (Bombay, 1969), p. 138.

* Owned funds are equivalent to share capital and reserves. Owned resources include share capital, reserves, and deposits.

mobilize resources for lending activities was very limited. Owned funds, including share capital and reserves, did not amount to more than Rs. 165 crores. Although the Third Plan target for short-term loans was set at Rs. 530 crores, the cooperatives in 1966/67 advanced loans totaling Rs. 325 crores. More than one-half of this amount was financed by outside borrowings from higher institutions whose own lending resources were significantly dependent on government contributions to share capital. Even then, the ability of agricultural credit cooperatives to command outside borrowings was actually eroding, as the percent of overdues to loans outstanding increased to over 33 percent in 1966/67, and a growing number of societies failed to meet the Reserve Bank's standards for "non-overdue cover" in qualifying for maximum credit accommodations. Altogether, loans advanced by the cooperatives probably did not amount to more than 15 or 20 percent of the total funds borrowed annually by cultivators. Of this limited amount, the data showed that "the small cultivators continue to be handicapped over large parts of the country" in obtaining their fair share because of "one or more factors, viz., exclusion from membership, insistence on landed security, and restrictions on the size of loans which may be made to tenants."[110]

There were few links between the agricultural credit societies and marketing cooperatives. Well over one-third of all village credit societies were not even members of the area (taluka) marketing society, and fewer than ten percent of all loans advanced by credit cooperatives were recovered through the sale proceeds of marketing societies.[111] This absence of an effective linkage between agricultural credit and marketing undermined the determined efforts by the Reserve Bank in 1966 to introduce a crop-based system of production loans as an instrument for helping small and medium farmers to participate in the high-yielding varieties program.[112] Under conditions in which the credit agency rarely had any control over the sale proceeds of members' crops, "crop loans" came to mean little more than a paper exercise to determine production costs for each crop per acre, and to establish the maximum amount for which a member was eligible according to the value of his gross produce. In prac-

[110] *Ibid.*, p. 176.          [111] *Fourth Five Year Plan, A Draft Outline*, p. 142.

[112] The crop-based system of agricultural credit was supposed to provide each participant with sufficient finance from the cooperative to meet his full production needs by determining repayment capacity according to the value of gross product rather than ownership of property or other assets. The production loans, advanced in cash and kind components, with a major share provided in the form of fertilizers, were generally subject to an individual maximum borrowing limit of Rs. 2,000 in order to ration scarce funds equitably. Supplementary "special credit limits" were sanctioned by the Reserve Bank for use by central cooperative banks in providing advances to agricultural societies to ensure the full credit needs of all participants. They allowed cooperatives to lend a larger proportion of the credit requirements of participants in the high-yielding varieties program than would have been possible if the Reserve Bank maintained restrictive regulations such as non-overdue cover as a condition of sanctioning maximum credit limits to central banks and agricultural credit societies. At the core of the crop-loan system, however, was the provision that loans advanced by the credit society must be recovered from the sale proceeds of the crop. In theory, each borrower was obligated to sell to the cooperative marketing society to which the credit agency was affiliated the quantity of produce necessary to meet the principle and interest of the loan. For a description of the crop-loan system recommended by the government, see Reserve Bank of India, Agricultural Credit Department, "Manual on Short-term and Medium-term Loans for Agricultural Purposes" (Bombay, 1966), Part I.

tice, the actual limit of each individual's loan, as in the past, was calculated according to the value of the security—land or jewelry—he offered.

Actually, small farmers, for their part, frequently failed to use their maximum borrowing power, even at the modest rate of finance provided. Their absorptive capacity for modern inputs in the absence of assured supply of water was very low. They were, in particular, reluctant to draw the full fertilizer component of crop loans for fear of incurring large debts that might prove difficult to repay if inadequate water caused crop losses. Indeed, between 1966 and 1969, the cooperatives often found it difficult to use funds available for production loans under special credit accommodations for the high-yielding varieties program, as a result of "lack of demand" by borrowers.[113]

Large farmers, by contrast, began a process of capital accumulation that allowed them to pyramid their gains. Profits earned from the introduction of high-yielding varieties[114] were used to buy more land, improve land already under cultivation, purchase modern equipment for mechanization of farm operations that allowed double and triple cropping, and diversification of cropping patterns to include more profitable commercial crops. The biggest wheat farmers were, in addition, the major beneficiaries of the central government's new price policy.[115] During 1967-1969, procurement prices set at incentive levels approached the inflationary wholesale prices prevailing in the open market during the period of extreme shortage in the preceding drought years. The increase in 1968 procurement prices over 1965 levels reached more than 81 percent in Haryana, 23 percent in Madhya Pradesh, 46 percent in Punjab, 58 percent in Rajasthan, and 31 percent in Uttar Pradesh.[116] Indeed, in 1968 and again in 1969, the official procurement price for Mexican wheat at Rs. 76 per quintal was actually above the open-market price by about 18 percent to 26 percent.[117] Government purchasing agents were virtually

[113] This was the situation in the IADP districts of West Godavary, Tanjore, Palghat, and Burdwan, for which data was collected in 1969. See Frankel, *India's Green Revolution*, pp. 66-68, 96-97, 131-34, 170-72.

[114] In the most advanced areas of the wheat belt, it is possible for farmers adopting the new technology to double their output and increase their net income on the average by over 70 percent. Gains from the new paddy techniques are more modest, but on the average may exceed net returns on local varieties by 25 to 30 percent. *Ibid.*, pp. 24, 51.

[115] According to S. S. Johl, the biggest-size farms in the Punjab not only had larger aggregate quantities of grains to sell, but also managed larger surpluses per acre. Those with farms of 57 acres and above increased their marketed surplus per acre by more than 44 percent over the increases achieved by farms in the smallest-size group of 14 acres or below. S. S. Johl, "Gains of the Green Revolution (How They Have Been Shared in Punjab)," 1971, mimeographed, Table 5.

[116] Ministry of Food, Agriculture, Community Development and Cooperation, Department of Agriculture, *Report of the Agricultural Prices Commission on Price Policy for Rabi Foodgrains for 1968-69 Season* (March 1968), p. 24.

[117] "Country Crop Paper—Wheat."

inundated by the large quantities of Mexican wheat offered for sale, and procurement for government stocks had to be doubled over the official target. This heavy drain on government finances, moreover, forced a reexamination of retail issue prices through the food distribution system. As projections of the cost of food subsidies at existing rates increased from Rs. 130 crores to Rs. 190 crores in 1968,[118] the government shifted the burden of higher procurement prices to consumers by raising the issue prices of wheat distributed by the fair price shops. The increase in 1968 over 1965 prices was estimated at 88 percent in Haryana, 41 percent in Rajasthan, and 31 percent in Uttar Pradesh.[119]

This general tendency toward economic polarization occurred in a transformed political environment. By 1969, all of the dangers antici-pated from the failure of peaceful reform were already at hand. After twenty years of socialist rhetoric, new principles of legitimacy based on equality and participation were slowly taking hold, even as the demo-cratic political framework failed to provide effective organizational devices for translating these ideals into action. Plan policies that offered little hope of benefit to the majority of the population risked serious dan-gers that discontent would spill over into disorder and violence. Against the background of economic failures that increased the pressure of pro-liferating demands on fixed resources, populist and Marxist parties emerged, committed to a strategy of mass mobilization for a direct attack on the propertied classes and the constitutional system that buttressed their privileged position. In fact, the National Development Council it-self was no longer a homogeneous group. The chief ministers of Kerala and West Bengal, representing Marxist-led coalition governments, sat as full members. They argued forcefully for fundamental institutional change to increase the quantum of resources subject to government con-trol. E.M.S. Namboodirapad, then chief minister of Kerala, denounced the entire Fourth Plan, to insist that "all economic policies need rethink-ing to reach the objective of a socialist society, all the instruments and means of production, distribution and exchange had to be socially owned."[120] At the very time when conservative groups believed they had won a final victory in reorienting the basic principles of economic policy toward a free enterprise model, the opportunity for achieving a national political consensus around a capitalist approach had already passed.

[118] *Ibid.*, p. 32.
[119] *Report of the Agricultural Prices Commission, 1968-69 Season*, p. 24.
[120] The Twenty-Sixth Meeting of the National Development Council, *Summary Record*, p. 25.

# NINE

# Crisis of Political Stability

By the mid-1960s, the combination of food shortages, rising prices, and increasing income disparities threatened to undermine much of the hard-won gains in political stability achieved since Independence. Sections of the population normally immune to agitational appeals were mobilized for *bandhs* or general work stoppages to protest the "anti-peoples policies" of the government. Illegal strikes for higher salaries and dearness allowances were called by government employees ranging the gamut of doctors (in Bihar, Orissa, and Delhi); teachers (in Kerala); engineers (in Punjab); and junior-grade civil servants (in West Bengal, Maharashtra, and Uttar Pradesh). Trade union leaders, protesting rising prices, launched lightning strikes for higher wages that tied up industries and services in large parts of the country. Students, frustrated by outdated curricula and spiraling fees, vented their resentment in burning and looting of shops, buses, post offices, railway equipment, and the destruction of college buildings and laboratories. Potential for violent protest was also evident in the countryside, especially in regions where communist agitators were actively organizing among the peasantry. In West Bengal, the Communist parties took the lead in organizing mob attacks on district procurement offices, rice mills, and markets, which expanded to destruction of railway stations, banks, telephone and telegraph equipment, before culminating on March 10, 1966, in a statewide total strike or Bengal Bandh. The public disorder in Calcutta and the surrounding countryside on that day was so widespread that the police were inadequate to control the mobs. Only the entry of army troops, called in by a frightened administration, was able to restore order.

Events showed, moreover, that mass protest movements could be mobilized around regional, ethnic, or communal cleavages through appeals that combined promises of protection for the economic interests with promotion of the socio-cultural aspirations of threatened groups. The first notable instance of success in fusing populist and parochial demands was provided by the ability of the DMK in Madras to launch a statewide movement of student protest against the central government's promulgation in January 1965 (according to constitutional provisions) of Hindi as the official language of the Union. The student strikes, which drew on longstanding resentment against northern Brahmin domination of Tamil language and culture, were all the more incendiary when sparked by fears among the educated unemployed that introduction of Hindi as the national language would further diminish their chances of securing appointment in the central government public services. Despite the large-scale intervention of the police, including the arrest of about 10,000 persons and police firings in twenty-one towns (that left over fifty persons dead), the government could not restore public order until the Center agreed to an indefinite continuation in the use of English in addition to Hindi as the language of government administration.

Other popular discontents, compounded of economic grievances and ethnic aspirations, sparked rebellions that were more difficult to pacify. On the politically sensitive northeast border with China and Pakistan, tribal groups in the hill areas of Assam, charging economic discrimination by the people of the valley, resorted to violent struggles for independence that were only partially defused by the creation of separate states of Nagaland (in 1963) and Meghalaya (in 1967). In March 1966, moreover, Mizo tribals, demanding complete independence, launched a bloody guerrilla war with the suspected help of China and Pakistan. The rebel leaders organized the Mizo National Front, went underground, and succeeded in establishing their authority over rural base areas in a direct appeal to ethnic nationalism that emphasized economic exploitation of hill peoples by the Assamese.

The potential scope for activating social discontent through organization around communal groupings was even greater. The Hindu-oriented Jan Sangh enjoyed a natural recruiting ground that extended to the whole of the Hindi-speaking heartland in north India. In November 1966, crowds estimated in the hundreds of thousands, and believed to be organized by the RSS, went on a rampage in front of the Lok Sabha in New Delhi, attacking government offices, burning cars, and killing a policeman in the cause of extracting government promises for a total ban on the slaughter of cows. Altogether, eight persons were killed and more than forty injured when riot troops had to be called in to restore order.[1]

The communists, meanwhile, did not lag behind in devising their own methods of mass organization to tap discontents expressed in more traditional forms. In December 1966, E.M.S. Namboodiripad, then the leading theoretician of the CPI (Marxists), formally advanced a new thesis on the national question that justified communist support for regional, linguistic, and tribal "struggles" against the central government when they were carried out to win greater equality and political autonomy for the most "socially oppressed" groups. According to Namboodiripad,

---

[1] For a vivid description of the "atmosphere of pervasive violence" that set in by the beginning of the summer of 1966, see Pran Chopra, *Uncertain India*, pp. 365–80.

The dominant ruling group at the centre tried to establish a fake "unity of the nation" by denying the right of every nationality and social group to have equality of opportunity and status in a democratic set-up . . . the so-called "struggle between nationalism and the fissiparous forces"—the struggle in the name of which the leaders of the ruling party are trying to beat the opposition forces into submission—is a fake "struggle." It is the means through which the dominant section of the bourgeoisie is trying to maintain its domination not only over the working people but even sections of their own class. The slogan of "national unity" is thus the weapon with which the dominant monopoly group tried to bring their competitors into submission.[2]

The new thesis allowed the Marxists to interpret the demands of the various nationalities, linguistic groups, and tribes for greater resources and political power as "perfectly legitimate democratic demands [which] are part of the platform on the basis of which the democratic revolution is to be completed and the soil prepared for the socialist revolution."[3] This formulation quickly revealed its potentiality for political disruption when, in November 1966, the communists helped to organize student demonstrations in fourteen cities and towns of Andhra Pradesh to agitate for central acquiescence in setting up a steel mill in the state's coastal city of Vizagapatnam. The demonstrations, which deteriorated in many places into mob violence, forced police firings in three cities and claimed several lives.

At the same time that dissatisfied regional, communal, and ethnic groups departed from methods of parliamentary competition to embrace tactics of violent protest in imposing their claims on government, the Congress party, confronted by new demands on an already strained patronage system, was losing its capacity to function as an umbrella organization. Bitter internal disputes over the allocation of party tickets at the states led to large-scale defections that splintered the organization around the factional and caste groupings at its core. Meanwhile, the ruling party's advantage in a divided opposition was reduced by efforts of the two communist parties on the one hand, and the conservative and communal parties on the other, to arrange electoral adjustments and alliances.

The dramatic losses suffered by the Congress party in the 1967 elections were interpreted as a political watershed signaling the demise of the one-party dominant system. At the national level, the emerging pattern

[2] E.M.S. Namboodiripad, "The Programme Explained," Calcutta, December 1966. Reprinted as Appendix III in Fic, *Kerala, Yenan of India*, p. 481.
[3] *Ibid.*

showed Congress occupying the place of political center from a contracting base of popular support against growing challenges to its hegemonic
position from communists on the left and a conservative and communal
alignment on the right. At the state level, heterogenous anti-Congress
combinations came to power in unstable coalitions that created a
semipermanent condition of Cabinet crisis and administrative paralysis.

At a time when the ability of the Congress party to provide political
consensus and stability declined, the CPI (Marxists)—and a small group
of communist revolutionaries that splintered off to follow Maoist
methods of armed agrarian struggle—enjoyed growing success in organizing peasant agitations around class divisions that coincided with
traditional cleavages of region, tribe, community, and caste. As incidents
of agrarian violence multiplied throughout the country, the Marxists'
approach of using existing social units as political building blocks for an
attack on the constitutional system appeared to have broad scope for
radicalizing Indian politics. Uneven agricultural modernization, increasing disparities, incomplete land reforms—all were eroding traditional
patron-client ties to uncover the economic conflicts at the core of caste
divisions. Vertical factional allegiances cross-cutting caste and class lines
began to weaken in the face of contradictory appeals to the common economic interest of low caste/class groups.

As the nation prepared for the fourth general elections, Mrs. Gandhi's
credibility as an effective national leader was seriously impaired. The
sudden wave of lawlessness provided evidence that the prime minister's
independent position on the basis of popular support was still uncertain.
Indeed, the 1967 election appeared to offer opposition parties the first favorable opportunity since Independence of defeating Congress at the
polls.

Prominent faction leaders having a political base in regional or caste
followings, and dissatisfied with the share of their supporters in the allocation of party tickets, announced their resignation from the party. In
Madhya Pradesh, the conflict over this question between the dominant
group headed by the chief minister, D. P. Mishra, and dissidents, including the powerful Maharani Vijaya Scindia of Gwalior, led to large-scale
defections that saw thousands of party workers at various levels of the
organization leave the Congress to join the newly formed Jana Congress
or to contest the elections as independents. Similarly, in Bihar, failure of
the dominant group led by Chief Minister K. B. Sahay to satisfy the
claims of the former PCC president, Mahamaya Prasad Sinha, and the
Raja of Ramgarh prompted defections of both leaders and the formation
with their followers of a new party, the Jan Kranti Dal. In Rajasthan, two
factions led by the Maharaja of Jhalawar and the revenue minister, Kum-

bharam Arya, left the Congress party to form their own Janta party, with other defectors contesting the elections either as independents or on the Jan Sangh and Swatantra tickets. In Orissa, the disgruntled former chief minister, Harekrushna Mahtab, took eleven MLAs with him into the opposition to serve as the nucleus of a new Jana Congress party.

The most embittered intraparty factional dispute occurred in West Bengal. In that state, the followers of Atulya Ghosh, Pradesh Congress Committee secretary and long the undisputed leader of the state organization, confronted a challenge to their control from a group aligned with Ajoy Kumar Mukherjee, president of the Pradesh Congress Committee. The Mukherjee faction charged Ghosh with "corrupt and dictatorial" practices. They demanded as their price for remaining inside the party an intervention by the Working Committee to supersede the PCC and appoint an ad hoc committee with Mukherjee's followers in the dominant position. Relations between the two senior leaders were finally exacerbated to the point that Mukherjee publicly supported the Bengal Bandh organized by the left opposition against his own (Congress) government's food policy in March 1966. Expelled for "indiscipline" from the Congress party on June 18, Mukherjee, joined by the influential Muslim Congress leader Humayun Kabir, took his own followers out of the party and formed the Bangla Congress. The split in West Bengal was reminiscent of an earlier defection in Kerala that had already proved disastrous for the electoral fortunes of the Congress party. In that state, the struggle between the organizational and ministerial wings, dating from 1963, had also featured acrimonious charges by the organization leadership of corruption against its own party members in the ministry. The dissidents, who formed the Kerala Congress, contested the 1965 midterm poll as a separate party. The result was that the Congress rebels siphoned off about thirteen percent of the vote of the undivided party, depriving it of a majority, and setting the stage (after a period of President's Rule) for a drive by the communists to return to power in the state.

The rising defection rate did, in fact, provide strong incentives to opposition leaders for combining in coalitions that could destroy the weakened Congress party's advantage in a fragmented opposition. The two communist parties, despite the fact that they were divided on basic questions of strategy and tactics, shared a broad policy perspective that allowed them to explore the possibilities of closer cooperation. Both parties took their point of departure from a blanket indictment of Congress economic policies.[4] They denounced the Planning Commission for "yielding to and helping the right offensive against planning itself" in

---

[4] The election manifestoes of the CPI and CPI(M) are published in Chandidas et al., *India Votes*, pp. 37-78.

relying mainly on foreign aid, particularly "U.S. imperialist aid" to finance development; and attacked the Draft Outline of the Fourth Plan for following the capitalist path in giving free play to market forces, "which means a free hand to foreign and Indian exploiters."[5] Both parties attached the highest importance to restoring the priority of capital-goods industries to the "pride of place" in Indian planning, and to expanding the public sector in order to achieve a commanding position for the state in economic development. Indeed, each party advocated extensive nationalization of key sectors in the economy, both to curb concentration of economic power in private hands, and to provide additional domestic resources for large public investment. The proposals included pledges for nationalization of banks, foreign-owned industrial enterprises, export and import trade, as well as state takeover of the wholesale trade in foodgrains. The CPI called for the break-up of the seventy-five largest business houses in the private sector and nationalization of "some sections of private industry and capital," including oil and petroleum, coal mining, nonferrous metals, electricity, cars, and trucks. The Marxists endorsed "nationalization of the concerns of monopolists and of such industry as is immediately necessary to the interest of the people."[6]

There was also general agreement on the agricultural strategy. Both parties concentrated on institutional change as the primary requirement of advance in agriculture, especially far-reaching redistribution of land. The Marxists, already committed to the organization of peasant revolutionary movements, were most detailed in calling for drastic reductions in rents; abolition of all cesses and taxes on uneconomic holdings; cancellation of debts; and "the taking over of the land of the big landlords and their distribution gratis among agricultural workers and peasants."[7]

Both parties also explored the implications of a radical domestic program for India's foreign policy. Both argued the necessity of ending dependence on American foreign aid, the Marxists going so far as to call for a moratorium on repayment of all outstanding loans until "we get out of the crisis."[8] Both urged an "independent" foreign policy based on strong resistance to American aggression (with Vietnam in mind) and a policy of "firm friendship with the socialist camp."[9] The CPI registered its disapproval of Communist China in breaking away from the world communist movement, and reiterated its solidarity with the international socialist camp led by the Soviet Union. Indeed, as a technique for strengthening Indo-Soviet ties beyond solidarity on questions of international affairs, and to reduce India's dependence on the "world imperialist market," the CPI advocated the progressive diversion of Indian trade (on the basis of rupee payments) toward the socialist states.

[5] *Ibid.*, p. 47.
[6] *Ibid.*, pp. 46, 66.
[7] *Ibid.*, p. 64.
[8] *Ibid.*, p. 63.
[9] *Ibid.*, pp. 70-71.

Most significant, the two parties served public notice they would no longer be willing to accept the constraints of the existing constitutional framework in pursuing their goals. On the contrary, they gave warning of a concerted attempt to change the rules of the political game. Two bulwarks of the conservative social order protected by the constitution were singled out for attack—the privileges of former princely rulers and the prerogatives of the British-trained members of the Indian Civil Service, many of whom had occupied top administrative posts since Independence. In the first case, they pledged to annul all constitutional guarantees for the princes; in the second, to enforce the immediate retirement of all ICS officers, overriding constitutional guarantees of tenure.

An even more far-reaching attack on fundamental principles of the constitution was launched in a challenge to the preeminent position of the Center under the federal division of powers. The major target of the combined left assault was the provision allowing proclamation of President's Rule in any state after determination that conditions existed that prevent the government from carrying out its constitutional responsibilities. Both leftist parties strongly insisted on abolition of the emergency powers of the president. They argued that only parliament should be able to declare a national emergency, and then solely in the event of foreign invasion. Nor was the central government to continue to use the Defense of India Rules or acts of preventive detention to arrest persons suspected of subversion. Finally, the two parties advanced proposals for fundamental change in the electoral system. Both gave highest priority to ending the system of single-member constituencies based on plurality vote, and proposed to replace it with the principle of proportional representation. This was not all. The Marxists, at least, did not hesitate to say they would use nonelectoral and extraparliamentary techniques to enforce these changes. Declaring that the road to socialism would be opened only through "the establishment of a State of People's Democracy, replacing the present bourgeois-landlord state led by the big bourgeoisie," they argued this could be achieved only by developing "determined mass struggle."[10]

The two parties, moreover, were encouraged by considerations of political expediency to overlook their differences on questions of strategy and tactics. The CPI still endorsed an approach to winning political power that aimed at participation in a national coalition. The 1964 party congress accepted the leadership's program for "united front from above tactics" to bring together all the "patriotic forces in the country, including the working class, the entire peasantry, the rich peasants and the agricultural laborers, the intelligentsia and the non-monopolist bourgeoisie" in a National Democratic Front. The core of the united front

10 *Ibid.*, p. 75.

from above tactic was, in fact, a coalition with the "progressive section of the Congress" in order to attract the "vast mass following of the party"—still the largest electoral force in the country.[11] CPI theoreticians envisaged that the NDF could come to power either through an electoral alliance with Congress or a split inside the party that would force its left wing to bring communists into the central government in order to maintain a majority. The leadership of the CPI (Marxists), by contrast, were just as firmly convinced of the necessity of replacing the existing "bourgeois-landlord" government of the Congress party as a basic precondition for carrying out radical economic and social change. They were powerfully influenced by the Kerala experience and the failure of the communist-led ministry to convert the governmental machinery into an instrument of socialist transformation once the Congress-controlled central government invoked emergency powers to impose President's Rule. The Marxists rejected any possibility of a coalition with elements of the ruling party. They were, on the contrary, convinced that left parties joining a national coalition in cooperation with the Congress would be submerged by the dominant bourgeois elements.

Yet each party encountered serious constraints in carrying out its preferred approach under conditions of the 1967 elections. The CPI found it impossible to pursue its goal of a National Democratic Front in the face of the refusal by Kamaraj as Congress party president to consider entering into discussions of an electoral alliance. At the same time, evidence of internal decay inside the ruling party prompted reassessment of the tactic of an anti-Congress alliance. Under the new conditions, it offered a promising method of eroding Congress strength to the point that the national leadership would have little choice but to seek communist allies against both extremes of the right and left. The CPI leadership even speculated that such an alliance might "prepare the ground for a new alignment at the Centre which will halt the present trend and make possible decisive policy shifts toward the left."[12] The Marxists, for their part, conceded that a left front could not come to power at the Center in the absence of Congress support. They therefore assigned primary importance to strengthening the regional bases of communist power in Kerala and West Bengal, and to forming "People Democracies" at the state level. According to CPI(M) theoreticians, the correct road to power at the Center lay through formation of as many left united front state governments as possible, in order to increase political pressure for con-

[11] "The Programme of the Communist Party of India, as Adopted by the Seventh Congress of the Communist Party of India," Bombay, December 13-23, 1964 (New Delhi, 1965). Cited in Marcus F. Franda, *Radical Politics in West Bengal*, pp. 216-17.

[12] "The Present Political Situation," Resolution of the National Council of the Communist Party in India, Hyderabad, June 9-15, 1966 (New Delhi, July 1966). Cited in Fic, *Kerala, Yenan of India*, p. 345.

cessions to greater state autonomy. The electoral strategy required by this approach was one of alignments with all groups and parties willing to fight against Congress, so that "the opposition vote may not get split and the defeat of the Congress party may be ensured in the maximum number of constituencies thereby facilitating the formation of alternative governments wherever possible."[13] At the outset, the CPI(M) hoped to protect the united front ministries from central intervention by working within the limits of the constitution to press for recognition of trade unions, unemployment relief, minimum wages for agricultural laborers, and legislation for redistribution of land, all at the same time as they educated public opinion about the obstacles to fundamental social reform under the existing distribution of Central and state powers. Gradually, by expanding its organizational capability for militant agitations and extraparliamentary campaigns, the Marxists aimed at building the potential in a number of states for mass movements among the peasantry and workers that would bring irresistible pressure on the central government for structural change.

Serious discussions of electoral adjustments between the two communist parties got underway by July 1966. The consultative committees of the left opposition parties agreed to avoid mutual contests in as many constituencies as possible. Predictable differences between the two parties over the correct assessment of the relative strength of each in the constituencies to be contested imposed limitations on the agreements reached. In Andhra, negotiations completely broke down. The rivals did, however, achieve significant cooperation in their regional strongholds of Kerala and West Bengal. In Kerala, where the 1965 elections had already demonstrated the superior relative strength of the CPI(M) over the CPI, negotiations were faciliated by the willingness of the latter to accept a subordinate position in conceding the returns as the basis of allocating seats between the two parties.

Negotiations in West Bengal proved more difficult. The CPI, which had taken the lead since 1952 in promoting leftist electoral coalitions, refused to accept the CPI(M)'s claim that it was much the stronger party as measured by the yardstick of organizational strength. While negotiations for a united front including the two parties eventually broke down, substantial progress was made in reducing the area of mutual contest. Ultimately, two electoral coalitions were created: the United Left Front, a seven-party alignment dominated by the CPI(M); and the Peoples United Left Front, in which the CPI played a leading role. Confrontation between members of the ULF and the PULF was limited in practice to about one-third the constituencies of the state. The CPI and CPI(M) engaged in direct conflict in only thirty-eight constituencies—approxi-

---

[13] "On Ideological Discussion," *People's Democracy*, 2:36 (June 26, 1966).

mately fifteen percent of the total—representing communist strongholds neither party was prepared to concede to the other.[14] From the point of view of the CPI, moreover, the creation of the PULF represented an historic turning point. The CPI's major partner, and in fact the dominant member measured by the allocation of seats, was the Bangla Congress, the first rebel Congress group ever to be willing to cooperate with a communist party to defeat its parent organization. The CPI, heralding the event as dramatic proof of the correctness of its long-term strategy, predicted this type of coalition would ultimately project the communists into power at the Center and in the majority of states.

Conservative groups enjoyed more modest success in overcoming their differences to strike advantageous alliances. Nevertheless, Swatantra did manage to arrange limited electoral adjustments in Madhya Pradesh with Congress defectors, the Jan Sangh, and regional groupings; found a congenial ally in Orissa in the Jan Congress; and joined the DMK-led electoral alliance in Madras. It also enjoyed other advantages. In Rajasthan, Madhya Pradesh, Bihar, and Gujerat, the defection of influential princes from the Congress party often meant a groundswell in support for Swatantra. Most important, the business community organized in FICCI met for the first time since Independence to consider a proposal for creating a large election fund to support a business party. Although the larger business houses eventually vetoed the idea as unnecessarily provocative, and FICCI did not openly endorse any party, the result was a substantial intervention by its membership on behalf of individual candidates, most of whom were running on the Swatantra ticket. As funds were channeled to the Swatantra party, moreover, financial contributions from the business community to Congress sharply declined. Even those funds contributed to Congress were not offered through the party's Central Election Committee, as in the past, but to individual central and state leaders prepared to promise more direct influence to the business community over the formulation of government policy.[15]

Meanwhile, the Swatantra and Jan Sangh attempted to find common ideological ground that might serve as the basis for more extensive cooperation in the future. The election manifestoes of both parties[16] revealed growing convergence on major principles of economic policy. Asserting that the priorities, techniques, and strategies of the five-year plans had

[14] John Osgood Field and Marcus F. Franda, "The Communist Parties of West Bengal," in Myron Weiner and John Osgood Field, eds., *Electoral Politics in the Indian States*, Vol. 1, 45–46.

[15] See Stanley A. Kochanek, "The Federation of Indian Chambers of Commerce and Industry in Indian Politics," *Asian Survey*, 11:9 (September 1971), 866–85.

[16] The election manifestoes of the Swatantra party and the Jan Sangh are published in *India Votes*, pp. 19-32.

dismally failed in improving facilities and employment for the common man, the two parties proposed to rely primarily on incentives to private investment for the achievement of development goals. They endorsed the new strategy in agriculture, recommending, in addition, assurances to cultivators against any changes in land tenure laws, either to lower ceilings on landownership or introduce cooperative farming. Swatantra, underlining the necessity of following a predominately free enterprise approach in industry, reiterated its longstanding view that government should confine itself to providing "infrastructure"—power, highways, railways, waterways, ports, posts, telegraphs, and telephones. The Jan Sangh, in turn, moved closer to this position, stressing the general principle that "while assigning responsibility for developing a particular industry the government should be guided by merit rather than doctrinaire principles of socialism." The party leadership went further, moreover, to declare that during the three plans the public sector had already expanded so much that it mainly needed "consolidation." Except in power, mineral oils, and defense industries, ordinarily "no program of expansion in the public sector should be undertaken for some years to come."[17] The consensus extended to negative recommendations, as well. Neither party favored nationalization, whether of the banks or any other section of private industry or trade. Both opposed physical controls to regulate prices, and preferred to rely on monetary and fiscal measures. Each argued for the delicensing of a wide spectrum of industrial enterprises, with Swatantra calling for the complete end of "Permit-Quota-License Raj."

There were some areas of difference, although mainly in emphasis. The more militantly nationalistic Jan Sangh was less enthusiastic than Swatantra about taking further Western aid or inviting foreign equity capital to play a significant role in developing Indian industry. Yet, while cautious about greater economic dependence, the Jan Sangh, concerned about providing a defense against Pakistan and China, and committed to liberating occupied areas, did see some merit in Swatantra's view that "proper defense alliances with reliable powers were necessary to deal with the realities of the international situation."[18] The Jan Sangh, observing that "non-alignment can neither be our creed nor a permanent basis of our foreign policy," recognized that "when we are aggressed we must have allies." Their solution was to "follow an independent foreign policy and enter into bilateral alliances with countries irrespective of their allegiance to the two power blocs on the basis of reciprocity and mutuality of interest."[19]

The most revealing, because obvious, attempt of the two parties to achieve a common approach came in Swatantra's special statement on the

[17] *Ibid.*, p. 29.                                    [18] *Ibid.*, p. 17.
[19] *Ibid.*, p. 21.

role of religion in Indian development. While restating its support for the right to religious freedom guaranteed by the constitution, Swatantra nevertheless argued the necessity of strengthening moral and spiritual values as a motive and sanction of "right conduct" more powerful than any provided by the laws and regulations of the state. In what appeared to be a startling departure from secular norms, it went on to link the commitment of restoring religious values to their "legitimate place in life," with pursuit of spiritual goals defined in traditional Hindu terms of *dharma*. Swatantra concluded its election manifesto, in fact, with special recognition of the "role of Dharma as a God-oriented inner law to be resuscitated and welcomed and fostered by the Government of the country," and assured the voters that it "seeks to restore to the body politic the Gandhian principle of giving first priority to the rule of Dharma as the true basis for enduring moral progress and material prosperity."[20]

On the eve of the 1967 elections, neither the left nor the conservative opposition any longer felt politically inhibited from launching an open attack on the basic principles of policy set down by the national leadership under Nehru's direction. On the one hand, the leftist parties, seeking legitimacy by identifying themselves with Nehru's socialist goals as embedded in the official program of the Congress party, questioned the very possibility of implementing them through the constitutional framework. Instead, they demanded sweeping changes to facilitate confiscation of the property of the industrial and landed classes. The Marxists were prepared to rely on tactics of extraparliamentary "mass struggles" as the major instrument for bringing about the pressure from below that would provide the sanction for radical social change. The CPI hoped to capture power at the Center through a National Democratic Front of antiimperialist, antifeudal and antimonopolist elements, in a transitional arrangement leading to the exclusive leadership of "the working class." On the other hand, the Swatantra party and the Jan Sangh, professing allegiance to the democratic political processes enshrined in the constitution, rejected virtually all the substantive social goals Congress pledged to achieve through gradual and peaceful change, including planned development, socialism, secularism, and nonalignment.

The Congress party, immobilized by internal personal and factional disputes, did not even try to present a coherent defense of its policies or a new strategy for improving on past failures in implementation. The election manifesto (drafted by a subcommittee of the Working Committee, headed by Mrs. Gandhi and Kamaraj) did little more than reiterate support for the old principles of planning, socialism, secularism, democracy, and nonalignment, while attempting to placate dissidents inside the party

---

[20] *Ibid.*, pp. 18-19.

at both ends of the ideological spectrum. In an effort to conciliate critics of planning, the manifesto avoided any mention of the Draft Outline of the Fourth Plan as the main economic program of the party. At the same time, it tried to mollify the strident socialist minority who pressed for a specific commitment to bank nationalization by a compromise pledge to "bring most of these banking institutions under social control in order to serve the cause of economic growth and fulfill our social purposes more effectively."[21] As before, the platform of the Congress party was largely irrelevant to its electoral strategy. More than ever, it relied on its now reduced political capital earned during the leadership of the nationalist movement, and on the mass appeal of a national leader identified with those glorious days by her direct personal link with Nehru's charisma. Political observers, assessing the prospects of the Congress party in the 1967 election, raised the same general question: "Will [Mrs. Gandhi] as her father so very often did before her, so charm the crowds, reaching out to them over the heads of the party bosses and faction leaders, that the party admits she is indispensable to it."[22]

In the event, Mrs. Gandhi's link with Nehru's rule proved too weak to reverse the downward trend in popular support for the Congress party. Its share in the total vote for the Lok Sabha dropped to 41 percent, down almost 4 percent from 1962. The percentage of voter support for Congress at the state level declined to 42 percent, down over 3 percent from the previous poll. Changes in the distribution of voter support among critical elements of the electorate, first apparent in 1962, were reinforced in 1967. According to the analysis prepared by the Indian Institute of Public Opinion, "the broad generalization remains true that the young, the 'under-matrics' and the lowest income groups have been since 1962 or even earlier rewriting their basic loyalties to the Congress."[23] The party could win only one out of four additional votes polled at the national level in 1967, compared to one in three in 1962. The dominant trend in the states reflected the same pattern—a declining share in additional votes cast over 1962 levels—with the three exceptions of Madhya Pradesh, Rajasthan, and Uttar Pradesh.[24]

Survey data, while limited in extent, strengthened the general impression of progressive erosion in the Congress vote among groups that had

[21] The manifesto of the Indian National Congress is published in Chandidas et al., *India Votes*, pp. 5-19. The pledge to establish social control of banks is found on p. 8.

[22] Pran Chopra, "The Next Hundred Days of Mrs. Gandhi," *The Statesman*, November 28, 1966.

[23] Indian Institute of Public Opinion, *Monthly Public Opinion Surveys, 139, 140, 141*, Vol. XII, Nos. 7, 8, 9 (April, May, June 1967), 3.

[24] *Ibid.*, p. 12.

provided the broad base of the party's following. Between 1957 and 1967, the level of support for Congress among the lowest income groups, the uneducated, and religious minorities all showed a decline. In addition, Congress was failing to attract the younger generation who came of voting age in the post-Independence period as the party's vote in the age group between 21 and 35 deteriorated.[25] There were other disturbing trends. In the cities, the vote for the Congress party, which had remained relatively stable during the previous three national elections, plunged downward in 1967 for the first time. The major opposition parties, both of the right and left, increased their poll at the expense of Congress rather than independents and small opposition parties. The greatest gains were registered by the Jan Sangh, which sharply increased its vote in the urban centers of the Hindi region, and also expanded into the urban constituencies of Andhra and Maharashtra. The communists, meanwhile, made modest increases in West Bengal and Bihar.[26] In the urban areas, at least, in a pattern apprehended by some Congress socialists, the electorate was becoming polarized around the Communist parties on the one hand, and the communal and conservative parties on the other, while Congress appeared as the party of the "center," fighting both extremes from a contracting base of support.

More dramatic than any statistical trends or survey data in creating the impression of precipitous decline were the defeats suffered by the most prominent leaders of national and state governments and party organizations. At the Center, nearly a dozen central ministers and deputy ministers were repudiated at the polls, including the prime minister's closest economic advisers, C. Subramaniam, minister of food and agriculture, and Sachindra Chaudhuri, finance minister. In addition, Syndicate boss S. K. Patil, powerful head of the Bombay party organization then serving as railways minister, also went down to defeat, as did Syndicate member Atulya Ghosh, who lost his Lok Sabha seat from West Bengal. "In a class by itself," however, was the "fantastic fall of Mr. Kamaraj hitherto considered invulnerable,"[27] defeated in his home-town Madras constituency. At the state level, the casualty lists were similarly headed by leading party figures including chief ministers, among them K. B. Sahay of Bihar; P. C. Sen of West Bengal, and Bhaktavatsalam of Madras.

Most spectacular of all was the disastrous loss of seats by the Congress party, both at the Center and in the states. Not only did the party's decline in average vote level erode its capacity to win pluralities in multi-

---

[25] Ibid., p. 23.

[26] Myron Weiner and John Osgood Field, "India's Urban Constituencies" in Weiner and Field, eds., Electoral Politics in the Indian States, vol. 3.

[27] Inder Malhotra, "India's Voters Throw Out the Old-Timers," The Statesman, February 24, 1967.

lateral contests, but the electoral impact of its waning popularity was magnified by alliances among opposition parties that reduced the fragmentation of the anti-Congress vote. Under these conditions, a relatively small decrease of 4 percent in the Congress party's vote for the Lok Sabha produced a loss of over 21 percent in seats. A comparison of percentages of total votes polled and seats won by each major party in the 1962 and 1967 elections presented in Table 9-1 shows how the small aggregate shift in voter preference away from Congress benefitted almost all opposition parties, including independents, with only small splinter groups suffering significant losses.

The combination of declining average vote levels and alliances among opposition parties produced a much more serious debacle in the states. The party was reduced to a minority in the legislative assemblies of Kerala, Madras, Orissa, Punjab, Rajasthan, Uttar Pradesh, and West Bengal. In four of the eight states in which Congress was defeated, the party suffered large declines of voter support, as shown in Table 9-2, ranging from −6.3 percent in West Bengal to −8.2 percent in Punjab, −8.5 percent in Bihar, and −12.5 percent in Orissa. In Uttar Pradesh, where the votes polled by Congress decreased between 1962 and 1967 at a more modest rate of −4.2 percent, the decline, coming on top of a progressive erosion in popularity from a peak of 47.9 percent in 1952, had an equally unfavorable effect.

The magnitude of the defeat suffered by the Congress party was not, however, explained simply by the decrease in votes polled. Another critical factor was the presence—or absence—of opposition election alliances. In the states in which Congress polled less than 40 percent of the popular vote, the decrease in its percentage of seats relative to the decline in its percentage of votes was higher where the opposition had arranged electoral adjustments. In Bihar, Punjab, and Uttar Pradesh, where the Congress faced a divided opposition, its percentage loss of votes was reflected in seats lost by multiples of 2, 1.3, and 2.6, respectively. In Orissa, where Congress confronted the Swatantra-Jan Congress alliance, its loss of seats relative to the decrease in its popular vote was multiplied by a factor of 3. The most dramatic example of the multiplier effect occurred in Kerala, where the left parties, concentrating on local strongholds, transformed relatively small popular followings into much larger proportions of seats. Although the distribution of the popular vote among the Congress and the individual opposition parties changed very little between 1965 and 1967—with Congress actually registering a slight increase in its poll—the seven-party united front coalition led by the CPI(M) and the CPI inflicted very large losses on the Congress party, at the same time as it won spectacular gains for the communists. As shown in Table 9-3, the Congress party, which improved its poll from 33.5 percent in 1965 to 35.4 percent in 1967, suffered a devastating loss of seats

## TABLE 9-1

### Percentage of Total Vote Polled and Seats Won by Major Parties in the Lok Sabha Elections, 1962 and 1967

| Name of party | Votes polled 1962 | % | Votes polled 1967 | % | Seats won 1962 | % | Seats won 1967 | % |
|---|---|---|---|---|---|---|---|---|
| Congress | 51,509,084 | 44.72 | 59,538,197 | 40.92 | 361 | 73.07 | 284 | 54.60 |
| Swatantra | 9,085,252 | 7.89 | 12,332,316 | 8.48 | 18 | 3.64 | 42 | 8.08 |
| Jan Sangh | 7,422,766 | 6.44 | 13,693,682 | 9.34 | 14 | 2.83 | 35 | 6.73 |
| CPI | 11,450,037 | 9.94 | 7,063,115 | 4.85 | 29 | 5.87 | 23 | 4.42 |
| CPI(M) | — | — | 6,502,608 | 4.47 | — | — | 19 | 3.65 |
| Socialist★ | 3,099,397 | 2.69 | — | — | 6 | 1.21 | — | — |
| SSP★ | — | — | 7,223,499 | 4.96 | — | — | 23 | 4.42 |
| PSP | 7,848,345 | 6.44 | 4,480,224 | 3.05 | 12 | 2.43 | 13 | 2.50 |
| DMK | 2,315,610 | 2.01 | 5,524,514 | 3.79 | 7 | 1.42 | 25 | 4.82 |
| Other parties | 12,795,579 | 11.11 | 8,226,276 | 5.66 | 27 | 5.46 | 13 | 2.50 |
| Independents | 12,749,813 | 11.08 | 21,044,892 | 14.47 | 20 | 4.05 | 43 | 8.27 |

SOURCE: Indian National Congress, *The Fourth General Elections, A Statistical Analysis* (June 1967), pp. 2-3.

★ The Socialist party, led by Rammanohar Lohia, was organized on the eve of the 1962 elections by defectors from the PSP. Subsequently, in 1964, Lohia's Socialists and the PSP briefly merged to form a united socialist party, the Samuykta Socialist party (SSP). This merger unraveled in February 1965 when disgruntled elements decided to reconstitute themselves as an independent party. The Socialists retained the name of the briefly united Socialist party.

## TABLE 9-2

### Decrease in Percentage of Votes Polled and Seats Won by the Congress Party in the 1967 State Assembly Elections

| States | % of votes polled in 1962 | % of votes polled in 1967 | Increase or decrease in % of votes | % of seats won in 1962 | % of seats won in 1967 | Increase or decrease in % of seats |
|---|---|---|---|---|---|---|
| Bihar | 41.35 | 32.84 | −8.53 | 58.1 | 40.3 | −17.8 |
| Kerala★ | 33.58 | 35.40 | +1.82 | 27.1 | 6.8 | −20.3 |
| Madras | 46.14 | 41.49 | −4.65 | 67.2 | 21.4 | −46.0 |
| Orissa | 43.28 | 30.73 | −12.55 | 58.6 | 22.1 | −36.5 |
| Punjab | 45.63 | 37.42 | −8.21 | 57.5 | 46.2 | −11.3 |
| Rajasthan | 40.02 | 41.44 | +1.42 | 50.0 | 48.4 | −1.6 |
| Uttar Pradesh | 36.33 | 32.13 | −4.20 | 57.9 | 48.8 | −11.1 |
| West Bengal | 47.20 | 40.97 | −6.32 | 62.3 | 45.4 | −16.9 |

SOURCE: AICC, *The Fourth General Elections*, p. i.

★ Percentage of vote for Kerala is given for the 1965 mid-term election.

TABLE 9-3

Congress Party Performance Relative to Opposition Parties Contesting
Individually in 1965 and as Part of the United Front in 1967 (Kerala)

| | 1965 | | 1967 | |
| | Votes % | Seats % | Votes % | Seats % |
| Parties | | | | |
|---|---|---|---|---|
| Congress | 33.03 | 27.07 | 34.22 | 6.77 |
| CPI(M) | 19.55 | 30.08 | 22.62 | 39.01 |
| CPI | 8.02 | 2.25 | 8.24 | 14.29 |
| Muslim League | 3.71 | 4.51 | 6.51 | 10.61 |
| SSP | 8.00 | 9.79 | 8.08 | 14.29 |
| RSP | 1.30 | — | 2.61 | 4.51 |
| KTP | 1.19 | 0.75 | 0.65 | 1.50 |
| KSP | — | — | 0.51 | 0.01 |
| *Sub-Total*: opposition parties contesting separately and as part of United Front | 41.77 | 47.38 | 49.22 | 84.22 |
| Kerala Congress | 13.11 | 18.04 | 7.31 | 3.76 |
| Independents | 10.30 | 7.51 | 4.36 | 4.51 |
| Others | .27 | — | 1.29 | 0.74 |
| Invalid | 1.52 | | 3.60 | |
| Total | 100.00 | 100.00 | 100.00 | 100.00 |

SOURCE: Victor M.Fic, *Kerala, Yenan of India*, pp. 499, 518.

which reduced its strength in the legislative assembly from over 35
percent to 7 percent of the total. By contrast, the communist parties,
which improved their performance at the polls from 27.5 percent in 1965
to 30.6 percent in 1967—still below Congress levels—managed to increase their share of seats in the legislative assembly by 11 percent, raising their overall strength from 32 percent to 43 percent of the total.
Combined with substantial gains in seats won by other members of the
united front, the coalition that together won 49 percent of the popular
vote was able to amass over 87 percent of the seats.

The ability of opposition parties to use electoral alliances as efficient
techniques for gaining a majority of seats, even when Congress sustained
vote levels of more than 40 percent—levels that previously had been sufficient to win assembly majorities—was demonstrated in the three states
of Rajasthan, Madras, and West Bengal. In Rajasthan, where Congress
faced an informal Swatantra-Jan Sangh alliance, and actually improved
its poll performance marginally over 1962 levels, its strength in the state
assembly declined from 50 percent to 48.4 percent—sufficient to destroy
its majority. The debacle was much worse in Madras. There, Congress

polled over 41 percent of the vote, a decline of less than 5 percent over 1962 levels, but suffered a staggering loss of 46 percent in seats, gaining 50 compared to 139 in the previous election. By contrast, the DMK, which also polled approximately 41 percent of the vote, was able to win 138 seats, a clear majority in a House of 234, as head of an electoral alliance that included Swatantra, CPI(M), PSP, SSP, and the Muslim League.

Once again, however, it was the communist parties, this time in West Bengal, that demonstrated the greatest skill in using united front alliances to gain a larger proportion of seats from a relatively fixed base of popular support, to prevent Congress from converting a substantial plurality into a majority of assembly seats. Indeed, in 1952, 1957, and 1962, Congress pluralities of 40 percent, 46 percent, and 47 percent, respectively, had been sufficient to form stable governments. On the basis of past experience, the party's vote in 1967 of 41 percent should have led to the same result. But this time the opposition was concentrated in the CPI(M) United Left Front, and the CPI-led Peoples United Left Front. The outcome, as shown in Table 9-4, was that Congress suffered a 17 percent loss of seats relative to its 6 percent loss in votes, winning only 127 seats out of 280 in the legislative assembly, to fall substantially short of a majority. The two Communist parties, by contrast, which won virtually the same proportion of the vote in 1967 as had the undivided CPI in 1962, about 25 percent of the total, were able to improve slightly their combined strength from about 20 percent to 21 percent of seats, winning in 59 out of 280 contests. More important, by forming a coalition between the two fronts after the election, they gained control of 45 percent of assembly seats—126, or more then twice the number won by the two parties alone. Coopting the members of three nonelectoral front parties and one independent, the leftists succeeded in establishing the first non-Congress government in West Bengal and the second communist-dominated united front government in India since Independence. The victory, moreover, had wider implications. The CPI felt confirmed in the correctness of its general strategy for combining with Congress dissidents to rally mass support behind a progressive political alignment favorable to formation of a National Democratic Front. Indeed, Ajoy Mukherjee, the leader of the Congress dissidents and president of the Bangla Congress, was selected to form the new government as the only politican who could command support from communist and noncommunist groups.

Although the results of the 1967 elections revealed a dramatic erosion in the dominant position of the Congress party, the meaning of this decline for the ideological direction of Indian politics was less clear. The conservative parties, both absolutely and in terms of marginal rates of

TABLE 9-4

Congress Party Performance Relative to Opposition Parties Contesting
Individually in 1962 and as Part of the United Front in 1967
(West Bengal)

| | 1962 | | 1967 | |
| | Votes % | Seats % | Votes % | Seats % |
| Parties | | | | |
|---|---|---|---|---|
| Congress | 47.2 | 62.3 | 41.2 | 45.3 |
| United Left Front | | | | |
| CPI(M) | — | — | 18.1 | 15.4 |
| SSP | — | — | 2.1 | 2.5 |
| RSP | 2.5 | 3.5 | 2.1 | 2.1 |
| SUC | .73 | — | .72 | 1.4 |
| Workers party | .28 | — | .34 | .009 |
| Forward Bloc | | | | |
| (Marxist) | .32 | — | .41 | .003 |
| Total | 3.83 | 3.5 | 23.77 | 21.41 |
| Peoples United Left Front | | | | |
| Bangla Congress | — | — | 10.0 | 12.1 |
| CPI | 24.9 | 19.8 | 6.5 | 5.7 |
| Forward Bloc | 4.6 | 5.1 | 3.8 | 4.7 |
| Total | 29.5 | 24.9 | 20.3 | 22.5 |
| PSP | 4.99 | 1.9 | 1.88 | 2.5 |
| Lok Sevak Sangh | .72 | 1.0 | .68 | 1.8 |
| Gorkha League | .40 | .008 | .45 | .007 |
| Jan Sangh | .45 | — | 1.33 | .003 |
| Swatantra | .57 | — | .81 | .003 |
| Independents | 10.8 | 4.3 | 8.9 | 4.0 |

SOURCES: Victor M. Fic, *Kerala, Yenan of India*, pp. 408-410; Marcus F. Franda, *Radical Politics in West Bengal*, pp. 116-118.

growth, made the greatest gains.[28] The Jan Sangh was, nevertheless, still predominately centered in urban areas and in constituencies confined mainly to the Hindi-speaking region. Swatantra, although more success-ful in rural areas, generally drew on traditional rather than modern con-servative sentiment, by continuing to build its electoral following on the vertical networks controlled by former princes and zamindars. The communist parties, by contrast, while increasing their overall support only modestly over 1962 levels, had succeeded in building regional

[28] The marginal turnout that calculates the distribution of additional valid votes cast from one election to the next favored both the Jan Sangh and the Swatantra party in 1967, using the previous election in 1962 as a base of comparison. The ratio was highest for the Jan Sangh (3.27) followed by Swatantra (1.38). By contrast, the marginal growth rate for the Congress party was less than unity (.69). The Indian Institute of Public Opinion, *Monthly Public Opinion Surveys* (April, May, June 1967), p. 5.

strongholds that, when combined with shrewd manipulation of electoral alliances, carried communist-led United Front coalitions to power in two states. At the same time, in Madras, a regional party, the DMK, combined a militant anti-Hindi appeal with promises of subsidized rice for the cities and land redistribution in the countryside to build a political base among the urban poor and smaller farmers that effectively dislodged one of the best organized Congress party machines in India.

On the whole, most observers agreed with the assessment of the Indian Institute of Public Opinion that it was "almost impossible . . . to read the choice of an ideology in the electorate's choice except on the negative evidence that it is approving less and less of the Congress party."[29] The AICC's appraisal was similarly bemused. The official review found it pertinent to ask

> to what extent the manifestoes of the Congress and other parties influenced the thinking of the electorate. It is the view of many competent observers that the ideologies as such or the manifestoes did not play a considerable part. The question is more complex than the answer would suggest. The country is broadly familiar with Congress thinking and had by and large accepted its basic stand in regard to many vital issues. The anti-Congress vote did not exactly represent opposition to the Congress ideology. It is true that opposition parties, particularly the Jan Sangh, the Swatantra and the Communists stand for views and policies which are far from identical with the views and policies of the Congress in many vital matters. But a vote for the Jan Sangh was not necessarily a vote for the Jan Sangh ideology nor was the vote for the Swatantra necessarily a vote for the ideology of the Swatantra party. This was also true to a considerable extent of the Communist parties. There were certainly sections among voters for those opposition parties who supported the ideologies which these parties preached but there were those among their supporters who just wished to express their resentment against the Congress for the hardships they suffered and for other reasons.[30]

The analysts were, however, agreed on one point. The 1967 election was perceived as a watershed in Indian political development, an event that marked the "end of an era." Although Congress continued to be the single largest party in the nation, and to enjoy a firm majority at the Center, the demise of the one-party dominant political system was thereafter accepted as virtually inevitable. Faced with the prospect of increasingly efficient opposition alliances, and projections that Congress would have to regain at least 1962 vote levels to win a majority of seats in the next

[29] *Ibid.*, p. 7.
[30] Indian National Congress, *The Fourth General Elections, A Statistical Analysis*.

national election scheduled for 1972,[31] the outlook appeared bleak. Most experts, in fact, anticipated a continued decline. They predicted that Congress would never again be able to win a majority of Lok Sabha seats on its own, but could "only come to power again with a substantial alliance either with the Right or the Left." Indeed, they saw the "inevitability of coalition governments everywhere in the country."[32]

Yet the likelihood of stable coalitions in the states based on programmatic realignment of political parties toward the right and left was slim. The 1967 elections revealed a very uneven pattern of development. Princes in Madhya Pradesh, Rajasthan, Gujerat, and Bihar were voted into office, along with radical Marxists in Kerala and West Bengal. Hindu communalists roused enthusiastic support in the towns and cities of the Hindi heartland, while militant anti-Hindi parties captured power in the towns and villages of the south. The Congress, as the only national force in India, appeared beleaguered on all sides and destined to decline further in competition with regional parties clamoring for greater autonomy to the states. At the same time, with the exception of the Marxists in Kerala and West Bengal, and to a lesser degree, the DMK in Madras,[33] the regional parties continued to rely mainly on vertical patterns of political mobilization, building electoral support by combining the networks of followers and factional alliances commanded by local notables on the basis of caste and economic ties. Where class-based peasant mobilization did occur, moreover, it was rarely the natural outgrowth of an evolutionary change in which the poor peasantry generated their own leadership and electoral organization to challenge the vertical power structures managed by local elites. Rather it was the result, as Gandhi long ago had feared, of the "cleverness and maneuvering of non-labor leaders" committed to an agitational approach that openly questioned the value of the electoral system for purposes of socialist reform.

Assessing future prospects, fears of political instability and even national disintegration, quiescent since Independence, quickly revived. Misgivings were heightened in the aftermath of the election by a number

[31] This projection was based on two assumptions: the inability of the Congress party to win significantly greater numbers of seats than votes when the number of candidates declines to four or fewer; and the prospect that Congress would face two alliances, one of the right and one of the left. Indian Institute of Public Opinion, *Monthly Public Opinion Surveys* (April, May, June 1967), p. 10.

[32] *Ibid.*, p. 10.

[33] The original mainstay of DMK support was students who responded to the party's anti-Hindi platform as well as promises of generous educational scholarship programs. After the 1962 elections, however, the DMK, advocating lower ceilings on landownership, began to organize in the villages, recruiting directly from the smaller peasant farmers, the two and three-acre people belonging to the backward castes. By 1967, the party had developed a strong local cadre that succeeded in challenging upper-caste landlords aligned with the Congress party for control of village panchayat and cooperative institutions, providing the rural base for the party's drive to political victory in the state.

of ominous signs: the onset of chronic political instability at the state level, accompanied by disregard for parliamentary norms and the abuse of constitutional powers; a resurgence of linguistic and tribal nationalism; the outbreak of "class struggles" between landowners and laborers, and industrial managers and workers in states governed by communist-led united front coalitions; and sharp increase in the country as a whole of incidents of rural violence.

In several states, the disruption of democratic processes and procedures was virtually simultaneous with the results of the election. The Congress party won a clear majority in the legislative assemblies of only seven states—Andhra Pradesh, Assam, Gujerat, Haryana, Madhya Pradesh, Maharashtra, and Mysore. Congress did, however, still constitute the single largest party in five other states—Bihar, Punjab, Rajasthan, West Bengal, and Uttar Pradesh. In two of these states, Rajasthan and Uttar Pradesh, both Congress and opposition alliances claimed the support of a majority of legislators in the assembly, and requested the governor to give them the opportunity of forming a coalition government. The conflicting claims provoked unanswered questions about the discretion of state governors under Article 164 of the constitution in appointing the chief ministers of states when no party had secured an absolute majority in a general election. Leading jurists consulted on the question by the home minister failed to reach a consensus on specific guidelines that supported either the convention of inviting the leader of the largest single party or the leader of the opposition (or next largest party) in the legislature to form a government. The view therefore prevailed that "the Governor should make endeavors to appoint a person who has been found by him as a result of his soundings, to be most likely to command a stable majority in the Legislature."[34] Such wide discretionary powers conceded to state governors appointed by the president of India on advice of the central government, that is, the leadership of the ruling party, proved to carry considerable potentiality for abuse.

Both in Uttar Pradesh and Rajasthan, where the governor invited the leader of Congress as the single largest party to form a government, charges of political favoritism were immediately raised. They were less persuasive in the case of Uttar Pradesh. There, the opposition parties formed a United Legislator's party, Samuykta Vidhayak Dal or SVD, which claimed a strength of 215 members in a House of 423, and re-

---

[34] This was originally set down as the "third view" by the home minister, Y. B. Chavan, in soliciting opinion for constitutional experts about authoritative guidelines for governors in situations where no party enjoyed a clear majority in the assembly. A copy of Chavan's letter, dated May 17, 1967, is published in Subhash C. Kashyap, *The Politics of Power*, pp. 621-22.

quested an opportunity to form a non-Congress government. The governor, in inviting C. B. Gupta, the leader of the Congress legislature party, to form the government, justified his decision on grounds that both groups had claimed the support of the same independents, but only Congress was actually able to produce such legislators in person. In Rajasthan, however, the charges of favoritism were more difficult to refute. In that state, the governor, Dr. Sampurnanand (a former Congress chief minister of Uttar Pradesh) called on the Congress party leader Mohanlal Sukhadia to form the government, although the combined opposition organized in the Samuykta Vidhayak Dal claimed a majority with the support of independents. The governor's explanation of his decision, that he had followed "convention" in calling upon the leader of the largest single party, was weakened further by his revelation that he had "not counted" the independents in the SVD coalition on grounds that parties contest elections on the basis of their programs, but in the case of independents, "the people do not know their policies."[35] The decision triggered four days of street violence by partisans of the united front, during which 324 persons, including prominent members of the opposition, were arrested. Confrontations between stone-throwing mobs and the police finally ended in a firing that killed several persons and wounded at least 40 others. Order could be restored only by calling in army troops. The legislative assembly, suspended under a proclamation of President's Rule on March 13, was not recalled until six weeks later, when on April 26 the proclamation was revoked and a new government installed. By this time, Dr. Sampurnanand had been replaced as governor—tacitly conceding the opposition's charges of improper conduct—and the Congress was able to demonstrate a clear majority in the legislature, but only because the interregnum provided additional time to arrange defections to Congress of legislators elected as independents or on the Jan Sangh or Swatantra tickets.

The events in Rajasthan were, in fact, only the beginning of a disruptive phenomenon at the state level of political defections and counterdefections from Congress to the opposition and from opposition coalitions to the Congress. The defections created chronic uncertainty about party strength from one day to the next, and increasingly politicized the role of the state governors, who had to decide as "a result of their soundings" not only the person most likely to command a majority, but the point at which the prospect of obtaining a stable government became so doubtful as to justify a recommendation for imposition of President's Rule. A crisis of political stability erupted in Haryana only one week after the Congress ministry assumed office. The Congress government

[35] *Ibid.*, p. 138.

was defeated in the assembly when twelve dissidents left the party to form the Haryana Congress, and joined with independents and other opposition parties in constructing a united front that was invited to form a new government. In Uttar Pradesh, the Congress ministry lasted three weeks. On April 17, eighteen Congressmen defected to form a new group, the Jan Congress, and joined hands with opposition parties to create a United Legislator's party, Samuykta Vidhayak Dal, or SVD, which led a new coalition government. In Madhya Pradesh, a major defection from Congress to the opposition occurred on July 29, 1967, when thirty-six MLAs crossed the floor to establish an SVD government. By the summer of 1967, eight of India's seventeen states and the majority of the population were governed by coalitions, either communist-led united front regimes or SVD ministries.

Whereas the two united front governments in Kerala and West Bengal had an initial advantage of a dominant ideological perspective, the SVD coalitions were formed solely as anti-Congress combinations. They variously included defectors from the Congress party, MLAs elected on the tickets of such divergent parties as Jan Sangh, Swatantra, SSP, PSP, and the two communist parties, as well as regionally based caste and communal splinter groups that represented no more than the political extension of the personal followings of former princes and ex-zamindars. Causes for disagreement among such unmatched partners were myriad. They ranged the entire ideological spectrum of contention over controversial policy issues, including such questions as abolition of land revenue, compulsory procurement of foodgrains, release of persons detained under preventive detention acts, and the status of Urdu as an official language in the north Indian states. The most chronic dissatisfaction occurred, however, over the distribution of portfolios among constituent parties and individual leaders of the legislators' alliances. In most cases, the SVD coalition governed only by the slimmest majority. It therefore became possible for dissident factions to promote their own power by the practice of defection either to join the Congress or to form a new party of their own, in order to hold the balance between the two groups and bargain for ministerial positions as the price of support. The result was the development of a "fairly typical pattern of cabinet crisis":

> After the formation of each government, it became known that a prominent individual belonging to a faction in the Congress or in a non-Congress party was disaffected with the government because he was not satisfied with his place in the government or was not given a position in it. The disaffected leader then began to gather supporters, while criticizing the government in general terms for "corruption" or for failure to implement portions of the program

rapidly enough. Finally a prominent public event occurred or an issue was found which provided the leader with an immediate cause for defection with his loyal supporters.

The defecting leader was then given the opportunity to form a government, which . . . was either a non–Congress coalition or a minority government with Congress support. In either event, the defecting leader became the new Chief Minister, most of those who defected with him received ministerial office and a new crisis began. In the interim between the two governments the opposing forces in the legislature continually bargained for the support of independents and potential party defectors. The game came to an end . . . when the governors became convinced that no stable coalitions were possible and that the Assembly should be dissolved and new elections should be called.[36]

All parties, in their frenzied competition to win this "game," resorted to flagrant violation of parliamentary and constitutional norms. SVD leaders wooed Congress dissidents with promises of ministerial posts for themselves and their followers in expanded coalition governments that far exceeded the size justified by administrative considerations, and amounted to an abuse of constitutional authority for purposes of partisan advantage. Leaders of the Congress party similarly encouraged defections from SVD coalitions with promises of assembly support short of a formal alliance, which led to the installation of minority governments composed entirely of defectors. Both sides, moreover, raised charges against the other of using less subtle means to induce MLAs to cross the floor, including bribery and intimidation, extending to kidnappings, beatings, and methods of "gangsterism and terrorization." In several states, as a result of all these techniques, there were almost daily defections in both directions. According to calculations by the home ministry, during the first twelve months after the election, there were 438 defections in the various state assemblies, and in some states the same individuals crossed back and forth several times.[37] The politics of defection gained momentum in succeeding years. Overall, between March 1967 and March 1970, defections in the states reached the astounding figure of 1,827, compared to the total number of seats in all the assemblies of 3,487.[38]

The two-way traffic produced constant claims and counterclaims by Congress and non–Congress coalitions that each enjoyed majority support in the assembly. Altogether, in the years between 1967 and 1970

[36] Paul R. Brass, "Coalition Politics in North India," *American Political Science Review*, 62:4 (December 1968), 1182.
[37] *New York Times*, May 17, 1968.          [38] Kashyap, *The Politics of Power*, p. 37.

twenty-three governments were constituted and then collapsed in the seven states of Bihar, Haryana, Kerala, Madhya Pradesh, Punjab, Uttar Pradesh, and West Bengal.[39] Politicians in pursuit of these transitory gains were not restrained by parliamentary norms of behavior. Motions of no confidence by the opposition against the government frequently occurred amid scenes of "unprecedented pandemonium and hurling of unprintable abuses" by one side against the other, with the dissatisfied sections engaging in such "unruly scenes" that the assembly found it impossible to function.[40] There were also more serious improprieties— those involving questionable interpretations of constitutional powers by the speaker of the assembly and/or the governor in rulings that had the effect of advancing the prospects of one side or the other in the continuous struggle for power. In the Punjab, in March 1968, after a defection from the united front paved the way for the formation of a Congress-backed minority government composed almost entirely of defectors organized in the Punjab Janta party, a motion of no confidence against the speaker (who had been elected to his post during the united front regime) introduced by the Congress-Janta party alliance was ruled unconstitutional by the speaker. When this ruling provoked "unruly scenes," the speaker, on March 7, declared the House adjourned for two months. The controversial decision, which came before the annual budget could be passed, created a constitutional crisis. The governor, urged by the united front to recommend dissolution of the assembly and imposition of President's Rule, and by Congress to prorogue and resummon the assembly (thereby preserving the Congress-backed government in power) followed the second course. The action not only provoked a challenge in the courts, but set the stage for worse violations of parliamentary procedure. As soon as the assembly reconvened, the speaker, ruling the action of the governor in proroguing and resummoning the assembly "illegal and void," once again adjourned the House. The session could then be held only with the deputy speaker in the chair. This questionable expedient produced such outrage among partisans of the united front that "several men jumped onto the Speaker's rostrum and grappled with the opposition members there. A hand to hand fight followed and continued for quarter of an hour when the rostrum was cleared. . . . Amidst deafening noise and thumping of tables and shouting of slogans, all the financial business before the House—passing of the supplementary estimates for the current year and the budget for 1968/69 and related appropriations bills—was reported and completed under the Presidentship of the Deputy Speaker."[41] This was accomplished, however, only after the chief minister had ordered the police to occupy the assembly.

[39] Ibid., pp. 11-12.                         [40] Ibid., pp. 323-24.
[41] Ibid., p. 413.

Similar events occurred in West Bengal. The united front's majority in that state was called into question in November 1967, after the food minister, Dr. P. C. Ghosh, resigned and along with seventeen other defecting MLAs formed the Progressive Democratic Front with the backing of the Congress party. The refusal of the chief minister, Ajoy Mukherjee, to heed the governor's advice in calling an unscheduled "early" session of the assembly in order to test the government's strength, provoked a proclamation by the governor dismissing the united front ministry. Amid charges by the united front that the governor had exceeded his powers, and, in fact, "murdered" democracy in the state, a new minority government headed by Dr. Ghosh was sworn in—but only after precautionary security measures were taken, including ordinances forbidding public assemblies in Calcutta and the surrounding areas, and a military alert. When, however, the assembly met on November 29, the speaker, in an "unprecedented ruling" adjourned the House sine die, arguing that the governor's dissolution of the united front government in the absence of a vote of no confidence by the assembly, the appointment of the Ghosh ministry, and the summoning of the assembly on the advice of that ministry were unconstitutional and invalid. The governor, despite demands from the united front for dissolution of the assembly and new elections, decided instead to prorogue the assembly, thereby encouraging the two sides to settle their dispute in the streets. By the time the Ghosh ministry was finally installed on December 23, some 4,800 people had been arrested, while daily confrontations between the police and demonstrators in Calcutta reduced to routine events spectacles of mob protest, police tear-gassing, lathi-charges, and firings. Even then, when the governor resummoned the assembly on February 14, the speaker once more adjourned the session on grounds that it had been illegally convened. Meanwhile, arrests during the three months of the Ghosh ministry had mounted to a total of 30,000.[42]

In the neighboring state of Bihar, a less dramatic but more flagrant instance of abuse of the governor's power in favor of the Congress party revealed the extent to which constitutional norms were being undermined. In that state, the chosen instrument of Congress attempts to topple the SVD ministry was B. P. Mandal, an ex-Congressman expelled from the party in 1965 for indiscipline, who subsequently joined the SSP and in 1967 was elected to the Lok Sabha. Mandal, who had preferred to join the state ministry rather than take his Lok Sabha seat, and was not a member of the legislative assembly, ignored orders from the Central Paliamentary Board of the SSP directing him to resign from the Bihar Cabinet and take his seat at the Center—even though he was nearing the

---

[42] Ibid., pp. 542-51.

six-month limit prescribed by the constitution as the period during which an individual may remain a minister without becoming a member of the legislature. Ten days before the six months was to expire, on August 26, 1967, Mandal resigned from the Bihar Cabinet—and the SSP—to form a new party, the Shoshit Dal (Party of the Exploited), with the backing of the Congress party. The combined Shoshit Dal-Congress alliance succeeded in defeating the SVD government on a motion of no confidence on January 19. Subsequently, the leader of the Congress party advised the governor that his party pledged support to a minority Shoshit Dal ministry, and suggested that B. P. Mandal be invited to form a new government. The fact that Mandal was not a member of the legislature and therefore ineligible to become chief minister was solved expeditiously, if cynically. Mandal's nominee, S. P. Singh, was sworn in as chief minister on January 28. On January 29, the governor, on the advice of Singh, nominated Mandal to the Bihar Legislative Council, the upper house of the assembly. Chief Minister Singh thereupon submitted his resignation, and on January 31, Mandal was invited to form a new government.

The cost of these and similar maneuvers to the legitimacy of the democratic process—in growing public contempt for politicians of all parties, increasing popular disorders, more frequent recourse by state governments to political arrests under preventive detention acts, police teargassings, lathi-charges, and firings, and rule by executive ordinances as legislatures were rendered incapable of functioning and/or were prorogued—was of course very high. Yet, in the end, the gains to the legislators responsible for this descent into almost unlimited opportunism were quite transient. The continuing large-scale and frequent defections by MLAs on both sides, with some legislators defecting three and four times, finally convinced the governors in several states and the government in New Delhi that no stable ministry could be formed without holding fresh elections. President's Rule was imposed first on Haryana on November 21, 1967. This was followed by the imposition of President's Rule and dissolution of the legislative assembly in four other states: in West Bengal on February 20, 1968; Uttar Pradesh, on February 25, 1968; Bihar, on June 29, 1968; and Punjab on August 23, 1968.

The full toll of the politics of defection on the prospects of democratic development is impossible to estimate, but it went beyond the weakening of constitutional norms. Constant preoccupation with political survival reduced further the capacities of shaky state governments to formulate policies and implement programs for accomplishing national goals. The "minimum programs" accepted by SVD alliances were limited to generalities that provoked the least controversy among their ill-assorted partners, while attempting to invoke the maximum popular support.

They offered, on the one hand, promises of benefit to all groups and classes from "clean and efficient" administration, elimination of corruption, intensified efforts of agricultural and industrial development, and general improvement in conditions of the poor. They attempted, on the other, to solidify the coalition's position by cementing the loyalties of strategic interests and groups, variously promising to abolish land revenue and urban land taxes, to grant free irrigation facilities, to increase the wages and allowances of government employees, to provide scholarships for poor students, to bring down food prices through government subsidies and/or rationing of foodgrains, all of which drained further the financial capacity of the state governments to carry out development programs. As a substitution for the rewards (and costs) of economic growth, they increasingly relied on providing less tangible but more easily achieved symbolic satisfactions of collective regional grievances and aspirations. Indeed, as central power eroded, regional sentiments found more militant expression.

Plans to establish Hindi as the national "link" language were delayed indefinitely after the new DMK government in Tamil Nadu (renamed from Madras after the 1967 election) lent tacit support to large-scale student rioting against Hindi. The Official Languages (Amendment) Bill adopted by the Lok Sabha in December 1967 provided for the continued use of English in official communications between the Union and non-Hindi states, and non-Hindi and Hindi states, as well as for its use in parliament. Confronted with DMK charges, moreover, that non-Hindi speakers would still be at a disadvantage in having to learn either English or Hindi in addition to their mother tongue in order to compete in the Union Public Services Commission examinations, the home ministry, starting in 1968, began preparations for a progressive transition to the regional language in most subjects. The national "consensus" on the language problem ultimately hammered out by the Union Cabinet envisaged a three-language formula for recruitment to the central services, with all candidates expected to know English, Hindi, and one regional language other than Hindi. Similarly, the national education policy, approved in July 1968, endorsed the three-language formula, with students required to study their own mother tongue as a regional language, Hindi (or when this was the mother tongue a second modern Indian language, preferably South Indian), and English, with gradual transition to the regional language as the medium of university instruction.

There were signs of interregional tension. The appearance of DMK-led Tamil Senas (Tamil armies) in several districts of Tamil Nadu— although organized to counter intensive anti-DMK political propaganda by Congress youth organizations—also assigned considerable importance to the role of protecting the interests of Tamils against non-Tamils in the state. At the same time, in Gauhati (Assam), riots against "outsiders," particularly Marwari industrialists and traders with family origins in Rajasthan, resulted in large-scale destruction and looting of property. The conflict underlined the growing antagonism of the poor and unemployed toward prosperous owners of factories and well-paid managers and technicians, especially when the two groups were also separated by traditional ethnic and caste boundaries. A particularly virulent expression of this phenomenon erupted in Maharashtra, where the Marathi working classes, organized in the Shiv Sena (Army of Shivaji) took to the streets in violent demonstrations against employment of South Indians and non-Marathis in Bombay.

Such antagonisms, compounded of economic discontent and cultural nationalism, provided the possibility of mass political organization around natural social building blocks of region, caste, and tribe. The communist parties, which already enjoyed control over strategic levers of government power in two states, gained the greatest advantages from the new opportunities for mass mobilization at the grass-roots level. In Kerala and West Bengal, they set out to create a new form of political awareness among the poorest caste, communal, and tribal groups based on recognition of common class interests, which was then used to build up peasants' and workers' associations for direct confrontation with landowning upper and middle castes and business and trading communities.

The CPI(M), which dominated the united front government of Kerala in 1967, immediately set out to expand its organizational capacity for mounting extraparliamentary mass campaigns aimed at mobilizing popular pressure for radical social reforms. The situation was particularly favorable. The Marxists had inherited the major part of the undivided CPI's organization in the state among tenants and laborers of the low-caste Ezhavas and the Harijans. The Kerala land reforms act, approved in 1963, had, in addition, sharply eroded ties between landlords and tenants. The new legislation converted the customary rights of hereditary tenure enjoyed by the majority of tenants[43] into legal occupancy rights. Many landlords who had met their obligations under the traditional system, accepting customary rates of rent even as land values appreciated, and advancing other facilities to tenants in time of need, felt themselves betrayed by the apparent preference of longtime clients for impersonal

[43] In Kerala, unlike the rest of India, the majority of tenants not only had enjoyed hereditary rights by the "custom of the locality"—with informal relationships sometimes extending over two and three generations—but many cultivators also had proof of possession. For a brief description of the land tenure system in Kerala prior to the land reforms, see Frankel, *India's Green Revolution*, pp. 127-28.

legal assurances and guarantees. Some reacted by withdrawing all customary facilities from tenants, including advances for production costs,
and other loans in time of emergency, illness, or marriage. The embittered tenants, in their turn, responded by refusing to recognize any right
of the landlord beyond that of collecting rent. They ignored the landowners' advice about proper cultivation practices. Some even went to
the extent of prohibiting the landlord from visiting his fields.

The social tension was heightened by the introduction of the omnibus
Kerala Land Reforms (Amendment) Bill in 1968. The new legislation
lowered the upper limit on landownership from 25 to 20 acres per family;
vested ownership to house sites in tenants; and provided that on a date to
be designated by the government all intermediary rights in land, including those enjoyed by Hindu temples and landlords, would vest in the
government, subject to compensation at sixteen times the fair rent. Subsequently, rights of ownership were to be assigned to occupancy tenants;
and rents payable to the landlord would be collected by the state and adjusted toward the purchase of land.

Simultaneously, the united front government enacted measures to
strengthen its appeal among Harijan, low caste, and Muslim farm laborers. The Agricultural Minimum Wages Act of 1969 lent statutory authority to the workers' demands for higher minimum cash wages for day
labor and payments in kind received for harvesting. Landlords once
again responded with plans to stop traditional bonus payments of paddy
and other articles in kind at the time of festivals and religious occasions,
and withdraw other facilities such as loans and advances, adding further
to rural tensions.

In Kerala, the CPI(M)'s capacity for peasant organization around implementation of land reform laws was enhanced by its growing ability to
protect those who joined Marxist-sponsored peasants' associations or
laborers' unions from retaliation. The party, which already had a statewide network of district and taluka branches, set out to establish village cells wherever possible. The village units were headed by younger
agricultural workers, many of whom found they could use their new
prestige as political cadres of a powerful party in the state government to
assert their personal independence of the landowner. In addition, the
Marxists, who controlled the portfolios of both land and home (including the police), ensured that local authorities would not intervene to protect landowners from strikes or other harassment by tenants and laborers
engaged in "legitimate and democratic" class struggles. Village-level
"popular committees" led by members of united front parties, and usually dominated by local Marxists, increasingly acted outside the law, ostensibly helping the administration's food procurement drive by stopping at will persons carrying or transporting rice, and distributing it to

the public on the spot at "fair prices." Plans of the Kerala government to vest the "popular committees" with statutory powers to seize "hoarded" grain were inhibited only by the refusal of the central government under its powers of ratification on a Concurrent Subject (of local government) to advise presidential assent. Even so, the police did not intervene to prevent unlawful raids on private homes, or to stop large-scale encroachments on government land and uncultivated lots of absentee landlords. Indeed, the Marxists made plans to neutralize the police by creation of local volunteer forces of their own at the district and village level to act as the militant arm of the popular committees.

Industrial disputes, although less virulent, were similarly handled. The police were instructed not to intervene in labor-management conflicts on behalf of employers, even when they were the victims of *gheraos* by their employees. The tactic, which involved surrounding senior management personnel to prevent their access to food, water, other amenities, or outside communication by telephone for periods ranging from a few hours to a few days, that is, until concessions were granted, became the normal method of settling disputes in the state, not only in industrial relations but in government administration. Indeed, by the time the united front government collapsed from internal defections in October 1969, patterns of deference rooted in ritual and/or status hierarchies were breaking down in all areas of life. Relations between landlords and tenants, landowners and laborers, factory management and workers, senior administrative officers and junior personnel, were transformed into adversary conflicts based on new notions of class division.

In West Bengal, a similar process was set in motion. The united front ministry at the outset adopted the policy of "recognizing the rights of workers and peasants to voice their just demands and grievances," and pledged "not to suppress the democratic and legitimate struggles of the people."[44] The disruption arising from this policy was initially felt mainly in the cities, where the undivided CPI had concentrated most of its organizational efforts on the trade union front. One of the first initiatives taken by the labor minister after the election was to announce a "break with the past" in legalizing *gheraos* as a legitimate tactic in labor-management disputes. As the Marxists and other parties of the united front joined in intense competition to unionize workers and increase their political influence at the expense of the CPI, *gheraos* became an everyday occurrence. Altogether, during the six months between March and August 1967, 583 establishments were subjected to 1,018 *gheraos*, while the police, instructed not to intervene, stood aside.[45] In

[44] *The Statesman*, March 7, 1967.

[45] Nitish R. De and Suresh Srivastava, "Gheraos in West Bengal," *Economic and Political Weekly* (Bombay), November 18, 1967, p. 2015.

West Bengal, as in other parts of the country, the labor-management disputes were all the more bitter for the feeling of the workers that business, especially in Calcutta, was dominated by "outsiders"—Marwaris, other non-Bengali Indians, and British industrialists.

At the same time, the Marxists who held the Land and Land Revenue portfolio made plans to emulate the Kerala pattern in the rural areas. The land revenue minister announced in 1967 that the policy of the state government would be to recover land held illegally in violation of ceiling laws, and that the police in rural areas would not suppress the "democratic and legitimate struggle of the people" to identify and transfer such lands. The Marxists then began the process of organizing the low-caste, Harijan, and Muslim peasantry against the predominately upper-caste, landlord, and *jotedar* (large farmer) classes. Although the peasants were initially skeptical that the left parties of the united front could protect them if they gave evidence against the landlords, some gained courage from the growing strength of the Krishak Sabhas (peasants' associations) organized in the villages by the Marxists, and the special camp courts backed up by additional police contingents set up to decide cases on the spot and enforce the magistrate's ruling. Within a few months, moreover, the united front government announced further measures that suggested a serious intention to act against the *jotedars*. They proclaimed the abolition of the private wholesale trade in rice and paddy in the state, and made preparations to procure paddy by levy on large farmers and rice mills at fixed prices. In those districts where the Krishak Sabhas were well established, these moves began to embolden sharecroppers in other efforts to enforce the law, especially provisions that the crop be divided between the sharecropper and the landlord in the ratio of 60 : 40 percent rather than the customary 50 percent still exacted. On the eve of the harvest, fear was widespread that sharecroppers would withhold the crop, and that clashes with *jotedars* would trigger large-scale rural violence. At the last moment, however, in November 1967, the united front government, suffering defections, lost its tenuous one-vote majority and was replaced by a noncommunist minority government enjoying Congress support. The levy orders on *jotedars* and rice mills were subsequently sharply reduced. Police protection for the sharecroppers in confrontation with local landlords was withdrawn. Yet, support for the Marxists in rural areas continued to rise as tenant-cultivators and landless laborers became convinced that a future communist government would redistribute land on a large scale.

The fact was that despite the fate of any particular united front government, objective conditions were emerging—extending to areas outside the regional strongholds of the communist parties—that favored extraparliamentary tactics of peasant mobilization. In one year, 1967/68, reported cases of agrarian conflict more than doubled. The overwhelming majority of the agitations, over eighty percent, were led by the landless against landowners over demands for increased agricultural wages, security of tenure, larger crop shares, and most important, redistribution of land. The causes of the growing agrarian tension were complex. According to the home ministry, "predisposing factors" were failure of land reforms to provide tenants with security of tenure or fair rents, or to correct inequalities of landownership through redistribution of land. "Proximate" causes, the factors that actually converted latent discontent into open conflict, were located in the new agricultural strategy and the green revolution.[46]

The proliferation of scattered enclaves of modern agriculture, coexisting alongside much larger subsistence sectors, upset customary patron-client ties in a number of small pockets across the rural hinterland. Except for the heartland of the wheat belt, where the average size of farm holding was large enough to extend opportunities for modern farming to a large number of cultivators, the ability of the land-poor and the landless to share in the gains of the new technology was very limited. Larger farmers, by contrast, were increasingly alert to opportunities for pyramiding their gains by investing the profits from the high-yielding varieties to buy more land, improve land under cultivation, or to mechanize farm operations and double or triple-crop part of their holdings. As a result, they quickly adjusted their attitudes toward agricultural production from a subsistence way of life to a profitable set of business activities. Landowners began to make rough calculations of opportunity costs in determining whether or not to lease out part of their land or cultivate directly, rather than be guided by traditional sentiments of personal obligation to customary tenants. They did not hesitate to raise rentals in line with appreciating land values and/or evict tenants having longstanding cultivating possession of the land. These changes were superimposed on the strains already created by the land reform laws, which while abortive in most states, caused landowners to view tenants as potential adversaries. The tenants, shifted from plot to plot, and cultivating always in fear of losing some part of their holding to another tenant or to the landlord, for their part sloughed off traditional feelings of deference and obligation toward the landlord.

The same tendency toward erosion of traditional attitudes of mutual dependence and obligation emerged in relations between landowners and laborers. Although more intensive cropping and diversification of the cropping pattern tended to create more employment opportunities for farm workers, and in most cases the level of cash wages also increased,

---

[46] For a summary of the contents of the home ministry's report, see P. C. Joshi, "A Review Article," in *Seminar* (New Delhi, May 1970).

rising prices generally left laborers with little improvement in real income. In some cases, they actually experienced deterioration over previous years. Their main hope, in fact, of sharing equally in the benefits of
the new technology was to maintain the traditional system of proportional payments in kind for major agricultural operations. But the landowners, calculating that their own economic interests lay in converting
all kind payments to cash, denounced the traditional system as exploitative and moved to introduce a cash wage for all kinds of farm work.
Where mechanization was feasible, large farmers were anxious to buy
machinery as quickly as possible, partly to reduce their dependence on
agricultural laborers. As customary patron-client relationships were replaced by bargaining arrangements in the recruitment of farm labor, old
ideas of reciprocal obligation between the landed upper and landless
lower castes were replaced by new notions of opposing economic interest. The emerging social tension was transformed into open class conflict
in several pockets of rural India. By the late 1960s, both communist parties saw sufficient scope to launch a nationwide "agrarian struggle"
around "land-grab" agitations that were carried out in several states, including Punjab, Uttar Pradesh, Rajasthan, Andhra Pradesh, Tamil
Nadu, and Kerala.

The potentially explosive implications for political order in the rural
areas of the convergence of all these factors—rapid and uneven agrarian
modernization, the erosion of traditional patron-client ties, growing economic disparities, and class-based peasant organization—burst on the
public mind through the violent events set in motion during a bitter
wage dispute in Tanjore district of Tamil Nadu. Shortly after the 1967
elections, Marxists who had entered the DMK ministry as junior partners of the winning electoral alliance, and who counted on police neutrality,
started to organize Harijan farm workers into unions in order to demand
higher wages. Large parties of Marxist-led farm workers entered the
paddy fields of recalcitrant landowners to prevent farm operations from
being carried out by imported laborers or nonunionized local laborers
who remained loyal to the landowners. Although the landowners conceded modest gains to the striking workers, the 1967 agitations proved to
be only the first round of a prolonged and increasingly violent confrontation.

Actually, from the beginning, the labor agitations involved more fundamental issues than the limited demand for higher wages. Farm laborers
participating in *gheraos* shouted the standard Marxist slogans of "the land
belongs to labor," "landownership should go," "let the landlord be put
out." After the police failed to offer adequate protection to victims of
*gheraos* in 1967, moreover, the landlords banded together to organize
their own security forces, drawn mainly from non-Harijan farm work-

ers. Subsequently, the confrontation was transformed into open "class struggle" in which attempts made to dissuade Harijan farm workers from joining Marxist-led unions relied on strong-arm methods, such as abductions, beatings, and arson. By 1968, the ruling DMK, which enjoyed an absolute majority in the state assembly, and did not need Marxist support in order to govern, became increasingly alarmed. As a result, the police were no longer restrained from taking action against trespassing farm workers. The Marxists, in turn, citing police failures to protect the laborers from "attacks by goondas of the landlords" raised their own volunteer force. By December, numerous beatings, abductions, incidents of arson, and even murder were reported on both sides. Finally, on the night of December 25, accumulating hostilities exploded. In the village of Kilvenmani, 25 huts of Harijan farm workers were set afire; inside one hut, 43 persons, mainly the wives and children of striking laborers, were burned alive. Among the 200 attackers reportedly involved were some of the richest Brahmin landowners in the district.[47] In Tanjore, the traditional self-enforcing mechanisms of social control based on the mutual acceptance of ascriptive inequalities in the rights and duties sanctified by caste had collapsed. Subsequently, abductions, arson, and beatings became a common feature of rural life. Relations between landowners and laborers settled into a permanent adversary pattern. The hostility between the two groups found organizational expression in the rival private armies or volunteer forces commanded by both sides. In Tanjore, as in other parts of India, the increasing class enmity largely coincided with the traditional cleavages rooted in caste. The landless farm worker was most commonly a Harijan; the landlord he confronted, a Brahmin.

The tactic of organizing the poor peasantry around traditional tribal and caste cleavages was also used by small groups of revolutionaries committed to Maoist methods of armed agrarian uprising and guerrilla war. In Andhra Pradesh, communist revolutionaries, continuing in the tradition of the Telengana revolt, had been experimenting with tribal or-

---

[47] The immediate circumstances leading to the attack on the Harijans of Kilvenmani are uncertain. According to one version, laborers imported from nearby villages for harvest operations were returning from work on the evening of December 25 when they were waylaid and attacked by local laborers. Their leader was taken to Kilvenmani and stabbed to death. Two hours later, the landlords led loyal workers in a retaliatory raid, and set fire to the huts in the Harijan quarter. *The Statesman*, December 27, 1968. According to a second account, fighting broke out between Harijan laborers of Kilvenmani and laborers loyal to the landowners after the latter had abducted a Harijan leader in order to coerce striking laborers to abandon their agitation. On December 25, the Harijans attacked the landlords' camp and succeeded in forcing the release of their leader. In the fighting, however, a loyal laborer was killed and his body taken to Kilvenmani. That evening the landlords retaliated. Leading a large band of workers, they entered Kilvenmani, fired a few shots, and then put torches to the huts of the Harijans. *New York Times*, January 15, 1969.

ganizations that sought to harness resentment against exploitation by landlords from the plains for purposes of militant agrarian struggle. Operating in the Girijan tribal reserve in the district of Srikakulum since 1959, local communist leaders, some of whom lived with the tribals in the mountainous and forested regions of the Andhra-Orissa border, established the Girijan Sangham and began a large-scale organizational effort.

The Girijans, numbering about 80,000, had long been victimized by plainsmen who moved into the reserve as merchants, moneylenders, and contractors, and then, as the tribals sank ever deeper into debt, "purchased" their holdings for small sums. The new landlords subsequently employed Girijans as farm laborers at such low wages that they lived in conditions bordering those of serfdom. The communists, concentrating on the political education of a Girijan cadre, combined agitation for agrarian reform under a "new democratic revolution" with promises of a Girijan "autonomous region." The movement gained momentum gradually. Tribals were pressed to attend organized meetings, exposed to sustained Marxist propaganda, and initiated in the tactics of processions and demonstrations outside the homes of landlords, which finally succeeded in winning significant wage increases. Subsequently, the Girijan movement progressed to a "higher stage," with the tribals actually seizing crops and occupying about 2,000 acres from the landlords. The landlords responded by organizing their own security force to resist further demands for the restoration of land. As both sides armed—the Girijans mainly with country-made guns, bows, arrows, and axes—the confrontation escalated into violent struggle. By early 1968, the state government had lost effective control of scores of isolated mountain villages to the local Marxist leadership. The Girijan Sanghams started to function as soviets, leading the tribals in seizing grain and money, redistributing government land, and establishing their own administrative machinery for the "liberated area." Daily raids by armed police operating from special camps in the plains resulted in the arrest of several hundred Girijans and the seizure of scores of country-made weapons, although without capturing the leadership, who turned to terrorist tactics aimed at killing individual landlords. The Central Reserve Police, which was sent into Srikakulum in 1969 after the government declared it a "disturbed area," was more effective, arresting or killing key leaders and slowing down the momentum of the movement.[48]

A more alarming outbreak of peasant violence, one that potentially threatened the national integrity of India, occurred in the nothern portion

[48] See V. M. Nair, "Girjan Revolt—I, II," *Statesman*, April 11 and 12, 1968. Also V. M. Nair, "Time to Wean the Girijans from the Naxalites—I, II," *Statesman*, December 10 and 11, 1969. The movement in Srikakulam is described in greater detail in Mohan Ram, *Maoism in India* (New York, 1971), pp. 89-136.

of West Bengal in the Naxalbari subdivision of Darjeeling district. The area, a narrow border region between Nepal and East Pakistan, formed the only territorial corridor between the northeastern states and the plains below. It also had a predominately tribal population in addition to large numbers of Harijans, most of whom were landless. The agrarian economy was dominated by large tea plantations, often owned by foreigners and exempt from state ceiling legislation, even though at any given time extensive sections of the total lands were held fallow or leased out on crop-share for the cultivation of paddy. Clashes between the tea plantation managements and local *jotedars* on the one side, and share-croppers and landless laborers on the other were frequent. Landless peasants attempted to lay claim to the uncultivated area, and in some cases held back the landlord's share of the crop. Landlords, for their part, engaged in forcible eviction of tenants.

The Naxalbari area, as the scene of sustained peasant agitation since 1959, was one of the few regions in India to generate an indigenous leadership from among the members of the tribal, low-caste, and Muslim peasant communities. The organizers, embracing communist ideology, concentrated on building up strong peasant associations that brought them a position of popular support and trust. Eventually, they became valuable allies of the Marxists in the state. Indeed, in 1967, the communists in Naxalbari were absorbed into the CPI(M)'s Darjeeling and Siliguri district committees and the local Krishak Samiti. Yet, when the Marxists decided to enter the united front government, they withdrew support from a previously planned peasant agitation in Naxalbari, rather than risk their strategic position in the ministry either through a confrontation with coalition partners that could topple the government or provide provocation to the Center for imposition of President's Rule. The Krishak Samiti nevertheless decided to pursue the agitation on its own. By March 1967, they began to organize tribal bands for "direct action" against landlords. Initially, the demonstrations were peaceful. The homes of individual landowners charged with evicting tenants or hoarding foodgrains or cultivating land in excess of ceiling limits were selected as targets for demonstrations. Occasionally, there were instances of forcible possession of the uncultivated lands of the tea estates. Then, on May 23, a policeman was killed in a clash with the tribals. Subsequently, the agitation took on all the characteristics of armed struggle. Between June and August 1967, the Samiti waged open war on local landlords, seizing guns from people in the area, arming small bands of tribals with bows, arrows, and other homemade weapons, and engaging in the murder of landlords, arson, and the seizure of foodgrains.

This time, the police were not restrained. Ajoy Mukherjee, then chief minister, also held the portfolio of Home Affairs. Echoing the urgent concerns of the Center about the threat to national security of an unchecked "pro-Chinese" agrarian uprising in a strategic border area, he responded with strong counterforce. The Marxists, although protesting the "conspiracy" between the central government and the West Bengal government to quash a popular movement, did not resign. Rather, they acquiesced in government orders sealing the borders with East Bengal and Nepal to isolate the rebels, banning the use of bows, arrows, and spears in the region, and conferring full powers on the local administration to open fire in order to put down the agitation. Ultimately more than 1,500 police were dispatched to help local law and order forces in rounding up the rebels. Between August and September 1967, police arrested about 1,300 men, including most of the top leadership of the movement—although Kanu Sanyal, the foremost revolutionary hero of the rebellion—managed to escape. The survivors, however, had to go underground, and the movement was effectively suppressed within a few weeks.[49]

The Naxalbari revolt had a radicalizing effect on large numbers of young students and urban intellectuals. Many had supported the CPI(M) as a revolutionary force only to see it apparently succumb, as the CPI before it, to the blandishments of the electoral system in the rewards of office. As the party leadership dissociated itself from the Naxalites, dissolving the Darjeeling and Siliguri units, expelling nineteen members from the party, and acquiescing in the state government's decision to use the police against the rebels, dissident left factions of the CPI(M) formed an ad hoc All-India Coordination Committee of Communist Revolutionaries (AICCCR) to pressure the party into denouncing parliamentary tactics in favor of class struggle. The radicals, buoyed by attacks on the CPI(M) leadership in the Peking press, charging the Marxists with revisionist tendencies in suppressing the agrarian revolutionary struggle, were by September 1967 prepared to leave the party rather than continue to endorse an electoral strategy. Defections occurred in several states. Revolutionary communists, collectively identified as Naxalites, left the CPI(M) in large numbers in Andhra Pradesh and West Bengal. Naxalite factions also emerged in Kerala, Uttar Pradesh, Punjab, and Tamil Nadu.[50] By May 1969, the number of Naxalite activists in the states was estimated at between 15,000 and 20,000, with approximately one half of their ranks drawn from CPI(M) defectors.[51] Sporadic terrorism by Naxalites, including raids on the homes of landlords, murder and arson, and more spectacular attacks on police stations, occurred in widely separate parts of the country. Naxalite groups were reported to be gaining

[49] For an extended analysis of the Naxalbari movement, see Franda, *Radical Politics in West Bengal*, pp. 149-62; also Moham Ram, *Maoism in India*, pp. 38-71.

[50] The origin of the split of the CPI(M) is described in detail in Fic, *Kerala, Yenan of India*, pp. 421-43.

[51] "Naxalites," *The Times of India Magazine*, May 18, 1969.

ground among landless peasants and youth in the rice-growing coastal areas of Andhra Pradesh, Kerala, West Bengal, and Orissa. The home ministry, in June 1970, found it necessary formally to caution six states—West Bengal, Bihar, Punjab, Orissa, Uttar Pradesh, and Kerala, about the activities of Naxalites, who were said to be planning a "new, democratic" revolution on Maoist lines involving extensive class violence in rural areas.[52]

The Naxalites, although weakened by internal differences on the structure of a revolutionary party, that saw rival centers of influence emerge in the leadership of the two main West Bengal and Andhra contingents, did succeed, at least as a formal exercise, in founding the first Indian communist party openly committed to techniques of rural class war. On May Day 1969, the Bengali Naxalites, led by Kanu Sanyal, announced formation of a new "Communist Party, Marxist-Leninist,"[53] which rejected outright the "hoax of parliamentarism" in a commitment to "immediate revolution . . . through revolutionary peoples war." The basic task of the party was to "liberate the rural areas through revolutionary armed agrarian revolution and encircle the cities, and finally, to liberate the cities and thus complete the revolution throughout the country."[54] The party, which had an estimated all-India membership of 20,000 to 30,000,[55] and attracted activists from among college students and the urban middle class, proposed to work underground in a two-pronged organizational effort aimed at educating students on the need to organize the peasantry, and in turn to convince the peasantry of the need for revolution. Although weakly organized and limited in practice mainly to terrorist activities, the CP(ML) received immediate recognition by China as the only true revolutionary force in India. It did, moreover, endorse for the first time the Chinese path of agrarian revolution as the correct model for India. Affirming the dictum that political power grows out of the barrel of a gun, the CP(ML) called on communist revolutionaries to "study Chairman Mao's thought, for it is only Chairman Mao's thought that can bring the peasants into the revolutionary front, and Chairman Mao's theory of peoples' war is the only means by which an apparently weak revolutionary force can wage a successful struggle against an apparently powerful enemy and win victory. The basic tactics of the struggle of the revolutionary peasantry led by the working class is guerrilla warfare."[56]

[52] *The Statesman*, June 29, 1970.
[53] The events surrounding the formation of the CP(ML) are described in Fic, *Kerala, Yenan of India*, pp. 443-52. See also Mohan Ram, *Maoism in India*, pp. 137-69; and Franda, *Radical Politics in West Bengal*, pp. 168-76.
[54] Cited in Franda, *Radical Politics in West Bengal*, p. 173.
[55] *Link*, May 25, 1969, p. 11.
[56] "Political Resolution of the Communist Party of India (Marxist-Leninist)," cited in Fic, *Kerala, Yenan of India*, p. 22.

By 1969, the intensification of tribal discontent, combined with the outbreak of agrarian conflicts in diverse parts of the country, actually lent a certain credibility to the Maoist strategy. Some observers believed that "from the speed with which the Naxalite movement is spreading to all parts of India, it can be concluded that objective conditions really exist in India, for an armed uprising, its dynamism fed by twin forces of the national and tribal unrest on the one hand, the agrarian upsurge on the other."[57]

The state governments, paralyzed by internal factional conflicts, were completely incapable of providing democratic solutions for the deep social causes of the growing agrarian discontent. Instead, they handled each new outbreak as a problem of law and order, responding with reinforcements for police action, including contingents deputed from the Central Reserve Police. The Center, no less than the states, attempted to meet the "extraordinary situation" existing in the country by acquiring stronger powers. A few weeks before the five-year old State of Emergency was terminated, lifting the Defense of India Rules, government pushed through the Lok Sabha a new Unlawful Activities (Prevention) Bill. The legislation declared illegal all activities and organizations aimed at disrupting the sovereignty or territorial integrity of the country, and conferred "extraordinary powers" on the government to identify, arrest, or proscribe such individuals and organizations, subject only to review by a one-man judicial tribunal. Members of the CPI(M) and other left opposition parties walked out of parliament rather than vote on a measure they believed was directed against them for suspected Chinese ties. The national leadership, meanwhile, looked forward to the mid-term elections as an opportunity for restoring stability to state politics and the predominant position of the Congress party.

Five mid-term elections, one in Haryana in May 1968 and four in Bihar, Punjab, West Bengal, and Uttar Pradesh in February 1969, did little, however, to reestablish confidence in the efficacy of democratic institutions. The Congress, campaigning primarily on the slogan of political stability, barred the nomination of defectors, those who either left the Congress to join other parties or joined the Congress from other groups. The opposition, chastened by the rapid collapse of SVD alliances, either contested alone or attempted electoral adjustments with similarly oriented parties.

The outcome in Haryana at first appeared hopeful. Congress increased its popular vote somewhat, and won exactly the same number of seats (48 out of 81) as it had in the 1967 elections. The new chief minister, Bansi Lal, seemed to enjoy the support of all factions in the state party

[57] *Ibid.*, p. 451.

organization. However, before the end of the year, the Haryana Congress was once again a "divided house." Dissidents loyal to the former chief minister, Bhagwat Dayal Sharma, resigned from the party to join the opposition. Sharma, who was immediately elected head of a new SVD coalition, claimed a majority in the assembly and presented a memorandum to the governor requesting he be allowed to form a new government. The Congress, citing the support of independents, denied it had lost the majority, and asserted a counterclaim. A "fierce battle of body-snatching" between the two sides began anew.[58] Assembly proceedings were once again marked by "defections, uproarious scenes, walkouts, and adjournments."[59] The Bansi Lal ministry survived, but only by putting into play the full arsenal of weapons perfected during the previous round of political warfare. Assembly sessions were variously prolonged, adjourned, prorogued, and resummoned, depending on estimates of the momentary balance of power between Congress and the SVD coalition. Major business of the House was often conducted in the absence of opposition parties that had walked out in protest. The problem of a clear majority for the government was for the time being solved when, on April 9, 1970, Bansi Lal expanded his Cabinet to appoint ten more ministers, including several of the original Congress defectors.

The situation in Bihar, where the Congress High Command took direct charge of the election campaign was, if anything, less reassuring. The poll itself was marred by incidents of violence and attempts at some places to prevent voters from casting their ballots, as well as to tamper with the ballot boxes. Congress emerged as the largest single party in the state legislature (with 118 seats in a House of 318), but with ten fewer seats than in 1967. The Working Committee, moreover, for the first time conceded requests by the state leadership to participate as a full partner in a Congress-led multiparty coalition government, including not only small regional groupings, but also the Swatantra party. Even so, within less than four months, on June 19, the ministry was defeated in the assembly after "violent dissensions among the coalition partners and rival factions within the Congress over the distributions of ministerial offices and allocation of portfolios."[60] An alternative government formed by the opposition lasted no more than ten days before it, too, collapsed over internal disputes on the allocation of offices. On July 4, 1969, the assembly was suspended and President's Rule once more imposed on Bihar.

Elsewhere, the Congress was defeated by regional coalitions. In the Punjab, the Sikh-based Akali Dal arrived at an "electoral adjustment" with the Jan Sangh to win less than 39 percent of the popular vote but a majority of seats. The Congress, which polled more votes than in 1967,

[58] Kashyap, *The Politics of Power*, p. 203.
[59] *Ibid.*, p. 205.                                   [60] *Ibid.*, p. 353.

and achieved a total popular vote somewhat higher than that of the two parties combined, did not win more than 36 percent of the seats. A similar picture emerged in West Bengal. This time the Congress faced a 13-party United Front Alliance, including both Communist parties as well as the Bangla Congress. Although the Congress vote remained virtually unchanged at about 40 percent, outstripping the total won by the three major parties in the coalition (who together gained less than 35 percent), the front secured almost four times as many seats as the Congress (214 compared to 55 in a House of 280) to inflict a decisive defeat on the party.

The most favorable outcome occurred in Uttar Pradesh, but even this fell short of the Congress party's expectations. The Congress, which once again concentrated on the issue of political stability, appeared determined to secure a clear majority in the keystone state of all-India politics, representing about one-sixth of the electorate. The senior leadership campaigned extensively. Mrs. Gandhi spent fifteen days traveling to all major regions of the state; in one three-day tour alone she addressed about fifty election meetings.[61] Yet the results were in the end disappointing. The Congress did achieve an incremental gain in the popular vote statewide, and succeeded in increasing its number of seats in the state legislative assembly from 168 to 180. But it could not manage to win a decisive victory, falling two seats short of a majority. The government formed by the leader of the Congress legislative party, C. B. Gupta, took office with a shaky majority dependent on the support of Swatantra and independents.

On the whole, the 1969 mid-term elections were read as confirmation of earlier trends. Congress appeared in permanent decline, failing to win a majority in any state. At the same time, no national alternative appeared on the horizon. Indeed, the 1969 election suggested that the "national parties" were in decline. Apart from the Congress, the national parties that suffered losses included the SSP in Bihar, and the Swatantra and Jan Sangh in Uttar Pradesh. The Jan Sangh, which had enjoyed the position of second largest party in Uttar Pradesh since 1962, was in fact pushed from that place by the unexpected success of a new regional party, the Bharatiya Kranti Dal (Indian Revolutionary party).

The prospect of further Congress decline and proliferation of regional parties refueled fears of national disintegration. The united front governments in Kerala and West Bengal, as well as the DMK regime in Tamil Nadu, were already demanding structural changes in the federal system that would seriously weaken the power of the national government. The CPI(M), taking the lead, proposed a "radical and immediate" change in Center-state relations, designed to rally maximum support from potential allies among noncommunist state governments, many of

[61] *Times of India*, January 14, 1969.

which were chafing at the Center's financial powers. The party program, adopted in 1969, called for a number of far-reaching reforms, including transfer of all Concurrent List Subjects in the constitution to the exclusive jurisdiction of the states; devolution of seventy-five percent of Central revenues to the states; and state management of all centrally administered agricultural, industrial, educational, social, and welfare enterprises. The strategic reform, however, from the point of view of the Marxists, was the demand for effective state control over the all-India services, especially the IAS and the police, including transfer of control to the states of all central security forces, industrial security forces, the Central Reserve Police, and the Border Security Forces. Meanwhile, the Kerala state leadership of the CPI(M) no longer hesitated to proclaim publicly that the party's purpose was to "capture power by making the fullest use of the constitutional machinery so that we can break the Constitution from within."[62] Indeed, the victory of a Marxist-dominated coalition in the sensitive border state of West Bengal once again led to the outbreak of large-scale disorders and violence.

After the 1969 elections in West Bengal, CPI(M) ministers not only controlled the critical portfolio of land and land revenue, but the major departments of the home ministry, including general administration and police. One of the first actions of the united front government was to order the release of all Naxalites and other persons detained under the preventive detention act. At the same time, the police were instructed to "consult officers of the Land Revenue Department before they decided to act on the basis of the *jotedars'* complaints."[63] Marxist political workers subsequently concentrated their organizational efforts in the rural areas, recruiting sharecroppers and landless laborers for membership in the Krishak Sabhas. The land revenue administration then took advantage of the "popular movement from below" to convince sharecroppers they would be protected against retaliation for coming forward to give information to local revenue officers against landlords holding land in excess of the ceiling limit. By early 1970, the Marxist land and land revenue minister claimed that more than 300,000 acres of *benami* land had been identified in this way and registered by revenue officers as available for legal transfer. The result, however, was a sharp increase in incidents of forcible seizure of land. Constituents of the united front, unwilling to trust the outcome to judicial procedures, fought among themselves to "grab" the land and settle their own supporters on it. The technique used by the Marxists of organizing volunteer forces at the local level composed of party members and their sympathizers, in order to "assist" the government in carrying out the distribution program, was followed by

[62] *The Statesman*, July 12, 1969.          [63] *The Statesman*, November 11, 1969.

most other members of the united front. Incidents of arson, kidnapping, and even murder rapidly multiplied as poor peasants killed other poor peasants in conflicts over *benami* land, and *jotedars* clashed with share-croppers.

By the beginning of 1970, law and order in West Bengal had seriously deteriorated. Ajoy Mukherjee, the chief minister and head of the Bangla Congress, the major non-Marxist constituent of the united front, lost all control over the adminstration and the police in his own government. According to Mukherjee, in some rural areas of West Bengal "murders, violent clashes, looting, *gherao* and forcible occupation of land have become the order of the day."[64] In early February, the Bangla Congress withdrew its three ministers from the government; the assembly subsequently became an arena in which CPI(M) and Bangla Congress MLAs settled their disagreements by exchanging blows. Finally, on March 16, 1970, the chief minister, charging that the CPI(M) was establishing a "reign of terror" in the state, submitted his resignation. This time, however, it brought little immediate improvement in law and order. Non-communist leaders charged that the administration had been permanently infiltrated by the Marxists, and the police were still inactive in protecting *jotedars* against attacks by landless workers. The Naxalites, moreover, sharply increased their terrorist activities, murdering political opponents and *jotedars* in rural areas, and launching bomb attacks in the towns on educational institutions and printing presses considered symbolic of bourgeois domination.

The mid-term elections, however, did more than confirm previous tendencies. They helped clarify a new trend in political development that illuminated the question of the direction of ideological change. In the welter of confusion that saw regional, communal, communist, and conservative groups all win positions of power, there was a common pattern in the use of "economic leftism" to attract popular support. Parties ranging the entire spectrum of political opinion sought and gained advantage from populist slogans for the abolition of land revenue, minimum wages for workers, higher dearness allowances for government employees, and lower prices for foodgrains and other essential commodities. In the key state of Uttar Pradesh, the first clear signs emerged that appeals to economic interest could be effective as a principle of horizontal electoral organization of the Backward Classes, eroding the hold of local elites over their low-caste followings.

The mid-term poll in Uttar Pradesh was distinguished from previous contests in several ways. First, a new party emerged, the Bhartiya Kranti

[64] *The Statesman*, November 11, 1969.

Dal or Indian Revolutionary party, with the ability to field candidates in almost all the constituencies of the state. Second, the leader of the BKD, Charan Singh—the man who had precipitated the collapse of the Congress ministry in 1967 by leading his followers outside the party to form the Jan Congress and serve as the chief minister of the successor SVD government—was the first member of a nonelite caste to hold the highest political office in the state and head a major party. Although a Jat, the one peasant caste in Uttar Pradesh not officially listed as "Backward," Charan Singh belonged to that part of the Jat leadership that preferred to think of themselves as the natural leaders of the smaller peasant farmers among the Backward Classes. His popularity as the longtime leader of the Congress organization in Meerut district was built on a reputation for championing the interests of peasant cultivators of diverse agricultural castes, including low-ranking Ahirs, Kurmis, and Gujars, and also the Muslim farming population.

The BKD as a political party was a new phenomenon in the politics of Uttar Pradesh for other reasons. Until the 1969 elections, established political patterns mirrored those in many other states. Political leadership was the near monopoly of upper-caste landowning families, mainly the elite Brahmins and Thakurs. At the district level, political mobilization occurred in a vertical pattern: leaders of the elite landed communities constructed multicaste political factions with support from families of low-status dependent groups to create "an organization based upon the ties between a leader and his followers, an economic patron and his dependents."[65] The BKD, by contrast, decided on a strategy of peasant mobilization that emphasized a direct appeal to the common economic interests of the Backward Classes throughout the state. Well over sixty percent of the candidates it fielded had no previous experience in electoral contests.[66] Well over one-half of its nominees belonged to the Backward communities; "scores" were Muslims, and nine belonged to the Jat caste.[67]

There were other innovations in campaign style. The BKD relied less on public meetings in cities and towns, and more on house-to-house canvassing in the villages to reach voters. Charan Singh raised his election fund of Rs. 15 lakhs in his own constituency of Chaprauli, and managed to attract another Rs. 15 lakhs in Meerut district as a whole through solicitations that concentrated not so much on local traders and merchants as on peasant farmers.

[65] Paul R. Brass, *Factional Politics in an Indian State*, p. 236.
[66] According to data compiled by Craig Baxter, of the 402 candidates fielded by the BKD, 146, or approximately 36 percent, had contested previous elections. Craig Baxter, "The Rise and Fall of the Bhartiya Kranti Dal in Uttar Pradesh" in Weiner and Field, eds., *Electoral Politics in the Indian States*, vol. 4.
[67] *Times of India*, January 30, 1969.

Populist themes characterized the party's election appeals. In contrast to Congress, which deliberately emphasized issues that cut across class lines in promising to restore stability to state politics as the condition for achieving progress for all, the BKD concentrated on winning support of the Backward Classes by identifying Congress rule not only with corrupt government but with biased administration that served only the special interests of the "capitalists."

The surprising success of the BKD in emerging as the second largest party in the state, surpassing the Jan Sangh, indicated deep currents of social change, amounting to evidence that "the dominance of the upper castes seemed to have been broken."[68] Although traditional patron-client ties still exerted primary sway on voting preference in the more backward eastern and central regions of the state, considerations of common economic interests appeared to exercise an independent influence on electoral behavior in the highly advanced western region that formed part of the heartland of the "green revolution." The Jan Sangh's support, which declined in all areas of the state in 1969 relative to 1967 levels, suffered the greatest loss in forward momentum in the western region. The Congress party, similarly, showed comparatively greater strength in the least developed eastern and central districts of the state. The BKD, by contrast, scored its highest popular vote in the western region, exceeding its overall average for all rural constituencies by about nine percentage points to win more than thirty percent of the poll. Analysis of the data to examine linkages between economic change and electoral behavior[69] showed interesting contrasts in the western districts between the pattern of support of the Congress party and the Jan Sangh on the one hand, and the BKD on the other. In that region, the vote for the Jan Sangh as well as for the Congress party was inversely related to the vote for the BKD, and also to a wide range of indicators of agricultural modernization. One unexpected result of the Uttar Pradesh election was that it signaled the first signs of changing patterns of peasant participation toward new forms of horizontal alignments, as customary ties between upper-caste landlords and low-status peasant cultivators and landless groups began to erode. The long-term viability of vertical patterns of political mobilization was called into question within the Hindi-speaking heartland itself.

[68] Kashyap, *The Politics of Power*, p. 271.
[69] For a systematic analysis of the changing relationships between electoral behavior and agrarian modernization during the 1962, 1967, and 1969 elections in Uttar Pradesh see Francine Frankel, "The Problems of Correlating Electoral and Economic Variables."

# TEN

# The Congress Split
# and the Radicalization
# of Indian Politics

By the late 1960s, India was caught up in a double crisis of economic stagnation and political instability. Liberal economic policies adopted during the Shastri years appeared unlikely to solve the problems of the economic decline and certain to aggravate the difficulties of political disorder.

The new agricultural strategy made rapid production gains only in limited areas of the country, where large consolidated holdings were able to provide economies of scale essential for profitable investment in costly modern inputs. Meanwhile, diversion of scarce public finances and foreign exchange to the agricultural sector threatened the modest momentum in industrial growth. As aid levels declined, it became difficult to ensure even the minimum imports of raw materials, components, and spare parts necessary to achieve the full utilization of existing capacity. A wide array of incentives to the private sector, including relaxing licensing provisions, lifting price controls, and stepping up credit from government financial institutions, gave little sign of generating much higher levels of investment. Many businessmen found it more attractive to divert often undeclared and untaxed "black money" into speculative activities ensuring quick, high profit and low-risk returns.

The liberal economic policies, moreover, widened existing inequalities. Concentration of economic power in the larger business houses perceptibly heightened glaring disparities between the opulent life style of prosperous factory owners and their executives and the marginal existence of the masses of the urban poor and unemployed. The new agricultural strategy exacted even higher social costs, exacerbating both regional and class inequalities. A few well-placed states, primarily in the irrigated wheat areas, made spectacular progress. A small minority of larger landowners doubled and trebled their incomes from a variety of more efficient techniques. The bulk of agriculturists, however, fell further behind. Within the vast rural sector, forty to fifty percent of the population, those with no land or small fragments, continued to live at such marginal levels that their condition was officially described at below the level of poverty.

The strength of the Congress party and its capacity to secure national integration and provide stable government at the Center and in the states dramatically eroded. The dissatisfied young, the lower income groups, the uneducated, the religious minorities—all of whom had provided the party with its broad-based following—turned to diverse local opposition parties. Yet the heterogenous coalitions that replaced Congress governments in several states after 1967 proved incapable of creating stable majorities around a common economic and political program. They led a precarious existence punctuated by defections and counterdefections that produced conditions of quasi-permanent cabinet crises.

As the economic situation deteriorated, popular discontent spilled over into political violence. Marxist and Naxalite revolutionary groups scored striking successes in organizing extraparliamentary "mass struggles" that fused appeals to regional, linguistic, and tribal aspirations with promises of ending economic exploitation. In West Bengal, coercive industrial strikes and land-grab agitations paralyzed normal economic and political life, even while posing a national security threat in a sensitive border region. At the same time, the growing incidence of spontaneous agrarian outbreaks suggested large scope for organizing land-grab movements among the peasantry in widely separate areas of the country. The question of the viability of democratic processes of government under conditions of increasing political unrest was for the first time seriously debated.

Economic stagnation, compounded by problems of political instability and disorder, seemed to make it inevitable that questions of fundamental economic and social transformation, set aside since Nehru's death, would once again be raised. But renewed demands that Congress carry out longstanding promises of economic reform were advanced in a political setting that had become much less favorable to accommodative methods of social change. The unresolved controversies over the direction and pace of social transformation were, moreover, revived in the immediate context of a complex power struggle inside the Congress party.

The conflict had two separate but ultimately intertwining strands. The prime minister and the senior leaders of the Congress party organization—known collectively as the Syndicate—were engaged in an embittered battle for preeminence in the conduct of governmental affairs. At the same time, the older party bosses—some of whom belonged to the Syndicate—were caught up in a confrontation with a younger group of socialist radicals determined to wrest control of the organization from their hands and shape it into an effective instrument of reform. The intersection of these two factional battles, in which the radicals offered support to Mrs. Gandhi and she accepted their help after it became evident that the Syndicate was preparing to replace her as prime minister, led directly to the split of the Congress party in 1969. It also transformed the nature of Indian politics. The split was subsequently justified solely as an ideological conflict between those with a vested interest in the status quo and those committed to socialist change. As a result, even the appearance of political consensus that had established the Congress as a party of national unity was shattered. Political rhetoric emphasizing slogans of class struggle replaced the pragmatic language of accommodation. Compromise, once lauded as the expression of India's national genius in political life, was denounced as nothing more than collusion with the vested interests. Political action increasingly tended toward confrontation.

The conflict between Mrs. Gandhi and the Syndicate surfaced immediately after the 1967 elections. It was prompted by fears among the party leaders that they were fast losing their former position of influence under the principle of collective leadership established during the Shastri years. The electoral disasters experienced by the party, and the humiliating personal defeats suffered by S. K. Patil, Atulya Ghosh, and Kamaraj, critically weakened the prestige of the organizational wing. Kamaraj, in particular, found little opportunity to reenact his role as arbiter in the selection of the new prime minister. Instead, the chief ministers of those states where Congress was returned to power united around the candidacy of Mrs. Gandhi. This time, in fact, Mrs. Gandhi's election was taken for granted. There was no succession contest and no secret ballot at the meeting of the Congress parliamentary party on March 12, 1967, which unanimously elected Mrs. Gandhi leader and prime minister.[1]

The new ministry announced on March 14 further reflected Mrs. Gandhi's independence of party guidance. The list of Cabinet members was shown to Kamaraj only as a courtesy shortly before the formal announcement. It excluded N. Sanjiva Reddy, the only eligible member of the Syndicate previously holding a ministerial post. Instead, the Congress party boss of Andhra Pradesh was "elevated" to speaker of the Lok Sabha. Otherwise, places were found for the prime minister's political supporters and personal allies, including Jagjivan Ram (Food and Agriculture); Y. B. Chavan (Home); Asoka Mehta (Petroleum and Chemicals); Fakhruddin Ali Ahmed (Industrial Development); and Dinesh Singh (Commerce). Others accommodated were drawn from among the

---

[1] According to interview data reported by Michael Brecher, Congress MPs were reinforced in their preference for Mrs. Gandhi by the election setbacks at the states. They believed that Mrs. Gandhi's national image, reputation for flexibility, and acceptability to minorities were decisive qualifications for leadership at a time when both party unity and national integration might depend on the central government's overall credibility in its dealings with disparate state coalitions. See Michael Brecher, *Political Leadership in India*, pp. 57-58, 71-94.

nominees of those chief ministers who had supported Mrs. Gandhi's candidacy as prime minister.[2]

The Syndicate, however, did manage to execute an unexpected maneuver that gained them a foothold in the new government. Rumors of defections from the ruling party in the Lok Sabha provided the rationalization for arguments that a close working relationship between Mrs. Gandhi and Morarji Desai was necessary to assure political stability at the Center. Desai was, in fact, the only credible rallying point for dissidents inside the national party. Kamaraj, in his capacity as Congress president, initiated the move toward a rapprochement with Desai. He took the lead in urging that the senior leader be included in the Cabinet as the best guarantee of party unity. Although Mrs. Gandhi's personal allies were opposed to any such arrangement, the fact that her major backers among the chief ministers insisted on the accommodation constrained her to agree.[3] Desai was more difficult to convince. He considered the prime minister's first offer to him of the finance ministry both a thankless task, and one inferior in status to the home ministry held by Chavan, a man junior to him in age, experience, and years of service to the party. Kamaraj, acting as an intermediary, eventually prevailed on Desai to join the Cabinet, but only under a new formula that made him both deputy prime minister and finance minister.[4]

The active role played by Kamaraj in securing Desai's entrance into the government created the impression that the new deputy prime minister was the Syndicate's representative inside the Cabinet for the purpose of "keep[ing] a check on Mrs. Gandhi"[5] in the ongoing power struggle. This notion easily merged with the broader idea, encouraged by the radicals, that Desai acted as spokesman for the Syndicate in conflicts over questions of policy. Actually, Kamaraj as well as other members of the Syndicate were at various times distressed by Desai's inflexible posture on economic and social policy. They supported him almost entirely for cynical reasons. Desai, limited by age, could not monopolize political power very long even if he was permitted to realize his longtime ambition of becoming prime minister. Mrs. Gandhi, by contrast, was still a young woman. She could, like her father before her, establish herself indefinitely as the authoritative head of government, ending all prospect of

---

[2] See Zareer Masani, *Indira Gandhi, a Biography*, pp. 175–76.

[3] The chief ministers of Madhya Pradesh, Uttar Pradesh, Andhra, and Mysore, having a strong hold on the votes of 178 of the 283 members of the Congress parliamentary party, threatened to withdraw their support from Mrs. Gandhi unless she agreed to Desai's terms. *Ibid.*, p. 174.

[4] Desai's interpretation of his powers as deputy prime minister, which he said he expressed to Mrs. Gandhi before accepting the post, was that "I must be able to speak on your behalf without asking you." Interview, Morarji Desai, New Delhi, August 30, 1973.

[5] Kuldip Nayar reported that Kamaraj used this phrase in describing his satisfaction at Desai's return to the Cabinet. See Nayar, *India, the Critical Years*, p. 28.

restoring the Syndicate's preferred style of collective leadership. Desai himself had no illusions about the Syndicate's motivations. He attributed their sudden support for him to the fact that "Indira put all the Syndicate members on the scrap heap" and called it an "irony of fate that I am with the Syndicate now."[6]

Mrs. Gandhi, counseled that Desai was the Syndicate's "Trojan horse in the Cabinet,"[7] reacted by seeking out new allies inside the party in an effort to build an independent base of power. The prime minister's natural constituency, both as Jawaharlal Nehru's daughter and in the context of her own "progressive" image, had long been thought to rest with the younger socialists among the party's rank and file. Yet, since assuming power in 1966, Mrs. Gandhi's credibility among this group and the wider left outside was seriously compromised by dependence on economic advisers counseling technocratic growth strategies that could be accomplished only through greater incentives to private enterprise. Such an approach, moreover, was predicated on receiving higher levels of Western, particularly American, aid. But even before devaluation, growing dependence on American assistance created widespread anxiety among the Congress rank and file that India was losing her independence in foreign affairs. The decision to devalue in obvious response to Western pressure was denounced as the ultimate step in national humiliation. The left, in particular, excoriated Mrs. Gandhi for her action. The CPI, which for years had taken pains to support Nehru in distinction to other "reactionary" elements inside the Congress party, no longer made the same discrimination in relation to his daughter. The National Council of the CPI, meeting on June 9-15, 1966, adopted a formal resolution to demand "the immediate resignation of the Central Government headed by Indira Gandhi because it had proved itself wholly unworthy of any national trust and thereby forfeited its moral and political right to be placed at the helm of national affairs."[8]

Notwithstanding the flood of political abuse pouring in on the prime minister in the wake of devaluation, she still enjoyed one crucial advantage in tapping the deep public sentiment that had been revealed against dictation or the appearance of any dictation from the West on questions of national policy. Mrs. Gandhi, after all, was the daughter of Nehru— India's architect of nonalignment. Her opponents in the Syndicate were, by contrast, publicly identified with pro-American sentiments. Desai, a fierce antagonist of communism and the Soviet Union, was by default associated with a personal preference for the West. S. K. Patil, long outspoken in his admiration for the capitalist system, made no secret of his sympathies for the United States.

[6] Interview, Morarji Desai, New Delhi, August 18, 1973.
[7] Nayar, *India, the Critical Years*, p. 28.
[8] Cited in Fic, *Kerala, Yenan of India*, p. 341.

There were signs that Mrs. Gandhi was tentatively edging into a more critical posture toward the United States. As early as July 1966, she used the opportunity of her visit to the Soviet Union to sign a joint communiqué demanding an immediate and unconditional halt in American bombing of North Vietnam. After the 1967 elections, moreover, the government made it known that a proposal for a joint Indo–American Education Foundation in India, announced during the prime minister's 1966 visit to the United States, would be dropped.[9] The government's attitude toward foreign private investment, especially toward collaboration by international oil companies in fertilizer projects favored by the World Bank, became almost entirely negative. Asoka Mehta, then minister of petroleum and chemicals, and until the debacle of devaluation one of the prime minister's closest economic advisers, found his proposals for joint ventures between foreign investors and Indian firms, though framed in terms he considered mutually beneficial, "shot down one by one" at Mrs. Gandhi's behest in the Cabinet. Disillusioned, he resigned in August 1968.[10]

A more critical stance toward the United States was perhaps inevitable as the 1960s drew to an end. Disillusionment, frustration, and anger were all feelings that ran deep. There had been multiple sources of disappointment. The Kennedy administration, which at the time of the Chinese attack in 1962 responded immediately to India's crisis request for transport planes, light equipment, and infantry weapons, was unprepared for the entanglements and massive expenditures envisaged in meeting follow-up proposals for a joint air defense or for providing arms manufacturing capacity, raw materials, tanks, and fighter planes required to create a modern air force. The price tag on assistance of this magnitude, vaguely estimated at some "billions of dollars" by the American ambassador,[11] was sharply reduced in negotiations to about $500 million worth of arms and equipment. The major portion of this amount was

[9] The proposal envisaged that the foundation would fund higher education and research projects in India, using an initial endowment of 300 million dollars drawn from U.S. holdings of PL 480 rupees. At the AICC meeting on May 21, 1966, a debate on a nonofficial resolution to discuss the proposal for the establishment of the Indo–U.S. Education Foundation revealed widespread concern over the potential for American penetration of India's educational system. The venture was denounced for "bartering away the minds of the people"; apprehension was also expressed about operatives of the CIA, who went to foreign countries "masquerading as education experts." *Congress Bulletin*, Nos. 4, 5, and 6 (April–June 1966), pp. 169, 171.

[10] The formal reason given by Mehta for his resignation from the Cabinet was dissent from India's decision to abstain on the United Nations resolution condemning Russia for the invasion of Czechoslovakia in August 1968. Privately, he dated his estrangement from the government to the end of 1967, when Mrs. Gandhi, relying on new advisers, especially P. N. Haksar and Dinesh Singh, withdrew her support from growth-oriented economic policies to follow a more populist approach. Interview, Asoka Mehta, New Delhi, June 15, 1973.

[11] Galbraith, *Ambassador's Journal*, p. 471.

never delivered. The United States suspended all military aid to both Pakistan and India during the 1965 war, at a time when deliveries to India were well under $100 millions. By contrast, Pakistan had already received military aid from the United States—dating from the 1954 SEATO alliance—valued at a minimum of $672 millions,[12] including Patton tanks, Sabre jets, and supersonic fighters. Some of this equipment was used against India in the 1965 war, compounding the sense of outrage experienced by the government and public at the sudden cut-off of aid.

Similar disappointments developed on matters of economic assistance. After years of pressure by USAID and the World Bank for higher investment priority to agriculture and a larger role for private enterprise in industrial development, India's reorientation of the development strategy in line with Western advice did not secure the higher aid levels promised to finance the necessary imports of fertilizers, industrial raw materials, components, and spare parts in support of the new approach. Instead, the Johnson administration, preoccupied with the war in Vietnam and unable to surmount Congressional opposition to additional expenditures on foreign assistance, cut back on earlier pledges. The reduced contributions by the United States had an immediate impact on Consortium aid. This fell to about one-half of the total amount projected during discussions on devaluation between India and the World Bank.

The government found it necessary to look in other directions. After 1965, the Soviet Union became India's most important source of defense equipment, supplying the manufacturing capacity for building advanced fighter aircraft as well as a wide range of other modern arms, equipment, ammunition, and spare parts. At about the same time, the Russians also greatly increased aid commitments for India's development plans, providing badly needed finance for heavy industry projects in the public sector. As the prospect of nonproject aid from the Consortium powers declined, reducing the availability of free foreign exchange for imports, moreover, the idea of expanded trade agreements with the Soviet Union based on commodity payments—including provisions specifying that the Russians would take an increasing share of its imports from India in manufactured goods—became particularly attractive. A major Indo-Soviet trade agreement based on these arrangements was signed in January 1966. It raised expectations of a hundredfold increase in trade between the two countries by 1970 to make the USSR India's second largest trading partner. Further, it established the principle of setting up industrial capacity in each country to meet the requirements of the other.

[12] Pran Chopra, *India's Second Liberation* (Delhi, 1973), p. 28. Figures used by the Defense Department and other American officials to estimate the value of arms deliveries to Pakistan until the suspension of military aid in 1965 have ranged from $672 million to $2,000 million.

The gradual decline in Indo–American ties and the corresponding strengthening of Indo–Soviet relations was as a general phenomenon related to overall shifts in international power alignments. The sharpening conflict between China and the USSR caused the superpowers to reassess their policies toward the subcontinent. In the case of the United States, this reassessment ultimately led to attempts at rapprochement with China. In the case of the USSR, it enhanced the value of closer cooperation with India as a bulwark against Chinese expansion, and contributed to a situation in which the interests of India and the Soviet Union more frequently converged. These changing alignments no doubt would have influenced the foreign policy of any Indian government in a similar direction during this period. Indeed, the military, aid, and trade agreements that provided the building blocks of a closer Indo–Soviet friendship all had their origins in initiatives taken during the Nehru and Shastri years. Nevertheless, the rhetoric of antiimperialism that was employed by the Indian government after 1967 as a rationalization for the shift was at least partly designed to influence the outcome of the emerging struggle for power inside the party, as a means of building the prime minister's popular support. It was this rhetoric—charges that Western powers were determined to prevent India from becoming a strong, industrialized state—rather than the shifting alignment itself, that created the worst personal and political animosities, which slowly began to corrode Indo–American relations. It did, however, permit Mrs. Gandhi to reassert her national image as a "progressive" leader inside the Congress party, and also to mend her political fences with the CPI. This last was not a minor consideration in the aftermath of the 1967 elections. It allowed the prime minister to renew her ties with communist leaders in those states in which Congress was in a minority, and it helped to broaden the base of her personal support in parliament.

It was not, however, on questions of foreign policy, but over domestic economic and political issues, that rival groups inside the party started the process of confrontation that threatened Congress unity. The immediate impetus for the growing division originated in differing interpretations of the reasons for the 1967 election defeats. Small teams sent around the country by the AICC to investigate at first hand the causes of electoral failures came back with broadly similar conclusions. The setbacks were due mainly to the gap between Congress policies and implementation in the economic field. Opposition parties of all shades of opinion had been able to convert popular disappointment into anti-Congress votes at the polls.

The note on "Lessons of the General Election"[13] submitted by G. L. Nanda on April 10, 1967, to the Working Committee did not stop at

[13] G. L. Nanda, *Lessons of the General Election* (New Delhi, 1967), p. 2976.

such general observations. It went on to consider the reasons why Congress programs were not carried out, as well as the direction of needed reforms if these failures were to be reversed. According to Nanda, the source of Congress inability to implement basic plan policies could be found in the nature of the party organization itself. The leadership did not share any common socialist outlook or set of ideals. Rather, it viewed the party primarily as an arena in which to advance personal power and economic interests. Mass contacts were neglected. Power was exercised on behalf of a small section of the community. Committed workers were excluded from leadership positions inside the party. Entrenched bosses manipulated party elections by voting millions of bogus or fictitious names on behalf of their own factional candidates in contests to local bodies that, in turn, elected all higher organs of the party.

The analysis advanced two broad conclusions. It was, of course, necessary to reaffirm party principles and programs, especially the pledges of Bhubaneswar to provide a national minimum standard of food, clothing, housing, education, and health. Even more essential, however, the party organization had to be thoroughly reformed. There had to be an end to bogus membership. Primary members had to be recruited on the basis of an understanding of Congress principles and a willingness to promote its policies. A cadre of trained, full-time workers had to be created for the purpose of mobilizing the general membership and the masses for implementation of specific tasks in a scheme of constructive work. Most important, the responsibility for this kind of transformation could not be left solely in the hands of the senior leadership, by implication the very party bosses who had been manipulating bogus memberships to establish their control. The task had to be placed in the hands of younger men elevated to leadership positions according to criteria of commitment to Congress policies.

These themes, sounded as early as 1962 by the Congress Forum for Socialist Action, but shut out in the years since Nehru's death by the dominant conservative leadership, met with a divided response. They found a resonant echo among socialist members of the rank and file, many of whom had some association with the Forum. But the leadership at all levels of the party organization were reluctant to endorse such a sweeping indictment of their own stewardship. PCC presidents and secretaries, while acknowledging that failures in economic policy had been very important in accounting for election defeats pointed to a multitude of other factors. They cited the effects of a united opposition; shortages of campaign funds; the role of ex-rulers who suddenly joined the opposition; and regional issues ranging from the language problem in the south to drought in Bihar, Orissa, and Uttar Pradesh.[14]

[14] See the proceedings of the Conference of Presidents and Secretaries of PCCs and DCCs, April 9, 1967, New Delhi. *Congress Bulletin*, Nos. 4-5 (April-May 1967), pp. 46-62.

The high command was divided. At the AICC meeting in June 1967, where the election results were debated,[15] Kamaraj endorsed the view that the major factor explaining election losses was the gap between Congress policies and implementation in economic matters, and that it was urgently necessary to fulfill past promises. S. K. Patil, by contrast, found the election results no more than "a normal change in a democracy because people get tired with the same leader and party."[16] Morarji Desai reacted angrily at what he considered a campaign to "malign" the older leadership.[17] Mrs. Gandhi endorsed the arguments for immediate action to "curb the tendency which sought to perpetuate the privileged and the underprivileged." She also expressed concern about the problem of bogus membership in the organization and the need to recruit students and youth and elevate them to responsible positions inside the party. She was unwilling however, to join in the attacks on the older leadership.[18]

The Working Committee, although divided on the exact causes and cures for the Congress decline, nevertheless felt the need for some symbolic action to dramatize the commitment of the party to implementation of Congress programs. Atulya Ghosh took the first step in proposing a new initiative on May 12, 1967, when he introduced a note declaring that the privileges of princes were "incongruous to the concept and practice of democracy" and necessary steps should be taken to remove them.[19] Subsequently, the high command, incorporating the proposal in a "Resolution for Implementation of Congress Programmes" approved a more comprehensive "Ten-Point Programme"[20] to accelerate the attainment of a socialist society. These stated:

1. Government should take steps to implement social control of banking institutions, and;
2. Nationalize general insurance.
3. Export and import trade should be progressively undertaken through State agencies.
4. A national policy of public distribution of foodgrains particularly to the vulnerable sections of the community should be worked out and the F.C.I. and cooperative agencies should be utilized to the maximum extent.
5. Consumer cooperatives should be organized to cover urban and rural areas for supply of the more essential commodities to the community at fair prices . . . processing and manufacturing in-

---

[15] A full debate on the results of the general election was conducted at the AICC meeting in New Delhi, June 23, 1967. For the proceedings, see *Congress Bulletin*, Nos. 6-7 (June-July 1967), pp. 83-133.

[16] *Ibid.*, p. 87.                    [17] *Ibid.*, p. 94.

[18] *Ibid.*, p. 133.

[19] *Congress Bulletin*, Nos. 4-5 (April-May 1967), p. 37.

[20] The text of the Ten-Point Program is published *ibid.*, pp. 38-39.

dustries in the State and cooperative sector should be established on an extensive scale.

6. The Working Committee welcomes the decision of the Government to implement the Monopolies Commission report[21] and hopes effective steps would be taken to curb monopolies and concentration of economic power.

7. A positive step should be taken towards the provision of minimum needs to the entire community.

8. Limitations of urban income and property.

9. Rural works program to give employment to the landless; improved implementation of land reforms; credit against personal security of assets that are to be created to agricultural laborers; drinking water.

10. The privileges other than privy purses enjoyed by the ex-rulers are incongruous to the concept and practice of democracy. Government should examine it and take steps to remove them.

The Ten-Point Program, apart from the proposal to remove privileges enjoyed by ex-rulers, did no more than reiterate longstanding policies of the Congress party. Nevertheless, the resolution provoked a sharp ideological debate when it was submitted for approval to the AICC on June 23, 1967. K. D. Malaviya, spokesman for the Forum's point of view, revived earlier criticism of the Working Committee's "feeling shy" of the word nationalization when it referred to banks. Efforts to change the wording from a proposal for "social control" to one calling for nationalization of banks were, however, again defeated. But this time, the radicals scored a highly visible victory. Mohan Dharia (then general secretary of the Maharashtra Pradesh Congress Committee and a member of the Congress Forum for Socialist Action) offered an amendment of the resolution demanding abolition of the privy purses as well as the privileges of former princely rulers. The amendment, introduced at the end of the session, when most delegates had already departed, was passed by a vote of seventeen to four. Even so, it automatically became part of the Ten-Point Program, which was adopted by unanimous vote of the AICC. Reaction to the amendment and the way it was passed revealed substantial ideological disarray among the senior

[21] The Monopoly Inquiry Commission was appointed by the government in April 1964 to "enquire into the existence and effect of concentration of economic power in private hands." The report pointed out that the big business houses had important advantages over smaller firms in securing licenses for the establishment of new industries or expansion of existing capacity. The larger business houses were considered more credit-worthy by banks and other financial institutions; they were also the main beneficiaries of the system of controls that restricted freedom of entry into most industries and favored those firms that were already established. See India, *Report of the Monopolies Inquiry Commission*, 1965, Vols. 1 and 2 (Delhi, 1966).

party leaders. Y. B. Chavan and Atulya Ghosh were both pleased. S. K. Patil described the move as "stark madness." Morarji Desai repudiated it as a breach of faith with the princes. Mrs. Gandhi was mainly disturbed at the way in which the resolution was passed.[22]

The party as a whole was rapidly growing more divided. The younger radicals grew insistent on immediate action to implement the Ten-Point Program. Their demands, along with renewed arguments for the complete takeover of the banking system, was urged on the national leadership on the eve of the Jabalpur AICC Session in October 1967. Although the radicals relied on supporters both inside the Cabinet and the Working Committee, they came up in both bodies against the rock-like opposition of Morarji Desai. The deputy prime minister prevailed in winning a commitment from his colleagues to consider bank nationalization only after social control had been given a fair trial for at least two years. In addition, he won an agreement to proceed slowly on the abolition of privy purses through negotiations with former rulers, aimed at reaching a consensual solution.

At Jabalpur, the radicals, dubbed "Young Turks" by the press, greeted these decisions with protests that questioned the government's sincerity in implementing the Ten-Point Program. This time the senior leadership closed ranks. Mrs. Gandhi, urging that nothing should be done to jeopardize Congress unity, extended her support to Morarji Desai. Her lead was followed by Kamaraj, and by Chavan and Jagjivan Ram, the two Cabinet ministers on whose support the Young Turks had counted.[23]

Over the next year, government policy reflected the deputy prime minister's views. Legislation imposing "social control" over commercial banks was passed by the Lok Sabha.[24] General insurance was submitted to similar regulation.[25] Meanwhile, in November 1967, the Cabinet approved the first round of negotiations between the representatives of government and the Concord of Princes.

The party remained sharply divided. After Jabalpur, the Working

---

[22] See Kunhi Krishnan, *Chavan and the Troubled Decade*, pp. 256–59.

[23] For an account of the proceedings at the Jabalpur AICC meeting, see *Congress Bulletin*, No. 10 (October 1967), pp. 203–17.

[24] The scheme for "social control" of commercial banks relied heavily on administrative reforms to reconstitute and diversify the boards of directors of each bank in order to dilute the controlling power of the larger business houses. The plan included provisions for Reserve Bank approval in the appointments of full-time chairmen and the selection of directors from diverse sectors of the economy, ranging from small-scale and medium industries to cooperatives and agriculture. In addition, the banks were to be guided in credit policy by a newly created National Credit Council and by the already nationalized State Bank of India, including targets for opening branches in rural areas and expanding deposits. See *The Statesman*, December 11, 12, 22, 23, 1967.

[25] See *The Statesman*, April 9, 1968.

Committee placed only "explanatory statements" on economic policy before the AICC, rather than risk the divisive debates that would have accompanied voting on a formal resolution. The Congress could not, in fact, agree on any resolution on economic policy for two years, the period between the adoption of the Ten-Point Program in June 1967 and the Bangalore session of the AICC in July 1969, which presaged the split in the party.

The Syndicate, divided on issues of policy, remained welded together by their common aim of curbing the independent power of the prime minister. Although the strain between Kamaraj and Mrs. Gandhi finally resulted, in November 1967, in a decision to elect a new president of the Congress, the Working Committee mandated that the nominee be named as the common choice of Kamaraj and Mrs. Gandhi. The two compromised on S. Nijalingappa, then chief minister of Mysore, a member of the Syndicate, but a politician without any personal animus toward Mrs. Gandhi.

The 1968 Hyderabad session of the AICC revealed a rough balance of power between the followers of the Syndicate on the one hand, and those of the state chief ministers who were generally identified with Mrs. Gandhi on the other. The outcome of the election for the seven elective seats in the twenty-one-member Working Committee indicated that the Syndicate's ability to elect their own supporters was matched by the capacity of Mrs. Gandhi's allies to get elected without Syndicate help. Nijalingappa, in appointing the thirteen nominated members of the Working Committee, preserved roughly the same factional balance. The new Central Parliamentary Board elected by the Working Committee also appeared equally divided between the two groups.

Relationships among the senior leadership remained uneasy. Mrs. Gandhi, hemmed in by Morarji Desai, attempted to maintain a balance in the Cabinet by cultivating the support of lesser leaders. Increasingly, she sought advice from trusted personal advisers, first Dinesh Singh, who was elevated to foreign minister, and then P. N. Haksar, who succeeded L. K. Jha as head of the prime minister's secretariat in early 1968. She appeared, moreover, to condone—through silence—attacks on conservative Syndicate members launched by Congress MPs aligned with the Forum group. Nijalingappa's repeated threats of disciplinary action against the radicals did not elicit any expressions of support. On the contrary, Mrs. Gandhi failed to come to the defense of Morarji Desai when Chandra Shekhar, a prominent Forum MP, impugned the personal integrity of the deputy prime minister on the floor of the Lok Sabha. When evidence for the charges appeared unconvincing, Mrs. Gandhi did not censure Chandra Shekhar, although the Congress parliamentary party authorized her to do so.

Such incidents only increased the personal animosity of some Syndicate members toward Mrs. Gandhi. In addition, the conservatives were
alarmed at the prime minister's growing reliance on P. N. Haksar as a
political adviser. A career civil servant who had held important diplomatic posts in Germany, Eastern Europe, and Great Britain, serving for a
time as secretary in the Ministry of External Affairs, Haksar was known
to be a dedicated socialist. Since his student days, when he participated in
communist labor front organizations and by some accounts became a
member of the CPI, he had believed that social change in India would
require more radical political methods than democratic processes were
likely to allow. Staunch conservatives such as S. K. Patil did not find it
difficult to imagine that Haksar served as a channel of communication
between Moscow and New Delhi, via the Soviet embassy, and actually
passed on directives from the Russians to Mrs. Gandhi.[26] Desai, already
convinced that Mrs. Gandhi was capable of adopting any tactics "which
are necessary to preserve herself in power," also came to credit charges
that the prime minister would "sell India to the Russians."[27]

As early as August 1968, all of these irritants convinced Desai,
Kamaraj, and Patil that Mrs. Gandhi should be removed. Yet they initially met with an unenthusiastic response from Nijalingappa, who was
concerned that the prime minister's enforced resignation would "break
the party and the whole country would be in chaos."[28] The Congress
party president nevertheless grew increasingly alienated by Mrs. Gandhi's failure to consult him or the Working Committee on matters of
government policy, and also by his suspicion that she was keeping for
her own political use funds collected in the name of the party through
Dinesh Singh.[29] By April 1969, Nijalingappa was converted to the view
of other Syndicate members that Mrs. Gandhi did not deserve to continue in office and should be removed.[30] By that time, moreover, both
Kamaraj and S. K. Patil had successfully contested by-elections from
their home states, and were once again in the Lok Sabha, actively asserting their influence within the Congress parliamentry party.

The first public indication that the Syndicate was prepared for a direct
confrontation with Mrs. Gandhi came at the April 25-27 Faridabad
session of the Congress. The struggle inside the top leadership found expression in the Congress president's open challenge to the prime minister's authority in the key area of government economic policy. The substance of the policy disagreement paralleled the ongoing ideological debate between the senior conservative leadership and the younger radicals
among the rank and file, and paved the way for an alliance between Mrs.
Gandhi and the radicals.

[26] Nayar, *India, the Critical Years*, p. 3.
[27] Interview, Morarji Desai, New Delhi, August 2, 1973.
[28] Nayar, *India, the Critical Years*, p. 3. The citation is taken from Nijalingappa's diary.
[29] *Ibid.*, p. 31.                                          [30] *Ibid.*, p. 32.

The Faridabad session was held under circumstances that virtually guaranteed that the process of internal polarization would be accelerated. Publication of the Fourth Plan Draft Outline in March 1969 made it impossible to postpone further a general discussion of the government's economic priorities and approach to development. The Working Committee, meeting on April 25, 1969, decided that the prime minister should present a broad outline of the Fourth Plan to the AICC, followed by a general discussion of "consideration of social, political and economic programs with special reference to the implementation of the Ten Point Program adopted by the A.I.C.C. and approach to the Fourth Plan."[31] The attempt to integrate the two documents was, however, an impossible task. They were the very embodiment of the ideological contradictions immobilizing the party.

The Ten–Point Program was on the face of it designed to accelerate the implementation of policies aimed at achieving a socialist pattern of society. The instruments envisaged for accomplishing this goal all involved greater state regulation and control over key sectors of the economy, as well as measures to curb economic concentration. But the Draft Outline of the Fourth Plan, prepared by the Planning Commission in consultation with the finance ministry, endorsed an entrepreneurial approach that required increased incentives to private investment for those classes of people who already had the capability of responding to "growth opportunities." The strategy explicitly proposed a relaxation of government regulation over the economy, extending to recommendations for almost complete removal of industrial licensing and other controls over the private sector. It also directly recognized that such policies must inevitably increase disparities.

The AICC session was soon paralyzed. Delegates, divided for discussions among three panels on the political situation, party reorganization, and economic policy, were drawn into bitter debate. Only the Panel on the Political Situation could come up with an agreed report for presentation before the AICC. Even that resolution was more an exercise in wish fulfillment than a statement of political reality. Its main burden was to condemn "all attempts at polarization and splitting of the party on the basis of extreme right or left ideologies as a disruptive process that would not only weaken the party but also hinder the political and economic development of the country."[32] The Reorganization Subcommittee's report dealt only with peripheral issues of party reorganization, sidestepping the controversial proposals for creation of a full-time trained cadre. That report was sent back to the PCCs for reconsideration, since "no unanimous opinion could emerge in the Panel discussions."[33] Debate

---

[31] *Congress Bulletin*, Nos. 4–5 (April–May 1969), p. 20.
[32] *Ibid.*, p. 30.                                    [33] *Ibid.*, p. 55.

was most acrimonious in the Economic Panel, chaired by Morarji Desai. This time, demands by Forum leaders for a restatement of economic policy calling for outright nationalization of banks and legislative measures to curb the growth of monopolies was supported by several members of the senior leadership, including Kamaraj, Atulya Ghosh, Sanjiva Reddy, Y. B. Chavan, and Subramaniam. Although the majority attending the meeting also endorsed the recommendation for bank nationalization, Desai as chairman of the panel refused to draft an economic resolution accepting the proposal, on the ground that social control, started only three months previously, had not been given a fair chance. Arguing that the Congress did not function by majority but by consensus, he further ruled that the matter should be decided later on by the high command in New Delhi.[34]

The AICC met in full session on April 27. It unanimously passed the political resolution, the only formal agenda item before it. As previously arranged, the prime minister then addressed the members on basic issues involving the priorities and approach to the Fourth Plan. Asserting that "many countries were trying to influence India" because the nation was not self-sufficient, Mrs. Gandhi went on to identify India's independence in foreign affairs with the development of a strong industrial base, and to declare her conviction that "more and more" investment was required in the public sector.[35] The remarks, which were consistent with her own past statements, and had on other occasions been endorsed by conservative economic advisers such as Asoka Mehta, should normally have passed unnoticed. But Nijalingappa chose that same evening to use his presidential address to the plenary session for a general attack on the inefficiency of the public sector. The unusual intervention, especially under circumstances of sharp ideological cleavage on basic issues of development policy inside the party, was interpreted as support by the Congress president for Morarji Desai and a direct challenge to Mrs. Gandhi's authority as arbiter of the government's economic policy.

Nijalingappa, whose speech otherwise commended the Ten-Point Program, expressed strong doubts about the utility of establishing additional large-scale industrial projects in the public sector. He observed:

> While we should encourage the development of industries, we must see that big industries are not established in the public sector without due regard to demand and the capacity to produce. I am told that some industries in the public sector are so badly managed that the full capacity is not utilized and that they are run on very unscientific methods. The labor employed in some of them is so large that the

[34] This account of the debate in the Economic Panel is based on an interview with C. Subramaniam, New Delhi, August 20, 1973.

[35] *Congress Bulletin*, Nos. 4–5 (April–May 1969), p. 64.

result can only be loss and no profit. I am of the view that the public sector should yield profits. . . . If production of articles in the private sector can be achieved more economically we can even encourage the private sector. There is a case for reviewing the public sector attempt at establishing large scale industries.

There are lots of complaints about the delays in granting licenses, resulting in corruption. Where there are controls and licensing, there is always corruption and the sooner we do away with licensing and controls the better it would be unless there is compelling necessity.[36]

The remarks produced outrage among the radicals in the rank and file. Forum leaders introduced two different amendments to censure Nijalingappa's statements on the public sector, or to delete them from the address. Both were disallowed by the president as improper in asking for a debate on a presidential address. Mrs. Gandhi, however, who talked to the plenary session following the president's speech, was under no procedural constraints. The prime minister, reiterating the need for more and more investment in the public sector to ensure national self-reliance, challenged Nijalingappa's assertions on the shortcomings of the public sector almost point by point. If there was a delay in granting industrial licenses, this was warranted "by the paramountcy of India's political and economic interests." If the public sector failed to make profits, "profit was not the sole motive for organizing this sector of industry." Rather, "the public sector was conceived as the base of Indian industry so that the country might have more machines, more steel. It also ensured India's freedom. It catered to defense and agricultural needs. To the extent India depended on imports, its independence was compromised, encroached upon."[37] The prime minister, for the first time, took a clear public position that appeared to support the Forum group against the senior leadership of the party.

The open antagonism between Mrs. Gandhi and the Syndicate, and the growing identification of the Syndicate with Morarji Desai, provided an opportunity for the radicals to represent the conflict as an ideological struggle in their aim of "purging" the reactionary elements from the party. By 1969, the membership of the Congress Forum for Socialist Action (CFSA) had substantially changed. Only a few veteran Gandhian and socialist Congressmen remained from the Nehru years. They were joined by a younger generation of socialist militants who were impatient at the party's failures to implement economic reforms, and worried

[36] A. M. Zaidi, *The Great Upheaval, '69-'72*, p. 70. Nijalingappa's speech is published in part *ibid.*, pp. 67-71, and in full in *Congress Bulletin*, Nos. 4-5 (April-May 1969), pp. 70-86.

[37] *Congress Bulletin*, Nos. 4-5 (April-May 1969), pp. 65-66. Also Zaidi, *The Great Upheaval*, pp. 71-73.

about the political costs in the growing alienation of youth from Congress. This militant core had been strengthened in 1963 when Asoka Mehta, then a leading figure in the Praja Socialist party, brought a number of his followers back into the Congress.

The most important changes in the composition of the Forum, however, stemmed from another source. Starting in the late 1950s and early 1960s, a small number of socialists and longtime members or sympathizers of the CPI began to seek membership in the Congress party. The move paralleled a reassessment of the weakness of the left relative to Congress, that saw the CPI acknowledge its tactical error in attempting to establish a Government of Democratic Unity as a non-Congress or anti-Congress government. The dominant reality in the Indian situation, the communists conceded, was the influence of the Congress among all classes of people. By December 1964, at the first post-split meeting of the party, the CPI officially recognized the vital role of the "progressive forces inside the Congress" as potential allies in the formation of a National Democratic Front.[38]

The revised tactical line did not, however, convince all communist intellectuals that the party leadership had developed the concrete elements of a new program for collaboration with the progressive forces inside Congress. The dissidents were concerned that the CPI still accepted, in principle, the thesis that conditions in some states might be favorable for formation of a non-Congress united front government. Such an assumption had, in fact, dictated the electoral strategy of the party both in 1962 and 1967.

Unsatisfied critics of the revised party line found a cogent political thesis in the arguments of Mohan Kumaramangalam, whose "A Review of Party Policy since 1947"[39] questioned that the leadership had either completely understood or fully corrected the basic weakness of its approach. According to Kumaramangalam, the national line had to recognize that the large sections of the petty bourgeoisie, the majority of the peasantry and the working class "follow the bourgeois Congress leadership not because they support that leadership's real programme of developing capitalism in India, but because they are supporters of the proclaimed programme of the Congress—the Jaipur, Avadi and Bhubaneswar decisions of the Congress to build 'Socialism.' "[40] Any anti-Congress approach, therefore, only played into the hands of the ex-

[38] See Fic, *Kerala, Yenan of India*, pp. 164–81, for a detailed discussion of the proceedings of the December 1964 Congress.

[39] See Satindra Singh, *Communists in Congress, Kumaramangalam's Thesis*. The thesis was published in full, with an introduction by Singh, a journalist and former member of the Communist party. Singh wrote that he hoped its "exposure" might "help Mrs. Gandhi see the light before it is too late for her as well as for democracy" (p. xxiii).

[40] *Ibid.*, p. 91.

treme anticommunist right inside the Congress, and allowed them to rally the masses against any communist-led movement for national advance. Even in Kerala and West Bengal, where the CPI succeeded in coming to power, Kumaramangalam argued, the replacement of the Congress government by a "democratic" government had ignored the large numbers of the "Congress-minded" masses whose loyalty could still be used by the right-wing leadership of the Congress, both in the states and at the Center, to undermine the stability of the united front regimes.

The more effective tactic, described at length in the thesis, was an approach aimed at building up a powerful movement around the progressive declarations of the Congress itself, and then attacking the extreme right of the leadership for failure to implement the *"programme of the nation* for their betrayal of their own proclaimed programme."[41] Not only would such a tactic enable the communists to unify all the antiimperialist masses until then splintered behind Congress, the CPI, and socialist parties, but it would eliminate lingering doubts about the loyalty of the communists by placing them squarely within the "great traditions of the national liberation movement."[42] Indeed, all of the immediate program of the Communist party was found in one or another of the economic resolutions of the Indian National Congress. The Communist party, therefore, should adopt the approach of being "ready to support the Congress and even to participate in a United Front National Government *if the Congress would implement its own proclaimed policy*."[43]

Kumaramangalam, arguing from this thesis, criticized the CPI leadership for its imprecise definition of the political struggle as between "right reaction" on the one hand and the "democratic forces" on the other. He preferred to characterize the conflict as between "the national forces on the one side and anti-national forces on the other, the national democratic front and the enemies of the nation." Stated in its most basic form, the correct line for the communists to follow was that

> the anti-national forces are anti-national because they stand in the way of the *implementation of the national programme*. In contrast, the national forces are national because they stand for the implementation *of the national programme* developed over the years of the national liberation struggle . . . the attack on the enemies of the national democratic front has to be launched on them as enemies of national progress, of the nation's tradition, of the nation's programme. . . . This correct approach in my opinion, would enable us to ressurect the old fire of the great Indian liberation movement and base our-

[41] *Ibid*., p. 71.                                    [42] *Ibid*., p. 27.
[43] *Ibid*., p. 27. Emphasis in original.

selves squarely in its rich and glorious traditions. . . . Then our immediate demands . . . can be directly related to the national tradition and the national programme. And the attack on the Congress leadership and in particular on the extreme right in that leadership must be for their failure to implement the *programme of the nation*, for the betrayal of their own programme.[44]

The thesis envisaged a two-pronged electoral and extraparliamentary offensive. Electoral campaigns should aim at uniting all the democratic masses around the CPI and those parties, particularly the Congress party, which endorsed the implementation of the national economic program. Extraparliamentary "mass struggles" should be organized to intensify pressure on government for implementation of these demands as the first step toward the creation of National Democracy and development along the noncapitalist path. Over the long term, the communists would replace the Congress party as the dominant element in the National Democratic Front. According to Kumaramangalam, the new tactic would actually enable the working class, led by the party, "increasingly to assume leadership over the very sections of the petty bourgeoisie and the peasantry who are today supporting the Congress leadership because of its 'socialist' policy and aim. . . . And the more powerful and widespread these struggles, the more swiftly the working class and the Communist Party will attain the leadership of the National Democratic Front."[45]

Kumaramangalam's political thesis, presented to the CPI leadership as a confidential document in 1964—and unknown to outsiders until it was "leaked" for publication in 1972—failed to persuade the Politburo to make a complete break with its past oscillations in policy between the old practices and the new line. But it contributed to a curious reprise of the strategy adopted by the CPI in the 1930s, when many of its members joined the socialist wing of the Congress in an attempt to use slogans of left unity for penetrating the nationalist movement and capturing its top policy-making organs. This time, the stratagem was not adopted as a general CPI tactic. Instead, individual communists, including Kumaramangalam, disillusioned with the CPI's anti-Congress electoral strategy in 1962 and again in 1967, allowed their membership in the party to "lapse." They then joined the Congress party. Kumaramangalam, a

[44] *Ibid.*, pp. 70-71. Emphasis in original.
[45] *Ibid.*, p. 90. According to Kumaramangalam, prospects for the success of the tactical line aimed at building the National Democratic Front for implementing the National Program were enhanced by two "positive aspects" in the current situation. The first was improving relations between India and the Soviet Union as Indians "are able to see in concrete action the selfless aid given by the Soviets." The second was the "growth of a radical trend inside the Congress itself which has found expression in pressing forward for a consistent turn to the left in Congress policy." *Ibid.*, p. 83.

prominent laywer in Madras, left the CPI in 1966 at the invitation of Kamaraj to become advocate general of Madras and then chairman of Indian Airlines.[46] Others sought nomination as Congress candidates to the Lok Sabha. In the 1967 election, some—fewer than a dozen—were successful. They continued to adhere to Kumaramangalam's tactical line, with the difference that they intended to pursue the goal of a national democratic front from inside the Congress party.

Such an adaptation of the political thesis required organization of the more radical rank and file inside the Congress for application of pressure on the conservatives among the national leadership, in order to dislodge them from key party posts and force the implementation of the national economic program. The ex-communists, in pursuing this strategy, continued as in the past to look toward the Soviet Union for political support.[47] They maintained their links with Moscow through membership in "front" organizations (such as the Indo-Soviet Cultural Society, the All-India Peace and Solidarity Organization of the World Peace Council, and the Afro-Asian Solidarity Council). They bolstered these ties with periodic trips abroad to Moscow and to international peace conferences, which in the latter 1960s were generally called to protest American policy in Vietnam.

Just as the Congress Socialist party had served as the vehicle for CPI infiltration into Congress during the mid-1930s, the Congress Forum for Socialist Action provided a ready-made instrument for the same purpose during the mid-1960s. Struggling for survival during the conservative post-Nehru years, the Forum's leadership had already hit on the tactic of claiming exclusive ideological inspiration from Nehru's thinking and writing. Between 1962 and 1967 the Forum organization, including the parliamentary, state, and district units, had confined themselves mainly to the discussion of Nehru's ideas. This was also the format followed at the periodic regional conferences and during the all-India meetings of Forum members held at the time of the annual Congress session. The result was that the Congress Forum for Socialist Action (like its predecessor, the Congress Socialist Forum) lapsed into a discussion and study group that was ineffective in mounting pressure on the party leadership for implementation of Congress policies. Under G. L. Nanda's leadership,

---

[46] The 1967 elections resulted in the defeat of the Congress party in Madras and the end of Kumaramangalam's tenure as advocate general, a post-filled by political appointment.

[47] In general, the ex-communists believed that India and the USSR shared a mutual interest in seeing developing countries become strong economically, inasmuch as this weakened the U.S. hold on these economies. By contrast, they considered that the United States was bent on following a global strategy of imperialism that prospered primarily through the cooperation of weak, petty dictatorships.

the organizational side of the Forum was for the most part not well taken care of and as the nation approached the IVth General Elections in January 1967, the Forum was not a really organized force and could not effectively influence either the formulation of far-reaching election policies or selection of Congress candidates. . . . Because of the lack of consolidation of the socialist forces in the Congress, and weakness of the Forum organization, the undesirable trend in the selection of Congress candidates could not be prevented and bossist influence had its sway and very few real socialist minded Congressmen got tickets.[48]

Yet, the Forum had one crucial political asset. Its activities had been explicitly endorsed by Nehru to confer legitimacy on the functioning of a separate socialist group inside the Congress party. Its aim of training party workers to carry out Congress policies had received the public "blessings of Prime Minister Jawaharlal Nehru."[49] It was, for this reason, the natural focus of attempts by the ex-communists to establish legitimate positions of influence inside the Congress party. As in the 1930s, moreover, Congress socialists, whether longtime members or recent recruits, frustrated with the national leadership's failure to implement party promises, lulled by the CPI's "patriotic" response in the wake of the Chinese invasion, and unaware of the political tactic inspired by Kumaramangalam's thesis, once again called for an approach of left unity to strengthen the "progressive forces" inside the country.

The "committed" MPs discovered one another quickly, through mutual friends among journalists and former colleagues in the CPI who had taken the same route earlier. Once the postelection Lok Sabha was called into session, their first step was to open up communications with the ex-PSP group and other radical Congress backbenchers. In May 1967, the two groups joined forces for the first time in the Rajya Sabha debate on the Hazari Report to demand an investigation into the functioning of the industrial licensing system, in the light of data showing a disproportionate number of licenses issued to Birla enterprises. The alliance was fruitful on two counts. It provoked an announcement by the

---

[48] Congress Forum for Socialist Action, *Short History of the Congress Forum for Socialist Action*, p. 8.

[49] *Ibid.*, p. 5. At the time the Forum was organized, Nehru endorsed it as "a good idea" in a letter to G. L. Nanda, and then sent a special message to the inaugural issue of the quarterly journal, "Congress Forum." The message stressed the educational, rather than the organizational, role of the Forum. It asserted: "The Congress Forum for Socialist Action is meant to spread socialistic ideas and outlook among our people. More specifically, it is meant to help the study of various aspects of socialism in order to give intellectual background to our people's thinking." *Ibid.*, p. 6.

minister of industrial development that the government would appoint a three-man Industrial Licensing Policy Inquiry Committee—one member of which was Mohan Kumaramangalam—to investigate the working of the licensing system over the past three years. It also set in motion frequent consultations between the former communists and the socialist backbenchers that led to a common plan for more effective pressure on the party leadership. The strategy decided upon was to "take over" the Congress Forum for Socialist Action in order to consolidate the radical elements inside the party, and weld them into a cohesive organizational force for challenging the control of the conservative leadership.[50]

The apparatus of the Forum under Nanda's guidance was considered hopelessly inadequate. There were no specific criteria of membership. "Opportunists" often joined as long as they perceived some personal advantage of being part of a group close to a powerful Cabinet minister. There were no clear rules for the election of leaders. The parliamentary unit was headed by a steering committee of three or four persons selected by consensus. Nanda himself, more a Gandhian than a socialist, hesitated to risk confrontation with the established state leadership in setting up a separate organizational chain of command. Instead, conveners of Forum units at the state level were appointed by the presidents of the Pradesh Congress Committees.

The plan to "capture" the Socialist Forum was set in motion in August 1967, when Congress radicals convened a national conference in New Delhi on "Principles of Democracy, Socialism, National Integration and a policy of peace and non-alignment which emphasized the basic tenets of Nehru's thought." Simultaneously, a meeting of the Forum was called at which a large number of delegates attending the conference were present. The left elements at that meeting in effect organized a coup. They argued that the Forum had to have proper rules amounting to a constitution, and to have elections to form a leadership. The left infusion at this point was about forty MPs, and they "carried the election and captured the Forum."

The new steering committee, which did not include G. L. Nanda, set out to accomplish a "qualitative transformation" of the Forum. At a general body meeting symbolically scheduled on the occasion of Nehru's birth anniversary on November 14, 1967, the new Scheme was un-

[50] The details of the strategy worked out by party radicals for organizing themselves as a cohesive political group from their vantage point in the Congress Forum for Socialist Action has been constructed from interviews conducted in 1973 in New Delhi with leading members of the CFSA, and supplemented by published materials wherever available. Most of these persons are still active in politics and requested anonymity in freely expressing their views. I have not, therefore, usually attributed specific information to particular individuals in my account of the Forum's activities.

veiled.[51] The organizers, who followed the tactical line earlier sketched out by Kumaramangalam, identified the Forum's objectives entirely with the path of planned development set down by Nehru, especially the "strategy of the creation of a self-generating economy through growth of basic industries and ever-expanding public sector, through land reforms and cooperation, so that after some time the public sector could attain the commanding heights in the economy and lead it towards a socialist society."[52] They took care not to go beyond party policy in protesting the "distortions" in this strategy, calling only for corrections in the process of planned development to restore the people's faith in planned efforts, and to realize the "great objective of building an India of Nehru's dreams."[53] The substance of the immediate steps endorsed by the Forum for these purposes were almost identical to the "national" Ten-Point Program adopted by the Congress, with the exception of demands for outright nationalization of banking, general insurance, and foreign trade.[54]

Major changes were, however, approved in the Forum's organizational Scheme. The new guidelines amounted to plans for establishing a parallel organization at all levels of the party, based on a socialist and cadre-style core of workers responsive to the Forum leadership rather than to the regularly constituted District and Pradesh Party Committees. The suggestion of a parallel party operating inside the national organization was sought to be obscured by semantic devices. The framework for Forum activities was called a Scheme rather than a constitution; the structure of the association was described as its working rules rather than its organization. But the aspiration, if not the reality, was clear.

The "working rules"[55] of the reorganized Congress Forum for Socialist Action envisaged the establishment of Forum units in village, municipal, district, state, and national organs of the Congress party. At the local or village level, at least twenty members had to be enrolled to constitute an active Forum unit having authority to call an annual meeting and elect a convener and local steering committee. Similarly, each district was required to have a minimum of three local units to call an annual district convention and elections for a chairman, conveners, and a district steering committee. As soon as steering committees had been formed in at least one-fifth of the districts of a state, an annual state convention was to be called to elect its own chairman, deputy chairman, conveners, and central steering committee. The district, state, and cen-

---

[51] See Congress Forum for Socialist Action, *Scheme*, published by H. D. Malaviya, Convener, Central Steering Committee.

[52] *Ibid*., p. 8.                                    [53] *Ibid*., p. 12.

[54] *Ibid*., pp. 9-10.                    [55] See Congress Forum for Socialist Action, *Working Rules*.

tral steering committee were to meet at least once in three months and "govern and direct the functioning of the Forum at their respective levels." Every state convention, moreover, was expected to set up a number of subcommittees, including those for women, weaker sections, trade unions, agrarian affairs, youth, and education in order to guide members in attempts to establish Forum units in mass organizations with which they were affiliated. Finally, all Forum members in a state Congress legislative party or the Congress parliamentary party were to organize themselves as the legislative/parliamentary wing of the Forum, and "meet as often as possible to discuss various Legislative measures and steps to be taken by the Forum members in the legislatures."

Important changes were also approved on criteria of membership. All members of the Indian National Congress were eligible for membership in the CFSA, but membership was not automatic. Persons desiring to become Forum members had to apply to the convener of the local steering committee on a prescribed form, which included a declaration signifying commitment to active work on behalf of Forum objectives and programs. They had, in addition, to be recommended by at least two members of the Forum who had already completed two years of membership. All new members, moreover, had to be approved by the central steering committee or an authority appointed by it.

The "working rules" set down for the Forum were at the same time advanced as a model for the "revitalization" of the Congress party consistent with "Nehru's Guide-lines for the Congress."[56] Asserting that the "present method of registering 'Active Members' has proved not only utterly useless, but has also led to organizational decay, corruption and factionalism,"[57] the Forum recommended criteria for party recruitment based on ideological commitment to socialism, active participation in study circles, and seminars on party principles and policies. They stressed, in particular, that party work at the local and district levels should concentrate on preparation and implementation of the Plan, mobilization of popular support for the implementation of Plan programs, organizational work among students, youth, Harijans, women, peasants, and other mass fronts, and training of cadres through study circles.

Despite these ambitious aims, however, the newly elected central steering committee of the Forum was aware of the need to proceed very cautiously. They were, in particular, careful to avoid any appearance of acting as a parallel organization, "because we would have been smashed." They nevertheless began to organize a chain of command out-

<hr>

[56] See Congress Forum for Socialist Action, *Congress Revitalization and Reorganization*, published by H. D. Malaviya, Convener.
[57] *Ibid.*, p. 6.

side the existing leadership of the party. Organization was carried out from the top down. The national conveners of the central steering committee nominated conveners at the state level after consultations with party members known to be sympathetic to Forum aims. State units organized in this way usually produced a nucleus of forty or fifty "friends." State conveners, in turn, traveled to the districts, consulting with sympathetic workers to locate district conveners. After having identified core members informally through such consultations, district and state conferences were called to which all members of the Congress party were invited. The PCC president or secretary, or the chief minister, was asked to address the meeting to "emphasize the impression that this was an all-party group." Forum speakers at such meetings did not go beyond the limits of official party policy in calling for implementation of the national program.

The technique had its advantages, both in attracting support of non-Forum MPs and Congressmen, and neutralizing any complaints by the senior leadership. When, on August 9, 1967, a small group of Forum MPs drafted a memorandum to the Congress president and the prime minister demanding the immediate implementation of the Ten-Point Program, they were able to get the signatures of 118 Congress members of parliament.[58] Indeed, the Ten-Point Program was successfully used by the Forum as "an instrument of struggle" against the senior party leaders. A handful of Forum MPs, taking the program as its platform, toured the country to attack Morarji Desai and other conservative leaders openly for failures in implementation of established party policies. Although the general secretary of the AICC sent a circular to the Pradesh Congress Committees directing that party facilities be denied the touring MPs, they were able to use their own networks in the PCCs and DCCs to publicize their activities in local newspapers. Those who made the tour recalled that "we were well received and aroused enthusiasm with the image that we were the people fighting the vested interests. We were met at railway station stops by very large crowds of people, especially of young people. Our pictures were all over, and we were received as heroes who had prevailed against the reactionary forces in the Working Committee."[59]

The approach also had its limitations, however. Between 1967 and 1969, growth in Forum membership was slow. State conventions normally drew about five hundred persons, and district conventions little more than a hundred. There was, moreover, almost no progress in penetrating the villages. Indeed, after the Jabalpur session of the AICC,

---

[58] For the text of the memorandum, see *Young Indian*, Special Independence Number (New Delhi, 1972), pp. D 139-40.

[59] Interview, Mohan Dharia, New Delhi, July 13, 1973.

when the Forum's offensive on behalf of the immediate implementation
of the Ten-Point Program was turned back by the Working Committee,
its leaders became convinced that a purge of the conservatives from positions of power inside the party was essential for implementation of the
national program. In particular, they found it impossible to overcome
the dominant influence of Morarji Desai and other state bosses on the
delegates of the AICC and the members of the Working Committee.
Yet, as late as the April 1969 Faridabad session, "while the task was clear,
what was not clear was who would undertake this work." In retrospect,
Forum leaders could say with satisfaction and not a little surprise that it
was "a sign of the vitality of the Congress that within a few months the
party discovered in Indira Gandhi a leader with the courage of principles
and the integrity of purpose necessary for fulfilling this task."[60]

Forum MPs, from the beginning, pressed their views on those senior
leaders who appeared sympathetic to arguments that Congress election
losses could only be recouped by closing the gap between policies and
implementation. Chavan, Swaran Singh, Fakhruddin Ali Ahmed, Subramaniam, all were canvassed on the idea that the older reactionary
elements had to be purged from key positions in the party. These arguments were also carried to Mrs. Gandhi by diverse intermediaries, including Subramaniam, Haksar, and Kumaramangalam.

The first sign that Mrs. Gandhi might consider an alignment with the
radicals did not come until April 1968, when at the Faridabad session of
Congress she challenged the criticism of the public sector raised by
Nijalingappa in his presidential address. But her intention was not clear.
It is plausible that the prime minister, sensing the Syndicate's determination to remove her from office, was simply serving notice of the possibility that she could mobilize countervailing support through an alliance
with the left—a step toward transforming the power struggle into an
ideological battle in which the Syndicate, cast as reactionaries, would
have to fight on unfavorable ground. Yet, if this was meant as a warning
signal, it went unheeded.

Only one week after the Faridabad session, the Syndicate found the
opportunity they were seeking. The death of Zakir Husain, president of
India on May 3, 1969, became the occasion for a test of strength between
the two sides as they maneuvered to select the new Congress candidate
for the presidential election scheduled on August 16. Although previous
practice favored the nomination of the vice president as president, and
Vice President V. V. Giri was sworn in as interim president, neither side
was enthusiastic about his continuation in office. Instead, over a period of
weeks, discussions on the party nominee were pursued in the Working

---

[60] *Short History of the Congress Forum for Socialist Action*, p. 23.

Committee and through informal consultations among the senior leadership. A final decision was left for a meeting of the Congress Parliamentary Board scheduled to coincide with the special session of the AICC called at Bangalore on July 10-13, 1969.

The prime minister was noncommittal throughout the party discussions. She did not object when Kamaraj suggested the candidacy of N. Sanjiva Reddy, then speaker in the Lok Sabha. Yet the nomination soon appeared to have an ominous purpose. At the end of June, while on tour in Japan, Mrs. Gandhi received word from two of her personal allies in the Cabinet that the Syndicate was mounting a conspiracy to install Reddy as president, with the purpose of removing her from office and electing Morarji Desai as the next prime minister.[61]

The loyalty of the next president of India to Mrs. Gandhi was in fact critical to her prospects of remaining prime minister. Under the constitution, important formal powers were vested in the office of the president, including the right to appoint the prime minister and the council of ministers, all of whom held office "during the pleasure of the President." The Cabinet, while in office, was, moreover, directed to "aid and advise the President in the exercise of his [executive] functions."[62] Although the president, in practice, had been guided since Independence by the advice of his ministers, there was nothing in the constitution that bound him to do so. If, for example, the Syndicate, controlling large blocs of votes in parliament, and enjoying the refurbished power and prestige of electing their own nominee as president, moved to question the majority of the prime minister in the Lok Sabha, a sympathetic president could direct the government to secure a vote of confidence. He could, in the event that the government failed to command a majority, reject the prime minister's advice to dissolve the Lok Sabha and call new elections. Indeed, he was empowered to invite the dissidents to form a new government and, in effect, thwart any attempt by Mrs. Gandhi to appeal to the country over the heads of the party leadership.

When Mrs. Gandhi returned to India on July 3, one week before the scheduled meeting of the Congress parliamentary party at Bangalore, it seemed certain that the Syndicate's support for Reddy was part of a conspiracy against her. Yet she had neither opposed Reddy's candidacy, nor indicated a preference of her own. The only stratagem at that point for avoiding a defeat that would reinforce rumors of her removal was to postpone the final decision. The prospect that at least this much could be accomplished rested on the possibility of stalemating the Congress Par-

[61] See Kunhi Krishnan, *Chavan and the Troubled Decade*, p. 303.
[62] The powers were conferred by Articles 74 and 75 of the 1950 constitution. Article 53 was the foundation of more sweeping formal powers. It vested "the executive power of the Union" in the president, and also the "supreme command of the Defense Forces of the Union."

liamentary Board by introducing a new name at the last moment that
would automatically find support from the prime minister's allies.
Among these, on the eight-member board, she included Fakhruddin Ali
Ahmed and Jagjivan Ram. She also assumed that Y. B. Chavan, when
pressed, would dissociate himself from the "reactionary" members of
the Syndicate, that is, Nijalingappa, Desai, Patil, and Kamaraj, and protect his progressive image by coming down on her side.

There was also an outside chance of persuading the Syndicate to pull
back from a confrontation. The Bangalore session, in fact, provided an
ideal opportunity for an object lesson in the danger to the party—and the
position of the Syndicate—if the power struggle were converted into an
ideological dispute. Outstanding policy issues that had divided the
Faridabad session were again on the agenda at Bangalore. In particular,
the official economic resolution provided a target for the expression of
bitter controversy inside the party. Senior leaders, intent on avoiding a
divisive political debate, once again closed ranks in support of a bland
statement reiterating previous goals. The draft resolution reaffirmed the
broad objectives of the Bhubaneswar resolution; deplored the problems
of persistent poverty, inequalities, and "different disturbances," pledged
implementation of the Ten-Point Program, and proposed to meet the
minimum needs of all Indians through the spread of "green revolution"
techniques for increasing food output.[63] By contrast, a small Forum
group presented their own "Note on Economic Policies"[64] to the Working Committee as an amendment to the official resolution in a position
paper that called for "a radical change in these [financial and fiscal]
policies" pursued since Independence. They demanded, once again, immediate nationalization of private commercial banks and general insurance companies. This time, however, they did not stop at these immediate aims. On the contrary, they insisted on fundamental changes in
public policy toward the corporate sector that directly challenged the
terms of accommodation worked out between government and the big
business houses.

The Forum's "Note on Economic Policies" drew its inspiration from
the newly published report of the Industrial Licensing Policy Inquiry
Committee. Among the measures endorsed by the report and advanced
by the Forum to limit concentration of economic power were the appointment of a Monopolies Commission to monitor all new applications
by the larger business houses for industrial licenses; a ban on the entry of
larger business houses in new industrial projects involving more than Rs.
1 crore outlay and in consumer goods industries; a ban on intercorporate

---

[63] *Congress Bulletin*, Nos. 6-7 (June-July 1969), p. 15.
[64] The text of the Forum's statement on national economic policies is published in *Young Indian*, Special Independence Number (New Delhi, 1972), pp. D 153-58.

investments and loans to restrict the growth of industrial empires; limitations on the entry of foreign capital to those industrial fields where technical know-how was not available in India; and special efforts to build up a professional management cadre for public-sector projects. The recommendations did not stop at proposals to restrict the *future* expansion of the larger business houses. They also included measures to increase government direction and control over the profits and ownership structure of existing enterprises. These focused on proposals to impose ceilings on perquisites of directors and other senior personnel, and to introduce progressive rates of taxation in the corporate sector, similar to the taxation of personal incomes. The most radical departure from previous policy, however, was the Forum's endorsement for the concept of the "joint sector," an arrangement that appeared to provide an entering wedge for the eventual nationalization of the larger business houses. According to their resolution, "the assistance given to the monopoly Houses by the Government should be converted into equity holdings so that economic advantages of the monopoly Houses were shared by the public financial institutions which have provided most of the project finance to these industrial houses."

The two resolutions reflected in sharp relief the extreme ideological positions increasingly immobilizing the party on issues of economic policy. The first reiterated existing incremental approaches favored by the Syndicate (and the high command); the second advocated a program of radical change in the economic structure. The conflict was in one sense, however, politically opportune. It provided the occasion for an intervention by the prime minister aimed at endorsing some elements of the radicals' program in order to project a populist image in the ongoing battle with the "reactionary" Syndicate for public support. Such a tactic promised an additional advantage. The Forum itself offered an auxiliary political base inside the party in the allegiance of the younger rank and file. Indeed, Forum leaders, assessing the opportunities provided by the power struggle, early concluded that their best tactic was to come down unequivocally on the side of Mrs. Gandhi. Their messages, conveyed to her by diverse intermediaries, had one recurrent theme, that the Forum was a group on whom the prime minister could depend at any point of time for absolute support, and could rely upon in any difficult period. Even more, the Forum stood ready to mobilize support on behalf of Mrs. Gandhi from the wider left outside the Congress through its links with the CPI.

The initial indication that Mrs. Gandhi was considering a de facto alliance with the Forum group in her struggle with the Syndicate came on the first day of the Bangalore session. Indisposed in New Delhi, the prime minister, without warning, sent her own "Note on Economic Policy" to the Working Committee for consideration as an alternative to Subramaniam's draft. Remarking that these were "just some stray thoughts rather hurriedly dictated" after reviewing Subramaniam's suggestions and "glanc[ing] through the Forum M.P.'s 'Note,'" Mrs. Gandhi went on to suggest "full or partial" action on a number of policies that took their inspiration—as well as some of their wording—from the dissidents' proposals.[65] Her detailed suggestions, however, drew on the least radical recommendations in the Forum's program. She endorsed proposals to appoint a monopolies commission; ban the entry of big business in most consumer goods industries; restrict foreign capital to fields in which local know-how was not available; build up a professional management cadre for public-sector projects; reorient the credit policies of public financial institutions to favor new entrepreneurs in less developed regions; and impose a ceiling on unproductive expenditures by private corporations. The political salience of the "Note," however, derived from one other provision. The prime minister, this time breaking ranks with the senior party leadership, indicated she was willing to reopen the issue of bank nationalization. The initiative both served notice that the power struggle could be converted into an ideological confrontation unfavorable to the Syndicate, and left room for a conciliatory outcome. Mrs. Gandhi noted, "There is a great feeling in the country regarding the nationalization of private commercial banks. We had taken a decision at an earlier A.I.C.C. but perhaps we may review it. Either we can consider the nationalization of the top five or six banks or issue directions that the resources of the banks should be reserved to a larger extent for public purposes."[66] The Working Committee—startled at the sudden arrival of the prime minister's "Note" and divided among themselves by the policy issues raised in it—was not, however, disrupted. The ambiguity of the proposal on bank nationalization, as well as the general nature of the other recommendations on industrial policy, provided a path that allowed the Syndicate to steer clear of any traps set for it in exposing their reactionary intentions. The Working Committee, which met on July 11, merely appended a covering resolution to Mrs. Gandhi's "Note" for presentation to the AICC, declaring that, "it sets out the policies to be pursued and steps to be taken for the purpose of improving the performance of our economy in industry and agriculture and at the same time ensure that the process of economic development does not lead to the concentration of wealth and power in a few hands." The high command further called upon the central and state governments "to take the necessary steps to expeditiously implement the various points mentioned

---

[65] The text of the prime minister's note on economic policy is published in Zaidi, *The Great Upheaval*, p. 81.

[66] *Ibid.*, p. 82.

in the note."[67] The next day, on July 12, Morarji Desai introduced the "Resolution on Economic Policy and Program" in the AICC session, affirming that he supported the prime minister's "Note" "without any reservation."[68]

The Syndicate's attention was fixed on something more important, the meeting of the Congress Parliamentary Board directly following the AICC session. They confidently expected to win a majority at the meeting for their selection of Sanjiva Reddy as the Congress candidate in the upcoming presidential election—the first step in their strategy for replacing Mrs. Gandhi. Their calculations proved correct. When the prime minister, just minutes before the meeting, informed Chavan she intended to support the candidacy of Jagjivan Ram in opposition to Sanjeeva Reddy, Chavan told her what the Syndicate already knew, that he had made an earlier commitment to vote for Reddy which at this late hour could not be changed. At the meeting a short while later, when Fakhruddin Ali Ahmed introduced Jagjivan Ram's name, Mrs. Gandhi stood defeated. The vote in favor of Reddy was 4-2, Kamaraj, Patil, Deasi, and Chavan in support; Mrs. Gandhi and Fakhruddin Ali Ahmed opposed. Nijalingappa, as chairman, and Jagjivan Ram both abstained.[69]

Opinion on all sides was unanimous that the decision represented a blow for Mrs. Gandhi which "reopened the whole question of the Prime Minister's position inside the party."[70] Mrs. Gandhi, convinced she had been deliberately outvoted as a challenge to her authority, angrily warned at a press conference that the party bosses would "have to face the consequences." Foreshadowing the strategy of her counterattack, she characterized the board's action in forcing a candidate on her that she opposed as an assault "related to my views and attitudes and my social and foreign policies. When one holds certain views one expects to be attacked."[71]

Between July 12, when Reddy was first nominated by the Congress Paliamentary Board, and August 16, the date of the presidential election, Mrs. Gandhi devised a counterattack that put into action the implied threat of Faridabad and Bangalore of turning the power struggle into an ideological confrontation in an appeal for popular support over the heads of the party leaders. The first round in a political blitzkrieg against the Syndicate was fired only two days after the Bangalore session. On July 16, Mrs. Gandhi summarily relieved Morarji Desai of the finance portfolio, predictably precipitating his resignation as deputy prime minister and departure from the government. On July 21, less than

[67] *Congress Bulletin*, Nos. 6-7 (June-July 1969), p. 20.      [68] *Ibid*., p. 74.
[69] See Kunhi Krishnan, *Chavan and the Troubled Decade*, pp. 307-309.
[70] *The Statesman*, July 13, 1969.      [71] *Ibid*.

forty-eight hours before the Lok Sabha was scheduled to meet, the government announced that fourteen of the largest commerical banks in India (accounting for 56 percent of total deposits and over 52 percent of total credit in the economy) had been nationalized by presidential ordinance.[72]

The ideological tone that subsequently came to characterize the confrontation was established at the outset by the prime minister. Her brief letter of dismissal to Morarji Desai omitted any reference to a power struggle. The note mentioned only the ongoing debate on the policies for socio-economic change necessary to give the poorest sections "a real feeling of hope," and the decision, taken at Bangalore, to "put the responsibility on the Government for the early and effective implementation of the new economic policies" sketched out in the resolution approved by the AICC. The operative part of the letter continued:

> As a disciplined soldier of the party you lent support to the resolution which was adopted, even though I know that in regard to some of the basic issues that arise, you entertain strong reservations and have your own views about the direction as well as the pace of change. You have expressed your views clearly in the Working Committee and on other occasions. I have given deep thought to this matter and feel that in all fairness, I should not burden you with this responsibility in your capacity as Finance Minister, but should take it directly upon myself.[73]

The prime minister's assertion that her differences with the Syndicate had all along centered around issues of social change gained popular credibility from the almost miraculous rapidity with which bank nationalization was accomplished once Desai's tenure as finance minister was ended. The decision to carry out bank nationalization by presidential ordinance with immediate effect had an additional political advantage. It identified a striking "progressive" measure—favored by many other senior leaders—exclusively with the prime minister.

The notion that Mrs. Gandhi was the personal embodiment of a new direction in economic policy aimed at benefitting the poor was meanwhile promoted through large rallies and demonstrations in New Delhi. The young, unemployed, and the most humble of the city's citizens surged toward the prime minister's house in a mood of high excitement. Although the demonstrations were, in part, organized by the CPI, the sentiments they tapped were clearly spontaneous. Ordinary people responded with exhilaration to the explanations of agitators on the meaning of bank nationalization that the money in India's largest commercial banks had now been transferred into their hands.

[72] *The Statesman*, July 22, 1969.          [73] Zaidi, *The Great Upheaval*, pp. 92–93.

Such tactics, however, were resented not only by the Syndicate but other party leaders, who felt robbed of the credit they would have shared if the normal legislative process had been followed. In addition, they stirred apprehension among the noncommunist opposition as the harbinger of "dictatorial trends."[74] Misgivings were reinforced when the government—despite a stay order that set August 12 as the date for hearings on petitions challenging the constitutionality of bank nationalization—rushed to submit legislation replacing the ordinance. Opposition protests at the "indecent haste" with which the presidential ordinance had been promulgated and the new bill introduced had no effect. On the contrary, the speed of the legislative process was accelerated by unprecedented procedural shortcuts.[75] The bill, passed by a voice vote in the Lok Sabha on August 5, 1969—after a walkout by Jan Sangh and Swatantra MPs, who charged the government with "murdering" parliamentary procedure[76]—was signed into law by the acting president on August 10, two days before the Supreme Court's hearings.

The popular outpouring of enthusiasm that followed the promulgation of bank nationalization in itself accelerated the momentum toward political confrontation. The conservative opposition parties were profoundly alarmed at the ability of the prime minister to arouse an apathetic mass public, and her willingness to take politics into the street in a tacit alliance with the CPI. They did not hesitate to label Mrs. Gandhi "a Communist fellow-traveler, who in the company of communists has set her foot on the slippery path to dictatorship."[77] The charges, moreover, were echoed by the prime minister's opponents inside the Congress party, who also accused her of "brinksmanship" in economic policies as a means of winning the power struggle with the Syndicate.[78]

The attacks brought responses in kind from the prime minister. Addressing the rallies that daily gathered before her house, she pointed out the hypocrisy of Congressmen who for years had voted for socialist programs and were now labeling her a dictator "when I am trying to implement these programs." She questioned the credibility of press criticism when a few monied individuals owned the newspapers and they were "able to raise their voice against the common man, against me and

---

[74] *Hindustan Times*, July 26, 1969.

[75] *Ibid*. The Bank Nationalization Bill was introduced within three days of the beginning of the new session of the Lok Sabha. Rules of procedure requiring a notice period of seven days before a bill could be introduced, and another two days of study prior to its consideration, were suspended by the House. The speed of the legislative process was accelerated further by eliminating the normal one-day pause between amendment of a bill and the final reading.

[76] *The Statesman*, August 5, 1969.          [77] *The Statesman*, August 7, 1969.

[78] *The Statesman*, August 13, 1969. This criticism was levied by Asoka Mehta. Mrs. Sucheta Kripalani, among others, also charged that Mrs. Gandhi was "under the influence of Communists and fellow-travelers." *Ibid*.

against the women of this country through their newspapers." As for charges that "I am trying to promote Communism," Mrs. Gandhi asserted, "if I wanted to become a Communist, nothing could have prevented me from doing so. I am all for the Congress and its programs and I have always been in the Congress. It does not sound reasonable to say that by implementation of Congress policies and programs I have become a Communist."[79]

The popularity of such arguments with the mass public led to an immediate tactical victory for the prime minister in her struggle with the Syndicate. The possibility that Y. B. Chavan might yield to growing Syndicate pressures for his resignation from the Cabinet as the first step in splitting the Congress parliamentary party—thereby paving the way for a no-confidence vote against Mrs. Gandhi—was averted. After bank nationalization, Chavan informed Nijalingappa he was not resigning, and "as far as I am concerned, there was absolutely no question of disassociating myself from the bold and dynamic policy of the Prime Minister."[80]

The Syndicate, denied Chavan's support, became more and more vulnerable to charges of reaction and collusion with vested interests. This was, in fact, the tactic ultimately used by Mrs. Gandhi to repudiate Sanjiva Reddy, the presidential candidate endorsed by her own party, and to discredit countercharges that she was working to defeat the Congress nominee from considerations of personal advantage in a power struggle.

On July 22, at Nijalingappa's request, Mrs. Gandhi had signed the nomination papers of Sanjiva Reddy as the Congress candidate. The move was a prelude—in the normal course—to a whip directing Congress MPs and MLAs (members of the electoral college of both houses of parliament and the legislative assemblies of the states), to vote for Reddy as the party's nominee. But Mrs. Gandhi was convinced that if Reddy were elected she would certainly be overthrown. Her advisers, moreover, were persuaded that the prime minister's support for the prinicple of a "free vote" represented the best chance of defeating Reddy in the election.

There was, moreover, an alternative candidate that could be supported with some credibility as the representative of the "progressive forces" in the contest. On July 13, V. V. Giri, the former vice president and acting president, announced his decision to stand for election as president in a statement that criticized the Congress Parliamentary Board for a "partisan approach" in selecting the party's nominee. He explained his step as "a moral struggle against any injustice irrespective of the consequences,

[79] *The Statesman*, August 5, 1969.
[80] Kunhi Krishnan, *Chavan and the Troubled Decade*, p. 314.

necessary to provide an alternative candidate concerned for the good of the nation" and the need to keep the office of the president "scrupulously above party considerations."[81] Giri, a self-described "ardent follower of the Father of the Nation"[82] since 1913 and a trade union organizer, attracted the support of several opposition parties, including important regional groups such as the Akali Dal, DMK, and the Muslim League. The two communists parties, calculating that their best hope of "thwart[ing] the forces of reaction" was to build up political opposition to Reddy, also endorsed Giri's candidacy.[83] CPI leaders, in particular, viewed Giri's victory as essential to prevent "a right reactionary takeover of power at the Center."[84] The Swatantra and Jan Sangh, for their part, contributed to the growing sense of ideological polarization rapidly building up around the rival candidacies of Reddy and Giri by describing the nation as at a "crossroads," involving nothing less than the choice between "a democratic constitution and free way of life and Communism."[85] Although both conservative parties decided to support C. D. Desmukh, a former finance minister, as their official nominee, they did so with the knowledge he had no serious chance of victory. More significant was their decision to cast second-preference votes for Reddy in a contest that most observers expected to be very close.

It was, indeed, Nijalingappa's discussions with Jan Sangh and Swatantra party leaders in the first week of August on the question of such second-preference support for Reddy that provided Mrs. Gandhi's forces with the opportunity they were seeking. Individual MPs associated with the Forum had already sought permission from Nijalingappa to "follow their conscience" in the presidential vote. Yet a large-scale effort to organize Congress MPs and MLAs in favor of Giri, despite formal endorsement by their own party leadership for Reddy, required that leading members of the government known to have the confidence of the prime minister publicly endorse such a demand. On August 9, moreover, Nijalingappa addressed a request to Mrs. Gandhi for "an appeal from you to the Members of the party" on behalf of the Congress nominee.[86] The request, less than one week before the election, underscored the necessity of taking a clear position.

On August 11, at a meeting at the prime minister's house, Jagjivan Ram and Fakhruddin Ali Ahmed drafted the letter to Nijalingappa that prepared the ground for a "free vote." The two ministers informed the Congress president that "considerable confusion exists in the minds of numerous members of our Parliamentary Party regarding the talks that

---

[81] Giri's statement announcing his candidacy is published in Zaidi, *The Great Upheaval*, pp. 89–91.

[82] *Ibid.*, p. 90.

[83] *The Statesman*, July 15, 1969.

[84] *Ibid.*

[85] *The Statesman*, August 7, 1969.

[86] Zaidi, *The Great Upheaval*, p. 122.

you had, on your own initiative, with some leaders of the Jan Sangh and Swatantra Party. It is claimed that as a direct result of your talks, the Jan Sangh Executive decided to extend support to Shri Sanjiva Reddy. What is agitating the minds of members of our Party is the basis on which you could possibly have had these talks. All kinds of ugly rumors are afloat and situation has worsened because those who you have approached have openly demanded the removal of the Prime Minister." The letter ended with the warning of "grave repercussions on the Presidential election" unless the "whole position is fully clarified and the basis of your talks and their readiness to support Shri Sanjeeva Reddy is satisfactorily disclosed."[87]

Nijalingappa's reply that the talks were part of the "usual practice" of approaching all parties and voters for support, "done in the past by all of us including the Prime Minister," was of no avail.[88] Nor were stronger denials in response to subsequent, more accusatory, letters from Ram and Ahmed. The Congress president's characterization of rumors that "I had talked with Jan Sangh and Swatantra for a coalition" as "an unadulterated lie," and his constant reiteration that no negotiations, "covert or overt," for sharing power with the Jan Sangh and Swatantra parties ever occurred[89] were met by replies expressing regret that the basis of the talks with the two parties had not been revealed. According to Ram and Ahmed, it was becoming more difficult than ever "for us to convince our members in Parliament and the State Legislatures that it is not a matter of conscience for them as to how they should vote in the coming election."[90]

On August 13, Mrs. Gandhi finally made her own position public. Referring to "the strong feelings of Congressmen, Members of Parliament as well as Members of State Legislatures, regarding the steps taken to make electoral arrangements with the Jan Sangh and Swatantra party in the forthcoming Presidential election," and expressing "deep anguish" that "our colleagues and leading members should be convinced that attempts are now being made to compromise with political parties totally opposed to our principles and accepted programmes," Mrs. Gandhi informed Nijalingappa that in these circumstances "I do not think . . . it would be right for me to have whips issued."[91] The letter freed Mrs. Gandhi and her supporters to mount a furious campaign on behalf of Giri. The Forum, in particular, became the "storm troopers in the fight against the reactionary forces, the main fighters of the Giri election."

The results, announced on August 20, revealed that Giri had won a narrow victory. Although the outcome was hailed by Mrs. Gandhi's

[87] *Ibid.*, pp. 123-24.                          [88] *Ibid.*, pp. 124-25.
[89] *Ibid.*, p. 126.                               [90] *Ibid.*, p. 127.
[91] *Ibid.*, pp. 132-33.

supporters as a "peoples triumph," the battle for primacy between the prime minister and Syndicate within the ruling party had not yet been won. An analysis of the vote showed that the large majority of Congress MPs and MLAs (estimated at 62 to 65 percent of MPs and 66 to 75 percent of MLAs) had followed the organization's lead in supporting Reddy.[92] It was clear that Giri had won his modest victory with a minority of Congress votes, in combination with those of diverse opposition parties.

After the presidential election, both sides set out to win a decisive test of strength. The intricate maneuvers that characterized the struggle between Mrs. Gandhi and the Syndicate between August and November 1969 were designed not only to achieve a strategic advantage in key party organs, but to demonstrate that the opposing side was to blame for the imminent rupture. On both counts, Mrs. Gandhi and her allies emerged victorious.

The Syndicate found it impossible to counter the prime minister's initial advantage in her identification with the "progressive forces." On August 14, Nijalingappa did serve notice on Mrs. Gandhi (as well as on Jagjivan Ram and Fakhruddin Ali Ahmed) that their conduct during the presidential election was inconsistent with party discipline and would be considered by the Working Committee. But the fact that Giri's election sparked another outpouring of popular support for the prime minister immobilized the party leaders in their plans for disciplinary action. At the Working Committee's meeting on August 25, S. K. Patil, the Syndicate's most conservative member, argued in favor of dropping all charges against the prime minister and her allies. The loss of Chavan's support, he was convinced, had made it impossible to wage a public battle against Mrs. Gandhi on the issues posed by her before the country. The only satisfaction the Syndicate could extract from the prime minister and her supporters was a brief unity resolution conceding "allegations made against the President [of an electoral understanding with the Jan Sangh and Swatantra parties] were on wrong assumptions based on information available at that time and therefore they are untenable."[93]

The struggle subsequently shifted to maneuvers for control of the party machinery. The immediate events leading to the final denouement of a formal split were triggered by the resignation on September 27 of C. Subramaniam as president of the Tamil Nadu Congress Committee after a majority of members (loyal to Kamaraj) presented a petition of no confidence in his leadership. The resignation created an opportunity for the Syndicate to upset the delicate balance of forces inside the Working

[92] *Ibid.*, p. 491. Also see Nayar, *India, the Critical Years*, p. 56.
[93] Zaidi, *The Great Upheaval*, p. 157.

Committee by challenging Subramaniam's right to continue as a member. The ground for questioning Subramaniam's status was that he owed his membership on the AICC—a prerequisite for membership on the Working Committee—to his ex-officio standing as a Pradesh Congress president.

Information passed on to Mrs. Gandhi by Shankar Dayal Sharma, then general secretary of the AICC, that Nijalingappa was preparing such a move spurred an immediate counterattack. On October 9, Mrs. Gandhi and five of her supporters (this time including Chavan) sent a letter to Nijalingappa charging the Congress president with issuing "arbitrary orders" in removing Subramaniam and demanding an early meeting of the Working Committee (by October 15) and of the AICC (by November 17) to "consider the entire political situation."[94] Nijalingappa, who had not actually mailed a dismissal notice to Subramaniam, denied in reply "any action taken by me which need have caused the concern you have shown in your communication."[95] On that account, he informed the prime minister, it was unnecessary to call a meeting of the Working Committee before the regularly scheduled date of November 1.

Mrs. Gandhi's next challenge, however, was more difficult to brush aside. The Congress president, within days, was confronted with a signature campaign among AICC members to requisition a special meeting of the AICC for the purpose of electing a new president. The move aimed to reverse a resolution passed at the Faridabad session extending Nijalingappa's term of office one year beyond December 1969, the date it would otherwise have expired. The reason given was that Nijalingappa had violated the spirit of the unity resolution in moving against Subramaniam, and had exposed the difficulty of implementing declared policies of the Congress "unless the Congress organization as a whole is attuned to this purpose and gives its wholehearted cooperation particularly at its top level." The requisition notice, formally submitted to the Working Committee on October 19, bore the signatures of 405 members of the AICC, indicating a clear majority for Mrs. Gandhi in the larger executive body.[96]

On the day before the scheduled November 1 meeting of the Working Committee, Nijalingappa took the actions that hardened factional cleavages into a party break. He removed both Subramaniam and Fakhruddin Ali Ahmed from membership in the Working Committee. He informed Subramaniam that "you have lost the basic eligibility for being an elected member"; and he indicted Ahmed for "embark[ing] upon a course of action that is calculated to subvert the constitution of the organization, engineer a split in the organization, and disrupt the democratic functioning

[94] *Ibid.*, p. 159.                              [95] *Ibid.*, p. 161.
[96] *Ibid.*, pp. 161–62.

of the organization."[97] On November 1, Nijalingappa further requested the resignation of Shankar Dayal Sharma as general secretary of the AICC, and removed him from membership of the Working Committee for lack of "basic loyalty that the President is entitled to receive from the General Secretary."[98]

The response of Mrs. Gandhi and her allies was not only to boycott the scheduled meeting of the Working Committee, but to set up a parallel Working Committee by calling for a meeting at the same hour in the prime minister's residence. On November 1, the two factions, one headed by Nijalingappa and the other by Mrs. Gandhi, held separate meetings that revealed the Working Committee was almost evenly divided between the two groups. The ten members of the Working Committee meeting under the chairmanship of Mrs. Gandhi assumed executive authority in deciding to convene a meeting of the AICC on November 22 and 23 in New Delhi in response to the requisition notice. The eleven members of the Congress Working Committee meeting under the chairmanship of Nijalingappa rejected the requisition notice as "out of order" on grounds that it amounted to a no-confidence motion against the president that only the plenary session, not the AICC, was competent to consider. At the same time, Nijalingappa served notice on Mrs. Gandhi that only office bearers of the AICC had authority to convene a meeting of the AICC. He characterized the prime minister's action in calling for a special session as "an unpardonable act of gross indiscipline, a flagrant violation of the Constitution of the Congress calculated to disrupt the unity of the organization."[99]

As the conflict reached the point of no return, Mrs. Gandhi, on November 8, circulated a six-page letter[100] to all members of the AICC explaining "the background" of the requisition. She described it as "a crisis building over a long time" that was unrelated to a "mere clash of personalities," a "fight for power," or a "conflict between the Parliamentary and organizational wings." The conflict, according to the prime minister, was between "those who are for Socialism, for change and for the fullest internal democracy and debate in the organization on the one hand, and those who are for the status quo, for conformism and for less than full discussion inside the Congress." The conflict, Mrs. Gandhi continued, was one between "two outlooks and attitudes in regard to the objectives of the Congress and the methods in which the Congress itself should function." It had existed at least since Independence "and even before." It was manifested in the "lip service" paid to Congress ideals of socialism, democracy, secularism, and nonaligment by a group that did

---

[97] *Ibid.*, pp. 177-82.  [98] *Ibid.*, p. 203.
[99] *Ibid.*, pp. 192-93.
[100] The text of Mrs. Gandhi's letter is published in *The Statesman*, November 12, 1969.

CONGRESS SPLIT

not have faith in these objectives, but "knew that if they openly expressed their reservations they would lose the power and influence they had derived from the party." This same group, Mrs. Gandhi asserted, had attacked Nehru's preeminence inside the party during the last years of his leadership. "I know," she stated, that

> this group constantly tried to check and frustrate my father's attempts to bring about far-reaching economic and social changes. . . . In his last years, my father was greatly concerned that the Congress was moving away from the people and that there were people inside the Congress who were offering resistance to change. . . . To consolidate their hold and in the name of discipline they pushed out of the Congress many honest and devoted workers whose loyalty to the organization and its ideals was beyond question . . . the party registers were packed with bogus names. Recently, the tendency to acquire factional control of the organization has become more intense. This is linked up with the desire to control the direction of Government policy and economic life in line with the narrow purposes and interests of a limited section. This is the background of the present crisis.

On November 12, Nijalingappa, speaking for the Working Committee, offered an entirely different interpretation of the political crisis. He insisted that the party split had been created solely by the prime minister's "basic and overriding desire to concentrate all power in her own hands." He then declared that Mrs. Gandhi had been removed from primary membership of the Congress party for "her deliberate act of defiance of the decision of the Working Committee and her actively sponsoring the setting up of a rival Working Committee and a rival AICC and her other attitudes and actions spreading indiscipline in the Congress organization." The Working Committee further declared that "with the removal from membership of the Congress, Smt. Indira Gandhi ceases to be the leader of the Congress Party in Parliament. The Working Committee directs the Congress Party in Parliament to take steps immediately to elect a new leader."[101] This "directive" was followed by sixty Congress members of the Lok Sabha, who met on November 16 and elected Ram Subhag Singh as leader in place of Mrs. Gandhi. The Congress parliamentary party was split.[102]

The requisitioned meeting of the AICC on November 22 and 23 completed the formalities of the final break. The session, with Mrs. Gandhi in the chair, passed resolutions removing Nijalingappa as Congress president, invalidating all disciplinary action previously taken against the prime minister and her supporters, and providing for the election of a

[101] Zaidi, *The Great Upheaval*, pp. 234–38.  [102] *Ibid.*, p. 248.

new president on the basis of present delegates to the plenary session scheduled for the last week of December. The AICC further elected Subramaniam interim president for the intervening five-week period.

Subramaniam's first action was to constitute an Interim Working Committee that would "bring in the younger and radical elements in the Congress and displace the old faces to project a radical new image."[103] The names of those members of the Working Committee who had met at Mrs. Gandhi's residence on November 1 (with the addition of D. P. Mishra) were submitted as the official slate for election by the AICC, thereby giving maximum leverage to the president in the appointment of new members. Of the ten appointees, three, K. R. Ganesh, Chandrajit Yadav, and Nandini Satpathy, belonged to the ex-communist contingent associated with the Forum. Forum leaders, however, were the first to realize the largely symbolic nature of their new status in the party organization. Observing that "groupings in any political party are never fully ideological and the present situation in the Congress is in no way an exception," they asserted, "we must accept the painful reality that many who do not subscribe to the socialist objectives have taken position on our side because of political expediency."[104]

The fact that the Congress split originated in a power struggle during which Mrs. Gandhi's faction made an expedient alliance with party radicals as a means of evoking popular support did not mean that the leadership was able to return to its previous accommodative style. The decisive round in the battle between Mrs. Gandhi's Congress, styled Congress (R) or Requisition, and the Syndicate's party, known as Congress (O) or Organization, was still to come in the confrontation during the national elections scheduled for 1972. The limitations of organizing electoral support through vertical patterns of peasant mobilization—evident as early as 1962—appeared much more severe in the wake of the split, when large numbers of local notables who had served the Congress as "link men" in the constituencies defected to the Congress (O). Despite the substantial majority won by Mrs. Gandhi in the AICC, the Congress (R) had lost about forty percent of its organizational strength compared to that of the undivided party.[105]

[103] Interview, C. Subramaniam, New Delhi, August 20, 1973.

[104] Zaidi, *The Great Upheaval*, p. 257. Their assessment was presented in "Congress M.P.'s Note on Socialist Objectives of the Congress Submitted to the A.I.C.C." at the November 1969 Requisition Meeting. The note was signed by Chandra Shekhar, Mohan Dharia, Krishna Kant, R. K. Sinha, and Chandrajit Yadav.

[105] The AICC session held in Bombay in December 1969 revealed that 423 out of 707 elected members (approximately 60 percent) and 56 out of 95 nominated members (59 percent) holding these positions in the pre-split session at Faridabad had stayed with the Congress (R). Similarly, 2,870 of 4,690 delegates (61 percent) entitled to vote in the plenary session at Faridabad attended the Bombay session. See Zaidi, *The Great Upheaval*.

Support for the Congress (R), moreover, was unevenly distributed among the states. While the party remained more or less intact in Andhra Pradesh, Haryana, Madhya Pradesh, Maharashtra, and Rajasthan, it was virtually decimated in Gujerat (Morarji Desai's home state); it lost three-quarters of the membership in West Bengal; and two-thirds to one-half in Bihar, Kerala, Mysore, Tamil Nadu, and Uttar Pradesh.[106]

The position of the Congress (R) was also considerably weakened in the state legislative assemblies. Except for Assam, Kashmir, Madhya Pradesh, and Punjab, there were defections in all states. In the Syndicate strongholds of Gujerat, Mysore, and Tamil Nadu, the overwhelming majority of MLAs went over to the Congress (O).[107] The biennal election to the Rajya Sabha in March 1970, moreover, exposed a serious erosion of party discipline among Congress (R) MLAs, many of whom engaged in cross-voting to defeat their own party's candidates endorsed by the Central Parliamentary Board.[108] The post-split period, in fact, saw a renewed frenzy of defection politics. Both the Congress (R) and the Congress (O) attempted to compensate for their truncated strength by trying to wean away or regain supporters from the other side, or to arrange alliances with other parties as well as independents. In most cases, the two Congress parties competed for the same MLAs, attracting defectors from each other and from such diverse groups as the Swatantra party, the Akali Dal, BKD, SSP, and independents. The most fierce and prolonged battle occurred in the key state of Uttar Pradesh. There, after renewed and grave violations of democratic, parliamentary, and constitutional norms, the struggle was temporarily decided in favor of a five-party SVD ministry, representing an alliance between the Congress (O), BKD, Jan Sangh, SSP, and Swatantra.[109]

The organizational disarray of both sides made clear that the final (electoral) victory would go to the party capable of rallying public opinion to its side in settling the competing claims of each to be the "real" Congress. There was, therefore, a premium on the use of publicity, propaganda, and simple slogans to arouse emotional support among the mass public.

Each side escalated its charges against the other. The Congress (O), tarred by the Syndicate brush, had little scope—or desire—for invoking popular enthusiasm as the vanguard of the "progressive forces." While it endorsed the undivided party's Ten-Point Program elaborated in June 1967 as its own, this was not the major thrust of its propaganda. Rather, it concentrated on discrediting Mrs. Gandhi personally and the Congress

---

[106] *The Statesman*, November 23, 1969.
[107] Zaidi, *The Great Upheaval*, pp. 465-66.
[108] See *The Statesman*, March 29, March 31, April 3, 1970.
[109] See Kashyap, *The Politics of Power*, pp. 275-304, 653-72.

(R) politically for opportunist policies aimed at winning power, even at the price of destroying India's democratic foundations and her independence of foreign influence.

Nijalingappa, who continued as president of the Congress (O) until December 1970, charged Mrs. Gandhi with using the aura of radicalism to stir up a "politics of mass hysteria." He accused the prime minister of cynical exploitation of government media of communication, and the willful erosion of democratic procedures of functioning in the Congress organization and the Congress parliamentary party, all of which split the party and endangered the country's political stability. In her "urge for total personal power," Nijalingappa charged, the prime minister had not only made parliamentary alliances of convenience with religious and obscurantist elements, but in effect, came close to treason. He asserted, "she has not hesitated to subordinate some of India's policies to the Soviet Union in order to gain for herself the support of the Communists. She has deliberately encouraged former cardholders in the administration and the party and in all her actions she had acted in a partisan manner, where the partisanship has favored those acceptable to the Communists. The softening process that the Communists favor of organizations and administration has been acquiesced in by Smt. Indira Gandhi."[110] All of this, according to Nijalingappa, had been accompanied "by the influx of foreign money and the growing interference of a foreign power in the internal affairs of our country," so much so that India was being reduced to "the position of a Soviet satellite."[111] Such tactics were meant to set the stage for the subversion of democracy. In particular, the Congress (O) warned against a "deliberate attack on the fundamental rights of the citizen to his property which threatens to develop into an attempt to amend the Constitution in a manner that would give the government the right to expropriate arbitrarily even the poor peasant's modest amount of land."[112]

Mrs. Gandhi's allies, for their part, did not hesitate to invoke even more radical rhetoric to rally public support and establish her version of the split as a "conflict between the established and entrenched bosses and the progressive forces."[113] The services of Forum MPs and their supporters were once again enlisted, this time to draft the political resolutions adopted at the AICC and plenary sessions of the party as authoritative statements of the conflict.

The charges against the Syndicate were broadened. They were accused not only of using their position as "bosses" inside the undivided party to

---

[110] Zaidi, *The Great Upheaval*, p. 309.      [111] *Ibid.*, pp. 370, 394.

[112] *Ibid.*, p. 394.

[113] See "Welcome Address of Mr. Fakhruddin Ali Ahmed at the Requisitioned Meeting of A.I.C.C., New Delhi, November 22, 1969," *ibid.*, pp. 266–74.

protect the vested interests by obstructing implementation of progressive policies, but of allying with outside forces of "right reaction and communalism" to defeat the new tendencies toward change inside the Congress. According to the political resolution adopted by the requisitioned AICC meeting at Delhi (November 22-23, 1969),[114] this alliance, pursued secretly at first, was responsible for splitting the party organization and the Congress party in parliament. Subsequently, open attempts were made to form a "grand alliance" of the Syndicate, Jan Sangh, and Swatantra to function as a combined force inside parliament aimed at toppling the Congress government. All of these acts exposed the Congress (O) as "nothing but an ally of the forces of right reaction and communalism." These forces, moreover, were represented as particularly ruthless enemies. Once confronted with the challenge of "change and extinction," they could not afford a posture of magnanimity, but were starting to operate "with all their vigour, using all means at their disposal" to protect their privileges. Their efforts to slow down the rate of social transformation included use of the "monopoly press" to raise the bogey of communism and spread confusion; and appeal to communal emotions to divert attention from basic social tasks; and unspecified collusion in the advancement of "political interests on the national and international plane."

Actually, the political resolutions went further, to attack virtually all opposition groups other than the CPI. The June 1970 AICC session in New Delhi criticized the regional parties because they diluted the unity necessary for carrying out national tasks of social transformation, and castigated the Naxalites—and those in the CPI (Marxists) supporting them—for inciting violence and chaotic action that diverted attention from "constructive" policies. Indeed, the very principle of legitimate opposition was at least implicitly challenged by repeated assertions that "Congress alone" with its heritage and commitment to multiple goals of secularism and socialism could carry out the "historic task" of providing direction to revolutionary processes of social and economic transformation.[115] Even moderates inside the party allowed themselves to imply that opposition to Mrs. Gandhi's leadership was by itself suspect. Subramaniam, in appealing for the support of the Congress rank and file, declared that "the Prime Minister today represents the forces which stand for dynamism in our economic and social policies and programmes, not merely in formation but also in implementation."[116]

[114] The text of the Resolution on Political Situation adopted at the plenary session of the Congress (R) at Bombay, December 28-29, 1969, is published in AICC, *From Bombay to Delhi*, pp. 204-208.

[115] The text of the resolution adopted at the June 1970 AICC session in New Delhi is published in AICC, *From Delhi to Patna* (New Delhi, October 1970), pp. 192-97.

[116] Subramaniam made this remark when, as interim Congress president, he appealed to

Such language, moreover, could not simply be dismissed as rhetorical excess. The Congress (R), as the governing party, enjoyed ready access to the press, and more important, control over the government-owned All-India Radio. After 1969, Marxist polemics were routinely used in the government media by the ruling party to discredit their opposition. The result was that the political idiom was quickly transformed from one of conciliation to one of conflict. Notions that the time had come to "fight a crucial battle against these forces of reaction"[117] blended easily into a new criterion of political morality. "Commitment to socialism" and the advance of the social and economic program adopted in its name became the touchstone for judging the legitimacy of political action by persons and groups. Mrs. Gandhi, dramatizing the ideological dimensions of the conflict, lent her personal authority to the principle that Congress would no longer accommodate all shades of opinion. On the contrary, she asserted, "our doors will be shut to those who are working against our policies, our way of thinking and our ideology. We have to close our door to such forces."[118] Jagjivan Ram, Subramaniam's successor as Congress president in December 1969, welcomed a "polarization of political forces," and went on officially to "invite all progressive forces believing in our ideology to join the organization.[119] After 1969, large numbers of former members of the CPI did respond to this invitation by seeking membership in local units of the Congress party. The split, and its aftermath, opened the way for the socialists and communists who left the Congress in the 1930s and 1940s to reenter the party. It reestablished the left as an important political faction inside the successor Congress (R).

---

Congressmen for support on the eve of the December 1969 plenary session at Bombay. See Zaidi, *The Great Upheaval*, p. 298.

[117] See text of the Resolution on Political and Economic Situation adopted at the Patna AICC Meeting, October 13-14, 1970, published in All-India Congress Committee, *Congress Marches Ahead—III*, p. 147.

[118] See "PM Mrs. Indira Gandhi's Speech at the Requisitioned Meeting of the A.I.C.C. (Extract)," in Zaidi, *The Great Upheaval*, p. 278.

[119] Jagjivan Ram extended the invitation during his presidential address to the plenary session at Bombay, December 28, 1969. *Ibid.*, pp. 331-32.

# ELEVEN

# Reprise: Class Accommodation or Class Struggle?

There is little evidence to suggest that the national leadership initially intended to go beyond the use of Marxist rhetoric of class struggle to discredit the opposition and justify the party conflict as a fight between the "progressive forces" and the "forces of right reaction." They did, however, endorse one major departure from the previous approach to democratic methods of social change. Senior leaders accepted the arguments advanced by socialists inside Congress since 1962 that the tactical separation between an accommodative party ideology and organization aimed at conciliating the propertied classes on the one hand, and economic plans and institutions designed to accomplish social reform on the other, could not be maintained. The gains of political unity and stability earlier ascribed to the approach had been purchased at the price of effective implementation of economic reforms. The continued failure to carry out these programs could only encourage the "extremisms of the left and the right" that had already undermined the previous achievements of political consensus, stability, and order. At the same time, the endorsement of even more radical policies without any ability to implement them risked further damage not only to the credibility of the Congress party, but to the entire democratic political system. The primary need, according to this reasoning, was not for more and more radical pronouncements, but for party organization that could reach down into the villages and among the depressed classes, to involve the peasantry in the implementation of Congress programs.

Despite the intention of the national leadership to relate promises of economic reform to the party's capacity for implementation, pressures exerted by short-run calculations of maintaining political power worked in the opposite direction. The prime minister, in particular, was caught up in a complex set of compulsions. She had, on the one hand, to maintain her personal credibility as a committed socialist against charges of political opportunism advanced by the Congress (O) and other conservative parties. She had, on the other, to neutralize her most potent rivals on the extreme left, the CPI (Marxists) and the Naxalites. Even while containing her opponents on the right and left, she still had to construct an independent base of popular support to establish her paramount position inside the Congress party. On all counts, Mrs. Gandhi was pushed into the continuing use of populist appeals that promised radical social changes without the revolutionary costs of large-scale violence.

The political expediency of following such an approach could, of course, be rationalized. Once established as the preeminent national leader, the prime minister might find it possible to impose the changes in party organization that were necessary to make Congress an effective instrument of social change. The risks of taking such a road, however, were so great as to be virtually overwhelming. There was the pitfall, fully appreciated by the national leadership since the early days of the independence movement, that inflation of radical rhetoric would increase demands on the political system for economic reforms at a rate far exceeding the ability of the leadership to establish effective organizational channels for implementing these claims within the democratic framework. Another danger was perhaps not as well understood. It derived from the deliberate strategy pursued by the Forum to organize support from inside the Congress party, in the name of the socialist ideology endorsed by the prime minister, for adoption of radical policies that could not be carried out within the constitutional framework; and then to use these commitments to challenge the credibility of both the national leadership and the democratic political system.

The prime minister gave little impression of resolving this contradiction between the long-term risks and short-run benefits to be expected from continuing to pursue political power through populist appeals. Instead, she followed an ad hoc approach that aimed at solving the immediate problem of establishing her preeminent personal position as leader of the "progressive forces."

The approach was a gamble that also suited the aspirations of the Forum and the CPI. It cemented the alliance struck on the eve of the Congress split between the prime minister and the CFSA, and opened the way for their entry into key policy-making positions inside the party and the government. The CPI also anticipated tangible benefits from an alignment with the prime minister and her party. At the least, an alliance with the "progressive" section of Congress held out the prospect of neutralizing the CPI (Marxists), their own main rival on the left, in the regional strongholds of Kerala and West Bengal. At best, it promised success for the CPI's strategy of coming to power at the Center as a member of a Congress-led coalition. The main counterpoint of the political struggle in the years immediately following the split was provided by these attempts of Mrs. Gandhi to make use of the support of radical socialists (including the CPI) in containing the Marxists, while establishing her own independent power as popular leader of the progressive forces; and of the left, to exploit the leverage they acquired inside the party as Mrs. Gandhi's most faithful allies for radicalizing Congress policies against which the prime minister's performance would ultimately be measured.

Differences between the national leadership and the socialists inside Congress on the endorsement of radical policy goals and methods surfaced immediately after the split. Economic resolutions adopted by the Working Committee did no more than reiterate the piecemeal reforms of the 1967 Ten-Point Program. By contrast, resolutions ̩assed by the Central Steering Committee and all-India conventions of CFSA advanced measures and programs that added up to a revolutionary change in the foundations of India's economic and political life since Independence.

The two key policy issues that revealed major differences in approach were those relating to nationalization of private business enterprises, and the future of constitutional provisions establishing the right to property as a fundamental right coequal with political freedoms.

During 1969/70, the Forum launched a strenuous attack on the private sector to challenge the legitimate role of the larger business houses in India's economic development. They urged an extensive program of nationalization to generate the vast investment funds required to mount larger public-sector plans. Among the business enterprises and activities targeted for immediate government takeover were foreign trade, general insurance, tea, coffee and rubber plantations, jute mills, cotton textiles, mines and chemicals, and other "core sectors of the economy crucial for earning foreign exchange." They proposed, in addition, that government undertake a "selective" nationalization of nonessential industries to capture the "lucrative heights" in cases where large profits would subsequently become available to the state. Other appropriate areas for state intervention were identified as consumer goods industries and the distribution system. The remaining parts of the economy were earmarked for incremental nationalization. This was to be accomplished through three related techniques: government participation in the management of private-sector enterprises in proportion to its holdings of share capital; the conversion of loans or debentures advanced to the corporate sector by the government or public financial institutions into equity; and pursuit of a "judicious policy" aimed at raising state holdings in the enterprise "so as to reach the commanding position, thus gradually bringing the private enterprise of today under public control."[1]

Government policy during the same period, while "radical" when judged against the liberal economic measures inherited from the Shastri years, fell far short of the Forum's program. Starting toward the end of

[1] Congress Forum for Socialist Action, *Two Years of CFSA, Decisions and Resolutions*, pp. 27-31.

1969, and continuing through the next year, several new measures were adopted to prevent further concentration of economic power in the hands of the larger industrial houses. Legislation was passed, with effect from April 1970, to abolish the managing agency system. New government orders issued by the Company Law Department also prohibited individuals from holding the managing directorship of more than one company; made future appointment of paid directors subject to approval by the Company Law Board; and reduced the maximum salaries, allowances, and other perquisites that could be paid to company directors and managers.

The most far-reaching changes arose from government's efforts to implement selected recommendations of the 1969 report of the Industrial Licensing Policy Inquiry Committee. The new licensing policy, announced in February 1970,[2] entirely reversed the trend toward decontrol started in the mid-1960s and endorsed by the Planning Commission in the Draft Outline of the Fourth Plan. All previous exemptions (of forty-one industries) from licensing requirements were withdrawn, so that applications from the larger business houses for new undertakings or substantial expansion might be specially screened. The government proposed to apply specific restrictions on companies belonging to the "larger industrial houses,"[3] "dominant undertakings,"[4] and to foreign firms and their subsidiaries. Undertakings belonging to any of these groups were normally to be confined in their new investments to participation in the "heavy investment sector." This included the list of "core" industries drawn up by the Planning Commission to identify "basic, critical and strategic industries" for which detailed industrial plans were still prepared, as well as new investment proposals involving outlays of Rs. 5 crores or more. The government, in addition, accepted the concept of the joint sector "in principle" for application to the heavy investment sector. Public financial institutions providing "substantial" assistance for

[2] The government's new industrial licensing policy was distributed as a press note, "Industrial Licensing Policy, Government's Decisions," dated February 18, 1970, in the form of background for the press, mimeographed. The basic features of the licensing policy are summarized in Planning Commission, *Fourth Five Year Plan, 1969-74* (July 1970), pp. 307-309.

[3] The Industrial Licensing Policy Inquiry Committee defined "large industrial house" to include "those business concerns over which a common authority holds sway," and which in 1964 owned assets in the aggregate of more than Rs. 5 crores; large independent companies with assets above Rs. 5 crores; and foreign-owned and controlled companies, including Indian subsidiaries and branches of foreign companies. The criteria used to determine the composition of a Large Industrial House and a list of the seventy-three Large Industrial Houses identified by the committee are presented in Department of Industrial Development, *Report of the Industrial Licensing Policy Inquiry Committee (Main Report)*, pp. 11-20.

[4] A "dominant undertaking" as defined in the Monopolies and Restrictive Trade Practices Act, 1969 is an undertaking which by itself or along with interconnected undertakings produces, supplies, distributes, or otherwise controls at least one-third of the total goods and services of any description produced, supplied, distributed, or rendered in India. *The Monopolies and Restrictive Trade Practices Act, 1969* (Allahabad, 1973), p. 1.

major projects were directed to insert conversion clauses into loan agreements, allowing them to exercise an option of converting loans and debentures either wholly or partly into equity within a specified period of time. Starting in August 1970, the government also decided to take over voting rights of shares pledged to public financial institutions for the purpose of securing loans, and to appoint representatives to the boards of directors of such companies.

There were other regulations. All undertakings with total assets of Rs. 20 crores or more had to register with the newly established Ministry of Company Affairs, and in making applications for expansion satisfy the requirements of the new Monopolies and Restrictive Trade Practices Act that "the proposed expansion or the scheme of finance with regard to such expansion is not likely to lead to the concentration of economic power to the common detriment or is not likely to be prejudicial to the public interest in any other manner."[5] The act, which was expected to affect the future applications of about 1,200 companies,[6] set up a Monopolies and Restrictive Trade Practices Commission appointed by the central government to advise the Ministry of Industrial Development on questionable applications.

The new bureaucratic apparatus for the control of the private sector was, in fact, formidable. Applications for licenses by larger industrial houses and foreign firms had to pass through multiple checkpoints on a long journey toward clearance. An interministerial licensing committee, with members of all concerned ministries, including industrial development, company affairs, finance, and the Planning Commission had to be satisfied before any application could be forwarded to the Ministry of Industrial Development for final approval. Those applications that were considered problematical, moreover, could be referred for advice to the Monopolies Commission and/or to the Economic Affairs Committee of the Cabinet, a procedure that in the last analysis required the larger business houses to get personal approval of the prime minister and her closest advisers for new ventures.

Yet the intent of the new licensing policies, for all their complicated regulations and procedures, was still ambiguous. Leading members of the business community were predictably opposed to the measures as a major reversal of the gains made since 1966. Some saw in them the entering wedge in the progressive government takeover of ownership and control of private-sector companies. Congress radicals, by contrast, were suspicious that the government was not serious in seeking fundamental reform. The measures did not directly advance their aims of nationalization. At best, the new industrial licensing policy made it possible to convert *future* loans to private enterprise into equity. Meanwhile, it

---

[5] *Ibid.*, p. 10.                                    [6] *The Statesman*, August 14, 1970.

appeared to endorse a premise that was antithetical to nationalization, namely that only the larger business houses had sufficient resources to invest in major projects. Indeed, the scheme did not impose an outright ban on investments by the big houses in any area of the economy (save those industries already reserved for the public sector). On the contrary, it seemed to encourage economic concentration by directing larger firms to invest in massive projects involving outlays of Rs. 5 crores or more.

This latter interpretation was buttressed after publication of the final version of the Fourth Plan in July 1970. Public-sector outlay—even taking into account the improved prospect for mobilizing additional savings after bank nationalization—showed only a modest increase from Rs. 14,398 crores provided in the March 1969 Draft Outline to Rs. 15,902 crores in the final Fourth Plan. The total amount was roughly the same as originally projected in the 1966 Fourth Plan Draft Outline, without any adjustment for inflation. Public outlay in organized industry and mining was similarly increased by a small amount, from about Rs. 2,800 crores to Rs. 3,048 crores. The major proportion of this outlay, as before, was earmarked for projects already under implementation, with scope for new schemes only in a few high-priority fields. The estimate of investment outlay in the private sector of Rs. 2,250 crores—a moderate reduction from the 1969 target of Rs. 2,400 crores—still represented a "considerable step-up over current levels" and about twice the Third Plan private investment program.[7] The revised figures, in fact, did little more than accomplish the public relations goal of demonstrating an apparent gain in the public sector's share of new industrial investment now accounting for about sixty percent, "which is broadly in line with the proportion of investment between the public sector and the private sector envisaged in the Third Plan."[8]

A more striking difference between the Congress leadership and the CFSA surfaced in respect to the key issue of constitutional change raised by obstacles to economic and social reform in existing provisions that protected the right to property as a fundamental right. The original provisions required government to pay compensation for all property taken possession of or acquired in the public interest, and allowed individuals to challenge compensation awards in the courts as inadequate or in violation of the right to equal protection under the law.

During the 1950s, such comprehensive guarantees were modified by constitutional amendments enacted primarily to protect the zamindari abolition and land ceiling laws. The First Amendment (1951) specifically removed existing zamindari abolition laws from the protection of the

---

[7] Planning Commission, *Fourth Five Year Plan, 1969-74* (July 1970), p. 316.
[8] *Ibid.*, p. 314.

fundamental rights section of the constitution. The Fourth Amendment (1954) was more far-reaching. It qualified an individual's right to compensation in cases of compulsory acquisition of private property by providing that "no such law shall be called into question in any court on the ground that the compensation provided by that law is not adequate." Nevertheless, after Nehru's death, conservative elements inside the Congress party succeeded in reversing the earlier trend. The Seventeenth Amendment (1964) was specifically aimed at impeding the implementation of a substantial land redistribution program. Although it allowed existing land ceiling laws to stand, it provided that in all future land reform acts, cultivating owners of land would be entitled to compensation for loss of land or any rights therein on the basis of full market value. Then, in 1967, the Supreme Court by a narrow majority of six to five delivered a stunning ruling in the Golak Nath case,[9] which reversed the entire direction of constitutional development since 1950. The court asserted, in effect, that fundamental rights were part of the basic structure of the constitution, and could not be amended under the ordinary amendatory process provided in Article 368.[10] According to the majority opinion, fundamental rights could be abridged or taken away only by convocation of another Constituent Assembly. Invoking the doctrine of "prospective overruling," the court allowed the earlier amendments to the property right to stand, but ruled that in the future parliament would have no power to amend, abridge, or take away any fundamental rights.

The dilemma created by the Supreme Court's judgment in the Golak Nath case was an acute one. The reinstatement of virtually an absolute right to property proved a major bottleneck in the government's ability to carry out even piecemeal economic and social reforms to which it had already committed much of its prestige. On February 10, 1970, the Supreme Court, acting on writ petitions challenging the validity of bank nationalization, ruled (this time by an overwhelming majority of ten to one) that the Banking Companies (Acquisition and Transfer of Undertakings) Act of 1969 was in violation of fundamental rights under the constitution. The court's judgment[11] asserted that shareholders in the nationalized banks had been deprived of guarantees under Article 14 for equality before the law and equal protection of the law by "hostile discrimination" against the fourteen named banks prohibited from carrying

[9] The Supreme Court's judgment on the Golak Nath case is published in P. L. Lakhanpal, ed., *Two Historic Judgments*, Part I, pp. 13–150.

[10] The amendment procedure provided in Article 368 of the constitution required introduction of a bill for the purpose of constitutional amendment in either house of parliament and passage in each house of the bill by majority of the total membership of that house and by a majority of not less than two-thirds of those present and voting. Once the bill was passed it was presented to the president for his assent, and after his signature the constitution stood amended.

[11] See Lakhanpal, *Two Historic Judgments*, Part II, pp. 33–112.

out banking business in the absence of any explanation of their special selection. Further, and more far-reaching in its implications, the court asserted that guarantees under Article 31(2) for payment of compensation had been impaired on two grounds: (a) the principles provided by the act to determine the amount of compensation awarded to shareholders were not "appropriate to the determination of compensation for the particular class of property sought to be acquired";[12] and (b) although any one of a number of principles might actually be relevant, the overriding criteria was that the principle selected must satisfy the "basic guarantee" of the constitution for compensation as "an equivalent in money of the property compulsorily acquired."[13] Otherwise, the expropriated owner could challenge the award in the courts.

Although the government was able to meet the Supreme Court's particular objections to the existing legislation by drafting a new ordinance and Bank Nationalization Bill (passed during the March 1970 Budget Session of the Lok Sabha), the ruling represented a major obstacle to further nationalization. It reopened the entire question of an individual's right to "adequate" compensation, declared nonjusticiable by the Fourth Amendment, and imposed prohibitive financial obligations on the state in future plans for acquiring large properties and enterprises.

The government experienced an even greater setback as the result of Supreme Court rulings under fundamental rights provisions in its efforts to abolish the privy purses and privileges of the ex-princely rulers. Legislation to terminate the privy purses and privileges of the former rulers of the Indian States was voted in the Lok Sabha on September 2, 1970, winning the requisite two-thirds majority of members voting and present for a constitutional amendment. Three days later, on September 5, the bill was defeated in the Rajya Sabha (the upper house), when it failed by one-third of one vote to win a two-thirds majority. The defeat, in itself, was a serious blow to the government's already shaky position. The Cabinet, meeting the same evening in emergency session, resorted to an unprecedented use of executive power "as the only possible way out for us"[14] in avoiding the demoralization of the ruling party and the government. They approved a recommendation to the president of India advising him to issue an order "derecognizing" the princes with immediate effect. The government asserted that it was competent to abolish the privy purses and privileges of the ex-rulers without constitutional amendment on several counts: the rights of ex-rulers to receive privy purses and privileges were derived from political agreements or "covenants" entered into by each ruler of an Indian State and the Government of India at the time of Independence; these rights were nonjusticiable in-

---

[12] *Ibid.*, p. 98.                          [13] *Ibid.*, p. 108.

[14] This account of the Cabinet's decision was related by Y. B. Chavan, then finance minister, to his biographer. See Kunhi Krishnan, *Chavan and the Troubled Decade*, p. 271.

asmuch as Article 363(1) of the constitution specifically removed disputes arising from such covenants from the jurisdiction of the Supreme Court; and the president as "a matter of State policy" was competent to pass a derecognition order under the provisions of Article 366(22) of the constitution, which specified that the successor of the ruler who signed such a covenant was only that person "who for the time being is recognized by the President as the Ruler of the State."[15]

The outcome was predictable. The Supreme Court, on December 15, 1970, ruling on petitions brought by the princes, declared the presidential order withdrawing recognition of the princes unconstitutional and invalid. According to the majority, "an order merely derecognizing a ruler without providing for continuation of rulership which is an integral part of the Constitutional scheme is plainly illegal."[16] The court, in addition, ruled that the princes derived their rights to privy purses and other privileges not from the original covenants of accession barred from judicial review, but under separate provisions (in Articles 291 and 362),[17] which independently accepted the obligations of government to pay privy purses and recognize other personal rights and dignities guaranteed under separate legislation. The court did not stop there. It ruled that the princes' right to privy purses must be construed as a right to "property" within the meaning of the constitution, and was fully protected by the articles on fundamental rights.

The verdict appeared to make inevitable some form of confrontation between the Supreme Court and the parliament over legislative powers to amend fundamental rights as the condition for even moderate social reforms. The prime minister, in reacting to the ruling, limited her statement to general assurances that government would abide by the judgment, but seek to abolish privy purses by "appropriate constitutional means."[18] The Congress party as a whole maintained a studied vagueness in endorsing the need for such "constitutional remedies and

[15] The government's case was argued before the Supreme Court in response to challenges by the princes, and is summarized in press reports of the proceedings. See *The Statesman*, December 16, 1970.

[16] *Ibid*.

[17] According to Article 291, "Where under any covenant or agreement entered into by the Ruler of any Indian State before the commencement of this Constitution, the payment of any sums, free of tax, has been guaranteed or assured by the Government of the Dominion of India to any Ruler of such State as privy purse—(a) such sums shall be charged on, and paid out of, the Consolidated Fund of India; and (b) the sums so paid to any Ruler shall be exempt from all taxes on income." Article 362 further provides, "In the exercise of the power of Parliament or of the Legislature of a State to make laws or in the exercise of the executive power of the Union or of a State, due regard shall be had to the guarantee of assurance given under any such covenant or agreement as is referred to in Article 291 with respect to personal rights, privileges and dignities of the Ruler of an Indian State." See V. N. Shukla, *The Constitution of India*, 4th edition (Delhi, 1963), pp. 412, 492.

[18] *The Statesman*, December 16, 1970.

amendments as are necessary to overcome the impediments in the path of social justice."[19] The CFSA, by contrast, responded to the court's decision with the demand for comprehensive constitutional revisions to amend the amending process of the constitution and take away the right to property as a fundamental right. They insisted that a new Constituent Assembly must be convened for the purpose of "drastically" revising the existing constitution, so that "a second Republic, a Democratic Socialist Republic of India, a Republic with live, vital, responsible democratic institutions be set up." They urged government to call a new election to seek a mandate for "bringing about fundamental social changes," including the convening of a Constituent Assembly. They further endorsed, albeit indirectly, the formation of a National Democratic Front on the ground that "the challenge of consolidated right reaction cannot be met by Congress alone." The Forum argued: "The Congress must invite and join hands with all other progressive, democratic, socialist parties and forces in order to unleash a mighty movement of the people which alone can foil the conspiracies of right reaction. The members of the CFSA must take necessary initiative in the direction of consolidating all the democratic socialist forces against the right reaction."[20]

The members of the Forum who pressed their recommendations for comprehensive constitutional changes on the national leadership were met with restatements of the Congress party's commitment to democracy. In reply to party radicals who urged, among other measures, restrictions on communal political parties and government curbs on the press to remove important obstacles to more rapid economic reform, Mrs. Gandhi rejected any shortcuts that bypassed democratic processes. She asserted:

> We cannot proceed very much for the time perhaps and go faster than we are going; but we cannot go very much faster without changing the whole system. And it is up to us to weigh whether the price of changing the system will not ultimately come to the same cost, the same as slightly slower progress along the path of democracy.
>
> I believe there is no short-cut. The only sure real short-cut is more efficient functioning, a clear cut path, a clear cut ideology, a programme and more speedy and effective functioning to implement it. That is the only short-cut. But there is no short-cut of bypassing democracy. And what is especially sad and dangerous is that we, many of us, use the word democracy in order to try and defeat de-

[19] Indian National Congress, *Election Manifesto 1972/1971* (New Delhi, 1972), pp. 5-6.
[20] *Two Years of CFSA, Decisions & Resolutions*, p. 33.

mocracy, to weaken democracy. And here again, it is on both sides, it is in the name of economic betterment and many other names.

. . . It is not just one or two parties that can be considered opposed to democracy. Anybody who believes that any one section of the people does not have the right that other people have, they are undemocratic. It does not matter by what name they go. I am not against one party or another. I am against certain attitude of mind, certain methods of functioning. If the communists use them, I am against them, if the Congress uses them, I am afraid I am against those Congressmen also.[21]

Jagjivan Ram, then Congress party president, also insisted that the lesson of past failures to carry out socialist policies was not, as the radicals suggested, to restrict democracy, but on the contrary to expand it. He urged that "the Scheduled Castes, Scheduled Tribes, other backward classes and all the minorities should be drawn in larger numbers into the Congress and involved directly in its activities. A sense of participation in the decision-making bodies at all levels should be ensured to them."[22] Expanded participation, moreover, had to be accompanied by "culturalization."[23] It was not enough to politicize larger and larger numbers of people when the end result was to strengthen the desire of each segment to maintain or secure new benefits for its own narrow group in the access to political power. Instead, participation had to be organized around common economic and social interests, crosscutting traditional caste lines. The first prerequisite was for Congressmen themselves to have a clear ideology and program and a genuine commitment to the party's principles of democracy, socialism, and secularism. The party organization itself had to be reshaped to carry out the new goals.

Plans to "reorganize and revitalize" the party were drafted as early as January 1970. The Congress Working Committee, endorsing the goal of making the organization a "suitable instrument for social transformation," announced a number of steps aimed at "building cadres at all levels of the Organization."[24] They included directives for the reorganization of the AICC office into advisory committees and cells to look after the special problems of minorities, scheduled castes, backward classes, and labor; to publish official weeklies in Hindi and English, and literature on Congress ideology and programs. In addition, a new AICC Committee for Cadre Building and Training Program was created with the mandate to draft detailed plans for the organization of seminars, meetings, and camps at which district and state party workers would be trained to ex-

[21] AICC, *From Delhi to Patna*, pp. 148-49.
[22] AICC, *From Bombay to Delhi*, p. 199.
[23] *Ibid.*, p. 198.                          [24] *Ibid.*, pp. 9-13.

plain party programs as part of a movement of mass contact in villages throughout the country. The Pradesh Congress Committees were similarly directed to follow the new organizational pattern in reconstructing state and district level party units. The Working Committee also authorized the appointment of central advisory committees for organization or reactivation of a number of mass fronts including, most urgently, the Youth Congress.

Such plans for party building could only be carried out over a long period of time. They contrasted sharply with the continuing disarray of state and district units. During the period immediately after the split, the Working Committee had to improvise—extending the term of office of all Congress committees and office bearers by one year, authorizing PCCs to fill "vacancies" from among their own members, and instructing the Congress president to appoint ad hoc Pradesh Congress Committees wherever necessary. Subramaniam, then interim president, did try to select state conveners, that is, de facto presidents of the ad hoc Pradesh Congress Committees, who were "personally known as sympathetic to Congress policies." Even so, he was guided by the "consensus" of the state leadership in appointing the full executive committee.[25] In practice, moreover, the membership of the ad hoc committees were drawn exclusively from among PCC members who had attended the requisition AICC or the plenary Bombay session in 1969. Such Congressmen were by definition accepted as "committed" party workers dedicated to progressive policies. Six months later, Jagjivan Ram had to report to the AICC that in several states "it has not been possible yet to constitute Congress Committees at various levels." The new party machinery, moreover, was functioning in the old way. According to Ram, "in certain areas, in some places, efforts are being made to see that Congress Committees are so constituted that some persons and some leaders keep their control over them. Elements which may be more useful, more dynamic, more energetic, but which are not likely to be under the thumb of a set of persons are not readily admitted to the Congress."[26]

Indeed, the drive for enrollment of new members started in the early months of 1970, although ostensibly following central directives to focus on agricultural laborers, scheduled castes, scheduled tribes, students, youth, minorities, and women, did little to solve the longstanding problem of bogus membership. Pending revision of the Congress constitution, there was still a premium on enrolling fictitious persons with the object of voting large blocs of names in election to local committees, which in turn selected the more powerful District and Pradesh Congress Committees. Even then, the local party organizations were so disrupted

[25] Interview, C. Subramaniam, New Delhi, August 20, 1973.
[26] AICC, *From Delhi to Patna*, pp. 84–90.

that as late as mid–December 1970, "a number of P.C.C.'s has not even sent membership figures," fees, or delimitations of delegate constituencies to the AICC office. As a result, the Working Committee felt compelled to postpone for "an indefinite period" the organizational elections scheduled at the end of December, and to cancel the plenary session of Congress in 1971.[27]

Constitutional constraints and the limitations of weak party organization meant that radical economic reforms could not be implemented. Yet the upsurge of mass enthusiasm for Mrs. Gandhi's leadership rested precisely on evocation of hopes by slogans of socialist rhetoric for redistributive policies extending to basic structural change. Despite the reluctance to make promises of radical reform that could raise expectations beyond the capacity of the Congress party and government to satisfy, the immediate problem of maintaining political credibility placed an even greater premium on the use of ideological appeals. Over the short term, such tactics helped to solve Mrs. Gandhi's most pressing problems. These included the need to maintain her personal image of commitment to socialism; attribute slow progress to opposition by vested interests grouped in the Congress (O) and other reactionary parties, and make credible her promises to carry out radical changes through peaceful and parliamentary means once the vested interests were defeated.

The prime minister's need to establish her socialist commitment found expression in a closer association with the Forum group inside the Congress party. Within the Forum, moreover, Mrs. Gandhi tended to gravitate toward the ex-communist faction, partly in response to their own posture of absolute support for her leadership. Less interested in the immediate implementation of socialist economic reforms than in securing influential political posts inside the government and party, they fully reciprocated Mrs. Gandhi's concern that committed Congressmen maintain a posture of complete loyalty to the prime minister. Their policy of being "absolutely, fanatically loyal to Mrs. Gandhi"[28] was rewarded. Noncommunist socialists inside Congress (many of whom did not hesitate to launch public attacks on the government's failure to implement even the modest Ten-Point Program) were often passed over in favor of their ex-communist colleagues in appointments to key Congress committees and senior posts inside the government.

Considerations of political expediency were also an important factor in

[27] AICC, *Congress Marches Ahead—III*, pp. 133-34.
[28] The account of the Forum's strategy for advancing their influence inside the Congress party in the period following the split draws on interviews conducted in 1973, supplemented by published material wherever available. Although I occasionally use direct quotations as indicated in the text, the individual source has not been named since many of those persons interviewed are still active in politics.

a closer alignment between the Congress (R) and the CPI. The possibility of an electoral understanding between the two parties held out the
prospect of important political benefits to both sides. The most serious
challenge to the Congress by an organized opposition group had been
mounted by the party that was also the most formidable rival of the CPI
for leadership of the left, the more radical CPI (Marxists). The Marxists
had handed both parties significant setbacks. Marxist-led anti-Congress
united front electoral alliances had already displaced Congress as the
dominant party in two states, Kerala and West Bengal, and brought
Marxist-dominated united front governments to power. Once in power,
moreover, the Marxists had not hesitated to neutralize the police and use
control of key portfolios to increase their own influence at the expense of
coalition partners, including the CPI. Marxist-led land grab movements
and industrial strikes in both states paralyzed production and created
law-and-order problems of serious concern to the central government,
even while they established the CPI (Marxists) relative to the CPI as the
dominant leader of the left.

Yet, for all of this, the effectiveness of the Marxists, both as an electoral force and after coming to power, depended in large measure on the
margin of support provided by the CPI. In both Kerala and West Bengal,
the Marxists were able to put together a parliamentary majority and to
maintain their narrow margin only with the cooperation of the CPI and
its allies. If communist support were withdrawn and/or transferred to the
Congress (R), the challenge of the Marxists might be neutralized. Congress, as the single largest party in both states, could expect to regain its
dominant role. At the same time, the CPI could claim a share of power in
a political coalition that excluded the Marxists from all governmental
posts and prevented them from using official levers to advance their
power.

A test case of the utility of an alignment to both parties occurred during the Kerala mid-term election of June 1970, the first statewide poll to
be called in the aftermath of the Congress split. The uneasy alliance between the CPI(M) and the CPI in the Marxist-dominated united front
government had broken down months earlier, when the communists
joined an anti-Marxist grouping inside the ruling coalition in what
amounted to a vote of no confidence. The successor mini-front government led by the CPI (with informal support from the Congress [R])
operated with a razor-thin majority in constant danger of collapse from
defection. The decision to seek a new mandate in calling for a mid-term
election set the stage for talks between the CPI and the Congress aimed at
establishing an overall electoral adjustment that stopped short of a formal
alliance. The final agreement provided that Congress would put up candidates in only 56 out of 133 constituencies in the state. The CPI-led

mini-front contested 71 constituencies, with the CPI fielding its own candidates in 30 contests.

The arrangement satisfied the objectives of both parties in putting the Marxists at an initial disadvantage by having to face a combined Congress (R) mini-front opposition in most constituencies of the state. The Congress (R), meanwhile, protected by electoral adjustments that prevented splitting of the anti-Marxist vote, was able to concentrate on those constituencies where it had a reasonable chance of success, and to carry its slogan of "Defeat Marxists" to the rural strongholds of the CPI(M). The reduced effort, moreover, permitted the prime minister to campaign personally in as many as fifty of the fifty-six constituencies in which Congress candidates were contesting, and to experiment with an appeal that at once denounced class struggle and promised radical change. Attacking the Marxists for their strategy of confrontation between the Center and the states, and the poor and the rich social classes, Mrs. Gandhi promised to solve Kerala's problems of poverty and unemployment through close cooperation between the national and state government, and by means of programs that would accomplish "great changes" without the revolutionary costs of "cutting off peoples heads."[29]

The promises once again evoked an unusual outpouring of popular enthusiasm, especially among young people and students long alienated from the Congress leadership. In Kerala, the Kerala Students Union (KSU) organized in 1957 by Vyalar Ravi, had previously played an important political role in orchestrating student agitations that helped topple the first united front government. By the early 1960s, the KSU, acting as the student wing of the Pradesh Youth Congress, had emerged as the biggest force in Kerala's high schools and colleges. Under Ravi's leadership, the Youth Congress did not hesitate to use the same strong-arm tactics often employed by rival communist agitators to win over the uncommitted and to discourage the opposition. Yet KSU leaders had long opposed the leadership of their own Pradesh Congress Committees as "rich men using the administration for their own advantage." Their efforts, however, to "join Congress at local levels and to infiltrate and capture power and turn the older leadership out" had been unsuccessful. Student nominees were easily defeated in local party elections by their elders, who used bogus membership lists in voting large numbers of fictitious names to elect their own hand-picked candidates. After the 1969 split, when many of the older state leaders joined the Congress (O), Ravi and his associates finally saw a chance of coming to power inside the Congress (R). During the 1970 state election, in return for party tickets,

---

[29] AICC, *Kerala Mid-Term Election, 1970—An Analysis*, p. 12.

they led the KSU and the Youth Congress in enthusiastic support of Mrs. Gandhi. These students, many of whom had their family homes in the countryside, operated as the "real election machinery" of the Congress (R) in the villages.[30]

The results of the poll offered powerful support to those inside both the Congress (R) and the CPI arguing the potential benefit to their own party of pursuing the tactic of a united front. The electoral returns[31] produced a serious setback to the CPI(M). Although the Marxists managed to maintain roughly the same share of the total popular vote in 1970 as in 1967—about 23 percent—they won only 28 seats, compared to 52 in the previous election. By contrast, even though the Congress vote shrank to 19 percent in 1970, compared to 35 percent in 1967, the number of seats won jumped to 32 instead of 9 in 1967. Seventeen of the 27 seats gained from the opposition, moreover, were at the direct expense of the Marxists. At the same time, despite official party statements claiming a "spectacular victory for the Congress party,"[32] the fact was that Congress had fallen short of the majority needed to form a new government. This margin could be provided only by its electoral allies in the CPI-led minifront. The CPI, which won only 9 percent of the popular vote (a full percentage point less than its 1967 level) and even fewer seats in 1970 than in 1967 (16 compared to 19), provided along with its mini-front allies the assembly majority necessary to deny the Marxists any role in the new government. Indeed, when the Congress (R) decided against a formal coalition with the communists, another CPI-led mini-front government returned to power.

In Kerala, each party succeeded in using the other to further its own advantage. The CPI, relegated to the role of a junior partner in Marxist-dominated political coalitions since the 1964 split in the undivided Communist party, was able to exclude the Marxists from power by denying them the support of other left parties. A small minority, both in terms of popular support and seats won, they achieved a strategic position in providing the Congress (R) with the necessary margin to put together a majority in the legislative assembly, and actually headed the new government. The outcome suggested that the CPI's favored strategy of coming to power at the Center through an alignment with the progressive section of Congress had much wider scope under the new conditions of a truncated ruling party, one that might easily fall short of a majority in parliament at the next national election.

The Congress (R), for its part, found the electoral adjustment with the

---

[30] This account of the KSU's activities in Kerala is based on an interview with Vyalar Ravi in New Delhi, August 28, 1973.

[31] See *Kerala Mid-Term Election, 1970—An Analysis*, pp. 12-23.

[32] *Ibid.*, p. 14.

CPI in Kerala equally useful. It permitted them to consolidate the anti-Marxist vote and win a much larger number of seats from a smaller base of electoral support. The Marxists, the largest single party in the state in terms of the popular vote, were neutralized in their own regional stronghold. The new government, moreover, although led by the CPI, could not function without Congress (R) support. The practical result was that Congress restored its dominant role in the politics of the state.

The CPI's leverage at the Center, however, presented a more difficult problem as long as Congress remained at the head of a minority government. The Center had already deferred to communist opposition in allowing its powers of preventive detention to lapse throughout the country when existing legislation expired on December 31, 1969. The concession to the communists was a costly one. It compounded the difficulties of containing activities of communist and Naxalite agitators suspected of organizing the peasantry in land-grab movements and carrying out acts of political murder and sabotage in the cities.

The prime minister once again improvised to strengthen her personal position. In June 1970, Mrs. Gandhi succeeded in carrying out a far-reaching reorganization of the government that concentrated important new powers in her hands. As part of a Cabinet reshuffle,[33] she transferred 60 of the 100 sections of the home ministry (and 7 of the 14 joint secretaries) to the Cabinet secretariat. The move brought under her personal control the major administrative, police, and intelligence services of the national government. The All-India Administrative Service, the Intelligence Bureau, and the Central Bureau of Investigation were transferred from the Ministry of Home Affairs to the Cabinet secretariat. At the same time, plans were drawn up to consolidate and expand the intelligence services under the Research and Analysis Wing (RAW) of the prime minister's secretariat, with an enlarged role in carrying out domestic political surveillance. The prime minister did not stop there. After transferring Y. B. Chavan to Defense, she personally took charge of the truncated Ministry of Home Affairs. This move gave her personal control of the central police units (including the border security force, the central industrial security force, the central reserve police, and the home guards), all of which were subsequently greatly strengthened in numbers.

The political stakes for each partner of participation in the new pattern of alliances were considerably raised after the announcement on December 27, 1970, that the Fourth Lok Sabha had been dissolved. Mrs. Gandhi, explaining her decision to go to the electorate one year earlier than the expiration of the normal five-year term, was clearly hoping to regain

[33] See *The Statesman*, June 26 and 27, 1970.

freedom of political maneuver in a decisive mandate from the electorate.[34] The Forum, as the first group to call for an early election, was buoyed by the hope of advancing their strategic position inside the Congress party and the government.

The close political association between Mrs. Gandhi and the ex-communist faction did, in fact, allow them to make substantial gains. The Congress Parliamentary Board, which was authorized to carry out the functions of the Central Election Committee for selecting candidates and conducting the election campaign, was instructed to seek out "committed" candidates. Although all MPs who had attended the Requisition AICC and/or the plenary session at Bombay in 1969 were still accepted as "committed" by definition, other guidelines that emphasized the need to select larger numbers of nominees from among youth, women, Harijans, Muslims, and other minorities offered some scope for discretion. Overall, the Forum was able to win party tickets for about eighty candidates that satisfied its own more rigorous standards of socialist commitment, and for another thirty or so considered to be sympathetic.

The Forum was less successful in persuading the senior leadership to head a united front of leftist forces, including the CPI. Mrs. Gandhi and Jagjivan Ram did, however, enter into negotiations at the state level for regional electoral understandings. Altogether, the Congress set up no candidates in seventy-eight constituencies as part of ad hoc electoral alliances that were expected to improve the CPI's chances of winning additional seats in the Lok Sabha. The CPI reciprocated by drawing a clear distinction in their election manifesto[35] between Mrs. Gandhi and the "forces of progress" inside the Congress (R), on the one hand, and the "vested interests and their representatives" within the party, on the other. This time, moreover, the communists openly attacked the Marxists for "equat[ing] the Congress (R) and other parties which are today fighting the Rightist axis with the parties of the axis." They expressed their own desire of uniting with the progressive faction of the ruling party against the forces of right reaction, and defined the goal as a "new Lok Sabha which has a [more] firm left and democratic orientation than the last one."

The CPI's aim appeared almost within reach. Informed observers gave the Congress (R) virtually no chance of regaining its previous position of dominance. The grass-roots organization of the party in 1971 was much weaker than that of the undivided Congress in 1967, which managed to

---

[34] Mrs. Gandhi, in a broadcast on the eve of the dissolution of the Fourth Lok Sabha, explained her decision to seek an early election in the desire to get a fresh mandate from the people that would restore the party's majority and allow the government to go ahead with its proclaimed program. AICC, *People's Victory, An Analysis of 1971 Elections*, pp. 1-3.
[35] The election manifesto of the CPI is summarized in *The Statesman*, February 2, 1971.

win little more than 40 percent of the vote and 284 seats in the 520-member Lok Sabha, about 55 percent of the total. In addition, the majority of princes, angered at the government's assault on privy purses and privileges, turned their backs on the Congress (R). Some decided to stand as independent candidates in their local strongholds in Orissa, Rajasthan, and Madhya Pradesh; others attempted to come to an ad hoc electoral understanding on a state-to-state basis with the opposition party best placed to defeat the Congress (R), primarily Swatantra in Orissa and Rajasthan, and the Jan Sangh in Madhya Pradesh.

The potential benefit to the Congress (R) of division of votes among the conservative parties was also reduced by opposition electoral alliances. The Congress (O), Jan Sangh, Swatantra, and SSP participated in a "Grand Alliance" to set up a joint Democratic Front. The electoral understanding allowed the four parties to put up agreed candidates in 300 of the 518 Lok Sabha constituencies. At the same time, the CPI (Marxists) attempted to break out of its narrow regional bases in West Bengal and Kerala. They managed to put up 84 candidates (compared to 59 in 1967) in several states across the country. As in earlier elections, moreover, the Congress still had to contend with regional party groups that had important popular followings. On the basis of all of these limitations, the "rational" estimate of political experts assessing the strength of the Congress (R)—even after superimposing Mrs. Gandhi's countrywide appeal as compensation for weaknesses in party organization—did not give the party much more than one-third of the popular vote and a bare majority of 50 percent of the seats.[36]

Mrs. Gandhi's method of confounding such "rational" estimates was precisely not to rely on the existing party apparatus in carrying out her election campaign. Instead, she concentrated on building up a new organizational machinery that pledged its support not to the party but to the policies identified with her personal leadership. A beginning was made by efforts to revive the largely moribund Youth Congress at all levels of the party organization, and to set up a separate National Students Union to carry out political work in colleges and universities.

The potential of the Indian Youth Congress as the organizational arm of the prime minister was substantial. Except in a few states, Pradesh

---

[36] See S. Nihal Singh, "Congress (R) Nearing Its Moment of Truth," *The Statesman*, February 26, 1971. According to Singh, "any rational estimate, superimposing Mrs. Gandhi's countrywide appeal on the regional, State, local, caste and minority factors and the candidates' calibre, does not give the party more than 240 seats at the outside," that is, nineteen seats short of a majority. The Indian Institute of Public Opinion in its pre-poll forecast was only slightly more encouraging. It estimated that the Congress (R) would win 36.2 percent of the valid votes cast, and about 50 percent of the seats. Indian Institute of Public Opinion, *The Fifth Lok Sabha Elections* (New Delhi, 1971), p. 4.

Youth Congresses had been dormant since the 1950s. The new units had to be constituted as ad hoc committees nominated by the AICC's newly appointed National Youth Advisory Council. The state conveners recruited to set up the Pradesh units were mainly newcomers to Congress, drawn to party work by their allegiance to Mrs. Gandhi as the embodiment of the renewed socialist commitment. They pledged their direct support not to the party but to "Smt. Indira Gandhi and her associates."[37] Under their leadership, the All-India Conference of the Youth Congress, convened in January 1970, similarly "gave a call to the Youth of the Country to march towards Democratic Socialism under the leadership of Jagjivan Babu and Smt. Indira Gandhi."[38]

The newly organized National Students Union of India provided more tangible benefits to Mrs. Gandhi's campaign. Vyalar Ravi, the Keralan student leader who by then had been placed in charge of the AICC's students wing, set out to establish branches of the National Students Union at colleges and universities throughout the country. Such efforts were most successful in West Bengal, where young radicals opposed to the communists had long been active in the universities to develop an organizational alternative to the CPI. By the mid-1960s this group, organized in the West Bengal Chhatra Parishad (Students Association) succeeded in "capturing" the students' union at Calcutta University. The militants, led by Priya Ranjan das Munshi, adopted the same strong-arm tactics that Ravi had earlier found useful in Kerala to contest the control of communist organizers over student associations. In West Bengal, after 1969, the Chhatra Parishad and the reconstituted Youth Congress functioned as separate organizations with different missions. The Pradesh Youth Congress Executive, which maintained formal links with the Pradesh Congress Committee through the appointment of some common members, concentrated on organizational work among youth other than students that gave the appearance of conforming to democratic norms. The Chhatra Parishad, with more tenuous ties to the Pradesh Congress Committee, provided the party (in the person of the prime minister) with its own storm troops in the confrontation with the Marxists and Naxalites. Supplied with weapons and adept at street fighting, they did not hesitate to counterattack against Naxalites who had previously broken up Congress meetings, and they even made important inroads into the youthful membership of Marxist and Naxalite groups. Together, the Youth Congress and the Chhatra Parishad largely compensated for the defections from the undivided Congress party after the

---

[37] AICC, *Report of the General Secretaries* (December 1969-May 1970) (New Delhi, 1970), p. 40.

[38] *Ibid*.

split. They became the dominant influence in the reconstituted party organization at the state and district levels.[39]

If Mrs. Gandhi largely ignored the regular party machinery and encouraged the formation of new youth organizations that pledged their
full support to her leadership, these were still mainly limited to urban
areas. During the 1971 campaign, the primary substitute for organization
in the vast rural hinterland still had to be the prime minister's personal
image. The campaign strategy followed in broad outline the pattern that
had already proved successful in Kerala. Congress (R) tacticians and their
supporters concentrated on projecting their greatest asset, the image of
Mrs. Gandhi as a symbol of change for something better, among the
"dispossessed and the poorer sections and a proportion of the young."[40]
Campaign techniques were designed to tap this emotional factor through
an unprecedented barrage of publicity materials from the AICC office.
Millions of posters and badges imprinted with Mrs. Gandhi's picture fil-
tered down from large urban centers to small towns and into the villages.
The prime minister herself, making extensive use of government planes
and helicopters, undertook a "whirlwind tour" across the nation aimed
at marginal constituencies in key states. Altogether, Mrs. Gandhi campaigned for forty-one days, addressing over 250 mammoth public meetings and hundreds of smaller wayside crowds.[41]

The message that the prime minister delivered strengthened the impression among the electorate that she personally, rather than the Congress party, represented the renewed commitment to economic and
social reform. The complex ideological and political conflicts that had
divided the Congress party were explained in terms of her own struggle
as a weak and frail woman to improve the lives of the poor in the face of
plots by powerful party bosses determined to protect the vested interests.
Mrs. Gandhi turned aside the opposition's charges against her of unprincipled methods by pointing out that the "Syndicate Congress" had
joined hands with the parties of right reaction for the sole purpose of fulfilling what they themselves called their One-Point Program of Indira
Hatao, that of removing her from office. She personalized the difference
between the Grand Alliance and the Congress (R) on complex issues of
rapid economic reform in a simple slogan that came to define the choices
confronting the electorate in the campaign:

> Kuch log kehtai hai, Indira hatao
> Mai kehti hu, garibi hatao.

[39] This account of the relationship between Youth Congress and Chhatra Parishad activities in West Bengal is based on an interview with Priya Ranjan das Munshi in New
Delhi, August 19, 1973.

[40] See Singh, "Congress (R) Nearing Its Moment of Truth."

[41] *Congress Marches Ahead—III*, p. 103.

(Some people say, get rid of Indira
I say, get rid of poverty.)

The slogan, which implied a program of radical social change, was combined with attacks on those who resorted to class struggle methods in order to carry out economic reforms. The prime minister explained the slow progress of her own government in implementing the party's promises by the minority position of the Congress (R) in parliament and the crippling compromises it had to make with the vested interests in order to survive. She appealed to the electorate to "strengthen my hands" by giving the Congress (R) an absolute majority in parliament. Given such a popular mandate, Mrs. Gandhi pledged she would redeem her promises of radical change through peaceful means.[42]

If the 1971 general election was a political gamble by Mrs. Gandhi that she could defeat both her opponents in the conservative Grand Alliance and her competitors on the communist left through a direct class appeal that promised radical economic reform through parliamentary methods, then the prime minister handsomely won that gamble. The results of the election[43] confounded both Mrs. Gandhi's opponents and her supporters. The "astonishing wins" nationwide that gave the Congress (R) 350 seats in the 518-member Lok Sabha—a clear two-thirds majority—at once decimated the right opposition, turned the tables on the CPI, and neutralized the Marxists in their own regional stronghold.

Overall, the Congress (R) increased its share of the popular vote from 40.7 percent won by the undivided party in 1967 to 43 percent in 1971—despite the fact that it contested in only 85 percent of the constituencies.[44] The fact was, as shown in Table 11-1, the Congress (R) inherited virtually the whole of the Congress undivided vote. The Congress (O) was routed. It managed to win only 10 percent of the popular vote and 16 seats, losing 47 of the 63 seats it held at the time of the dissolution of the Lok Sabha. The same fate overtook other members of the Grand Alliance. Swatantra saw its popular vote decline from over 8 percent in 1967 to 3 percent in 1971, winning only 8 seats in the Lok Sabha, a loss of 27 over its position in December 1970. The Jan Sangh suffered a smaller decline in its popular vote from over 9 percent in 1967 to somewhat over 7 percent in 1971, but it also lost 11 of its 33 seats in the Lok Sabha. The SSP was virtually destroyed. Its popular vote declined from approxi-

---

[42] See Sydney R. Schanberg, "For Mrs. Gandhi, Awesome Responsibilities," *New York Times*, March 13, 1971.

[43] *People's Victory, An Analysis of 1971 Elections*, pp. 7-19.

[44] A comparison of the Congress party's performance in 1967 and 1971 in the 434 constituencies contested in both elections showed a substantial increase of over 10 percent in the popular vote, from an average of approximately 42 percent to 53 percent. *Ibid.*, p. 14.

TABLE 11-1

Comparative Analysis of Seats Won and Votes Polled
by Various Parties in the 1967 Elections,
Seats Held at the Time of Dissolution of the Fourth
Lok Sabha (December 1970), and Seats Won and Votes Polled in 1971
Elections

| Party | 1967 | | Seats held at time of dissolution of the Lok Sabha (December 1970) | 1971 | |
|---|---|---|---|---|---|
| | No. of seats won | % of valid votes polled | | No. of seats won | % of valid votes polled |
| Congress (R) | 283 | 40.73 | 221 | 350 | 43.66 |
| Congress (O) | | | 63 | 16 | 10.47 |
| Jan Sangh | 35 | 9.41 | 33 | 22 | 7.39 |
| Swatantra | 44 | 8.68 | 35 | 8 | 3.08 |
| SSP | 23 | 4.92 | 17 | 3 | 2.43 |
| PSP | 13 | 3.06 | 15 | 2 | 1.09 |
| CPI | 23 | 5.19 | 24 | 23 | 4.73 |
| CPM | 19 | 4.21 | 19 | 25 | 5.14 |
| DMK | 25 | 3.90 | 24 | 23 | 3.85 |
| Others | 20 | 6.15 | 5★ | 32 | 11.08 |
| Independents | 35 | 13.75 | 51★ | 11 | 7.08 |

SOURCE: *People's Victory, An Analysis of 1971 Elections* (New Delhi, April 1971), pp. 10, 17.

★ Figures for these categories in December 1970 are not comparable to those for 1967 and 1971. Seats listed as belonging to other parties include only those held by the Muslim League and RSP. Seats held by other small opposition parties are included as part of the number for independents.

mately 5 percent in 1967 to 2.4 percent in 1971, and it lost 14 of its 17 seats in the Lok Sabha.

The defeat of the "forces of Right Reaction" brought little benefit to the CPI, however. Against the overwhelming superiority enjoyed by the Congress both in terms of popular votes and seats won, the CPI's strength at less than 5 percent of the vote and 23 seats in the Lok Sabha (one fewer than in 1970) indicated the absence of any momentum. Not only was the CPI's support unnecessary to the Congress majority, but it was superfluous even for the purpose of the two-thirds majority required for constitutional amendment. The calculations of the communists that they could achieve a strategic political position at the Center through an alignment with a weakened Congress (R) proved to be totally misplaced. The influence of the CPI, in contradistinction to their earlier expectations, subsequently depended upon the willingness of the party to confine its activities to actions acceptable to the prime minister.

This lesson was driven home almost immediately after the election. In early May, the government, once again resorting to presidential ordinance, resumed its powers of preventive detention throughout the country. The ordinance, later introduced into the Lok Sabha and passed as the Maintenance of Internal Security Act (MISA), empowered the government at the Center and in the states to issue detention orders for a period of up to one year against any person to prevent him from acting "in any manner prejudicial" to the defense of India, the security of the state, the maintenance of public order, or the maintenance of essential supplies and public services.[45] The CPI, whose spokesman opposed the legislation "lock, stock and barrel" as an attempt to stifle the opposition, found no other recourse than to join a general walkout by opposition parties during the debate, in alliance with Jan Sangh and Swatantra.[46]

Possibly the most disastrous consequences of the Congress (R)'s election sweep were suffered by the CPI(M), even though they were the only opposition party at the Center that improved both their percentage of votes polled and seats won. The Marxists were neutralized in their own regional stronghold of West Bengal, and prevented from converting growing popular support into government power. Altogether, the Marxists made impressive electoral gains in West Bengal. They won about one-third of the popular vote and 111 seats (compared to 80 at the time of dissolution), to emerge as the single largest party in the legislative assembly. Along with their allies in the United Left Front, they commanded a total of 123 seats in the 277-member legislative assembly. Yet the Congress (R), which lagged slightly behind the Marxists in the number of seats won, nevertheless made a dramatic improvement in their position from 38 seats at the time of dissolution to 105 seats in the 1971 election.[47] The gains proved sufficient for Congress to form a six-party coalition government (with the Bangla Congress, Muslim League, Gorkha League, PSP, and SSP) that also received support from the CPI. Within three months, moreover, the chief minister, Ajoy Mukherjee, citing the deterioration of law and order and the influx of refugees from East Bengal,[48] advised the governor that President's Rule should be im-

[45] Under the MISA legislation, détenus had to be informed about the grounds of their detention within fifteen days of arrest. The act also set up three-man advisory review boards whose members had the status of High Court judges. The government was required to place before the board the grounds on which detention was made within thirty days of the order. The board was mandated to submit its report to government within ten weeks of the detention order, advising whether there was sufficient cause to detain. See *The Statesman*, May 8, 1971.

[46] *The Statesman*, June 4, 1971.

[47] *People's Victory, An Analysis of 1971 Elections*, p. 48. See also *The Statesman*, March 16, 1971.

[48] The refusal of the Government of Pakistan to permit the National Assembly elected in December 1970 to meet after Bengali nationalists organized in the Awami League won a majority led to a rebellion in East Bengal. Efforts by the Pakistani army, beginning in March 1971, to suppress the guerrilla forces of the separatist movement led to mass killings and other atrocities that forced millions of Bengalis to seek refuge across the border of India.

posed. The proclamation, signed by President Giri on June 29, 1971, was
followed by appointment of Sidhartha Shankar Ray as Union minister
without portfolio to exercise the presidential power of "superinten-
dence, control and direction" over the affairs of West Bengal.[49] One of
Ray's first acts was to request the deployment of the army to assist the
civil authorities in dealing with law and order in the most disturbed parts
of the state. By the end of the year, as the number of killings reached into
the thousands and the number of political prisoners climbed into the tens
of thousands,[50] official spokesmen reported that West Bengal had become "one of the most peaceful States in India."[51]

The importance of the Congress party's overwhelming victory, however, went far beyond the unprecedented setbacks suffered by almost all
opposition political parties. It represented a landmark event in the political development of post-Independence India. The national leadership of
the Congress party, and in particular Mrs. Gandhi herself, succeeded on
a large scale in breaching the strategic position of local factional leaders
and intermediate elites as the political mobilizers of the poor peasantry.
In a significant sense, it can be said that large numbers of the peasantry
directly participated in the national political process for the first time.

Results in the three state elections, although complicated by local issues and regional party groups, reinforced the impression of a departure
from previous patterns of vertical mobilization at the village and constituency levels. In Tamil Nadu, where the Congress (R) agreed not to contest any state assembly seats, but supported candidates endorsed by the
Dravida Munnetra Kazhagam,[52] the DMK was expected to have difficulty maintaining its majority after local elections to village and town
panchayats gave the Congress (O) 46 percent of the seats, compared to
34 percent for the DMK. Notwithstanding the alignments at the village
level, however, the DMK won a "sensational victory" in the state, increasing its dominant position in the 234-seat legislative assembly from
138 in 1967 to 184 in 1971. By contrast, the Congress (O) suffered a rout,

[49] *The Statesman*, July 4, 1971.
[50] The army's combing operations were undertaken on top of large-scale arrests in the
state during the period of President's Rule preceding the March 1971 elections, when over
3,000 people were detained for suspected Naxalite activities. *The Statesman*, July 9, 1971.
There are no official figures to establish the actual number of persons subsequently killed or
arrested during the combined police and army action against the Naxalites. A "low" estimate, offered by a senior civil servant under Ray's command, is that 15,000 to 17,000 persons were rounded up in 1971, of whom approximately 2,000 were killed and the remainder sent to prison. Others have estimated that much larger numbers were detained in prison
under MISA and other preventive detention laws, and that by 1973, there were 30,000 to
50,000 political détenus in West Bengal. See "Calcutta Diary," *Economic and Political
Weekly*, May 19, 1973, p. 889.
[51] *The Statesman*, December 12, 1971.
[52] This arrangement was made in return for an electoral adjustment with the DMK to
support Congress (R) candidates in 10 of 39 Lok Sabha constituencies.

declining to 15 seats from its previous total of 49. Analysis of available postelection data concluded that increased support for the DMK came from "among the less affluent sections of society—that is to say among the predominant majority of the masses" in the rural and semiurban areas.[53]

A similar phenomenon occurred in Orissa. In 1967, old patterns of vertical mobilization were sufficiently strong to make Swatantra the single largest party in the state legislative assembly. Based on its strength in the highlands area, where the party was organized by former princely rulers commanding the loyalty of a predominately tribal population, Swatantra was able to win 49 out of 140 seats, while the undivided Congress party, with 31 seats, was relegated to second position. But in the 1971 elections, the Congress (R) was able to reverse this relationship. Relying mainly on Mrs. Gandhi's preelection visits to marginal constituencies, the Congress (R) won a total of 51 seats, becoming the largest single party in the legislative assembly, while Swatantra, with 36 seats, was reduced to second place. The Congress also managed to turn back the challenge from the Utkal Congress in Orissa, which based its appeal on regional interest.

Even in West Bengal, where all parties resorted to political violence in order to influence the outcome, and Congress owed a good part of its improved showing to the heavy majorities it polled in Calcutta, critical gains came from unprecedented victories in the rural constituencies of northern Bengal. The area was one where Congress organization was virtually nonexistent, but which had been targeted for Mrs. Gandhi's personal campaign on the eve of the elections, and repetition of her promise to eradicate poverty.

This turning point in the political process was clearly recognized. Experts, assessing where their earlier projections had gone wrong, noted evidence that previous patterns of clientelist politics had broken down not only in urban constituencies, but also in rural areas. They observed that "the estimates went wrong because no one anticipated that Mrs. Gandhi's simple message would get across to the bulk of voters and compulsively superimpose itself on the caste, local and regional factors. Not only did this message get across—obviously by word of mouth rather than through recognized channels of communication—but her appeal also momentarily swept away caste and regional prejudices."[54]

The Congress Working Committee took official note of "this new historic situation" which "brought into the national mainstream vast masses of the weaker sections of society who cutting across barriers

[53] *The Statesman*, March 13, 1971.
[54] S. Nihal Singh, "Mrs. Gandhi's Task of Redeeming Her Promises," *ibid.*, March 19, 1971.

of caste, religion and regional loyalties voted for democracy, socialism, secularism and non-alignment."[55] Mrs. Gandhi, commenting on the election results, also stressed the popular character of the party's victory, cutting across all caste, religious, and other cleavages to convert the Congress campaign into a "people's campaign."[56]

The results were received with optimism. They were interpreted as a direct mandate given to the government for rapid economic changes through parliamentary means. Hopes for achieving the multiple aims of economic growth and social reform through democratic methods revived. The Working Committee, meeting immediately after the election results became known, cited signs of "this new consciousness of the people," and defined the tasks before the party primarily in terms of organizing the weaker sections in order to institutionalize popular participation and pressure at the grass roots, in a sanction for the "social transformation of India." They authorized the president to set up a committee to recommend changes in the party constitution "in order to make the party an effective instrument for the fulfillment of the aspirations of the people."[57]

The dangers inherent in the unprecedented Congress victory were at least as great as the opportunities, however. There was for the time being no popular organization in place. On the contrary, the most salient feature of the new political situation was the supersession of all party organization, including that of the victorious Congress (R), as an important source of power. The massive vote for the party was recognized on all sides as "Mrs. Gandhi's fantastic victory." Her own supporters were reported to be stunned and embarrassed by the size of their party's majority, conscious of the fact they had been "swept into the new Lok Sabha on [Mrs. Gandhi's] coattails."[58] Overnight, the prime minister's position appeared transformed. She succeeded at one swoop in making her leadership indispensable to the Congress party as the only figure with a personal following transcending regional, communal, and caste lines. She had become, according to some observers, the most powerful prime minister since Independence, excelling even her father. Her paramountcy was rooted directly in popular support. It did not need or derive strength from the consensus of the state party bosses.

The personal power of the prime minister was reinforced within the year as the result of her leadership role during the third Indo-Pakistan War in December 1971.[59] The onset of the crisis virtually coincided with

[55] AICC, *Congress Marches Ahead—IV*, p. 5.
[56] *Ibid.*, p. 71.                              [57] *Ibid.*, p. 5.
[58] See Singh, "Mrs. Gandhi's Task of Redeeming Her Promises."
[59] For an extended analysis of the government's strategy during the 1971 Indo-Pakistan War, see Pran Chopra, *India's Second Liberation*, chs. 3, 4, 5. Mrs. Gandhi's leadership role during the crisis is described in Masani, *Indira Gandhi, a Biography*, pp. 234–56.

Mrs. Gandhi's election triumph. On March 25, 1971, the Pakistani army began a campaign of repression in East Pakistan designed to quash the Bengali secessionist movement led by the Awami League. The nationalists responded with a declaration announcing the formation of an independent nation of Bangladesh. They organized their own guerrilla army, the Mukti Bahini, and prepared for a protracted conflict with the regular troops of West Pakistan. As the conflict escalated, the army repression became so severe that in some areas it bordered on genocide. Thousands and then millions of refugees streamed across the border into India, where they were provided with food and other minimum facilities in temporary camps that eventually drained government resources by about $3-$4 million per day.

Mrs. Gandhi played a key role from the beginning in deciding the government's strategy. At the outset, she resisted the growing clamor for war with Pakistan as the only way to force recognition of Bangladesh and repatriate the refugees. Instead, she embarked on a highly visible world tour to explain India's growing financial and political difficulties to the major powers, and appeal for their intervention to put pressure on Pakistan in negotiating a settlement of the Bangladesh conflict. At the same time, she approved measures to undermine the Pakistani army in its efforts to pacify East Bengal by providing the Mukti Bahini with military training, arms, funds, and a sanctuary across the Indian border. Although the prime minister's diplomatic forays elicited little more than expressions of sympathy, the delaying tactics provided time for the nation's armed forces to prepare for another conflict. When Pakistan launched a surprise air attack against India on December 3, the army went into action with a plan for the speedy conquest of East Bengal. They achieved complete victory in less than two weeks. On December 16, the Pakistani army surrendered unconditionally to India. Shortly after, Bangladesh was established as an independent country. Pakistan lost her entire eastern wing and any aspirations to equality with India as a military power in the subcontinent. India, under Mrs. Gandhi's leadership, had achieved a decisive victory over her foremost enemy that neither Nehru nor Shastri had been able to accomplish. The success was hailed as another personal triumph for the prime minister. It even suggested to some of her supporters access to divine sources of energy. As Mrs. Gandhi's biographer, Zareer Masani, observed:

In a country . . . where mysticism mingles with politics, Indira Gandhi appeared as an omnipotent Mother Goddess who had protected her people and liberated another from the forces of evil. The idea that a woman should lead her country to victory did not appear incongruous in a country where Durga, the Goddess of War, is widely worshipped. Hindu mythology has it that Durga was created by the gods after their explusion from the heavenly heights by the demons. Armed with divine weapons, Durga, according to the legend, had fought alone against the demon hordes, vanquishing them and restoring the Gods to their rightful place. Many Indians saw Indira Gandhi as an incarnation of the same Shakti or female energy.[60]

The analogies used to describe Mrs. Gandhi's power at the end of 1971, ranging from the regal ("Empress of India") to the religious (incarnation of Shakti) were in a sense correct, but not in the meaning of absolute power that such phrases normally convey. Like an empress, Mrs. Gandhi became the source from which all legitimate authority flowed, the indispensable leader of the Congress party as the personal symbol of the nation. Like Durga, she wielded enormous power for destroying her enemies, whether those in the conservative opposition or revolutionary communist parties. On her own, however, she had neither the ideological conviction nor the organizational capacity for attempting the creative tasks of party reform that were necessary to redeem promises of socialist change through peaceful means. And after the 1971 elections, those best placed inside the party to take maximum advantage of the new opportunities for political organization among the vast peasantry were members of the Forum, who had other priorities. They were mainly interested in bypassing the established leadership to build up a cadre directly responsive to their own control, and capable of pushing the party into more and more radical policy commitments that could only be carried out at the expense of the existing constitutional framework.

According to CFSA leaders, between 1969 and 1972 "everything was on an ascendent scale in the influence of the Forum." The most striking gains were in states where the organization of the undivided party remained largely in the hands of the Congress (O). In Mysore, immediately after the split, the Congress Forum and the Pradesh Congress Committee was "completely the same." The same was true in Gujerat, where the PCC and the Forum were "synonymous," and Forum units spread to all the northern districts of the state. Similarly, in Bombay, the PCC was converted into a Forum body following an influx of radical intellectuals into the Congress party. Meanwhile, Forum leaders at the Center took the initiative in organizational work where defection of local leadership of the undivided party left a political vacuum. A strong Forum contingent was in this way built up at the state and district levels of the Congress party in Uttar Pradesh, Rajasthan, Delhi, Bihar, and Orissa. By October 1970, the Forum was able to hold its Fourth All-India Convention at Madras, independently of the timing of the annual Congress

[60] *Ibid.*, p. 250.

session, and to attract 1,000 delegates. Its newly elected 55-member Central Steering Committee had representatives from all parts of the country reflecting the establishment of Forum units in all states and membership of "thousands of active Congress workers."[61]

The Forum's most important gains, however, were registered at the Center in the aftermath of the 1971 general election. CFSA leaders estimated that sixty to eighty "staunch supporters" had been elected to the Lok Sabha. Attendance at postelection meetings of the parliamentary unit reached about a hundred MPs.[62]

Members and associates of the Forum were appointed to senior posts both inside the government and the Congress party. Mrs. Gandhi, who continued to consolidate her own power (adding the portfolio of Information and Broadcasting to her other responsibilities as minister of home affairs, planning, and atomic energy) left the four senior members of the Cabinet undisturbed. Jagjivan Ram, Y. B. Chavan, Swaran Singh, and Fakhruddin Ali Ahmed retained their respective charges of defense, finance, external affairs, and agriculture. At the same time, other ministers of Cabinet rank were dropped to make way for new nominees. The most dramatic rise of a newcomer inside the party was accomplished by Mohan Kumaramangalam, named minister of steel and heavy engineering. He was joined by Sidhartha Shankar Ray, minister of education, social welfare, and culture, a longstanding ally of the Forum in the Congress party of West Bengal. At the sub-Cabinet level, eight of the twenty-two ministers of state were members or permanent invitees of the CFSA.[63]

There were other points of direct access. P. N. Haksar, head of the prime minister's secretariat, was in direct operational control of the reorganized "super-ministry" with its expanded secretariat coordinating appointments and policies in all other ministries. D. P. Dhar, like Haksar a "committed" Marxist and former ambassador to the Soviet Union, served as chairman of the Policy Planning Committee of the Ministry of External Affairs. The Forum's views were also directly represented in the highest executive organs of the Congress party. Chandrajit Yadav held a key post as member of the Working Committee and general secretary of the AICC. Sidhartha Shankar Ray and Chandra Shekhar found places as members of the Working Committee. Ray also sat on the eight-member Central Parliamentary Board. He and Chandra Shekhar were members of the fifteen-person Central Election Committee.

[61] *Short History of the Congress Forum for Socialist Action*, p. 28.

[62] *Ibid.*, p. 4.

[63] A list of the members and permanent invitees of the Congress Forum for Socialist Action is published in *Two Years of CFSA, Decisions & Resolutions*, pp. 59-63. The names of the ministers of state appointed to Mrs. Gandhi's government in May 1971 are published in *The Statesman*, May 3, 1971.

There was, in addition, an informal caucus among a small group of the ex-communist faction that acted as a kind of mini-Cabinet in charting out the political strategies of the Forum inside the government and the Congress party. Led by Mohan Kumaramangalam, this inner circle[64] remained careful to avoid the appearance of functioning as a party within the party, working directly through "committed" members who occupied key policy-making roles inside the government and the party. They continued to follow the tactical line of identifying CFSA policies with the national program of the Congress party.

The approach brought spectacular success within less than one year. Evoking Mrs. Gandhi's election pledge to end poverty by peaceful means and the egalitarian and socialist directive principles of state policy in the constitution (principles explicitly linked by Nehru to the work of the Planning Commission), the Forum mounted a campaign to mobilize support inside the Congress parliamentary party for comprehensive constitutional amendments of fundamental rights.

The issue of constitutional amendment to restore parliament's power of amending fundamental rights to the position held before the Supreme Court's 1967 ruling in the Golak Nath case was raised immediately after the 1971 election. Mrs. Gandhi, in her first press conference after the Congress party's landslide victory, suggested that the constitution might be amended to remove guarantees for property as an unalterable right, but within a framework accepting the right to property.[65] Draft legislation subsequently prepared by the government did not go beyond provisions to restore to parliament the authority to amend the fundamental rights chapter of the constitution. This was advanced in the context of a "step-by-step" approach that envisaged subsequent amendments, through which the right to property would be extricated from the fundamental rights chapter, replaced by a general right to property subject to regulation in the public interest, and with restrictions against judicial review of compensation as inadequate or in violation of other constitutional guarantees.[66]

The government's "piecemeal" approach, which actually approximated the Forum's December 1970 position that after extending parliament's powers of amendment to include fundamental rights, the right to property must be removed as a fundamental right, no longer satisfied the demands of the stronger radical faction. In May 1971, the Central Steering Committee of the CFSA unveiled a new set of proposals on amendments to the constitution that more accurately reflected their intention of weakening not only the fundamental right to property, but the other

---

[64] The core group included, in addition to Kumaramangalam, two junior Cabinet ministers and a leading member of the AICC.

[65] *The Statesman*, March 12, 1971.          [66] *The Statesman*, July 14, 1971.

basic political rights (including freedom of speech, expression, assembly, and association) protected from amendment under Part III of the constitution.

The Forum's proposals envisaged a series of related amendments. These included revisions in Article 368 to broaden explicitly the amending powers of parliament extending to modification of the fundamental rights provisions; amendments to Articles 31 and 31(a) to put a ceiling on "property of any description and to take over the property in excess of such ceiling without payment of any compensation"; amendment to Article 19 ensuring that such laws could not be challenged under provisions for equal protection under the laws; and amendment to Article 32 to prevent any appeal of compensation awards in the courts. Further, according to the Forum, it was necessary to ensure that policies aimed at implementing the directive principles of the constitution could not be impeded by court challenges based on other fundamental rights. In particular, they demanded that "Article 32 and 226 be amended to take away the jurisdiction of the Supreme Court and the High Courts respectively to exclude judicial review of any law which is in consonance with the directive principles of State policy or any step taken in pursuance of such a law."[67]

The new proposals were used as a program around which to rally Congress MPs for pressure on the prime minister to recast the government's legislation. The parliamentary unit of the CFSA formally endorsed the recommendations for more radical constitutional amendments on June 25.[68] Within less than three weeks, Forum leaders submitted a memorandum to Mrs. Gandhi urging that "a comprehensive Bill to amend the Constitution must be brought forward in this very Session of Parliament. This will convince our people that we mean business, that we stand by our election pledges and that we shall not let people's enthusiasm change into frustration." The memorandum was signed by 210 Congress MPs—sixty percent of the Congress parliamentary party.[69] The Forum's strategy of building up support inside the party around the national leadership's own socialist declarations, and then challenging the credibility of the leadership for failing to implement its own program—a threat implicit in the backing of the majority of the CPP—worked to good effect. The two bills introduced to amend the constitution shortly afterward followed almost entirely the Forum's proposals.

The Constitution (Twenty-Fourth Amendment) Bill inserted a new clause under Article 13, which removed from judicial review any amendment of the constitution made under Article 368 that had the effect of abridging or taking away fundamental rights protected by Part III of

[67] *Two Years of CFSA, Decisions & Resolutions*, pp. 35-36.
[68] *The Statesman*, June 26, 1971.                    [69] *The Statesman*, July 14, 1971.

the constitution. The same bill also inserted an additional clause to Article 368, specifying that the ordinary procedures provided for amending the constitution were sufficient to confer constituent powers on parliament extending to those of amending "by way of addition, variation or repeal" any provision of the constitution.[70] The bill, which was passed by an overwhelming majority of 384-23 on August 4, 1971, was described by Mrs. Gandhi as "a milestone in the progress of democracy."[71]

The Constitution (Twenty-Fifth Amendment) Bill went further to establish the supremacy of parliament over the constitution as the arbiter of fundamental rights. The first part of the Twenty-Fifth Amendment altered the language of Article 31 to delete the word "compensation" from provisions for payment in the case of the compulsory acquisition of property. The new formulation provided only that any law for the compulsory acquisition of property must provide "for an amount which may be fixed by such law or which may be determined in accordance with such principles and given in such manner as may be specified in such law"; and reiterated the prohibition against calling such a law into question in any court on the grounds that the amount fixed was not adequate.

The second part of the Twenty-Fifth Amendment inserted an entirely new Article 31(c) to establish the superior legal force of the directive principles of state policy of the constitution over the provisions of Part III protecting fundamental rights. It provided:

> Notwithstanding anything contained in article 13, no law giving effect to the policy of the State towards securing the principles specified in clause (b) or clause (c) of article 39 shall be deemed to be void on the ground that it is inconsistent with, or takes away or abridges any of the rights conferred by article 14, article 19 or article 31. And no law containing a declaration that it is for giving effect to such policy shall be called into question in any court on the ground that it does not give effect to such policy.
>
> Provided that where such law is made by the Legislature of a State, the provisions of this article shall not apply thereto unless such law, having been reserved for the consideration of the President, has received his assent.[72]

The Twenty-Fifth Amendment was passed by the Lok Sabha on December 1, 1971, with another massive majority of 353-20.[73] It was followed

---

[70] The text of The Constitution (Twenty-Fourth Amendment) Act, 1971 is published in Lakhanpal, *Two Historic Judgments*, pp. 180-81.

[71] *The Statesman*, August 5, 1971.

[72] For the text of The Constitution (Twenty-Fifth Amendment) Bill, 1971, see Lakhanpal, *Two Historic Judgments*, pp. 182-83.

[73] *The Statesman*, December 2, 1971.

on the next day by passage of the Constitution (Twenty-Sixth Amendment) Bill, abolishing the privileges and privy purses of the princes.[74]

The constitutional changes, as critics in the judiciary, the press, and the opposition political parties pointed out, reduced the constitution to "tatters." Its original framework and political philosophy was drastically transformed. Two of the directive principles, Article 39(b) and (c), which had previously been broad guidelines to state policy and nonenforceable in the courts, were elevated into the paramount principles of the legal order. These provided that "the State shall, in particular, direct its policy toward securing . . . (b) that the ownership and control of material resources of the community are so distributed as best to subserve the common good; (c) that the operation of the economic system does not result in the concentration of wealth and means of production to the common detriment." The fundamental rights, which since Independence had prevailed in any clear conflict with the directive principles, thus establishing that legislation for economic reform must be accomplished through measures consistent with the preservation of the "sheltered rights of the citizen," were declared nonenforceable.[75] This inroad on fundamental rights extended far beyond the right to property or to compensation in the case of compulsory acquisition of property by government as guaranteed in Article 31. It also removed constitutional guarantees of fundamental political rights when these came into conflict with legislation whose declared purpose was implementation of the directive principles. Among the rights affected were those at the heart of the democratic political order, including the right to equality before the law and equal protection of law, and those of freedom of speech, assembly, association, and movement.

The official defense of the Congress party's decision to press for comprehensive constitutional changes was written by Mohan Kumaramangalam. It explicitly defended this reversal of the original relationship between economic reform and political rights. According to

[74] The 26th Amendment deleted Articles 291 and 362 of the constitution, guaranteeing the privy purses and privileges of the Rulers of Indian States. It "derecognized" the princes and abolished all privy purses and other rights and privileges of the former rulers in the following language: "A prince, chief or other person who at any time before the commencement of the Constitution (26th Amendment) Act, 1971 was recognized by the President as the successor of such a ruler, shall on and from such commencement cease to be recognized as such a ruler or the successor of such rulers. On and from the commencement of the Constitution (26th Amendment) Act, 1971, the privy purse is abolished and accordingly, the ruler or, as the case may be, the successor of such rulers, or any other persons shall not be paid any such privy purse." See *The Statesman*, August 6, 1971.

[75] A judicial critique of the "drastic change from the original ideology of our constitution" was developed by M. Hidayatullah, a former chief justice of India in the Eighth Shri Ram Memorial Lecture. The text, "The Constitution: The Parliament and the Court" is published in Indian Institute of Public Opinion, *Monthly Public Opinion Surveys*, 27:5 (February 1972), 6–14.

Kumaramangalam, the "clear object" of Article 31(c) under the Twenty-Fifth Amendment was "to subordinate the rights of the individual as expressed in the Fundamental Rights conferred under articles 14, 19 and 31, to the urgent needs of society as expressed in these Directive Principles."[76] The immediate needs of society for which such powers were sought included "major reforms in nationalizing big monopolies, for Article 31(c) deprives these monoplies of the possibility of resort to Articles 14, 19 and 31 to protect them from radical legislation designed to nationalize the vast holdings in industry."[77] Otherwise, Kumaramangalam argued, deprived only of fundamental right to property, "it may well be that the men of property will fall back on the other Fundamental Rights in order to protect their interests."[78] From this point of view, the Twenty-Fourth, Twenty-Fifth, and Twenty-Sixth Amendments together made up "a single whole."[79] That single whole was an entirely new constitutional doctrine of the "sovereignty of the people" that vested in them and their representatives in parliament "the power to determine where the line is to be drawn between the preservation of private rights on the one hand and the assertion of the rights of the community on the other." This power could not be entrusted to the judiciary, Kumaramangalam concluded, because "this is a delicate matter, essentially political in content which can only be decided on political grounds."[80]

This new doctrine that the political views and desires of the people, as expressed through their representatives in parliament, were supreme over the fundamental rights of the constitution did ease the central government's path in moving against some segments of the private sector. In May 1971, the management of general insurance companies was vested in government by presidential ordinance, preparatory to nationalization in August 1972 by act of parliament. A similar sequence was followed when government took over the management of 214 coking coal mines in 1971, and then nationalized them in May 1972. The entire coal-mining industry, including the noncoking coal mines, was nationalized in January 1973.

Other legislation was also approved by parliament to curb the perquisites or power of independent institutions considered unfriendly to the progressive forces. Some had mainly symbolic value. Others chipped away at the main supports of the democratic political system.

The passage of the Former Secretary of State Service Officer (Conditions of Service Bill) by the Lok Sabha in September 1972 fell into the

[76] S. Mohan Kumaramangalam, "Constitutional Amendments: The Reason Why," (New Delhi, November 1971), p. 22.
 [77] *Ibid.*, p. 21.                               [78] *Ibid.*, p. 12.
 [79] *Ibid.*, p. 29.                               [80] *Ibid.*, p. 9.

first category. The special retirement and pension privileges guaranteed to the officers of the Indian Civil Service (ICS) under Article 314 of the constitution were withdrawn and substituted by the pattern set for the successor Indian Administrative Service (IAS). The changes came at a time when barely eighty ICS officers were still active, and six years before the last of the cadre was scheduled to retire.[81] They represented mainly "a psychological boost to the image of the Congress."[82] Perhaps of greater significance was removal shortly thereafter of the longstanding ban on recruitment into the IAS of persons with a background of affiliation with the CPI.

More serious was the first inroad against the freedom of the press, carried out through an act aimed at diffusing ownership of major newspapers and news agencies. The new legislation, passed in 1973, prohibited any individual or corporate body from holding more than five percent of the paid-up equity share capital of the company, either by himself or in the aggregate with any other shareholder who was his relative or nominee. The act also required all major newspaper companies to reconstitute their board of directors so that fifty percent of the members were chosen in elections by working journalists and other staff, and only the remaining fifty percent appointed by the general meeting of the company. The new boards, moreover, were assigned the ambiguous responsibility of promoting the directive principles of the constitution.[83]

Other major policy goals advanced by the CFSA leadership in foreign affairs were aided by the unexpected opportunities created in the wake of the Bangladesh conflict. The likelihood that India would inevitably be drawn into a third military confrontation with Pakistan inflamed fears of diplomatic and military isolation. The United States, which revealed the secret Kissinger-Chou talks in Peking during July 1971, was clearly moving toward a rapprochement with China within the perspective of a global strategy that not only denied India a central role in the emerging balance of power in Asia, but recognized the "legitimate interests" of China in the subcontinent. The prospect that China might come to the aid of Pakistan in the event of armed conflict between India and Pakistan was sufficiently alarming to cause serious concern about finding a counterweight. The diplomatic and military assurances sought by India were available only from the Soviet Union.[84] In the summer of 1971, Mrs. Gandhi, on the basis of positive recommendations from both D. P. Dhar

---

[81] *The Statesman*, September 20, 1972.

[82] Krishnan, *Chavan and the Troubled Decade*, p. 274.

[83] *The Statesman*, August 19, 1971.

[84] For a discussion of the strategic considerations on both sides, see Ashok Kapur, "Indo-Soviet Treaty and the Emerging Asian Balance" in *Asian Survey* (Spring 1972), pp. 463-74; and Robert H. Donaldson, "India: The Soviet Stake in Stability," in *Asian Survey* (Spring 1972), pp. 475-92.

and P. N. Haksar, authorized negotiations for a formal treaty. On August 9, 1971, India and the Soviet Union signed a Twenty-Year Treaty of Peace and Friendship[85] that altered the nation's policy of nonalignment pursued since Independence. Although the USSR did affirm its respect for India's policy of nonalignment, and the treaty stopped short of automatic provisions for mutual defense, it nevertheless defined a wide area of consultation and coordination in military policies. In particular, Article IX specified that "each high contracting party undertakes to abstain from providing any assistance to any third party that engages in armed conflict with the other party. In the event of either party being subjected to an attack or a threat thereof, the high contracting parties shall immediately enter into mutual consultations in order to remove such threat and to take appropriate effective measures to ensure peace and the security of their countries."

This operative part of the treaty was buttressed by more general provisions for regular contacts between the two countries to establish "mutually advantageous and comprehensive cooperation" over a wide area, including the fields of economic, scientific, and technological cooperation, as well as "the fields of science, art, literature, education, public health, press, radio, television, cinema, tourism and sports."

The influence of the Soviet Union in India, reinforced as it was by the vanishing presence of the United States, greatly increased in the aftermath of the treaty. A new Indo-Soviet Commission, established in November 1972, began the process of institutionalizing the treaty provisions for economic, scientific, and technical cooperation in order to provide a permanent framework for discussions between the two countries, aimed at coordinating selected production and trade programs of the Russian and Indian economic plans. In November 1973, the two countries signed a fifteen-year agreement for more rapid development of economic and trade relations.[86] The accord, described by Soviet party chief Leonid Brezhnev as a "qualitatively new, positive advancement in Indo-Soviet relations," projected a 150-200 percent increase in trade by 1980; major Soviet assistance to India for installation of new capacity and expansion of existing capacity in steel, power generation, coal mining, and oil exploration; and closer coordination between the Indian Planning Commission and the State Planning Committee of the USSR.

Within a year of the 1971 election, the CFSA leadership had good reason to feel satisfied with its role in radicalizing the Congress party's "national program." Even so, the Forum had not achieved its goal of radicalizing the party organization. Its gains in the states were piecemeal

---

[85] The text of the treaty is published in *The Statesman*, August 10, 1971.
[86] See *The Statesman*, November 29, November 30, 1973.

and disproportionately concentrated in areas where the bulk of the undivided party remained in the hands of the Congress (O) after the split. These strongholds, moreover, were threatened in the aftermath of the massive election victory won by the Congress (R), when large numbers of Congress (O) members and even entire Congress (O) units expressed their desire to return to the "real" Congress.

The Central Parliamentary Board, which discussed the issue on March 22, 1971, decided that as a general principle "the entry of the members belonging to the Syndicate, particularly its office bearers . . . should be discouraged." Yet it placed no outright prohibition on their return. It allowed each PCC to take its own decision "after making thorough scrutiny and on merits," applying as one of the main criteria "commitment to the progressive policies and programs of the Congress party."[87] The same principle was also enunciated with respect to screening the large numbers of MLAs from the opposition parties seeking to enter the Congress legislative parties. Within the next few months the influx of new members, primarily from the Congress (O), was so great that the Forum found itself in danger of being overwhelmed. The Central Steering Committee of CFSA was so alarmed at the "unprecedented influx of a large number of opportunistic and reactionary forces into the Congress" that it departed from its customary prudence in addressing a formal appeal to its own members to "consolidate and equip itself fully to smash the threat of consolidation of the forces of right reaction within the Congress Party, so that this Forum continues to play the role of a vanguard of the Congress Party in the march toward socialist society."[88]

The Forum had, in fact, begun to operate as a faction in the intraparty disputes that once again plagued state and district party organizations. Warring groups, variously composed of entrenched party factions, new alignments put together by defectors from opposition parties, or the personal followings of powerful individuals capable of holding the balance between two or more larger rival groups, advanced claims for key positions inside the party and the government. The Forum, using labels of "reactionary" and "progressive" to villify their opponents and exalt their supporters, made opportunistic alliances with one or the other rivals to advance their own claims to key party and ministerial posts. Anxious to demonstrate their strength on the eve of the 1972 general elections to the state legislative assemblies, and eager to influence the selection of party candidates, they set out to organize state and district conventions throughout the country. The meetings, which variously attracted 500 to 1,500 delegates,[89] and were addressed by members of the Forum's own Central Steering Committee, inevitably aroused accusations that the

---

[87] *Congress Marches Ahead—IV*, p. 147.
[88] *Short History of the Congress Forum for Socialist Action*, p. 49.      [89] *Ibid.*, pp. 33-35.

CFSA was attempting to promote its own power at the expense of the regular party leadership.

Charges that the Forum was a parallel organization and a party within a party were raised in the Executive Committee of the Congress party in parliament, and repeated in the press. By November 1971, the CFSA leadership found it necessary to issue an extended statement affirming that "we always remember that the Forum is no tribune for carving out careers. No tickets can be demanded in the name of the Forum. The impression that our critics may like to create that the Forum is a faction has to be vigorously fought by adhering to policies in preference to persons."[90] The public assurances were coupled with a personal letter to the prime minister, reiterating that "we are not a faction but a group devoted to the furtherance of ideologies. Our stand has been that we have the fullest faith in you as the pre-eminent leader of our party and the policies pursued by you."[91]

The fact that the Forum's role had become a matter of party and public debate was, however, an indication that it had fallen into the very trap of appearing to act as a parallel organization that the leadership sought at the outset to avoid. Attacks against the Forum were all the more effective because they coincided with renewed opposition charges of communist influence on Mrs. Gandhi in the wake of the Indo-Soviet treaty. Opponents denounced the agreement as a departure from nonalignment that had pushed India into the Russian orbit.

The worst possible outcome, from the point of view of the Forum, occurred. The attacks started what the CFSA leadership perceived as a "rethinking in the Prime Minister." The first indication of what the Forum leadership considered a reversion by Mrs. Gandhi to "status quo policies" came on the eve of the 1972 general elections in the selection of the party's candidates.

The CFSA, in October 1971, had set down its own norms for selection of the Congress nominees. These stressed the necessity of giving tickets to youth, representatives of labor, peasants, women, backward and minority communities, and above all, "known person[s] committed to progressive, Radical, Socialist thoughts and implementation and possessing unblemished public character and integrity." Conversely, they insisted that party tickets should be denied to members of the Congress (O) who joined the party after the mid-term poll, and all those "generally known to be opposed to the party's fundamental policies, programs and principles irrespective of their resourcefulness to win elections." They suggested that places should be found for committed candidates by denying tickets to one-third of the members of the party in the outgoing assembly; and that chief ministers be excluded from meetings

---

[90] *Ibid.*, p. 38.                                    [91] *Ibid.*, p. 35.

of the Central Election Commission, which approved the final lists, in order to prevent them from vetoing progressive candidates.[92]

A less stringent set of procedures and criteria for the selection of candidates was adopted. The Central Election Committee made no effort to exclude the chief ministers from its deliberations. They did agree that "as far as possible," one-third of the sitting members of the Congress legislative parties should retire; fifteen percent of all seats should be allotted to women; and minorities, intellectuals, youth, labor, and the weaker sections of society should receive "adequate representation." No ban was placed on giving party tickets to recent defectors from the Congress (O) or other opposition parties.[93]

The guidelines were sufficiently broad to provide considerable room for discretion at the level of the DCC executives and the Pradesh Election Committees in making recommendations to the Central Election Committee. In any case, the DCCs and PECs were often unable to come up with an agreed list of candidates, and in many cases forwarded panels of names representing diverse candidates of local faction groups. Even when this was not so, the Central Election Committee, which played a more important role than in previous elections, often rejected recommendations by the PECs. Yet the Forum found that it could not prevail on the senior leadership, and in particular on Mrs. Gandhi, to endorse their own list of candidates. On the contrary, the Forum experienced "a major setback with the 1972 elections." The prime minister, who they hoped would be accessible to their advice through the membership of S. S. Ray on the CEC, instead turned to other advisers. These included old-time family friends, especially Uma Shankar Dikshit, then AICC treasurer, and Yashpal Kapoor, personal secretary to the prime minister. Both men counseled that it was necessary to make concessions to established factional groups in the different context of state elections, where local issues and loyalties would assume more critical importance in the decisions of the electorate. The result was that the Forum got very few of its candidates approved by the CEC, no more than two to three hundred by their own estimate, out of the almost twenty-seven hundred seats contested by Congress.

The setback to the Forum at the state level did not mean that Mrs. Gandhi had recovered her freedom to reconstitute the party as an instrument of popular participation in the tasks of carrying out Congress policies. After 1971, the influx into Congress of defectors from opposition parties, ranging the entire political spectrum, left the organization without any cohesive ideological core, and even less capacity for popular mobilization than that of the undivided party.

[92] *Two Years of CFSA, Decisions & Resolutions*, pp. 50-51.
[93] AICC, *Congress Marches Ahead—V*, pp. 147-55.

The prime minister continued to undercut the position of established party bosses at the state level. On the eve of the 1972 general elections, Mrs. Gandhi removed or otherwise arranged the resignation of no fewer than four chief ministers, among them men who had dominated the party machinery since the early years of Independence. Starting in June 1971, moreover, the central leadership announced its intention of "revitalizing" the party's organizational apparatus by superseding the Pradesh Congress Committees in "problem states,"[94] and reconstituting ad hoc Pradesh Congress Committees and Pradesh Election Committees.

The reconstituted party organizations were even more ineffective as instruments of social transformation than the undivided party had been.[95] The fact was that while the prime minister could weaken the personal hold of individual party bosses on the political machinery of the states, she could not replace the old political patterns of caste and factional alignments in reconstituting district and state committees. The new aspirants to power inside the party usually had no more ideological commitment to socialism than their predecessors, and with only few exceptions in the states, they represented the same socio-economic groups. Younger and less experienced than the established leadership, they enjoyed an even more narrow and tenuous base of popular support.

The "major overhaul of the organizational set-up" carried out under these circumstances only opened up new possibilities of factional infighting by inflaming the ambition of lesser leaders for key positions in the party and the government. At the same time, the hold of established state party bosses on the political machinery was neither completely destroyed nor replaced. On the contrary, in most cases the new executives were selected as the "consensus" choice of Mrs. Gandhi and the outgoing leadership. At best, the changes momentarily refurbished the image of the party by bringing in new faces. Even then, they diminished its organizational cohesion by accommodating the claims of a burgeoning number of "groups" that now demanded direct representation in the distribution of party and ministerial posts. Worse still, even though Mrs. Gandhi, by virtue of her preeminence inside the party, was able to override objections by powerful local leaders to changes in the personnel of Pradesh Congress Committees and state ministries, the "unanimous" decisions reported at the end of Center-state consultations on the composition of new party and government executives were artificial. No sooner

[94] These included the states of Tamil Nadu, Gujerat, Bihar, Madhya Pradesh, Rajasthan, West Bengal, Orissa, Andhra Pradesh, and Assam.

[95] See S. Viswam, "The Congress (R) in Disarray," *The Statesman*, October 8, 1971; and by the same journalist, "Patchwork Unity in Congress (R)," *The Statesman*, January 7, 1972; also, Zareer Masani, *Indira Gandhi, a Biography*, pp. 291-96.

had Pradesh Congress Committees been "reconstituted" and ministries "reshuffled" on the basis of "agreed" lists, than the struggle for power among rival groups resurfaced. The party organization and government at the state level were soon caught up in a paralysis of factional infighting that required periodic interventions by the prime minister to redistribute party and government posts that, at best, produced only a temporary truce.

The appearance of a large number of new faces among state and government leaders did not signify the "revitalization" of the Congress party. Rather, it indicated a growing organizational vacuum. The new chief ministers and PCC presidents selected by Mrs. Gandhi owed their position entirely to the favor bestowed by her. Often, they were political "outsiders" lacking a personal base in the complex caste and factional alignments that still continued to operate at the district and state level. They were, on this account, less dangerous than their predecessors as potential rivals to the prime minister. But, weakened by an uncertain tenure and the absence of an autonomous organizational base, they lacked the capacity to mobilize local followings on behalf of national policies. They were also easy prey for other aspirants to leadership positions inside their own party. This was especially true in the case of rivals who were prepared to use bribes and other less innocent means of intimidation for rallying defectors from the dominant group in order to demonstrate a new "majority" inside the party, and convince the prime minister once again to intervene and "reconstitute" party committees and "reshuffle" state ministries. The net result was a premium on bribery and intimidation that undermined the stability of Congress ministries, and ultimately exposed the democratic process to charges of political fraud.

Indeed, political corruption grew so pervasive that some critics came to perceive it as constituting the "milieu of the Indian polity."[96] It went beyond abuse of office by individual ministers and party officials for personal advantage and enrichment. The entire electoral process was compromised by the growing importance of "black money" in financing election campaigns. The Congress party, which could no longer rely on intermediaries to "deliver" the peasant vote, but failed to build a substitute grass-roots organization that might have generated funds through collection of numerous small donations, became more and more dependent on the "black-moneyed elite" for campaign finances. As the Congress switched over to a direct mass appeal, its needs for election funds to finance massive publicity campaigns and mammoth public meetings greatly expanded. By 1972, although direct verification was impossible,

---

[96] Dev Dutt, "In Politics," in Suresh Kohli, ed., *Corruption: The Growing Evil in India*, p. 78.

it was believed that the Congress party and the prime minister personally had become the main recipient of illegal contributions by the larger business houses (in response to political blackmail implicit in threats of nationalization), and from leading smugglers (in return for political protection over a wide range of illegal transactions) that sparked rumors of growing ties between the government and "black professions" of the underworld.[97]

At the time of the 1972 general elections to the state legislative assemblies, organizational degeneration and moral decay were so far advanced that the realistic possibilities of party reform had diminished almost to the vanishing point. Yet the national leadership once again contested the poll on a platform that described Congress as the only party with the capacity to achieve a "socialist revolution which is peaceful and democratic and embraces all our people and permeates all spheres of national life."

The election strategy closely paralleled the successful campaign of 1971. Mrs. Gandhi once again embarked on an extended tour that involved a month of nonstop electioneering in all the states where assembly elections were scheduled. "Theme" posters, films, records, cinema slides, tracts, leaflets, hoardings, and "publicity materials of all kinds" were produced by the AICC[98] in the various regional languages, and distributed among all sections of the electorate to establish the salience of broad national issues over local and state problems stressed by the opposition. Mrs. Gandhi, in her speeches across the country, asserted the need for strong and stable government not only at the Center but in the states, and pressed the argument that only the Congress party could provide such governments. Although there were recurrent references to the need for national vigilance against another Indo-Pakistani war, the main focus was on returning to "the bigger war—the war against poverty."[99] This time, moreover, Mrs. Gandhi elaborated the pledges of Garibi Hatao with promises to improve the income of the masses of the rural poor through new legislation to lower ceiling limits on landownership. The proposal for another round of agrarian reform was specific. It called for a ceiling on family holdings at 10 to 18 acres of perennially irrigated land or irrigated land capable of growing two crops, or the equivalent amount for other categories of land. According to the election manifesto, the Congress party, recognizing that the "mere passing of legislation is not enough," pledged to "lend its organizational support to the Government in carrying out reforms at the grass-roots level."[100]

[97] *Ibid.*, pp. 82-101.              [98] AICC, *People's Victory—Second Phase*, pp. 13-15.
[99] *Ibid.*, p. 17.
[100] Indian National Congress, *Election Manifesto 1971-72*, pp. 9-13.

The result of the election[101] was another massive victory for the Congress party and a "virtual massacre" of the opposition. Although Congress did not contest in 7 percent of assembly constituencies, primarily as a result of electoral adjustments with the CPI, it nevertheless won over 70 percent of the total number of seats. Overall, the party registered a net gain of 549 seats, compared to its position on the eve of elections. It captured seats from opposition parties and independents ranging across the entire ideological spectrum.

The party's share of the popular vote also showed a marked improvement. It climbed to 47 percent, compared to 42 percent in 1967, the highest percentage ever polled by Congress in assembly general elections.[102] The strength of this popular support, with the exception of Bihar (and the small newly created states of Manipur and Meghalaya and the Union territory of Goa) was evenly distributed. As shown in Table 11-2, Congress won either a large plurality or a majority of valid votes polled, and an overwhelming majority of seats in the major states where elections were held.

TABLE 11-2

Congress Votes and Seats Won in the 1972 Election

| State | Percentage of valid votes polled | Percentage of seats won |
|---|---|---|
| Andhra Pradesh | 52.17 | 76.31 |
| Assam | 53.26 | 83.33 |
| Bihar | 32.30 | 52.52 |
| Gujerat | 45.84 | 83.33 |
| Haryana | 46.90 | 64.20 |
| Himachal | 51.16 | 78.46 |
| Jammu and Kashmir | 55.89 | 77.00 |
| Madhya Pradesh | 47.95 | 74.32 |
| Maharashtra | 56.47 | 82.22 |
| Meghalaya | 9.95 | 15.00 |
| Manipur | 30.02 | 28.33 |
| Mysore | 52.24 | 76.39 |
| Punjab | 42.84 | 63.46 |
| Rajasthan | 49.29 | 78.81 |
| West Bengal | 48.99 | 77.14 |
| Tripura | 44.94 | 68.33 |
| Goa | 13.72 | 3.33 |
| Delhi | 48.55 | 78.57 |

SOURCE: *People's Victory—Second Phase (An Analysis of the 1972 General Election to State Assemblies)* (New Delhi, June 1972), Appendix II, IV.

[101] *People's Victory—Second Phase*, pp. 19–38.
[102] Congress vote totals actually reached an average of 50.74 percent when calculated as a percentage of total valid votes cast in the constituencies where Congress candidates contested.

Among the opposition parties, only the CPI, which had profited from its electoral adjustment with Congress, was able marginally to improve its position. The communists won about 4 percent of the popular vote, increasing its share of seats to 4 percent in 1971 from 3 percent in 1967. They emerged as the second largest party in Andhra Pradesh, Bihar, Punjab, and West Bengal. Swatantra, by contrast, decimated by defections, was destroyed as a national party. It polled less than 2 percent of the vote in 1971, compared to 7 percent in 1967, winning 0.59 percent of the seats, in contrast to its earlier victories in almost 7 percent of assembly constituencies. Other opposition parties were routed in their regional strongholds. The Congress (O) managed to win only 6.6 percent of the total vote, compared to 10 percent polled by it during the Lok Sabha election. They captured only 3 percent of the total seats, and were reduced to a splinter group in both Gujerat and Mysore. Even the Jan Sangh, which managed to maintain its 1967 vote level of about 8.5 percent, suffered a serious loss of seats from 7.7 percent in 1967 to 3.8 percent in 1972, losing strength in Delhi and Madhya Pradesh. Most startling, the CPI (Marxists) were pushed back in West Bengal. They suffered a setback in their share of the popular vote from almost 33 percent in 1971 to less than 27 percent in 1972, and a staggering loss of seats from 111 in the 1971 assembly election to 14 seats in 1972.[103]

The outcome of the 1972 elections only helped to underscore a paradox of India's political development. Perhaps at no other moment had conditions been more favorable for the realization of Gandhi's and Nehru's original vision of social transformation through democratic and constitutional methods. The awakening of large numbers of the rural poor to a desire for the implementation of new principles of equality and participation had taken political form. The outpouring of support across regional, linguistic, communal, and caste lines held out the possibility of creating a strong party organization that could institutionalize popular participation at the grass-roots level, and provide an effective nonviolent sanction from below for agrarian reform. The almost total rout of the opposition, both right and left, the formation of Congress majority governments at the Center and in the states, the elimination of virtually all constitutional impediments to the redistribution of property, all made it seem as if the popular endorsement for "Garibi Hatao" was the first step in the fulfillment of Nehru's strategy for democratic social transformation.

Yet what at an earlier time might have been a beginning was, under the

---

[103] Marxist leaders challenged the validity of the electoral results on grounds that the central government had unleashed a reign of terror in the state, using the police, Central Reserve Police, and the Army to kill, arrest, and intimidate party workers. See Field and Franda, "The Communist Parties of West Bengal," in Weiner and Field, eds., *Electoral Politics in the Indian States*, vol. 1, 14–19.

conditions of the early 1970s, the end of Nehru's democratic design for the creation of a socialist pattern of society. The enormous organizational effort at the state level that would have been needed to involve the poorer castes and classes in the implementation of Congress promises for social and economic reform was never attempted. On the contrary, the national party organization was itself immobilized by ideological cleavages that threatened to harden into a new split.

After the 1972 elections, the "committed" Congressmen inside the party were increasingly exposed and attacked as a communist faction seeking to advance their own control over the organization. Chandra Shekhar, one of the most influential radical MPs inside the party, spoke for the non-communist socialists as a whole when he publicly denounced the CFSA leadership for functioning as a cell in an attempt to gain power. He charged:

> Once the struggle against the Syndicate was over, a section of the so-called Left started having different ideas about their role in the new organization. The members, hailing from the C.P.I. started functioning as a clique. Apparently they turned themselves into a cell. Old habits die hard indeed. They started having secret meetings to plan their strategy to reach positions of power. Their strategy was solely to achieve personal ends and their tall talk of Leftism was just a cover to camouflage their opportunist role in the party. Their second strategy seems to have been to denigrate and isolate those Congress Socialists who did not have their Communist background. Their third line of operation has been to spread rumors that they alone enjoyed the confidence of the Prime Minister, as they were the only loyal adherents to the Congress ideology. . . .
>
> The Forum which embraced all shades of progressive opinion in the Congress was pressed into service for such a power game. While holding the leadership of the Forum in their hands, they sought to exploit others by associating them with the organization. The State units were formed for factional considerations. This did not go unnoticed by the leadership. Besides, the group started moving towards capturing the party apparatus.
>
> In this sordid game, they used Afro-Asian Solidarity and Peace Council organizations besides a host of other friendship organizations of the Communist countries for their ends. It was so easy to entrap members of Parliament and other Congress workers. The dictum was like that in the old British navy: Join these organizations and see the world. Some of them had managed to become Ministers or party bosses.[104]

[104] *The Statesman*, June 7, 1972.

By May 1972, moreover, the Forum's bid for hegemony over the Congress parliamentary party was directly challenged by the sudden appearance of a rival Nehru Study Forum led by senior Congress members of parliament. The immediate provocation for starting the Nehru Forum was described as concern at criticism of Nehru's approach to social transformation through democratic and peaceful methods by "so-called radicals and pseudo socialists."[105] The main activity of the new group was defined in terms of studying and explaining the meaning of Nehru's philosophy, policy, and program of "democracy, democratic socialism meaning thereby Planned development of the Indian society within the framework of the Indian Constitution, Secularism and Non-Violence."[106] Although the leaders of the Nehru Study Forum did not actually name the CFSA in their attacks, they set out to organize a show of strength in the Congress parliamentary party in order to exert counterpressure on the national leadership to silence and radicals.

The MPs of the Nehru Forum were alarmed at the infiltration of ex-communists into the party, their domination at CPP meetings, their close links with those committed to a "foreign type of scientific socialism," and their use of propaganda in the name of the prime minister to pressure the party into the adoption of radical policy goals that could not be carried out within the democratic process. Above all, they feared that if unchecked, CFSA activities would "bring about a situation [of popular discontent] leading to confusion and chaos in which only a Marxist solution was possible. There would be a suspension or liquidation of the democratic order, probably in the name of restoring law and order, and a method of telling people what they must do, rather than persuading them to do it. So India would be converted from the path of democratic socialism to some kind of dictatorship with a Marxist left orientation of the kind seen in other countries."[107]

Shortly after the formation of the Nehru Study Forum, publications appeared that detailed the communist affiliations and contacts of prominent members of the Congress party organization and the government. Excerpts from Kumaramangalam's Thesis were printed, and the document was published in full in July 1973, along with an allegation that it had been resubmitted for consideration to the leadership of the CPI in early 1969, and that on this occasion, in contrast to the disinterested response of 1964, "the Party leadership plumped for it."[108]

Mrs. Gandhi publicly maintained a detached posture in her relation-

[105] R. D. Bhandare, "Thoughts of Jawaharlal Nehru," *Seminar on Jawaharlal Nehru, 14th and 15th November, 1972* (New Delhi, Nehru Study Forum, 1972), p. 5.

[106] *Ibid.*, p. 8.

[107] These fears were expressed by a founding member and executive officer of the Nehru Study Forum during an interview in New Delhi, August 21, 1973.

[108] Satindra Singh, *Communists in Congress, Kumaramangalam's Thesis*, p. vii.

ships with both groups. But she did not attempt to stop one of her closest advisers, U. S. Dikshit, from voicing his public support for the Nehru Forum by addressing one of its meetings. Shortly after the 1972 elections, moreover, Mrs. Gandhi herself suggested privately to prominent members of the CFSA that it was unnecessary to have a separate Congress Forum for Socialist Action inside the party, when the split had already assured that all party members were committed to socialism. As the activities of the Nehru Study Forum intensified and threatened to cause a confrontation amounting to a split in the Congress parliamentary party, the subject of the continuation of both forums was raised in the Congress Parliamentary Board. On April 3, 1973, the board reported "the consensus of opinion of the members [that] Congress having decided to vigorously pursue its well-established policy of democratic socialism, continuance of various forums within the Party is unnecessary and is proving to be against the interests of the party."[109] The CFSA, advised of the board's view, immediately announced its decision to wind up all its activities. The only other alternative would have been to fight against Mrs. Gandhi and "to play into the hands of our enemies." The Nehru Study Forum, its main goal accomplished, dissolved its own organization soon after.

Neither group, however, ceased to function as an informal caucus inside the Congress parliamentary party. Indeed, each put up its own "unofficial" slate of candidates for the first time in elections to the Executive Committee of the Congress parliamentary party in May 1973. The results showed that the party was almost evenly divided between the two groups, with seats in the executive going in about equal numbers to the nominees of each forum. The outcome demonstrated that the CFSA enjoyed "much wider support in the party than most people had even suspected."[110] It also provided evidence "if any proof were needed that the Congress Parliamentary Party is split in its attitude toward implementing socialism," and " if the two groups go their own way, there is every danger of a physical split."[111]

The ideological cleavage paralyzed the national party organization. Proposals for changes in the Congress constitution languished inside a divided Working Committee for three years. The nine-man Constitution Subcommittee appointed by the Congress president in April 1971 at the height of the Forum's influence had been dominated by party radicals. Their proposals for reform revived elements of the communists' strategy in the 1930s for capturing power inside the party organization. They rec-

[109] AICC, *Report of the General Secretaries*, June 1972-August 1973 (New Delhi, September 1973), pp. 11-12.
[110] *Times of India*, May 19, 1973.
[111] See S. Viswam, "The Lessons of the C.P.P. Elections," *The Statesman*, May 18, 1973.

ommended that active members be required to take up organizational
work in "functional" mass organizations; that such fronts be given institutional membership in the Congress; and that executive committees
at all levels of the party organization include a fixed number of coopted
members from the affiliated institutions.[112] Such recommendations were
passively resisted by senior leaders of the Working Committee, who continued to postpone action by insisting that further consideration was required. By January 1973, the opponents of such changes were strong
enough to win an enlargement of the subcommittee that succeeded in
neutralizing the radicals. The constitutional changes, finally adopted in
May 1974 on the basis of new proposals by the enlarged Constitution
Subcommittee, made piecemeal changes in the organizational structure
of the party.[113] The recommendations for institutional affiliation and
ex-officio representation on party executive committees of active workers in mass fronts were watered down. They provided that "special elements not adequately represented" should be coopted as members of the
DCCs, PCCs, and All-India Congress Committee, including representatives of women, trade unions, scheduled castes and Tribes, the Indian
Youth Congress, and the National Students Union, although with an
upper limit of fifteen percent on the proportion of the coopted membership. No change at all was allowed in the procedure for enrolling
primary members through payment of a nominal fee (of Rs. 1 bien-
nially), or in their voting rights to elections of local units of the Congress
party. At the same time, the ability of party bosses to manipulate organizational elections at the upper tiers of the party structure was reduced by
new provisions requiring the direct election of members of the Pradesh
Congress Committees by all active members in the constituency voting
on the basis of simple majority. Another amendment to the Congress
constitution required all active members to participate in a "training program of political and ideological study as directed by the Working
Committee from time to time"—the only concession to the enthusiasm
of the radicals for building "cadres" at all levels of the organization.

The condition of the party was nevertheless rapidly deteriorating. The
first organizational elections since the 1969 split, held in December 1972,
had been accompanied by a flood of complaints to the AICC office of
massive bribery, intimidation, and manipulation of bogus membership
lists by rival factions. Order could be restored only when the prime
minister personally intervened to impose a "consensus" choice for the
party leadership. The new executive committees, whether elective or ap-
pointive, ignored directives from the AICC office to set up special cells
for active recruitment of minorities, Harijans, peasants, landless laborers,

---

[112] *Two Years of CFSA, Decisions & Resolutions*, pp. 45-47.
[113] AICC, *Congress Marches Ahead—10*, pp. 33-62.

and other disadvantaged groups. Although record targets for the enrollment of ten million primary members were met by 1973, approximately
sixty percent of the membership was believed to be "bogus."[114] Organizational elections under the revised constitution scheduled for early
January 1975 were cancelled. Instead, the Working Committee instituted
routine recourse to the appointment of new ad hoc committees, authorizing the Congress president to "take necessary steps to strengthen the organization and wherever deemed necessary to restructure the PCC's by
appointing ad hoc Committees."[115]

The achievements of the AICC's Political Training and Cadre Building Department were no better. K. D. Malaviya initially took up the
program in 1971, with hopes of building up a grass-roots organization of
one million trained workers who could be mobilized within their own
area at short notice to organize the population to implement Congress
policies. His plans met with continued resistance by the Working Committee. Malaviya, who actually recruited most of the candidates for the
training camps from "highly motivated" young persons who were outside the Congress party, managed to hold no more than four camps with
about a thousand recruits before he finally resigned as convener of the
cadre building program. He found that the "members were forever
postponing the convening of these camps out of fear that they would be
used to create a Marxist-style cadre that would not be bound by methods
of democratic operation."[116] His successors, working inside the regular
party apparatus, organized only three central camps for about 300 workers in three years, and were almost completely frustrated in attempts to
convince local party committees to take up political training activities.[117]

The Indian Youth Congress, for the time being, remained an urban-
based organization with a greater capacity for political disruption than
popular organization. As their links with international youth organizations of Eastern Europe and the USSR expanded, they devoted most of
their energies to organizing mass demonstrations, protests, and rallies,
invoking Marxist slogans of exploitation to rouse public anger against
the failures of popularly elected governments to carry out promises of
economic reform.

The prime minister, whose credibility had become identified with the
implementation of peaceful and democratic socialist revolution, appeared
helpless against the organizational decay in her own party, but was unable to admit these internal limitations without exposing the hollowness

---

[114] Masani, *Indira Gandhi, a Biography*, p. 292.
[115] *Congress Marches Ahead—10*, p. 77.
[116] Interview, K. D. Malaviya, New Delhi, June 20, 1973.
[117] AICC, *Report of the General Secretaries*, June 1972-August 1973 (New Delhi, September 1973), pp. 47-48.

of her promises. Instead, through her speeches and those of senior party leaders appointed at her command, she encouraged the political climate in which Congress workers officially blamed failures of implementation on the "forces of reaction which are again active today."[118] Shankar Dayal Sharma, whose loyalty to Mrs. Gandhi during the 1969 split was rewarded by his appointment as Congress president in May 1972, advanced the theory of a "deep-seated conspiracy of the opposition parties against the interests of the country"[119] to explain growing incidents of communal, linguistic, and regional violence as planned outbreaks intended to weaken national unity and divert national attention from basic issues of socialist reform. Mrs. Gandhi, angered by the opposition attacks against her, pointed to the "forces gathering against us" and to the dangers coming both from "within and without."[120] The result was a further acceleration in the process of polarization that strained democratic consensus to the point of breakdown.

The decisive confrontation between the government and the opposition was joined in the wake of yet another adverse ruling by the Supreme Court, which called into question the most radical elements of the sweeping constitutional changes pushed through by the ruling party after the 1971 elections. On April 24, 1973, a Special Constitution Bench of thirteen judges of the Supreme Court, acting on writ petitions challenging the validity of the Twenty-Fourth and Twenty-Fifth Amendments, handed down their judgment on the case of Keshavananda Bharati vs. State of Kerala.[121] The judges, in a unanimous opinion, reversed their previous ruling under the Golak Nath case to uphold the validity of the Twenty-Fourth Amendment. They affirmed the right of parliament to amend any provision of the constitution, including all of the fundamental rights. They also held that the first part of the Twenty-Fifth Amendment was valid in substituting the word "amount" for "compensation" in cases of compulsory acquisition of property by the government, and that any challenge based on the inadequacy of the amount could not be heard by the court. The Special Constitution Bench, however, was closely divided on the validity of the second part of the Twenty-Fifth Amendment inserted as a new Article 31(c). A majority of seven to six upheld the first provision of the section that no law giving effect to the directive principles as specified in Article 39(b) and (c) could be deemed void on

[118] See "Resolution on Political Situation," summary of the proceedings of the North Zone Conference of AICC, Patiala, March 23 & 24, 1973, All India Congress Committee, *Congresses Marches Ahead—VIII*, p. 224.

[119] *Ibid.*, p. 205.                                    [120] *Ibid.*, p. 193.

[121] The court's judgment and the opinions of the individual judges are summarized at length in *The Statesman*, April 25, 1973. The issues involved in the case are analyzed in H. P. Raina, "The Judgment," in Kuldip Nayar, ed., *Supersession of Judges*, pp. 137-56.

the grounds that it abridged or took away the fundamental rights conferred by Articles 14, 19, and 31. But a larger majority struck down the second section of the article, namely, the provision that "no law containing a declaration that it is for giving effect to such policy shall be called into question in any court on the ground that it does not give effect to such policy."

The judgment, as reported in the English-language press was interpreted as a personal defeat for Mrs. Gandhi. The prime minister, who by her efforts had come to embody the Congress party's renewed commitment to economic reform, was also persuaded that the court's ruling was designed as a direct challenge to her power. Her supporters among the ex-communists inside the party were, in addition, convinced that the opinion foreshadowed future attacks on the legality of social legislation that could stymie efforts to carry out sweeping constitutional changes in the name of the directive principles. Once again, the prime minister and the "committed" socialists inside the Congress party discovered a mutual interest in joining forces against common enemies on the court who posed a challenge to their preeminent position.

The court, in fact, was deeply divided on the fundamental constitutional question of the scope of parliament's amending power. Six judges, including the chief justice, S. M. Sikri, rejected the government's interpretation of the unlimited scope of parliament's amending power extending to repeal or abrogation of any article in the constitution, including the preamble, the directive principles, and the amending power itself, subject only to the limitation that the word "amendment" prevented parliament from repealing the whole constitution. These six judges agreed that parliament could amend every article of the constitution and abridge any of the fundamental rights, but they insisted that this power could not extend to damaging or destroying the essential features of the constitution. According to this interpretation, the constitution had been given by the people to themselves and remained supreme over parliament. Parliament was required to act as its functionary, and had no competence to destroy any of its fundamental parts. The fundamental rights, in this view, were among the essential features of the constitution. They could be amended or abridged, but they could not be damaged, abrogated, or destroyed. On this interpretation of parliament's amending powers, the judges were prepared to join their colleagues in upholding the Twenty-Fourth Amendment, stating that it did not enlarge the amending power of the constitution as it stood prior to the Golak Nath case. Similarly, they agreed with the other members of the bench on the validity of the first part of the Twenty-Fifth Amendment, asserting that its provisions did not abrogate the right to property in requiring the state to pay an "amount" for the compulsory acquisition of property, since this could not be so arbitrary or illusory that it amounted to an abrogation of the right to property. Using the same line of reasoning, however, the six judges held the second part of the Twenty-Fifth Amendment or Article 31(c) invalid on the grounds that it empowered parliament and the state legislatures to make laws that, in effect, would permit abrogation of the fundamental rights under Articles 14, 19, and 31, which were essential features of the constitution.

The doctrine that the powers of parliament to amend the constitution were inherently limited by the requirement to preserve the fundamental features of the constitution, including the fundamental rights, was rejected by six other members of the Special Constitution Bench. Their opinions followed the arguments of government that parliament's power of amendment was unlimited; that it extended to powers of abrogating any part or parts of the constitution, and that there could be no distinction for the purpose of the amending power between essential and nonessential features. Accordingly, they upheld the validity not only of the Twenty-Fourth Amendment and the first part of the Twenty-Fifth Amendment, but also the next section of the Twenty-Fifth Amendment, establishing the legal superiority of the directive principles of state policy over the provisions protecting fundamental rights, breaking ranks to strike down only the final provision prohibiting judicial review of such legislation upon the simple declaration by the legislature that it was designed to give effect to directive principles of state policy.

The statement of constitutional doctrine as it emerged in the majority judgment of the court was an uneasy compromise between these two views, derived in large measure from the intermediate position taken by the tie-breaking member of the Special Bench, Justice Khanna. According to the majority opinion, parliament's power to amend the constitution was limited in the sense that it could not abrogate the constitution or alter the "basic structure or framework" of the constitution. The meaning of this restriction was that parliament could not use its power of amendment to make such drastic changes that the constitution lost its identity. Parliament's plenary power, for example, did not extend to abolishing the states or the federal structure or the democratic political system. At the same time, according to this compromise formulation, the right to property and the other fundamental rights were not included in the "basic structure" of the constitution. They fell, therefore, within the power of parliament to amend, abridge, or repeal.

The court's ruling established that legislation undertaken in the name of the directive principles was still subject to judicial review, and that it could be challenged on the grounds that it impaired the "basic structure" of the constitution. The Supreme Court, moreover, was so closely divided on the issue of fundamental rights that it might easily shift once again toward a more restrictive interpretation of the amending power. Under the circumstances, the role of the chief justice suddenly assumed special importance. Not only did he often give a lead to other members of the court, but he also appointed the members of each bench before which a particular case was heard. The sitting chief justice, S. M. Sikri, moreover, was scheduled to retire only two days after the court's judgment on the fundamental rights cases had been announced. His successor, under established conventions of seniority, would have been J. M. Shelat, one of the six judges favoring a restricted interpretation of the amending power to include fundamental rights as an essential feature that could not be destroyed. K. S. Hedge and A. N. Grover, the two next most senior judges, had joined Shelat in taking this position.

On April 25, one day after the Supreme Court's judgment, the president of India, on advice of the Cabinet, superseded the three most senior judges to appoint Justice A. N. Ray chief justice. The new chief justice had ruled on the side of the government on all questions of law raised by the fundamental rights issues. The decision to depart from the established convention of seniority followed the recommendations advanced to the prime minister by H. R. Gokhale, the law minister; S. S. Ray, then chief minister of West Bengal; and Mohan Kumaramangalam, minister of mines and steel, all of whom were agreed that the legal philosophy of the three judges would stand in the way of progressive legislation.

The decision set off a major explosion of criticism against the government, which raised the issue of India's future as a democracy in stark terms. The legal community was virtually unanimous in its condemnation. The three superseded judges resigned in protest. Along with the outgoing chief justice, they boycotted the swearing-in ceremony of A. N. Ray as the new chief justice. K. S. Hedge, one of the superseded judges, citing Kumaramangalam's role in the appointment, raised the alarm that it was part of a continuing scheme, first launched in 1969, by the communists to infiltrate the Congress party, and from this position undermine the constitution from within. Hedge warned that

the supercession of the Judges is not an isolated act. It is part of a scheme. Ever since the Congress split in 1969, several important Communists have entered the ruling party in pursuance of a policy adopted in 1964, viz., to capture Congress from within and pervert the Constitution. The various steps taken by our Government since the 1971 elections bear testimony to the enormous influence wielded by the Communists. . . . The people are being systematically cheated of their rights. They are deprived of their freedoms one by one. The destruction of the independence of the judiciary is an act of treachery and a fraud on our Constitution. The profession of faith in democracy by some of our leaders is a mere cloak to hide their real intentions. Their acts belie their profession. Unless the people shake off their lethargy and find out the realpolitik behind the recent developments, they will soon find themselves deprived of all their rights. We are on the way to dictatorship.[122]

The Supreme Court Bar Association, which refrained from endorsing the conspiracy theory, nevertheless voted overwhelmingly to condemn the government for taking a "purely political" act in a "blatant and outrageous attempt at undermining the independence and impartiality of the judiciary" and to "make the judiciary subservient to the executive and subject to political pressures and dependent on Government patronage and influence."[123]

The decision, which was debated in the Lok Sabha, also produced an "unprecedented uproar" among non-Communist members of the opposition, who charged that it was an effort to make the Supreme Court into a "mouthpiece of the Government."[124] The major intervention on behalf of the government during the Lok Sabha debate was not by the law minister, but by the minister of mines and steel, Mohan Kumaramangalam, reflecting the key role he had played in the Cabinet's action. His speech was forthright.[125] It explained the background against which the decision to abandon the established principle of seniority was taken, and the new criteria on the basis of which the chief justice had been selected. Citing the confrontation between the government on the one hand and the Supreme Court on the other during the six years since the Golak Nath case, Kumaramangalam at the outset defended the right of government to "think in terms of a more stable relationship between the Court and ourselves." One important requirement in putting an end to the confrontation, he argued, was an examination of the basic outlook, attitude toward life, and politics of the man appointed to the office of chief justice. According to Kumaramangalam, it was "entirely within the discretion of the Government of the day to appoint the person considered in its eyes as the most suitable, as having the most suitable philosophy or outlook," and it was this "prerogative as a Government" that had been exercised. He described in the following way the approach followed by the Cabinet in making the appointment of the new chief justice:

Read the 1,600 page judgment of the Supreme Court that has recently been delivered and all of us will know the opinions of each one of these judges. The six Judges who have upheld the 24th, 25th and 26th amendments, each one of them puts directive principles a

---

[122] *Ibid.*, pp. 52-53.                          [123] *Ibid.*, p. 28.
[124] *The Statesman*, April 27, May 3, 1973.
[125] Kumaramangalam's speech is reproduced in Nayar, *Supercession of Judges*, pp. 78-92.

little higher, fundamental rights a little lower; the due rights of a society a little higher and the rights of an individual a little lower. Then you go to the other six who have, on the contrary, said that they are the basic essential features of the Constitution which should not be violated. Fundamental Rights are sacrosanct things which must be protected, must be protected from the evil hand of the executive and everything must be done to implement the directive principles. You can see the philosophy, the outlook. Certainly, we as a government have a duty to take the philosophy and outlook of the Judge in coming to the conclusion whether he should or should not leave the Supreme Court at this time. It is our duty in the Government honestly and fairly to come to the conclusion whether a particular person is fit to be appointed the Chief Justice of the Court because of his outlook, because of his philosophy as expressed in his expressed opinions, whether he is a more suitable or a more competent Judge. This is our prerogative as a Government and I say that the Constitution has entrusted that to us.

The law minister endorsed Kumaramangalam's explanation in the Lok Sabha as the "basic understanding" of the government shared "by my other colleagues and myself."[126] The statement crystallized the "real issue" of the debate: should the judge uphold the laws of the constitution or the social philosophy of the ruling party?[127]

The clear threat to the supremacy of the constitution and the rule of law contained in the doctrine of a "committed judiciary" endorsed by the government provided an issue around which the opposition parties began to reorganize. Leaders of all opposition groups, except the CPI, this time spanning the entire ideological spectrum from the CPI (Marxists) to the Jan Sangh, began a process of consultation aimed at coordinating an attack on the government. The opposition spilled beyond organized party groups to rally prominent members of the legal profession and the press. An unlikely leader, moreover, was emerging. Jayaprakash Narayan, virtually the last remaining link with the giants of the national Independence movement, his reputation for integrity undimmed after twenty years of political retirement in the service of the Gandhian Sarvodaya Samaj, was so "deeply distressed and worried by the recent happenings" that he addressed a personal appeal to Mrs. Gandhi.[128] His appeal was directed to two counts: the need to provide constitutional safeguards preventing parliament from "abrogating the fundamental freedoms of the citizen except for suspending them for temporary periods and in clearly specified circumstances," and the necessity of ensuring the independence of the judiciary. Otherwise, Narayan warned, the pro-

[126] *Ibid.*, p. 94.  [127] *Ibid.*, pp. 36-37.
[128] The text of Narayan's letter, written on May 16, 1973, is reproduced *ibid.*, pp. 69-72.

claimed aim of the national leadership to establish socialism by peaceful means would be defeated, and "the very foundations of our democracy will be in danger of being totally destroyed."

Mrs. Gandhi no longer appeared to understand the argument Narayan raised, or his question: "if establishment of socialism necessitates the abrogation of the people's fundamental freedoms, what remains of democratic means?" On the contrary, the prime minister denied that democracy was at all endangered. Dismissing accusations that she was preparing to subvert the judiciary, censor the press, do away with civil liberties, and undermine the authority of parliament, Mrs. Gandhi once again attributed such charges to persons and groups hostile to social change and the economic policies of her government. She countered that the "cry" raised against her was the same as raised "throughout my father's time" and "it is a concerted attempt to decry me and the very policies and ideas for which Jawaharlal Nehru stood."[129] Replying to Narayan, she observed blandly, "You have spoken about the competing rights of democracy and socialism. It has been our endeavor throughout our struggle for freedom and during these 25 years as an independent nation to reconcile the two. I am perhaps more confident than you that we can achieve this reconciliation. Democracy, independence of the judiciary and fundamental rights are not in danger. They would be threatened if we were to allow our faith to be eclipsed by defeatism and if we help alliances of the extreme left and right."[130]

Mrs. Gandhi, in the end, was hopelessly entrapped. If the Forum appeared captive to her leadership as the source of their influence, she was no less a prisoner of the radical policies initiated by them and endorsed by the national party in her name. The sudden death on May 31, 1973, of Mohan Kumaramangalam in an airplane crash did not alter the qualitative change in the legitimacy of her leadership. It merely deprived the Forum of their master strategist and the prime minister of any adviser with a broad ideological vision and an overall political plan for achieving basic socialist transformation. Yet Mrs. Gandhi's own credibility, and by extension that of the democratic political process over which she presided, had become inextricably linked to promises for the implementation of radical economic reform through parliamentary means. Under the best circumstances, these promises could not be easily reconciled. Under conditions of an organizational vacuum in the states and ideological polarization at the Center, both within the ruling party and between the government and the opposition, such pledges were impossible to redeem.

[129] *Times of India*, May 5, 1973.
[130] The prime minister's reply to Narayan, dated June 9, 1973, is reproduced in Nayar, *Supersession of Judges*, pp. 73-74.

# TWELVE

# Impasse

The national leadership's inability to carry out radical social change through peaceful and parliamentary means led India into an economic and political impasse that prevented progress toward goals of growth and social justice, even while destroying the political consensus that provided the foundation of stable democratic government. Pledges of the prime minister and the Congress party to eliminate mass poverty and accelerate economic progress could not be redeemed within the existing structure of economic and political power. On the contrary, the attempt to achieve both economic development and reduction of disparities in the absence of basic institutional changes led, inevitably, to the pursuit of contradictory policies that were bound to result in the worst of both worlds, achieving neither growth nor redistribution. Yet, as Mrs. Gandhi herself realized, the transformed political environment of increasingly politicized discontent, both among the educated unemployed in the urban areas and the landless agricultural laborers in the countryside, demanded some improvement in the conditions of the most desperate sections of the population, "not only to help the people directly but also to get peace in the country which is prerequisite to any kind of progress."[1]

The central government, which had no party organization in place to provide sustained popular support from below for implementing land reforms and other redistributive measures essential for achieving growth *through* social justice, temporized by following separate economic and "socio-political" policies. The first set of programs aimed at maximizing economic growth, and the second at "reaching the benefits of development to the numerically larger but weaker sections of the rural areas."[2] On the one hand, the growth strategy required policies based on incentives to private investment that inexorably increased disparities still further; on the other, equity considerations dictated the introduction of a new array of central sector schemes to provide some technical training for the educated unemployed, and subsidized loans and public employment to marginal and small farmers and landless laborers to increase their income and consumption. Yet it was impossible to mobilize additional

[1] Planning Commission, Twenty-eighth Meeting of the National Development Council, May 30 and 31, 1972, *Summary Record*, excerpt from speech by Indira Gandhi, p. 17.

[2] Ministry of Agriculture, Department of Agriculture, *Central Sector Schemes for Small Farmers, Marginal Farmers and Agricultural Laborers* (New Delhi, March 1973), p. 2.

resources on the scale required, or to devise many productive schemes involving the very poor under the existing pattern of extreme concentration in economic assets. Even a substantial diversion of development resources in favor of the most impoverished groups offered only the prospect of marginal changes in the pattern of inequalities of income and consumption. But such expenditures, which could not significantly reduce the enormous numbers of the population living below the poverty line, could siphon off scarce funds to depress still further rates of growth.

Worse still, government failures to make any progress toward the promise of growth with social justice compounded the feelings of cynicism among the educated classes about the capacity of the democratic system to provide any solutions at all for the fundamental problems of the economic and political order. Growing unemployment, soaring prices, shortages of foodgrains and essential commodities, all of which imposed the most severe hardships on the poorer sections of the population, converted the slogan of *"garibi hatao"* into a bitter joke. Those who went to government ration shops and were turned away for lack of supplies, while the administration and police did nothing to prevent black-marketeering in the hoarded stocks, concluded that *"garibi hatao"* did not mean the elimination of poverty (*garibi*) but the elimination of the poor (*garib*). The urban lower-middle and middle classes, who could not find relief from the rampant inflation that eroded their living standards (even as state leaders elected on promises to meet the basic needs of the common man indulged in intraparty factional struggles and blatant corruption to advance their own interests), took their grievances into the streets. Spontaneous uprisings aimed at forcing the resignation of corrupt, repressive, and "anti-peoples" ministries, provided evidence of popular disillusionment and discontent not only with particular state governments, but with the process of party politics and the parliamentary system. On the extreme left, Marxist revolutionaries denounced the national leadership's incremental approach to social reform as falling far short of promises to carry out basic socialist transformation. On the right, opposition parties, alarmed at the growing ties between Congress and the CPI, and the continued reliance of the national leadership on populist rhetoric to hold on to the support of the rural poor, assaulted the Congress for creating a situation of frustrated expectations that could push the country toward chaos and a communist takeover.

Both sides focused their attacks on the prime minister as the personal embodiment of the Congress party's promises to carry out an accelerated socialist transformation. The need to conciliate these extremes proved all the more difficult for Indira Gandhi. Unlike Mahatma Gandhi or Jawaharlal Nehru, she was not a charismatic leader whose popularity transcended conventional criteria of performance. She had, moreover, sacrificed—and indeed never earned—the personal esteem of her opponents. As the opposition turned to extraparliamentary agitations aimed at forcing elected governments from office, and as the Center responded with the ruthless suppression of the agitators, the shared consensus on legitimate methods of conflict disintegrated, destroying the essential condition for preserving accommodative politics.

At the time that Mrs. Gandhi made her promise to "abolish poverty," absolute poverty (defined in terms of per capita consumption of less than Rs. 40 per month at 1972 prices) afflicted at least two-fifths of the population, a minimum of 220 million people.[3] The vast majority of those living below the poverty line were concentrated in the rural areas, drawn about equally from the ranks of small and marginal cultivators and agricultural laborers.

Data collected for India's first agricultural census in 1970/71 revealed that the number of very small holdings had recorded a significant increase over 1961/62 levels. As shown in Table 12-1, one half of all opera-

TABLE 12-1

Size Distribution of Operational Holdings*
1961/62 and 1970/71

| Category of holding | Size group (acres) | 1961/62 | | 1970/71 | |
|---|---|---|---|---|---|
| | | Number % | Area % | Number % | Area % |
| Marginal | less than 2.5 | 39.07 | 6.86 | 50.6 | 9.0 |
| Small | 2.5–4.99 | 22.62 | 12.32 | 19.0 | 11.9 |
| Semi-medium | 5–9.99 | 19.80 | 20.70 | 15.2 | 18.5 |
| Sub-total: small & semi-medium | | 42.42 | 33.02 | 34.2 | 30.4 |
| Medium | 10–24.99 | 13.99 | 31.17 | 11.3 | 29.7 |
| Large | 25 acres and above | 4.52 | 28.95 | 3.9 | 30.9 |

SOURCES: The National Sample Survey, Number 140, *Tables with Notes on Some Aspects of Landholdings in Rural Areas (State and All-India Estimates)*, Seventeenth Round, September 1961-July 1962 (Calcutta, 1966), p. 60; India, Ministry of Agriculture and Irrigation, Department of Agriculture, *All India Report on Agricultural Census, 1970-71* (New Delhi, 1975), p. 26.

* An operational holding includes all land used for agricultural production as part of the same technical and economic unit, regardless of title, size, or location.

tional holdings were less than one hectare (2.5 acres) in size, putting them in the category of "marginal and sub-marginal" units. Altogether, this bottom one-half of cultivators operated just nine percent of the area. This distribution contrasted with the relatively more favorable pattern of 1961/62, when about 39 percent of all holdings had been less than one hectare, accounting for about 7 percent of the land. The additional 19

[3] Planning Commission, *Towards Self-Reliance, Approach to the Fifth Five Year Plan*, p. 4.

percent of all cultivators who operated "small farms"—holdings between one and two hectares in size—accounted for almost 12 percent of the area. The size of this group, whose prospects of becoming viable producers were most favorable with the help of government-subsidized loans for the adoption of improved methods and/or ancillary farm occupations, by contrast, was slowly shrinking in number. Another major limitation on the spread of agricultural modernization imposed by the agrarian pattern was the high incidence of tenancy. An estimated one-quarter of the total cultivated land continued to be operated by share-croppers, with this proportion reaching as much as 40 percent in the densely populated rice regions.[4]

Data on agricultural laborers as a percentage of the total work force, although not strictly comparable from the 1961 census to the 1971 census, nevertheless suggested that the numbers of landless workers, like those of marginal farmers, were also on the rise. Even if a major part of the increase were to be discounted as an artifact of the changing definitions used from one census to the next,[5] it is clear, as shown in Table 12-2, that in absolute terms over 25 percent of all workers were agricultural laborers; and in the rice-growing areas, with the highest population densities (including Andhra Pradesh, Bihar, West Bengal, Kerala, and Tamil Nadu) the proportion of agricultural laborers had either reached or was approaching that of farmer-cultivators.

An official survey of unemployment and underemployment conducted in 1972/73 showed that the numbers of unemployed wage-seeking laborers were approximately twice the size anticipated according to statistical projections based on 1961 census data. These earlier calculations had projected levels of "surplus" manpower at about 17 percent of the agricultural work force. The new studies revealed that chronic underemployment affected as many as one-third of all agricultural laborers.[6]

    [4] Estimates of the extent of sharecropping still rely heavily on the 1961 census. Experts on land tenure do not believe that the situation has changed significantly in recent years. See A. M. Khusro, *Economics of Land Reform and Farm Size in India*, p. 26.

    [5] The data collected for the 1961 and 1971 censuses are not strictly comparable because the definition of "cultivators" and "agricultural laborers" underwent some change from one enumeration to the next. In 1961, persons who were basically agricultural laborers but cultivated a tiny plot of land for some part of the work day were classified as "cultivators" under a criterion that stated, "the basis of work will be satisfied in the case of seasonal work like cultivation, if the person has had some regular work of more than one hour a day throughout the greater part of the working season." In 1971, the criterion of work was changed to mean "the main activity of the person," i.e., "how he engages himself mostly." Registrar General and Census Commissioner, *Provisional Population Totals*, pp. 27-28.

    [6] These data were generated through the Pilot Intensive Rural Employment Project launched by the Department of Community Development in 1972/73 as part of the government's Crash Scheme for Rural Employment. A survey of unemployment and underemployment was conducted in fifteen selected Blocks, each in different states, to get data representative for the country as a whole. India, Ministry of Agriculture, Department of Community Development, unpublished.

## TABLE 12-2

Agricultural Laborers and Cultivators as a Percentage
of Total Workers according to the 1961 and 1971 Censuses

|  | 1961 | 1971 | 1961 | 1971 |
|---|---|---|---|---|
|  | Agricultural laborers | | Cultivators | |
| INDIA | 16.71 | 25.76 | 52.78 | 42.87 |
| STATES |  |  |  |  |
| Andhra Pradesh | 28.59 | 37.40 | 40.12 | 32.23 |
| Assam | 3.59 | 9.35 | 63.18 | 56.41 |
| Bihar | 22.97 | 38.02 | 53.87 | 42.38 |
| Gujerat | 14.77 | 22.06 | 53.33 | 43.01 |
| Haryana | 6.90 | 16.23 | 63.87 | 49.28 |
| Himachal Pradesh | 1.41 | 4.25 | 80.68 | 71.60 |
| Jammu & Kashmir | 1.21 | 3.12 | 75.70 | 64.01 |
| Kerala | 17.38 | 30.68 | 20.92 | 17.97 |
| Madhya Pradesh | 16.63 | 26.31 | 62.68 | 52.13 |
| Maharashtra | 23.80 | 28.98 | 46.11 | 35.09 |
| Mysore | 16.42 | 25.73 | 54.13 | 39.73 |
| Nagaland | 1.14 | 1.44 | 88.22 | 78.19 |
| Orissa | 17.01 | 27.79 | 56.82 | 48.51 |
| Punjab | 9.65 | 20.03 | 46.24 | 42.75 |
| Rajasthan | 4.11 | 9.10 | 73.61 | 63.59 |
| Tamil Nadu | 18.42 | 29.13 | 42.07 | 30.97 |
| Uttar Pradesh | 11.30 | 19.35 | 63.88 | 55.99 |
| West Bengal | 15.30 | 25.75 | 38.50 | 31.75 |

SOURCE: India, Registrar General and Census Commissioner, *Census of India 1971*, Paper 1 of 1971—Supplement Provisional Population Totals (Delhi, 1971), pp. 30–33.

No solution to the problem of mass poverty was in sight from more rapid progress in the growth of the industrial sector. On the contrary, there was general agreement that "no foreseeable acceleration in the pace of industrial development in India [was] likely to produce enough jobs to make even a slight dent on rural unemployment and poverty over the next decade."[7] Indeed, there was the likelihood of an increase in the absolute number of persons dependent on agriculture for their living, with the possibility that the pace of industrial growth might not be able to keep up with growing urban unemployment. By the mid-1970s, the total number of jobs generated within the organized sector both by public and private enterprises had stagnated at about 500,000 per year.[8] By contrast, estimates made in 1971 on the basis of population increases that had already occurred projected an additional 65 million entrants into the

[7] B. S. Minhas, "Mass Poverty and Strategy of Rural Development in India" (Economic Development Institute, International Bank for Reconstruction and Development, March 1971), mimeographed, p. 3.

[8] Planning Commission, *The Fourth Plan Mid-Term Appraisal*, I, 50.

labor force by 1986.[9] There was, in addition, a backlog of unemployment estimated at 18 million persons.[10]

It had become increasingly difficult even to maintain the momentum of the earlier industrial expansion. Organized industry and mining still represented only 15 percent of Gross Domestic Output.[11] Although public investment accounted for over 50 percent of paid-up share capital in the corporate sector, including the strategic areas of steel, heavy engineering, petroleum, and banking,[12] the government's drive to overtake the private sector as the primary engine of industrial growth was perceptibly slowing down. The Center's growing difficulty in mobilizing additional resources for outlays in core sectors of the economy was reflected in declining rates of aggregate real investment after 1966[13] and failures to meet expenditure targets in industry and mining during the Fourth Plan.[14] Preliminary projections for the Fifth Plan aimed at achieving industrial growth rates of about 8 percent per annum required not only that public investment more than double in size, but that private investment increase by almost three times previous levels.[15] It was, however, unlikely that the private sector would step up investment in core industries at the rate required. Over 50 percent of the assets of organized private industry were controlled by the approximately 1,200 business houses whose expansion government was committed to restrict in the interests of achieving the objective of social justice. Leaders of the business community, citing the "fear, uncertainty and discouragement to growth" created by the government's stringent licensing policy (adopted in 1970 to prevent further economic concentration in the industrial sector), plainly advised that "there is no alternative to Government reviewing their present industrial policy" as the condition of higher investment levels by private enterprise.[16]

[9] Planning Commission, *Draft Fifth Five Year Plan, 1974-79*, Part I, p. 3.

[10] *Fourth Five Year Plan, A Draft Outline*, pp. 106-108.

[11] Agriculture still accounted for almost 46 percent of GDP; social services for another 28 percent, and electricity, transport, and construction for the remainder. *Draft Fifth Five Year Plan, 1974-79*, Part I, p. 10.

[12] Lawrence Veit, *India's Second Revolution*, p. 276.

[13] The increase in aggregate real investment dropped from an average of over 8 percent annually between 1960 and 1966 to under 2 percent per year between 1967 and 1972. See A. Vaidyanathan, "Constraints on Growth and Political Options," *Economic and Political Weekly*, 12:38 (September 17, 1977), 1643.

[14] Actual Plan outlay under this head was Rs. 2,864 crores, compared to the original target of Rs. 3,377 crores. Ministry of Finance, *Economic Survey 1975-76* (New Delhi, 1976), p. 80.

[15] *Draft Fifth Five Year Plan, 1974-79*, p. 85. The ratio of public to private investment in the key mining and manufacturing sector on the basis of these projections would not have been more than 52 : 48, the lowest level since the early years of planning.

[16] "Suggestions for Accelerating Industrial Growth" (memorandum submitted by Tata Industries on May 17, 1972 at the request of the Government of India as to how best industrial growth could be stepped up within the framework of the government's socio-economic policies and programs with special reference to the joint sector concept), p. 16.

Even then, incentives to higher private investment in the industrial sector offered only the prospect of containing the problems of unemployment and underemployment already endemic in the rural areas. There was no possibility of gaining ground except through new policies that could create additional job opportunities within the agricultural sector.

Such calculations were at the core of the new rural development programs hastily incorporated in the Fourth Plan. At the prime minister's initiative—and over the objections of the Planning Commission—a central committee consisting of representatives from the finance ministry, the food and agriculture ministry, and the Planning Commission agreed to approve a number of new central sector schemes. As early as July 1970, when the final version of the Fourth Plan was belatedly accepted, the pilot experiment in establishing five-year projects for Small Farmer Development Agencies (SFDA) to provide central assistance for potentially viable farmers had already been expanded in coverage from 20 to 45 selected districts. Under these projects, participating farmers became eligible for a wide array of subsidized loans from cooperative and/or commerical lending institutions, usually at the rate of 25 percent of the cost of production credit; investment capital (for minor irrigation, land improvement, and soil conservation schemes); and the introduction of subsidiary animal husbandry enterprises.

The Planning Commission's argument that it would be uneconomic to take up similar programs for submarginal farmers and agricultural laborers was set aside for political considerations. An additional forty projects for Marginal Farmers and Agricultural Laborers (MFAL) were subsequently authorized in different districts throughout the country, these projects to provide participants with subsidies of one-third the cost of adopting improved production practices and/or taking up subsidiary farm occupations, especially cattle raising, poultry farming, piggery, and goat and sheep raising.

Other central sector schemes soon followed. A three-year experimental Crash Scheme for Rural Employment (CSRE) was started in April 1971 to generate employment for one thousand persons per year in every district of the country. This was followed in December 1971 by a new Drought-Prone Areas Program (DPAP) which aimed at mitigating the hardships of the rural population in the seventy-four chronically afflicted districts by providing subsidies on the cost of wage-labor works in irrigation, soil conservation, and road construction and individual subsidized loans to small and marginal farmers for land improvement schemes.

The central sector schemes, which involved the government in additional financial commitments of Rs. 371 crores[17]—at a time when the re-

[17] Each of the 40 MFAL agencies was budgeted at Rs. 1.5 crores per district for the proj-

sources position under the Fourth Plan was already severely strained—were clearly inadequate by themselves to redeem the Congress party's election pledges of improving the income and consumption of the "large masses of people." Funds provided for all the SFDA/MFAL projects were sufficient to reach a total of little more than 3 million agriculturists over a five-year period. By contrast, the number of small and marginal farmers operating holdings of less than five acres totaled over 49 million. The central sector rural works projects, whether under the CSRE or DPAP schemes, suffered from similar financial limitations. Compared to budgeted outlays of Rs. 150 crores over three years of CSRE, and Rs. 161 crores during the Fifth Plan for DPAP, the cost to government of mounting a full employment program in the rural areas was estimated at Rs. 10 lakhs for each of India's 5,265 Blocks, or well over Rs. 500 crores per year.[18]

Even if it had been possible to provide funds of the required magnitude, moreover, it was extremely unlikely that the expenditure would have resulted in higher levels of productivity that could permanently increase the income and consumption of the poorest classes.[19] The possibility of using loan subsidy programs to achieve the long-term economic viability of large numbers of marginal farmers and agricultural laborers was quite small in an agro–economic environment where the majority of agriculturists had no land or very little land to offer as security for loans. As in earlier credit schemes, participating farmers could receive subsidized loans above an upper limit only against mortgages on land. Similarly, all sharecroppers were ineligible for subsidized irrigation loans, and only recorded sharecroppers could qualify for subsidized production credit. At the same time, the small size and fragmentation of individual holdings prevented even eligible small landowners from taking advantage of subsidized rates for installing tubewells or other minor irrigation works in areas with plentiful groundwater supplies. Even in cases where a group loan was arranged to create an efficient operational unit among contiguous holdings, the main purpose of the scheme in benefitting small and marginal farmers was diluted by the practical necessity of including neighboring "medium" and "large" farmers as participants.

ect period. The total cost of the CSRE and DPAP schemes was budgeted at Rs. 150 crores and Rs. 161 crores, respectively.

[18] This estimate was derived from the data collected by the Pilot Intensive Rural Employment Project conducted by the Ministry of Community Development in 1972/73 and cited above (note 6).

[19] The assessment of the SFDA/MFAL projects on criteria of economic viability, presented in the following paragraphs, is based on data for farm budgets collected in my interviews with participants in SFDA and MFAL projects, Summer 1973, in Madurai (Tamil Nadu), Cuddapah (Andhra Pradesh), Purulia (West Bengal), and Mathura (Uttar Pradesh). The field trips were authorized by the Planning Commission, and were arranged at the local level by the project officer.

The prospect of ensuring the economic viability of marginal cultivators through subsidized loans for subsidiary occupations in animal
husbandry was not much more favorable. The economics of many of
these enterprises were problematical at the outset. The profitability of
such activities (such as raising milch cattle, poultry, goats, and/or
piggery), was reduced by a number of factors, including scarcity of improved breeds, lack of large-scale scientific facilities for feeding and
treatment of disease, financial inability of many small farmers to afford
optimum levels of feed, or even to keep their stock for sale until they
matured in size and weight, and not least of all by the marketing structure in the hands of local middlemen who absorbed a major share of the
profit. Those participants who did make some gains after expenses on
the new enterprises, moreover, tended to spend their additional income
for some modest improvement in consumption and/or to repay loans
taken from private moneylenders. On the whole, the central sector
SFDA/MFAL projects could not be distinguished from social welfare
programs that temporarily—for the duration of the subsidy scheme—
increased the consumption of impoverished participants, but could not
create additional opportunities for productive employment to raise their
income permanently.

The central sector rural works projects came up against similar constraints of the agrarian structure in accomplishing basic improvements in
agricultural infrastructure that could spur a more rapid rate of growth
and generate higher levels of permanent employment. The majority of
rural works taken up for construction under the CRSE and DPAP
schemes were make-work projects—usually roads—with site selection
determined on the criteria of where workers were located, not where a
project was especially needed. Such a limitation was inevitable so long as
laborers—some of whom owned tiny fragments of land—remained tied
to their villages and could only work on schemes within walking distance, at most a radius of two or three miles. It was, moreover, virtually
impossible even within the village area to take up productive overhead
labor investment projects in soil conservation and water development so
long as land was cultivated within an agrarian pattern of small and scattered individual holdings.

The conflict between economic goals of increasing aggregate growth
rates and political priorities of raising mass consumption levels paralyzed
the planning process. The planners, already alarmed by the reversal of
liberal industrial licensing policies in 1970, soon became convinced that
the proliferation of new central sector schemes in agriculture would
siphon off sufficient funds to jettison their entire growth strategy. But
they could not prevail against the prime minister. Immediately after Mrs.
Gandhi's landslide election victory in March 1971, all the members of the

Planning Commission, including its deputy chairman, D. R. Gadgil, submitted their resignations.

The way was clear, once again, for Mrs. Gandhi to reconstitute the Planning Commission. This time her choice for the position of deputy chairman, C. Subramaniam, the architect of the new agricultural strategy, met no opposition. The new Commission continued to emphasize its limited advisory role. Those appointed to membership included eminent economists who fulfilled their mandate to function as an "expert" body. Nevertheless, in contrast to their predecessors, the new members took their point of departure from the overriding political objective set down by Subramaniam in his dual capacity as deputy chairman and minister of planning, that of redeeming the Congress party's election pledge to remove poverty.

The government began to cast around for "new directions" in economic policy. Mrs. Gandhi, arguing that an "increase in GNP must be considered only as one component of a multi-dimensional transformation of society,"[20] assigned highest priority to the political task of carrying out a "speedier program to usher in socialism." Otherwise, she warned, evolutionary improvements based on the "gradual percolation of better living" to the lowest income groups would take a long time and wear thin the patience of the poor.[21] Such pronouncements amounted to a political directive for reorienting economic policy to ensure basic minimum standards of consumption to the poorest sections of the population.

The Planning Commission's May 1972 paper, "Towards Self-Reliance, Approach to the Fifth Five Year Plan," dutifully restated "the basic premise of our Five Year Plans" as "development along socialist lines to secure rapid economic growth and expansion of employment, reduction of disparities in income, wealth, prevention of concentration of economic power and creation of the values and attitudes of a free and equal

[20] Mrs. Gandhi, in April 1972, delivered what was considered a landmark speech to FICCI, apparently accepting the view then being advanced by Mahbub al-Haq, a senior adviser to the Economics Department of the World Bank, that "hot pursuit of GNP growth" by the underdeveloped countries, on the assumption that distribution could be adjusted later, had led to worsening poverty and explosive political discontent. Although Mrs. Gandhi did not mention Haq's name in her speech, her thesis closely paralleled his argument in asserting that " 'growthmanship' which results in undivided attention to the maximization of GNP can be dangerous for the results are almost always social and political unrest." For a report of Mrs. Gandhi's speech, see Sarwar Lateef, "The New Economics—1 Disenchantment with Growth," The Statesman, April 12, 1972. Haq's views were published under the title "Employment in the 1970's: A New Perspective," International Development Review (December 1971), pp. 9-13.

[21] Twenty-eighth Meeting of the National Development Council, May 30 and 31, 1972, Summary Record, excerpt from remarks by Indira Gandhi, p. 49.

society." It also elaborated a strategy of development that was "directly anchored to the objective of removal of poverty in the Fifth Plan."[22]

The policy framework advanced by the Planning Commission for reconciling goals of economic self-reliance and removal of poverty once again raised the insoluble issues of institutional changes set aside in the decade since Nehru's death. The "new" directions in planning required policies that in several aspects were virtually indistinguishable from the proposals for basic social transformation incorporated into the Second and Third Five-Year Plans. There was, to begin with, the need to provide the maximum possible productive employment in the rural areas "in a way that the assets created increase productivity and the welfare of the people."[23] This criterion necessarily incorporated land reforms. It involved "redistribution in favor of the poor, in part by providing the self-employed with the wherewithal to achieve greater productivity from land and also through a program of land redistribution and other transfers."[24] Subramaniam, who formulated the Approach document with a ceiling in mind of ten acres on the best-irrigated, double-cropped land, and a maximum in other categories of not more than 20 or 30 acres, hoped that the new legislation might yield some 40 million acres for redistribution, about 12 percent of the cultivated land.[25] These expectations went far beyond reforms that had been previously achieved through the legislative process. By 1972, a total of only 2.3 million acres of surplus land had been formally transferred from private landowners to government under land ceiling legislation enacted by the states.[26] Yet even under conditions of a land reform on the scale projected, the number of rural people living below the poverty line would be directly reduced from about two-fifths to one-third.[27]

The remaining one-third of the rural poor were expected to improve their level of living as a result of a gain in employment opportunities generated in the wake of agrarian reform. Although the Planning Commission carefully refrained from linking land reforms to the formation of cooperative farms, it was nevertheless clear that the employment program required some degree of change in agrarian organization to provide

[22] *Towards Self-Reliance, Approach to the Fifth Five Year Plan*, pp. 3-4.

[23] *Ibid*., p. 7.                                    [24] *Ibid*., p. 7.

[25] Subramaniam became persuaded that a land reform of this magnitude was possible after Mrs. Gandhi's landslide election victory created the impression that the central government could use its popular mandate to carry out meaningful reform. Interview, New Delhi, June 15, 1973. Also see Sarwar Lateef, "Land Ceiling," *Statesman*, May 22, 1972.

[26] Planning Commission, *Report of the Task Force on Agrarian Relations*, p. 96.

[27] This estimate is a projection for 1969/70 computed by the Indian economist B. S. Minhas on the assumption that a ceiling is placed on household ownership holdings of twenty acres. B. S. Minhas, "Mass Poverty and Strategy of Rural Development in India," p. 7.

opportunities for land and water development schemes that cut across the boundaries of individual fragments and farms. The planners proposed to accomplish this goal by redefining the unit of agricultural planning—although not of ownership—as an area having homogenous land and water resources; and then integrating the various development schemes into a "comprehensive program of land consolidation, land and water development, drainage and other infrastructural activities in the rural areas."[28] These technocratic schemes were themselves to be combined with the central sector programs like SFDA, MFAL, CSRE, and DPAP in order to ensure that "the large mass of the rural people, particularly the small farmers, marginal farmers, agricultural laborers are enabled to participate in development and share the benefits of such development."[29]

The new proposals, like the earlier policies that preceded them, rested on recommendations for the creation of a "parallel organization of a credit system"[30] to meet the developmental needs of small farmers, marginal farmers, agricultural laborers and artisans. According to the scheme approved by the minister of agriculture[31] and circulated for comment to the chief ministers of the states in August 1972, Farmers Service Societies were to be organized to serve a minimum population of 10,000 persons and provide integrated credit services for both agriculture and ancillary farm enterprises to small and marginal cultivators, agricultural laborers, and artisans. All cultivators within the new society's jurisdiction were to be eligible for membership—except those individuals who were already members of another primary cooperative. But two-thirds of the management of the new societies were to be selected from among members defined by the registrar as small farmers, marginal farmers, agricultural laborers, or rural artisans. According to government guidelines, only the new Farmers Service Societies were in the future to be eligible for financial contributions from state governments toward share capital, salaries of managerial and technical personnel, and construction of facilities such

[28] *Towards Self-Reliance, Approach to the Fifth Five Year Plan*, p. 8.

[29] Planning Commission, "Integrated Agricultural Development Projects in Canal Irrigated Areas, Interim Report by the Task Force on Integrated Rural Development" (September 1972), mimeographed, p. 6.

[30] D. P. Dhar, who succeeded Subramaniam as minister of planning, proposed to redirect the flow of facilities and inputs to the rural areas from the larger agriculturists to the landless laborers and small and marginal farmers by having a parallel organization of credit cooperatives "because the present cooperative movement, in many places, is in the hands of richer sections of the rural society." All India Congress Committee, AICC Central Training Camp, Narora: November 22-24, 1974, "The Economic Outlook" (New Delhi, January 1975), pp. 41-42.

[31] India, Ministry of Agriculture, Department of Agriculture, "A Note on Recommendations of the National Commission on Agriculture in their Interim Report on Credit Services for Small and Marginal Farmers and Agricultural Laborers," April 16, 1973, mimeographed.

as godowns. The societies were expected to provide all categories of credit—short, medium, and long-term loans; procure, purchase, and supply scarce agricultural inputs, especially fertilizers, funneled to them from government stocks; procure, purchase and sell agricultural, dairy, and animal husbandry products directly or through marketing societies; operate processing units, maintain godowns, and organize common services, particularly the hiring of agricultural machinery. Over the long run, the agriculture ministry anticipated that the new societies would displace the existing primary cooperatives as new members or nonborrowing members of the existing societies became "persuaded to join the Farmers Service Society."[32]

The recommendations for large-scale land redistribution and formation of Farmers Service Societies were combined with renewed proposals for a comprehensive scheme of state trading in foodgrains and other essential commodities. The Planning Commission envisaged the takeover of the wholesale trade in wheat and rice, and the buildup of additional machinery for public procurement and distribution of standard cloth, sugar, and edible (cooking) oils. Such a public procurement and distribution system provided the keystone of the Fifth Plan's effort to achieve conditions of price stability essential to planned growth, even while raising the purchasing power of the poorer sections by ensuring the availability of basic consumption items at controlled prices. These recommendations for a substantial expansion in the public-sector role in trade and distribution were linked with proposals to reorient industrial output away from "elitest" items of consumption toward products of mass consumption. Not only would such new production priorities satisfy the basic needs of the poorer classes, but they would also provide a needed stimulus in a wider home market for higher investment levels in industry.

The policy frame of the Fifth Plan, including plans for land redistribution, organization of Farmers Service Cooperatives, public procurement and controlled distribution of essential commodities, and a pattern of industrial output aimed at providing the basic consumption requirements of the poor, was similar in several respects to the development strategy adopted in the first three Five Year Plans. Still, there was a significant difference in approach. The planners' sense of political realism, their own lack of ideological commitment to cooperation as a social ideal, and not least important, their confidence in the powers of modern technology to make small farmers into viable producers once they were provided with low-cost credit, services, and complementary public infrastructure, led them to endorse an agrarian pattern based on small family farms. But in the absence of joint village management and/or any effective village in-

[32] *Ibid.*, p. 3.

stitutions to coordinate the economic activities and recover the costs of area development schemes from local contributions in capital and manpower, the new proposals required an extraordinary infusion of administrative and financial resources into the rural sector. Not only survey and design, but also the construction of land and water development projects had to be carried out from above, under the direction of the district development administration and the state governments. The costs of carrying out these rural development works on a village-by-village basis had to be squeezed out of Plan allocations for agriculture and irrigation.

The financial requirements of the new policies were raised further by recognition that even if all these schemes succeeded in generating substantial new employment opportunities for the poor, they would still not carry out a sufficiently sweeping redistribution of income to permit the majority of workers to buy all their essential goods and services. The planners therefore argued that the program for providing larger income and employment for the rural poor would have to be augmented by "a national plan for the provision of social consumption in the form of education, health, nutrition, drinking water, housing, communications and electricity up to a minimum standard."[33] Yet, as the planners also pointed out, the cost of these programs, while essential for making a substantial impact "on the progress toward the objective of 'Garibi Hatao,' " represented only a comparatively small part of the total Plan. New investments to achieve an adequate rate of growth in agriculture, industry, transport, and communications still had to be taken into account.

The Draft Fifth Five Year Plan, completed by the Planning Commission in late 1973 under the direction of D. P. Dhar, Subramaniam's successor,[34] was more specific in assessing the financial implications of the new policies. Overall, the minimum outlays required to make some progress toward goals of social equity, while maintaining a moderate rate of growth of GNP at 5.5 percent per annum (including sectoral growth rates in industry of about 8 percent, and in agriculture of approximately 4 percent annually) amounted to Rs. 31,400 crores for investment and Rs. 5,850 crores for current expenditure. The total sum of Rs. 37,250 crores represented more than twice the size of Fourth Plan outlays. According to the planners, at least 95 percent of this amount had to be financed from domestic resources. They did not believe, moreover, that economic conditions over the next several years would permit the

[33] *Towards Self-Reliance, Approach to the Fifth Five Year Plan*, pp. 3-4.
[34] Subramaniam stepped down as deputy chairman of the Planning Commission in August 1972 to assume a new Cabinet post as minister of industrial development. He was succeeded by D. P. Dhar, then chairman of the Policy Planning Committee in the external affairs ministry, a Marxist who advocated higher priority for public investment in basic and heavy industry and closer economic ties to the Soviet Union as a source of assistance.

use of deficit financing. Yet, estimates of resources for the public sector from all sources, including balances of current revenues, surpluses of public enterprises, market borrowings, small savings and loans, and credits from financial institutions and banks—although flawed as usual by overly optimistic assumptions—still left a gap of Rs. 6,850 crores. This remainder had to be filled by additional resource mobilization, estimated at Rs. 4,300 crores at the Center and Rs. 2,550 crores at the state level.[35]

Possible measures for increasing government revenues had all been recommended in previous Plans. They included proposals to raise the surpluses of public-sector enterprises by price increases in electricity, commercial irrigation, freights, and fares; measures to streamline tax administration in order to minimize evasion and avoidance; and directives for the adoption of "stringent measures" to prevent the further accumulation of black money.

The major instrument for augmenting the stream of disposable income at the government's command, however, remained that of additional taxation. Between 1965/66 and 1973/74, tax revenues had increased only slightly, from 14.1 percent to 14.8 percent of GNP.[36] Repeated recourse to indirect taxation had reduced the scope of further increases from this source. The yield from indirect taxes in 1973/74 had reached 11.8 percent of GNP, compared to the yield from direct taxes of no more than 3 percent of GNP.[37] During the Fifth Plan, a "major thrust"[38] of additional resource mobilization had to be toward raising the low yield of direct taxes.

Apart from proposals to increase taxes on urban property, the planners came back to the necessity of measures for imposing direct taxes on agriculture. Indeed, the greatest limitation on the government's ability to mobilize adequate domestic resources for development was its almost complete lack of success in siphoning off a significant proportion of additional income generated by large development outlays in agriculture. Although agricultural income still accounted for about 45 percent of GNP at the end of the Fourth Plan, the share of total tax revenues contributed by direct agricultural taxes was less than 1 percent.[39] Once more, the planners proposed measures for tapping a part of the additional incomes of agriculturists, ranging from a graduated agricultural holdings tax to imposition of a surcharge on land revenue, cesses on commercial crops, and collection of a betterment levy.

Even before the Draft Fifth Five Year Plan had been completed, it became clear that the government lacked the organizational capacity to

[35] *Draft Fifth Five Year Plan, 1974-79*, Part I, pp. 56–59.
[36] *Ibid.*, p. 46; *The Fourth Plan—Mid-Term Appraisal*, p. 38.
[37] *Ibid.*, pp. 44–45.                    [38] *Ibid.*, p. 44.
[39] *Ibid.*, p. 59.

carry out economic reforms required for the implementation of its social policies. The familiar political pattern of the Nehru years reappeared. The national Congress party approved, without dissent, resolutions endorsing the outline of the Planning Commission's approach to self-reliance and removal of poverty[40]—and then failed to provide the leadership required at the state level to implement the policy framework essential for achieving these goals.

There was, perhaps, no more clear yardstick for measuring the government's capacity to carry out policies aimed at reducing inequalities than its explicit promise during the March 1972 state elections to revise existing land ceiling legislation and implement a substantial land redistribution program.[41] After the elections, however, by the time the Center's land reform proposals had worked their way through an extensive consultative process, involving several rounds of negotiation with the state chief ministers and presidents of the Pradesh Congress Committees, the new formulas accepted once again provided considerable latitude. The promise of the 1971 election manifesto to impose a ceiling range of 10 to 18 acres on family holdings of perennially irrigated land or land capable of growing two crops, was redeemed. Yet, much more liberal ceilings were permitted for other classes of land, which made up the overwhelming proportion of the cultivated area. Apart from an exception for orchards, ceiling limits were established at 27 acres for land having irrigation facilities for one crop, increasing to a maximum of 54 acres for the most inferior dry land holdings. The upper limits, moreover, were applied to a family of five persons, while allowing an allotment for each additional minor child up to a maximum of two times the ceiling limit, and an additional unit up to the size of the ceiling level for each unmarried adult child.[42]

[40] The AICC's "Resolution on Economic Policy," adopted at Gandhinagar (Gujerat) in October 1972, endorsed the main elements of the increased employment strategy set down in the 1972 *Approach to the Fifth Five Year Plan*. It put a deadline of December 31, 1972, for enacting legislation to lower ceiling limits on land; gave full approval for government takeover of the wholesale trade in foodgrains and organization of an extensive public distribution system for selected essential commodities; reiterated the highest priority in industrial development for the full utilization and creation of new capacity in basic industries, and recognized that "there can be no escape from a massive taxation effort to finance rising levels of public investment." AICC, *Congress Marches Ahead—VII*, pp. 63-72.

[41] The model preferred by the central government for the new state ceiling laws was the West Bengal Land Reforms (Amendment) Act, 1972, introduced by the Center under the emergency powers vested in it during the period of President's Rule. The act had established an upper limit of 17.5 acres on ownership of all classes of agricultural land (except orchards) for a family of five persons, allowing 1.7 acres for each additional minor child up to an absolute ceiling of 23.5 acres. It provided an additional 8.7 acres for each adult unmarried family member.

[42] Department of Agriculture, Land Reforms Division, "Salient Features of Laws on Ceiling on Agricultural Holdings," undated, mimeographed. The major features of the new land ceiling legislation were reported in the press. See *The Statesman*, July 23 and 24, 1972; October 9, 1972.

The revised land ceiling acts, passed by the state legislatures in 1972 and 1973, were something less than the "important advance"[43] claimed for them. The relatively generous levels allowed for ownership of partially irrigated and dry farm land, combined with additional allotments for minor children and unmarried adult family members, all superimposed on a landownership pattern that had already been transformed by partitions and transfers of holdings to avoid the first round of ceiling legislation in the 1960s and the impact of the new laws that were first signaled in 1971, resulted in a modest amount of land for redistribution. Altogether, a maximum of four million acres—about one percent of the cultivated area—was expected to become available for redistribution.[44] In practice, slow implementation of ceiling laws, as landowners questioned the validity or the specific application of the new laws in the courts, meant that by 1975 only 62,000 acres had actually come into the possession of the states.[45]

Other proposals by the Ministry of Agriculture to establish Farmer Service Societies for providing integrated credit, supplies, and other common services at subsidized rates to small and marginal farmers and agricultural laborers languished amid delays by the chief ministers in providing comments to the Center. Under an agreement ultimately worked out in 1973, the scheme was taken up on a pilot basis in a few selected areas, with the expectation that only a few hundred would be organized during the Fifth Plan. The Center's recommendations to the states for raising the yield from direct taxes by imposing a graduated tax on agricultural income were not so much rejected as ignored.

The most dramatic—and costly—defeat suffered by the government, however, was on the policy of state trading in foodgrains. The state chief ministers, placed under constant pressure from the prime minister and her closest economic advisers to make a beginning in taking over the wholesale trade in foodgrains, gave "unanimous approval"[46] to the Center's plans for banning the private wholesale trade in wheat and rice from the 1973/74 season. Under the plan introduced for the procurement of the wheat crop during the spring and summer of 1973,[47] all private dealers were "delicensed and banned" from the wholesale wheat trade; each surplus wheat state or surplus district within a deficit state was established as a separate trading zone to facilitate government procurement; only the FCI or other public agencies could purchase wheat in wholesale quantities at the fixed government procurement prices, or move stocks across zonal boundaries into the major consuming centers of deficit states.

[43] *The Statesman*, November 28, 1974.     [44] *Ibid*.
[45] *The Statesman*, March 31, 1975.     [46] *The Statesman*, February 27, 1973.
[47] A vivid account of the scheme's objectives and the reasons for failure in the procurement campaign is provided in Wolf Ladejinsky, "The Failure of the Wheat Trade Takeover," August 13, 1973, mimeographed.

The scheme met with immediate resistance. It had been introduced, partly by inadvertence, at a particularly unfavorable time. Wheat production, which over the previous four years had been increasing by three to four million tons per annum, unexpectedly began to stabilize at the existing level of about 26 million tons. The smaller than expected wheat crop of 1973 came on the heels of declining levels of production in coarse grains and rice during the previous two years, spurring a sharp rise in the prices of all foodgrains. The procurement price of Rs. 76 per quintal for Mexican varieties, which had matched open market prices for wheat in previous seasons, fell far short of black market rates of Rs. 120 to 170 per quintal prevailing in many areas in 1973. Farmers who were unwilling to sell their grain at the fixed procurement price, moreover, had other alternatives. Many private traders continued to operate illegally. Some wholesalers advanced funds to the larger producers, who kept stocks on their behalf until they could be gradually smuggled out of the villages. Others took advantage of loopholes in the law to apply for licences as retail dealers, and carried out their trading operations in several small transactions.

The state governments, by contrast, had no organizational apparatus at the village level to enforce a producers' levy against hoarders or to move against smugglers. Indeed, many of the ruling party's own workers, including MLAs and MPs, were actively circumventing government controls, abetted by state inspectors stationed along the routes into market towns who turned a blind eye toward smuggled stocks in exchange for the appropriate sum.

Inevitably, as the government procurement effort faltered in achieving little more than half of its original target, wheat started to disappear from the market. Supplies for the public distribution system dramatically declined. Rations from fair-price shops had to be reduced to minimal levels, and even these small amounts could often not be supplied in scarcity areas. Foodgrain prices, which had risen only moderately during the first three years of the Fourth Plan, jumped by 13 percent between 1972 and 1973, and by 29 percent between 1973 and 1974.[48] The central government, which had delayed in arranging adequate imports to supplement depleted stocks, had no alternative but to retreat. Proposals for state takeover of the wholesale trade in rice were abandoned by September 1973. The return to private trade in wheat was announced in March 1974. As a result, government procurement prices for both major foodgrains had to be substantially increased in light of inflationary open market prices, making it necessary to impose another increase in issue prices from fair price shops to reduce the drain on government finances of

[48] Ministry of Finance, *Economic Survey, 1975-76*, p. 92.

higher subsidies. The poorest sections of the population, those who were the intended beneficiaries of the government's public distribution policy, became the first victims of its failures of implementation.

The government's capacity to carry out a planned development effort aimed at achieving goals of growth and distribution was dramatically declining. During the 1960s and early 1970s, the average rate of growth of Net National Product at constant prices was somewhat less than the level that had been reached in the early years of planning. Annual increases during the First Plan (1951-1956) and the Second Plan (1956-1961) of 3.4 percent and 4 percent, respectively, contrasted with gains during the Third Plan (1961-1966) of 2.6 percent, and after a three-year Plan holiday, with the progress during the Fourth Plan (1969-1974) of 3.3 percent.[49] These reverses were accompanied by a sharp deceleration in the rate of industrial production—from an average annual increase of over 8 percent in 1956-1961 to less than four percent per annum during 1969-1974.[50] This picture was brightened by two important achievements. Public-sector enterprises as a whole broke even for the first time in 1972/73, and in subsequent years earned modest pretax profits. Exports also recorded a rising trend that reflected a growing capacity to compete in markets for nontraditional products, promising long-term improvements in the balance of payments position.

Nevertheless, the stimulus to the industrial sector from the creation of heavy industries under the import-substitution strategy had been largely exhausted. By the early 1970s, the logic of rapid industrial growth dictated a substantial diversification of output in the direction of mass consumer goods. The prospect of altering the production pattern in this manner depended on increasing agricultural productivity, both to solve the problems of raw materials shortages and to generate additional demand. Higher rates of employment, income, and consumption in the rural sector had come to constitute the conditions of accelerated economic growth, no less than social justice. Even the most enthusiastic advocates of the new agricultural techniques acknowledged that "the benefits of growth have to be diffused among a much wider population. Otherwise, all that you get are small pockets of affluence with very little spread effect to the rest of economy, and in Indian social conditions, no assurance that even this small class will use their additional income for productive purposes."[51]

[49] *Ibid.*, p. 59.
[50] Ministry of Finance, *Economic Survey, 1974-75* (New Delhi, 1975), p. 10.
[51] Interview, B. Sivaraman, member, Planning Commission, June 18, 1973. Sivaraman, as secretary of agriculture in the food and agriculture ministry under Subramaniam's tenure, supervised the implementation of the new agricultural strategy and was one of its most enthusiastic advocates inside the goverment.

Indeed, by the end of the Fourth Plan, the clear outlines of an enclave pattern was emerging that threatened to harden into a permanent separation between a small high-productivity sector, both in industry and agriculture, and a vast agricultural hinterland in which the majority of the work force struggled with primitive techniques to meet their subsistence requirements. In industry, a substantial segment of the modern sector was suffering from under-utilization of capacity. There was a steep drop in the production of coal and lignite, and stagnation in several major industries, including textiles, iron and steel, industrial machinery, fertilizers, petro-chemicals, petroleum, and railroad and other transport equipment. Apart from declining demand for capital goods as the level of public investment stagnated, other bottlenecks to the efficient use of industrial capacity were created by shortages of agricultural raw materials, unstable supplies of power, and transportation problems. Not least important, as inflation eroded the real income of factory workers, a growing spate of industrial strikes by 1974 cost industry more than 31,000,000 man-days lost per year.[52]

Above all, however, it was the unsatisfactory performance of agriculture that provided the "most important factor contributing both to the stagnation of national income as well as to the inflationary pressures of the economy."[53] The relatively rapid gains in agricultural production generated by the improved technology introduced during the mid-1960s soon slowed down. Wheat production, which more than doubled in size between 1965/66 and 1971/72 began to show a declining trend after 1972/73,[54] in the face of depleted soil fertility, shortages and rising prices of fertilizers, problems of rust disease, and power cutbacks that shut down electric pumps. Rice output which increased at an annual compound trend rate of 2 percent during 1961/62 to 1973/74[55] did not show any visible impact from the introduction of the new agricultural strategy, despite the fact that targets for steady expansion of the area under the high-yielding varieties of paddy were fulfilled. After a dramatic initial spurt in foodgrains production, which reached a record level of 108 million tons in 1970/71, output declined. Harvests in 1973/74—following a succession of poor-weather years—were somewhat smaller than in 1970/71.[56] The overall rate of growth in foodgrains production at 2.7 percent per annum[57] was well below the Fourth Plan target of 5 percent. In retrospect, the planners felt compelled to acknowledge the validity of

[52] Ministry of Planning, *Basic Statistics Relating to the Indian Economy, 1950-51 to 1974-75*, p. 55.

[53] *Economic Survey, 1975-76*, p. 5.

[54] *Basic Statistics Relating to the Indian Economy, 1950-51 to 1974-75*, p. 25.

[55] Planning Commission, *Fifth Five Year Plan 1974-79*, p. 5.

[56] Production of foodgrains in 1970/71 reached a peak level of 108.4 million tons, but dropped back to 103.6 million tons in 1974/75. *Economic Survey, 1974-75*, p. 6.

[57] *Ibid.*, p. 6.

the earlier emphasis on institutional changes rather than larger investments in intensive agricultural areas as the better approach to achieving
more rapid gains. Assessing the record of agricultural progress over the
period of the Five Year Plans, when growth rates declined from 3.3 percent per annum in the 1950s to 2.1 percent per annum in the 1960s,[58] they
could find "little evidence to suggest that a rural development strategy
that is somewhat concentrated and selective in geographical spread is
more effective. Our agricultural performance was superior in the first
decade of planning when with the community development scheme we
deliberately spread out resources thinly in order to reach as large an area,
as large a group of persons as was possible."[59]

Longstanding arguments that had stressed the necessity of land reforms "not merely to secure social justice but also to raise productivity"
were revived. Recommendations for institutional change to facilitate
cooperative forms of crop management were renewed, as the planners
became aware that the new agricultural technology, with its need for
very careful area water management, pest prevention, and disease control required steps to be taken "particularly at the political level" to ensure that such cooperative efforts would be forthcoming. On the whole,
they concluded, "There is very little evidence that spending more money
is the answer to our agricultural problems. The answer seems to be
mainly institutional and organizational changes and a redirection of effort."[60]

Yet the reality was that a more egalitarian agrarian pattern as the foundation of a cooperative agricultural economy had receded even further
into the distance. Data collected by the Planning Commission for the
trienniums 1962/63 to 64/65 and 1970/71 to 72/73 showed that the upper
29 percent of districts had achieved compound growth rates of more than
3 percent annually. By contrast, the bottom 37 percent of all districts recorded either negative growth rates or gains of less than 1 percent per
annum. The middle one-third of districts, meanwhile, managed to
realize increments in growth between 1 percent and 2.9 percent annually.[61] Within these areas, the gains from development had been unevenly distributed in favor of the dominant landowning castes. Indeed,
as prices skyrocketed and per capita availability of cereals in 1973[62]
slipped back to levels achieved in the early 1960s, the ranks of the popula-

[58] These estimates are taken from A. Vaidyanathan, "Constraints on Growth and Policy
Options," p. 1644. They are based on five-year averages for the index of agricultural production for 1950/51 to 1954/55, 1960/61 to 1964/65, and 1970/71 to 1974/75.
[59] "The Economic Outlook," AICC Central Training Camp, Narora: November 22-24,
1974, p. 17.
[60] Ibid., pp. 26-28.                                    [61] Fifth Five Year Plan, 1974-79, pp. 6-7.
[62] Economic Survey, 1975-76, p. 69. The per capita net availability of cereals and pulses per
day in 1973 was somewhat less than 15 ounces, compared to levels of 14.4 ounces and 14.1
ounces in the near-famine years of 1966 and 1967, and 16.5 ounces achieved in 1961.

tion living below the official poverty line once again began to swell with additional numbers of landless agricultural laborers and marginal farmers.

The outlook for economic growth in the future offered little hope of reversing these tendencies. The expectation that the Fourth Plan would reestablish a rising trend in the rate of saving and investment was disappointed. During the five-year period, net saving as a proportion of net domestic product managed to exceed the peak level of approximately 12 percent achieved in 1966/67 only by minimal amounts, hovering at about 12 percent during the first four years, and showing some improvement to 12.8 percent in 1973/74, the last year of the Plan.[63] Similarly, the ratio of net investment to net domestic product remained at levels between 12.5 percent and 13.5 percent for the five years of the Plan, representing a drop from the record level of 15.4 percent achieved in 1966/67, as the net inflow of foreign resources began to decline.[64] Changes in fiscal policy alone were unlikely to provide a corrective.

The factors responsible for the stagnant saving rate were built into the structure of the political economy. On the one hand, the government's inability to prevent large-scale evasion and avoidance of income taxes levied on individuals and firms in the urban sector, and on the other its almost complete lack of success in persuading state governments to impose direct taxes on agricultural income to widen the tax base, restricted the possibilities for increasing real resources for development. At the same time, weak governments were unable to ignore rising political pressures for steady increases in non-Plan outlays. Apart from rising debt service charges and higher outlays on defense, they were compelled to find funds for increases in pay and dearness allowances of government employees, and rising subsidies for foodgrains. Meanwhile, many of the state governments, attempting to build up larger reservoirs of popular support, actually set about eliminating or reducing land revenue taxes. Between 1965/66 and 1973/74, the public sector's share in Gross Domestic Product increased only slightly, from 13.4 percent to 14.7 percent of GNP. The ratio of public saving to public disposable income actually fell from approximately 22 percent in 1965/66 to 19 percent in 1973/74. In the aggregate, public saving as a percentage of GNP was no more than 2.8 percent.[65] The private sector, which still accounted for over 85 percent of GNP, and achieved a saving rate of 11 percent of private disposable income, provided the larger share of domestic saving at 9.4 percent of GNP.[66]

Even if the government had been so inclined, there were serious prob-

[63] Ministry of Finance, *Economic Survey, 1977-78* (New Delhi, 1978), p. 59.
[64] *Ibid.*
[65] *Basic Statistics Relating to the Indian Economy, 1950-51 to 1974-75*, p. 15.
[66] *Draft Fifth Year Plan, 1974-79*, pp. 12-13.

lems in relying mainly on the growth of private savings in any perspective savings strategy. The household sector, which provided the major component of private saving, was stabilized at a saving rate of about 7 to 8 percent of household disposable income.[67] Despite gains to the larger landowners after the mid-1960s from the adoption of improved techniques, and a sharp inflationary rise in foodgrains prices, household saving did not go up, but registered a modest decline. Indeed, there was "every evidence that non-functional consumption like that in ceremonials, rituals and superstitious practices [was] on the increase."[68] The private corporate sector did not offer any better prospect for generating a higher rate of saving. Apart from the fact that the public sector's draft on private savings (through market borrowings, small savings and contributions by government employees to state Provident Funds) reduced the pool of investible resources available, there was little incentive for private enterprise to step up the level of its economic activity. Corporate profits in 1971 showed a "sizeable fall"[69] over the estimates projected at the beginning of the Fourth Plan. Meanwhile, the stringent licensing policies introduced in 1970, along with the implicit threat of nationalization, dulled much of any remaining entrepreneurial enthusiasm for taking up new ventures.

The solution, especially in the context of political priorities for reducing inequalities in wealth and income, pointed to a policy of primary expansion of public saving. Such a savings strategy, requiring a substantial improvement in the public sector's share of GNP and a major increase in the ratio of public saving to public disposable income, had been endorsed by the Planning Commission as the keystone of its approach to the Fifth Plan. But this solution only restated the political constraints that were crippling the entire development effort. A review of the reasons for the inability to mobilize sufficient amounts of public savings for investment plainly revealed that

> the first reason for this weakness lies in the fact that a substantial proportion of incomes arising from development have accrued to farmers and traders. The incidence of taxation on farm incomes is particularly low. A substantial proportion of incomes accruing to traders escapes taxation, a tendency which is reinforced by the fact that some part of these incomes arises from illegal transactions. Moreover, it is also known that there is a substantial amount of tax evasion in other sectors also. Thus a large proportion of the surpluses generated by economic activity escape taxation.[70]

[67] *The Fourth Plan Mid-Term Appraisal*, i, 43.
[68] *Ibid.*, p. 43.                                     [69] *Ibid.*, p. 24.
[70] "The Economic Outlook," AICC Central Training Camp, Narora: November 22-24, 1974, p. 19.

Even if it were possible to plug tax loopholes arising from evasion, and black marketing and smuggling in the urban sector, there was no way to get around the basic problem that "practically no country in the world has succeeded in developing without mobilizing agricultural surpluses and it is unlikely that India would be an exception to this rule."[71] Further, there was little likelihood of increasing the proportion of public savings to public disposable income as long as inflationary pressures, stimulated by shortages of foodgrains and essential commodities, and compounded by the absence of a public distribution system, pushed up the costs of government administration and the burdens of nondevelopmental expenditures.

Such additional charges on domestic resources, occurring in tandem with unexpected increases in foreign exchange costs, had already inflated budgetary deficits beyond the reach of conventional fiscal controls. During the first years of the Fourth Plan new expenditures on central sector schemes, as well as steady increases in non-Plan outlays for dearness allowances, food subsidies, and relief to refugees from Bangladesh, all eroded current balances expected to be available for the Fourth Plan. Early warning signals of a resource crisis were converted into a full-scale alarm by a series of events that also had devastating consequences for the balance of payments position. War broke out with Pakistan in December 1971, imposing larger financial burdens for defense and assistance to Bangladesh, at the same time as the United States once again suspended all economic aid; drought in the summer of 1972 created widespread food shortages that had to be met in part by high-priced imports of grain; the steep increase in the price of crude oil set by the OPEC countries after 1973 increased India's import bill for petroleum and other lubricants by over four times.

The level of real resources available to finance annual outlays could not be maintained against these mounting financial pressures. Fourth Plan expenditures reached Rs. 16,160 crores, somewhat more than the original outlay of Rs. 15,902 crores. But this level of spending had been achieved only with unprecedented amounts of deficit financing at Rs. 2,060 crores—compared to an original estimate of Rs. 850 crores considered safe over the five-year period.[72] The expansion of the money supply in such large amounts, at a time when the economy was stretched by shortages of foodgrains and other essential commodities, contributed to unprecedented levels of inflation. The wholesale prices of all commodities including food articles, industrial raw materials, and manufactures, which had been increasing at about 3 to 6 percent per annum during the first three years of the Plan, jumped by about 13 percent between

[71] *Ibid.*, p. 20.
[72] *Basic Statistics Relating to the Indian Economy 1950-51 to 1974-75*, p. 125.

1972 and 1973, and then shot up by almost 30 percent between 1973 and 1974.[73] Over the five-year period 1969-1974, the price index had climbed almost 58 percent, creating a shortfall in the level of development expenditure in real terms of more than 17 percent.[74]

The projection of resources for the Fifth Plan appeared increasingly problematical. By June 1973, D. P. Dhar had to admit that the abnormal rise in prices and shortages of foodgrains and other materials had made some reduction in financial outlays inevitable. The Fifth Plan, scheduled to begin on April 1, 1974, could not be implemented. The Planning Commission was once again "reconstituted," this time with P. N. Haksar as chairman. In April 1975, the planners publicly conceded that the Draft Fifth Plan, including the program for minimum needs, had become obsolete because of the sharp rise in domestic prices and the increase in international prices of crude oil.

The rise in prices threatened the future of the entire development effort. The government was convinced that something drastic had to be done immediately to contain inflation, or "things would go completely out of hand."[75] Mrs. Gandhi, disillusioned with her closest economic advisers after the failure of the state takeover of the wholesale trade in wheat, appeared newly wary of "certain cliches, for instance, what is leftism, what is radical and what is not"[76] in setting economic policies that under Indian conditions could not be implemented. The central government, moreover, was once again confronting pressures from the International Monetary Fund to carry out a "stabilization" program that would bring inflation under control as the condition of a credit line to cover the massive balance of payments deficit. The IMF recommended stringent fiscal discipline to reduce the money supply and complementary economic policies to freeze wages, increase imports, promote exports, and provide incentives to private investment. These recommendations were also taken up by the World Bank as part of the negotiations on development aid then in progress between the Consortium countries and India. The Bank pressed even harder for a complete overhaul of the economy that would mark a departure from socialistic policies in order to "open up the economy along western lines."[77] The convergence of these sets of domestic and international pressures led yet once again to a reorientation

[73] *Economic Survey 1975-76*, p. 92.

[74] *Ibid.*, p. 92; "The Economic Outlook," AICC Central Training Camp, Narora: November 22-24, 1974, p. 18.

[75] This was the assessment of the Finance Minister, Y. B. Chavan, in his speech to the AICC on July 21, 1974. All India Congress Committee, *Congress Marches Ahead—10*, p. 234.

[76] AICC, *Two Exclusive Interviews, Prime Minister Indira Gandhi on Questions Facing India and the World*, pp. 13-14.

[77] See Jeremiah Novak, "The Role of IMF, World Bank," *Times of India*, July 1 and 2, 1977.

of economic policies that was tantamount to a growth strategy with no more than marginal adjustments in the interests of more equitable distribution. This time the new approach was adopted without open debate.

In July 1974, the president, acting on the advice of the Cabinet, promulgated a series of antiinflation ordinances[78] that mandated compulsory deposit by all salaried employees of any wage increases won through strikes or collective bargaining, as well as one-half of all additional dearness allowances; placed a ceiling on dividends that could be distributed from after-tax profits by private companies; and imposed compulsory deposits on all income-tax payers with earnings of more than Rs. 15,000 per year of 4 to 8 percent of their income. The ordinances were combined with a dear money policy by the Reserve Bank that announced a sharp rise in the lending rate and substantial increase in the interest rate for various categories of savings instruments. Shortly after, the government adopted new procedures to ensure "automatic" import licenses to eligible industries as a means of reducing the domestic price level and undercutting smuggling and black marketing activities. At the same time, measures were taken for the rapid clearance of industrial licenses, including permission for larger business houses to expand production in selected industries that had been closed to them under the 1970 licensing policy. All of this was accompanied by the government's decision to enlarge its extraordinary powers under MISA to make smuggling and evasion of foreign exchange controls grounds for preventive detention. In September 1974, the scope of MISA was extended by presidential ordinance, and in December 1974, the ordinance was replaced by a new Act of Parliament (Conservation of Foreign Exchange and Prevention of Smuggling Activities) that permitted the government to carry out "dehoarding" raids in Delhi and some of the states and arrest suspected hoarders and smugglers.

The combination of the wage freeze and suspension of cost-of-living adjustments, the tight credit policy, and some amount of dehoarding brought about by the raids (including "precautionary withdrawal of black money from the trade")[79] did begin to show the first signs of reducing the rate of inflation by late 1974. But this economic gain was purchased at the political cost of further alienating the urban lower-middle and middle classes, who bore the brunt of the antiinflation measures even as growing unemployment, soaring prices, and shortages of essential commodities eroded their living standards, and a climate of political cor-

---

[78] The text of the antiinflation ordinances is published in *The Statesman*, July 8 and 18, 1974.

[79] "The Economic Outlook," AICC Central Training Camp, Narora: November 22-24, 1974, p. 14.

ruption destroyed their confidence in normal democratic processes to solve India's basic problems.

During the years following the prime minister's landslide election victories, the credibility of her leadership and that of the Congress party rapidly declined. Mrs. Gandhi appeared to dissipate her energies in efforts to protect her position from any challenge within the party, and to prevent the emergence of rival centers of power by any means that came to hand. She perfected a style of coterie politics that saw a slide toward the political abyss of corruption and abuse of power. Ministers, chief ministers, and party functionaries who had no political base beyond their personal acceptability to the prime minister vied with one another in declaring their loyalty to her and in establishing their socialist credentials through radical statements and slogans. Such persons, using the prime minister's name, often gave the impression of being beyond accountability. Members of the middle-class intelligentsia did not find it difficult to believe that

> a minister can be corrupt and know he will get away with this corruption; can grab the poor people's land and know he will get away with it; can collect money through patently illegal means from all and sundry, and know he will get away with it. Nobody dares cross-examine him, accuse him, pillory him. Even if someone dares, it would be an instance of infructuous impetuosity. For, doesn't he shout, full throatedly, each of the slogans the Prime Minister has added lustre to? He belongs to the Prime Minister's parlor; he can cock a snook at the world.[80]

The stain of corruption spread until it tainted the reputation of the prime minister's younger son. In 1969, after years of debate, the government decided to approve the production of a low-priced "people's" car and awarded the license to Sanjay Gandhi. Sanjay, then 22 years old, had completed only one year of training at a Rolls Royce plant in Great Britain when he was chosen over seventeen others who had also submitted proposals for the project. Subsequently, charges were raised in parliament that he had acquired hundreds of acres of prime agricultural land as the site of his factory on the Delhi-Gurgaon road, at an artificially low price—and in violation of government regulations prohibiting plant construction within 1,000 meters of a defense installation—through the intervention of Bansi Lal, then chief minister of Haryana and one of Mrs. Gandhi's closest allies. It was also rumored that Sanjay had raised large sums of capital for his firm, Maruti, Ltd., by a variety of illegitimate and

[80] *Economic and Political Weekly*, July 7, 1973, p. 1175.

illegal methods, using his mother's position to persuade businessmen to invest in dealerships, and even accepting subscriptions from *benami* or nonexistent firms set up for the purpose by the Birlas. The Maruti car itself proved unsuccessful. Structural faults in the prototype could not be corrected to put the "people's car" into mass production. Yet, even as Maruti sank into debt, the nationalized banks provided additional infusions of funds to keep the firm afloat. Meanwhile, subsidiaries of Maruti set up to provide consulting services and to manufacture road rollers attracted lucrative government contracts despite serious questions about the capacity of the company to fill them—all of which spurred additional charges of corruption.[81]

In the states, meanwhile, the Congress governments, almost all of which enjoyed massive majorities after the landslide electoral victories of 1972, were soon paralyzed once again by factionalism. Although the prime minister's hand-picked nominees for chief minister in each state had been accepted "unanimously" by the Congress legislature party, the fact that they lacked a secure base at home made them easy targets for attacks by rival aspirants to power. In several states, there was a complete breakdown of party discipline as dissidents maneuvered "day and night" to oust the leadership from office. Factional infighting and defections from the ruling party brought about the collapse of the Congress ministries and the imposition of President's Rule in Andhra (January 1973) and in Orissa (March 1973). In Uttar Pradesh, a mutiny by the provincial armed constabulary, and the ineptness and corruption of state administration revealed by it, precipitated the resignation of the ministry and a spell of President's Rule in June 1973. In other states, including Bihar, Gujerat, and Mysore, the struggle for power among rival groups led to renewed toppling activities that saw the reshuffling of ministries to accommodate rival factions. Worse still, in West Bengal, feuds erupted between leaders of the Youth Congress and Chhatra Parishad, which led to a general situation of lawlessness in which each side resorted to political murders in their efforts to annihilate the other.

As the politics of defection and counterdefection drained the energies of elected Congress governments and left them impotent to solve the problems of food shortages, rising prices, and unemployment pressing down on their constituents, Congress was defeated by opposition alliances and by the CPI in a number of by-elections. The defeats called Mrs. Gandhi's own popularity into question, and they reduced her margin for political maneuver. The CPI, capitalizing on the government's waning credibility, made more effective use of its two-pronged electoral

---

[81] For a summary of the charges raised against Sanjay Gandhi in connection with the Maruti car project see Nayar, *The Judgement*, Annexure, Maruti.

and extraparliamentary strategy to apply renewed pressure on the Congress party to "end the government policy of status quo and force a shift to the left."[82] CPI leaders once again called for the unity of all left and democratic forces inside and outside the Congress on principles of the ruling party's own national economic program, especially for price controls and state takeover of wholesale trade in foodgrains and essential commodities. They mounted meetings, processions, sit-ins, *gheraos* and other forms of "mass struggles" state by state, and used antiprice-rise agitations and "dehoarding" drives to bring pressure on Congress governments for the implementation of their own policies. In a number of states, including Assam, Bihar, West Bengal, Tamil Nadu, and Karnataka, the tactic brought special political dividends. In those states, "either the state-level leadership of the Congress or sections of it [had] agreed to joint campaigns and sometimes participated in joint or convergent actions."[83]

The national leadership, moreover, also found it more difficult to keep their distance from the CPI once declining popular support created fresh doubts about the ability of the Congress party to win state elections on its own. Two important state elections were scheduled for February 1974, one in Uttar Pradesh, the other in Orissa. In Uttar Pradesh, the keystone state of the Congress party's national power, the credibility of the state government had been undermined by food agitations, the police revolt, rampant student violence, corruption, the resignation of the state ministry and imposition of President's Rule. The opposition parties, which could not manage to agree on the terms of an electoral alliance, were nevertheless convinced that Congress was completely discredited and would be defeated at the polls. Similarly, in Orissa, where the state Congress party was divided by bitter factional disputes, and in addition was confronted by a combined opposition of the Utkal Congress, Swatantra, and the SSP organized in a new Pragati party, the prospect for the ruling party appeared bleak. In both states, the Congress party decided to take the precaution of entering into an electoral alignment with the CPI. In the event, despite a significant erosion of its popular vote,[84] in Uttar Pradesh Congress was able to secure a slim majority of

[82] Communist Party of India, "Resolutions and Reports Adopted by the National Council of the Communist Party of India, New Delhi, 1-4 September 1973" (New Delhi, September 1973), p. 10.

[83] *Ibid.*, p. 58.

[84] The popular vote for Congress declined from more than 48 percent in 1971 to less than 33 percent in 1974, while the combined vote of the Jan Sangh, BKD, Congress (O), and SSP went up from 37 percent in 1971 to more than 47 percent in 1974. The results of the 1974 election in Uttar Pradesh are published in Communist Party of India, "Report and Resolutions of the National Council of the Communist Party of India, New Delhi, 23-26 March 1974" (New Delhi, April 1974), pp. 31, 33.

seats on its own. Yet the Congress government, weakened by internal dissent and ruling with a bare majority, conferred a special status on the CPI as its most firm ally inside the assembly. In Orissa, where Congress actually increased both its popular vote and the number of seats won over its performance in the previous election of 1971,[85] it was nevertheless unable to form the government without the support of the CPI.

The Congress party's growing ties to the CPI created further suspicions among anticommunists inside the Congress party and outside its ranks about Mrs. Gandhi's motives. Such fears of the noncommunist Congress left and the right opposition parties alike were inflamed by boasts of the CPI leadership, which interpreted the results of the U.P. and Orissa elections as once again "prov[ing] the correctness of the party's policy and tactics."[86] Indeed, the National Council of the CPI publicly declared that the party's "central political perspective" was to replace the present government at the Center by " a government of left and democratic unity" in which power would be shared by the "parties and forces representing the working class peasantry, radical middle class and patriotic nonmonopolistic sections of the national bourgeoisie." They described their own tactics as a plan to "force mass sanctions, build up unity of left and democratic forces, including the progressive sections within the ruling Congress, and raise it to such a political level as to change the correlation of class forces in the country in favor of the working class and the worker-peasant alliance."[87] They even spoke openly of their hopes for creating a "Kerala-style" coalition government at the Center, a goal widely interpreted to signal stepped-up communist pressure on the central government, to expose Congress failures of implementation in order to divide the party on ideological lines and speed up the process of another split.

Opponents of the communists, both inside the Congress party and in the opposition, appeared increasingly ineffectual to counter these political thrusts. On the contrary, ex-communists within the national Congress party reasserted their influence. Factional infighting among the members of the dissolved Congress Socialist Forum and Nehru Forum resurfaced, even while the anticommunist socialists coalesced around their own spokesmen, especially Chandra Shekhar and Mohan Dharia. But although the majority of the rank and file remained opposed to their party's growing links with the CPI, they were losing ground, perhaps not least because "all of them, including senior Ministers, now hide their

[85] The Congress vote in Orissa increased from 26.5 percent in 1971 to 37.4 percent in 1974, while its share of the seats in the 146-member state legislature increased from 51 to 69. *The Statesman*, March 8, 1974.
[86] "Report and Resolutions of the National Council of the Communist Party of India, 23-26 March 1974," p. 5.
[87] *Ibid.*, pp. 16-17.

opinions lest they be accused of lacking a sense of 'commitment.' "[88] There was, indeed, no open protest even from the leaders of the Nehru Forum when, following the resignation of S. D. Sharma as party president in August 1974, the Working Committee unanimously appointed D. K. Barooah, the declared choice of the Socialist Forum, as provisional president of the Congress.

Outside the Congress, the right opposition appeared demoralized. Although some of their leaders feared that Mrs. Gandhi was taking the country in the direction of personal dictatorship, and that the "unholy alliance between the Congress and the CPI was gradually making India a camp follower of Soviet Russia,"[89] they felt powerless to prevail against the ruling party at the polls. The Congress victories in Uttar Pradesh and Orissa appeared to offer persuasive evidence on that point. The victories, especially the success in Uttar Pradesh—which even ardent Congress supporters had considered doubtful—were tainted by what political observers and members of the opposition considered unfair use of the state machinery and illicit funds "which vitiated the electoral mechanism on which the system's legitimacy was based."[90]

In Uttar Pradesh, the Congress High Command had financed the campaign with subscriptions received from the "oil kings" of Gujerat (in return for decontrol of the groundnut oil industry in that state),[91] and had refurbished the image of the state government by diverting food supplies from other deficit states to Uttar Pradesh in order to maintain rations from the public distribution system. The prime minister, using government helicopters, maximized the impact of these political resources by personally addressing hundreds of meetings that took her into remote villages. Congress party workers, sometimes with jeeps at their disposal, and amply supplied with posters and streamers embossed with Mrs. Gandhi's picture, once again relied on her appeal for the minorities and land-poor peasants among the Harijans and backward castes. The party's main slogan throughout the state, as in 1971, was "give your precious vote to the Congress to strengthen Indira Gandhi's hands."[92]

The appeal, moreover, must have had some credibility to many of the rural poor. Largely oblivious to the factional infighting that was paralyzing the state Congress party, insulated in some degree from the worst impact of rising prices, voters belonging to the Harijans and Backward

[88] *The Statesman*, January 29, 1974.

[89] This was the assessment of the Jan Sangh in the party's resolution on the internal situation adopted at the Kanpur session in February 1973. See S. Viswam, "The Jan Sangh at the Crossroads," *The Statesman*, June 23, 1973.

[90] Ram Joshi, "India, 1974: Growing Political Crisis," *Asian Survey*, February 1975.

[91] See Dawn E. Jones and Rodney W. Jones, "Urban Upheaval in India: The 1974 Nav Nirman Riots in Gujerat," pp. 1016-17.

[92] *The Statesman*, February 22, 1974.

Castes were impressed by the bounties that had come their way and others that had been promised. Some small and marginal farmers and landless laborers had personally received subsidized loans from cooperatives or nationalized banks, or jobs on government work projects under the central sector schemes. Others looked forward to the distribution of government-owned land for house sites, and even surplus agricultural land under new state legislation. Those who benefited or hoped to benefit from such new programs attributed their good fortune directly to "Indiraji." They did not blame the prime minister for other government failures in carrying out promises to control prices of foodgrains or supply essential commodities. It did not seem reasonable to expect Mrs. Gandhi to do everything by herself. The people "making the trouble," they concluded, were the moneylenders and traders standing in her way, and the corrupt officials who pandered to them in the implementing agencies of the party and government (sarkar).[93]

Efforts by the noncommunist opposition parties to merge into a single party after the 1974 state elections and offer a national alternative to the Congress bogged down. Not only were the Jan Sangh, Congress (O), and the Socialist party reluctant to abandon their separate identities, but all of the conservative opposition parties were confronted with the dilemma of having to devise a popular appeal that simultaneously endorsed equality and social justice, but rejected the principles of centralized economic planning or basic socialist reform. The new Bharatiya Lok Dal (Indian Peoples party) launched in July 1974 by seven of the smaller opposition parties (including the BKD, SSP, Swatantra, and the Utkal Congress), hit on the tactic of rooting their alternative "in Indian soil, both physically and spiritually" and drawing "inspiration and guidance from Indian thought, experience and culture, build[ing] an ethos embodied in the teachings and aspirations of Mahatma Gandhi."[94] Even so, the opposition as a whole was stymied in their "search of an identity which is eluding them"[95] and which would permit them to take advantage of the deteriorating economic situation to mount a major offensive against the Congress party. The weaknesses of the noncommunist opposition were clearly exposed in the new presidential election called in August 1974, when President Giri stepped down from office. Not all of the parties could agree on a common candidate to oppose the Congress Parliamentary Board's nominee, Fakhruddin Ali Ahmed, known as one of the prime minister's closest allies. Ahmed actually won the election with

[93] Such attitudes were commonly expressed by landless workers and farmers in selected villages outside Lucknow and in Mathura district of Uttar Pradesh during my field trips in the late summer of 1973.

[94] *The Statesman*, July 3, 1974.

[95] S. Nihal Singh, "Shadow Boxing by the Opposition?" *The Statesman*, July 11, 1974.

a sizable section of the non–Congress vote, garnering more than eighty percent of the total in the electoral college of the state assemblies and parliament, where Congress enjoyed a two–thirds majority.[96]

The spectacle of inept national and state Congress governments, crippled by factionalism and tainted with corruption, unable to cope with mounting economic problems despite massive legislative majorities, even while the national Congress party strengthened its ties to the CPI, and the anticommunist opposition appeared completely ineffectual in offering any alternative, produced growing despair about the efficacy and legitimacy of the party system and the parliamentary process. Touring the country in the early months of 1974, Kuldip Nayar, the prominent journalist, reported the widespread belief that "the present system of parliamentary democracy cannot deliver the goods. People openly talk in terms of military dictatorship or communist revolution. Mismanagement at every step has led even the most conservative to talk about revolution because the whole system is held to be rotten to the core."[97]

Such speculations went beyond the theoretical musings of middle-class intellectuals to take on a terrifying immediacy. In January 1974 there was a spontaneous uprising throughout the cities and towns of the western state of Gujerat, directed at forcing the resignation of the chief minister and the dissolution of the legislative assembly for following corrupt and "anti-peoples" policies.

In Gujerat, Morarji Desai's home state, the undivided Congress party had aligned itself with the Congress (O) after the 1969 split, and the New Congress party's organization had splintered into rival and unstable groups of widely disparate backgrounds. The intraparty rivalries were particularly embittered by the enduring resentment of the local ex-communist and socialist Congressmen affiliated with the Socialist Forum who had been pushed aside during the 1972 elections, when the central leadership allowed former members of the Congress (O) and Swatantra to enter the party and stand on the Congress ticket. Their anger was intensified when Mrs. Gandhi's nominee to the chief ministership in Gujerat, Ghanshyam Oza, a reform-minded member of parliament, virtually ignored the Forum in selecting his Cabinet. The leftists in the state Congress reacted by becoming "completely opportunistic," subsequently working with Oza's main rivals in the government to topple the chief minister from office. Ultimately, in late June 1973, this dissident faction led by Chimanbhai Patel, then minister of industries and planning (dubbed a "kulak" by his enemies because of his political base among the affluent farmers of the dominant Patidar landowning caste), and Kantilal

[96] *The Statesman*, August 21, 1974.
[97] Kuldip Nayar, "Accommodating Various Interests," *The Statesman*, April 24, 1974.

Ghia, a businessman enjoying the support of Ahmedabad industrialists, succeeded in winning over 70 of the 138 members of the Congress legislature party. Yet the vote of no confidence engineered against the chief minister was accomplished only after sensational stories had appeared in the press that Chimanbhai Patel, spending over Rs. 30 lakhs, purchased defections from the Oza government. Stories circulated that Patel had kept his own supporters sequestered on a farm near Ahmedabad city, where all sorts of "unbefitting methods were used to win over MLA's." Some MLAs were said to have been actually "kidnapped, rescued and hidden as if they are cattle."[98]

The ascent to the chief ministership of Chimanbhai Patel following the collapse of the Oza ministry did not end the factional conflict. On the contrary, the two allies, Patel and Ghia, had by this time fallen out. In addition, Oza and his supporters inside the ministry turned their own energies to overthrowing the Patel government. As part of this struggle, prominent Congressmen took the lead in denouncing their own party leaders for corruption in failing to act against hoarders and black marketeers, to halt a precipitous price rise.

Indeed, by the end of 1973, during the time that Congress energies were absorbed in the internal fight for power, the state of Gujerat, a food deficit area, had suffered a drastic cut of about two-thirds in central foodgrains supplies to the ration shops, and price increases of cooking oil and foodgrains of a hundred percent or more in less than one year. In both cases, price rigging by politicians and traders was blamed. Chimanbhai Patel, in fact, had made a deal with the oil trade allowing prices to rise in return for subscriptions to party funds; and despite a bumper crop of rice and millet, the state failed to make up the deficits in central deliveries by an active grain procurement program.

The contempt for party politics and the entire political system induced by the spectacle of elected officials concerned only with their own gain even while the economic plight of the people they had pledged to help precipitously worsened finally exploded in a spontaneous popular upheaval.[99] In early January 1974, students at the L. D. Engineering College in Ahmedabad, protesting rising charges for mess bills, set fire to the college canteen and attacked the rector's house. The chief minister ordered riot police into the campus. About thirty-five percent of the stu-

[98] Kantilal Ghia, who subsequently broke with Chimanbhai Patel, made these charges public in a press statement. Cited in AICC (Congress O), "Note" on Gujerat Nav Nirman Movement, January 9, 1977, mimeographed, p. 4.

[99] This account of the uprising in Gujerat is based on newspaper reports of the period and detailed analyses published in: Ghanshyam Shah, "The Upsurge in Gujerat," *Economic and Political Weekly*, 9:32-34 (Special Number, 1974), 1429-53; John R. Wood, "Extra-Parliamentary Opposition in India: An Analysis of Populist Agitations in Gujerat and Bihar," *Pacific Affairs*, 48:3 (Fall 1975), 313-34; Jones and Jones, "Urban Upheaval in India," pp. 1012-33; and AICC (Congress O), "Note" on Gujerat Nav Nirman Movement.

dent body was arrested, and several students were severely beaten. The police action triggered the formation of a Vidyarthi Lagni Parishad (Students Strike Association) by other college and university students in Ahmedabad, which called for the release of those arrested, a reduction in mess charges, resignation of the education minister, and a strike to shut down colleges and secondary schools from January 7 until these demands were met. At the outset, the students linked their demands to popular economic grievances, calling upon the state government to arrest the hoarders and profiteers responsible for the sharp rise in the prices of foodgrains, cooking oil, and other essential commodities.

Student confrontations with the police broke out almost immediately. Gangs of young people stoned municipal buses and attacked and looted a number of foodgrains shops in Ahmedabad. The agitation quickly drew in several elements of the disaffected middle classes. The citywide trade union organizations of white collar employees of the state and city governments—including those who worked in the national banks and insurance companies and primary and secondary schools—approved the call for an Ahmedabad *bandh* on January 10 to protest police brutality against students and rising prices. The powerful college and university teachers' associations, which had strong grievances of their own against the chief minister (for his intervention in elections at Gujerat University to impose his own nominee as vice chancellor), also expressed sympathy for the students and announced support for the Ahmedabad *bandh*. The strike, in addition, received the support of the opposition parties, the Jan Sangh, and Congress (O), and dissident members of the Patel ministry.

On the day of the *bandh*, Ahmedabad was almost completely shut down. Looting of food and oil shops and arson of municipal milk booths broke out immediately. Confrontations between the demonstrators and police escalated into full-scale riots and spread into the middle-class areas of the city. The police who entered the narrow lanes of the residential sections in the old walled city became "targets for stones and flaming rags thrown from balconies and windows and their discipline broke down."[100] By the twelfth, rioting had spread to Baroda and most other urban areas of the state. Police lathi charges, the use of tear gas, and finally, "shoot-at-sight" orders had only a temporary effect in controlling the rioters.

This time, the succession of demonstrations, strikes, looting, rioting, and arson of public and private property was more than just an outlet for feelings of frustration and anomie. The agitations acquired a sharp political focus, one that revealed just how precarious the consensus supporting parliamentary processes of government had become. On January 10, the Vidyarthi Lagni Parishad dissolved and reconstituted itself as the Nav

[100] Jones and Jones, "Urban Upheaval in India," p. 1025.

Nirman Yuvak Samiti (Youth for Reconstruction Association), which declared a program to wage a nonviolent struggle to purify and rebuild society. Nav Nirman Committees sprang up in all important cities of Gujerat. Their uncompromising demand was for the resignation of the chief minister, Chimanbhai Patel, and the dissolution of the state assembly. The demand was supported by the college teachers, who had themselves promoted it, and the major white-collar unions. Rioting and serious bloodshed once again erupted in cities throughout the state. Although curfews were imposed on 106 cities and towns on January 25, and the state police was reinforced by contingents from the Border Security Forces and the Central Reserve Police, the escalation of mob violence made it impossible to restore public order. "Every day some new effort was made to express popular anger—'peoples curfews,' processions with empty oil tins and grain sacks, silent marches, the beating of thalis [metal eating plates], relay fasts, bus hijackings, mock courts, and mock funerals [of Patel and later of Indira Gandhi]."[101] On January 26, after doubts had arisen about the reliability of the police, the state government finally asked for Indian army units to be sent in. Even the army, however, could not defuse the political agitations for the resignation of the Chimanbhai Patel ministry. Fresh rioting swept the state after February 4. On February 9, after four dissident ministers in his own government had demanded he resign, the chief minister, on orders from New Delhi, submitted his resignation. The Gujerat assembly was suspended and President's Rule was imposed on the state.

The agitation had still not run its course. During the next five weeks the state was kept in constant turmoil by renewed demonstrations for the dissolution of the legislative assembly that began to spread into the rural areas. The demand received additional impetus as the opposition parties, especially the Congress (O) and Jan Sangh, lent their support to the agitation. Sarvodaya workers, including Jayaprakash Narayan, announced that they also supported the demand for dissolution.

Despite the fact that leaders of the agitation continued to emphasize nonviolent methods of protest, the second phase of the movement directed at dissolution of the assembly was particularly violent. Riots and looting continued in many towns and cities. In addition, mob pressure was directed at forcing the resignation of Congress politicians from municipal councils and the legislative assembly. In some instances, legislators "were attacked, their houses and properties set on fire, their relatives kidnapped in order to terrorize them to resign."[102]

Mrs. Gandhi, determined not to bow to coercion, at first refused to dissolve the assembly. She appeared hopeful that firm action, includ-

[101] Wood, "Extra-Parliamentary Opposition in India," p. 318.

[102] AICC, *Congress Marches Ahead—IX*, excerpt from "Resolution on Political Situation," pp. 39-40.

ing the arrest of 200 Nav Nirman leaders, would ultimately defeat the movement. But on March 11, her longtime adversary, Morarji Desai, announced a "fast unto death" in Ahmedabad. Within a few days, moreover, a majority of MPs, ignoring central directives to stand firm in the fact of new threats against their families, had submitted their resignations. The possibility that the Congress legislature party could provide a new government disappeared. Mrs. Gandhi, left with no alternative, announced on March 15 dissolution of the state assembly. The agitation had lasted for more than ten weeks. It had taken 103 lives, injured another 310 persons, and spurred arrests of more than 8,000 demonstrators.

The Gujerat uprising can be considered a political watershed. It marked the collapse of shared consensus on legitimate methods of conflict resolution between the government and opposition groups. Leaders of the Congress party charged the opposition with acting as "the protagonists of vested interests" both at home and abroad in their support for extraparliamentary agitations that were creating conditions for the establishment of a fascist dictatorship in the country.[103] Senior leaders of the opposition accused the prime minister of using extraordinary police powers to curb the expression of popular discontent in a plan to take the country toward authoritarian rule in collusion with the Soviet-backed Communist party. Each side became convinced that the other would no longer abide by the rules of democratic politics. Each side justified its own excesses in the name of safeguarding democracy from the assaults mounted on it by the other.

Mrs. Gandhi and other leading members of the Congress party were, in fact, already apprehensive that the central government and, in particular, the prime minister, had become a target of a conspiracy by "external elements in India's affairs in collusion with some internal groups."[104] The press in Gujerat had published charges in April 1973 that the political adviser to the U.S. consul in Bombay had been meeting regularly with "certain elements" in the Gujerat ministry in order to "cause a political setback to Mrs. Gandhi."[105] Mrs. Gandhi herself, in September 1973,

[103] According to the Congress Working Committee: "right reaction and vested interests have resorted to naked and systematic violence because the common people have in free elections repeatedly frustrated their attempts to capture power. Frustration in the camp of reaction has increased because of repeated reaffirmation of people's faith in the principles of democracy, secularism and socialism and their support to programs which the Congress party under the leadership of Prime Minister, Smt. Indira Gandhi, is pledged to implement. The Congress, the chosen instrument of the people for accomplishing fundamental and radical changes in society, stands as an obstacle in the path of vested interests. Hence, the verdict of the ballot box is being sought to be thwarted by extra-parliamentary and fascist methods of coercion and duress." *Ibid.*, p. 40.

[104] Excerpt from Mrs. Gandhi's speech to the AICC, September 15, 1973, *ibid.*, p. 101.

[105] An account of this is given in H. D. Malaviya, *CIA, Its Real Face* (Delhi, 1975), pp. 57-58.

warned the AICC about the danger of foreign intervention in India's internal affairs. She appeared to believe that the same fate that had overtaken President Allende of Chile—when his elected Marxist government was overthrown and he was murdered in a military coup after CIA agents had intervened to aggravate domestic economic difficulties— might also be planned for her by her enemies in the opposition acting in cooperation with "outsiders."[106]

Such fears were intensified by the growing recourse of opposition parties to extraparliamentary agitations for giving expression to popular economic and political discontent. Immediately after the dissolution of the Gujerat assembly, student agitators in Bihar, protesting soaring prices, shortages of essential commodities, mounting unemployment, and outmoded educational curricula had launched plans for a mass *gherao* of the state legislative assembly to press their demand for the resignation of the ministry and dissolution of the Assembly. This time, moreover, the movement was dominated by members of the Jan Sangh's student front, the Vidyarthi Parishad, in alliance with the student wing of the Samuykta Socialist party. The Student Action Committee, formed by leaders of noncommunist student organizations across the state, attracted the support of opposition parties ranging from the communal and conservative Jan Sangh and Congress (O) to the radical CPI (Marxists). Once again, the agitation sparked large-scale civil violence. On the opening day of the Assembly's budget session on March 18, looting and arson in the capital city of Patna was so widespread that army troops had to be called out to contain the mobs. This time, moreover, Jayaprakash Narayan did more than lend his prestige in support of the students' demands. He announced that he would reenter political life to lead their movement, while expanding its goal to root out corruption from public life by waging "a struggle against the very system which has compelled almost everybody to go corrupt."[107] A dialogue between Narayan and Mrs. Gandhi broke down as each questioned the good faith of the other, Mrs. Gandhi charging that the "J. P. Movement" was being financed by "wealthy friends" under the influence of American capitalists, and Narayan accusing the prime minister of leading India toward a Soviet-backed dictatorship.[108]

Even as the Bihar agitation gained momentum, the central government was confronted with a call for a general strike of India's approximately 1.7 million railway workers, a strike it believed was part of a deliberate attempt, this time by the left opposition parties, to create eco-

---

[106] *Congress Marches Ahead—IX*, pp. 103-104.          [107] *The Statesman*, April 10, 1974.

[108] Mrs. Gandhi and Jayaprakash Narayan each aired their grievances against the other in separate interviews with *Blitz*, the prime minister in December 1974 and "J. P." in January and February 1975. See R. K. Karanjia, *Indira-J.P. Confrontation, The Great Debate*, pp. 38-71.

nomic and political chaos. The National Coordination Committee for Railwaymen's Struggle, the union coordinating group formed to lead the approximately two hundred separate unions of railway employees in a national work stoppage, had been convened by the Socialist party leader George Fernandes. Fernandes, then president of the All-India Railwaymen's Federation (the only recognized national federation of railway unions apart from the larger Congress-dominated National Federation of Indian Railwaymen), managed to win the support of other trade union fronts allied to the CPI, CPI (Marxists), and even the Jan Sangh, and accommodated their representatives on the National Coordination Committee. The demands of the workers, which centered around a doubling of wages, additional dearness allowance, payment of annual bonus, and provision of foodgrains and other essential commodities at subsidized prices, would have required, according to government estimates, additional expenditures of about Rs. 450 crores at a time when inflation was already crippling the Center's economic growth plans.[109]

The national leadership, convinced that the Gujerat and Bihar agitations signalled the beginning of a "combined attack by extreme Right and Left on all Government policies,"[110] and apprehensive that the railway strike was "politically motivated" and engineered by "certain extreme elements"[111] to interrupt production and aggravate economic difficulties, became determined to resist all further concessions to opposition demands. When discussions between union leaders and the railway minister, L. N. Mishra, threatened to reach an impasse less than one week before the scheduled date of the strike (called for May 8, 1974), the central government suddenly withdrew from all negotiations and invoked the Defense of India Rules (DIR) under the 1971 Emergency Proclamation still in force to declare the strike illegal; and used its powers of preventive detention under the Maintenance of Internal Security Act (MISA) to arrest Fernandes, other members of the National Coordination Committee, and abut six hundred railway employees. The unprecedented use of extraordinary powers to arrest leading members of the trade union movement and opposition was characterized by members of the Action Committee negotiating with government as a "heinous step" and in "violation of all democratic values."[112] But the Congress parliamentary party, strongly endorsing the government's decision to use such extreme measures, retorted that "since it is a political issue the challenge has to be met on the political plane."[113] Once the strike was actually underway, and it became apparent that more than fifty percent of all railway workers were absent from their jobs despite division within the

---

[109] *The Statesman*, April 30, 1973.     [110] *Ibid*., March 22, 1974.
[111] Excerpt from AICC, "Resolution on Political Situation," *Congress Marches Ahead—* 10, p. 16.
[112] *The Statesman*, May 3, 1974.     |     [113] *Ibid*., May 5, 1974.

union leadership, the government moved decisively to crush the strike. Altogether, at least twenty thousand striking workers were arrested under DIR and MISA provisions. The strike was withdrawn after twenty days in what was considered a personal triumph for Mrs. Gandhi. Union leaders, admitting defeat, grimly conceded that they could not hold out in the face of the government's "miniwar" against the railway workers.[114]

If the prime minister appeared persuaded that recourse to extraordinary powers was essential to cope with the growing incidence of extraparliamentary agitations and political violence that disrupted the functioning of democratic governments, the opposition was no less convinced that only direct people's intervention provided a corrective to the growing abuse of power by corrupt and unprincipled politicians. This climate of political mistrust, in which each side accused the other of attempting to pull down democratic institutions, was poisoned still further in early January 1975 by the shock of the first assassination since Independence of a Cabinet minister. The Union railway minister, L. N. Mishra, was killed and several others injured when a bomb exploded at the Samastipur railway station in Bihar as the minister inaugurated a new branch line. The murder of Mishra brought charges both by leaders of the opposition and government that the other side was responsible. Mishra, an important fund-raiser for the Congress party, had been the target of opposition demands for a parliamentary investigation into an import licenses scandal[115] that appeared to have been set in motion at the time when Mishra had been foreign trade minister. The opposition, which believed that an open inquiry into the case would have led to exposure of corruption at the highest levels of the Congress party, did not shrink from speculation that the Congress leadership had arranged the assassination to prevent further damage to its image and that of the prime minister. The Congress party leadership, for their part, were equally convinced that Mishra had been " a victim to the cult of violence, intimidation and coercion which is being spread in the country by fascist and anti-democratic elements and groups out to undermine democracy and create chaos."[116] Indeed, by the time of the Mishra murder, Mrs. Gandhi was persuaded that a "dangerous and calculated plan" against democracy

[114] Bernard Weinraub, "India's Rail Walkout Collapses, A Major Triumph for Mrs. Gandhi," *New York Times*, May 29, 1974.

[115] According to a Central Bureau of Investigation (CBI) report, import licenses had been approved for several blacklisted and nonexistent firms by Mishra's successor as foreign trade minister on the basis of a memorandum of support earlier submitted to Mishra and ostensibly signed by 21 members of parliament. On examination, 20 of the 21 signatures proved to be forgeries. The one authentic signature was that of Tulmohan Ram, MP, known as a protégé of L. N. Mishra.

[116] Congress Working Committee, Condolence Resolution, *Congress Marches Ahead— 10*, p. 73.

was underway and that the Mishra assassination was only a "rehearsal" for an open assault aimed at removing her from power. She commented bitterly on opposition charges that members of the ruling party might be behind the bomb explosion: "When I am murdered they will say I arranged it for myself."[117]

The breakdown of consensus between the government and the opposition had in fact crystalized into an open confrontation between Mrs. Gandhi and her allies inside the Congress on the one side, and Jayaprakash Narayan and his own array of widely disparate supporters on the other. "J.P.," at the age of 72 (in 1974), ailing and disappointed at the failure of the Sarvodaya Samaj to bring about the nonviolent social revolution to which he had devoted his life's work, had seen in the spontaneous student uprising of Gujerat the best hope for a populist movement to awaken public opinion and apply pressure from below for economic and political reform. Student leaders in Gujerat, claiming ideological inspiration from Mahatma Gandhi, had sent messages to "J. P." asking for expressions of support. Youthful agitators in Bihar—Narayan's home state—had also come to him with arguments that a Gujerat-style movement should be started there.

The political situation in Bihar reproduced the same conditions of unstable factional coalitions and political corruption that had ignited the Gujerat upheaval. If anything, conditions in Bihar—long accorded the melancholy distinction of being the most impoverished and worst governed state in India—were more desperate. Unlike Gujerat, with its sizable urban sector, Bihar remained almost entirely dependent upon a subsistence agricultural economy. About two-thirds of the state's population were believed to be living below the poverty line, enmeshed in debt to local landowners and moneylenders, and victimized by the "army of corrupt officials with whom they come into contact." Spiraling prices and shortages of essential commodities superimposed on this abject poverty pushed many of the rural poor to the very brink of starvation. Yet, after years of nepotism and corruption, both under the Congress party and the revolving united front ministries that followed, "the people [had] lost faith in the government as well as the political parties." Hopes stirred by Mrs. Gandhi's apparent commitment to social justice and the return of Congress rule in the state after the 1972 elections were quickly dissipated by revival of a "no-holds barred struggle between rival factions to capture public office with the object of making money, enjoying official privileges and distributing jobs and patronage among relations, friends and hangers-on."[118]

[117] *The Statesman*, January 8, 1975.
[118] Ajit Bhattacharjea, "Despair and Hope in Bihar," *Times of India*, September 17, 1973.

"J. P.'s" decision to lead the student agitation in Bihar endowed the protest with national political significance. Narayan was the only leader still in Indian political life cast from the Gandhian mold, a nationalist hero with the prospect of becoming prime minister who had renounced power to devote his life in service of the poor. Narayan, like Gandhi, also had a broad social vision, one that impelled him at the outset of the Bihar agitation to proclaim that the goal of the movement he was heading went far beyond a change in the ministry or dissolution of the state assembly, to encompass *Sampurna Kranti* (Total Revolution). Although the components of Narayan's "total revolution" were not articulated into a clearly integrated ideology, still the broad range of social reforms they included went beyond the rhetoric of a simple slogan to invoke Gandhian principles of social and political reorganization. His long-term goals of a "communitarian society" and a "partyless democracy" built on the reconstructed Indian village were a reaffirmation of the validity of Gandhi's vision of a "truly nonexploitative social order," that was neither the "present feudal-capitalist structure" nor "State Capitalism, miscalled Socialism."[119] Such an order, according to Narayan, required "institutional changes all around," including the "elimination of caste and communalism, participatory democracy at the village and panchayat levels, implementing land reforms, changes in the cultural patterns as also a campaign against corruption in the private sector industries." His advocacy of political and economic decentralization,[120] employment-oriented growth, labor-intensive village and small industries, primary education, and basic agricultural development echoed Gandhi's practical approach to village reconstruction.

Yet, the differences between "J. P." and Gandhi were at least as important. Narayan, who had spent twenty years in constructive work activity to spearhead the *bhoodan* movement in Bihar, without accomplishing the conditions of peaceful agrarian reform, had run out of time. He no longer hesitated to proclaim his ultimate goals in explicit terms as "an allround revolution, political, economic, social, educational, moral and cultural."[121] He was, moreover, finally prepared to risk a confrontation with rural elites by organizing directly among the poor. What was needed, "J. P." emphasized over and over again, were "permanent institutions of peoples power"[122] to convert the Bihar agitation from a Gujerat-style upheaval with no staying power into a sustained populist movement.

In Bihar, where Sarvodaya workers had been preparing public opinion for more than twenty years, the program of "total revolution" included "educating the people, building grass-roots organizations, launching

---

[119] *Everyman's Weekly*, May 18, 1975.   [120] *Ibid.*, December 8, 1974.
[121] *Ibid.*, December 22, 1974.   [122] *Ibid.*, December 8, 1974.

struggle against corruption and other social evils and initiating constructive action to usher in a new value system for the new social order to be
built." This process was to be started with the organization of Students
and People's Struggle Committees at the village and Block levels, incorporating all sections of the population, but concentrating particularly on
religious minorities, Harijans and members of the Backward Classes.
Formation of the committees would be followed by the establishment of
Janata Sarkars, people's governments that would not only "carry on the
day to day affairs of the people"[123] through its public office, public fund,
people's court, and army of specially recruited youth, but would carry
out a minimum program aimed at effective implementation of land reforms; fair distribution of essential commodities; elimination of caste
evils, especially payment of dowry; a campaign for cleanliness; and verification of electoral rolls. Outside of Bihar, the struggle was to be more
focused on more narrow economic and political reforms. These included
the elimination of corruption, economic policies to meet the problems of
high prices and growing unemployment, and programs for radical
changes in education. Such goals were supplemented by proposals for
electoral reform aimed at curbing the use of black money in campaigns;
and strengthening the basis of popular participation in elections by providing for the selection of (Janata) candidates for every assembly constituency from lists drawn up by village councils rather than political
parties.

Yet, for the time being, Bihar remained the political center of the
movement, and in Bihar, as in Gujerat, all of these long-term goals were
symbolized in the immediate demand of the "J. P. Movement" to remove the state ministry as the embodiment of corrupt party politics. Between March and November 1974, the "J. P. Movement" paralyzed the
administration of the state, variously mounting a three-day Bihar *bandh*
(March), a Paralyze the Government Agitation (April), a march of one-
half million people on Patna (June), another three-day Bihar *bandh* (October), and a second massive demonstration in Patna (November). But in
Bihar, the government replied to the agitator's demands with unexpected force. Convinced that it had to resist the Bihar agitation or face a
movement for dissolution of elected governments in other states
throughout the country, the central leadership refused to consider the
demands for resignation of the ministry (then headed by Abdul
Ghafoor). Students, youth, and women demonstrators, peacefully
obstructing the work of government offices, were arrested en masse by
the police. Train and bus services were canceled to prevent demonstrators from converging on Patna in support of strike calls. When
large-scale mob violence erupted and police firings could not secure pub-

[123] *Ibid.*, May 18, 1975.

lic order, the central government responded by garrisoning the state with approximately 40,000 security forces drawn primarily from the Central Reserve Police and the Border Security Forces to gather intelligence, arrest agitators, prevent sabotage on the railways, and otherwise maintain order. By August 1974, Bihar was "like an armed camp with police and military guarding all major governmental and educational institutions at a reported cost of Rs. 100,000 per day."[124] This show of force was effective. Once assured of their personal security, the overwhelming majority of legislators in the Bihar assembly proved immune to moral appeals for their resignation. By November 1974, unable to achieve his immediate goals of overthrowing the Bihar ministry, "J. P." agreed to take up the challenge directed at him by Mrs. Gandhi of letting the next general elections, scheduled for March 1976, determine which side enjoyed the people's mandate.

Even so, the Center had only succeeded in converting the Bihar movement from a state agitation to a movement of all-India scope. "J. P.'s" student followers in Bihar demonstrated very little staying power. Further, the logic of the fight against corrupt state governments—the popular rallying point for the movement—dictated a shift of focus to the Center. It was clear, as "J. P." argued, that "Mrs. Gandhi has reduced the autonomy of the States to near zero, so that all decisions of any importance are made in Delhi rather than in Patna or the other State capitals."[125] The chief minister of Bihar, and indeed, the majority of chief ministers of the states, had been selected by Mrs. Gandhi and were propped up at her command. There was little more to be gained from attacking the periphery; but rather, it was necessary to strike at the source.

Narayan was also responding to broader political considerations in his decision to mount an all-India movement. Leaders of the noncommunist opposition, including such disparate groups as the Jan Sangh, Congress (O), SSP, BLD, and such regional parties as the DMK and Akali Dal, saw in Narayan, with his capacity to attract unprecedented crowds by a moral appeal that transcended divisive social and economic issues, a godsend in their attempt to overcome problems of finding a credible popular alternative to Congress and mount an offensive against the government. "J. P.," for his part, had to concede that he could not solve the organizational problems inherent in accepting Mrs. Gandhi's challenge to convert the conflict into a contest at the next Lok Sabha poll, simply by relying on students without the help of organized political parties. Even in Bihar, the Students and People's Struggle Committee had relied heavily on the work of student cadres from the Jan Sangh's youth wing (Vidyar-

---

[124] Wood, "Extra-Parliamentary Opposition in India," p. 322.
[125] Karanjia, *Indira-J.P. Confrontation*, p. 63.

thi Parishad), augmented by the much smaller student fronts of the SSP and Congress (O).

The "J. P. Movement," in the last months of 1974, began to change its character. The grass-roots organizational work in Bihar that would have been necessary to establish the institutional base for a sustained populist movement in that state was neglected, even while the energies of "J. P.'s" followers were diverted toward the opposition's purpose of defeating the Congress party and removing Mrs. Gandhi from power. A twenty-member National Coordination Committee, including Sarvodaya leaders and leaders of the Jan Sangh, Congress (O), BLD, Socialist party, and Akali Dal, formally endorsed Narayan's long-term goals for "basic social, economic, political, cultural and educational changes leading ultimately to total revolution,"[126] at the same time as they shifted the immediate focus of the struggle to an assault on the central government in their decision to organize a massive people's march on parliament. Subsequently, Narayan, at mammoth public meetings in several states, gave his approval for the extension of the movement to Haryana, eastern Uttar Pradesh, Gujerat, West Bengal, and Andhra. Although he denied charges that the Bihar movement had been converted into another Grand Alliance in an "Indira Hatao" campaign, because it was "not against any individual but against a system," "J. P." issued an unmistakable warning to the prime minister: "If Mrs. Gandhi does not take steps to change radically the system and persists in standing in the way of revolutionary struggle, she cannot complain if, in its onward march, the movement pushes her aside with so much else."[127]

As the huge processions and public meetings succeeded one after the other, and Narayan called on his followers to engage in *gheraos*, sit-ins, and protest fasts; appealed to legislators to resign their posts; advised students to boycott the universities and admonished the police and army not to obey orders that were "unconstitutional, illegal or against their conscience,"[128] he accumulated a moral authority that challenged Mrs. Gandhi's effective power. Within a few months, the press was full of reports that " 'J. P.' rather than any Congress leader today symbolizes the traditional values of the party bequeathed by Gandhi and Nehru. He is insisting on probity in public life and in the task of governing the country. He is raising his voice against a growing tendency towards authoritarian forms of rule."[129]

The "J. P. Movement" polarized the supporters and opponents of Mrs. Gandhi, pushing political antagonists beyond the point of reconcili-

[126] *The Statesman*, November 27, 1974.
[127] Karanjia, *Indira-J.P. Confrontation*, pp. 63-64.
[128] *Everyman's Weekly*, April 20, 1975.
[129] N. Nihal Singh, "An Anniversary to Remember," *The Statesman*, March 22, 1975.

ation. Within the Congress party, the cleavage between the ex-communists on the one hand, and noncommunist socialists and other Congressmen on the other, hardened almost to the point of an open division.

In Bihar, the center of the "J. P. Movement," this division had become impossible to disguise. The Bihar PCC was torn between the pro-CPI faction, which argued that "the Congress cannot exist alone," and those who asserted that "Congress had been successfully fighting reactionary forces even when the so-called progressive forces were not born yet in this country."[130] In fact, the Congress had had to rely heavily on the CPI in Bihar as the only party capable of mounting large-scale pro-government demonstrations in solidarity with the Center's refusal to concede the dismissal of the state ministry.

The polarization in the Bihar Congress was reproduced at the Center. Within the Cabinet, two Bihari ministers, L. N. Mishra and Jagjivan Ram, each threw his support to one of the rival factions in the state. Mishra, regarded as the partisan of the pro-communist faction, appeared to have the advantage over Jagjivan Ram in enjoying the special confidence of Mrs. Gandhi. Within the AICC, the pro-CPI faction similarly used its influence with the prime minister to convert the party executive into a forum for constant attacks on "J. P." Crediting rumors of CIA involvement in the Bihar agitation, they argued that behind the slogan of partyless democracy was a conspiracy of the vested interests to subvert democratic institutions. At the height of their influence, in November 1974, they were able to commit the national leadership to the official view that

> behind the facade of partyless democracy lurk the dark and violent forces of Indian fascism, well-organized and well-poised to destroy the democratic institutions and impose their reign of terror. The Jan Sangh, the RSS and the Anand Marg are the driving forces behind the assault on the citadel of democracy. When it falls they will move in quickly to occupy the vantage positions. The result can be predicted. A naked dictatorship of the propertied classes will come into existence. It will appeal to the most regressive tendencies in our social and political life. Communalism, regional chauvinism, fanaticism of all kinds and a narrow, life-denying cultural revivalism, will thrive.[131]

[130] *The Statesman*, October 25, 1974.

[131] AICC Central Training Camp, Narora: November 22-24, 1974, *Present Political Situation*, p. 19. The Ananda Marga Pracaraka Samgha (Organization for the Propagation of the Path of Bliss) was founded in Bihar in 1955 by Prabhat Rainjana Sarkar, then an accountant at the Railway Workshop in Jamalpur. Ananda Margis profess an ideology combining commitment to the highest spiritual ideals of Hinduism with devotion to revolutionary so-

Prominent exponents of this view, including D. K. Barooah, then president of the Congress party, began to convey their advice to the prime minister that she would have to take strong measures, including the arrest of major opposition leaders.

By contrast, a pro-Narayan section emerged among the noncommunist socialists in the Congress parliamentary party. They not only defended "J. P.'s" patriotic motives, but argued in favor of a dialogue between the prime minister and the Sarvodaya leader to bridge the growing gulf between the government and opposition parties, and thwart the "sinister attempts and machinations" of the pro-CPI elements to create another split in the Congress party as the prelude to establishing an "alternate" government of left and democratic unity.[132] Led by Chandra Shekhar and Mohan Dharia, with an effective strength of thirty to forty MPs, this group kept up its own persistent demands for negotiations between Mrs. Gandhi and "J. P." on basic issues of unemployment and corruption that "needed to be tackled rather than sidetracked."[133] Mrs. Gandhi, who argued that only two points were actually at issue, namely, the Bihar agitation aimed at destroying democracy and the opposition alliance to remove her from office, professed bewilderment about "what negotiations mean." She asked rhetorically, "What do you negotiate about? How to destroy democracy? Is that negotiable? . . . The other main point is to remove Indira Gandhi. How can I negotiate about that?"[134]

The conflict could not be contained behind the scenes, but broke out into the open. In January 1975, Jagjivan Ram, the most senior member of the Cabinet, threw his influence on the side of Chandra Shekhar and his group by publicly warning against the grave danger to Congress from infiltration of former communists.[135] Ram's warning "set many alarm bells going in the ruling party."[136] It emboldened other Congress leaders to assert openly that the CPI had been the main beneficiary of the confrontation between Narayan and the ruling party. These sounds of dissent among senior leaders resonated within the rank and file. Shortly after, the pro-CPI faction suffered a serious attrition in its support from members of the Congress parliamentary party. Elections for office bear-

---

cial transformation aimed at ending economic exploitation. According to Sarkar, revered by his disciples as a great spiritual leader, only a popular uprising against the "structure of inequality and inequity" established by capitalism can reverse the moral decay that divert rich and poor alike from the path of spiritual virtue. By the mid-1970s, the Ananda Marga had attracted a large following in Bihar and neighboring West Bengal, especially among members of the disaffected middle classes. Olav T. Oftedal, "The Birth of an Ideology, The Ananda Marga Controversy in India," 1974, unpublished.

[132] *The Statesman*, November 24, 1974.     [133] *Ibid.*, February 20, 1975.
[134] Karanjia, *Indira-J.P. Confrontation*, p. 38.     [135] *The Statesman*, January 13, 1975.
[136] *Ibid.*, February 6, 1975.

ers held in May 1975 demonstrated that a "silent majority" inside the CPP preferred candidates allied with Chandra Shekhar and the advocates of a dialogue with "J. P." over nominees of factions supporting the anti-"J. P." position of the ex-communists.[137] Yet Mrs. Gandhi, who had peremptorily dismissed Mohan Dharia (then minister of state for works and housing) in March 1975 for his insistence on talks with "J. P.," gave no indication that she intended to change her position. Indeed, it was hardly reasonable to expect her to do so.

Any doubt that the "J. P. Movement" had been converted into an opposition alliance aimed at removing Mrs. Gandhi from office was dispelled by the show of solidarity between Narayan and Morarji Desai when the latter, charging the central government with "unwarranted extension" of President's Rule in Gujerat and "blatant refusal" to hold new elections after dissolution of the Gujerat assembly, announced "an indefinite fast from April 7 [1975] at my residence in Delhi for restoring the people's right of electing their representatives before the end of May and removal of the state of emergency in the country and thus stopping the accelerating process of negation of democracy."[138] Desai, who subsequently conceded he had begun the hunger strike to "start the battle I had been dreaming of ever since 1969,"[139] received strong support from Narayan. In a public statement that challenged the central government's credibility in twice postponing elections for the Gujerat assembly until September 1975 at the earliest—first for reasons of completing delimitation of constituencies, and then on grounds of extreme scarcity and drought conditions in the state—he asserted, "I am . . . fully inclined to agree with Morarjibhai that the decision of the Prime Minister was politically motivated to suit the interest of her party and that the promise to hold elections in September was a cleverly designed political rape."[140]

The ties between Narayan, prominent leaders of the opposition, and dissidents inside the Congress party were, moreover, self-evident. More than forty Congress MPs meeting at the home of Mohan Dharia expressed the consensus of the meeting that demands for an early election in Gujerat should be met and that "the Government should save Mr. Desai's life."[141] Mrs. Gandhi, who apparently did fear the political consequences of being held responsible for the aging leader's death, gave assurances on April 13 that elections to the Gujerat assembly would be held by June 10. The concession marked the beginning of a dramatic erosion in the prime minister's power to contain the assault on her position by the combined forces of the opposition and dissidents inside the party.

---

[137] Ibid., May 10, 1975.                                        [138] Ibid., April 3, 1975.
[139] Morarji Desai to Oriana Fallaci, June 25, 1975, an interview published in The New Republic, July 1975.
[140] The Statesman, April 7, 1975.                    [141] Ibid., April 14, 1975.

During the next few weeks, Mrs. Gandhi suffered a series of setbacks that could not have been anticipated either by her or her allies. On the morning of June 12, 1975, after a four-year litigation challenging the legality of her 1971 election—in a court case considered to present no more than a minor political embarrassment for the prime minister—Justice Jagmohan Lal Sinha of the Allahabad High Court ruled that Mrs. Gandhi had committed "corrupt practices" under the Representation of the People Act (1951) in her campaign for the Lok Sabha from Rae Bareli constituency in Uttar Pradesh. The charges, filed in an election petition by the defeated candidate, Raj Narain, challenged the legality of Mrs. Gandhi's use of Indian air force planes for transportation to her constituency; the use of local administrative and police officers and engineers to make arrangements for election meetings, including the construction of speakers' rostrums, the supply of loudspeakers, and electric power to operate them; and the provision by state authorities of government vehicles, telephones, and police security at election rallies. According to the petition, all these practices violated statutory prohibitions against the use of official machinery for the purpose of advancing the election prospects of a candidate. They had provided advantages of mobility and communication to the prime minister over her opponent that reduced the election to a "farce."[142] The petition argued further that the cost of such arrangements had been improperly charged to the central and state governments, and should be assessed instead against the prime minister's personal campaign to place her in violation of the $5,000 legal limit on election expenditure. Added to these charges were additional complaints alleging the prime minister had actually bribed voters with gifts and offered free rides to the polls; and that she had used a "religious symbol"—a cow and calf—to further her election prospects. Another charge in the complaint specifically accused the prime minister of using the services of her personal secretary, Yashpal Kapoor, while he was still a government officer on special duty in the prime minister's secretariat to launch her campaign in Rae Bareli.

Justice Sinha did exonerate Mrs. Gandhi on the most serious charges, particularly those of bribing voters and of exceeding the legal limit on campaign expenditure. Nevertheless, he found the prime minister guilty of two lesser charges. He ruled that she had authorized Yashpal Kapoor to carry out election work on her behalf in Rae Bareli, before his resignation from government service to act as her election agent could become effective. He also found Mrs. Gandhi guilty of using the services of local officials to construct rostrums and provide loudspeakers and power, arrangements which added to the effectiveness of her campaign but could

[142] *Times of India*, April 23, 1975.

not be justified strictly in terms of security arrangements essential to the protection of the prime minister.

The conviction on "corrupt practices," even in the case of such minor offenses, automatically invalidated Mrs. Gandhi's 1971 election from Rae Bareli. Under India's electoral law, it also debarred Mrs. Gandhi from holding any elective office during the next six years. Once deprived of a seat in parliament, Mrs. Gandhi could constitutionally continue as prime minister only for a period of six months, and during that time she would not have been able to vote in the Lok Sabha. It appeared that she had no alternative but to resign. At the same time, Justice Sinha had allowed a clear "stay order" delaying execution of the judgment for twenty days, permitting time for Mrs. Gandhi to file an appeal in the Supreme Court.

Even before the prime minister had time to absorb the full implications of the court decision, other news reaching New Delhi the same evening indicated an upset in the Gujerat election. In Gujerat, the Lok Sangharsh Samiti, set up in March 1975 to launch a "J. P."-type movement in the state, had organized a Janata Front under the "stewardship" of Morarji Desai to oppose the Congress in the Assembly elections. The front, composed of a four-party alliance between the Congress (O), Jan Sangh, BLD, and Socialist party, agreed to Narayan's proposals for selecting "clean" Janata candidates from lists drawn up by the constituent parties, and to abide by Desai's decision in the case of any differences among them. The notion that the non–CPI opposition alliance "would have the disadvantages of a Grand Alliance which the Congress would find it relatively easy to demolish"[143] was disproved at the polls. Despite the fact that the Congress leadership had been determined to defeat the front as the forerunner of another opposition electoral alliance at the 1976 Lok Sabha poll—and notwithstanding extensive election appearances by Mrs. Gandhi at nearly a hundred meetings during the campaign—Congress suffered a serious loss of seats from 140 in 1971 to 75 in 1975. The Janata Front, campaigning on charges of government corruption, commanded a clear majority of 87 out of 168 seats.[144] It ousted the Congress from power and formed the new government in the state.

The two virtually simultaneous reverses dramatically eroded both Mrs. Gandhi's legal position and her moral authority. The noncommunist opposition parties immediately demanded her resignation. They sent a joint deputation to President Fakhruddin Ali Ahmed, requesting him to order Mrs. Gandhi from office. The major Indian newspapers took up a similar position. They insisted that democratic propriety demanded she must step down at least temporarily until the Supreme Court could exonerate her from wrongdoing on appeal.

[143] S. Nihal Singh, "New Jauntiness in Congress," *The Statesman*, May 2, 1975.
[144] Norman D. Palmer, "The Crisis of Democracy in India," *Orbis*, xix:2 (Summer 1975), 385.

Mrs. Gandhi had finally exhausted the possibilities of political maneuver within the limitations of the existing parliamentary process.
Although the Congress parliamentary party put up a show of public solidarity to reiterate the party's "fullest faith and confidence" in Mrs. Gandhi's leadership, the arguments of the opposition were being echoed by a
growing number of MPs.[145] Indeed, Chandra Shekhar and Mohan
Dharia were actively canvassing support in the parliamentary party
around the demand that Mrs. Gandhi temporarily resign until the Supreme Court could rule on her appeal. Yet it was not likely that the
prime minister could regain her power, even if the Supreme Court
finally ruled in her favor. Initial probes aimed at exploring the political
consequences if Mrs. Gandhi chose to step down indicated irreconcilable
differences inside the Congress parliamentary party on the question of
even a temporary successor. Supporters of Jagjivan Ram, the most senior
member of the Cabinet, and the only national leader with an autonomous base of support (in the Harijan community), made it known that
he would contest any effort by the prime minister to impose her own
choice as head of a caretaker government. The prime minister, who was
receiving intelligence reports that Chandra Shekhar and his group were
in close communication with Ram, did not trust him to step aside even if
she was successful on appeal. This fear also animated the discussions of
the ex-communists, who preferred the choice of a "safe and pliable" col-
league as caretaker, but were equally worried that any slight to Jagjivan
Ram might cause him to leave the party. The specter of another split
raised the possibility of political disaster. The Forum and its allies could
not command a majority inside the Congress parliamentary party; an alternative government of left and democratic unity had to be ruled out.
Instead, the dominant faction, led by Jagjivan Ram, would seek out its
allies among the conservative opposition groups; or, in case a stable coalition government was not possible, it was even conceivable that the
army would have to step in. In either case, the ex-communists would
have lost everything because they would have lost their access to the
source of power after the departure of Mrs. Gandhi. They could not see
any alternative to her continuation in office until the Supreme Court had
time to review the case. This was also the assessment of the communists
outside the party. A resolution adopted by the CPI on June 13 offered
unequivocal support to the prime minister against the forces of "right
reaction" calling for her resignation.

The Congress party president, D. K. Barooah, who gave expression
to this consensus with the hyperbolic slogan, "Indira is India and India is

[145] The most detailed account of events preceding the decision to invoke emergency pro-
visions of the constitution is provided in Nayar, *The Judgement*. See also Marcus F. Franda,
*India's Double Emergency Democracy, Part I: Transformations*, South Asia Series XIX:17
(American Universities Field Staff, 1975).

Indira," found his allies where he could. There was, in fact, a great deal of support for the prime minister from Cabinet ministers and chief ministers at the states who owed their power to her. Perhaps equally important, at the moment when Mrs. Gandhi appeared to some to be "on the verge" of resigning, there was probably no one with a more compelling personal interest in her continuation as prime minister than her younger son, Sanjay, whose Maruti venture continued to attract opposition demands for a parliamentary probe. Indeed, although Sanjay's pro-business views made him antagonistic to the ex-communist faction inside the party, he and Barooah did share a common interest in pulling together to convince Mrs. Gandhi not to resign. Meanwhile, Mrs. Gandhi herself was leaning more and more on advice from her son, "who was giving her all the strength from wilting under pressure and who had told her not to resign when some of her staunchest supporters appeared to be faltering."[146]

Sanjay, who had begun to exercise some political influence through his friendships with R. K. Dhavan, the prime minister's additional private secretary (in the prime minister's secretariat) and Bansi Lal, the chief minister of Haryana, worked with Barooah to orchestrate "spontaneous" popular demonstrations of loyalty to Mrs. Gandhi. They requisitioned trucks and government buses to go into nearby villages and bring crowds into New Delhi to shout their approval in front of the prime minister's house. They directed the chief ministers in the neighboring states to organize similar rallies. Yet, if Mrs. Gandhi quickly came around to their view that she should not resign even temporarily, still evidence was mounting that she could not continue in office for the several months required until the Supreme Court ruled on her case, and hope to govern effectively. The discontent within her own party was growing. Some members of the CPP began to have doubts that they could fight the upcoming February 1976 Lok Sabha elections with Mrs. Gandhi as leader. The legal situation, moreover, was discouraging. There was little reason to believe that the Supreme Court—which was expected to exonerate Mrs. Gandhi in the final ruling, would grant an absolute stay of execution of the Allahabad verdict. All legal precedent suggested the prime minister would receive a conditional stay only, allowing her to remain in office, but not to function as a full voting member in Lok Sabha debates. Her own lawyers, moreover, argued that unless Mrs. Gandhi was allowed to function as prime minister without restrictions during the three or four months required for a Supreme Court review, a "stigma" would attach to her name and office. It was not difficult to foresee that under such conditions agitations already being planned by the opposition to intensify popular pressure on Mrs. Gandhi

[146] *Ibid.*, p. 24.

to resign—especially when their impact on public opinion would be magnified by sympathetic coverage in the press—would foment even further discontent inside the Congress parliamentary party. All of these considerations made it appear that Mrs. Gandhi could not continue in office unless her opponents both outside and inside the party were prevented from carrying out agitations against her leadership, and—equally important—the press was curbed from carrying partisan reports of such opposition activities that could influence public opinion in favor of her enemies.

On June 15, Sanjay began his work on "some plan to set things right."[147] As initially conceived, it called for the arrest of important opposition leaders and the imposition of censorship on the press. It was within the government's powers to carry out the arrests under MISA, and such arrests had actually been rumored since January 1975, but it was not clear under which laws press censorship could be imposed. The advice that Mrs. Gandhi received from the West Bengal chief minister, Sidhartha Shankar Ray, a lawyer, and one of the few people taken into confidence about the action contemplated against the opposition was that the only way legally to arrest the opposition leaders and apply stringent press censorship was to declare an "internal" emergency under Article 352 of the constitution, so that government could assume sweeping powers.

Even as the prime minister considered the implications of such a step, her position became more untenable. On June 24, the Supreme Court refused her application for an absolute stay. Justice Krishna Iyer ruled that Mrs. Gandhi could continue as prime minister, but that during the period pending her appeal she would not have the right to vote in the Lok Sabha. The five-party Janata Front (its ranks augmented by the Akali Dal) seized on the Supreme Court's decision to insist that "the stigma of corruption continues" and that the interests of "political propriety and democratic convention" demanded Mrs. Gandhi step down from office. If the prime minister refused to resign, they warned, "we have no choice but to launch a countrywide movement, including satyagraha, demanding her resignation."[148] On June 25, at a mammoth rally in New Delhi, Jayaprakash Narayan announced plans of the opposition parties to launch a nationwide satyagraha for Mrs. Gandhi's resignation. He called upon the army, police, and government employees not to obey any "illegal" orders, and to protect the constitution; asked students to leave their classes; and appealed to his supporters not to cooperate with the government and refuse to pay any tax. On the same day, the national executives of the Congress (O), Jan Sangh, BKD, Socialist party, and Akali Dal set up a Lok Sangharsha Samiti (People's Struggle Committee),

[147] Ibid.          [148] *Times of India*, June 25, 1975.

headed by Morarji Desai, to organize a nationwide "struggle" beginning June 29, including rallies in all state capitals, tehsils, and Block headquarters. As part of this struggle, in New Delhi volunteers in groups of about a hundred were to defy police bans on demonstrations in the area around the prime minister's house, and march on her residence daily, asking Mrs. Gandhi to resign. Morarji Desai, in an interview with a foreign journalist on the evening of June 25, described the opposition's determination to oust Mrs. Gandhi from office through these tactics in unequivocal language:

> We intend to overthrow her, to force her to resign. For good. The lady won't survive this movement of ours. She won't be able to because it is on a national scale and includes all possible political trends, and even some members of her own party. Some Ministers she got rid of because they demanded social reforms, for instance. We are strong at last and we proclaimed a Satyagraha. . . . Satyagraha means civil disobedience. It consists in ignoring every prohibition, every law, every arrest, every police attack. You stand there, the police charge into the crowd and beat you up and you don't retreat. You don't yield an inch. You don't need strength to do this, you don't need to eat. It was Mahatma Gandhi who launched the first Satyagraha effort against the British. With them, it worked. They were compelled to leave. She will be forced to go too. Thousands of us will surround her house to prevent her going out or receive visitors. We'll camp there night and day shouting to her to resign.[149]

Even as Desai spoke, however, arrangements had been completed to impose an internal emergency starting at midnight, June 25. Whatever reservations the prime minister initially may have had were outweighed by the growing conviction that she was confronted with an opposition conspiracy to "paralyze the Government and indeed all national activity and to walk to power over the body of the nation."[150] The upheaval in Gujerat, the national railway strike, the agitation in Bihar, had all contributed to a feeling of chaos, with the "J. P. Movement" making it appear that pressures from the right and left would coalesce. The unexpected outcome of the Gujerat election and the stunning surprise of the High Court's decision increased the sense of threat, even sparking fears about the prime minister's physical safety as the first demonstrators prepared to take up their vigil outside her house after Narayan's inflammatory speech on June 25.

The danger to public order presented by the opposition's call for a countrywide satyagraha, moreover, was potentially serious. The op-

---

[149] Morarji Desai to Oriana Fallaci, *The New Republic*, July 1975.
[150] *New York Times*, July 5, 1975.

position's plans for paralyzing the Central (and state) governments by popular demonstrations inevitably evoked apprehension about large-scale battles between the demonstrators and the police. Against the background of unpredictable crowd violence since the Gujerat uprising, the feeling grew that "anything could happen." Several chief ministers had conveyed their own concern that local police forces would not be sufficient to maintain law and order in the event of popular agitations. In New Delhi itself, where tens of thousands had turned out to applaud "J. P.," and where the Jan Sangh with its RSS cadre was well entrenched, peaceful demonstrations could easily turn violent. Indeed, popular demonstrations could provoke such large-scale disorders that army troops might have to be called out. Under such circumstances, the civil authority, and in particular the power of the prime minister, whose credibility was already seriously suspect, would become dependent upon the goodwill of the military.

Still, no one, neither her opponents united around Narayan, nor her supporters inside the Congress party and the CPI, anticipated the full force of Mrs. Gandhi's reaction to her desperate situation. On the evening of June 25, the prime minister, accompanied by S. S. Ray, called on President Fakhruddin Ali Ahmed to inform him of their plan to impose an internal emergency. Before midnight the same day, the president, on the basis of a formal request from the prime minister signed a Proclamation of Emergency. In the early morning hours of June 26, Mrs. Gandhi, operating through "handpicked officials in the Prime Minister's Secretariat and a few Chief Ministers"[151] authorized the arrests of opposition leaders and dissidents inside the Congress party. Jayaprakash Narayan and Morarji Desai from the first group, and Chandra Shekhar and Mohan Dharia from the second were among the first taken into custody. Only after the Emergency Proclamation had been issued and the arrests carried out was the Cabinet summoned for a meeting at 6:00 A.M. to consider Mrs. Gandhi's decision. Stunned by news of the arrests, and particularly by the detention of Chandra Shekhar as Mrs. Gandhi's most influential opponent inside the party, and convinced that if Chandra Shekhar could be arrested, anybody could be arrested, they acquiesced in Mrs. Gandhi's action. At 8:00 A.M., one hour after President Ahmed publicly proclaimed the State of Emergency, Mrs. Gandhi went on All India Radio to explain her action as a response to "the deep seated and widespread conspiracy which has been brewing ever since I began to in-

---

[151] *Times of India*, June 26, 1977. Officials who would be loyal to the prime minister were moved into key posts in the Home Ministry and the intelligence bureau a few days before the Emergency. Among the chief ministers, only Bansi Lai (Haryana) and Sidhartha Shankar Ray (West Bengal) had advance knowledge of the decision to impose an internal Emergency. The other chief ministers were merely informed of plans to carry out arrests of opposition leaders under MISA and the DIR. See Nayar, *The Judgement*, pp. 35-45.

troduce certain progressive measures of benefit to the common man and woman in India."[152]

The proclamation placed unlimited authority in the hands of the central government, suspending both the federal provisions of the constitution and guarantees for fundamental rights. The Center acquired the power, either through parliament or by presidential ordinance to make laws for the states, and direct state officials to execute these laws. The right of citizens to move the courts in order to challenge the validity of laws in conflict with the fundamental rights provisions was no longer recognized. Presidential orders, moreover, gave specific content to these blanket powers. On June 29, "the right of any person [including a foreigner] to move any court for the enforcement of the rights conferred by Article 14, Article 21 and Article 22 of the Constitution" was revoked.[153] Subsequent decrees authorized the government to arrest political opponents without formal charges or court hearings, and to detain them for two years without the right to petition for release. The numbers of those ultimately arrested under these sweeping powers reached more than a hundred thousand.[154] This assault on the opposition was carried out under the most rigorous censorship imposed on the press to prevent reports of political arrests or any other news likely to "denigrate the institutions of the Prime Minister, President, Governors, and Judges of Supreme Court and High Courts . . . or bring into hatred and contempt the Government established by law in the country."[155] In addition, twenty-six political organizations affiliated with communal and extremist groups were banned, including the RSS on the right and the CP (ML) on the extreme left.

All of this "checkmated" the "J. P. Movement." Deprived of the top layer of its leadership, the movement had no grass-roots organizational apparatus in place to provide direction. There were few popular outbreaks and no mass upsurge in protest at the arrests. Even in Bihar, the opposition, which never had gone beyond its lower-middle and middle-class base, "melted away."[156]

Mrs. Gandhi followed a well-worn path. She justified her decision to suspend constitutional processes as a new opportunity to go ahead with economic reforms. Indeed, the Proclamation of Emergency was fol-

---

[152] Nayar, *The Judgement*, p. 42.

[153] The three articles guaranteed the right to equality before the law, protection of life and liberty, and protection against arrest without formal charges or appeal.

[154] Incomplete data released by the Home Ministry in July 1977 indicated that arrests under MISA and DIR totaled 74,462. Arrest figures from Andhra, Madhya Pradesh, Orissa, and Uttar Pradesh were not yet available. The best estimate of the total number of persons detained during the Emergency is 100,000-110,000. *Times of India*, July 8, 1977.

[155] The censorship guidelines are published in Nayar, *The Judgement*, Annexure II, pp. 204-206.

[156] *New York Times*, July 4, 1975.

lowed in only five days by announcement of a Twenty-Point Economic Program that promised to use the government's sweeping new powers to enforce longstanding policies for basic social change. The government pledged, among other things, to implement agricultural land ceilings, provide housesites for landless laborers, abolish bonded labor, liquidate rural debt, increase agricultural wages, bring prices down, step up agricultural and industrial production, socialize urban land, prevent tax evasion, confiscate the properties of smugglers, provide cheaper books for students, and enlarge overall employment.[157] The Congress party leadership hailed these promises as the "beginning of a renewed and vigorous battle against poverty, for laying the foundation of a new social order."[158]

Yet, while the Emergency enormously increased the personal power of the prime minister and the coterie that gathered around her, it could not augment the capacity of the central government to carry out basic social change. Mrs. Gandhi's word was law for the national administrative services and the police, and all other agencies of the state directly at her command—and at her mercy—under the centralized powers of the expanded prime minister's secretariat. Even so, the central government still had no direct administrative apparatus reaching down into the villages. Neither was there any functioning Congress party at the grassroots level that could rally the support of the rural poor around the administration's efforts to carry out agricultural reforms. Institutional changes, in particular, would have had to be implemented in the villages through the existing local authorities, that is, the very rural elites against whose power they were directed. At the villages, the loudest voices still belonged to leading members of the dominant landowning castes.

[157] For a full description of the Twenty-Point Program by an enthusiastic supporter, see J. S. Bright, *Emergency in India and 5 + 20 Point Programme* (New Delhi, 1976).
[158] *New York Times*, July 3, 1975.

# THIRTEEN

# Conclusion:
# Emergency and Beyond

An analysis of the performance of India's political economy over the past thirty years suggests at least three broad conclusions. The first is that adequate progress toward the multiple economic, social, and political goals of development cannot be accomplished in the absence of radical agrarian reform. Whether the aim is to achieve sustained economic growth, or to reduce social disparities, or to consolidate strong political institutions that can bypass local elites to penetrate the villages, it is essential to alter the pattern of economic concentration in the rural sector. This involves some significant redistribution of productive assets, particularly land, to ensure minimum levels of viability to larger numbers of small holdings. It also requires some degree of change in agrarian organization from individual to cooperative patterns of economic activity, both to augment capacities for investment on capital projects as well as ancillary agricultural enterprises, and to create additional employment opportunities for the growing numbers of marginal farmers and landless laborers.

Second, solutions for reconciling accommodative politics and radical social change through "non-political" organizational changes at the village level have proven unworkable. In particular, the assumption that cooperative and panchayat institutions introduced into the villages as instruments of community development, and constituted on principles of universal membership and adult suffrage, would operate to shift gradually the balance of economic and political power away from the dominant landed castes rested on a serious misunderstanding of the potentiality for reconstructing the village as the basic unit of social action in the countryside. Village cohesion, even at Independence, had already been eroded by growing class differentiation and economic disparities. The more affluent members of the dominant landowning castes had turned their resources to profitable new opportunities for participating in commercial farming provided by the wider market economy. Over time, they found fewer compelling reasons, either of economic interest or social status, to use their surpluses for meeting traditional obligations under the network of patron-client ties that had bound together the high-status landowning castes, and low-caste tenants, laborers, and artisans in the more self-contained and interdependent subsistence village economy. At the same time, the much larger numbers of marginal farmers and landless laborers, still splintered along traditional allegiances to family, caste, and faction, found it all the more difficult to present a united front against the larger landowners in the contest for control over the new community development bodies: many landless and land-poor families were faced with "economic crisis"[1] that could be contained only by safeguarding even attenuated dependency relationships with more affluent members of the landowning castes. The richer landowners, who were already better placed in the village social hierarchy, had little difficulty in manipulating a fragmented and dependent peasantry to maintain control of the cooperative and panchayat institutions. From this vantage point, they were able to exploit increased access to production credit, improved methods of cultivation, and more secure markets for further augmenting their resources. The politics of accommodation, under such conditions, actually operated to strengthen the power of these dominant peasant castes. They were able to rely both on strength of numbers (relative to the much smaller ranks of the elite upper castes) and growing economic affluence, to strike the most advantageous alliances with external sources of power in the ruling party and administration, which, in turn, further bolstered their strategic position as intermediaries between the land-poor peasantry and the wider economic and political system.

Third, unless countervailing efforts are made to organize the peasantry in new forms of class-based associations that can build their own direct relationships with outside power centers in the political parties and the administration, the superior numbers of the poor cannot be converted into a potent political resource. By definition, such an approach to political organization involves a departure from accommodative politics, and invites polarization of the political process. Yet, there does not seem to be any alternative if the basic advantage of the poor in their strength of numbers is to be brought to bear from below in effective application of pressure for the implementation of social reform.

Finally, even if such analytical conclusions appear unpersuasive to political elites who must ultimately cope with the consequences of a mobilized peasantry, they are likely to be impressed by a more irresistible fact. The last thirty years has seen a major transformation in Indian politics. Large numbers of the illiterate and the impoverished have become active participants in the political arena. They are aware of their

[1] An extremely useful analytical framework for understanding the differential impact of new opportunities in the wider market economy on village cohesion (by increasing opportunities for wealthier peasants to pursue profits and achieve recognition in the larger system, while intensifying the economic crises of the poorest families with neither the resources nor the orientation required for change) is presented in Joel S. Migdal, *Peasants, Politics and Revolution*. See especially the summary statement of his argument in chapter 1.

political rights, and increasingly of their political power. There is a great deal of evidence to suggest that substantial numbers of landless laborers and dispossessed tenants are also angry at government failures to carry out promises of basic agrarian reform. Even conservative parties, if they remain committed to a competitive political system, will have to satisfy new criteria of legitimacy based on the promise of removing mass poverty within the foreseeable future as the price of popular support at the polls. For reasons of political self-interest, if on no other grounds, it will be increasingly impossible to maintain the separation between issues of social reform and principles of political organization.

This chapter explores some of the implications of these broad conclusions for India's pattern of development, against the background of the brief experiment with authoritarian rule during the period of the national Emergency between June 1975 and March 1977. It concludes with an assessment of the prospect, after the restoration of parliamentary processes, for mobilizing popular support and expanding government power to carry out essential institutional change within the framework of democratic politics.

The Emergency, which concentrated unlimited formal powers in the hands of the central government, revealed in sharper relief than ever before the obstacles in the basic structure of the rural political economy to effective implementation of growth and distribution policies. The Twenty-Point Program, described by Congress party leaders as a "direct assault on poverty"[2] had as its primary purpose helping the vast mass of rural poor. It gave highest priority to rapid implementation of land ceilings; stepped-up provision of housesites for landless laborers; abolition of bonded labor; a moratorium on the recovery of debts from landless laborers, small farmers and rural artisans—including a plan to liquidate rural indebtedness; and legislation to establish higher minimum wages for agricultural workers. Constitutional federalism and legal guarantees for individual rights no longer prevented the central government from making laws on any of these matters or from directing state governments to do so. Yet, as the prime minister acknowledged, "in reality, it was the Chief Ministers who would have to do so."[3]

In fact, the chief ministers could not do it on their own. Guidelines issued by the Congress president in August 1975 for "speedy implementation of the 20-Point Economic Program and involvement of Congress organization" directed the states to set up a "new result-oriented and commitment-based Agency functioning in several tiers" starting from the state level down to district and subdistrict (Revenue Circle or Block)

[2] AICC, *Congress Marches Ahead—12*, p. 203.
[3] AICC, *Congress Marches Ahead—11*, p. 5.

level.[4] Although the state committee was to be headed by the chief minister, and to include senior members of the government, the Congress party and administration, the most important operational units, of necessity, were those at the district and subdistrict level. In the case of rural reforms, the greatest responsibilities were assigned to subdistrict or local-level committees. These committees were to be composed of Congress MPs, MLAs and MLCs; Congress presidents or other Congress members of Panchayat Samitis; prominent Congress workers from the area; experienced constructive workers; a Youth Congress worker and a representative from the National Students Union; and the appropriate official at the concerned level nominated by the district committee.

The powers conferred on the local committees were virtually unlimited. They extended to the right of inspecting government records; evaluating the work of individual officers and communicating these evaluations to state authorities; undertaking tours within the area of their jurisdiction; holding hearings; recording evidence of a "summary nature" and "not subject to the elaborate procedure and criteria of the Evidence Act"; and taking decisions "on the spot" whenever feasible.[5] The jurisdiction of the local committees extended to the implementation of land ceilings, abolition of bonded labor, liquidation of rural indebtedness, the enforcement of minimum agricultural wages, and verification of possession of government lands. An "aggrieved person" was allowed just one appeal on any ruling, and this to the next higher committee.

Such "guidelines" from the Congress president to the state chief ministers could not possibly have been carried out. They amounted to quixotic commands for putting in place a grass-roots organization for popular mobilization by fiat from above. There was no institutional infrastructure in the rural areas on which to build the implementation committees. Sixteen months after the Proclamation of Emergency, the Working Committee still had "difficulty in collecting lists of Active Members from different States," and had to consider deputing "important persons" from the AICC to the districts in order to "activise the working of the DCCs."[6] Neither was there any possibility of mobilizing the rural poor through the panchayat institutions, which were either moribund or in the hands of the dominant landed castes.

The most that some states attempted was appointment of "Political Implementation Committees" for the limited purpose of enforcing land ceiling legislation that had been passed in 1972 and 1973, but held in abeyance by the absence of accurate land records and large numbers of writ petitions filed in the High Courts, citing one or another error by the implementing authority in the application of law. On the basis of guide-

[4] *Ibid.*, pp. 110–18.                      [5] *Ibid.*, p. 116.
[6] AICC, *Congress Marches Ahead—13*, p. 18.

lines issued by the Congress president, several states established spe-
cialized machinery at the Revenue Circle composed of revenue officials
and nonofficials exclusively concerned with land reform work. These
local committees were charged with expediting the implementation of
land ceiling laws—scrutinizing returns filed under the law to detect un-
derreporting or fraudulent transfers, taking evidence, including oral testimony, and pronouncing decisions "on the spot." As part of the same
field operation, the committees were authorized to calculate the surplus
area of land in respect to each family's holdings; issue a notice to the
landowner that he identify the particular area to be surrendered; and take
possession of the surplus land for government. Actual distribution was
to be carried out immediately on the basis of lists of intended beneficiaries drawn up for each village.

Even such summary enforcement procedures were not entirely successful. Many of the "nonofficials" on the Political Implementation
Committees were outsiders. They lacked intimate knowledge about
local land arrangements, and were unable to provide much help in un-
covering cases of nonfiling of returns or fictitious transfers. Some progress in implementation, however, was achieved. This was attributable
mainly to the disability placed on landowners in moving the courts for a
stay against the committee's award, and the determination of the local
authorities to reduce the time lag between scrutiny of landholdings, surrender of surplus area, government takeover of the land, and distribution. This ability to circumvent the courts and cut down on red tape did
significantly speed up implementation in some states. Compared to
62,000 acres that had come into possession of government between 1972
and 1975, an additional 1.7 million acres were vested in government by
the end of December 1976, and approximately 1.1 million acres had been
distributed.[7]

Similarly, in a number of states, the administration was able to speed
up the implementation of the central sector scheme, introduced from
1972/73, to provide over 4 million housesites to landless laborers in rural
areas by 1979. Most of the state governments, secure against court challenge, passed legislation conferring homestead rights on landless laborers
in possession of housesites. Altogether, the states, aided by central financial assistance to cover the cost of acquiring and developing the housesites, succeeded in distributing, according to official estimates, over three
million housesites in the first year after the Emergency.[8]

[7] Estimate provided by the Director of Land Reforms, Ministry of Food and Agriculture,
interview, New Delhi, January 8, 1977.

[8] J. S. Bright, *Emergency in India and 5 + 20 Point Programme*, p. 62. The impact of this
achievement was, however, reduced by the extremely uneven progress among the states.
The great bulk of the number of housesites allotted was accounted for by two states,
Gujerat and Uttar Pradesh.

Notwithstanding such accomplishments, the implementation of the Twenty-Point Program fell far short of the leadership's claim that it would "open up immense possibilities of changing the face of rural India, for liberating the rural poor from the age-old chains of exploitation and poverty."[9] Implementation of basic agrarian reform remained out of reach, as the central government continued to be almost entirely dependent upon the administrative machinery at the district level to carry out its economic reforms. Even during the Emergency, as Mrs. Gandhi complained, there were still "a large number of persons in places of authority who have no feeling for this program or any other program which the Congress has put forward."[10] More to the point, no administrative machinery, however "committed," could have implemented agrarian reforms that at their base required organized peasant participation and/or an institutional infrastructure to provide alternatives to local landlords and moneylenders as souces of credit and other services to the rural poor.

A case in point was the promise to abolish bonded labor. Although the Bonded Labor System (Abolition) Ordinance was promulgated by the President with effect from October 25, 1975 (and later passed by both Houses of Parliament in February 1976), the Center was entirely dependent upon the states for the identification of bonded laborers whose numbers were finally placed at about 98,000 persons. At the state level, the district collector had formal responsibility for carrying out the provisions of the act for rehabilitation of bonded laborers. Yet, the district collectors were ill-equipped to enforce these directives without the help of village committees consisting of members drawn from the poorest sections of the community to supervise the "liberation." There were, however, few such active village committees. Reports by states to the Center of the number of bonded laborers estimated to have been "freed"—amounting to about 47,000—represented mainly official targets whose achievement could not be verified.[11]

Similar problems of implementation reduced the effectiveness of the action of several states in raising minimum agricultural wages. The official responsibility for enforcing the new laws devolved on the Block Development staff and the staffs of the Revenue Departments or Labor Departments. But the real work of implementation had to be done in the villages and required the organization of unions of agricultural laborers. This task was formally entrusted by the Congress leadership to its trade-union affiliate (All-India Trade Union Congress), which formed the Indian National Rural Workers Federation. But as the president of the new Federation pointed out, "it is, indeed, a stupendous task. It will re-

[9] From a statement by D. K. Barooah, Congress President, cited by Sankar Ghose, *Indira Gandhi, The Resurgent Congress and Socialism*, p. 53.
[10] *Congress Marches Ahead—13*, p. 70.     [11] *Ibid.*, p. 120.

quire sustained effort by dedicated and committed band of workers with the active support of the Party."[12] The statement was one of simple fact, but an admission, at the same time, that the task could not be accomplished.

Other deficiencies of institutional infrastructure limited the effectiveness of the government's effort to carry out plans for liquidating rural debt. The states did take legislative action to impose a moratorium on the recovery of debts from landless laborers, marginal and small farmers, and in some cases, to scale down and even liquidate debts of the most impoverished agriculturists. Yet, as district officials started to receive and decide applications for liquidation of debts, they were confronted with the problem of "virtual drying up of the traditional source of credit, in particular for consumption purposes."[13] Cooperative institutions were clearly too weak to provide an alternative source of credit; the rural branches of the nationalized banks were too limited in the type of loans they could make, that is, advances for commercial ventures and on conventional criteria of credit-worthiness. Indeed, the share of all institutional credit in meeting rural needs was still not much more than one-third of the total.[14] An entirely new scheme had to be proposed by the central government, one that envisaged the establishment of regional rural banks at the rate of 50 banks for 10 million people, each of which was eventually to open 1,000 branches in order to meet the credit needs of small and marginal farmers, landless laborers, and small artisans. But only 18 rural banks were actually established during the Emergency, and the problems of providing adequate financing from share capital subscribed by the Reserve Bank, the state governments, and nationalized banks precluded any possibility of meeting the requirements for consumption loans of the rural poor.

The inability to implement basic elements of the rural economic program was for the time being (and under conditions of press censorship) obscured by reports of dramatic "gains of the Emergency" occurring in urban areas. In the cities, the full force of the Center's power could be applied to control illegal or undesirable activities. Special squads were set up in major urban centers to carry out house-to-house investigation of undisclosed and/or undervalued investments in the contruction of luxury houses, estimated by October 1976 to total about Rs. 17 crores.[15] At the same time, the Urban Land (Ceiling and Regulation) Act, 1976, passed at the Center and adopted in several states, placed an upper ceiling on

[12] *Congress Marches Ahead—11*, p. 101.
[13] Bright, *Emergency in India and 5 + 20 Point Programme*, p. 80.
[14] Ministry of Finance, *Economic Survey, 1975-76*, p. 7.
[15] V. B. Singh, *Economics of 20 Point Programme* (India, Ministry of Information and Broadcasting, New Delhi, 1976), p. 23.

ownership of vacant urban land, and laid down maximum size limits on the construction of new individual dwellings to discourage future speculation in real estate.

Campaigns against tax evasion and smuggling were even more successful. Under a "voluntary disclosure scheme," 250,000 persons reported income and wealth of Rs. 1,600 crores, yielding additional tax revenues to the central government of Rs. 249 crores. Indeed, during the first year of the Emergency, collection of direct taxes increased by over 27 percent achieved in the corresponding period of the previous year.[16] At the state level, campaigns against evasion of sales taxes also yielded additional revenues. The ability of the states to meet planned targets for mobilizing additional resources showed a marked improvement: more efficient collection by the Center of income taxes increased the value of the state's share in central taxes; higher receipts from better collection of sales taxes directly augmented the states' revenues. In some cases, state governments even imposed higher electricity rates, land revenue taxes, and levies on irrigation.

Another major achievement was the campaign against smugglers. A presidential ordinance, promulgated in July 1975, provided that persons detained in connection with violations under the Conservation of Foreign Exchange and Prevention of Smuggling Activities Act, 1974, need no longer be informed of the grounds for their detention, and further, could not have charges raised against them reviewed by an advisory board. In addition, any "illegally acquired property" held by them or their relatives was subject to confiscation by the government. Within a year, by July 1976, implementation of the act in Bombay, Delhi, and Madras had resulted in imprisonment of over 2,100 purported smugglers and attachment of property worth more than one crore of rupees. Meanwhile, over 60,000 raids on the premises of suspected smugglers, hoarders, and others engaged in black-market activities led to seizures of goods valued at tens of crores of rupees.[17]

All of this (including a more zealous effort by the Customs Service to intercept smugglers on land and at sea) "completely disorganized the smuggling syndicates."[18] As opportunities for illegal transactions in foreign exchange were reduced, and there was a favorable impact on the strength of the rupee in international money markets, the margin between official and black-market exchange rates began to narrow. In addition, as smuggling and other illegal foreign exchange dealings became much more high-risk ventures, the government acted to provide financial incentives for increasing the flow of private remittances in foreign

[16] Ibid., p. 24.
[17] Bright, Emergency in India and 5 + 20 Point Programme, pp. 40–43.
[18] Ibid., p. 43.

exchange into the country. In November 1975, a new scheme was introduced to permit Indians or aliens of Indian origin living abroad to maintain deposit accounts in foreign currencies, to earn tax-free interest up to 10 percent, and to claim repayment in the same currency, thereby providing a convertibility guarantee. As large numbers of Indian nationals—including those who had migrated to Persian Gulf countries in search of higher salaries—responded to these inducements, the gap in the balance of payments created by foreign trade deficits was reduced to a significant degree by an improvement in net receipts on invisible account from larger inflows of private remittances. At the same time, stepped-up disbursements of net aid by the Consortium countries, including the World Bank and IDA in 1975/76, further reduced the pressure on India's external resources.

The government's claim of economic gains of the Emergency was bolstered by a dramatic improvement in the price situation, and reappearance in the market of essential consumer goods. A declining rate of inflation had been in evidence since November 1974, after the government had promulgated its comprehensive antiinflation measures. By the end of March 1976, the wholesale price index had declined by 11.6 percent under the peak levels reached in September 1974.[19] In this case, however, the achievement could not be detached from the effects of a happy coincidence—the "best distributed rainfall" reported over the previous thirty-five years.[20] The extremely good weather conditions helped to lift agricultural production in 1975/76 to a new record level of almost 121 million tons, an increase of 15.6 percent over the previous year. As prices started to fall, the government mounted a major procurement effort, converting the purchase price into a "minimum support price" that was higher in some areas than the open market price. The price support program allowed government to buy nearly 13 million tons of foodgrains in 1975/76. Along with imports that were already on order, they succeeded in building up record stocks of foodgrains (at 17 million tons) that easily supplied the requirements of the public distribution system. Procurement of other basic items at incentive prices, particularly sugar, allowed the government to replenish consumer stocks for distribution through the fair-price shops.

There were other "gains." In the industrial sector, a dramatic reduction occurred in the number of man-days lost in strikes or lockouts. Compared to six million man-days lost during July-September 1974 alone, the corresponding figure for July-September 1975 was 1.56 million, with a progressive decline registered in work time lost for each successive month.[21] Labor peace, in turn, was accompanied by a significant

[19] Ministry of Finance, *Economic Survey, 1976-77*, p. 1.
[20] *Ibid.*, p. 4.                              [21] *Economic Survey, 1975-76*, pp. 12-13.

improvement in the production of several public-sector industries, particularly in electricity and coal, and allied industries that are heavy consumers of power—iron and steel, aluminum, copper, and nitrogenous fertilizers. Altogether, in 1975/76, the economy recorded its most impressive growth rate in several years, exceeding somewhat the spurt of 8 percent in 1967/68, when the return of favorable weather conditions after two drought years and a record crop had also spurred an economic recovery.

Notwithstanding all these "gains of the Emergency," the structural obstacles to achieving sustained economic growth had still not been removed. The recovery in industrial production, which increased to about 6 percent, was incomplete. Most consumer goods industries, especially the most important group of textiles, remained stagnant. The fact was that increases in aggregate real income originating in the rural sector during a record crop year remained skewed toward the minority of farmers with surpluses to sell. The broad-based "demand for more consumer goods which could reasonably have been expected to find markets in the rural sector of the economy did not increase appreciably."[22]

Further, the gain in agricultural production was itself only partially related to the (much slower) continuing progress of the green revolution in response to greater use of irrigation, high-yielding varieties, and fertilizers. It could not be sustained during the poor weather conditions of the following year. In 1976/77, foodgrains output showed a sharp drop of 5 to 6 percent; the overall rate of growth in GNP slumped to less than 2 percent. Although the industrial growth rate did manage an impressive 10 percent increase, this was attributed to a number of favorable circumstances, which "cannot be assumed to indicate a more cheerful trend."[23] Much of the increase in production occurred in public-sector manufacturing enterprises due to considerable improvement in use of existing capacity, and could not be sustained without stepped-up levels of public investment. At the same time, "lack of adequate internal demand"[24] consigned some of the increases in output to inventory accumulation. In other cases, particularly iron and steel, engineering goods, and cotton apparel, additional output was diverted toward the expansion of exports. Indeed, experts in the finance ministry began to give serious consideration to solving the problem of excess capacity at home by promoting rapid growth in the export of industrial products. In particular, they suggested the "need for a change in the outlook of business firms towards the overseas markets if our industrial capacity is to be more fully utilized."[25]

The Technical Development Fund created in March 1976 was charged

[22] *Economic Survey, 1976-77*, p. 10.          [23] *Ibid.*, p. 46.
[24] *Ibid.*, p. 47.                              [25] *Economic Survey, 1975-76*, p. 11.

with advancing export development in priority industries by providing finances for technological upgrading and modernization, and preferential treatment in the import of essential machinery. The government was even prepared to act favorably on proposals for foreign collaboration and consultancy agreements involving the import of sophisticated equipment and designs. In addition, they indicated their interest in exploring possibilities for Indo-U.S. business cooperation in setting up joint enterprises in third countries.

If, even under conditions of the Emergency, Mrs. Gandhi felt compelled to deny the "rumors that there was going to be a big change in Government policy, that the Government was drifting towards right,"[26] it was because such policies created rising concern that the basic principle of self-reliance was being compromised. The willingness of some of the larger business houses to consider expansion abroad in collaboration with the multinationals contributed to an apprehension that important segments of Indian industry could become dependent upon foreign technology, financing, and distribution, perhaps sliding into a satellite relationship with the major capitalist industrial powers. Yet, even if government had been willing to run such a risk in order to get greater access to overseas markets, its own experts had pointed out that a strategy of export-led growth, while successful in other countries, was not a "realistic possibility" in India, given the relative smallness of the export sector (at about 5 to 6 percent of the economy). There was, in practice, no escape from the fact that "in the final analysis, in a country like India, sustained growth of industrial production is really linked to the growth of agriculture which is a major determinant of the size of the local market for industrial goods."[27] Indeed, in 1976/77 continuing "consumer resistance" prevented any production breakthrough in the key group of textile industries. At the same time, extensive liberalization of industrial licensing policies, relaxation of price controls, and tax incentives for new investment did not produce "the kind of upsurge [in industrial investment] hoped for." Several reasons were cited: "Firstly, there was no great revival in construction, including industrial construction. Secondly, a large part of the revival seems to be in the form of expansions and additions rather than new projects, because being less resource intensive, industrial units can find a part of the necessary resources internally. Thirdly, for the first time a buyer's market seems to have emerged in many products . . . new investment would be undertaken far more cautiously than in the past."[28]

It was clear that the old problems had not been solved. Unemployment was large and growing. New jobs in the organized sector remained

<hr>

[26] *Congress Marches Ahead—12*, p. 102.
[27] *Economic Survey, 1976-77*, p. 46.          [28] *Ibid.*, p. 13.

stabilized at about 500,000 per year.[29] The wholesale price index once again showed an upward trend, partly due to price increases of food and industrial raw materials, climbing by almost 12 percent in 1976/77.[30] As state governments exhausted the possibilities of improving collection of sales taxes, and still made no effort to expand the tax base by imposing an agricultural income tax, deterioration in their finances once again led to problems of large overdrafts on the Reserve Bank.

Other anomalies emerged that created new and embarrassing problems. Another massive procurement effort (which over two years had absorbed Rs. 2,000 crores of government finances) brought up the stock of foodgrains to 18 million tons by the end of the year. But the low purchasing power of the large numbers of landless laborers and small cultivators most urgently in need of increasing their consumption converted the huge stocks into a "glut" on the market, creating such difficulties of finance and storage that government began to consider opportunities for exporting wheat as a solution to the food "surplus." Similarly, record increases in foreign exchange reserves, which grew to over Rs. 2,800 crores at the end of 1976/77, could not be used to spur higher levels of economic growth, despite policies that virtually lifted restrictions on the imports of raw materials and components required by industry—partly because of rupee shortages essential to finance the domestic costs of public-sector projects, and lack of interest by private manufacturers in expanding their enterprises as the demand recession continued.

The startling inability of the economy to make productive use of large stocks of foodgrains and record reserves of foreign exchange (both of which helped to boost the saving rate to about 15 percent of GNP by 1976/77) pointed to a "collapse" of effective urban and rural demand, the consequence of the skewed flow of benefits from investment (and institutional lending) to a small minority of businessmen, traders, and professionals in the cities, and large and middle farmers with surpluses for sale in the countryside.[31] Prospects for the future continued to depend—as they had over the past thirty years—on possibilities for achieving "substantial increases in agricultural development and small-scale and rural industries."[32]

But the planners were themselves skeptical that higher levels of agricultural growth could be achieved simply through much larger outlays on irrigation, electrification, extension, and modern inputs. Water resources in the most advanced areas had already been fully exploited: additional gains were expected to come primarily from better water

[29] *Ibid.*, pp. 79–80.          [30] *Ibid.*, p. 1.
[31] For a brief analysis of structural problems in the economy limiting demand, see Prem Shankar Jha, "Hurdles to Growth, Collapse of Urban and Rural Demand," *Times of India*, September 19, 1977.
[32] *Economic Survey, 1976-77*, p. 47.

management. Untapped water resources in the Ganges heartland did not appear to offer the prospect of comparable production gains so long as unsolved tenurial problems created basic institutional obstacles to economic modernization. Rather, the solution to problems of increasing agricultural growth no less than to the dilemmas of raising effective consumer demand required a development strategy that led directly to higher productivity, incomes, and consumption of all households in the rural sector, especially the marginal farmers and landless laborers whose numbers were steadily increasing. Inevitably, it meant that "land reforms will have to be implemented, and surplus land distributed to the landless. Fragmented land will have to be consolidated. The institutional framework for supplying inputs and marketing output will have to be improved."[33]

Veterans of the planning process in the Nehru years felt vindicated in their original approach. Tarlok Singh, reflecting on India's development experience (in 1974), argued that a "basic identity now exists between measures required to achieve adequate and sustained growth and those needed to secure substantial progress towards a more efficient rural economic structure." Reiterating the importance of implementing land policies to reduce disparities in ownership, turn tenants into owners, and assure expanded employment opportunities to small and marginal farmers and landless laborers, he wrote:

> It is sufficient to state summarily that without transformation of the rural economy into a *progressively* cooperative system (suited to the conditions of each region), it will be virtually impossible to put all of India's manpower resources to productive use, to raise the productivity of land, labor generally, and to bring about in every rural area the development of an agro-industrial economy. These . . . are among the essential conditions for eradicating extreme forms of poverty as it affects the masses of landless workers, marginal and small farmers and rural artisans. . . . There is no course open to India but to face up to the tasks involved in a thorough and systematic matter as an integral part of a total national plan for economic development and social change.[34]

Far from "facing up" to the tasks of basic social change the government appeared incapable of mounting the grass-roots organizational effort that was required, state by state, to transform nascent sentiments of economic solidarity among the rural poor into effective support from below to implement agrarian reforms. On the contrary, having sus-

[33] From a summary analysis of the 1976-77 *Economic Survey* published in *Times of India*, June 14, 1977.
[34] Tarlok Singh, *India's Development Experience*, p. 193.

pended the electoral process, which provided the only political necessity for appealing to the common economic interests of the poorest sections, the ruling party had become more than ever dependent upon the very local elites it was presumably committed to displace in order to carry out its "growth"-oriented policies.

The major economic document completed during the Emergency, the long-delayed *Fifth Five Year Plan, 1974-79*, published in 1976, vividly illustrated the continuing contradiction between political rhetoric and public policy. The Rs. 39,000 crore Plan—representing less than a 5 percent increase in total outlay over the Draft Fifth Plan of 1973—achieved even this modest increase by projecting much higher targets for additional resource mobilization, but also once again increasing India's reliance on external assistance to almost 15 percent of Plan outlay.[35] The overall targets, moreover, were significantly lower than the moderate growth rates projected in the Draft Plan. The average increase in GNP was estimated at 4.3 percent per annum, including average annual increases of 3.9 percent in agriculture and 6.5 percent in industry.[36]

The dual objectives of removal of poverty and achievement of self-reliance focused on strategies of growth in three basic sectors, those of agriculture, creation of additional employment opportunities, and energy and critical industrial intermediates. The Plan approached the problem of raising production in "the most vital [agricultural] sector"[37] through a technocratic strategy that once again emphasized the expansion of scientific methods, particularly the increase of area under irrigation, the spread of available high-yielding varieties for foodgrains and nonfood crops, and higher fertilizer use. Problems of interregional and interclass disparities were treated mainly as modifications of production yardsticks to see "how at the margins you can weave in institutional changes in growth policies."[38] Most important from the planners' point of view was the decision to mount a direct effort at improving incomes in agriculture by injecting a number of "growth centers" into the rural economy through larger and regionally dispersed investments in medium and major irrigation, scientific water management, and extension. The model in mind, provided by the Punjab, envisaged setting in motion an autonomous growth process, supported at its base by the spread of commercial farming, including multiple cropping and diversification of the cropping pattern to expand employment in agriculture and related activities. This approach, which had to be carried out particularly in the paddy producing areas (because the potential for

[35] Planning Commission, *Fifth Five Year Plan, 1974-79*, p. 32.
[36] *Ibid.*, p. 25.                                    [37] *Ibid.*, p. 5.
[38] Interview with Dr. Yogindar Alagh, Head, Perspective Planning Division, Planning Commission, New Delhi, January 17, 1977.

growth in wheat was gradually being exhausted), once again failed to come to grips with the obstacles to increasing agricultural productivity and employment in the patterns of land distribution and land tenure. By comparison with the Punjab, in the rice areas the initial problems of inequality in landownership, fragmentation of holdings, number of marginal holdings, incidence of sharecropping and percentage of landless laborers were all more extreme. Despite such conditions, the regional approach relied heavily on providing incentives (through guaranteed support prices for foodgrains and large subsidies on modern inputs, particularly fertilizer) for higher levels of individual private investment, apparently in disregard of the well-documented pattern that "large" landowners often operated small parcels of land while leasing out scattered plots under sharecropping arrangements. At the same time, direct programs for reducing interclass disparities by creating additional employment opportunities for marginal and small farmers and landless laborers still were visualized mainly in terms of central sector schemes for subsidized loans to individuals starting farm household ancillary activities. Such a solution was not reexamined, even though the numbers of marginal cultivators and agricultural laborers accounted for as many as seventy to eighty percent of rural households in some areas, while the possibility of using loan subsidy programs to achieve the economic viability of even a small proportion of these households had yet to be demonstrated.

Apart from new employment opportunities created in the rural sector as the result of the spread of commercial farming, and of central sector subsidy schemes for small and marginal farmers and agricultural laborers inserted at the margin of the growth strategy, there was little prospect of any significant improvement in job prospects for the rural poor. Certainly, Plan programs in industry and mining, which had been pared down to the basic minimum, did not offer any prospect of enlarged employment opportunities. On the contrary, public investments were targeted for capital-intensive projects, aimed mainly at expanding production of energy substitutes in coal, electricity, and crude oil (including development of the promising off-shore oil deposits at Bombay High), and maintaining adequate production of critical intermediates, especially steel and aluminum. The Planning Commission did propose to create additional employment in village industries and small-scale rural industries, by "de-urbanizing" and decentralizing industrial production, but without specifying the means through which these longstanding proposals were going to be carried out.

Tacit recognition that all of this was by no means a strategy for removing mass poverty within any foreseeable future was perhaps implied in the addition to the Twenty-Point Program, in July 1976, of the "Four-Point Program" advanced by the Youth Congress. The Four Points concentrated on noncontroversial social reforms that were considered necessary to carry out the ideals of social justice endorsed by the Congress party. These included a commitment by each member of the Youth Congress to "teach at least one to read and write"; "plant a tree"; abolish dowry and other evils of the caste system; and "take an active part in family planning."[39]

Actually, the Four-Point Program had special political significance. It was adopted by the Congress party in the wake of the meteoric rise to national prominence of Mrs. Gandhi's younger son, Sanjay, the power behind the rapid growth of the Youth Congress after the Emergency. Having been elected in December 1975 to membership of the Central Executive of the Indian Youth Congress, Sanjay Gandhi succeeded in using his influence[40] to have Priya Ranjan Das Munshi replaced as president by a "dependable Punjabi girl,"[41] and in carrying out a shake-up at all levels of the organization to displace many of the young radicals from leadership roles. Acting from this position—the only office that he held inside the Congress party—Sanjay set out to build up the Youth Congress as a rival of the regular party organization and a vehicle of his personal power. Between January 1976 (when the Four-Point Program was first announced) and January 1977, the organization claimed to have recruited over five million members between the ages of fifteen and thirty-five.[42] Block Youth Congress organizations had been formed in all 6,000 Blocks, all by nomination from above. Plans were in progress to have nominated Youth Congress Committees for every five villages; and to proceed with elections for local units from the Block level upwards in June 1977.

Much of this "organization," of course, was inactive. Most of its active membership was disproportionately centered in the larger towns and cities, and these in the northern states most closely controlled by the Center (especially Uttar Pradesh, Madhya Pradesh, Rajasthan, Bihar, and Punjab). But it did attract large numbers of volatile young people, many among the educated unemployed who had previously been available for violent agitations against the government. And it did acquire a reputation for "goondaism" that made its members feared, if not respected.

Sanjay himself, at the center of the small coterie that gathered around Mrs. Gandhi, was developing a similar reputation for arbitrary interference into the workings of the government and administration, exerting

[39] Bright, *Emergency in India and 5 + 20 Point Programme*, pp. 107-108.
[40] At the time Sanjay Gandhi was elected to the Central Executive of the Indian Youth Congress, Mrs. Gandhi was the Chairman of the Central Youth Advisory Committee, with powers to appoint a General Secretary to "coordinate the works between the C.Y.A.C. and the I.Y.C." *Draft Constitution of Indian Youth Congress*, p. 15.
[41] Kuldip Nayar, *The Judgement*, p. 109.
[42] *Times of India*, January 16, 1977.

his influence on matters ranging from appointments to ministerial posts and replacements of chief ministers, to postings of senior government officials. Indeed, in Delhi, where the elected Municipal Corporation had been superseded (in March 1975) and the powers of the Corporation vested in the commissioner, this senior officer was himself instructed to "function under the overall supervision and control of Sh. Sanjay Gandhi and to seek orders from him." The same practice was also followed by the vice chairman of the Delhi Development Authority, so that Sanjay acquired a predominant influence in the affairs of the Delhi administration. Although he occupied no official position, the notion that his "wishes and desires" had the approval of the prime minister, and his interference in the day-to-day working of the Corporation—including directives for the transfer and postings of "all officers," often accompanied by threats that those who failed to follow his instructions would be suspended or dismissed or arrested under MISA—created a climate in which the staff was "terrorized." In particular, "he used to send lot of his people to watch the activities of the Corporation, the members of the Youth Congress and some people from his own factory, who always gave him exaggerated account of the activities of the Corporation. Even on slightest pretexts and reports, he would ask for the suspension of even senior officers."[43]

Some of the worst "excesses" of the Emergency occurred as a result of the constant pressure placed on municipal officials through Sanjay, especially his demands to carry out a massive slum clearance program in order to make Delhi a modern and beautiful city. The officials of the Municipal Corporation and the Delhi Development Authority, operating with such a sense of urgency that they did not take time to issue written notices to the population in the affected areas, launched a massive scheme of demolition of unauthorized *jhuggis* (shacks), shops, and other structures in Delhi, in the predominantly Muslim neighborhoods around Jama Masjid mosque and Turkman Gate. Altogether, during the course of these operations, over 150,000 structures were demolished,[44] leading by one estimate to the eviction of 700,000 people.[45] At Turkman Gate, where local residents resisted the demolition of their houses, they were confronted with the massed force of the Delhi police, augmented by contingents of the Central Reserve Police. Persons who attempted to pre-

[43] This account of Sanjay Gandhi's role in the administration of Delhi was submitted to the Shah Commission (set up by the central government to inquire into the abuses of the Emergency) by B. R. Tamta, Commissioner, Municipal Corporation of Delhi during the period of Emergency Rule. *Times of India*, December 18, 1977.

[44] This estimate is taken from a summary of the case presented before the Shah Commission on large-scale demolitions in the capital during the Emergency, and published in *Times of India*, December 14, 1977.

[45] *Times of India*, October 23, 1977.

vent the forcible entry of policemen into their homes were beaten, and others were arrested. Altogether, by official estimate, six persons were killed in police firings. The slum dwellers, many of whom lost virtually all of their belongings, were subsequently "relocated" to new colonies, hurriedly constructed on the outskirts of the city, many of which did not have drinking water or other basic amenities.

Mrs. Gandhi's apparent approval of Sanjay's activities—including the accelerated slum demolition program—created the impression that Delhi was being used as a "training ground" in grooming him as the prime minister's successor. As talk of a Nehru dynasty spread, "no Chief Minister thought his visit to Delhi was complete until he had met Sanjay. They all vied with one another in inviting him to their state and to show through government sponsored rallies how popular he was."[46]

And after April 1976, when the central government announced a new National Population Policy to reduce the annual birth rate from about 35 per thousand to 25 per thousand by 1984, Sanjay took up the family planning drive as the major plank of his Four-Point Program. Moreover, if the central government lacked the grass-roots political organization to mobilize the rural poor behind policies of agrarian reform that could ameliorate, if not remove, poverty, it had much less difficulty in activating the administrative and police personnel directly at its command to carry out the population policy that, at least in the future, could "remove" some of the poor. At the outset, the program was conceived as a combination of incentives and disincentives for couples to limit families in size to three children. It included legislation to raise the minimum age of marriage, denial of certain concessions such as subsidized housing and medical care to government employees if they did not voluntarily undergo sterilization after the third child, and higher incentive payments to men who voluntarily underwent sterilization. All of these provisions, however, did not seem sufficient to transform the family planning campaign into the "mass movement" that the central leadership, and especially Sanjay, considered necessary. Inevitably, as the pressure on state officials to set higher targets for sterilization increased, and as district officials and government employees, including teachers and health personnel, were assigned quotas of numbers of persons they were to persuade to undergo sterilization—or risk their own jobs, salary increases, and promotions—the family planning program degenerated in many areas into a terrifying campaign of forced sterilization. As always, those who were most powerless were the most vulnerable to arbitrary power, to being pulled down from buses, or forced from their houses by district officials and the police and taken to makeshift sterilization "camps." The

[46] Nayar, *The Judgement*, p. 107.

tribals, the Harijans, the minorities, and other members of the Backward Castes and classes were the first victims of forced sterilization.

The population control program was the most spectacular success of the Emergency. Targets set by the Union government aimed at sterilizing about 23 million persons over a period of three years were well on their way to being overfulfilled. According to government statistics, in the first five months of the campaign alone—between April and September 1976—3.7 million Indians were sterilized.[47] Flare-ups of popular violence in protest against enforced sterilization, including riots that provoked police firings at several places, were dismissed by the government as isolated incidents of abuse that could not be avoided. But more than any other measure of the Emergency, the sterilization campaign undermined Mrs. Gandhi's credibility among her strongest supporters in the minorities, the Harijans, and other members of the Backward Classes. Among the middle-class intelligentsia, who had from the outset resented Sanjay's "extraconstitutional" power and his arrogant personal style, he and his "storm troopers" in the Youth Congress appeared to present much worse danger than Mrs. Gandhi to individual liberties and the rule of law.

On the whole, the Emergency was perhaps less remarkable for official "excess" against individuals, which followed the familiar dynamic of corruption and abuse of authority associated with unrestricted power, than for the limitations on government's ability to use such absolute powers in bringing about basic social changes. The authoritarian regime, for all its enforced "social discipline," could not lead India onto a new path that showed the way out of the economic and political impasse that had followed after years of failure in implementing basic institutional change within the framework of democratic politics. At most, it could suppress the disruptive consequences in popular discontent and disorder of the Congress party's inability to devise a peaceful substitute for a frontal assault on the strategic position of the dominant minority of propertied castes and classes.

It was, moreover, uncertain how long even this accomplishment of restoring political stability could be sustained. Even in the absence of efforts to carry out radical social change, ties of national solidarity were strained by suspending the political consensus at the core of the federal system, that of constructing all-India policies with the consent of major regional groups. Yet, if there appeared to be no way out down the path of authoritarian rule, it was equally unlikely that India could go back to the pre-1969 pattern of accommodative politics that claimed to advance

---

[47] Cited in Norman D. Palmer, "The Politics of Depoliticization," *Asian Survey*, February 1977, p. 174.

the welfare of the poor even while protecting the interests of all groups. Mrs. Gandhi, perhaps to some extent unwittingly, had herself played a major role in transforming the principles of political legitimacy by which the performance of future governments would have to be judged. Indeed, she gave every indication of recognizing that such a transformation had taken place.

The prime minister was finally freed from any need to protect her position against challenges inside the party, or from the opposition through populist appeals for mass support—and indeed, she actually encouraged an open attack on the CPI (by December 1976) that questioned its patriotism, even while isolating most of the ex-communist members of the Forum from positions of influence during the Emergency. She nevertheless felt compelled to justify government proposals for sweeping constitutional changes aimed at enlarging the powers of the central government, and by extension her own power, exclusively in terms of the overriding necessity to "give fuller expression to the democratic and egalitarian aspirations of our people."[48]

A series of legislative and constitutional changes adopted by Parliament immediately after the Emergency had already strengthened Mrs. Gandhi's personal power. The two Houses of Parliament had convened on July 21, 1975, and—working without most members of the opposition parties, who were either in detention or had decided to boycott the session—not only approved the Proclamation of Emergency, but passed the Constitution (Thirty-ninth Amendment) Act, which made the declaration of Emergency nonjusticiable. It also retroactively changed the provisions of the Representation of the People Act (1951), the electoral law under which Mrs. Gandhi had been convicted of corrupt practices, to remove any legal grounds for a challenge to her 1971 election.[49] In addition, Parliament passed the Constitution (Fortieth Amendment) Bill to remove all election disputes arising in relation to the president, vice president, and speaker of the Lok Sabha from the jurisdiction of the courts.

These acts were followed up in early January 1976 with legislation to apply permanent curbs on the press. The Prevention of Publication of Objectionable Matter Act prohibited publication, among other items, of articles or pictures "likely to bring into hatred and contempt or excite disaffection toward the Government, thereby cause or tend to cause public disorder"; and any material "defamatory to the President of India, the Vice President, the Prime Minister, the Speaker of the House or the gov-

---

[48] *Congress Marches Ahead—12*, p. 14.
[49] On June 12, 1976, the Supreme Court unanimously reversed Mrs. Gandhi's conviction on corrupt electoral practices, citing the amendments passed to the election law by Parliament in August 1975.

ernment of a State."[50] At the same time, the four independent Indian news services were merged into one news service (Samachar), whose governing council was nominated by the government. Immunity for journalists covering parliamentary proceedings was withdrawn; those journalists considered unsympathetic to the government were denied accreditation to cover the capital, and some, including Kuldip Nayar, were arrested.

All remaining opposition strongholds were also liquidated. In January 1976, the central government dismissed the DMK government of Madras, alleging widespread corruption; and in March 1976, President's Rule was also imposed on Gujerat, on grounds that political violence was increasing in the state.

All of this, however, was only a prelude to the omnibus (fifty-nine-clause) Constitution (Forty-second Amendment) Act introduced in Parliament and passed by an overwhelming majority in November 1976.[51] The constitutional amendments institutionalized the greatly expanded powers of Parliament and the central government at the expense of all other autonomous centers of authority, in the courts, the administration, the opposition parties, and the states. The sweeping changes, which established the conditions for consolidation of a permanent dictatorship, were justified by leading members of the government solely in terms of carrying out the "country's duty to remove hurdles in the way of achieving socio-economic objectives."[52]

One of the most important purposes of the Forty-second Amendment, according to the law minister, was to reverse the effect of the Supreme Court's 1973 judgment in the *Keshavananda Bharati* case, that Parliament could not amend the "basic structure" of the constitution. In another amendment of Article 368, the most unequivocal language was used to remove all doubt that there was any limitation "whatever on the constituent power of Parliament to amend by way of addition, variation or repeal the provisions of the Constitution." Having thereby disposed of the "dogma of the basic structure," other amendments greatly curtailed the powers of the courts, removing from their jurisdiction matters relating to recruitment and conditions of service of persons appointed to the public services (including the Indian Administrative Service and the Indian Police Service); and authorizing Parliament to create a hierarchy of administrative tribunals at the Union and state levels to decide disputes on tax matters; foreign exchange and import and export matters; industrial and labor disputes; land reforms; ceiling on urban property; and issues

[50] *New York Times*, January 30, 1976.
[51] The full text of the Constitution of India (Forty-second Amendment) Act, 1976, is published in *The Constitution of India* (Central Law Agency, Allahabad, 1977).
[52] Excerpt from the statement of the Law Minister, H. R. Gokhale, to the Lok Sabha, explaining the Constitution Bill, *The Statesman*, October 26, 1976.

relating to production, procurement, supplies, and distribution of foodstuffs and other essential goods. At the same time, the jurisdiction of the Supreme Court for the enforcement of fundamental rights was limited to consideration of the validity of central laws (with the legality of state laws to be challenged only in the High Courts), while imposing the requirement that a two-thirds majority of a minimum of seven judges was necessary to declare any law invalid. Other powers conferred on Parliament provided that notwithstanding the fundamental rights to equality under the law, political freedom, and the right to property, laws for the "prevention or prohibition of anti-national activities; or, the prevention of formation of, or the prohibition of, anti-national associations" could not be declared unconstitutional. Further provisions of the amendment increased the terms of the Lok Sabha and state assemblies from five to six years; made it mandatory for the president to act on the advice of the Council of Ministers; and authorized the Government of India to deploy central armed force in any state for dealing with a breakdown of law and order, without any authorization or supervision by the state government concerned.

Above and beyond all these changes, providing the new principles of legitimacy used by the government to defend the amendments, was the "historic" step taken to give superior legal force to the Directive Principles of State Policy over the fundamental rights provisions of the constitution. The new preamble to the constitution solemnly resolved to constitute India into a "Sovereign Socialist Secular Democratic Republic," replacing the language of the 1950 document to establish a "Sovereign Democratic Republic." Most important, Article 31c added to the constitution by the Twenty-fifth Amendment Act, 1971, was retained and strengthened, and the section struck down by the Supreme Court in the *Keshavananda Bharati* case (1973) was restored. According to the new version of Article 31c, "no law giving effect to the policy of the State securing *all or any of the principles laid down in Part IV* shall be deemed void on the ground that it is inconsistent with, or takes away or abridges any of the rights conferred by article 14, article 19 or article 31; *and no law containing a declaration that it is for giving effect to such policy shall be called in question in any court on the ground that it does not give effect to such policy*.[53] Government spokesmen described the purpose of the amendment in direct language. They argued it was necessary to "ensure that certain rights, particularly property rights, of individuals should not be

---

[53] Emphasis added. The first italicized section represents a substitution for the more limited provision of the Constitution (Twenty-fifth Amendment) Act to extend protection to all laws enacted for the purpose of giving effect to all or any of the Directive Principles, rather than only to the specific principles set down in clause (b) and clause (c) of Article 39. The second italicized section restored the portion of the Twenty-fifth Amendment held unconstitutional by the Supreme Court in the *Keshavananda Bharati* case, 1973.

allowed to stand in the way of the progress and well-being of society. The directive principles which embody social rights, have to over-ride those fundamental rights which are essentially private or individual rights."[54]

The Forty-second Amendment attacked the very foundations of the political order established at Independence. It imposed the new constitutional doctrine of absolute supremacy of Parliament and established the overriding importance of the Directive Principles for securing a social order to "promote the welfare of the people," in cases of conflict with the fundamental rights protecting individual political freedom and property. The meaning of this reordered set of priorities for the prospect of democratic social transformation in a political system that had previously allowed legislation for economic reform only through measures that preserved individual political freedoms and the right to property, was not explored. Indeed, the significance of the new principles of political legitimacy was obscured by pervasive cynicism about the government's motives in initiating the sweeping constitutional changes. It was unmistakable that Mrs. Gandhi did not intend to use the new powers to usher in a social revolution. Rather, they provided legal rationale for depriving dissidents of their political rights and property under the law, and recalcitrant officers in the public services of any guarantees for tenure. The provisions also immeasurably strengthened the Center's coercive power against opposition governments in the states.

Still, if there was widespread cynicism about the government's motives in introducing the Forty-second Amendment, and general opposition to the provisions aimed at emasculating democratic institutions, many persons, both inside Congress and among the left opposition, had come to accept the new *principle* of legitimacy invoked by the government to justify its actions. Indeed, it is at least arguable that growing popular anger as the Emergency was prolonged was directed not only at the suspension of fundamental rights in itself, but at the abuse of the unlimited powers granted to government, which were exploited to advance the personal interests of a small coterie, rather than to redeem Congress promises of far-reaching socio-economic changes to alleviate the misery of the poor.

The extent to which popular political awareness had been heightened as new principles of political legitimacy took hold was illuminated in the extraordinary sequence of events set in motion by Mrs. Gandhi's announcement on January 18, 1977, of a new Lok Sabha election. The prime minister's statement was accompanied by the release of political detainees, including leading members of the opposition, relaxation of

[54] Central Campaign Committee (All India Congress Committee), *The Congress and Constitutional Amendments*, by Sankar Ghose (New Delhi, undated), p. 17.

press censorship, and lifting of restrictions on normal electoral activities by recognized political parties.

Even so, the opposition clearly entered the elections with severe disadvantages. They had only fifty days to organize a national election campaign, find campaign funds, and explain the issues at stake to an electorate of over 300 million, the majority of whom were illiterate. At the same time, prodded by Jayaprakash Narayan, the Congress (O), the Jan Sangh, the Bharatiya Lok Dal, and the Socialist party—that is, the major constituents of the "Grand Alliance" that had been routed by the Congress party in 1971—agreed to constitute a joint electoral party, the Janata party, and to have a single list of candidates, a common electoral symbol, and a common flag. At the head of this unified opposition was Mrs. Gandhi's implacable opponent, Morarji Desai.

The Janata party attracted new recruits from among the anticommunist Congress left, in particular those socialists led by Chandra Shekhar who had supported Jayaprakash Narayan, only to be arrested along with opposition leaders. In addition, the Janata managed to arrange electoral alliances with the CPI(M); the Akali Dal in Punjab, and the DMK in Tamil Nadu. The Congress, by contrast, found allies in the CPI and the ADMK in Tamil Nadu—a dissident group that had defected from the parent DMK party after launching charges of pervasive corruption against the leadership. The contest was the first since Independence in which party competition in most constituencies was limited to two opponents, one representing the Congress or its supporters, and the other, the Janata or its allies.

The course of the campaign confounded all expectations. The assumption that the Congress party could use its manifold advantages to win reelection easily was put into question when on February 2 Jagjivan Ram, the most senior member of the Cabinet, resigned from the government and the Congress party. The defection of Ram, who had served at the Center almost continuously for thirty years, and was the only Congress leader apart from Mrs. Gandhi with a broad national following—among the more than 80 million-strong Harijan community—dealt a devastating blow to the prime minister. The loss was all the more damaging because of Ram's bitter denunciation of Mrs. Gandhi for her destruction of internal democracy inside the Congress party, and the perversion of democratic institutions into "convenient instruments for asserting personal power."[55] Ram's decision to form the Congress for Democracy spurred defections from the Congress party in key northern states, and added to Janata's strength when the CFD also decided to contest under the same election symbol and party flag.

The united opposition succeeded in making the Emergency into the

[55] *Times of India*, February 22, 1977.

major issue of the election campaign. Jayaprakash Narayan defined the
stark choice before the electorate as one between "democracy and dictatorship and slavery and freedom."[56] Arguing that despite the concentration of all powers in her hands, Mrs. Gandhi had been unable to solve
the pressing economic problems of the people, Janata leaders promised
"both bread and freedom."[57]

Mrs. Gandhi's arguments that Janata represented an opportunistic alliance between parties of different ideologies and interests, and that the
choice was between "stability, peace and progress" under Congress or
"confusion, chaos and instability"[58] under her opponents failed to generate enthusiasm. Nor did her rebuttal to charges of dictatorship that
pointed to the very fact of the elections taking place as proof of her democratic commitment carry much conviction. Although the prime minister campaigned in all states, addressing up to twenty meetings a day in
the course of a month, her assurances to the electorate that "I am not
threatening anyone" but rather was offering herself to the people as a
"sevika," a servant of the people,[59] no longer aroused credibility.

Indeed, in state after state, the most unexpected phenomenon of the
campaign was the palpable "anti-Congress wave." With the exception of
the prime minister, Congress leaders, either at the center or in the locali-
ties, could not draw crowds that were comparable either in size or enthusiasm to those who gathered to listen to "J. P.," Morarji Desai, Jagjivan Ram, and lesser leaders of the Janata. Opposition candidates, concentrating on the excesses of forced sterilization, as well as the failure of
Congress to carry out its promises for land redistribution, employment,
and reduction of disparities, evoked spontaneous support reflected in the
collections of hundreds of thousands of small donations that were used to
finance the Janata party campaign. Kuldip Nayar reported that

> people would wait for hours, often past midnight just to hear [the
> Janata leaders]. People would not mind if the leaders came late be-
> cause of other meetings and the delays that car or train travel could
> entail. Organizations supporting the opposition budded overnight;
> there was instant response to the call of volunteers and funds. The
> mood, at least in the Indo-Gangetic plain, was reminiscent of the
> days before Independence. At that time, whatever the Congress said
> was carried out enthusiastically; now it was the Janata's clarion call
> that the people obeyed.[60]

The election turned into an unprecedented debacle for the Congress
party.[61] Over sixty percent of those eligible to vote went to the polls,

[56] *Times of India*, February 21, 1977.      [57] *Times of India*, February 27, 1977.
[58] *Times of India*, March 2, 1977.      [59] *Times of India*, March 1, 1977.
[60] Kuldip Nayar, *The Judgement*, p. 173.
[61] The results of the election are reported in *Times of India*, April 3, 1977; and April 18,
1977.

almost as high as the record percentage in 1967. India's voters—that is, the poor, both rural and urban—once given the chance to express openly their opinion on the new political order set up under the Emergency, had little difficulty in drawing up a balance sheet of the economic gains and political costs of authoritarian rule. In a striking reversal of the 1971 election results, when the Congress party had won over 43 percent of the votes polled, in 1977, it could obtain little more than 35 percent of the total. In the Lok Sabha, the reverses were much greater. Congress was reduced from 352 out of 518 seats in 1971 to 153 out of 540 seats in 1977. The Janata, which won 43 percent of the popular vote and 270 seats, achieved sufficient strength on its own to form a new government. Together with its allies, it actually reached a two-thirds majority necessary to carry out its election pledge of amending the constitution to repeal the Forty-second Amendment. More remarkable, the Congress party was defeated by Janata in all its northern and central strongholds, including Uttar Pradesh, Bihar, Punjab, Haryana, Madhya Pradesh, Rajasthan, West Bengal, Orissa, Assam, and Gujerat. It sustained major losses in votes and a staggering loss of seats in all of these states. Most spectacular, Mrs. Gandhi was herself defeated by her opponent, Raj Narain, in her home constituency of Rae Bareli. Her son, Sanjay, nominated by Congress to stand in the neighboring constituency of Amethi, was also rejected by the voters. Indeed, the party failed to win a single seat in Uttar Pradesh, the keystone state of Congress politics.

This overall pattern was reversed only in the four southern states of Tamil Nadu, Andhra Pradesh, Mysore, and Kerala, where the Janata party was badly defeated by Congress or Congress alliances. A number of reasons were probably responsible. The excesses of the Emergency had not been so directly experienced in the south. In addition, fears were also aroused that a Janata party government based on the Jan Sangh might attempt to impose Hindi as the national language, despite the compromise formulas that had previously been reached. In Tamil Nadu, moreover, the Janata party had contested in alliance with the DMK, then under sharp opposition attacks for widespread corruption at the highest levels. In Kerala, the Congress–CPI coalition had won a measure of genuine support, largely as the result of its efforts to implement the radical "land to the tiller" agrarian reform drafted by its predecessor, a CPI (Marxist)-led coalition government.

On March 22, immediately after the election results became known, Mrs. Gandhi submitted her resignation. Just before stepping down from the office she had held for eleven years, the prime minister moved to lift formally the state of internal Emergency. Six days later, the proclamation of external Emergency, which had remained in force since the Indo-Pakistan War of December 1971, was also finally revoked. On March 24, in one of the truly extraordinary feats of personal will and political courage demonstrated in contemporary democratic politics, Morarji Desai, at the age of 81, achieved his long-thwarted ambition. He was selected by Janata MPs to be the leader of the party, and he became the fourth prime minister of independent India.

The general pattern of popular support for the Janata party, moreover, was repeated in elections to the legislative assemblies of several states held in June 1977. Janata once again won large majorities in Uttar Pradesh, Bihar, Madhya Pradesh, Rajasthan, Orissa, and Punjab, yielding only to the CPI (Marxists) in West Bengal, where it managed for the first time to gain an absolute majority in that state. Elections at the same time in Tamil Nadu confirmed the commanding position of the regional ADMK in the state. Shortly thereafter, following the death of President Fakhruddin Ali Ahmed, and in a final repudiation of Mrs. Gandhi's rule, Morarji Desai placed in nomination for the presidency the name of N. Sanjiva Reddy, the same candidate nominated by the Congress party in 1969, and whom Mrs. Gandhi had opposed as a tool of the "Syndicate"—even at the cost of splitting the Congress party. On July 22, 1977, Sanjeeva Reddy was elected unopposed to the office of President of India.

The euphoria that accompanied all of these events could not quell indefinitely the uneasy feeling that India's democracy still faced its most severe tests. The poor majority had responded, yet again, to the promise, this time of an anti-Congress coalition, of "both bread and freedom." This renewed vote of popular confidence in democratic methods appeared all the more poignant in the face of doubts about the efficacy of the democratic process still troubling not only the middle-class intelligentsia, but the leading architect of the opposition's momentous triumph. Jayaprakash Narayan, who became the most revered political figure in India after the resumption of normal democratic government, was not himself convinced that problems of mass poverty could be solved even if the opposition were to win. While still under detention during the Emergency, Narayan confided in his prison diary: "The question is can the picture be fundamentally altered through the ordinary democratic process? Even if the opposition wins, will the picture change? I fear no. Laws will be passed and applied, monies will be spent—even if all this is done, possibly without corruption creeping in, will the structure, the system, the 'order' of our society change? I think no."[62]

As the months passed, and the Janata party, reflecting divergent ideological commitments and social and economic interests, failed to achieve a consensus on an economic strategy, such fears were more

[62] *New York Times Magazine*, March 27, 1977, p. 88.

widely expressed, the more so after the leadership fell back on an old formula—"the need to develop an alternative both to capitalism and communism." The alternative they proposed was "treading the path of Gandhian socialism based on political and economic decentralization."[63] The *Janata Statement on Economic Policy*, adopted in November 1977, committed the party to concentrate public-sector investible resources on rural development, including creation of new job opportunities in the rural sector, and the development of small-scale and cottage industries using labor-intensive techniques of production. The *Statement*, which declared the party's opposition to "any system which is based on exploitation" and promised to "do away with the dual society as development would be oriented to the jobless and the homeless, the small and marginal farmers and laborers,"[64] was particularly vague about the policy implications of carrying out this reorientation. The "dynamics of the change-over" made no mention of radical agrarian reform. Instead, they were described in general terms as "utmost decentralization of the process of planning" and the "elevation of agriculture to the predominant position and finally by a mass-oriented industrialization."[65]

Narayan's question—the question that has bedeviled India's political leadership since Independence—has yet to be answered, but it will be increasingly more difficult for any elected government to ignore. Can democratic processes be adapted to carry out a significant redistribution of income, status, and power to alter the structure of society?

Certainly, the record is not encouraging. The national leadership's expectation that political democracy would build up a mass base for the application of powerful pressures on government to carry out peaceful change has proved misconceived in several respects. Not least important, perhaps, was the failure to understand the distinction between the appreciable ability of electoral politics (with its principles of universal suffrage and majority rule) to undermine old psychological commitments to ascriptively based social hierarchies; and the much more limited capacity of elected politicians dependent on local notables as "link men" in the constituencies to implement faithfully institutional changes aimed at augmenting the economic resources of the rural poor for independent political action.

Ample evidence does exist that the first process of social mobilization is well advanced. Since the landmark election of 1971, when Mrs. Gandhi, deserted by large numbers of local influentials in the wake of the Congress party split, still managed to win unprecedented majorities among the rural poor, cutting across regional, linguistic, and caste lines

---

[63] *Statement on Economic Policy*, adopted by the Working Committee of the Janata Party on December 14, 1977, p. 1.

[64] *Ibid.*, pp. 2, 4.                          [65] *Ibid.*, p. 4.

with a direct class appeal to "abolish poverty," the growth of political awareness among the Indian masses has transformed the nature of democratic politics. The 1977 national and state elections, which ironically brought about Mrs. Gandhi's crushing defeat and inflicted unprecedented losses on the Congress party, offered the most dramatic evidence that large numbers of the peasantry have begun to participate directly in the national electoral process in response to political issues that transcend religious, caste, and factional divisions. Citing the striking similarity between urban and rural areas in the pattern of voting, Weiner has pointed out that

> rural dwellers have extensive contacts with urban areas; that urban migrants frequently return to their rural homes; that many of India's secondary and college students living in the towns and cities come from rural areas and continue to maintain rural links; that school teachers, lawyers, and bureaucrats penetrate the countryside as well as the towns and cities; that the construction of paved roads, the spread of transistor radios, the growth of the regional language press, and the expansion of the bus system have all linked rural and urban India into a single communications and transportation network; and finally, that the party system has penetrated rural as well as urban India.[66]

Journalists covering the March 1977 campaign were astonished at the "truly remarkable" manner in which "village audiences in the remote countryside react[ed] to sophisticated arguments about civil liberties, fundamental rights and independence of the judiciary."[67] Indeed, the election results showed that the voters were capable of a fine discrimination in selectively defeating precisely those senior Cabinet ministers from Mrs. Gandhi on down who were personally responsible for the greatest abuses of the Emergency.[68] If anything, the Emergency itself accelerated the pace of politicization among the poorer sections of the peasantry, making it clear from their own experience that they were likely to be the first victims of arbitrary government at the hands of local police and government officials concerned only with pleasing those in still higher positions of arbitrary power above them.

[66] Myron Weiner, "The 1977 Parliamentary Elections in India," *Asian Survey*, July 1977, p. 624.

[67] See Inder Malhotra, "Political Atmosphere Free from Rancour," *Times of India*, March 7, 1977.

[68] Senior ministers directly linked with the abuses of the Emergency, such as forced sterilization and censorship of the press, were defeated at the polls, while others were reelected on the Congress ticket. In the first group were Bansi Lal, the defense minister and "the master mind, who directed the sterilization program"; V. C. Shukla, the minister of information; and H. R. Gokhale, the law minister who had provided a legal rationale for the Emergency and its abuses. In the second group were old stalwarts like C. Subramaniam and Y. B. Chavan.

Yet, if it is by now well established that competitive politics over the past twenty-five years has succeeded in creating a "critical level of political awareness"[69] among the illiterate and the impoverished, it is equally apparent that this heightened political consciousness has not yet resulted in the application of effective popular pressure from below to carry out peaceful implementation of social reform. In particular, changes in the "thinking of the masses" have not been followed by changes in the pattern of political alignments that can mount sustained pressure on elected governments to carry out promises of economic reform.

There have been many reasons for this failure of the rural poor to convert their greatest resource in superior numbers into effective political power. At the outset, of course, the decision to separate the techniques of party organization from the methods of social reform meant that not very much else might be expected. The Congress party's claim to represent the entire nation without excluding any group, and its decision to build up its organization on the dominant groups in the rural areas meant that the new electorate was inducted into politics by intermediaries recruited from among leading members of the landowning castes. Although political competition between local leaders did draw growing numbers of the poor peasantry into the political process, the lack of direct contact between the most depressed groups and outside centers of power in the ruling party and the administration reinforced vertical political ties that provided the only hope of the poor for access to the benefits of, and protection against the abuses flowing from, closer ties to the wider political system.

These vertical political ties did not prevent the transformation of political consciousness. They do not explain by themselves the inability of the rural poor after some thirty years to generate their own leadership and organize the larger part of their numbers to challenge the hegemony of the landowning elites. A good part of the explanation must still be sought in internal cleavages among the peasantry based on caste, above all that which divides Harijans from members of other Backward Classes. At the same time, there is little doubt that the dominant landed castes were able to use their position as intermediaries in relationships between the village and external sources of power at the district and state levels of government and administration to frustrate the national leadership's policies for social transformation through institutional change. In particular, well-placed landed elites—through their contacts in the state legislatures, the land revenue administration, the state departments of cooperation, the Community Development staff—were able to prevent effective implementation of national policies on land reforms, the reor-

[69] For an interesting analysis of growing politicization among the Indian masses, see D. L. Sheth, "Structure of Indian Radicalism," *Economic and Political Weekly*, Annual Number, February 1975, 319-34.

ganization of agricultural credit, marketing, and distribution along cooperative lines, and indeed, all other measures for "social" reform aimed at weakening the links of dependence binding the peasantry to the dominant landed castes.

Worse still, failures in implementation of institutional change left the weakest sections of the village population more than ever dependent upon good relations with leading members of the dominant landed castes. Half-hearted attempts to carry out land reforms only alerted landlords to their long-term interests in protecting their property rights through evictions of tenants that converted customary leasing arrangements into contingent sharecropping agreements. Meanwhile, marginal farmers, their number swelling in size as tiny farms became too small to provide subsistence to all family members, joined the growing numbers of landless laborers seeking supplementary employment. As larger landowners found it more profitable to substitute wages in cash for payments in kind, many landless workers were confronted with a choice between uncertain casual employment at inflated rates, or new forms of permanent contracts providing some additional security, but at the cost of personal independence. Almost all poor rural households, moreover, could not escape the unwelcome ties to richer landowners arising out of the chronic necessity for revolving loans to meet basic consumption needs.

Land, income, status, contacts, power—all of these political resources were more than ever concentrated in the hands of the dominant landowning castes. The poor peasantry, who had numbers on their side, found it impossible to build alliances across kinship, caste, and factional groups for common political action in larger arenas, when their own fortunes inside the village were still intimately tied to good relations with members of the landowing elites. Above all, it would have been foolish for peasant leaders to attempt to organize a common front unless, at the minimum, they were assured against physical retaliation through links with a wider regional or national organization having its own capacity for imposing sanctions.

It is not surprising that under such conditions the peasantry should have proved unable to take advantage of political democracy either to generate its own leadership or build up party organizations from below. The only realistic alternative appears to be for a cadre of political workers coming into the villages from outside to take up the task of grass-roots party organization.

Is this feasible? Certainly, there are serious difficulties and even dangers of attempting this style of peasant mobilization. The democratic political parties that profess a commitment to social reform have never been in a more weakened organizational condition. The Congress party, which failed to rebuild its organizational base after the 1969 split, was disrupted even further by Mrs. Gandhi's decision, following renewed challenges to her leadership after the debacle of the 1977 elections, to force the new split that once again created two rival Congress party organizations. At the same time, Mrs. Gandhi's aspirations for a political comeback will have to overcome the obstacles set up by the Desai Government which took the first steps in July 1978 toward prosecution of the former prime minister on criminal charges of abuse of authority during the Emergency. Meanwhile, ex-Forum members began organization of a broad-based Socialist Forum to function without any political affiliation, drawing upon intellectuals, political activists, trade unionists and youth workers to "consolidate the socialist forces for political action in the long run."[70]

The Janata party is hardly better positioned. All of its constituent groups did formally merge into one party in May 1977, but months later, the party had yet to enroll its own primary members and set up units at the district and state levels. Meanwhile, the president of the Janata party, Chandra Shekhar, presides over an organization that still relies heavily on the Jan Sangh and its militant Hindu nationalist RSS cadre.

The communist parties have also lost a good deal of their momentum. The CPI was reduced to less than 3 percent of the popular vote; and even the CPI (Marxists) suffered a small overall decline to about 4 percent of the poll nationwide in 1977. The defeat of the Marxists by the Congress-CPI coalition in Kerala, even when compensated by their striking victory in West Bengal, marks them as a regional party.

Even if these grave weaknesses of political leadership could be overcome, class-based peasant organization would admittedly run up against caste antagonisms between Harijans and other Backward Classes; and conflicting interests between agricultural laborers pressing for higher wages and owners of small and marginal holdings who are not able to absorb such increases. Further, even while the solidarity of the poor still cannot be taken for granted—although the increasing proletarianization of the peasantry constitutes a positive development from that perspective—efforts to organize the Harijans and other Backward Classes on caste lines would certainly meet the solid opposition of the more prosperous landed castes. This is all the more the case when peasant organization must take place under conditions of low overall growth, increasing disparities, and the zero-sum character of redistribution policies for leveling up the poor, which inevitably involve some leveling down of the rich.

Yet, having set out all the obstacles to class-based peasant organization, it is impossible to find a substitute for sustained political pressure by the potential beneficiaries for implementation of land reform policies that

[70] *Times of India*, November 26, 1977.

have been accepted by all governments since Independence, enacted into law, and yet ignored with impunity by the landowning castes. Indeed, Jayaprakash Narayan, observing bleakly that the structure of village society had not changed in the thirty years since Independence, and admitting that "earlier I had disliked the idea of organizing [the Harijans and the landless] on class lines," could finally find no alternative to recommend than organizing the rural poor in class-based associations.[71]

Despite all the difficulties and dangers that such an approach entails, it should be pointed out that in some crucial respects, the political conditions for a peaceful restructuring of India's agrarian economy are more favorable now than at any time since Independence. Much higher levels of political awareness and new egalitarian norms are eroding the old caste and factional loyalties that buttressed previous patterns of vertical political mobilization. Progress toward removal of mass poverty is becoming a new touchstone for evaluating the performance of elected governments. This criterion of legitimacy, moreover, is widely accepted among the educated middle classes, the result of heightened social consciousness no less than growing uneasiness that "we can no longer take for granted the endurance and patience of our over-burdened people" whose "unendurable circumstances can only lead them to desperation."[72] Indeed, the Janata party, whose major constituents are themselves drawn from the more affluent and conservative members of society, the shopkeepers, traders, and civil servants who are the backbone of the Jan Sangh in the cities, and the larger peasant cultivators in the BLD who have made the greatest gains from the green revolution, have had to give tacit recognition to rising popular expectations. Morarji Desai, in a radio broadcast to the nation shortly after becoming prime minister, renewed his pledge to achieve both "bread and freedom," promising to "end destitution within a decade."[73] The Janata party has made a formal commitment to remove unemployment by 1987, and even to reduce income differentials between the minimum and maximum after tax to 1:20, with the ultimate objective being to reduce the differential to 1:10.[74]

There is another circumstance that may ultimately prove favorable. The notion that the democratic system must be evaluated by its ability to lift every citizen above the poverty level is taking hold at a time of renewed debate on the basic principles of the political system, especially the relationship between constitutional guarantees for fundamental rights and the directive principles to secure a just social order. Although the Janata party was able to take immediate action to liquidate the most arbi-

---

[71] *Times of India*, August 11, 1977.

[72] Excerpts from President Reddy's Independence Day Message, *Times of India*, August 15, 1977.

[73] *Times of India*, May 12, 1977.                    [74] *Statement on Economic Policy*, p. 29.

trary measures of the Emergency, including the ban on the RSS and other organizations, and the curbs voted on the press (even dissolving Samachar to restore the four independent news services), it could not carry out its election promises to revoke the Forty-second Amendment in its entirety. The Congress party, which retained a majority in the Upper House or Rajya Sabha, agreed to support only a limited statute to remove the most "obnoxious" provisions from the amended constitution. The Forty-fourth Constitution (Amendment) Bill passed in the Lok Sabha on December 20, 1977, deleted the right of Parliament to make laws banning "anti-national" activities and associations, and restored the powers of both the Supreme Court and the High Courts to consider the constitutional validity of any state or central legislation (and to declare a central or state law invalid by simple majority). Among other measures, it struck out provisions permitting the central government to dispatch armed forces to any state without its consent; and the special procedure for handling writ petitions challenging the election of the president, the vice president, prime minister, and speaker. The amendment also restored the five-year terms of the Lok Sabha and state assemblies. Yet, the Janata party and the Congress party could not agree on the government's proposals to change Article 31c in order to restore the Supreme Court's powers of judicial review over legislation designed to give precedence to the directive principles over the fundamental rights provisions. Whatever the outcome of future negotiations, moreover, it seems unlikely that the right to property will be restored to its original position as coequal with fundamental political rights. Assuming that this is the case, it will become feasible in the future to carry out basic economic reform through parliamentary measures that cannot subsequently be overturned in the courts.

Finally, the organizational vacuum that is in the process of developing in the rural areas opens up the possibility of forging horizontal alignments that can provide a direct base in popular support for political parties that invest the time and effort necessary to organize in the villages among the very poor. This much has been demonstrated in two states, Kerala and West Bengal, where the Marxists succeeded in building up state party organizations by recruiting among landless laborers and sharecroppers, to provide a reliable core of support that eventually led to state power. Although, in both states class-based peasant organization did lead to a sharp increase in incidents of agrarian violence, it is also the case that these clashes were contained from spreading into large-scale civil disorder by the ability of the central government to impose President's Rule and send central armed forces to reinforce state police. Perhaps even more important than the superior political and military power available to the Center in containing class conflict that could spill over into regional or religious or caste confrontation to weaken the political unity of the nation, is the considerable progress toward social and economic integration that has occurred over the last thirty years. In any event, movements toward regional nationalism and greater autonomy for the states are likely to receive their greatest popular support under conditions of an ineffectual ruling party and central government that cannot keep its promises to provide the minimum needs of India's diverse social groups.

In the end, of course, it is impossible to calibrate finely the benefits and risks of political organization among the rural poor on class lines. But the alternative of not doing so is perhaps more certainly to end in the failure of hopes for a "gradual revolution" of India's society.

Polarization is proceeding, in any case. Since the end of the Emergency, in a number of states, a large proportion of the plots distributed to landless laborers under the Twenty-Point Program has been forcibly taken back by the landowners. Incidents of caste violence, particularly murders and other atrocities against Harijans by upper-caste Hindus angered at their attempts to assert rights to land or other benefits under the Twenty-Point Program, indicate a growing antagonism between landed and landless groups.

At present, the greatest dangers to long-term political stability do not appear to come from any attempt to build up effective political parties that can mobilize the poor peasantry and institutionalize their demands. Rather, the most serious threat to political order can be expected from the progressive loss of legitimacy of traditional power relationships, without putting any substitute structure in its place. Adversary groups, confronting and colliding with each other in the absence of any accepted rules, can trigger cycles of violence and repression that destroy the ability of existing democratic institutions to function, while failing to create the conditions for reconstruction of a more effective political order.

The middle-class intelligentsia professing a commitment to democratic socialism may yet have much to gain in attempting to organize the poor peasantry while it is still possible to bring them into politics in a way that will strengthen political stability, that is, by augmenting the capacity of elected governments to complete the second part of the gradual revolution for structural change. It does not require much imagination to visualize the conditions of another breakdown in the democratic processes of government. It is much more difficult to conceive that the extraordinary events of 1977, which restored the democratic political order after its all but complete collapse in the face of previous failures to carry out basic social reform, can be repeated a second time.

# BIBLIOGRAPHY

INTERVIEWS

Probably the most important insights in interpreting the mass of economic and political data available on India's development were generated during the course of numerous interviews conducted during several field trips starting in 1958. Over the years, I have been privileged to talk with prominent leaders of the Congress party and government, including the members of the Planning Commission and senior administrators both at the Center and in several states; and in 1969 and again in 1973 to carry out interviews at the village level with all classes of agriculturists in widely separate parts of India. All of these materials have been invaluable in penetrating behind formal statements of official policy to glimpse the reality of intentions and events as they have actually unfolded. I have drawn freely from them, making attribution in the case of discussions that no longer raise problems of political sensitivity. I have respected the anonymity of persons interviewed about events that still arouse controversy—for example, the Congress party split of 1969 and its aftermath—especially since most of those interviewed are still active in politics.

GOVERNMENT DOCUMENTS AND REPORTS

India. *The Constitution of India*, As Amended by the Constitution 42nd Amendment Act, 1976, with short notes. Allahabad, 1977.

————. Administrative Reforms Commission. *Report of the Study Team, Machinery for Planning*, Final Report. New Delhi, 1967.

————. *Report of the Monopolies Inquiry Commission, 1965*. Vols. I and II. Delhi, 1966.

————. Department of Industrial Development, Ministry of Industrial Development, Internal Trade and Company Affairs. *Report of the Industrial Licensing Policy Inquiry Committee, Main Report*. New Delhi, July 1969.

————. Directorate of Economics and Statistics. *Agricultural Legislation in India*. Vol. IV, Land Reforms (Abolition of Intermediaries). New Delhi, 1953.

————. Directorate of Economics and Statistics. *Area, Production and Yield of Principal Crops in India, 1949-50 to 1967-68*. Delhi, 1969.

————. Ministry of Agriculture and Irrigation (Department of Agriculture). *All India Report on Agricultural Census, 1970-71*. New Delhi, 1975.

India. Ministry of Finance. *Budget*. Delhi, annual.

———. Ministry of Finance, Direct Taxes Enquiry Committee. *Final Report*. Delhi, 1971.

———. Ministry of Finance. *Report of the Committee on Taxation of Agricultural Wealth and Income*. New Delhi, 1972.

———. Ministry of Finance, Economic Division. *Economic Survey*. Delhi, annual.

———. Ministry of Food and Agriculture. *Report of the Indian Delegation to China on Agriculture Planning and Techniques*. New Delhi, 1956.

———. Ministry of Food and Agriculture, Department of Agriculture. *Agricultural Development: Problems and Perspective*. New Delhi, 1965.

———. Ministry of Food and Agriculture, Department of Agriculture. *Agricultural Production in the Fourth Five Year Plan, Strategy and Programme*. New Delhi, 1965.

———. Ministry of Food and Agriculture, Department of Food. *Report of the Foodgrains Enquiry Committee*. New Delhi, 1957.

———. Ministry of Food and Agriculture and Ministry of Community Development and Cooperation. *Report of India's Food Crisis and Steps To Meet It*. New Delhi, 1959.

———. Ministry of Industry. *Industrial Planning and Licensing Policy, Interim Report to Planning Commission* by R. K. Hazari. New Delhi, 1967.

———. Ministry of Planning, Department of Statistics, Central Statistical Organization. *Basic Statistics Relating to the Indian Economy, 1950-51 to 1974-75*. New Delhi, 1976.

———. *National Sample Survey, Eighth Round: July 1954-March 1955*. Number 10. *First Report on Land Holdings, Rural Sector*. Delhi, 1958.

———. *National Sample Survey, Eighth Round: July 1954-April 1955*. Number 30. *Report of Land Holdings (2), Operational Holdings in Rural India*. Calcutta, 1960.

———. *National Sample Survey, Sixteenth Round, July 1960-June 1961*. Number 122. *Tables with Notes on Agricultural Holdings in Rural India*. Calcutta, 1963.

———. *National Sample Survey, Seventeenth Round, September 1961-July 1962*. Number 140. *Tables with Notes on Some Aspects of Landholdings in Rural Areas (State and All-India Estimates)*. Calcutta, 1966.

———. Planning Commission. *Annual Plan, 1966-67*. Delhi, 1966.

———. Planning Commission. *Annual Plan, 1967-68*. Delhi, 1967.

————. Planning Commission. *Annual Plan, 1968-69*. Delhi, 1968.

————. Planning Commission. *Appraisal and Prospects of the Second Five Year Plan*. New Delhi, 1958.

————. Planning Commission. *Draft Fifth Five Year Plan, 1974-79*. Part I. Delhi, 1973.

————. Planning Commission. *First Five Year Plan*. New Delhi, 1953.

————. Planning Commission. *First Five Year Plan, A Draft Outline*. New Delhi, 1951.

————. Planning Commission. *Fifth Five Year Plan 1974-79*. Delhi, 1976.

————. Planning Commission. *Fourth Five Year Plan, 1969-74*. New Delhi, July 1970.

————. Planning Commission. *Fourth Five Year Plan, 1969-74, Draft*. Delhi, 1969.

————. Planning Commission. *Fourth Five Year Plan: A Draft Outline*. New Delhi, 1966.

————. Planning Commission. *The Fourth Plan Mid-Term Appraisal*. Vol. I. New Delhi, 1971.

————. Planning Commission. *Fourth Five Year Plan—Resources, Outlays and Programme*. New Delhi, 1965.

————. Planning Commission. *Implementation of Land Reforms: A Review*. New Delhi, 1966.

————. Planning Commission. *Main Issues Relating to the Third Five Year Plan*. New Delhi, 1959.

————. Planning Commission. *Memorandum on the Fourth Five Year Plan*. New Delhi, 1964.

————. Planning Commission. *Notes on Perspectives of Development: India: 1960-61 and 1975-76*. New Delhi, 1964.

————. Planning Commission. *The Planning Process*. New Delhi, 1963.

————. Planning Commission. *Progress of Land Reforms*. New Delhi, 1963.

————. Planning Commission. *Report of the Indian Delegation to China on Agrarian Cooperatives*. New Delhi, 1956.

————. Planning Commission. *Report of the Task Force on Agrarian Relations*. New Delhi, 1973.

————. Planning Commission. *The Second Five Year Plan*. New Delhi, 1956.

————. Planning Commission. *A Study of Tenurial Conditions in Package Districts* by Wolf Ladejinsky. New Delhi, 1965.

————. Planning Commission. *Third Five Year Plan*. New Delhi, 1962.

————. Planning Commission. *Third Five Year Plan, A Draft Outline*. New Delhi, 1960.

India. Planning Commission. *The Third Plan, Mid-Term Appraisal*. New Delhi, 1963.

――――. Planning Commission. *Towards Self-Reliance, Approach to the Fifth Five Year Plan*. New Delhi, June 1972.

――――. Planning Commission, Panel of Economists. *Papers Relating to the Formulation of the Second Five Year Plan*. New Delhi, 1955.

――――. Planning Commission, Panel of Land Reforms. *Report of the Committee on Ceilings on Land Holdings*. New Delhi, 1961.

――――. Planning Commission, Panel on Land Reforms. *Report of the Committee on Tenancy Reforms*. New Delhi, 1961.

――――. Planning Commission, Programme Evaluation Organization. *Evaluation of the Gram Sahayak Program*. New Delhi, 1961.

――――. Planning Commission, Programme Evaluation Organization. *Evaluation Report on First Years Working of Community Projects*. New Delhi, 1954.

――――. Planning Commission, Programme Evaluation Organization. *Evaluation Report on Second Year's Working of Community Projects*. New Delhi, 1955.

――――. Planning Commission, Programme Evaluation Organization. *Evaluation Report on Working of Community Projects and N.E.S. Blocks*. New Delhi, 1956.

――――. Planning Commission, Programme Evaluation Organization. *Evaluation Report on Working of Community Projects and N.E.S. Blocks*. New Delhi, 1957.

――――. Planning Commission, Programme Evaluation Organization. *The Fifth Evaluation Report on Working of Community Development and N.E.S. Blocks*. New Delhi, 1958.

――――. Planning Commission, Programme Evaluation Organization. *Seventh Evaluation Report on Community Development and Some Allied Fields*. New Delhi, 1960.

――――. Planning Commission, Programme Evaluation Organization. *The Sixth Evaluation Report on Working of Community Development and N.E.S. Blocks*. New Delhi, 1959.

――――. Planning Commission, Programme Evaluation Organization. *Study of Utilization of Cooperative Loans*. New Delhi, 1965.

――――. Registrar General and Census Commissioner. *Census of India, 1971, Provisional Population Totals*. Paper 1 of 1971—Supplement. New Delhi, 1971.

Reserve Bank of India. *Report*. Bombay, annual.

――――. *Report of the All-India Rural Credit Review Committee*. Bombay, 1969.

――――. Report of the Committee of Direction. *All-India Rural Credit Survey, II, The General Report*. Bombay, 1954.

PROCEEDINGS, REPORTS, PAMPHLETS OF
THE CONGRESS PARTY AND AFFILIATED GROUPS

Congress Forum for Socialist Action. *An Approach to the Fifth Plan, Some Basic Considerations*. New Delhi, 1972.

———. *Congress Revitalization and Reorganization, Nehru's Guidelines for the Congress*. New Delhi, 1968.

———. *Scheme*. New Delhi, 1967.

———. *Short History of the Congress Forum for Socialist Action*. New Delhi, 1971.

———. *Two Years of CFSA, Decisions and Resolutions*. New Delhi, 1971.

———. *Working Rules*. New Delhi, 1967.

Congress Socialist Forum. *Keep the Flame Alive: A Thesis by a Group of Congress Workers*. New Delhi, 1957.

———. *Looking into the National Mirror, an Appraisal of the Third General Election*. New Delhi, undated.

Indian National Congress, All India Congress Committee. AICC Central Training Camp, Narora: November 22-24, 1974. *The Economic Outlook* and *Present Political Situation*. New Delhi, 1975.

———. *Bye-Elections Committee Report*. New Delhi, 1963.

———. *Congress Bulletin*. 1950-1969.

———. *Congress Marches Ahead—III*. New Delhi, October 1970.

———. *Congress Marches Ahead—IV*. April 1971-September 1971. New Delhi, 1971.

———. *Congress Marches Ahead—V*. October 1971-May 1972. New Delhi, June 1972.

———. *Congress Marches Ahead—VI*. June 1972-August 1972. New Delhi, September 1972.

———. *Congress Marches Ahead—VII*. September 1972-December 1972. New Delhi, December 1972.

———. *Congress Marches Ahead—VIII*. December 1972-August 1973. New Delhi, September 1973.

———. *Congress Marches Ahead—IX*. September 1973-June 1974. New Delhi, July 1974.

———. *Congress Marches Ahead—10*. July 1974-May 1975. New Delhi, 1975.

———. *Congress Marches Ahead—11*. May 1975-December 1975. New Delhi, 1975.

———. *Congress Marches Ahead—12*. December 1975-May 1976. New Delhi, 1976.

———. *Congress Marches Ahead—13*. May 1976-October 1976. New Delhi, 1976.

———. *The Fourth General Elections, A Statistical Analysis*. New Delhi, 1967.

Indian National Congress, AICC. *From Bombay to Delhi*. New Delhi, June
     1970.
———. *From Delhi to Patna*. New Delhi, October 1970.
———. *Kerala Mid-Term Election, 1970—An Analysis*. New Delhi, 1970.
———. *People's Victory, An Analysis of 1971 Elections*. New Delhi, 1971.
———. *People's Victory—Second Phase (An Analysis of the 1972 General
     Election to State Assemblies)*. New Delhi, 1972.
———. *Report of the Congress Agrarian Reforms Committee*. New Delhi,
     1949.
———. *Report of the Congress Planning Sub-Committee*. New Delhi, 1959.
———. *Resolutions on Economic Policy and Programme, 1924-54*. New
     Delhi, 1954.
———. *Two Exclusive Interviews, Prime Minister Indira Gandhi on Ques-
     tions Facing India and the World*. New Delhi, 1973.
———. Economic and Political Research Department. *A.I.C.C. Eco-
     nomic Review*. 1956-1962.
Indian National Congress, United Provinces Congress Committee.
     *Agrarian Distress in the United Provinces*. Allahabad, 1931.
Indian Youth Congress. *Draft Constitution*. Undated.

UNPUBLISHED OR RESTRICTED
DOCUMENTS AND PAPERS

India, Department of Agriculture (Land Reforms Division). "Salient
     Features of Laws on Ceiling on Agricultural Holdings." Un-
     dated, post-1973. Mimeographed.
India, Planning Commission. "Preparation of States' Plans, An Apprais-
     al of the 4th Plan Experience." Undated. Mimeographed.
———. *Summary Record*, Meetings of the National Development Coun-
     cil. 1955-1972.
———. Perspective Planning Division. "Perspective of Development,
     1961-1976, Implications of Planning for a Minimum Level of
     Living." August 1962. Mimeographed.
International Bank for Reconstruction and Development. Report to the
     President of the International Bank for Reconstruction and De-
     velopment and the International Development Association on
     *India's Economic Development Effort*. Vols. II, III, IV, Agricultural
     Policy and Appendices, 1964/65 Economic Mission Headed by
     Bernard R. Bell. October 1, 1965.
Nehru, Jawaharlal. *Fortnightly Letters to the Chief Ministers, 1948-63*.

NEWSPAPERS AND PERIODICALS

*Economic and Political Weekly* (Bombay)
*The Economic Times* (Bombay)

*The Eastern Economist* (New Delhi)
*Hindu* (Madras)
*The Hindustan Times* (New Delhi)
*Indian Express* (New Delhi)
*LINK* (New Delhi)
*Seminar* (New Delhi)
*The Statesman* (Calcutta)
*Times of India* (Bombay)


BOOKS AND ARTICLES

Baden-Powell, B. H. *Land Systems of British India*. Vols. I, II, III. Oxford, 1892.

Baxter, Craig. *The Jana Sangh: A Biography of an Indian Political Party*. Philadelphia, 1969.

———. "The Rise and Fall of the Bhartiya Kranti Dal" in Myron Weiner and John Osgood Field, eds. *Electoral Politics in the Indian States*. Vol. 4, *Party Systems and Cleavages*. Delhi, 1975.

Bhagwati, Jagdish N., and T. N. Srinivasan. *Foreign Trade Regimes and Economic Development, India*. Amsterdam, 1974.

Bhave, Vinoba. *Swaraj Shastra*. Wardha, 1945.

Blyn, George. *Agricultural Trends in India, 1891-1947: Output, Availability and Productivity*. Philadelphia, 1966.

Bose, N. K., ed. *Selections from Gandhi*. Ahmedabad, 1948.

Brass, Paul R. "Coalition Politics in North India," *American Political Science Review*, 42:4 (December 1968).

———. *Factional Politics in an Indian State: The Congress Party in Uttar Pradesh*. Berkeley and Los Angeles, 1965.

Brecher, Michael. *Nehru, A Political Biography*. London, 1959.

———. *Nehru's Mantle*. Westport, Conn., 1966.

———. *Political Leadership in India, an Analysis of Elite Attitudes*. New York, 1969.

Bright, J. S. *Emergency in India and 5 + 20 Point Programme*. New Delhi, 1976.

Centre for the Study of Developing Societies. Occasional Papers: Number 1. *Party System and Election Studies*. Bombay, 1967.

Chandidas, R., Ward Morehouse, Leon Clark, Richard Fontera. *India Votes*. New York, 1968.

Chopra, Pran. *India's Second Liberation*. Delhi, 1973.

———. *Uncertain India*. Cambridge, Mass., 1968.

*Cooperative Farming, The Great Debate*. Bombay: Democratic Research Service, 1959.

Dantwala, M. L. "Financial Implications of Land Reforms," *Indian Journal of Agricultural Economics*, 17 (October-December 1962).

Das, Durga, ed. *Sardar Patel's Correspondence, 1945-50*. Vol. 6. Ahmedabad, 1971.

Deshmukh, C. D. *Economic Development in India, 1946-1956*. Bombay, 1957.

Erdman, Howard L. *The Swatantra Party and Indian Conservatism*. Cambridge, 1967.

Federation of Indian Chambers of Commerce and Industry. *Second Five Year Plan: A Comparative Study of the Objectives and Techniques of the Tentative Plan Frame*. New Delhi, 1955.

Fic, Victor M. *Kerala, Yenan of India. Rise of Communist Power, 1937-1969*. Bombay, 1970.

Franda, Marcus F. "India's Double Emergency Democracy." Part I, Transformations, South Asia Series, 19:17. Hanover, New Hampshire, 1975.

————. *Radical Politics in West Bengal*. Cambridge, Mass., 1971.

Frankel, Francine R. *India's Green Revolution, Economic Gains and Political Costs*. Princeton, 1971.

————. "Problems of Correlating Electoral and Economic Variables: An Analysis of Voting Behavior and Agrarian Modernization in Uttar Pradesh," in Myron Weiner and John Osgood Field, eds. *Electoral Politics in the Indian States*. Vol. 3, *The Impact of Modernization*. Delhi, 1977.

Gadgil, D. R. *Planning and Economic Policy in India*. Poona, 1961.

Galbraith, John Kenneth. *Ambassador's Journal*. Boston, 1969.

Gandhi, Mohandas K. *An Autobiography, The Story of My Experiments with Truth*. Boston, 1957.

————. *Democracy: Real and Deceptive*. Ahmedabad, 1961.

————. *Hind Swaraj or Indian Home Rule*. Ahmedabad, 1938.

————. *The India of My Dreams*. Bombay, 1947.

————. *Socialism of My Conception*. Bombay, 1957.

————. *Towards Non-Violent Socialism*. Ahmedabad, 1951.

Ganguli, B. N. *Economic Development in New China*. New York, 1954.

Ghose, Sankar. *Indira Gandhi, the Resurgent Congress and Socialism*. New Delhi, 1975.

Ghosh, Atulya. *The Split in the Indian National Congress*. Calcutta, 1970.

Hanson, A. H. *The Process of Planning, A Study of India's Five Year Plans, 1950-1964*. London, 1966.

Harrison, Selig. *India: The Most Dangerous Decades*. Princeton, 1960.

Huntington, Samuel P. *Political Order in Changing Societies*. New Haven, 1968.

Jones, Dawn E. and Rodney W. Jones. "Urban Upheaval in India: The 1974 Nav Nirman Riots in Gujerat," *Asian Survey*, 16 (November 1976).

Karanjia, R. K. *Indira-J.P. Confrontation, The Great Debate*. New Delhi, 1975.

———. *The Mind of Mr. Nehru: An Interview*. London, 1960.

Kashyap, Subhash C. *The Politics of Power, Defections and State Politics in India*. Delhi, 1974.

Khusro, A. M. *Economics of Land Reform and Farm Size in India*. Madras, 1973.

Kohli, Suresh, ed. *Corruption: The Growing Evil in India*. New Delhi, 1975.

Kochanek, Stanley A. *The Congress Party of India*. Princeton, 1968.

Kothari, Rajni. *Politics in India*. Boston, 1970.

———. *Democratic Polity and Social Change in India*. New Delhi, 1977.

Krishna, Gopal. "The Development of the Indian National Congress as a Mass Organization, 1918-1923," *Journal of Asian Studies*, 25 (May 1966).

Kumaramangalam, S. Mohan. *Constitutional Amendments: The Reason Why*. New Delhi, 1971.

Kunhi Krishnan, T. V. *Chavan and the Troubled Decade*. New Delhi, 1971.

Lakhanpal, P. L., ed. *Two Historic Judgments*. Delhi, 1972.

Lewis, John P. *Quiet Crisis in India*. Garden City, N.Y., 1964.

Malaviya, H. D. *The Danger of Right Reaction*. New Delhi, 1965.

Mahalanobis, P. C. *Talks on Planning*. Bombay, 1961.

Masani, M. R. *The Communist Party of India, A Short History*. London, 1954.

Masani, Zareer. *Indira Gandhi, a Biography*. New York, 1976.

Mellor, John A. *The New Economics of Growth, a Strategy for India and the Developing World*. Ithaca, 1976.

Metcalf, Thomas R. "Landlords without Land: The U.P. Zamindars Today," *Pacific Affairs*, 40 (Spring and Summer, 1967).

Migdal, Joel S. *Peasants, Politics and Revolution, Pressures toward Political and Social Change in the Third World*. Princeton, 1974.

Minhas, B. S. *Mass Poverty and Strategy of Rural Development in India*. Washington, D.C., 1971.

Monteiro, John B. *Corruption*. Bombay, 1966.

Moore, Barrington, Jr. *Social Origins of Dictatorship and Democracy, Lord and Peasant in the Making of the Modern World*. Boston, 1966.

Moreland, W. H. *The Agrarian System of Moslem India*. Cambridge, 1929.

Myrdal, Gunnar. *Asian Drama: An Inquiry into the Poverty of Nations*. New York, 1968.

Nanavati, Manilal B., and J. J. Anjarai. *The Indian Rural Problem*. Bombay, 1944.

Narayan, Jayaprakash. *Towards Struggle: Selected Manifestoes, Speeches and Writings*. Bombay, 1964.

Nayar, Kuldip. *India, the Critical Years*. Delhi, 1971.
————. *The Judgement, Inside Story of Emergency in India*. New Delhi, 1977.
————, ed. *Supersession of Judges*. New Delhi, 1973.
Nehru, Jawaharlal. *An Autobiography*. London, 1936.
————. *The Discovery of India*. New York, 1946.
————. *India, Today and Tomorrow*. Azad Memorial Lectures. Calcutta, 1960.
————. *Nehru on Gandhi*. New York, 1941.
————. *Planning and Development*. New Delhi, 1956.
————. *Toward Freedom, The Autobiography of Jawaharlal Nehru*. New York, 1941.
————. *Whither India?*. Allahabad, 1933.
Overstreet, Gene D., and Marshall Windmiller. *Communism in India*. Berkeley and Los Angeles, 1959.
Palmer, Norman D. *Elections and Political Development: the South Asian Experience*. London, 1975.
————. *The Indian Political System*. Second edition. Boston, 1971.
Ram, Mohan. *Maoism in India*. New York, 1971.
Ranga, N. G. *History of the Kisan Movement*. Madras, 1939.
————. *Kisan Handbook*. Madras, 1938.
————. *Kisan Speaks*. Madras, 1937; Calcutta, 1952.
Rudolph, Lloyd, and Susanne Rudolph. *The Modernity of Tradition, Political Development in India*. Chicago, 1967.
Shah, Ghanshyam. "The Upsurge in Gujerat," *Economic and Political Weekly*, IX, Special Number (1974).
Singh, Jitendra. *Communist Rule in Kerala*. New Delhi, 1959.
Singh, Satindra. *Communists in Congress, Kumaramangalam's Thesis*. Delhi, 1973.
Singh, Tarlok. *India's Development Experience*. London, 1974.
————. *Towards an Integrated Society*. Bombay, 1969.
Sitaramayya, B. Pattabhi. *The History of the Indian National Congress, 1885-1935*. Delhi, 1935.
Srinivas, S. N. *Social Change in Modern India*. Berkeley and Los Angeles, 1967.
Streeten, Paul, and Michael Lipton, eds. *The Crisis of Indian Planning*. London, 1968.
Veit, Lawrence. *India's Second Revolution*. New York, 1976.
Weiner, Myron. *Party Building in a New Nation, The Indian National Congress*. Chicago, 1967.
————. *Party Politics in India*. Princeton, 1957.
————, ed. *State Politics in India*. Princeton, 1968.

————, and John Osgood Field. "India's Urban Constituencies," in Myron Weiner and John Osgood Field, eds. *Electoral Politics in the Indian States*. Vol. 3, *The Impact of Modernization*. Delhi, 1977.

Wood, John R. "Extra-Parliamentary Opposition in India: An Analysis of Populist Agitations in Gujerat and Bihar," *Pacific Affairs*, 48:3 (Fall 1975).

Zagoria, Donald S. "The Ecology of Peasant Communism in India," *The American Political Science Review*, 65:1 (March 1971).

Zaidi, A. M. *The Great Upheaval, '69-'72*. New Delhi, 1972.

# INDEX

LIBRARY OF CONGRESS CATALOGING IN PUBLICATION DATA

Frankel, Francine R.
  India's political economy, 1947-1977.

  Bibliography: p.
  Includes index.
    1.  India—Economic conditions—1947-
2.  India—Economic policy.    3.  India—Social
conditions—1947-    4.  Social conflict.
5.  India—Politics and government—1947-
I.  Title.
HC435.2.F7      330.9'54'04      78-51164
ISBN 0-691-03120-7
ISBN 0-691-10072-1 pbk